CW01160877

Drafting Copyright Exceptions

How should copyright exceptions be drafted? This question is of ongoing interest to scholarly and law reform debates, and often turns on claims regarding the respective merits of 'flexible' and 'specific' provisions. This book assesses drafting options using insights from the standards and rules literature, and a case study on the cultural institution sector in Australia, Canada, the United Kingdom and the United States. Drawing from thousands of hours of fieldwork conducted over fourteen years, it describes how staff engage with and interpret exceptions. It argues that sometimes practices are guided heavily by the 'law in books', but on other occasions are influenced by a variety of factors, ranging from ethical views and risk assessment through to prosaic matters in relation to copyright management. It discusses why practices change – sometimes dramatically. The book uses this detailed account of interpretative practices and the 'law in action' to draw lessons for the drafting of copyright exceptions.

EMILY HUDSON is Reader in Law at King's College London and has previously held posts at the Melbourne Law School, University of Queensland and University of Oxford. Her PhD at the University of Melbourne – from which this book derives – won the Harold Luntz Graduate Thesis Prize 2012 and the Chancellor's Prize for Excellence in the PhD Thesis 2013.

Cambridge Intellectual Property and Information Law

As its economic potential has rapidly expanded, intellectual property has become a subject of front-rank legal importance. *Cambridge Intellectual Property and Information Law* is a series of monograph studies of major current issues in intellectual property. Each volume contains a mix of international, European, comparative and national law, making this a highly significant series for practitioners, judges and academic researchers in many countries.

Series Editors

Lionel Bently

Herchel Smith Professor of Intellectual Property Law, University of Cambridge

Graeme Dinwoodie

Global Professor of Intellectual Property Law, IIT Chicago-Kent College of Law

Advisory Editors

William R. Cornish, *Emeritus Herchel Smith Professor of Intellectual Property Law, University of Cambridge*

François Dessemontet, *Professor of Law, University of Lausanne*

Jane C. Ginsburg, *Morton L. Janklow Professor of Literary and Artistic Property Law, Columbia Law School*

Paul Goldstein, *Professor of Law, Stanford University*

The Rt Hon. Sir Robin Jacob, *Hugh Laddie Professor of Intellectual Property, University College London*

Ansgar Ohly, *Professor of Intellectual Property Law, Ludwig-Maximilian University of Munich*

A list of books in the series can be found at the end of this volume.

Drafting Copyright Exceptions
From the Law in Books to the Law in Action

Emily Hudson
King's College London

CAMBRIDGE
UNIVERSITY PRESS

CAMBRIDGE
UNIVERSITY PRESS

University Printing House, Cambridge CB2 8BS, United Kingdom

One Liberty Plaza, 20th Floor, New York, NY 10006, USA

477 Williamstown Road, Port Melbourne, VIC 3207, Australia

314–321, 3rd Floor, Plot 3, Splendor Forum, Jasola District Centre, New Delhi – 110025, India

79 Anson Road, #06–04/06, Singapore 079906

Cambridge University Press is part of the University of Cambridge.

It furthers the University's mission by disseminating knowledge in the pursuit of education, learning, and research at the highest international levels of excellence.

www.cambridge.org
Information on this title: www.cambridge.org/9781107043312
DOI: 10.1017/9781107338012

© Emily Hudson 2020

The author hereby asserts their moral rights, including the right to be identified as the author of this work.

This publication is in copyright. Subject to statutory exception and to the provisions of relevant collective licensing agreements, no reproduction of any part may take place without the written permission of Cambridge University Press.

First published 2020

A catalogue record for this publication is available from the British Library.

Library of Congress Cataloging-in-Publication Data
Names: Hudson, Emily, author.
Title: Drafting copyright exceptions : from the law in books to the law in action / Emily Hudson, King's College London.
Description: Cambridge, United Kingdom ; New York, NY, USA : Cambridge University Press, 2020. | Series: Cambridge intellectual property and information law. | Includes bibliographical references and index.
Identifiers: LCCN 2019019441 | ISBN 9781107043312 (hardback) | ISBN 9781107618541 (pbk.)
Subjects: LCSH: Copyright–English-speaking countries.
Classification: LCC K1420.5 .H837 2020 | DDC 808.06/6346–dc23
LC record available at https://lccn.loc.gov/2019019441

ISBN 978-1-107-04331-2 Hardback

Cambridge University Press has no responsibility for the persistence or accuracy of URLs for external or third-party internet websites referred to in this publication and does not guarantee that any content on such websites is, or will remain, accurate or appropriate.

For Nicholas John Hudson
Orator; Publisher; Spycatcher
1933–2018

Contents

Preface	page ix
Table of Cases	xi
Table of Statutes	xvi
Part I Background	1
1 Introduction	3
2 Standards and Rules	28
3 Copyright and Cultural Institutions	63
Part II The Law in Action	103
4 Sector-Specific Exceptions	105
5 Functional Fair Use	160
6 Australian Section 200AB	207
7 Fair Dealing's Failures?	230
Part III The Future	263
8 New Norms and Practices	265
9 Drafting Copyright Exceptions	308
Appendix	339
Bibliography	349
Index	370

Preface

The genesis of this book can be traced back to a research project conducted between 2003 and 2005 at the University of Melbourne, supported by the Australian Research Council (ARC) and six leading cultural institutions.[1] The aim of the project was to gain an understanding of the digitisation practices of Australian museums, galleries, libraries and archives, and to consider the ways in which copyright was handled by institutions and how it impacted on their practices. The research methodology included fieldwork at a range of cultural institutions and other bodies.

Since that time I have retained an ongoing research interest in the copyright experiences of the cultural institution sector, including through my doctoral research, which formed part of a second ARC Linkage Project supported by twelve partner organisations.[2] Much of this later work has focused on unremunerated 'exceptions' to copyright infringement: provisions that permit uses of copyright works without the consent of, or payment of money to, the copyright owner. Despite such provisions being the subject of much scholarly analysis, there has been far less systematic analysis of how exceptions are used on a day-to-day basis. One aim of my work has been to consider what the interpretative practices of institutional users means for the drafting of copyright exceptions, including ongoing calls for 'flexible drafting' and the introduction of a US-style fair use defence in other countries. However, my research also

---

[1] Kenyon and Christie, LP0348534. Industry partners: Art Gallery of New South Wales, Australian Centre for the Moving Image, Australian War Memorial, Museum Victoria, National Museum of Australia and State Library of Victoria.

[2] Kenyon and Christie, LP0669566. Partner organisations: Arts Law Centre of Australia, Australian Centre for the Moving Image, Museum Victoria, Museums Australia, National Film & Sound Archive, National Gallery of Victoria, National Library of Australia, National Museum of Australia, National and State Libraries Australasia, Powerhouse Museum, Screen Australia and State Library of Victoria. My doctoral work was conducted independently from other aspects of this project, and the opinions and conclusions presented in this book are strictly my own.

connects to broader themes in relation to legal drafting, the law in action and its relationship with the law in books.

Many people have contributed to the intellectual development of this project. I would like to thank my doctoral supervisors, Andrew Kenyon and David Brennan, and my colleagues from my time as a research fellow and PhD candidate at the University of Melbourne, especially Jason Bosland, Andrew Christie, David Lindsay, Megan Richardson and Kimberlee Weatherall. I have benefited enormously from the thoughts and feedback of numerous members of the intellectual property community, including Graeme Austin, Barton Beebe, James Bennett, Lionel Bently, Pascale Chapdelaine, Kenny Crews, Pina D'Agostino, Melissa de Zwart, Dev Gangjee, Daniel Gervais, Jonathan Griffiths, Michael Handler, Peter Hirtle, Marta Iljadica, Yin Harn Lee, Chris Morrison, Wee Loon Ng-Loy, James Parish, Graham Reynolds, Sam Ricketson, Jane Secker, Martin Sentfleben, Brad Sherman, Janice van de Velde and David Vaver. I would also like to acknowledge the input of my former colleagues at Oxford, Timothy Endicott and Peter Kail, in relation to philosophical aspects of this book; Caoimhe Ring for her research assistance; and everyone at Cambridge University Press who worked on this book, in particular Matt Galloway, Joshua Penney, Vinithan Sethumadhavan and Elizabeth Stone (at Bourchier).

The empirical work in this book would not have been possible without the input of hundreds of people from the cultural institution sector in Australia, Canada, the United Kingdom and the United States. The individuals who participated in these interviews were extremely generous with their time, and I thank them for agreeing to contribute to this work.

Finally, I would like to thank Tanya Aplin, Robert Burrell, Graeme Dinwoodie, Sam Hudson and Tim Roman for their particular support and encouragement.

The law in this book is up to date to 31 July 2019.

Table of Cases

Australia

Collier Constructions *v.* Foskett (1990) 19 IPR 44, 42
CBS Records Australia Ltd *v.* Telmak Teleproducts (Aust) Pty Ltd (1987) 9 IPR 440, 279
De Garis *v.* Neville Jeffress Pidler (1990) 18 IPR 292, 28, 233–234, 237, 240, 241, 247, 288, 289
National Rugby League Investments Pty Limited *v.* Singtel Optus Pty Ltd [2012] FCAFC 59, 46–48
TCN Channel Nine Pty Ltd *v.* Network Ten Pty Ltd (2001) 108 FCR 235; (2002) 118 FCR 417, 28, 234, 289
Telstra Corporation Pty Ltd *v.* Premier Media Group Pty Ltd (2007) 72 IPR 89, 234, 289
University of New South Wales *v.* Moorhouse (1975) 133 CLR 1, 70

Canada

Alberta (Education) *v.* Canadian Copyright Licensing Agency (Access Copyright) [2012] 2 SCR 345, 268, 271–273, 303, 305
Bishop *v.* Stevens (1990) 72 DLR (4th) 97, 320, 322
BMG Canada Inc *v.* John Doe [2004] 3 FC 241, 242
Breen *v.* Hancock House Publishers Ltd (1985) 6 CPR (3d) 433, 320
Canadian Broadcasting Corporation *v.* SODRAC 2003 Inc. [2015] 3 SCR 615, 320
Canadian Copyright Licensing Agency *v.* York University [2018] 2 FCR 43, 6, 69, 173, 266, 275, 301–306
Canadian Wireless Telecommunications Association *v.* Society of Composers, Authors and Music Publishers of Canada [2008] 3 FCR 539, 242–243
CCH Canadian Ltd *v.* Law Society of Upper Canada [2000] 2 FC 451; [2002] 4 FC 213; [2004] 1 SCR 339, 4–6, 8, 26, 70, 127–128, 151, 173, 230–262, 265–268, 273–275, 288, 294, 298, 303, 305, 307, 312, 317, 320–323, 325, 340

Cie Générale des Etablissements Michelin-Michelin & Cie *v.* CAW-Canada (1996) 71 CPR (3d) 348, 321–322
Edutile Inc *v.* Automobile Protection Assn (1997) 81 CPR (3d) 338, 237
Entertainment Software Association *v.* Society of Composers, Authors and Music Publishers of Canada [2012] 2 SCR 231, 268
Euro Excellence Inc *v.* Kraft Canada Inc [2004] 4 FCR 410; [2006] 3 FCR 91; [2007] 3 SCR 20, 243–245, 252, 325
Hager *v.* ECW Press Ltd [1999] 2 FCR 287, 321
The Queen *v.* James Lorimer and Co Ltd [1984] 1 FC 1065, 320
Re:Sound *v.* Motion Picture Theatre Associations of Canada [2012] 2 SCR 376, 268
Robertson *v.* Thomson Corporation [2006] 2 SCR 363, 242–243
Rogers Communications Inc *v.* Society of Composers, Authors and Music Publishers of Canada [2012] 2 SCR 283, 268
Society of Composers, Authors and Music Publishers of Canada *v.* Bell Canada [2012] 2 SCR 326, 268
Society of Composers, Authors and Music Publishers of Canada *v.* Canadian Association of Internet Providers [2002] FCA 166; [2004] 2 SCR 427, 242, 243, 246
Statement of Royalties to be Collected by SOCAN for the Communication to the Public by Telecommunication, in Canada, of Musical or Dramatico-Musical Works, Tariff No 22A (Internet – Online Music Services) 1996–2006, Copyright Board of Canada, 18 October 2007, 243, 246–248, 325
Tele-Direct (Publications) Inc *v.* American Business Information Inc [1998] 2 FC 22, 237
Théberge *v.* Galerie d'Art du Petit Champlain [2002] 2 SCR 336, 239, 244, 245
Zamacoîs *v.* Douville and Marchand (1943) 2 CPR 270, 319

European Union

Davidoff & Cie SA *v.* Gofkid Ltd (C-292/00) [2003] 1 WLR 1714, 311
Deckmyn *v.* Vandersteen (C-201/13) [2014] ECDR 21, 22, 23, 290–292
DR and TV2 Danmark A/S *v.* NCB – deNordisk Copyright Bureau (C-510/10) [2012] ECDR 20, 22
Funke Medien NRW GmbH *v.* Germany (C-469/17) [2019] ECDR 1; [2019] All ER (D) 48 (Aug), 21, 22, 23, 278
Painer *v.* Standard Verlags GmbH (C-145/10) [2012] ECDR 6, 18, 22, 72, 146, 278
Pelham GmbH *v.* Hütter (C-476/17) [2019] ECDR 3; [2019] Bus LR 2159, 20, 21, 22, 146, 278–280, 291, 292

Table of Cases xiii

Soulier v. Premier Ministre (C-301/15) [2017] ECDR 23, 101
Spiegel Online GMBH v. Volker Beck (C-516/17) [2019] Bus LR 2787, 21, 22, 23, 278, 284
Technische Universität Darmstadt v. Eugen Ulmer KG (C-117/13) [2014] ECDR 23, 18, 122, 152–153

New Zealand

Longman Group Ltd v. Carrington Technical Institute Board of Governors [1991] 2 NZLR 574, 237

United Kingdom

Antiquesportfolio.com v. Rodney Fitch & Co [2001] FSR 34, 72
Ashdown v. Telegraph Group [2002] Ch 149, 42
British Oxygen v. Liquid Air [1925] 1 Ch 383, 309
CBS Songs Ltd v. Amstrad Consumer Electronics Plc [1988] AC 1013, 48
Designers Guild Ltd v. Russell Williams (Textiles) Ltd [2000] 1 WLR 241, 52
England and Wales Cricket Board v. Tixdaq [2016] EWHC 575 (Ch) 23, 292
Fisher v. Brooker [2009] UKHL 41, 76
Hawkes and Sons v. Paramount Film Service [1934] 1 Ch 593, 309
HRH Prince of Wales v. Associated Newspapers Ltd [2006] EWHC 522 (Ch), 283
Hyperion Records Limited v. Sawkins [2005] EWCA Civ 565, 72
L'Oréal SA v. Bellure NV [2010] EWCA Civ 535, 24
Lion Laboratories v. Evans [1985] QB 526, 42
Norowzian v. Arks (No. 1) [1998] FSR 394, 279
Norowzian v. Arks (No. 2) [2000] FSR 363, 279
Performing Right Society Ltd v. Hammond's Bradford Brewery Co Ltd [1934] Ch 121, 320
Pro Sieben Media AG v. Carlton UK Television Ltd [1999] FSR 610, 242
Reject Shop v. Manners [1995] FSR 870, 72
Sillitoe v. McGraw-Hill Book Company (UK) Ltd [1983] FSR 545 (Ch), 234, 237, 240, 247, 288–289
Temple Island Collections Ltd v. New English Teas Ltd [2012] EWPCC 1, 72
University of London Press v. University Tutorial Press [1916] 2 Ch 601, 247, 309

United States

A&M Records Inc v. Napster, Inc, 239 F 3d 1004 (9th circuit, 2001), 165, 166

American Geophysical Union v. Texaco Inc, 802 F Supp 1 (SDNY, 1992); 60 F 3d 913 (2nd circuit, 1993), 126, 164, 172, 199

Authors Guild, Inc v. Google Inc, 770 F Supp 2d 666 (SDNY, 2011); 954 F Supp 2d 282 (SDNY, 2013); 804 F 3d 202 (2nd circuit, 2015), 66, 192

Authors Guild, Inc v. HathiTrust, 902 F Supp 2d 445 (SDNY, 2012); 755 F 3d 87 (2nd circuit, 2014), 158, 161, 168, 192–194, 329

Basic Books Inc v. Kinko's Graphics Corporation, 758 F Supp 1522 (SDNY, 1991), 173, 196, 198

Bill Graham Archives v. Dorling Kindersley Limited, 386 F Supp 2d 324 (SDNY, 2005); 448 F 3d 605 (2nd circuit, 2006), 45, 164–167, 170, 172, 174, 176, 186, 192, 193, 260

Blanch v. Koons, 467 F 3d 244 (2nd circuit, 2006), 168, 170

Bridgeman Art Library v. Corel Corp, 25 F Supp 2d 421 (SDNY, 1998); 36 F Supp 2d 191 (SDNY, 1999), 72, 176

Cambridge University Press v. Albert, 906 F 3d 1290 (11th circuit, 2018), 161, 329, 204–205

Cambridge University Press v. Becker, 863 F Supp 2d 1190 (ND Georgia, 2012); 2016 WL 3098397 (ND Georgia, 31 March 2016), 150, 161, 197–200, 201, 202–204

Cambridge University Press v. Patton, 769 F 3d 1232 (11th circuit, 2014), 150, 161, 197, 200, 202, 203, 302

Campbell v. Acuff-Rose Music Inc, 510 US 569 (1994), 59, 166, 167, 168, 175, 176, 199, 200, 317

Cariou v. Prince, 784 F Supp 2d 337 (SDNY, 2011); 714 F 3d 694 (2nd circuit, 2013), 168–170

Castle Rock Entertainment, Inc v. Carol Publishing Group Inc, 150 F 3d 132 (2nd circuit, 1998), 167, 168

Field v. Google Inc, 412 F Supp 2d 1106 (D Nev, 2006), 176

Folsom v. Marsh, 9 F Cas 342 (CCD Mass, 1841), 167

Graham v. Prince, No. 15-CV-10160 (SDNY, 18 July 2017), 169–170

Harper & Row Publishers Inc v. Nation Enterprises, 471 US 539 (1985), 59, 174

Kelly v. Arriba Soft Corporation, 77 F Supp 2d 1116 (CD Cal, 1999); 336 F 3d 811 (9th circuit, 2003), 164–167, 170, 172, 176, 186, 193, 260

Kienitz v. Sconnie Nation LLC, 766 F 3d 756 (7th circuit, 2014), 169

Mannion v. Coors Brewing Company, 377 F Supp 2d 444 (SDNY, 2005), 72
Marcus v. Rowley, 695 F 2d 1171 (9th circuit, 1983), 196
National Basketball Association v. Motorola Inc, 105 F 3d 841 (2nd circuit, 1997), 202
New York Times v. Tasini, 533 US 483 (2001), 176
Perfect 10 v. Amazon.com, 487 F 3d 701 (9th circuit, 2007), 164, 166, 167, 170, 172, 174, 176, 186, 260
Perfect 10 v. Google, 416 F Supp 2d 828 (CD Cal, 2006), 164, 260
Princeton University Press v. Michigan Document Services, 99 F 3d 1381 (6th circuit, 1996), 172, 196, 198
Rogers v. Koons, 960 F 2d 301 (2nd circuit, 1992), 72
Salinger v. Random House Inc, 811 F 2d 90 (2nd circuit, 1987), 45
Sony Corp of America v. Universal City Studios Inc, 446 US 417 (1984), 59
Stewart v. Abend, 495 US 207 (1990), 317
Sundeman v. Seajay Society Inc, 142 F 3d 194 (4th circuit, 1998), 176
Suntrust v. Houghton Mifflin Co, 268 F 3d 1257 (11th circuit, 2001), 176
TCA Television Corp v. McCollum, 839 F 3d 168 (2nd circuit, 2016), 169
Williams & Wilkins Company v. The United States, 172 USPQ 670 (Court of Claims, 1972); 487 F 2d 1345 (Court of Claims, 1973); 420 US 376 (1975), 115–116, 164

Table of Statutes

Australia

Acts Interpretation Act 1901 (Cth)
 s. 15AA, 47
Copyright Act 1905 (Cth)
 s. 28, 233
Copyright Act 1968 (Cth), 17, 30, 43, 110, 233
 s. 10(1), 124, 131, 143
 s. 10(4), 124
 s. 18, 125
 s. 40, 233
 ss. 40–42, 233
 s. 41, 37
 s. 41A, 214
 s. 42(1)(a), 37
 s. 43(2), 233
 s. 43C, 46
 s. 47J, 46
 ss. 48–53, 105
 s. 49, 125, 147, 148, 149, 152
 s. 49(9), 125
 ss. 49–52, 107
 s. 50, 125, 147, 148, 149
 s. 50(10), 125
 s. 51, 38, 147, 150
 s. 51(1), 148
 s. 51A, 132, 333
 s. 51A(1), 131, 137
 s. 51A(1)(a), 130
 s. 51A(1)(b), 130
 s. 51A(1)(c), 130

Table of Statutes

s. 51A(2), 37, 113, 143
s. 51A(3), 113, 143
s. 51A(6), 143
s. 51B, 41, 113, 130, 132, 133
s. 51B(4)(a), 131
s. 65, 87
s. 103A, 37
ss. 103A–103C, 233
s. 103AA, 214
s. 103B(1)(a), 37
s. 109A, 46
s. 110AA, 46
s. 110A, 46, 105, 147, 148, 150
s. 110B, 132, 333
s. 110B(1), 131, 137
s. 110B(1)(a), 130
s. 110B(1)(b), 130
s. 110B(1)(c), 130
s. 110B(2), 137
s. 110B(2)(a), 130
s. 110B(2)(b), 130, 137
s. 110B(2)(c), 130, 137
s. 110B(3), 131
s. 110BA, 113, 130, 132, 133
s. 110BA(3), 131
s. 110BA(5), 131
s. 111, 46
s. 111BA, 41
s. 112AA, 41, 113, 130, 132, 133
s. 112AA(2), 131
s. 113E, 230
ss. 113G–113M, 105, 132, 133
s. 113H, 131
s. 113H(1), 128
s. 113H(1)(b), 131
s. 113H(2), 152
s. 113J, 148
s. 113J(2), 152
s. 113K, 37, 143, 144
s. 113M, 131
s. 113M(1), 41

s. 113M(1)(d), 131
s. 113M(2), 152
s. 183, 223
Part VA, 86
Part VB, 86, 111
s. 200AB, 8, 17, 19, 26, 44, 69, 87, 105, 113, 128, 138, 148, 151, 207–229, 230, 265, 281, 299, 300, 312, 314–315, 323–325, 328, 331–332
s. 200AB(1), 87, 208, 216
s. 200AB(1)(a), 223
s. 200AB(2), 208, 214, 216
s. 200AB(6), 208, 223
s. 200AB(6A), 208
s. 200AB(7), 87, 207
Copyright Amendment (Digital Agenda) Act 2000 (Cth), 113
  Schedule 1, item 21, 124
  Schedule 1, items 73–78, 132
  Schedule, item 75, 143
Copyright Amendment (Disability Access and Other Measures) Act 2017 (Cth), 12, 37, 41, 81, 86, 87, 111, 113, 128, 131, 132, 207, 333
  Schedule 1, items 1–2, 30 & 35, 132
Copyright Amendment Act 1980 (Cth), 113
  s. 5, 124
  s. 12, 132
  ss. 10–12, 124
Copyright Amendment Act 1986 (Cth)
  s. 12, 132
Copyright Amendment Act 2006 (Cth), 12, 113
  Schedule 6, 46
  Schedule 6, item 24, 143
  Schedule 6, items 26–29, 132

Canada

An Act to amend the Copyright Act (S.C. 1997, c. 24), 117, 235
Copyright Act (R.S.C. 1952, c. 55), 117
  s. 17(2)(a), 117
Copyright Act (R.S.C. 1921, c. 32), 117, 319
Copyright Act (R.S.C. 1985, c. C-42), 5, 117, 252
  s. 2, 127, 130
  s. 3(1)(g), 70

Table of Statutes xix

s. 27, 236
s. 27(1), 236
s. 27(2), 236
s. 27(2)(e), 243
s. 29, 5, 230, 332
s. 29.1, 230
s. 29.2, 230
s. 29.7, 86
s. 30.1, 105
s. 30.1(1)(a), 120, 130, 131, 136
s. 30.1(1)(b), 120, 151–152
s. 30.1(1)(c), 120, 128
ss. 30.1(d)–(f), 143
s. 30.1(2), 120, 130, 152
s. 30.2, 105, 147, 255
s. 30.2(1), 127, 238
s. 30.2(2), 147
s. 30.21, 105, 147, 255
s. 32.2(1)(b)(ii), 87
s. 77, 92–94
s. 77(1), 93
s. 77(2), 93
s. 77(3), 93
Copyright Modernization Act (S.C. 2012, c. 20), 12, 121, 268, 273, 307, 332
s. 21, 121, 273, 332
s. 28–30, 121

European Union

Directive 2001/29/EC of the European Parliament and of the Council of 22 May 2001 on the harmonisation of certain aspects of copyright and related rights in the information society, 14, 19–23, 24, 25, 112
recital 31, 22
recital 32, 20, 22
Art. 2, 19
Art. 2(c), 279
Art. 3, 19
Art. 4, 19
Art. 5, 14, 15, 17–18, 19–23, 25, 112, 275, 276, 333
Art. 5(1), 19

Art. 5(2)(a), 121
Art. 5(2)(b), 20, 121
Art. 5(2)(c), 20, 152
Art. 5(2)(d), 22
Art. 5(2)(e), 121
Art. 5(3)(a), 20, 285
Art. 5(3)(c), 21
Art. 5(3)(d), 20, 21, 276, 282
Art. 5(3)(k), 20, 22, 289, 291, 292
Art. 5(3)(n), 20, 152
Art. 5(2)–(4), 19
Art. 5(5), 18, 23, 122
Art. 6(4), 143
Directive 2006/116/EC of the European Parliament and of the Council of 12 December 2006 on the term of protection of copyright and certain related rights
Art. 6, 72
Directive 2012/28/EU of the European Parliament and of the Council of 25 October 2012 on certain permitted uses of orphan works, 94–101
Directive (EU) 2019/790 of the European Parliament and of the Council of 17 April 2019 on copyright and related rights in the Digital Single Market and amending Directives 96/9/EC and 2001/29/EC, 19, 20, 21, 23, 82, 83, 92, 113, 121, 130
recital 27, 132, 147
recital 29, 130
recital 30, 100
recital 37, 100
Arts. 3–7, 20
Art. 5, 122, 287
Art. 5(2), 287
Art. 5(4), 287
Art. 6, 105, 130, 132, 141, 142
Art. 7(1), 142
Art. 8, 82, 83, 92, 100, 105
Art. 8(2), 82
Art. 8(4), 101
Art. 8(5), 92, 100
Art. 10, 100
Art. 14, 72–73
Art. 24, 20
Art. 29, 20

Table of Statutes

United Kingdom

Copyright (Public Administration) Regulations 2014 (SI 2014/1385), 12
Copyright Act 1911, 9, 108, 230, 233
  s. 2(1)(i), 230, 309
Copyright Act 1956, 43, 109, 320
  ss. 6(1)–(3), 309
  s. 7, 107, 109–110
  s. 7(6), 38
  ss. 9(1)–(2), 309
Copyright and Related Rights Regulations 2003 (SI 2003/2498), 112
  reg. 14, 112
Copyright and Rights in Performances (Certain Permitted Uses of Orphan Works) Regulations 2014 (SI 2014/2861), 12
Copyright and Rights in Performances (Disability) Regulations 2014 (SI 2014/1384), 12
Copyright and Rights in Performances (Extended Collective Licensing) Regulations 2014 (SI 2014/2588), 81
Copyright and Rights in Performances (Licensing of Orphan Works) Regulations 2014 (SI 2014/2863)
  reg. 3(1), 96
  reg. 4(2), 97
  reg. 4(3), 97
  reg. 6(2), 96
  reg. 8, 96
  reg. 10(1)(a), 97
  reg. 10(2), 97
  reg. 13(1), 97
  reg. 13(2), 97
Copyright and Rights in Performances (Quotation and Parody) Regulations 2014 (SI 2014/2356), 12
  reg. 3, 275
  reg. 5, 275
Copyright and Rights in Performances (Research, Education, Libraries and Archives) Regulations 2014 (SI 2014/1372), 12, 148
  reg. 4, 275
  reg. 5, 113, 139, 275
  reg. 6, 113
Copyright, Designs and Patents Act 1988, 10, 69, 112, 123, 141, 143, 307
  s. 16, 282

s. 29, 10, 230
s. 29(3)(b), 289
s. 29A(5), 75
s. 30, 10, 230
s. 30(1), 37, 283
s. 30(1A), 282, 284
s. 30(1A)(b), 282
s. 30(1A)(d), 282
s. 30(1ZA), 37, 146, 275, 276–284, 313
s. 30(1ZA)(a), 281
s. 30(2), 37
s. 30(4), 75
s. 30A, 10, 230, 275, 287–291
s. 31A, 289
ss. 31A–31F, 10
s. 32, 10, 230, 275, 284–287
s. 32(1)(b), 285
s. 32(2A)(c), 285
ss. 33–36A, 10, 286
ss. 34–36A, 286
ss. 37–44A, 112
s. 38, 148
s. 38(2)(a), 112
s. 39, 148
s. 39(2)(a), 112
ss. 40A–44B, 10, 105, 113
s. 40A, 123
s. 40B, 123, 152–153, 154–156, 314
s. 40B(1), 155
s. 40B(3)(a), 154
s. 40B(3)(c), 154
s. 41, 123, 147
s. 41(2), 124
s. 41(5), 75
s. 42, 123, 128, 139–141, 146, 313
s. 42(1), 131
s. 42(1)(a), 129
s. 42(3), 130, 141
s. 42(4), 124
s. 42(7), 75, 142
s. 42A, 123, 147, 148
s. 42A(1), 124

s. 43, 123, 147
s. 43A(2), 123
s. 43A(3), 123
s. 43A(4), 124
s. 43(3)(a), 112
s. 44B, 123
ss. 45–50, 10
ss. 50A–50D, 10
s. 58, 10
s. 60, 10
s. 62, 87
s. 116A, 96
s. 171(3), 42
s. 175(6), 282
s. 178, 282, 285
Schedule ZA1, 94, 101, 123, 299
Schedule ZA1 para 1(1), 95
Schedule ZA1 para 1(2), 95
Schedule ZA1 para 2(1), 95
Schedule ZA1 para 2(2), 95
Schedule ZA1 para 2(3), 95
Schedule ZA1 para 2(5), 95
Schedule ZA1 para 2(6), 95
Schedule ZA1 para 3, 95
Schedule ZA1 para 5, 95
Schedule ZA1 para 5(9), 95
Schedule ZA1 para 6(a), 95
Schedule ZA1 para 7(3), 95, 100
Schedule ZA1 para 7(4), 95
Intellectual Property (Copyright and Related Rights) (Amendment) (EU Exit) Regulations 2019 (SI 2019/605), 101

United States

Copyright Act of 1909, 35 Stat. 1075, 107
Copyright Act of 1976, 17 USC, 9, 11, 114, 163
   s. 101, 71
   s. 106, 162
   s. 106(5), 70–71
   s. 106A, 162
   s. 107, 9, 12, 18, 58, 87, 145, 160–206, 207, 261, 309, 312, 322, 325–326, 331, 333, 334–336, 340

xxiv Table of Statutes

    s. 108, 9, 41, 59, 105, 107, 117, 125–126, 134–135, 143, 160, 334–336
    s. 108(a), 125
    s. 108(a)(1), 126
    s. 108(a)(2), 125
    s. 108(b), 41, 129, 131, 135, 143, 177
    s. 108(b)(2), 153
    s. 108(c), 128, 129, 131, 158
    s. 108(c)(2), 153
    s. 108(d), 147, 335
    s. 108(e), 147, 335
    s. 108(f)(4), 336
    s. 108(g), 41, 150
    s. 108(i), 147, 148
    ss. 108–122, 9
    s. 110(5), 16–17
    s. 110(5)(A), 16–17
    s. 110(5)(B), 16–17
    s. 412, 311
    s. 504(c)(2), 311
    s. 1201, 143
    ss. 1201(a)(1)(B)–(D), 45
Digital Millennium Copyright Act 1998, 112 Stat. 2860, 117
    s. 404, 131, 153

Germany

German Copyright Act 1965
    s. 72, 72

Israel

Copyright Act 2007
    s. 19, 13

Sri Lanka

Intellectual Property Act, Act No. 36 of 2003
    s. 11, 13

Singapore

Copyright Act 1987
    s. 35(1), 10
    s. 36, 10
    s. 37, 10

International legislation and bilateral treaties

Agreement on Trade-Related Aspects of Intellectual Property Rights 1994, 14, 16–18, 217, 324–325
    Art. 13, 14, 16–18, 207, 231
    Art. 17, 17
    Art. 30, 17
Australia–US Free Trade Agreement (Washington, 18 May 2004) [2005] ATS 1, 208, 209–211
    Chapter 17, 210
Berne Convention for the Protection of Literary and Artistic Works, 14–16, 284
    Art. 3(3), 283
    Art. 5(2), 76
    Art. 7(2), 283
    Art. 9(2), 14–16, 25
    Art. 10(1), 276–278, 282–284, 333
    Art 10(2), 285
    Art. 10(3), 276
Marrakesh Treaty to Facilitate Access to Published Works for Persons Who Are Blind, Visually Impaired or Otherwise Print Disabled (adopted 27 June 2013), 23, 105

Part I

Background

1   Introduction

I   Overview

The central tenet of this book is that we need a new paradigm through which to view the operation and drafting of copyright exceptions. There already exists a large body of literature that has made important contributions to our understandings of the history and judicial interpretation of such provisions. This literature has also explored justifications for exceptions and the role they should play in copyright law.[1] In comparison with these well developed areas of analysis, the attention given to actual understandings of creators, copyright owners and users has been more limited, often appearing as ad hoc examples or impressionistic

---

[1] Some significant contributions include W. Gordon, 'Fair Use as Market Failure: A Structural and Economic Analysis of the Betamax Case and Its Predecessors' (1982) 82 *Columbia Law Review* 1600; L. Patterson, 'Free Speech, Copyright, and Fair Use' (1987) 40 *Vanderbilt Law Review* 1; W. Fisher III, 'Reconstructing the Fair Use Doctrine' (1988) 101 *Harvard Law Review* 1659; P. Leval, 'Toward a Fair Use Standard' (1990) 103 *Harvard Law Review* 1105; L. Weinrib, 'Fair's Fair: A Comment on the Fair Use Doctrine' (1990) 103 *Harvard Law Review* 1137; N. Netanel, 'Copyright and a Democratic Civil Society' (1996) 106 *Yale Law Journal* 283; J. Griffiths, 'Preserving Judicial Freedom of Movement – Interpreting Fair Dealing in Copyright Law' [2000] *Intellectual Property Quarterly* 164; R. Burrell, 'Reining in Copyright Law: Is Fair Use the Answer?' [2001] *Intellectual Property Quarterly* 361; J. Hughes, 'Fair Use Across Time' (2003) 50 *UCLA Law Review* 775; D. Nimmer, '"Fairest of Them All" and Other Fairy Tales of Fair Use' (2003) 66 *Law and Contemporary Problems* 263; R. Tushnet, 'Copy This Essay: How Fair Use Doctrine Harms Free Speech and How Copying Serves It' (2004) 114 *Yale Law Journal* 535; M. Sag, 'God in the Machine: A New Structural Analysis of Copyright's Fair Use Doctrine' (2005) 11 *Michigan Telecommunications and Technology Law Review* 381; G. D'Agostino, 'Healing Fair Dealing? A Comparative Analysis of Canada's Fair Dealing to U.K. Fair Dealing and U.S. Fair Use' (2008) 53 *McGill Law Journal* 309; G. Austin, 'Four Questions about the Australian Approach to Fair Dealing Defenses to Copyright Infringement' (2010) 57 *Journal of the Copyright Society of the USA* 611; C. Geiger, 'Promoting Creativity through Copyright Limitations: Reflections on the Concept of Exclusivity in Copyright Law' (2010) 12 *Vanderbilt Journal of Entertainment and Technology Law* 515; P. Samuelson, 'Possible Future of Fair Use' (2015) 90 *Washington Law Review* 815; and M. Senftleben, 'The Perfect Match: Civil Law Judges and Open-Ended Fair Use Provisions' (2017) 33 *American University International Law Review* 231.

4   Introduction

descriptions of practices.[2] And yet by overlooking these understandings and practices we risk ignoring, to borrow Paul Goldstein's words, 'the submerged mass of the iceberg' in relation to the operation of exceptions.[3] Existing scholarship has paid considerable attention to the tip of the iceberg: the 'law in books'. Whether the tip is indicative of what lies beneath or is at odds with the 'law in action' has been less well elucidated.

To be clear, this is not to suggest that existing scholarship has not engaged with practical questions about copyright or how it might impact on creators, users and other stakeholders. On the contrary, copyright scholars have been highly active in debates about the adequacy of exceptions and whether they ought to be reformed.[4] However, much analysis has adopted a top-down approach in which legislation and case law is used to paint a picture of the workings of exceptions and, from that, an assessment made of the state of the law and options for change.[5] A key idea underpinning this book is that without an understanding of the practices of non-legal actors, both the descriptive and normative aspects of the resulting conclusions are open to question.

An example illustrates this point and is a focus of later chapters.[6] On 4 March 2004 the Supreme Court of Canada handed down its decision in *CCH Canadian Ltd* v. *Law Society of Upper Canada*,[7] a case brought by

---

[2] Exceptions include K. Crews, *Copyright, Fair Use, and the Challenge for Universities: Promoting the Progress of Higher Education* (Chicago: University of Chicago Press, 1993); L. Murray, S. Piper and K. Robertson, *Putting Intellectual Property in Its Place: Rights Discourses, Creative Labor, and the Everyday* (New York: Oxford University Press, 2014) and M. Iljadica, *Copyright Beyond Law: Regulating Creativity in the Graffiti Subculture* (Oxford: Hart, 2016); and we should note the empirical turn in copyright research.

[3] P. Goldstein, 'Fair Use in Context' (2008) 31 *Columbia Journal of Law and the Arts* 433, 433.

[4] Including via contributions to law reform processes: e.g., R. Deazley, 'Copyright and Parody: Taking Backward the Gowers Review?' (2010) 73 *Modern Law Review* 785 (article based on submission to the Intellectual Property Office in 2010); R. Burrell, M. Handler, E. Hudson and K. Weatherall, 'ALRC Inquiry into Copyright and the Digital Economy', submission in response to Issues Paper No. 42 (14 December 2012); J. Besek, J. Ginsburg, P. Loengard and Y. Lev-Aretz, 'Copyright Exceptions in the United States for Educational Uses of Copyrighted Works', submission in response to the ALRC Issues Paper (2012); G. Hinze, P. Jaszi and M. Sag, 'The Fair Use Doctrine in the United States – A Response to the Kernochan Report', submission in response to ALRC Discussion Paper 79 (26 July 2013).

[5] A further criticism of this scholarship is that it frequently relies on a limited or cherry-picked set of materials. In response a number of scholars have sought to undertake a more systematic approach to their analysis: see especially B. Beebe, 'An Empirical Study of U.S. Copyright Fair Use Opinions' (2008) 156(3) *University of Pennsylvania Law Review* 549; P. Samuelson, 'Unbundling Fair Uses' (2009) 77 *Fordham Law Review* 2537; N. Netanel, 'Making Sense of Fair Use' (2011) 15 *Lewis & Clark Law Review* 715; M. Sag, 'Predicting Fair Use' (2012) 73 *Ohio State Law Journal* 47.

[6] See Chapters 7 and 8.   [7] [2004] 1 SCR 339 ('*CCH*').

a consortium of legal publishers against the Law Society as operator of the Great Library at Osgoode Hall. One aspect of the case related to a photocopying service in which the Library made and supplied copies of legal materials in response to requests by Law Society members. The publishers argued that this resulted in systematic infringement of copyright, entitling them to declaratory and injunctive relief. In a unanimous decision, the Supreme Court held that there was no infringement as the Library's activities fell within fair dealing for the purposes of research or private study.[8] Central to the reasoning was the unambiguous desire of the Court to adopt a more liberal approach to the interpretation of exceptions, as seen in the observation of McLachlin CJC that:

The fair dealing exception, like other exceptions in the Copyright Act, is a user's right. In order to maintain the proper balance between the rights of a copyright owner and users' interests, it must not be interpreted restrictively. As Professor Vaver ... has explained ...: 'User rights are not just loopholes. Both owner rights and user rights should therefore be given the fair and balanced reading that befits remedial legislation.'[9]

Following the Supreme Court's decision there was a flurry of academic writing, much of which lauded the Court for its statements regarding the role and conceptualisation of exceptions.[10] For instance, *CCH* was described as a 'landmark'[11] and its dicta predicted to have 'far-ranging' effects.[12] To the extent concerns were expressed about the decision, these often focused on the next stages of the liberalisation project, such as buttressing the broad understanding of fair dealing through legislative reform. For instance, Carys Craig argued that for the Supreme Court's vision to be fully realised it would be necessary to transform fair dealing into a fully open-ended exception in the style of fair use.[13]

Much of the favourable academic commentary was predicated on the idea that the Supreme Court had recalibrated fair dealing in Canada, a claim that on one level was self-evident and correct. *CCH*, a binding decision of Canada's highest court, was an unambiguous step away from

---

[8] Copyright Act (R.S.C. 1985, c. C-42), s. 29 (in this book 'Canadian Copyright Act').
[9] *CCH*, n. 7 above, para. 48 citing D. Vaver, *Copyright Law* (Toronto: Irwin Law, 2000), p. 171.
[10] See Chapter 7, Section III.B.
[11] P. Esmail, '*CCH Canadian Ltd v Law Society of Upper Canada:* Case Comment on a Landmark Copyright Case' (2005) 10 *Appeal* 13, 13.
[12] T. Scassa, 'Recalibrating Copyright Law? A Comment on the Supreme Court of Canada's Decision in *CCH Canadian Limited et al v Law Society of Upper Canada*' (2004) 3 *Canadian Journal of Law & Technology* 89, 89.
[13] C. Craig, 'The Changing Face of Fair Dealing in Canadian Copyright Law: A Proposal for Legislative Reform' in M. Geist (ed), *In the Public Interest: The Future of Canadian Copyright Law* (Toronto: Irwin Law, 2005).

the narrow interpretations of exceptions in the case law and copyright texts of the 1990s.[14] However, there were also reasons for questioning its supposedly transformative effects. To what extent was the favourable response of legal academics representative of the reception elsewhere? Would lawyers change the way they advised clients, and would judges sitting on lower tier courts take seriously the philosophical framework urged by the Supreme Court? Would library staff and other users even be aware of *CCH*, let alone update their practices by reference to the decision? As an empirical matter, the statement that *CCH* was groundbreaking relied on a range of assumptions about existing fair dealing interpretations and the amenability of those interpretations to change.

Chapters 7 and 8 tell the story of *CCH* and its reception in leading Canadian cultural institutions. This narrative draws not only from publicly available sources but from interviews conducted with institution staff and representatives of peak bodies. These chapters explain that during the five years following the Supreme Court's decision, a significant gap emerged between the forward-leaning interpretations of fair dealing preferred by academics and, to some extent, applied by judges, and the muted response within institutions, where awareness of the case was mixed and there were very few changes to procedures that were attributable to the decision. This was captured by the observation of one university librarian that there was a real divide between the views of academics within the university and those in the library who must 'face the music'.[15]

This book investigates why such a marked divergence arose between the law in books and the law in action, and what happened in the subsequent period to spur academic libraries to introduce meaningful changes to their fair dealing practices.[16] However, this book is about far more than the story of *CCH*. For instance, one of its key goals is to explore what the law in action means for the drafting of copyright exceptions, a question it explores using tools from the academic scholarship on standards and rules. As explained in Chapter 2, this literature makes predictions about when a legal command is better drafted so as to specify the legal consequences of particular behaviour in advance (i.e., as a rule) or using language that leaves factual determinations *and* the appropriate legal response to the judge (i.e., as a standard). Whilst there are echoes of this literature in debates about exceptions, current accounts

---

[14] See Chapter 9, Section II.D.   [15] 141L.
[16] See Chapter 8. This process is ongoing, with the most recent development being the failure of the fair dealing defence in *Canadian Copyright Licensing Agency ("Access Copyright") v. York University* [2018] 2 FCR 43.

are often over-simplified and ignore the crucial role that empirical analysis has in helping to determine the better form of drafting.

Second, it is hoped that this book will add a new dimension to long-standing debates about reform to exceptions, and in particular the 'fair use panacea'.[17] As explained in Section II of this chapter, these debates often centre on the proposition that countries with a closed-list approach to exceptions – i.e., those with an exhaustive suite of specific exceptions – face ongoing problems that can only be remedied by far greater use of open-ended and 'flexible' language, with fair use often presented as the best candidate for reform. This book uses qualitative methods to explore how one constituency in the United States – leading cultural institutions – has managed copyright challenges, and how this compares with the experiences of equivalent bodies in Australia, Canada and the United Kingdom. This book therefore seeks to present an empirically grounded assessment of the operation of fair use and whether it can be replicated elsewhere. As discussed in Section III of this chapter, this book is predicated on the assumption that open-ended exceptions can be compliant with the three-step test from international copyright law. It does not, therefore, replicate the extensive work done by others that supports this proposition.

Finally, this book is a longitudinal study of the copyright management practices of leading cultural institutions in Australia, Canada, the United Kingdom and the United States. The empirical material in this book dates back to 2004, and comprises thousands of hours of fieldwork with hundreds of people. In presenting this work the goal is not to provide an up-to-the-minute account of what cultural institutions do, nor to suggest that the interviews produced a comprehensive survey of practices. Rather, this book aims to describe the decision-making processes at institutions, to explore why some practices changed but others did not, and to consider what this means for copyright exceptions. It is hoped that this analysis will be of relevance not just to copyright scholars and the cultural institution sector but to those with an interest in social norms, law and society, and legal drafting.

As seen in Chapter 5, the empirical work suggested that for participating US cultural institutions, fair use was a meaningful part of copyright practices and had been responsive to new technologies and changing ideas about how institutions should make use of online opportunities. These experiences did not accord with characterisations of fair use as uncertain and unknowable, and may lend weight to the proposition that

---

[17] This rubric is taken from R. Burrell and A. Coleman, *Copyright Exceptions: The Digital Impact* (Cambridge: Cambridge University Press, 2005).

other jurisdictions might usefully add fair use to their suite of exceptions. However, not all experiences with 'flexible' drafting were as positive, as illustrated by Australia's bespoke section 200AB for cultural institutions and other users (Chapter 6) and, to a degree, Canada's experiences with post-*CCH* fair dealing (Chapter 7). In Chapter 9 this book nevertheless supports the introduction of fair use in other jurisdictions, for instance observing that the Australian experience cautions us not against fair use but poorly drafted standards. That said, just as standards are not inevitably superior to rules, nor is fair use the endpoint of a mature legal system. As discussed in Chapter 8, developments in Canada and the United Kingdom give us pause to consider whether under-exploited flexibility can be found in purpose-specific fair dealing exceptions, allowing for new interpretations without a major reconceptualisation of the existing legislative framework. Furthermore, even if fair use or another standard is a desirable component of copyright law, there will always be a role for rule-like exceptions, with the precise mix varying from place to place and time to time.

II The Fair Use Panacea

As mentioned in Section I, we seem to be caught in a never-ending discussion of copyright exceptions and the respective merits of different forms of drafting.[18] The prominence of these debates would seem to be a by-product of the role that such provisions have come to play in copyright law, where they now operate as the key 'balancing' mechanism to ensure that copyright is appropriately limited, i.e., that rewards are granted to authors but not in such a way that re-use and new authorship are unduly impaired.[19] There are other ways that balance could be achieved. For instance, we might create a system where strong but short rights are granted in relation to a narrow range of subject-matter. In such a world

---

[18] See examples in P. Hugenholtz, 'Flexible Copyright: Can the EU Author's Rights Accommodate Fair Use' in R. Okediji (ed), *Copyright Law in an Age of Limitations and Exceptions* (New York: Cambridge University Press, 2017); M. Handler and E. Hudson, 'Fair Use as an Advance on Fair Dealing? Depolarising the Debate' in H. Sun, S. Balganesh and W. Ng-Loy (eds), *Comparative Aspects of Limitations and Exceptions in Copyright Law* (New York: Cambridge University Press, forthcoming).

[19] For criticism of use of the term 'balance' in copyright law, see, e.g., Burrell and Coleman, n. 17 above, pp. 187–191; C. Craig, 'Globalizing User Rights-Talk: On Copyright Limits and Rhetorical Risks' (2017) 33 *American University International Law Review* 1, 44–48. For instance, Burrell and Coleman observe that such terminology can be a truism to which we all agree but without guidance as to 'how weight is to be attributed to differing interests or even as to which interests are to enjoy a place on the scales': p. 190. In addition, the language of balance can suggest that interests of different stakeholders are oppositional rather than complex and interrelated.

there would be less need for exceptions because of the channelling work done at the subsistence and duration stages. For copyright, however, there has been an incremental expansion of subject matter, duration and rights from the early eighteenth century onwards.[20] With political and legal impediments to winding back rights, exceptions have emerged as the key counterpoint to help ensure that copyright does not overreach.

Interest in exceptions is also high due to the different forms that such provisions can take, notably free or remunerated, and open-ended or limited by purpose, subject-matter and/or user. For instance, Robert Burrell and Allison Coleman have argued that, broadly speaking, two approaches to drafting can be observed:

> The first approach is to provide a small number of generally worded exceptions. The second approach is to provide a larger number of much more specific exceptions, encompassing carefully defined activities. Although no country can be said to adhere rigidly to either approach, some countries lean towards one approach rather than the other. The United States, for example, leans towards the first approach. This is because US copyright law contains a broad 'fair use' defence.[21]

Pausing here, since the passage of the Copyright Act of 1976,[22] fair use has been codified in section 107 of that statute. At the heart of section 107 is the statement that 'the fair use of a copyrighted work ... is not an infringement of copyright'. Whilst section 107 contains guidance regarding when this might be the case, including via a non-exhaustive list of illustrative purposes and four factors that 'shall' be considered when determining whether a use is fair, its drafting is open-ended. In addition to fair use, the US statute contains other exceptions, many of which are highly detailed.[23] In this book, section 108 – pertaining to libraries and archives – is of particular interest.

Returning to Burrell and Coleman, they note that in contrast,

> the United Kingdom has a list of very specific exceptions, encompassing carefully defined activities. With the benefit of hindsight, it is possible to point to the Copyright Act 1911 as providing the template for this approach. ... Thus Australia, Canada, India, New Zealand, Singapore and South Africa delineate

---

[20] For examination of the British experience, see, e.g., B. Sherman and L. Bently, *The Making of Modern Intellectual Property Law* (Cambridge: Cambridge University Press, 2002).
[21] Burrell and Coleman, n. 17 above, p. 4; for similar, see S. Ricketson, 'Simplifying Copyright Law: Proposals from Down Under' (1999) 21 *European Intellectual Property Review* 537, 541.
[22] Copyright Act of 1976, 17 USC ss. 101 ff (in this book 'US Copyright Act').
[23] Ibid., ss. 108–122.

10   Introduction

the limits of copyright protection by way of an exhaustive list of specifically defined exceptions.[24]

The countries listed in this quote are all fair dealing jurisdictions. In its usual form, fair dealing is closed-ended, applying to dealings that are fair and conducted for one of the prescribed purposes. These purposes vary between different countries, but include such things as research, study, criticism, review and news reporting. There have been changes to the legal landscape since Burrell and Coleman wrote the above passage in 2005, including that Singapore has shifted to extended fair dealing by reframing one of its fair dealing provisions as open-ended.[25] However, their general point remains valid, and in countries such as Australia, Canada and the United Kingdom, the copyright statutes are still characterised by large numbers of closed-ended exceptions. To illustrate, when introductory and explanatory provisions are excluded, there are currently almost sixty operational sections covering 'permitted acts' in the Copyright, Designs and Patents Act 1988.[26] In addition to fair dealing[27] there are exceptions covering uses by and on behalf of disabled persons;[28] uses in education, by libraries and archives, and as part of public administration;[29] and acts with computer programs and databases.[30] Many of these provisions are lengthy and contain numerous sub-parts, often focusing on narrowly framed conduct, as exemplified by exceptions covering note-taking by journalists and the copying of abstracts to scientific and technical articles.[31] This level of specificity led Justice Hugh Laddie, writing extra-judicially in 1996, to observe that in the United Kingdom,

[r]igidity is the rule. It is as if every tiny exception to the grasp of the copyright monopoly has had to be fought hard for, prized out of the unwilling hand of the legislature and, once conceded, defined precisely and confined within high and immutable walls. This approach also assumes that Parliament can foresee, and therefore legislate for, all possible circumstances in which allowing copyright to be enforced would be unjustified. Based on this approach, we now have an Act in

---

[24] Burrell and Coleman, n. 17 above, p. 249; for similar, see M. Spence, *Intellectual Property* (Oxford: Oxford University Press, 2007), pp. 112–115.
[25] Copyright Act 1987 (Sing.), s. 35(1) (fair dealing for the purpose of research or study amended by the Copyright (Amendment) Act 2004 (Sing.) so that it covers any purpose other than those caught by ss. 36 and 37, namely fair dealing for the purposes of criticism, review and reporting current events).
[26] In this book 'CDPA'.
[27] CDPA ss. 29 (research and private study), 30 (criticism, review, quotation and news reporting), 30A (caricature, parody or pastiche), 32 (illustration for instruction).
[28] Ibid., ss. 31A–31F.   [29] Ibid., ss. 33–36A, 40A–44B, 45–50, respectively.
[30] Ibid., ss. 50A–50D.   [31] Ibid., ss. 58, 60, respectively.

which there are 49 sections of numbingly detailed exceptions to copyright infringement.[32]

The mere fact that exceptions are verbose and voluminous does not, without more, mean that something has gone wrong in relation to drafting.[33] As will be discussed in Chapter 2, there are instances where legal commands are best drafted using detailed rules. A more compelling criticism is that this drafting style has been executed poorly or, more radically, is fundamentally unsuited to the end for which it is being deployed. For instance, one recurring criticism of detailed, closed-ended exceptions is that they limit judicial discretion and risk being over- or under-inclusive, for instance where the words of a provision exclude conduct that is within its spirit. A related complaint is that such provisions are prone to redundancy due to technological change as they often have limited capacity to self-update, meaning that they require ongoing legislative reform. These issues could be seen as the flipside of certainty, but even this assertion has been challenged on the basis that specific exceptions often lack clarity and predictability because of drafting failures and other interpretative challenges.[34] Even fair dealing – which taken at face value would seem to utilise general rather than specific language – has come under criticism, for instance on the basis that judges have understood the prescribed purposes narrowly, making the defence more confined than its language requires;[35] and that judges have applied fair dealing in such ad hoc and impressionistic ways that it is difficult to glean any useful indications about its scope from the case law.[36]

If concerns about closed exceptions are made out, the next question is whether they can be resolved within the existing system or are an inevitable part of any model that involves an exhaustive list of closed

---

[32] H. Laddie, 'Copyright: Over-Strength, Over-Regulated, Over-Rated?' (1996) 18 *European Intellectual Property Review* 253, 258.

[33] Although it may cause us to wonder whether rationalisation is required: e.g., A. Christie, 'Making It Simple: How Copyright Legislation Can Be Simplified' (2011) 6 *New Zealand Intellectual Property Journal* 783. See also J. Hughes, 'Fair Use and Its Politics – At Home and Abroad' in R. Okediji (ed), *Copyright Law in an Age of Limitations and Exceptions* (New York: Cambridge University Press, 2017), pp. 239–240 (noting the length of exceptions in the US Copyright Act, and suggesting this illustrates how rules can become more precise as they are tailored to increasingly detailed fact patterns).

[34] This critique formed a key limb of the analysis of Burrell and Coleman, n. 17 above, p. 252.

[35] See Burrell and Coleman, ibid., pp. 259–267.

[36] See, e.g., M. Handler and D. Rolph, '"A Real Pea Souper": *The Panel Case* and the Development of the Fair Dealing Defences to Copyright Infringement in Australia' (2003) 27 *Melbourne University Law Review* 381; A. Sims, 'Strangling Their Creation: The Courts' Treatment of Fair Dealing in Copyright Law since 1911' [2010] *Intellectual Property Quarterly* 192.

exceptions. A central tenet of the fair use panacea is that a fully open-ended provision, perhaps following the wording of section 107 of the US Copyright Act, is the best way to deal with the drafting challenges and inefficiencies associated with specific exceptions. It therefore doubts the efficacy of reform efforts that have largely remained within the prevailing legislative framework, for instance as seen in Australia, Canada and the United Kingdom.[37]

However, for all those arguing in favour of fair use there are those who are opposed to such a reform. One argument is that fair use is unnecessary, either because existing exceptions are functioning adequately or because exceptions should, if anything, be narrowed in the digital era.[38] Another perspective says that even if exceptions require reform, fair use risks tilting the balance too far in favour of users and may introduce intolerable uncertainty into copyright law.[39] One reason for the latter concern is the centrality of case law to the interpretation of fair use. It has been said that even if there is some predictability to section 107, a non-US provision would lack the common law history that fair use had before

---

[37] In these countries reform instruments have introduced new fair dealing purposes, and new and amended detailed exceptions. For Australia, see the Copyright Amendment Act 2006 (Cth) (adding parody and satire as fair dealing purposes, and adding new exceptions for time shifting, format shifting and preservation copying by key cultural institutions); Copyright Amendment (Disability Access and Other Measures) Act 2017 (Cth) (adding a new fair dealing exception for assisting persons with a disability, and revising the preservation copying provisions for cultural institutions). For Canada, see the Copyright Modernization Act (S.C. 2012, c. 20) (adding education, parody and satire as fair dealing purposes, and adding new exceptions for non-commercial user-generated content, private copying, time shifting and the making of back-up copies). For the United Kingdom, see the Copyright and Rights in Performances (Research, Education, Libraries and Archives) Regulations 2014 (SI 2014/1372), the Copyright and Rights in Performances (Disability) Regulations 2014 (SI 2014/1384), the Copyright (Public Administration) Regulations 2014 (SI 2014/1385), the Copyright and Rights in Performances (Quotation and Parody) Regulations 2014 (SI 2014/2356) and the Copyright and Rights in Performances (Certain Permitted Uses of Orphan Works) Regulations 2014 (SI 2014/2861) (together introducing a range of reforms, including adding quotation, parody, pastiche, caricature and illustration for instruction as fair dealing purposes, and adding new exceptions for computational analysis, assisting people with disabilities and library copying).

[38] For instance, it has been argued that new technologies reduce many of the transaction costs that justify exceptions due to market failure: see, e.g., T. Bell, 'Fair Use vs Fared Use: The Impact of Automated Rights Management on Copyright's Fair Use Doctrine' (1998) 76 *North Carolina Law Review* 557; M. Fraser, 'Fair is Foul and Foul Is Fair: From Analogue to Digital Fair Dealing' (1998) 9 *Journal of Law and Information Science* 93. See also discussion in Burrell and Coleman, n. 17 above, pp. 168–180, 251–252.

[39] For discussion of the different types of uncertainty that surround fair use, see e.g. G. Austin, 'This Is a Complex Issue: A Few More Questions about Fair Use' (2018) 28 *Australian Intellectual Property Journal* 97.

its codification in 1976, and that such a provision would be applied by judges in legal systems very different to that in the United States and, in many instances, with much lower levels of copyright litigation.[40] Importantly, this concern has vexed not only those whose philosophy inclines towards stronger copyright but those who believe that robust exceptions are required to ensure that user interests are protected.[41] That is, even if fair use is accepted to function well in the United States, it has been questioned whether it can be transposed, intact, from one jurisdiction to another.

We therefore have a debate that focuses a great deal of attention on certainty and flexibility, often presenting these qualities as alternatives in a choice between closed-list drafting and fair use.[42] With polarised views being presented in relation to the desirability of fair use, and political and doctrinal challenges placed in the way of such a reform, only a handful of countries have introduced fair use.[43] One goal of this book is to help move this debate beyond over-simplified tropes about certainty and flexibility by providing a more rigorous and empirically focused framework through which to assess the fair use panacea and the drafting of copyright exceptions.

III The Supranational and International Context

Given this book's focus on drafting and the fair use panacea, an obvious question is the relevance of supranational and international influences, i.e., whether its analysis assumes a world where governments have a free hand to craft exceptions, or whether it takes into account drafting limitations that derive from intellectual property treaties, trade agreements and the like. Given the intellectual framework being developed, the focus of this book is mostly domestic, and examines the drafting of exceptions through the prism of efficiency and other lessons from the standards and rules literature. However, it would be remiss not to consider the relationship between this framework and the supranational regulation of exceptions. Whilst multilateral treaties were traditionally read as preserving the

---

[40] For discussion of challenges in implementing fair use in a non-US system, see D. Hunter, 'American Lessons: Implementing Fair Use in Australia' (2014) 24 *Australian Intellectual Property Journal* 192.
[41] See Burrell and Coleman, n. 17 above, p. 252.
[42] Burrell and Coleman, n. 17 above, pp. 249–250; see also Austin, n. 1 above.
[43] Examples include Sri Lanka (Intellectual Property Act, Act No. 36 of 2003, s. 11) and Israel (Copyright Act 2007, s. 19).

ability of member states to develop provisions most suited to local conditions,[44] developments from the 1990s onwards have changed that position. The analysis in this section focuses on three propositions: (1) that standards such as fair use are, or can be, compatible with the three-step test from international copyright law; (2) that for members of the European Union's Information Society Directive (ISD),[45] Article 5 contains meaningful parameters for the wording of exceptions and would seem to stand in the way of a fully open-ended provision; and (3) that insights from the standards and rules literature may help inform our thinking about the harmonisation of exceptions, including the degree to which treaties should seek to prescribe the drafting used by member states.

A   The Three-Step Test

One doctrinal objection that has been made to the introduction of fair use is that it does not comply with the three-step test in Article 9(2) of the Berne Convention, Article 13 of the Agreement on Trade-Related Aspects of Intellectual Property Rights (TRIPS) (both set out below) and other copyright treaties.[46] This book prefers the position, ventilated in detail elsewhere, that there are historical, doctrinal and normative reasons for adopting a more open-textured understanding of the 'test' in which fair use is or can be 'compliant'.

For instance, the history suggests that Article 9(2) was written as a legislative compromise to allow the reproduction right to be introduced into the Berne Convention.[47] This revision was made at the

---

[44] See, e.g., S. Stewart, *International Copyright and Neighbouring Rights*, 2nd edition (London: Butterworths, 1989), p. 80; J. Sterling, *World Copyright Law*, 3rd edition (London: Street & Maxwell, 1998), para 10.37; L. Helfer, 'World Music on a U.S. Stage: A Berne/TRIPS and Economic Analysis of the Fairness in Music Licensing Act' (2000) 80 *Boston University Law Review* 93, 147–148.

[45] Directive 2001/29/EC of the European Parliament and of the Council of 22 May 2001 on the harmonisation of certain aspects of copyright and related rights in the information society.

[46] Discussed in, e.g., Australian Law Reform Commission, *Copyright and the Digital Economy: Final Report*, Report No. 122 (November 2013), paras. 4.134–4.164. There has been doubt that fair use is Berne- and TRIPS-compliant: see, e.g., R. Okediji, 'Towards an International Fair Use Doctrine' (2000) 39 *Columbia Journal of Transnational Law* 75.

[47] For discussion of that history, see especially M. Senftleben, *Copyright, Limitations and the Three-Step Test: An Analysis of the Three-Step Test in International and EC Copyright Law* (The Hague: Kluwer Law International, 2004), pp. 43–82; S. Ricketson and J. Ginsburg, *International Copyright and Neighbouring Rights: The Berne Convention and Beyond Volume I*, 2nd edition (Oxford: Oxford University Press, 2006), paras 13.03–13.09.

1967 conference in Stockholm but had been complicated by the presence of a wide variety of exemptions in domestic legislation, being provisions that contracting states were keen to retain. It was recognised early on that the best way forward was to give states some leeway to legislate for exceptions, however this presented the challenge of how to draft an article that would cover such disparate laws. One approach was to list all permissible exceptions, but this was rejected by the pre-conference Study Group due to drafting challenges and the concern that such a list, when read cumulatively, would erode unacceptably the reproduction right.[48] Instead the Study Group recommended a general article that would permit states to enact exceptions for certain purposes where such use did not compete economically with the copied work.[49] Following debate at the 1967 conference, agreement was reached on a form of words that eventually became Article 9(2):

> It shall be a matter for legislation in the countries of the Union to permit the reproduction of such works in certain special cases, provided that such reproduction does not conflict with a normal exploitation of the work and does not unreasonably prejudice the legitimate interests of the author.

This history is significant because it suggests that Article 9(2) was never intended as a rigid test against which exceptions should be judged but was created to ensure that contracting parties would agree to the revision of Berne.[50] This required a formulation that preserved the ability of Member States to write copyright exceptions, and for many years the three-step test was read in this way. That said, it would be impossible to argue that the test never contained *any* normative content, and even if this could be made out historically, intervening developments would seem to have rendered such an argument futile. These developments include the World Trade Organization (WTO) Panel decision of 2000, discussed next, and the inclusion of three-step test language in Article 5 of the Information Society Directive (see Section III.B).

---

[48] See, e.g., M. Ficsor, *The Law of Copyright and the Internet* (Oxford: Oxford University Press, 2002), para. 5.51.

[49] See *Records of the Intellectual Property Conference of Stockholm, June 11 to July 14, 1967, Volume I* (1971), pp. 112–113; proposal also reproduced in Ricketson and Ginsburg, n. 47 above, para. 13.06.

[50] See, e.g., Senftleben, n. 47 above, p. 51; K. Koelman, 'Fixing the Three Step Test' (2006) 28 *European Intellectual Property Review* 407.

16 Introduction

The WTO Panel decision centred on section 110(5) of the US Copyright Act.[51] That provision originally permitted the use of home-style radios and televisions – i.e., equipment intended for private use rather than use as a commercial entertainment system – in public places such as restaurants and shops. The rationale behind this exception was that the impacts of such uses were *de minimis* and should not attract liability.[52] In 1998, section 110(5) was amended by the Fairness in Music Licensing Act to contain two limbs: sub-paragraph (A) (which largely followed the text of the original home-style exemption, albeit with wording said to narrow the subject matter covered[53]) and detailed sub-paragraph (B) (the business exemption, which permitted nondramatic musical works to be played in establishments meeting certain limits in relation to size and equipment used). The European Communities challenged the TRIPS-compliance of revised section 110(5). Relevant to this discussion, the Panel held that sub-paragraph (B) failed all three stages of the three-step test in Article 13 but that sub-paragraph (A) was compliant.

The WTO Panel decision was significant because its reasoning aligned with those who had been arguing – or warning – that Article 13 served as a meaningful test against which exceptions needed to be judged.[54] The language of Article 13 followed much of Article 9(2) of Berne but contained some changes, in particular referring to 'limitations or exceptions' and the 'right holder':

Members shall confine limitations or exceptions to exclusive rights to certain special cases which do not conflict with a normal exploitation of the work and do not unreasonably prejudice the legitimate interests of the right holder.

The Panel stated that each of the three 'conditions' of Article 13 must be given a 'distinct meaning', and that the 'tenor' of Article 13, as with Article 9(2), 'discloses that it was not intended to provide for exceptions

---

[51] For analysis of the Panel decision, see, e.g., J. Ginsburg, 'Toward Supranational Copyright Law? The WTO Panel Decision and the "Three-Step Test" for Copyright Exceptions' (2001) 187 *Revue Internationale du Droit D'Auteur* 3; J. Oliver, 'Copyright in the WTO: The Panel Decision and the Three-Step Test' (2002) 25 *Columbia Journal of Law and the Arts* 119.

[52] World Trade Organization, *United States – Section 110(5) of the US Copyright Act: Report of the Panel* (15 June 2000, WT/DS160/R) ('WTO Panel Report'), paras. 2.5–2.6.

[53] The parties accepted that the redrafting of s. 110(5) was such that the home-style exception in sub-paragraph (A) no longer applied to all types of work but only to works other than nondramatic musical works: ibid., paras. 2.7–2.8. The correctness of this interpretation has been challenged: e.g., Helfer, n. 44 above, FN7.

[54] See, e.g., N. Netanel, 'The Next Round: The Impact of the WIPO Copyright Treaty on TRIPS Dispute Settlement' (1997) 37 *Virginia Journal of International Law* 441, 455–456, 459–460; see also Helfer, n. 44 above, 103, 147–148, 183–184.

or limitations except for those of a limited nature'.[55] Pertinent to the themes in this book, this included the observation that the word 'certain' in 'certain special cases' required that exceptions be 'clearly defined', although 'there is no need to identify explicitly each and every possible situation to which the exception could apply, provided that the scope of the exception is known and particularised. This guarantees a sufficient degree of legal certainty.'[56] 'Special' added a further dimension, in that the exception 'must be limited in its field of application or exceptional in its scope', i.e., be 'narrow in [a] quantitative as well as a qualitative sense'.[57] Applying this to the business exception, the large number of establishments that fell within the exception was inconsistent with section 110(5)(B) being a certain special case.[58] In contrast, section 110(5)(A) satisfied this condition because of its much narrower application, despite some arguments regarding the ambiguity of the definition of home-style equipment.[59]

There are questions about how much precedential weight should be afforded the section 110(5) decision, being a report from a WTO panel.[60] However, the case has been significant as the first and only instance where Article 13 has been considered in detail as part of WTO dispute resolution procedures.[61] Since that time the attention paid to the three-step test has only grown, especially given its appearance in other instruments (domestic and international) and the extension of its audience to judges and not just legislators.[62] The most obvious example of the latter phenomenon has been the incorporation of three-step test language into domestic statutes, as seen in section 200AB of the Copyright Act 1968 (Cth) in Australia.[63] However, it may be that three-step test analysis is necessary even where no direct incorporation has occurred. In Europe, for example, the ISD states that the exceptions and limitations in Article 5 'shall only be applied in certain special cases which do not conflict with a normal exploitation of the work or other

---

[55] WTO Panel Report, n. 52 above, para. 6.97.   [56] Ibid., para. 6.108.
[57] Ibid., para. 6.109.   [58] Ibid., paras. 6.131, 6.133.
[59] Ibid., paras. 6.143, 6.145–6.148.   [60] See, e.g., Okediji, n. 46 above, 90.
[61] TRIPS also contains a three-step test in relation to patents (Art. 30) and a general test for trade marks (Art. 17). Those provisions have also been the subject of WTO analysis: see, e.g., G. Dinwoodie and R. Dreyfuss, *A Neofederalist Vision of TRIPS* (New York: Oxford University Press, 2012), especially pp. 58–71.
[62] See, e.g., C. Geiger, 'From Berne to National Law, Via the Copyright Directive: The Dangerous Mutations of the Three-Step Test' (2007) 29 *European Intellectual Property Review* 486, 486; J. Griffiths, 'The "Three-Step Test" in European Copyright Law: Problems and Solutions' [2009] *Intellectual Property Quarterly* 428, 429.
[63] In this book 'Australian Copyright Act'. Section 200AB is discussed in detail in Chapter 6.

18   Introduction

subject-matter and do not unreasonably prejudice the legitimate interests of the rightholder'.[64] Although indications from the Court of Justice of the European Union (CJEU) have not been consistent,[65] the better view seems to be that those words are directed not just to legislators drafting exceptions but also to judges applying them.[66]

It can therefore be said that whatever the history, the three-step test plays a meaningful role in the drafting of copyright exceptions and, in some instances, their interpretation by judges. This leads to the question of the content of the test, including the degree of latitude that should be afforded individual countries to determine the contours of copyright exceptions. For example, if we understand the WTO Panel's statements that exceptions should be 'clearly defined' to mean that drafting should tend towards the prescriptive and specify legal consequences in advance – i.e., that provisions should be drafted as rules – this would erode the ability of states to use standards when enacting copyright exceptions. Such an approach was rejected in the 'Declaration on a Balanced Interpretation of the "Three-Step Test" in Copyright Law', which pressed for an approach to the three-step test that 'does not prevent ... legislatures from introducing open ended limitations and exceptions, so long as the scope of such limitations and exceptions is reasonably foreseeable'.[67] It may also be that, as a political matter, comfort can be derived from the absence of any formal challenge to section 107 of the US Copyright Act by reference to Article 13 of TRIPS.

---

[64] ISD Art. 5(5).
[65] E.g., compare *Painer* v. *Standard Verlags GmbH* (C-145/10) [2012] ECDR 6 (Third Chamber), para. 110 (Art. 5(5) 'makes the introduction of the exception under art. 5(3)(e) ... subject to three conditions) and *Technische Universität Darmstadt* v. *Eugen Ulmer KG* (C-117/13) [2014] ECDR 23 (Fourth Chamber), para. 56 ('acts of reproduction [under a domestic exception transposing Art. 5(2)(a) or (b)] must observe the conditions set out in Article 5(5)').
[66] Discussed in R. Arnold and E. Rosati, 'Are National Courts the Addressee of the InfoSoc Three-Step Test?' (2015) 10 *Journal of Intellectual Property Law & Practice* 741.
[67] C. Geiger, J. Griffiths and R. Hilty, 'Towards a Balanced Interpretation of the "Three-Step Test" in Copyright Law' (2008) 30 *European Intellectual Property Review* 489. See also J. Füller, 'Article 13 Limitations and Exceptions' in P. Stoll, J. Busche and K. Arend (eds), *WTO—Trade-Related Aspects of Intellectual Property Rights* (Leiden: Brill, 2009) pp. 281–282 (a 'general balancing *formula* such as a "rule of reason" may be sufficiently certain ... as long as the interests to be balanced are transparent. The requirements of Art. 13 [of TRIPS] are fulfilled if the potential cases have been concretised by case law or interpretational guidelines. The so-called "fair use doctrine" pursuant to Section 107 of the US Copyright Act is therefore still sufficiently certain and compliant with Art. 13.')

This book prefers the view that the three-step test should be understood as setting broad rather than narrow parameters for the operation of exceptions.[68] This reading not only sits more comfortably with the history of the test but reflects the multitude of interests that are affected by copyright law and the importance of giving states leeway to respond to local conditions when crafting exceptions, including through rule-like and standard-like drafting. This chapter returns to this point in Section III.C, when it discusses what the standards and rules literature might teach us about the harmonisation of exceptions.

B   Article 5 of the Information Society Directive

Given that the United Kingdom is one of the jurisdictions analysed in detail in this book, the ISD has obvious relevance to its analysis, bearing in mind that the future relevance of European directives will depend on the outcome of Brexit negotiations.[69] Even if the United Kingdom is no longer bound by European copyright law, the ISD will remain relevant to other members of the European Union and may have residual effects in the United Kingdom for many years.

The ISD is one of a number of European directives that effect a partial harmonisation of copyright law across EU Member States, and which form part of the broader project of creating a single internal market.[70] The ISD harmonises three rights: the reproduction right, the right of communication to the public and making available, and the distribution right.[71] In Article 5, the ISD deals with exceptions and limitations, requiring all Member States to exempt from the reproduction right certain temporary copies made as part of technological processes.[72] It then identifies a series of 'cases' in which Member States may enact an exception or limitation.[73] These include such things as 'use for the sole

---

[68] There has also been support for including three-step test language in domestic statutes, because of the test's 'enabling' function: e.g., Senftleben, n. 47 above, pp. 280–281; C. Geiger, D. Gervais and M. Senftleben, 'The Three-Step Test Revisited: How to Use the Test's Flexibility in National Copyright Law' (2014) 29 *American University International Law Review* 581. The experiences described in Chapter 6 in relation to section 200AB of the Australian Copyright Act cast doubt on the desirability of such a move, a matter discussed further in Chapter 9, Section III; for a similar concern, see Griffiths, n. 62 above, 447–448.
[69] For a brief overview, see L. Bently, B. Sherman, D. Gangjee and P. Johnson, *Intellectual Property Law*, 5th edition (Oxford: Oxford University Press, 2018), pp. 29–31, 57.
[70] Ibid., pp. 12–29, 51–54. Analysis of the ISD must now include consideration of changes brought about by the new Directive on Copyright in the Digital Single Market: see pp. 56–57, and see n. 77 below and surrounding text.
[71] ISD Arts. 2, 3 and 4 respectively.   [72] Ibid., Art. 5(1).   [73] Ibid., Art. 5(2)–(4).

purpose of illustration for teaching or scientific research...',[74] 'quotations for purposes such as criticism or review...'[75] and 'specific acts of reproduction made by publicly accessible libraries, educational establishments or museums, or by archives, which are not for direct or indirect economic or commercial advantage'.[76] Article 5 has been amended by the new Directive on Copyright in the Digital Single Market (DSM Directive), which includes mandatory exceptions for text and data mining, illustration for instruction, and the preservation of collection items by cultural heritage institutions.[77] Member States have until 7 June 2021 to transpose the DSM Directive into domestic laws.[78]

It has been said by Justine Pila and Paul Torremans that '[t]aken together, [the] purpose-limited exceptions [in Article 5] can be read as comprising an EU "proportionate use" exception, corresponding to the "fair use" exception of other jurisdictions, including the United States'.[79] In making this claim, Pila and Torremans point to the breadth of cases that Article 5 countenances may be the target of exceptions.[80] That said, on current interpretations of the ISD, no Member State could pass a general exception stating that, for instance, 'the proportionate use of a copyrighted work is not an infringement of copyright'.[81] Article 5 refers to exceptions or limitations being made 'in the following cases', which suggests a closed list. This interpretation is bolstered by Recital 32 (describing the list of exceptions and limitations as 'exhaustive'), and in fact the CJEU has stated that Member States may not provide for exceptions and limitations outside those in Article 5.[82] Exceptions

---

[74] Ibid., Art. 5(3)(a). [75] Ibid., Art. 5(3)(d). [76] Ibid., Art. 5(2)(c).
[77] Directive (EU) 2019/790 of the European Parliament and of the Council of 17 April 2019 on copyright and related rights in the Digital Single Market and amending Directives 96/9/EC and 2001/29/EC, Arts. 3–7. Consequential amendments to the ISD and other directives are set out in Art. 24.
[78] Ibid., Art. 29.
[79] J. Pila and P. Torremans, *European Intellectual Property Law* (Oxford: Oxford University Press, 2016), p. 330.
[80] Ibid., pp. 334–335, citing Arts. 5(2)(b), (3)(a)–(e), (3)(j)–(n) (covering private use, illustration for teaching or scientific research, use by disabled persons, reporting of current events, quotation, public security and administration, the public exhibition or sale of artistic works, caricature, parody or pastiche, demonstration and repairs, and research use on dedicated terminals in certain institutions).
[81] Indeed, Pila and Torremans note the difference between the EU and US approaches: ibid., p. 343.
[82] See, e.g., *Pelham GmbH* v. *Hütter* (C-476/17) [2019] Bus LR 2159 (Grand Chamber), paras. 56–65 (German free use exception not compatible with ISD Art. 5) see also Hugenholtz, n. 18 above, pp. 276–277. In his submission to the Hargreaves review, Lionel Bently suggested that a case could be made that Art. 5 is not exhaustive, but that this would be 'a significant academic exercise, not feasible in the time available': L. Bently, 'Exploring the Flexibilities Available to UK Law', submission to the

reform in the United Kingdom has therefore proceeded on the basis that fair use is off the table, and that reforms such as a transformative use defence would require amendment of the ISD.[83] This understanding would not seem to have been displaced by the DSM Directive, which focuses on areas for which greater clarity and cross-border consistency are perceived as desirable.[84]

Despite the foregoing, there may be something in the argument that when the cases in Article 5 are viewed in aggregate, they approximate something close to fair use.[85] The degree to which this is correct empirically will depend on a systematic analysis of US and European legislation, case law and user practices.[86] For instance, whilst Article 5 may appear to be extensive, it originally only described one of the enumerated cases as mandatory; and even after the DSM Directive most of the cases remain optional. The degree of latitude afforded to users in any EU state will therefore depend on the extent to which that state has enacted exceptions that reflect the Article 5 list. In addition, it would seem that when the cases in Article 5 were being drafted, it was intended that Member States would enjoy varying levels of discretion in how they were implemented.[87]

Hargreaves Review (3 March 2011), FN1. It would seem that intervening developments have foreclosed this argument.

[83] I. Hargreaves, *Digital Opportunity: A Review of Intellectual Property and Growth* (May 2011), para. 5.19; *Gowers Review of Intellectual Property* (HM Treasury 2006), Recommendation 11.

[84] See the Explanatory Memorandum to the Proposed Directive, reproduced in European Commission, Proposal for a Directive of the European Parliament and the Council on Copyright in the Digital Single Market, 2016/0280 (COD).

[85] Pila and Torremans, n. 79 above, p. 343.

[86] For instance, a number of copyright scholars have pressed broad interpretations of exceptions for pastiche and quotation, which alone go a long way towards something that might have similar coverage to fair use: see E. Hudson, 'The Pastiche Exception in Copyright Law: A Case of Mashed-Up Drafting?' [2017] *Intellectual Property Quarterly* 346; L. Bently and T. Aplin, 'Whatever Became of Global, Mandatory, Fair Use? A Case Study in Dysfunctional Pluralism' in S. Frankel (ed), *Is Intellectual Property Pluralism Functional?* (Cheltenham: Edward Elgar, 2019); T. Aplin and L. Bently, 'Displacing the Dominance of the Three-Step Test: The Role of Global, Mandatory Fair Use' in H. Sun, S. Balganesh and W. Ng-Loy (eds), *Comparative Aspects of Limitations and Exceptions in Copyright Law* (New York: Cambridge University Press, forthcoming).

[87] E.g., *Funke Medien NRW GmbH v. Germany* (C-469/17) [2019] All ER (D) 48 (Aug) (Grand Chamber), paras. 39–54; *Spiegel Online GmbH v. Beck* (C-516/17) [2019] Bus LR 2787 (Grand Chamber), paras. 23–39 (both describing the discretion enjoyed by Member States in their implementation of ISD Arts. 5(3)(c) and (d), these being provisions that do not constitute 'measures of full harmonisation'). In explanatory material prepared by the Commission in relation to the ISD, the importance of harmonisation of exceptions and limitations was emphasised: Commission of the European Communities, *Proposal for a European Parliament and Council Directive on the harmonization of certain aspects of copyright and related rights in the Information Society*, 97/0359 (COD), pp. 29–33. However, it also appears that the level of harmonisation was intended to vary between different exceptions and limitations, with those perceived to

22   Introduction

Lest this seem wholly inconsistent with the logic of EU harmonisation, it should be emphasised that the CJEU has said that the level of discretion afforded Member States must be assessed on a case-by-case basis; and that there are various restrictions and imperatives in how exceptions and limitations operate, for instance where Article 5 language embodies autonomous European concepts and via interpretative canons such as 'fair balance'.[88] It would therefore seem that legislators are not required to follow the exact language of Article 5, although questions arise as to whether certain drafting choices or analytical approaches have been foreclosed by European copyright law.[89] In the United Kingdom, for

---

have the greatest impact on the Internal Market being compulsory or their application 'harmonized to a larger degree': p. 28. The Commission stated in relation to optional exceptions that 'Member States will be free to choose to keep or introduce these exceptions at their national level. If they so choose, they must then meet the conditions spelled out in the directive and in the international instruments, such as the "three step test"': p. 28. It concluded that this 'differentiating approach ... aims at enshrining a level playing field in copyright and related rights across Member States, whilst leaving Member States with sufficient room to keep their national legal and cultural traditions in place': pp. 29–30.

[88] See, e.g., *DR and TV2 Danmark A/S* v. *NCB – Nordisk Copyright Bureau* (C-510/10) [2012] ECDR 20 (Third Chamber), paras. 34–35 (considering the meaning of 'by means of its own facilities' in ISD Art. 5(2)(d), covering ephemeral recordings made by broadcasters); *Deckmyn* v. *Vandersteen* (C-201/13) [2014] ECDR 21 (Grand Chamber), para. 15 (considering the meaning of parody in ISD Art. 5(3)(k), covering caricature, parody or pastiche). In *Deckmyn*, the CJEU said at para. 16 that '[a]n interpretation according to which Member States that have introduced that exception are free to determine the limits in an unharmonised manner, which may vary from one Member State to another, would be incompatible with the objective of [the ISD]'). On fair balance, see ISD Recital 31; *Painer* v. *Standard Verlags*, n. 65 above, paras. 132–135; *Deckmyn*, paras. 26–32; Pila and Torremans, n. 79 above, pp. 338–359. For a systematic analysis of CJEU case law, see M. Favale, M. Kretschmer and P. Torremans, 'Is there an EU Copyright Jurisprudence? An Empirical Analysis of the Workings of the European Court of Justice' (2016) 79 *Modern Law Review* 31; H. Kalimo, T. Meyer and T. Mylly, 'Of Values and Legitimacy – Discourse Analytical Insights on the Copyright Case Law of the Court of Justice of the European Union' (2018) 81 *Modern Law Review* 282.

[89] It has been argued that CJEU case law, ISD Recital 32 and the wording of Art. 5 mean that Member States may not 'alter the scope of the exceptions and limitations that they have decided to transpose into their national regimes' unless expressly countenanced by Art. 5; and further that transposition must (generally) use the exact language of the ISD: E. Rosati, 'Copyright in the EU: In Search of (In)Flexibilities' (2014) 9 *Journal of Intellectual Property Law & Practice* 585, 592, 594. As noted above, it is now clear that Member States may not craft exceptions that extend beyond the reach of Art. 5: see the references in n. 82. But it would not seem that the European jurisprudence requires identity in wording between Art. 5 and the domestic exception. For instance, in *Funke Medien* and *Spiegel*, both n. 87 above, it was held in relation to Arts. 5(3)(c) and (d) that Member States have 'significant discretion' in the 'transposition of that provision and its application under national law', due to the open-textured nature of concepts like proportionality and fair practice: see paras. 43 and 28, respectively. See also *Pelham GmbH* v. *Hütter* (C-476/17) [2019] ECDR 3 (AG Opinion), para. AG 77, where Szpunar AG was of the view that Member States have latitude in the choice and

example, it might be argued that the fairness machinery in fair dealing reflects similar ideas and considerations to 'fair balance', although a more strident view might say that unless and until Brexit results in UK copyright law being severed from Europe, considerations from traditional fair dealing case law must be approached with caution or even abandoned.[90] Finally, the role and content of the three-step test language in Article 5(5) remains under-developed,[91] including whether it does any work additional to that performed by fair balance.[92]

In sum, whilst aspects of the drafting limitations provided by the ISD are clear – especially as regards the ousting of fair use – there remain questions about how far Member States may depart from the language of Article 5, and whether they may use homegrown infrastructure to implement European obligations. There are contradictions and ambiguities in the ISD and the CJEU case law, and perhaps the most that can be said is that further clarification may emerge as the CJEU jurisprudence continues to develop.

C   The Harmonisation of Exceptions

As noted above,[93] it was accepted for a long time that international treaties largely preserved the ability of member states to decide which exceptions they wished to enact and the structure and wording of those provisions. With shifts in understanding of the three-step test and the conclusion of more international and supranational instruments that give sustained attention to exceptions,[94] it must be asked whether treaties should set minimum

---

wording of exceptions, albeit that certain decisions might be limited, for instance because failing to introduce some exceptions may be incompatible with the Charter of Fundamental Rights of the European Union.

[90] See also J. Pila, 'Pluralism, Principles and Proportionality in Intellectual Property' (2014) 34 *Oxford Journal of Legal Studies* 182, 198–199 (noting the difference between fairness as applied in UK law and a European proportionality analysis).

[91] Statements from the CJEU have tended to be brief, and in the UK, almost all post-ISD fair dealing cases have proceeded without any consideration of Art. 5(5). Perhaps the longest treatment appears in *England and Wales Cricket Board Limited* v. *Tixdaq Limited* [2016] EWHC 575 (Ch), paras. 72, 88–92, per Arnold J.

[92] For instance, in *Deckmyn* v. *Vandersteen*, n. 88 above, no reference was made to Art. 5(5). In *Funke Medien* and *Spiegel*, both n. 87 above, Art. 5(5) and the need for fair balance were listed as separate restraints on the discretion of Member States (see paras. 52–53 and 37–38, respectively) but without any identification or explanation of the different considerations supplied by each.

[93] See n. 44 above and surrounding text.

[94] See, e.g., Marrakesh Treaty to Facilitate Access to Published Works for Persons Who Are Blind, Visually Impaired or Otherwise Print Disabled (adopted 27 June 2013); DSM Directive.

standards ('floors') in relation to exceptions, or whether their function should be more prescriptive and set 'ceilings' for what is permissible.

For instance, say our aim is to create a single integrated market, as per the European Union. If we take this seriously, we might form the view that: (1) Member States should not be able to craft their own bespoke exceptions but must adhere to a pre-approved list; and (2) these lists should be sufficiently prescriptive that domestic courts focus on factual determinations, lest judicial interpretations differ between different states. Taking these two imperatives together – i.e., that both the headline exception *and* its application are the same – then it would seem that either all exceptions must be drafted in such a way as to limit judicial discretion (i.e., as rules[95]) or that copyright cases are heard by a supranational body to ensure a uniform application.

Looking at the European Union, neither of these two things has happened. Article 5 is not drafted as a series of prescriptive commands whose application is known in advance; instead, its cases are written with greater and lesser degrees of generality. Whilst the CJEU operates as the highest court in relation to matters under the ISD, domestic courts are the key fora in which copyright claims are ventilated, and the final decision in cases referred to the CJEU for a preliminary ruling is made by the domestic court.[96] Significantly, the CJEU often interprets EU copyright law at high levels of generality, identifying broad interpretative principles to guide decision-making.[97] The current EU approach would therefore seem to cement the idea of domestic courts making legal and factual determinations, which may in turn lead to divergent approaches between Member States. This may change over time with the accrual of CJEU case law, although this will depend on how those cases are decided and the response of EU countries that do not subscribe to the ideas of precedent that characterise a common law system.

Does this mean that the use of general language is inevitable in any attempt to harmonise copyright exceptions? If considered purely through the lens of standards and rules, one might hypothesise that supranational and international instruments will have to make use of standard-like drafting unless there is a fundamental restructuring of the legal order. As will be seen in Chapter 2, it is difficult enough for domestic legislatures to draft copyright exceptions in rule-like ways, let alone for such a

---

[95] In the standards and rules sense of the term: see Chapter 2.
[96] Although the CJEU ruling may leave the domestic judge with no choice as to the outcome; for an example in the trade mark context that left the judge nonplussed, see *L'Oréal SA* v. *Bellure NV* [2010] EWCA Civ 535, especially paras. 7, 31 (Jacob LJ).
[97] For discussion, see Pila, n. 90 above (in relation to proportionality); Favale, Kretschmer and Torremans, n. 88 above (in relation to teleological reasoning).

task to be undertaken by negotiation teams in the context of states with diverse economies and cultural imperatives. One might therefore conclude that it is not surprising that many of the cases in Article 5 were written broadly, and that this, in turn, will reduce the likelihood of uniform application. That is, unless Article 5 strips from Member States all discretion about the legal content of exceptions through strict rule-like drafting, Member States may apply the same exception in different ways, even if they adopt the precise language of the ISD. The current approach under the ISD thus has some of the hallmarks of standards, with domestic judges considering European concepts (as guided by the CJEU jurisprudence) but also enjoying leeway in how they assess those concepts and apply them to particular facts.

It is open to question whether a regime with such latent flexibilities was intended. Writing in 2005, Burrell and Coleman argued that a paradox could be seen in the legislative history of the ISD: that the European Commission was not, for various reasons, motivated by a desire to protect user interests, but that Article 5 nevertheless had the potential to enable fairly generous copyright exceptions.[98] They suggested that this could be explained by inertia: that 'member states were keen to limit disruption to their existing arrangements'.[99] As discussed in Section III.B, whether Member States have in fact availed themselves of these flexibilities is an empirical question. This book will consider this question by reference to UK experiences, focusing in particular on leading cultural institutions.

IV Structure of this Book

The analysis in this book is presented in nine chapters (including this one) and can be divided into three broad parts. Part I is introductory, and describes the fair use panacea (Chapter 1), key insights from the literature on standards and rules (Chapter 2), the rationales and methodology for the empirical work (Chapter 3), and doctrinal matters in relation to copyright management and cultural institutions (also Chapter 3). It explains the relevance of this book to existing debates about the scope and drafting of exceptions, and provides context and an intellectual framework for its analysis of the law in action.

Part II focuses on institutional experiences in Australia, Canada, the United Kingdom and the United States in relation to free exceptions. This is not intended as a comprehensive survey or an up-to-the-minute

---

[98] Burrell and Coleman, n. 17 above, ch. 7.
[99] Ibid., p. 193. This has parallels with Article 9(2) of the Berne Convention.

account of practices. Rather, it is intended to highlight decision-making processes and their influences; how institutional thinking about copyright can change over time; and the degree to which practices are influenced by and consider the language of statutory provisions and interpretations in the case law. It starts by looking at sector-specific exceptions – many of which are written in rule-like form – and describes some instances where institutions have operationalised the detailed requirements of complex provisions, but others where practices have been driven by institutional ethics and other norms (Chapter 4). In the next three chapters it considers experiences in relation to general exceptions. It contrasts the positive reports around fair use in US law (Chapter 5) with the negative experiences in relation to section 200AB of the Australian Copyright Act (Chapter 6). With expansion to fair dealing also identified as a way to harness greater flexibilities,[100] this book considers experiences in relation to fair dealing, with particular focus on the reception given to *CCH* by Canadian cultural institutions (Chapter 7). Here it will be seen that in the five years following the decision, there were barely any changes to institutional practices. Considered alone, Chapters 6 and 7 might question whether it is possible to capture the benefits of fair use in any exception that does not adopt the language of section 107, and indeed raise a question mark over the ability of fair use to be transplanted elsewhere, and hence the fair use panacea.

But the story does not end there. Part III starts by describing three developments that might support greater utilisation of standard-like copyright exceptions, at least as suggested by the experiences of leading cultural institutions. These are: (1) the emergence of fair dealing as a meaningful part of the copyright management strategies of academic libraries in Canada; (2) the growing comfort of cultural institutions with risk, as seen in particular in fieldwork at Australian and UK institutions; and (3) the potential for new fair dealing purposes to effect a significant expansion to the ground covered by those provisions (Chapter 8). In Chapter 9 this book draws from its analysis of the law in action to ask what this means for the drafting of copyright exceptions. With observations about the changing nature of institutional norms and practices, an important question for the chapter is whether the introduction of new or enlarged standards should only occur when there is evidence that stakeholders *already* have the knowledge and practical infrastructure to embrace these provisions, or whether reform might operate as a signal to encourage the development of new processes. This book observes that

---

[100] For instance, this was the secondary recommendation of the ALRC, *Final Report*, n. 46 above, ch. 6; discussed in Handler and Hudson, n. 18 above.

an argument can be made in favour of fair use to future-proof the copyright statute, and in doing so recognises the signalling effect that fair use might provide. However, the book does not go so far as to say that this argument has universal applicability, as it recognises that different countries have different understandings of copyright (including greater acceptance of remunerated exceptions and extended collective licensing), and that even where a different normative understanding exists or were to emerge, a fair use provision may not be the best tool to effect that vision (compared with, say, expanded fair dealing). Finally, even though this book discusses the efficiencies of standards, it also describes areas of cultural institution practice that are well suited to complex rules.

In short, this book illustrates an important lesson from the standards and rules literature: that no particular form of drafting is inevitably superior. Instead, the way we draft copyright exception depends on a range of normative and practical considerations, many of which require a thorough understanding of not just the law in books but the law in action.

2   Standards and Rules

I   Introduction

As seen in Chapter 1, discussion of the drafting options for copyright exceptions is often framed around the respective merits of general and specific provisions. This, in turn, is often presented as a choice between flexibility and certainty. One of main propositions in this book is that this approach, whilst containing some truths, is ultimately counterfactual and oversimplified. It is counterfactual because many claims about how exceptions 'work' are based on analysis that lacks systematic study of how stakeholders understand and apply the law, instead being drawn exclusively from the law in books.[1] It is oversimplified because classification of a provision as general or specific is often undertaken with inadequate information and with certain characteristics simply asserted: flexibility, rigidity, certainty and so forth. As presented, it can seem that these characteristics are inevitable, invariable and mutually exclusive.

Whilst this book aims to address both of these issues, this chapter focuses primarily on the second concern – oversimplified thinking – through insights drawn from the literature on legal rulemaking.[2] This

---

[1] This approach is further weakened if judicial consideration of a provision has been sporadic, or if commentators focus on a subset of opinions. One example of the former is fair dealing in Australia, where most homegrown lessons come from two Federal Court cases: *De Garis* v. *Neville Jeffress Pidler* (1990) 18 IPR 292 and *TCN Channel Nine Pty Ltd* v. *Network Ten Pty Ltd* [2001] FCA 108; [2002] FCAFC 146. For concerns about cherry-picking, see B. Beebe, 'An Empirical Study of U.S. Copyright Fair Use Options, 1978–2005' (2008) 156 *University of Pennsylvania Law Review* 549, 553: 'like the "great men" approach to history, we pursue a "leading cases" ... approach to fair use. This anecdotal method, one essentially of connoisseurship, derives conventional wisdom about our case law from a limited aristocracy of hand-picked opinions appearing primarily in the U.S. Reports – or in the student casebooks. Whether these opinions have any influence on or are representative of the true state of our fair use doctrine as it is practiced in the courts remains an open, and strangely unasked, question.'

[2] For which two of the most prominent contributions are I. Ehrlich and R. Posner, 'An Economic Analysis of Legal Rulemaking' (1974) 3 *The Journal of Legal Studies* 257 and L. Kaplow, 'Rules versus Standards: An Economic Analysis' (1992) 42 *Duke Law Journal* 557.

scholarship compares the relative efficiencies of drafting legal commands in open-ended general terms (standards) and closed-ended detailed terms (rules).[3] Standards and rules analysis can trace its intellectual origins to the legal realist movement in the United States,[4] but in its modern guise has been strongly shaped by mainstream law and economics. This has inspired a sizeable body of literature, much of which has a broader intellectual foundation and has made significant additions to the insights offered by the Chicago school of economics and its legal offshoots.[5] Although concepts from the standards and rules literature would seem to be extremely relevant to any discussion of copyright law reform,[6] it has only been in relatively recent times that these concepts have appeared in any meaningful way in the analysis of exceptions.[7] Rather,

---

[3] As discussed in Section II of this chapter, there are further nuances in the definitions of each of these terms, and in the process of classifying a legal directive as a standard or rule.

[4] Identifying a single originating source for an intellectual movement is almost always artificial, but if one had to choose a single point of origin for standards and rules analysis, then the legal realists would seem to have a good claim: see, e.g., R. Pound, 'Hierarchy of Sources and Forms in Different Systems of Law' (1933) 7 *Tulane Law Review* 475; J. Dewey, *Theory of the Moral Life* (1932) (New York: Irvington Publishers, 1996), pp. 136–138. Describing Pound as a legal realist is somewhat controversial given his subsequent public break with the mainstream of the movement, but it is a label that suffices for present purposes. For discussion of the relationship between Pound's 'sociological jurisprudence' and other strands of legal realism, together with a description of his later disagreements with Karl Llewelyn and Jerome Frank, see N. Duxbury, *Patterns of American Jurisprudence* (Oxford: Clarendon Press, 1997), pp. 54–62.

[5] E.g., R. Korobkin, 'Behavioral Analysis and Legal Form: Rules vs. Standards Revisited' (2000) 79 *Oregon Law Review* 23 (using behavioural analysis to challenge some of the assumptions in standards and rules analysis that are based on rational choice theory); E. Posner, 'Standards, Rules, and Social Norms' (1997) 21 *Harvard Journal of Law and Public Policy* 101 (considering how factors such as signalling effects can also impact on the operation of the law. There are also those who approach legal drafting questions from other perspectives, for instance by reference to arguments regarding democratic principles: for a summary, see K. Sullivan, 'The Justices of Rules and Standards' (1992) 106 *Harvard Law Review* 22, 64–66.

[6] E.g., S. Ricketson, 'Simplifying Copyright Law: Proposals from Down Under' (1999) 21 *European Intellectual Property Review* 537, 541 ('[a]t one extreme, specific exceptions can be formulated on a case-by-case basis, through the application of broad general principles' and '[a]t the other extreme are detailed legislative solutions that embody clear and specific guidelines to deal with situations in advance').

[7] See, e.g., M. Sag, 'God in the Machine: A New Structural Analysis of Copyright's Fair Use Doctrine' (2005) 11 *Michigan Telecommunications and Technology Law Review* 381; E. Hudson, 'Implementing Fair Use in Copyright Law: Lessons from Australia' (2013) 25 *Intellectual Property Journal* 201; N. Elkin-Koren and O. Fischman-Afori, 'Rulifying Fair Use' (2017) 59 *Arizona Law Review* 161; J. Hughes, 'Fair Use and Its Politics – At Home and Abroad' in R. Okediji, *Copyright Law in an Age of Limitations and Exceptions* (New York: Cambridge University Press, 2017). Other copyright-related work to refer to standards and rules analysis includes D. Lindsay, 'Fair Use and Other Copyright Exceptions: Overview of Issues' (2005) 23 *Copyright Reporter* 4; Y. Tamura, 'Rethinking

the debate has tended to be evocative of aspects of the standards and rules literature but without its depth, at times relying on well-worn tropes that 'fair use is flexible but unpredictable' and 'detailed provisions provide certainty but are rigid'.

These issues can be illustrated by two examples from Australia. In 1996, the Copyright Law Review Committee (CLRC) was charged with considering 'how to simplify the *Copyright Act 1968* to make it able to be understood by people needing to understand their rights and obligations under the Act'.[8] This would seem to demand empirical and doctrinal analysis, as well consideration of what is meant by 'simplification' and how it would enhance user understanding.[9] In its 1998 report, the CLRC recommended the amendment and repeal of some existing exceptions, and the transformation of fair dealing into an open-ended provision. Significantly, the arguments presented by the CLRC in favour of reform – for instance, to introduce greater technological neutrality in the operation of exceptions and make them more responsive to change[10] – largely overlooked these foundational matters around the process and effects of simplification. The assumptions underlying the CLRC's analysis seemed to be that: (1) the operation of existing exceptions could be gleaned primarily from the statute book; (2) the proposed reforms would effect some rationalisation that would make exceptions easier to understand, leading to reformed stakeholder practices; and (3) a new open-ended fair dealing exception would be a simplification, despite its operation being tied to judge-made law. Whilst there was undoubtedly something in the argument that the existing exceptions were verbose and contained unprincipled limitations, it does not follow that all acts to consolidate

---

Copyright Institution for the Digital Age' (2009) 1 *WIPO Journal* 63, 70; D. Gervais, 'Fair Use, Fair Dealing, Fair Principles: Efforts to Conceptualize Exceptions and Limitations to Copyright' (2010) 57 *Journal of the Copyright Society of the USA* 499; G. Austin, 'Four Questions About the Australian Approach to Fair Dealing Defenses to Copyright Infringement' (2010) 57 *Journal of the Copyright Society of the USA* 611. Although not using the language of standards and rules, the analysis of vagueness in copyright law by Spence and Endicott tracks many of the themes in the standards and rules literature: M. Spence and T. Endicott, 'Vagueness in the Scope of Copyright' (2005) 121 *Law Quarterly Review* 657. Similarly, standards and rules thinking underpins arguments in D. Fagundes, 'Crystals in the Public Domain' (2009) 50 *Boston College Law Review* 139.

[8] Copyright Law Review Committee (CLRC), *Simplification of the Copyright Act 1968: Part 1 Exceptions to the Exclusive Rights of Copyright Owners* (September 1998), para. 1.03.

[9] As noted by Ricketson, n. 6 above, 537, the words 'simple' and 'simplify' 'have a number of dictionary meanings, most of which are hardly appropriate in the present context [i.e., copyright law reform]', e.g., 'unsophisticated', 'frank or artless' and 'ignorant'.

[10] CLRC, n. 8 above, especially paras. 6.01–6.09, 6.12–6.44.

and shorten the statutory text would improve user understanding, especially as regards open-ended fair dealing.[11]

In contrast, in its 2013 report recommending the introduction of fair use into the Copyright Act, the Australian Law Reform Commission (ALRC) showed greater engagement with stakeholder practices and understandings, and indeed referred to standard and rules in presenting its case for fair use.[12] The ALRC's description of the latter was mostly general statements of principle, for instance that standards and rules are points on a spectrum,[13] and that 'a clear principled standard is more certain than an unclear complex rule'.[14] Nevertheless, this use of standards and rules went some way to help explain the possibly contradictory propositions that fair use is 'flexible and technology-neutral' but also 'sufficiently certain and predictable.[15]

This chapter is structured as follows. Section II defines standards and rules, starting with a basic definition that focuses on the language of the relevant legal command, followed by further ideas that add nuance to the classification process. Section III discusses the relative efficiencies of each form of drafting, that is, when standard-like regulation is preferable to rule-like regulation and vice versa. Finally, Section IV synthesises this material to illustrate how standards and rules analysis provides a framework to assess the drafting of copyright exceptions.

II   Definitions

A   *Degree of Precision*

A starting point for differentiating standards and rules is by reference to the level of prescriptiveness – or flexibility – that inheres in a particular legal command. We can therefore say that rules give judges *less* discretion

---

[11] See also, Ricketson, n. 6 above, pointing at 540 to the 'significant substantive changes' imbued within the CLRC's proposals. Thus, although '[p]resented under the guise of simplification, the CLRC's approach is considerably more than just this': at 541. Nevertheless, Ricketson concluded at 549 that these changes would 'bring the existing multiplicity of exceptions into a coherent and orderly relationship' and 'will certainly simplify the existing law'.

[12] This author made two submissions to the review: R. Burrell, M. Handler, E. Hudson and K. Weatherall, 'ALRC Inquiry into Copyright and the Digital Economy: Submission in Response to Issues Paper No. 42' (14 December 2012) and R. Burrell, M. Handler, E. Hudson and K. Weatherall, 'ALRC Inquiry into Copyright and the Digital Economy: Submission in Response to Discussion Paper No. 79 (DP 79)' (31 July 2013).

[13] Australian Law Reform Commission, *Copyright and the Digital Economy: Final Report*, Report No. 122 (November 2013), para. 4.55.

[14] Ibid., para. 4.117.   [15] Ibid., paras. 3.126–3.130, 4.3–4.6, 4.39–4.64, 4.117–4.130.

to craft the response of the law to given facts, whilst standards permit *greater* context-dependent decision-making. This approach has long underpinned analysis of standards and rules. For instance, Roscoe Pound wrote in 1933 that rules are 'precepts attaching a definite detailed legal consequence to a definite, detailed state of facts',[16] whilst standards are 'general limits' in which 'no definite, detailed state of facts is provided for. No definite pattern is laid down.'[17] Similarly, Thomas Cowan observed in 1958 that a rule 'designates with some particularity the class of issues it proposes to deal with and purports to dispose of them in a forthright, uniform, if not mechanical, way'.[18] This was contrasted with the generalised guidance offered by standards, which Cowan described as 'resolving conflict among rules as well as critiques for changing rules or for refusing to apply them'.[19] Finally, in their seminal work on legal rulemaking in 1974, Isaac Ehrlich and Richard Posner defined a standard as 'a general criterion of social choice' that 'indicates the kinds of circumstances that are relevant to a decision on legality and is thus open-ended' and a rule as 'withdraw[ing] from the decision maker's consideration one or more of the circumstances that would be relevant to [the] decision according to a standard'.[20] They observed that '[t]he difference between a rule and a standard is a matter of degree – the degree of precision'.[21]

The difference between standards and rules is often illustrated by reference to speeding offences.[22] Such offences are commonly drafted as rules, for example that it is unlawful to drive above 40 miles per hour. Applying the definitions set out above, the judge in such a case has one factual matter to determine: how fast the motorist was travelling. Other factors that might conceivably be relevant to whether this speed was unsafe are withdrawn from consideration. In contrast, a standard might provide that it is unlawful for a person to drive at an excessive speed. Such a test would give the judge the overall criterion for adjudication (excessiveness) but leave it to them to determine what factors are relevant and how they will be weighed. Under this approach, the judge might also consider, say, the time of day, the weather conditions, the presence of other traffic and so on.

---

[16] Pound, n. 4 above, 482.   [17] Ibid., 485.
[18] T. Cowan, 'Rule or Standard in Tort Law' (1955) 13 *Rutgers Law Review* 141, 141.
[19] Ibid.   [20] Ehrlich and Posner, n. 2 above, 258.   [21] Ibid.
[22] E.g., Ehrlich and Posner, ibid., 257; Kaplow, n. 2 above, 560; J. Goebel, 'Rules and Standards: A Critique of Two Critical Theorists' (1992) 31 *Duquesne Law Review* 51, 55; Korobkin, n. 5 above, 23; Fagundes, n. 7 above, 145; Elkin-Cohen and Fischman-Afort, n. 7 above, 167; Hughes, n. 7 above, p. 238.

Michael Spence and Timothy Endicott, writing in relation to vagueness in copyright law, refer to two inter-related benefits of legal commands exhibiting precision.[23] The first is what they term 'guidance value', i.e., that precise laws give better *ex ante* information about the parameters of lawful conduct. The second, 'process value', posits that lawyers can advise with greater clarity and confidence under a precise law, and that judicial rulings are less likely to exhibit arbitrariness. Spence and Endicott also note that whilst precision carries benefits, there are circumstances where 'vagueness in the law is either inevitable or desirable'.[24] They centre on four ideas, which will be elaborated upon throughout this chapter: first, that precision can also be arbitrary due to over- and under-inclusiveness; second, that precision is not always possible, especially for 'widely varying conduct'; third, that there may be reasons to prefer judicial rather than legislative decision-making; and fourth, that vagueness can facilitate useful private ordering.[25]

The use of standards and rules analysis has been criticised by Pierre Schlag.[26] His central thesis is that debates about the form of legal regulation tend to rehearse similar themes,[27] being observations that are frequently 'nothing more than the unilluminating invocation of "canned" pro and con arguments'.[28] Thus 'the choice between adopting a rule or a standard is [often presented as] a choice between competing virtues and vices that we typically associate' with each style of regulation, i.e., that rules exhibit the virtues of certainty, stability and security but also the vices of intransigency, rigidity and closure, whilst standards are characterised by flexibility, open-endedness and dynamism but also manipulability, indeterminacy and adventurism.[29]

Schlag challenges the usefulness of this 'dialectic' for a number of reasons,[30] including its disregard of context: that 'no rule or standard (or any other piece of text) can control or determine the context within and from which it is interpreted'.[31] That is, determination of whether a rule exhibits certainty or whether a standard is desirable depends on our assumptions and other framing matters. Schlag gives the example of the reasonable person in tort law, and whether this standard could be

---

[23] Spence and Endicott, n. 7 above, 660–661.   [24] Ibid., 661.   [25] Ibid., 661–665.
[26] P. Schlag, 'Rules and Standards' (1985) 33 *UCLA Law Review* 379. For other critiques, see the references cited by Korobkin, n. 5 above, FN4.
[27] Schlag's working definitions are set out ibid. at 381–383: if we view any given legal directive as having two parts, namely a trigger (some phenomenon) and a response (the legal consequences), then a paradigm rule has a 'hard empirical trigger' and a 'hard determinate response', whilst a paradigm standard has a 'soft evaluative trigger' and a 'soft [guided] response'.
[28] Ibid., 380. Key propositions are summarised at 384–389.   [29] Ibid., 400.
[30] Ibid., 383.   [31] Ibid., 405.

replaced with a rule. Scholars often point to negligence concepts as illustrating the suitability, and at times inevitability, of standard-like legal commands. As noted by Spence and Endicott, for example, '[n]o precise standard of care could generally prescribe the degree of care that is to be taken, both because of the variety of ways in which lack of care can cause risks to others, and because of the variety of interests that would be damaged by requiring excessive care'.[32] Schlag states that this sort of reasoning

> seems true enough. But notice what has happened here: The reason we can say that a rule cannot adequately substitute ... is that we have left the context unchanged. The context remains 'the multitude of varied situations' in which the reasonable person standard applies. If we redescribed the context by breaking it down into component parts, for instance, automobile accidents, professional services, recreational activities, and so on, the possibility of establishing a regime of rules seems more plausible.[33]

The importance of context is also seen in Schlag's analysis of judicial techniques to avoid the application of rules and standards, such as 'factual distortion' (findings that oust the rule from the case at hand), the creation of sub-rules, rejection of a rule due to the 'grander purposive scheme', and insubordination.[34] He argues that these techniques have a dual character, being used 'not only to *subvert*, but to *preserve* the meaning of rules and standards', i.e., they 'are just as much incidents of legitimate interpretation as they are vehicles of misinterpretation'.[35] For example, the four techniques listed above each have a positive iteration: factual characterisation, elaboration of a rule through sub-rules, justification of an approach by appeal to the grander scheme, and judicial initiative.[36]

Schlag's critiques are significant and demonstrate the importance of framing questions and other contextual matters. In addition, his analysis casts doubt on any analysis that suggests that our drafting choice is between flexibility and certainty, with this division inhering in the statutory text. However, Schlag takes this further, arguing that 'our *dissatisfaction* with both rule-oriented and standard-oriented approaches is reflected in the tendency of rules to evolve or degenerate, depending upon our perspective, into standards, and standards to evolve or degenerate into rules'.[37] Whether this is a general phenomenon is open to question, but where it occurs may rest not on dissatisfaction but a natural

---

[32] Spence and Endicott, n. 7 above, 663; for similar remarks, see Kaplow, n. 2 above, 564.
[33] Schlag, n. 26 above, 415.   [34] Ibid., 416–417.
[35] Ibid., 417. Emphasis in the original.   [36] Ibid., 418.
[37] Ibid., 428–429. Emphasis supplied.

Definitions

evolution that is predicted in the standards and rules literature.[38] For instance, Carol Rose argues in the property law context that 'crystals' (rules) and 'mud' (standards) are a 'matched pair', reflecting different aspects of the bargaining process of individuals in long-term communities or relationships.[39] Her thesis is that 'the rhetoric of crystals focuses on the sense of predictability and security present in longterm dealings, while the rhetoric of mud focuses on the flexibility and willingness to make adjustments that longterm dealings normally offer'.[40] People in ongoing relationships need both 'upstream security' and 'downstream readjustment'.[41] In her view, crystals and mud – or rules and standards – are significant rhetorically because they reflect different ways of mediating relationships.

B Timing of Decision

Whilst one definition of standards and rules focuses on specificity in drafting, another says that the difference is better understood as the time at which the content of the law is developed. This approach underpinned Louis Kaplow's influential article on standards and rules, where it was argued that 'the only distinction between rules and standards is the extent to which efforts to give content to the law are undertaken before or after individuals act'.[42] Thus, when such content is determined *ex ante* – before the relevant conduct or circumstances occur – the regulation is a rule. When these determinations are made *ex post*, it is a standard. To return to the speeding example, a law making it an offence to drive above 40 miles per hour is a rule because one knows, in advance, the legal response if a motorist exceeds the speed limit.[43] A legal command that instead penalised 'excessive' speed would require the court to

---

[38] Indeed, there are those who support 'rulification' to help give greater content and predictability to standards like fair use: e.g., Elkin-Koren and Fischman-Afori, n. 7 above.

[39] C. Rose, 'Crystals and Mud in Property Law' (1988) 40 *Stanford Law Review* 577.

[40] Ibid., 605.   [41] Ibid., 609.

[42] Kaplow, n. 2 above, 560; see also Korobkin, n. 5 above, 25; Posner, n. 5 above, 101; Rose, n. 39 above, 603.

[43] This assumes that judges apply the law as set out in the statute book. One way in which such a rule might take on characteristics of a standard is through decision-makers or the police exercising discretion in enforcement, for instance in response to *de minimis* or normatively justifiable infractions. As noted by Sunstein, one problem with rules is to drive discretion underground as 'people in a position of authority may simply ignore them': C. Sunstein, 'Problems with Rules' (1995) 83 *California Law Review* 953, 994–995. Sunstein notes that some degree of discretion to revise rules may be desirable, for instance to help prevent unjust applications or to reflect changes in public sentiment: at 1008–1012.

determine factual matters *and* the legal question of whether a penalty should be applied, and would therefore be a standard. Whilst one could make predictions about the likely result, the legal consequences would only be known for sure following a judicial determination.

It has been said by Ehrlich and Posner that the choice between standards and rules is 'implicitly also a choice between legislative and judicial rulemaking'.[44] This statement reflects two important ideas that underpin any appraisal of the respective merits of standards and rules. First, as Ehrlich and Posner recognise, '[a] general legislative standard creates a demand for specification'.[45] That is, the question is not whether specificity is desirable but how it is achieved: is it more efficient for the legislature to write a series of rules that define legal consequences *ex ante* or is it preferable for those consequences to be determined by the courts *ex post*? Second, the accumulation of precedent, particularly from higher appellate courts, can lead to the emergence of a substratum of judge-made rules beneath standards.[46] This has ramifications for the accuracy of tropes regarding the uncertainty of standards: whilst standards require a judicial decision for a definitive statement of the legal response to particular facts, precedent can make those consequences more predictable than some analysis might suggest.

C Further Nuance: Gradations, Complexity and Clarity

Section II.B focused on the core differences between standards and rules, illustrated by reference to the regulation of speeding. This analysis was necessarily simplified to highlight the central features of this model. This sub-section builds on the foregoing by considering three further matters that provide greater nuance to standards and rules analysis: gradations, complexity and clarity.

First, whilst the speeding example describes a clear division between standards and rules, it is more accurate to imagine a spectrum in which decision-makers have increasing and decreasing capacity to determine the application of the law.[47] This can be illustrated by statutory exceptions to copyright infringement. For example, whilst fair use and fair dealing might be described as general exceptions, the latter contains

---

[44] Ehrlich and Posner, n. 2 above, 261.   [45] Ibid.
[46] See, e.g., Kaplow, n. 2 above, 577–579, 583–584, 611–614; Korobkin, n. 5 above, 29. The concept of precedent reflects a common law tradition, and it may be that aspects of standards and rules analysis operate differently in civil law systems.
[47] See, e.g., Ehrlich and Posner, n. 2 above, 258; Sullivan, n. 5 above, 58, FN231; Korobkin, n. 5 above, 26–28.

Definitions 37

purpose-based and other limitations – e.g., for a sufficient acknowledgement,[48] or that criticism or review relate to 'that or another work'[49] – that make them seem less standard-like than fair use.[50] Indeed, fair use would be a purer standard if it did not include indicative purposes and fairness factors, retaining only the central kernel that a 'fair' use is non-infringing.[51] At the other end of the spectrum, whilst sector-specific exceptions for cultural institutions often have the appearance of rules, some provisions contain language that would seem to be less prescriptive and have standard-like potential, such as the administrative purposes exception in Australian law.[52]

Second, rules and standards can be simple or complex, in other words, involve few or many considerations.[53] Thus, a pure rule may contain a single criterion whilst a complex one may have multiple components or be subject to exceptions.[54] Similarly, a standard may have a single overarching benchmark or be complex and set out a multi-factor balancing test. Complexity must be considered in addition to the form of a legal command. For instance, if we are of the view that a complex standard is superior to a simple standard, we must ask whether this is due to the former's complexity, *ex post* operation, or both.[55] Depending on the answer to these questions, it may be that a complex rule would be even better.[56] This illustrates a crucial point: because the operations of, say, a simple and complex rule are different, the merits and disadvantages of such rules are also different. This distinction can easily become

---

[48] Required in, e.g., CDPA ss. 30(1), (1ZA) and (2), and Australian Copyright Act ss. 41, 42(1)(a), 103A, 103B(1)(a).
[49] See, e.g., CDPA s. 30(1); Australian Copyright Act ss. 41, 103A.
[50] For instance, Lindsay states that as between fair use and fair dealing, the latter is more like a rule: Lindsay, n. 7 above, 8.
[51] See, e.g., Korobkin, n. 5 above, 27–28, distinguishing between 'pure standards' (e.g., the 'reasonable person') and 'less pure' multifactor balancing tests, which set out *ex ante* 'what facts are relevant to the legal determination'. For similar analysis, see Sunstein, n. 43 above, 963–965 (in relation to 'standards' and 'factors').
[52] For many years Australian Copyright Act s. 51A(2); following the Copyright Amendment (Disability Access and Other Measures) Act 2017 (Cth), now Australian Copyright Act s. 113K (applying to uses 'for purposes directly related to the care or control of the collection comprising the library or archives'). This provision contains many of the features of a rule as there are numerous acts that are unambiguously within its ambit. However, its language is sufficiently open that it could cover new ideas and practices.
[53] See, e.g., Kaplow, n. 2 above, 565–566, 586–596; Korobkin, n. 5 above, 25–30; L. Kaplow, 'A Model of the Optimal Complexity of Legal Rules' (1995) 11 *Journal of Law, Economics & Organization* 150.
[54] To return to the traffic example, a complex rule may use a multifactorial analysis to calculate the motorist's maximum permissible speed: Kaplow, n. 2 above, 565.
[55] Ibid., 566, noting some of the benefits of complexity in its own right.
[56] Ibid., 566–567, 589–590.

lost in discussions about legislative drafting. Consider the proposition that rules have a tendency to be over- and under-inclusive.[57] One reason for this concern is that rules, being set in advance, permit less fact-responsive decision-making than standards.[58] However, that may be to implicitly compare a complex standard with a simple rule.[59] A complex rule may contain many sub-parts, thus permitting quite fine-textured analysis.

Finally, one must consider the clarity of the language of a legal command, and the degree to which it facilitates *ex ante* decision-making. Thus, the inclusion in a rule of words that are ambiguous or do not reflect terms of art can reduce predictive value.[60] Similarly, a rule may contain language whose conceptual meaning is clear but whose application generates evidentiary challenges. For instance, the Australian Copyright Act allows libraries and archives to undertake certain acts with unpublished (but copyright-protected) works so long as fifty years has transpired since the year in which the author died.[61] Reliance on this rule therefore requires information about the identity and fate of the author of the work – information that might be difficult or impossible to obtain.[62] As noted by Ehrlich and Posner, 'the *concept* of legal precision is unambiguous – the fewer and simpler the facts to which definite legal consequences attach, the more precise is a legal obligation'.[63] But if these facts are hard to determine, a rule that looks precise may be impossible to apply with any confidence.

D   Empirical Matters

So far, the analysis in this section has focused on classification as a textual project, i.e., one focused on the statutory language. This is a logical first step, providing a series of hunches and hypotheses that can be the subject of further investigation. In the copyright context, for example, we might surmise that based on their drafting: (1) fair use is a standard, with its open-ended structure, utilisation of fairness factors and list of indicative purposes;[64] (2) fair dealing has standard-like qualities but is more limited that fair use, suggesting it is further down the spectrum towards rules;[65]

---

[57] See, e.g., Spence and Endicott, n. 7 above, 661.   [58] Kaplow, n. 2 above, 588–589.
[59] Ibid., 565, 593–596.   [60] See, e.g., Sunstein, n. 43 above, 984.
[61] Australian Copyright Act s. 51. This was modeled after the UK Copyright Act 1956, s. 7(6).
[62] See also S. Sterk, 'Property Rules, Liability Rules, and Uncertainty About Property Rights' (2008) 106 *Michigan Law Review* 1285.
[63] Ehrlich and Posner, n. 2 above, 261 (emphasis in original).
[64] See, e.g., Hughes, n. 7 above, p. 237.   [65] See, e.g., Lindsay, n. 7 above, 7–9.

Definitions

and (3) sector-specific exceptions for cultural institutions, many of which are highly particularised and delineate permitted conduct in detail, are often rules.[66]

In thinking about whether these classifications are accurate, it is important to remember that statutory provisions are not imbued with indelible meaning but are, like other texts, interpreted and operationalised by human beings. This raises questions about real-world interpretative processes: how people read and understand the law, and whether these processes differ between different actors. For instance, legal commands have two direct audiences: those whose behaviour is regulated by the law, and those who are involved in a professional capacity with advice and enforcement (e.g., judges and lawyers).[67] For those in the latter category, their formal legal training may have left them well versed in principles of statutory interpretation, the common law method and so forth. Obviously, there remains the question of whether a textual analysis will capture all the considerations that are, in practice, applied by such individuals. In contrast, those in the former category may include non-legal actors who have no technical legal training and whose day-to-day legal analysis is comprised mostly of best guesses and rules of thumb. Whether such individuals engage with the law in the same way as a legal professional is very much open to question.

These matters are recognised in the standards and rules literature, which notes that analysis of interpretative practices is essential to accurately understand and classify legal regulation. For instance, Cass Sunstein has written that classification

> cannot be decided in the abstract. Everything depends on the understandings and practices of the people who interpret the provision. Interpretative practices can convert an apparently rule-like provision into something very unrule-like. … The content and nature of a legal provision cannot be read off the provision. It is necessary to see what people take it to be.[68]

A similar point is implicit in Kaplow's reminder that the key question for classification is when 'information processing and acquisition' takes place.[69] He gives the example of a law prohibiting 'vulgar behaviour'. If the meaning of 'vulgar behaviour' is already well accepted, then such a

---

[66] See also Ricketson, n. 6 above, 541 (arguing that the Australian Copyright Act 'embodies *par excellence*' an approach to legislative drafting in which specific responses are set out in advance: the Act 'contains numerous detailed free use exceptions and compulsory licences directed to specific works, specific rights and specific technologies').
[67] Ehrlich and Posner, n. 2 above, 261.   [68] Sunstein, n. 43 above, 959–960.
[69] Kaplow, n. 2 above, 601.

law is more rule-like; if adjudicators must determine what is meant by the term, then it will be more like a standard. But such a conclusion rests on knowledge of the prevailing conditions, i.e., the law in action. This would seem to demand empirical analysis.

There are a number of forms such analysis can take. A more doctrinally oriented assessment might comprise a systematic analysis of judicial interpretations. For instance, rules can be less predictable and more standard-like if they contain numerous exceptions that are not applied in a coherent fashion by judges.[70] Similarly, a law that, on a plain reading, looks like is a complex standard may instead operate as a simple standard if judges invariably focus on only one or two elements.[71] Returning to copyright exceptions, a number of US scholars have analysed fair use case law and sought to challenge the notion that the doctrine is characterised by randomness and uncertainty.[72] For instance, Barton Beebe's empirical analysis reveals trends in how the four fairness factors are understood by judges and how outcomes for each factor impact on the success of a fair use defence;[73] Matthew Sag has used empirical techniques to analyse fair use case law, describing 'the uncertainty critique' as 'overblown';[74] and Pamela Samuelson has analysed fair use case law by reference to policy clusters, stating that such an approach 'will make fair use more rule-like without a concomitant loss in its utility as a flexible standard for balancing a wide range of interests in a wide variety of situations'.[75]

A further iteration of empirical analysis – albeit one that has been less common in the copyright literature – studies the interpretations of those subject to the law.[76] These interpretations are sometimes formalised in

---

[70] Korobkin, n. 5 above, 26–27.   [71] Kaplow, n. 2 above, 565–566.
[72] For examples of scholarship that emphasises the uncertainty said to surround fair use, see, e.g., W. Fisher III, 'Reconstructing the Fair Use Doctrine' (1988) 101 *Harvard Law Review* 1659; D. Nimmer, '"Fairest of Them All" and Other Fairy Tales of Fair Use' (2003) 66 *Law and Contemporary Problems* 263; M. Madison, 'Rewriting Fair Use and the Future of Copyright Reform' (2005) 23 *Cardozo Arts & Entertainment Law Journal* 391; Fagundes, n. 7 above, 151–153.
[73] Beebe, n. 1 above.
[74] M. Sag, 'Predicting Fair Use' (2012) 73 *Ohio State Law Journal* 47, 49 (pointing to 'consistent patterns that can assist individuals, businesses, and lawyers in assessing the merits of particular claims to fair use protection').
[75] P. Samuelson, 'Unbundling Fair Uses' (2009) 77 *Fordham Law Review* 2537, 2621. This use of policy clusters might be seen as an example of rule-like activity beneath a standard, as described by Schlag, n. 26 above, 396 (using the example of rules regarding freedom of speech).
[76] For some examples, see, e.g., K. Crews, *Copyright, Fair Use, and the Challenge for Universities: Promoting the Progress of Higher Education* (Chicago: University of Chicago Press, 1993); A. Kenyon and R. Wright, 'Whose Conflict? Copyright, Creators and

Definitions

industry guidelines, codes of best practice and internal policies,[77] whilst at other times exist as unwritten norms within a creative sector or a particular community. At times, such practices reflect the internalisation of ideas that are very different from those underpinning the relevant legal regulation, whether through a rejection of the law or apathy as to its content. They can reveal that a provision whose text suggests it is a standard in fact operates like a rule, and vice versa.[78]

To illustrate from the fieldwork in this book, consider the rule-like preservation copying exceptions for libraries and archives in Australia and the United States.[79] These provisions have contained various restrictions over the years, including, in some instances, a three-copy limit on the number of reproductions that may be made.[80] On the face of these provisions, once an institution makes a fourth copy it must turn to another exception or to licensing. And yet in interviews with staff at Australian and US institutions, it was reported that this restriction was ignored routinely, without a second thought. It seems that institution staff, having internalised norms about good preservation and archival practices, recognise that such practices – especially when performed with digital technologies – often require the production of more than three copies. They therefore seem to read the language of 'three copies' as a proxy for 'a reasonable number of copies'. Removal of the three-copy limitation in these provisions (as has happened in Australia) would simply be to bring the law up to date with existing practices.[81]

Cultural Institutions' (2010) 33 *UNSW Law Journal* 286; M. Iljadica, *Copyright Beyond Law: Regulating Creativity in the Graffiti Subculture* (Oxford: Hart, 2016).

[77] See, e.g., Ehrlich and Posner, n. 2 above, 261 (observing that the 'demand for specificity' can sometimes be met by rules developed by potential defendants, especially although not exclusively where legal regulation is drafted as a standard).

[78] See, e.g., the standard-like prohibition on 'systematic' reproduction in s. 108(g) of the US Copyright Act, which has been interpreted in rule-like ways in guidelines prepared by CONTU: National Commission on New Technological Uses of Copyrighted Works, *Final Report of the National Commission on New Technological Uses of Copyrighted Works, July 31, 1978* (Library of Congress, 1979).

[79] See Chapter 4, Section III.B.

[80] Australian Copyright Act ss. 51B, 111BA, 112AA (key cultural institutions); US Copyright Act s. 108(b) (libraries and archives). The Australian provisions were replaced with new provisions by the Copyright Amendment (Disability Access and Other Measures) Act 2017 (Cth). Under new s. 113M(1), the three-copy limitation has been removed.

[81] This move has also been suggested for the United States: see Section 108 Study Group, *The Section 108 Study Group Report: An Independent Report Sponsored by the United States Copyright Office and the National Digital Information Infrastructure and Preservation Program of the Library of Congress* (March 2008), p. 61; United States Copyright Office, *Section 108 of Title 17: A Discussion Document of the Register of Copyrights* (United States Copyright Office, September 2017), pp. 25–26.

To conclude, the standards and rules literature provides a richer account of drafting options than a mere binary division and identifies factors that imbue law with 'flexibility' and 'certainty', not all of which can be read off the statute book. It illustrates why we need to be cautious about any analysis of copyright law that provides an overly simplified account of the nature and characteristics of exceptions. On what basis did we determine that a provision operates as a rule or standard? Can a standard exhibit flexibility and certainty, for instance because it has the capacity for incremental change *and* areas where its application is predictable? Can a rule be applied in a manner that reads away the detail, such that compliance is with the spirit rather than the letter of the law? And how might the operation of legal regulation differ between different user constituencies, or be influenced by the preferences and behaviours of the legal profession?

This book explores how we might go about answering these questions and how the answers can change over time. It uses the cultural institution sector as a case study, comparing experiences in Australia, Canada, the United Kingdom and the United States. In order to translate its analysis to lessons for the drafting of exceptions, it also draws on other insights in the legal rulemaking literature in relation to the relative efficiencies of different forms of legal drafting. These are discussed, next, in Section III.

III Standard or Rule?

Section II focused on matters relevant to classifying a legal command as a standard or rule, including the importance of the interpretative practices of legal and non-legal actors. This section explores factors relevant to the choice of whether legal regulation should utilise rule-like or standard-like drafting, drawing from the model presented by Kaplow.[82] First, a statute is promulgated by the legislature.[83] This involves choices regarding, e.g., legislative priorities, how behaviour ought to be regulated, and how that regulation ought to be drafted. To effect any change, individuals targeted by the law must know about its content and respond accordingly. This

---

[82] Kaplow, n. 2 above, 568–570.
[83] This book focuses on statutory drafting because modern copyright exceptions are almost always located in copyright legislation, although some, such as fair use and fair dealing, originated as judge-made provisions. One example of a non-statutory exception is the public interest defence in British law (see, e.g., *Lion Laboratories* v. *Evans* [1985] QB 526; *Ashdown* v. *Telegraph Group* [2002] Ch 149), however, this defence would seem to be of limited scope and has received a frosty reception elsewhere (e.g., *Collier Constructions* v. *Foskett* (1990) 19 IPR 44 per Gummow J, rejecting the existence of the defence in Australia). It has also been said that its existence is recognised via s. 171(3) of the CDPA.

second stage therefore relates to choices by these individuals and has two parts: the ease or difficulty in learning about the law (including the costs of legal advice), and the factors that will influence decision-making (such as risk aversion and reputational concerns). Finally, the law must be enforced. Given the subject-matter of this book, this aspect focuses on civil rather than criminal measures. This section is divided into four parts, corresponding to each of these stages: promulgation costs; the costs of learning about the law; other decision-making factors; and enforcement costs. Like classification, these matters will be informed heavily by empirical analysis.

A   Costs of Promulgation

Recall that our question is not whether specificity is desirable but when the legal response to a particular set of facts should be ascertained. One option is for the legislature to fashion this response in advance. As discussed in Section II, this has a number of potential benefits. For instance, a comprehensive set of rules might establish a clear and immediate demarcation between illegal and legal behaviour, thus serving to incentivise desirable behaviour, disincentivise undesirable behaviour and enable non-legal actors to make cheaper and more accurate predictions about the legal consequences of particular conduct.[84] However, these potential benefits must be weighed against, amongst other things, promulgation costs. It is often said that rules require greater effort to draft than standards because decisions must be made upfront about their reach.[85] This may require a far higher degree of legislative time and resources than enacting a standard whose application will be determined by the courts.

In thinking about whether promulgation costs point towards a rule or standard, two factors are particularly relevant: the frequency and the homogeneity of the conduct to be regulated.[86] Where a particular fact pattern occurs regularly, it may be more efficient for the legislature to utilise rule-based drafting than leaves the legal response to be delineated by judges under a standard.[87] In contrast, where behaviour is highly

---

[84] Ehrlich and Posner, n. 2 above, 262–264; Fagundes, n. 7 above, 145.
[85] See, e.g., Kaplow, n. 2 above, 562–563; Korobkin, n. 5 above, 31–32. One way in which the costs of drafting a set of rules may be lowered is through copying the legislation of other jurisdictions: Kaplow, 569, FN19. For instance, many of the exceptions in Australia's first homegrown copyright statute, the Copyright Act 1968 (Cth), were modelled on the UK Copyright Act 1956: see Chapter 4.
[86] See, e.g., Korobkin, n. 5 above, 33; Spence and Endicott, n. 7 above, 662–663.
[87] Kaplow, n. 2 above, 563.

variable, it may be inefficient for the legislature to predict and determine the legal consequences of a vast array of scenarios, many of which will only occur infrequently.[88] This is not simply a matter of time and legislative bandwidth; the inevitable challenges in identifying and planning for every contingency lead to the risk that a catalogue of rules will be imperfect, being over- and under-inclusive.[89] As such, for variable fact patterns, the costs of creating and of amending the law may support promulgation of a standard.[90]

In addition to economic costs, there may be other costs to legislative rules. For instance, rule-based drafting may allow the Holmesian 'bad man'[91] to structure his affairs to take full and cynical advantage of his legal rights.[92] Furthermore, concerns might be raised about the legislative process and its capacity to become excessively politicised, polarised and influenced by certain well-organised interests.[93] In the copyright context, this has led to concerns about exceptions being narrowed at the behest of owner interests,[94] or being poorly conceptualised and drafted in an attempt to effect a compromise between different stakeholders.[95] Would outcomes be better under a standard? This will depend

---

[88] Ibid., 562–564, 572–573, 577, 599–601. Assessment of the frequency of behaviour refers not just to behaviour *as a class* but whether particular scenarios tend to recur that can be disposed of using the same consideration or set of considerations By way of example, Kaplow states at 564 that the circumstances that implicate laws of negligence cover a 'wide array of complex accident scenarios, many of which are materially different from each other and, when considered in isolation, are unlikely to occur'. Where individual scenarios are infrequent, it may be more efficient to defer precise determination of the law to the adjudication stage rather than bear them at the promulgation stage. This perspective was criticised by Schlag; see n. 33 above and surrounding text.

[89] See, e.g., Ehrlich and Posner, n. 2 above, 268; Korobkin, n. 5 above, 36. One way to deal with these problems is through including a standard that serves as a back-up for the rule, an approach suggested for copyright exceptions. However, as noted by Ehrlich and Posner, this approach can 'sacrifice some benefits from governance by rules'.

[90] See, e.g., Korobkin, n. 5 above, 33; Kaplow, n. 2 above, 564.

[91] See O. Holmes, 'The Path of the Law' (1897) 10 *Harvard Law Review* 457.

[92] See, e.g., D. Kennedy, 'Form and Substance in Private Law Adjudication' (1976) 89 *Harvard Law Review* 1685, 1773; Schlag, n. 26, 384–385. To illustrate, Korobkin, n. 5 above, 36, refers to the 'self-interested reveler' who responds to a prohibition on making noises above 100 decibels after 10:00 pm by 'play[ing] his stereo at ninety-nine decibels next to an open window six inches away from an adjacent sleeper'.

[93] See, e.g., Tamura, n. 7 above, 70; J. Litman, 'Copyright, Compromise, and Legislative History' (1987) 72 *Cornell Law Review* 857; M. Handler and E. Hudson, 'Fair Use as an Advance on Fair Dealing? Depolarising the Debate' in H. Sun, S. Balganesh and W. Ng-Loy (eds), *Comparative Aspects of Limitations and Exceptions in Copyright Law* (New York: Cambridge University Press, forthcoming).

[94] See, e.g., Tamura, ibid.

[95] See, e.g., D. Brennan, 'The Copyright Tribunal as Exception-Maker: Are both Flexibility and Certainty Achievable' (2018) 28 *Australian Intellectual Property Journal* 83 (discussing s. 200AB of the Australian Copyright Act). Experiences in relation to s. 200AB are discussed in detail in Chapter 6.

Standard or Rule?

on the capacity of judges and the litigation process to generate better results when compared with the legislature. For some legal matters there might be benefits of the litigation process that we wish to harness, for instance where judges have particular expertise in an area, or there are fast-paced changes to which judges can more readily respond.[96]

In the case of copyright exceptions, for example, an argument can be made that whilst certain categories of use occur regularly, variation in the manifestation of those uses make is difficult to create *ex ante* rules that distinguish conduct that is permissible from that which requires a licence. For example, whilst we may agree that facilitating historical scholarship is a laudable goal of the copyright system, this does not mean that *any* use for this purpose should be exempted. A range of factors may be relevant, which might be best situated beneath an overarching standard such as fairness.[97] In contrast, if there is consensus that libraries ought to be able to copy set quantities of print-based works for patrons engaged in research or study, then it may be efficient to record this in a rule.[98]

In addition to variation in the range of uses that can be made of copyright works, we must also consider 'chronological heterogeneity':[99] changes to such uses over time. For instance, one concern about statutory rules is that amendment requires fresh legislative intervention, whereas standards have a greater capacity to self-update as judges, especially those in higher appellate courts, can modify existing approaches or apply the law to new conditions.[100] Again, we need to take care in making absolute pronouncements as there are mechanisms that a legislature can use to facilitate the responsiveness of rules, for instance by delegating regulatory powers to a government agency.[101] For copyright exceptions, however, rapid advances in technology – most recently in

---

[96] See, e.g., Spence and Endicott, n. 7 above, 664 (discussing the benefits of the Unfair Contract Terms Act 1977 using vague terms such as reasonableness).

[97] See, e.g., *Salinger v. Random House, Inc*, 811 F 2d 90 (2nd circuit, 1987) (acceptance that use of unpublished letters in a biography falls within the illustrative fair use purposes of criticism, scholarship and research, although the fair use defence failed because of the second and third factors); *Bill Graham Archives v. Dorling Kindersley Ltd*, 448 F 3d 605 (2nd circuit, 2006) (fair use defence successful where small-scale images of concert posters and other ephemera used in a biography of the Grateful Dead). See also Samuelson, n. 75 above, 2568–2580 (discussing authorship-promoting fair uses).

[98] As happens in a number of countries; see discussion in Chapter 4.

[99] Korobkin, n. 5 above, 34.   [100] Kaplow, n. 2 above, 616–617.

[101] See, e.g., US Copyright Act s. 1201(a)(1)(B)–(D) (scheme in which the Librarian of Congress can declare exemptions from rules in relation to the circumvention of access controls). For a discussion of delegating some legislative power to the Australian Copyright Tribunal in relation to the making of exceptions, see Brennan, n. 95 above.

relation to digital and online uses – have led to concerns that specific exceptions are prone to redundancy, and that there is an inevitable lag between the emergence of new technologies and the legislative updating of exceptions to deal with those developments.[102]

These concerns can be illustrated by an example from Australia. In 2006, the Australian Copyright Act was amended to include new exceptions for time-shifting and format-shifting.[103] Before these amendments, these routine acts were not, by and large, accommodated within any existing copyright exceptions. In 2011, telecommunications company Optus launched a subscription service called TV Now. This system permitted time-shifting of free-to-air television programmes, with subscribers identifying programmes they wished to record, and these recordings being made on Optus's infrastructure and viewed by the subscriber at a time of their choosing via a computer, tablet or mobile telephone. Proceedings were instituted by the Australian Football League (AFL), the National Rugby League (NRL) and Telstra on the basis that Optus had infringed copyright by making unauthorised recordings of AFL and NRL matches. One question was the identity of the 'maker' of these recordings, which a full bench of the Federal Court concluded was Optus alone or Optus and the subscriber.[104] The second question was whether Optus could rely on the new time-shifting exception in section 111.[105] The facts raised the policy question of whether new forms of time-shifting, which involve a cloud service rather than a consumer making copies on their own infrastructure, ought to fall within private copying exceptions. However, the focus of the Federal Court was on the language of section 111, as informed by the legislative materials.[106] The Court concluded:

There is nothing in the language, or the provenance, of s 111 to suggest that it was intended to cover commercial copying on behalf of individuals. Moreover,

---

[102] See generally J. Litman, 'Copyright Legislation and Technological Change' (1989) 68 *Oregon Law Review* 275; J. Litman, 'Revising Copyright Law for the Information Age' (1996) 75 *Oregon Law Review* 19; B. Depoorter, 'Technology and Uncertainty: The Shaping Effect on Copyright Law' (2009) 157 *University of Pennsylvania Law Review* 1831.
[103] Copyright Amendment Act 2006 (Cth), Schedule 6, amending or introducing ss. 43C, 47J, 109A, 110AA and 111 into the Australian Copyright Act.
[104] *National Rugby League Investments Pty Limited* v. *Singtel Optus Pty Ltd* [2012] FCAFC 59.
[105] This section provides: '(1) This section applies if a person makes a cinematograph film or sound recording of a broadcast solely for private and domestic use by watching or listening to the material broadcast at a time more convenient than the time when the broadcast is made. (2) The making of the film or recording does not infringe copyright in the broadcast or in any work or other subject-matter included in the broadcast.'
[106] *NRL* v. *Optus*, n. 104 above, paras. 80–90.

Standard or Rule?

the natural meaning of the section is that the person who makes the copy is the person whose purpose is to use it as prescribed by s 111(1). Optus may well be said to have copied programmes so that others can use the recorded programme for the purpose envisaged by s 111. Optus, though, makes no use itself of the copies as it frankly concedes. It merely stores them for 30 days. And its purpose in providing its service – and, hence in making copies of programmes for subscribers – is to derive such market advantage in the digital TV industry as its commercial exploitation can provide.[107]

In coming to this conclusion, the Court did not ignore arguments regarding the justifications for time-shifting exceptions or the desirability of technologically neutral interpretations. The judges were

conscious that the construction which we are satisfied the language of s 111 requires is one that is capable of excluding, and does in fact in this instance exclude, a later technological development in copying. However, no principle of technological neutrality can overcome what is the clear and limited legislative purpose of s 111. It is not for this court to redraft this provision to secure an assumed legislative desire for such neutrality.[108]

The same problem arose for the argument that interpretation of section 111 could be informed by policy under a purposive construction:

[I]f the apparently confined words of a statute are to be given a more extended scope, not only must they be capable as a matter of language of sustaining such an extension, there must also be some indication in the legislation, its purpose and context of whether, and if so how, the legislature would wish to extend what, on its face, is the confined scope of the statute or of a section of it.[109]

This example is included not to interrogate the coverage of private copying exceptions[110] but to illustrate three matters. First, the language 'person makes ... solely for private and domestic use' was understood to refer *only* to copies made by the person who intended to watch the recording, not someone who facilitated this act by assisting with the making of the copy. Until recently this issue did not arise, as private

---

[107] Ibid., para. 89. It was possible that the subscriber might have been able to rely on s. 111; however, this did not save Optus, who was jointly and severally liable and needed to establish the s. 111 defence on its own merits: paras. 92–93.

[108] Ibid., para. 96.

[109] Ibid., para. 97, discussing the call for a purposive construction as permitted by s. 15AA of the Acts Interpretation Act 1901 (Cth).

[110] For such a discussion, see, e.g., N. Helberger and P. Hugenholtz, 'No Place Like Home for Making a Copy: Private Copying in European Copyright Law and Consumer Law' (2007) 22 *Berkeley Technology Law Journal* 1061; R. Giblin, 'Stranded in the Technological Dark Ages: Implications of the Full Federal Court's Decision in *NRL v Optus*' (2012) 34 *European Intellectual Property Review* 632; B. Hazucha, 'Private Copying and Harm to Authors – Compensation versus Remuneration' (2017) 133 *Law Quarterly Review* 269.

48   Standards and Rules

copying was undertaken by consumers using their own devices and media. There was still a commercial transaction, but this was the purchase of equipment rather than subscription to a service.[111] Second, with the High Court refusing an application to appeal from the Federal Court's decision,[112] it appears that section 111 will need to be amended by the legislature if the better normative view is that copying via cloud-based copying services is functionally equivalent to using a VCR or digital recorder, and that any free exception should extend to their use. Finally, this issue arose just five years after the introduction of section 111, consistent with the concern that for copyright, the use of rule-like exceptions can generate the need for regular rounds of legislative review.

B   *Costs in Learning about the Law*

In order for law to influence the 'primary behaviour'[113] of individuals, it is necessary that those people have knowledge of its content, whether through direct study, obtaining legal advice, reading industry guidelines, etc. With copyright relevant to many daily acts of intellectual and creative production, it can be questioned how much activity takes place in the absence of any meaningful knowledge of the law's operation – and not just in relation to exceptions. Jessica Litman, for example, has said that from her interactions with lay people and copyright experts, it would appear that 'copyright law is written by lawmakers unfamiliar with the process of authorship and that authorship is committed by innocents unversed in the details of copyright'.[114] She observes that much academic scholarship is written 'as if the authors to whom the statute speaks knew its provisions and modulated their authorship accordingly',[115] a matter that is especially problematic for those pressing an economic justification for legal intervention:

Much of the literature repackaging copyright in theoretical terms proceeds from the assumption that authors' creation of works is influenced by their awareness of the intricacies of the system. For those theorists who model the copyright law in

---

[111] This is not without legal exposure, as it has been argued that the sale of copying equipment or media can result in the manufacturer being liable under an authorisation analysis: for discussion, see, e.g., *CBS Songs Ltd* v. *Amstrad Consumer Electronics Plc* [1988] AC 1013 (sale of twin-deck cassette players held not to authorise any infringing activity by purchasers).
[112] See [2012] HCATrans 214.   [113] Ehrlich and Posner, n. 2 above, 261.
[114] J. Litman, 'Copyright as Myth' (1991) 53 *University of Pittsburgh Law Review* 235, 236. For the purposes of this discussion, Litman defines lay people as 'lawyers and non-lawyers and authors and non-authors; indeed, everyone but the copyright specialist': at 237.
[115] Ibid., 241.

economic or utilitarian terms, the assumption inheres in their approach: It is difficult to speak of the incentives supplied by a legal regime without relying on the convention that those whom the law seeks to prod are aware of the goodies that it offers as a bribe.[116]

Although Litman focuses on authorship, her underlying question – which centres on the possible disconnect between everyday understandings and the actual words of the law[117] – is relevant across the copyright system. It raises questions about lay knowledge of the law and the extent to which individuals adjust their behaviour to reflect that knowledge. This second aspect will be explored further in Section III.C.

The standards and rules literature says much about how and why individuals acquire legal knowledge, and what this means for different forms of drafting. According to Kaplow, self-interested individuals will 'acquire legal advice to guide their behaviour … only if its perceived value exceeds its perceived cost'.[118] Read in isolation, this may imply an unduly reductionist view of human decision-making, and it is important to recall insights from behavioural economics and other schools in relation to why people obey the law, including that we often behave 'irrationally' when compared with the cost-benefit analysis of *homo economicus*.[119] However, Kaplow's quote captures an important question for legal drafting: might the form of drafting change the likelihood that a person will invest resources in shifting from their default position (uninformed, and therefore complying with the law by way of best guess) to having actual knowledge of the law?

One may surmise that that the costs of learning will be lower for statutory rules because the content of the law is more certain and less open to interpretation.[120] This, in turn, may promote compliance with the law, as individuals will be more likely to understand its content.[121] To this picture we can add economies of scale: if a particular law is

---

[116] Ibid.
[117] Litman admitted that her perspective was impressionistic: ibid., 238. It may also be that public knowledge of copyright has changed since her article was published in 1991.
[118] Kaplow, n. 2 above, 571.
[119] One such example relates to the role of deterrence, i.e., that people will adjust their behaviour based on knowledge of the illegality of and/or likely sanction arising for particular conduct. For instance, Becker has argued that a person's decision to commit a crime is, like other decisions, based on a cost–benefit assessment: G. Becker, 'Crime and Punishment: An Economic Analysis' (1968) 78 *Journal of Political Economy* 169. Becker's rational choice model has been queried by behavioural economists, including on the basis that it does not chime with empirical evidence and everyday experience. This has led to a richer literature which seeks to identify the factors that influence dishonest behaviour: for an overview, see, e.g., D. Ariely, *The (Honest) Truth About Dishonesty* (London: Harper, 2012).
[120] Kaplow, n. 2 above, 563, 571.   [121] Ibid., 577.

relevant to many people, rules will be more efficient due to the reduction in legal costs incurred in the aggregate.[122] However, these propositions apply best to a well-drafted simple rule. The position may change if a rule is complex, as the level of detail may make the provision more time consuming to understand and necessitate the input of someone with specialist knowledge.[123] A complex rule may therefore cost just as much to understand as a standard. Furthermore, whilst some standards may require expert training to identify and interpret case law and to make predictions about a future decision – factors that may increase learning costs[124] – it is also the case that many standards are based on concepts readily accessible to non-experts. As stated by Ehrlich and Posner, standards often 'have a large intuitive element which makes them comprehensible without special training, while most legal rules are not understood unless studied'.[125] Thus, in considering learning costs, we must go beyond a basic demarcation between standards and rules to also consider matters such as the complexity and accessibility of relevant legal commands. This requires empirical assessment.[126]

Applying this to the copyright context, one might ask whether the costs to institutional users in learning about fair use or fair dealing are that much higher than those involved in familiarising themselves with the scope of specific exceptions, bearing in mind the complexities and drafting quirks often contained in the latter. Of course, some of these rules may be amenable to 'set and forget' decision-making; for instance, a library may produce standard-form documentation that reflects exceptions for external copying requests, thus facing an initial outlay in drafting and staff training but lower post-implementation costs. For a standard, on the other hand, there may be ongoing costs of legal advice if it is necessary to remain apprised of new case law or undertake fresh analysis regarding new applications of the provision. That said, some of these costs may be defrayed or shared through cooperation between institutions, and utilisation of a standard may be cheaper than other compliance options, such as paying for licences even though fair use or fair dealing arguments are available.

[122] Ibid., 574. [123] See, e.g., Korobkin, n. 5 above, 34.
[124] Kaplow, n. 2 above, 569.
[125] Ehrlich and Posner, n. 2 above, 270–271; see also Korobkin, n. 5 above, 35 (a standard that embodies community norms or commercial reasonableness might require less effort to understand than a complex rule); Kaplow, n. 2 above, 596–599 (suggesting that the costs of learning about a standard and a complex rule may be similar if the likely result for both is 'just as obvious' – i.e., individuals will only be motivated to put more effort into learning about a complex rule if they are 'materially uncertain about what the rules would say').
[126] See, e.g., Kaplow, n. 2 above, 597.

C   *Decision-Making Factors*

As just discussed, some degree of legal knowledge is a necessary requirement for individuals to adjust their behaviour in response to the law. But factors other than acquisition costs influence whether an individual will learn about the law and how they will respond to this information. This section focuses on three factors that are particularly relevant to cultural institutions: risk aversion, reputational concerns, and ethical views on the behaviours and characteristics of a 'good' institution.

Analysis of risk preferences is highly relevant to standards and rules because it recognises that different people have different need for certainty in their legal affairs. For instance, it is often said that uncertainty has a disproportionate effect on the risk averse as these individuals are more concerned by the possibility that conduct is unlawful, and therefore more likely to over-comply with the law or be over-deterred by it.[127] For instance, James Gibson has argued that the 'inherently ambiguous' divide between 'private entitlement ... and public privilege' in copyright law, combined with potentially 'severe remedies' such injunctions and statutory damages, can result in a default position of licensing, just to be on the safe side.[128] One analysis might therefore suggest that rules are preferable to standards when individuals are risk averse, on the basis that obtaining legal knowledge will be cheaper and more likely to result in *ex ante* certainty, thus reducing the likelihood that individuals will, out of an abundance of caution, adopt conservative interpretations or pay for unnecessary licences.[129]

There are counterpoints to this analysis. For example, we might give thought to the self-serving bias: the tendency of people 'to interpret ambiguous information in ways that resound to their benefit'.[130] It has been said that the in-built vagueness of standards cloaks users with greater freedom to adopt interpretations that confirm their view of what the law ought to say.[131] If right, this might mean that individuals – even

---

[127] See, e.g., Fagundes, n. 7 above, 146–147, 152–153.
[128] J. Gibson, 'Risk Aversion and Rights Accretion in Intellectual Property Law' (2007) 116 *Yale Law Journal* 882, 884; see, also, J. Rothman, 'The Questionable Use of Custom in Intellectual Property Law' (2007) 93 *Virginia Law Review* 1899, 1909–1916 (describing litigation-avoiding customs in intellectual property law, including clearance strategies); P. Jaszi, 'Copyright, Fair Use and Motion Pictures' [2007] *Utah Law Review* 715, 732–736 (describing the 'clearance culture' in documentary filmmaking, and the development of a best practices statement to help facilitate the making of fair use arguments).
[129] See, e.g., Ehrlich and Posner, n. 2 above, 262; Kaplow, n. 2 above, 605; Korobkin, n. 5 above, 37–38.
[130] Korobkin, n. 5 above, 46.   [131] Ibid.

the risk averse – are not as 'chilled' by standards as some analysis would predict. Furthermore, it has been suggested that vagueness is no bad thing to encourage negotiation between authors and users. For instance, Spence and Endicott argue that uncertainty about the 'scope' of copyright incentivises licensing activity, and that this 'must be preferable, whatever the underlying purpose of copyright'.[132] This argument would seem to respect the primacy of property-style transactions in the copyright system.[133] If we accept this premise, we may be comfortable with some vagueness around infringement principles – but perhaps not subsistence and ownership[134] – although this will depend on the suitability and functioning of the market. For instance, a Coasean analysis might suggest that the initial allocation is less important in a world with low transaction costs and no prohibitions on bargaining, and that the market in such a world will correct for over- or under-inclusive rules.[135] On the other hand, we might query whether equality of bargaining power exists between those at the negotiating table and any proposition that private outcomes are therefore preferable to those determined by legislators.[136]

Reputational concerns can also influence legal interpretations, for instance where strict compliance with the law is seen as important for reasons of relationship management with creators, funders, donors and so forth. This insight connects to the literature on law and social norms. This body of work recognises that law is just one way of influencing behaviour, and that people routinely cooperate and organise themselves

---

[132] Spence and Endicott, n. 7 above, 665. Given their focus on substantiality and the idea/expression dichotomy, which they discuss by reference to *Designers Guild Ltd v. Russell Williams (Textiles) Ltd* [2000] 1 WLR 2416, it would seem that 'scope' refers to infringement. Rose, n. 39 above, also discusses the tendency, if legal commands are 'muddy' (i.e., standard-like), for private actors to make their own 'crystalline' rules through negotiation and contract.

[133] See, generally, G. Calabresi and A. Melamed, 'Property Rules, Liability Rules, and Inalienability: One View of the Cathedral' (1972) 85 *Harvard Law Review* 1089; L. Kaplow and S. Shavell, 'Property Rules Versus Liability Rules: An Economic Analysis' (1996) 109 *Harvard Law Review* 713; and in the copyright context, W. Gordon, 'On the Economics of Copyright, Restitution, and "Fair Use": Systematic versus Case-by-Case Responses to Market Failure' (1997) 8 *Journal of Law and Information Science* 7; M. Lemley, 'Should a Licensing Market Require Licensing?' (2007) 70 *Law and Contemporary Problems* 185.

[134] It has been suggested that clarity around property entitlements promotes bargaining and hence efficiency, as there is clearer and more reliable information about the identity and rights of owners: for discussion, see Fagundes, n. 7 above, 146–147.

[135] See R. Coase, 'The Problem of Social Cost' (1960) 3 *Journal of Law & Economics* 1; Korobkin, n. 5, 40–41.

[136] See, e.g., Fagundes, n. 7 above, 163–164.

Standard or Rule? 53

in structured ways independently or in the absence of a legal framework.[137] The underlying insights behind social norms are longstanding, for instance appearing in the writings of philosopher David Hume,[138] and have been applied in various guises across different disciplines.[139] In the context of law, Robert Ellickson suggests that a focus on socialisation and social norms teaches us that

> [m]uch of the glue of a society comes not from law enforcement ... but rather from the informal enforcement of social mores by acquaintances, bystanders, trading partners, and others. These unofficial enforcers use punishments such as negative gossip and ostracism to discipline malefactors and bounties such as esteem and enhanced trading opportunities to reward the worthy. Informal systems of external social control are far more important than law in many contexts, especially ones where interacting parties have a continuing relationship and little at stake.[140]

A key feature of a social norm is not merely that a behaviour is common statistically but that it reflects community consensus regarding how people ought to behave, and that 'this agreement affects what people actually do'.[141] Robert Cooter illustrates this by reference to taking off one's hat in a boiler room and removing it in church, the former being done through inclination and the latter through obligation.[142] A social norm, in Cooter's view, is an 'effective consensus obligation', i.e., one that reflects widespread community agreement *and* influences the actions of individuals.[143] Social norms are but one influence on behaviour, as seen in Ellickson's identification of five 'controllers' that 'may be sources of both rules of behavior and sanctions that back up those rules':[144] personal ethics (which we exercise on ourselves), contracts (which are agreed between two or more parties voluntarily), norms (which derive from third parties, in this case social forces), organisation rules (coming from another third-party force, organisations) and law (which under this model comprises government control).[145] A 'rule' guiding behaviour can

---

[137] Key contributions to the social norms literature as it relates to law include R. Ellickson, *Order without Law: How Neighbors Settle Disputes* (Cambridge: Harvard University Press, 1991); E. Posner, *Law and Social Norms* (Cambridge: Harvard University Press, 2000).
[138] Hume has been classified by some as an early game theorist: see, e.g., P. Vanderschraaf, 'The Informal Game Theory in Hume's Account of Convention' (1998) 14 *Economics & Philosophy* 215.
[139] For a brief overview, see, R. Ellickson, 'Law and Economics Discovers Social Norms' (1998) 27 *Journal of Legal Studies* 537, 542–543, 546–549 and the citations therein.
[140] Ibid., 540.
[141] R. Cooter, 'Expressive Law and Economics' (1998) 27 *Journal of Legal Studies* 585, 587; see also R. McAdams, 'The Origin, Development, and Regulation of Norms' (1997) 96 *Michigan Law Review* 338, 350.
[142] Ibid.   [143] Ibid.   [144] Ellickson, n. 137 above, p. 126.   [145] Ibid., p. 127.

54   Standards and Rules

be proven 'only if the existence of the guideline actually influences the behavior either of those to whom it is addressed or of those who detect others breaching the guidelines'.[146] According to Ellickson, the application of sanctions is the best evidence that a rule exists; in contrast, a consistent pattern of behaviour is a more ambiguous indication.[147]

There are a number of explanations for the emergence of social norms,[148] but one way of understanding these processes – especially as they relate to cooperation and signalling – is by reference to game theory. Consider the iconic example of the Prisoner's Dilemma.[149] It has been said that a rational actor will always defect rather than cooperate, irrespective of whether the game is being played once or on a repeat basis.[150] However, further theoretical investigation suggests that inevitable cheating is not the best strategy,[151] a conclusion that chimes with

---

[146] Ibid., p. 128.
[147] Ibid., pp. 128–129. Ellickson uses the term 'sanctions' to refer to all rewards and punishments that might be imposed to encourage or discourage particular behaviour, and not merely the remedies or penalties one sees in legal systems. For instance, in one of the case studies presented by Ellickson in relation to residents of Shasta County, the norm that 'an owner of livestock is responsible for the conduct of his animals' was best seen through the response of the community to those who deviated from this rule, first with gossip and then with violent self-help: p. 130. Like the point made by Cooter, consistency in behaviour is not necessarily evidence of a rule, as it may not be 'normatively constrained' – Ellickson uses the example that the fact that most people sleep regularly does not, of itself, demonstrate that there is a rule that one must sleep: p. 129.
[148] See, e.g., McAdams, n. 141 above (esteem theory); Cooter, n. 141 above (internalisation theory).
[149] It has been argued that there has been almost myopic focus in law circles on the Prisoner's Dilemma, and that much would be gained from considering the lessons from other games: see R. McAdams, 'Beyond the Prisoners' Dilemma: Coordination, Game Theory, and Law' (2009) 82 *Southern California Law Review* 209.
[150] For a full account, see Posner, n. 137 above, pp. 13–15; Posner, n. 5 above, 107–110; McAdams, ibid., 215–216. In the classic Prisoner's Dilemma, the prosecutor has arrested two suspects. He or she can prove that they committed a misdemeanour but suspects them of a more serious crime. The prosecutor offers each suspect the same deal, and each suspect must choose – without any consultation with the other – whether to cooperate with one another by remaining silent, or defect (i.e., betray the other) through a confession. If one suspects confesses (defects) and the other does not, the confessor is rewarded with immunity (given an assigned value of zero) and the other is convicted of the serious crime and receives a longer jail sentence (to a value of –5). If both parties confess to the serious crime, they are given a reduction in this sentence to reward their candour (to a value of –3). If they both cooperate and remain silent, they are convicted of the minor crime only (to a value of –1). The key observation is that a suspect always does better by defecting, receiving zero rather than –1 if the other suspect cooperates, and –3 rather than –5 if the other suspect defects.
[151] See R. Axelrod, *The Evolution of Cooperation* (New York: Basic Books, 1984). Axelrod proposed that the best strategy for the iterated game is tit-for-tat, where the first move is to be nice (cooperate); after that, the player should mirror the previous move of his or her opponent. This can result in retaliation: if the opponent defected last time, the

everyday experience.[152] Indeed, it has been said that '[i]n cooperation ventures ... moral restraint can increase productivity, so people with good character may enjoy an advantage over people with bad character'.[153] In game theory terms, if mutual cooperation yields a higher payoff to both parties than mutual defection,[154] then 'good' types will want to seek out other good types with whom to cooperate. This goes some way to explain the efforts people make to signal their status as good: because there is only so much knowledge that an individual can acquire and retain about the past behaviours of others, there are things people do to signal their trustworthiness and other positive characteristics (e.g., via grooming, manners, gift-giving, working out of a fancy office, etc). Their effectiveness depends on whether they are perceived as signals and appreciated by their targets as positive indications. Indeed, in speaking about 'social norms', it is important to emphasise that 'the community' is not necessarily the general public but often a subset of individuals. Thus, the norms and signals of the residents of Shasta County (the focus of Ellickson's seminal work)[155] will be very different to those of the graffiti subculture in London (studied by Marta Iljadica[156]) and the cultural institutions, artists, donors, etc., in this book.

Applying social norms theory to standards and rules, we might ask whether reputational concerns influence how individuals engage with different forms of legal drafting. For instance, Eric Posner suggests that people may over-comply with standards relative to rules if reputation is important to them and they want to send signals that accord with how they believe a law-abiding person would behave.[157] If right, this might result in hesitancy around general exceptions like fair use (in case a forward-leaning interpretation is seen as playing fast and loose with rights) and greater comfort with forms of copyright compliance that, in theory at least, offer greater certainty. Bear in mind, though, that this assumes that the content of a rule is more predictable than that of a standard. Furthermore, it may be that compliance with the strict letter of the law is not the most important reputational concern.

Consider, for example, an art museum that is creating an online collection database that will operate primarily as a research tool and will

---

player will also defect. Tit-for-tat can involve a degree of forgiveness, where the player occasionally cooperates with an opponent who previously defected.

[152] See, e.g., Rose, n. 39 above, 602.   [153] Cooter, n. 141 above, 587.
[154] Which is the case in many coordination games; for discussion, see McAdams, n. 149 above, 218–225 (describing Assurance, the Battle of the Sexes and the Hawk-Dove game).
[155] Ellickson, n. 137 above.   [156] Iljadica, n. 76 above.
[157] See Posner, n. 5 above, 115–116.

be publicly accessible over the internet. The goal is for each entry to be accompanied by a low-resolution image of the work in question. The museum needs to determine whether it should obtain licences for this project. One reputational concern may be that cultural institutions, especially public ones, should respect the law; this may be bolstered by a concern that artists, donors and other supporters will be less likely to cooperate with an institution that is seen to disrespect copyright. If this norm is operational, then an institution may be inclined to secure permissions for all images, even if there are viable arguments that fair use or fair dealing is applicable. However, an alternative reputational concern may arise if artists expect institutions to undertake these sort of indexing uses and have no desire to be remunerated for them, a view that may mirror expectations of government and the public regarding the role of online technologies in modern museum practices. If this is the applicable norm then institutions may want to avoid any suggestion that they are technological luddites or are prioritising only some artists for online presence or do not take seriously their public interest missions of facilitating access and learning. This may make them more comfortable in relying on a general exception, despite its uncertainty; or perhaps even including some images by reference to 'pure' risk management.[158]

It is clear that for matters such as risk and relationship management, empirical work is essential to determine how institutions view risk, what social norms operate in the sector and whether either of these is in the process of change. However, as seen in Ellickson's controllers, there are other influences on behaviour. Of particular interest to this project is the ideas that cultural institution staff internalise about the characteristics of a 'good' museum or library, i.e., behavioural cues that come from personal ethics and organisation rules.[159] This may not be unrelated to reputation; for instance, Hume's work suggests that concern for reputation does not just encompass outwardly focused acts to build social relationships – what might cynically be termed virtue signalling performed out of self-interest and expediency – but can be honourable, reflecting a psychological transformation in which a commitment to justice is a moral obligation.[160] The empirical question for this book is

---

[158] See especially Chapter 3, Section IV and Chapter 8, Section III.B. The reference to 'pure' risk management is intended to cover instances in which institutions know that a use contravenes copyright law, or that arguments for a viable defence are weak, but nevertheless proceed with that use by reference to a risk assessment.

[159] See n. 144 to n. 145 above and surrounding text.

[160] See L. Besser-Jones, 'The Role of Justice in Hume's Theory of Psychological Development' (2006) 32 *Hume Studies* 253. Besser-Jones argues at 266 that the 'fully transformed, just individual ... has a concern for her reputation. She values meaningful

what happens when there is an actual or potential conflict between the law and what is perceived as the right thing to do. An example can be found in the best practice guidelines promulgated by industry bodies in relation to acquisition, conservation, access, disposal and so forth. Some of these ideas about excellence in collection management may sit uncomfortably with a strict reading of copyright, for instance where best practice demands that loaned artworks are photographed on entry and departure to record condition but there is no exception that seems to allow this activity.[161] When, if at all, do moral and ethical precepts regarding the actions of a 'good' institution oust consideration of copyright, or otherwise inform legal interpretations or adherence? And do the answers to these questions differ between different styles of drafting?

D Enforcement

The difference between rules and standards is also relevant to questions of enforcement. For instance, one may intuit that rules will lower enforcement costs because they reduce the likelihood of litigation and, should proceedings eventuate, the number of matters about which adjudicators must deliberate.[162] Indeed, given that standards reflect a preference for judicial rather than legislative decision-making, the administrative costs are intended to be back-loaded and, to a greater or lesser degree, borne by private parties.[163] This might be said to have consequences for access to justice: that those with fewer resources will be less able to bring or defend legal proceedings under a standard, rendering nugatory any suggestion that the individualised assessment of such laws achieves better justice between the parties.

As with the analysis of compliance costs, we must again take care with our assumptions and comparisons. To illustrate, many copyright disputes already turn on a large number of legal and evidentiary matters, including in relation to subsistence of rights, ownership and whether there was an infringing act. It is open to question whether the uncertainty and evidentiary demands of, say, a fair use or fair dealing defence makes litigation that much more costly or difficult than other elements of the

---

interactions with others, gauges her own worth in terms of these interactions, and so successfully regulates her behavior by the rules of justice.'

[161] See further Chapter 4. Although there are sector-specific exceptions for administration, these are often limited to items in the institution's own permanent collection.

[162] Ehrlich and Posner, n. 2 above, 265–266; Korobkin, n. 5 above, 32–33.

[163] Even for civil litigation, there must be state-funded infrastructure to pay the wages of judges and other staff, maintain court buildings, switch on the lights, etc. Furthermore, most enforcement actions will not proceed to trial, having been settled beforehand.

copyright system. Furthermore, the statement that fewer issues arise for rules assumes that the equivalent standard would be more complex, when complexity can be a feature of either form of drafting. Finally, other enforcement-related matters might be relevant to any comparative analysis of drafting options between different countries, for instance in relation to the award of legal costs and the availability of statutory damages. It has therefore been argued that any assessment of whether and how Australia should implement fair use must take into account the routine award of legal costs to the successful party, this being different from the US position.[164] It has been said that this may make Australian defendants more litigation averse, with the result that an Australian fair use exception would generate far less case law.

IV Synthesis and Illustration

So far, this chapter has described key lessons from the literature on standards and rules. The aim of this final section is to draw this material together and provide an indication of how it will help provide an intellectual framework for the analysis of the empirical work in this book. This will be done using fair use from US copyright law as a case study.

As noted throughout this chapter, the plain language of fair use shows all the hallmarks of a standard, being non-prescriptive and open-ended. This classification also accords with evidence regarding the legislative intent behind section 107, which was to codify the common law fair use doctrine that had emerged in US law.[165] For instance, the following passage from the House Report of 1976 shows a clear preference for judicial rather than legislative rulemaking, and a recognition that it would not be possible to delineate the application of section 107 beyond indications in the fairness factors and non-exhaustive list of purposes:

> The statement of the fair use doctrine in section 107 offers some guidance to users in determining when the principles of the doctrine apply. However, the endless variety of situations and combinations of circumstances that can arise in particular cases precludes the formulation of exact rules in the statute. ... Beyond a very broad statutory explanation of what fair use is and some of the criteria applicable to it, the courts must be free to adapt the doctrine to particular situations on a case-by-case basis.[166]

---

[164] See, e.g., D. Hunter, 'American Lessons: Implementing Fair Use in Australia' (2014) 24 *Australian Intellectual Property Journal* 192, 194.
[165] See, e.g., Elkin-Koren and Fischman-Afori, n. 7 above, 174–177.
[166] HR Report No 94-1476, 94th Congress, 2nd Session (1976), p. 66.

This statement has been cited by the US Supreme Court on a number of occasions,[167] including in *Campbell* v. *Acuff-Rose*, where it was observed that the application of fair use 'is not to be simplified with bright-line rules, for the statute, like the doctrine it recognizes, calls for case-by-case analysis'.[168] The House Report also warned of the futility of any attempt to set out some overarching principle underlying fair use:

> Although the courts have considered and ruled upon the fair use doctrine over and over again, no real definition of the concept has ever emerged. Indeed, since the doctrine is an equitable rule of reason, no generally applicable definition is possible, and each case raising the question must be decided on its own facts.[169]

Accepting that fair use utilises standard-like language and was intended by the US legislature to operate in standard-like ways, we can pose a number of questions. The first set of questions are empirical, and revolve around the operation of fair use in practice: is the doctrine interpreted in ways that suggest fixed or predetermined meanings, or in a manner that admits new applications? The second set of questions add a normative framework: is fair use fit-for-purpose, and if so, might it be attractive as a drafting option for other countries that are interested in exceptions reform?

For instance, we have seen the argument that standards are more responsive to new norms and technologies because they are self-updating through changes in the ways that general decision-making factors are applied – that judges can adjust these considerations to respond to new paradigms without further legislative intervention. To put this in the flexibility/certainty dichotomy, we might say that standards are more flexible and less prone to obsolescence than rules. If our classification of fair use as a standard is correct, we might predict that it will have the potential to apply to an array of uses by cultural institutions, including those outside the sector-specific exceptions in section 108 of the US Copyright Act. It may also be predicted that with technological innovation and changes to practices, reliance of fair use will also change over time.

However, we have also seen the argument that delays in the hearing and accrual of case law can lower predictive value when compared with a (well-drafted) rule, giving users less assurance about how they should structure their affairs.[170] Its perceived lack of certainty has been a

---

[167] See, e.g., *Sony Corp of America* v. *Universal City Studios, Inc*, 446 US 417, 448 (1984); *Harper & Row Publishers, Inc* v. *Nation Enterprises*, 471 US 539, 549 (1985).
[168] *Campbell* v. *Acuff-Rose Music, Inc*, 510 US 569, 577 (1994).
[169] HR Report, n. 165 above, p. 65.
[170] See, e.g., Sunstein, n. 43 above, 976 (noting that one of the stated benefits of rules is facilitating planning through predictable outcomes).

continued theme in criticisms of fair use.[171] For instance, Michael Madison has said that the propensity of fair use to be all things to all people has led to the doctrine becoming 'so fragmented as to make it useless as a predictive device for copyright owners, copyright consumers, and for the courts',[172] whilst *Nimmer on Copyright* states that 'what facts will be sufficient to raise this defense in any given case is not easily answered'.[173] Applying lessons from standard and rules, we might also hypothesise that issues with uncertainty will have a disproportionate effect on the risk averse, possibly leading to a feedback loop in which it becomes difficult to oust narrow interpretations of fair use because they are self-reinforcing for reasons of doctrine and practice.[174] Given the suggestion that cultural institutions tend towards risk-avoiding preferences,[175] one might predict that for this particular user group, fair use will not only fail to thrive but that the scope of reliance by institutions may retreat if they are challenged about their activities.

We therefore have two very different sets of predictions, the first highlighting the capacity for fair use to play a prominent role in institutional copyright practices, and the second suggesting that other options may be preferred because institutions will be discouraged by the uncertainty associated with *ex post* determination of the doctrine's application. According to the standards and rules literature, which plays out will depend not only on risk preferences but also on other factors such as the formation of precedent, information costs and the availability of legal advice. Thus, one might argue that because the content of fair use is informed by a vast body of case law and commentary, the costs of understanding the doctrine will be relatively high and require specialist input, due to the time and expertise to synthesise this body of jurisprudence. This might suggest that institutions that dedicate greater resources to copyright will be more likely to take a forward-leaning interpretation of fair use than those which dedicate fewer resources. That

---

[171] See the contributions cited in n. 72 above.
[172] See, e.g., Madison, n. 72 above, 1577.
[173] D. Nimmer, *Nimmer on Copyright*, Volume 4 (LexisNexis, online resource, accessed 15 January 2019), para. 13.05.
[174] See Gibson, n. 128 above, 885, arguing that this sort of 'doctrinal feedback' has the capacity to shape the law 'from the bottom up' because market practices in relation to licensing are often used by judges as evidence of the scope of the copyright owner's entitlement. For similar arguments, see Rothman, n. 128 above, 1902–1903; Fagundes, n. 7 above, 152–153. Whilst some judges have stated that the availability of a licence should not be determinative of whether fair use is applicable, Gibson's thesis has been described as highlighting a 'threat to fair use that is nevertheless real': W. Gordon, 'The "Why" of Markets: Fair Use and Circularity' (2007) 116 *Yale Law Journal Pocket Part* 358, 359.
[175] See especially Chapter 3, Section IV.

said, another plausible argument posits that standards make use of concepts that are more accessible intuitively and without legal training. In the case of fair use, one might therefore hypothesise that the doctrine can be meaningful even for users without extensive technical knowledge because the overarching criterion of fairness provides a strong normative compass for assessing when the doctrine should apply, and the concepts enumerated in the fairness factors can be readily understood by lay people. Of course, these intuitions are not free-standing and immutable, but are influenced by, amongst other things, views on the characteristics of a 'good' cultural institution and prevailing social and economic perspectives on the role of copyright and exceptions. Thus, we might predict that institutions that have internalised a narrow view of exceptions might rely on fair use in fewer circumstances than those that believe exceptions should play a prominent role.

In sum, it is not possible to accurately predict the role of fair use – or any other exception – from its wording. Additional analysis is required, including from empirical analysis of stakeholder practices. Standards and rules give us a useful framework to inform this work, thus creating a stronger base from which to draw conclusions about the drafting of copyright exceptions.

V   Conclusion

This chapter has provided a summary of insights from the standards and rules literature, matters that will help provide an intellectual framework to consider what the law in action means for the drafting of copyright exceptions. Perhaps the overarching lesson to come from this analysis is that the best form of drafting is context dependent, and will depend on factors such as the frequency and variability of the behaviour to be regulated, the learning costs of relevant users, decision-making factors such as risk aversion and reputational concerns, and enforcement costs. Another important lesson relates to how we assess different drafting options. For instance, in asking whether a fair use system is preferable to one involving many closed exceptions, the accurate comparison is not between US-style fair use and a perfectly drafted and comprehensive set of detailed rules, but between the sort of fair use that is likely to emerge and the rules that the legislature – with many demands on its time, and limits on its ability to predict future developments – is actually going to draft.

Whilst this book argues that, at least in some jurisdictions, a shift to fair use may be justified, fair use should not be seen as inevitably superior to specific exceptions or the endpoint of a mature copyright system. There will be times when the legal response is best captured in a simple rule; instances where a multi-factor standard is preferable; and still other times when the optimal approach is a well-drafted complex rule. As stated by Spence and Endicott, '[t]he challenge for lawmakers is to determine whether, in a given scheme of regulation, the arbitrariness resulting from precision is worse than the arbitrariness resulting from the application of a vague standard'.[176] This book illustrates this challenge using cultural institutions as a case study. In order to set up the empirical work, it turns in Chapter 3 to the final tranche of background material, which provides an overview of the empirical methodology and the relevance of copyright to cultural institutions. Later chapters will then focus in detail on practices in relation to copyright exceptions.

---

[176] Spence and Endicott, n. 7 above, 662.

3 Copyright and Cultural Institutions

I Introduction

One of the key messages in this book is the importance of empirical work for any analysis of the operation and drafting of copyright exceptions. In order to illustrate these ideas, it uses as a case study the experiences of cultural institutions in Australia, Canada, the United Kingdom and the United States. This material is the culmination of fieldwork at institutions and industry peak bodies from 2004 to the present day, including site visits, review of publicly-available documentation and interviews with hundreds of people. In some cases, it reveals significant changes in the knowledge, resources and decision-making practices of institution staff, including new roles for free exceptions. It illustrates how norms can change over time but in other cases be quite sticky, raising the question of whether law should be reformed mainly in response to current behaviours and activities, or whether statutory change might provide signals that encourage new practices to emerge.

This chapter has two main parts. In Section II it describes why cultural institutions are attractive candidates for empirical study and provides an overview of the methodology used in the fieldwork.[1] Section III then describes why copyright is relevant to cultural institutions, in particular as this relates to the use of third-party copyright in a range of institutional settings.[2] This section identifies four main compliance options. Three of these are products of the limited, property-style rights enjoyed by copyright owners,[3] and can therefore described as 'within' the copyright

---

[1] Fuller information in relation to the methodology is set out in the Appendix.
[2] Whilst this book focuses on activities involving works that are or were protected by copyright, intellectual property issues can arise for collections that fall outside copyright's ambit, as exemplified by the data surrounding natural and scientific collections: see, e.g., C. Alberts Carson, 'Laser Bones: Copyright Issues Raised by the Use of Information Technology in Archaelogy' (1997) 10 *Harvard Journal of Law & Technology* 281.
[3] Whether copyright is in fact a species of property is beyond the scope of this book, but has been addressed in detail elsewhere; see, e.g., M. Carrier, 'Cabining Intellectual Property

system: (1) selecting public domain works in order to avoid copyright issues; (2) acquiring rights through negotiation for a licence or assignment; and (3) reliance on an exception or compulsory licence. The fourth approach is a pure risk management decision to proceed with an activity despite an awareness that it does or might infringe copyright. Risk management is mostly 'outside' the copyright system (there being no general defence that the defendant acted in good faith or that the copyright owner was unlocatable), although there are ways it can be given more formalised effect, for instance via remedies limitations.[4] The section on risk management will include discussion of Canadian and UK schemes directed to orphaned works – i.e., those for which the copyright owner is impossible to identify or locate.[5]

Whilst this book focuses on free exceptions, it is important to understand this broader compliance framework. One reason is that exceptions will never constitute the sole mechanism for institutions to comply with their legal obligations. Unless there is a major shift in law and norms, there will always be activities for which permissions are required. Furthermore, an understanding of the array of compliance options is important because these strategies are inter-connected. For instance, if exceptions apply narrowly, there will be a greater body of activity for which other mechanisms must be invoked. Similarly, the availability and content of licences may influence decisions about whether to rely on exceptions.[6] This chapter therefore provides a snapshot of copyright management options in order to contextualise its later analysis of exceptions.

Through a Property Paradigm' (2004) 54 *Duke Law Journal* 1; A. Mossoff, 'Is Copyright Property?' (2005) 42 *San Diego Law Review* 29; S. Sterk, 'Intellectualizing Property: The Tenuous Connections Between Land and Copyright' (2005) 83 *Washington University Law Quarterly* 417; J. Cohen, 'What Kind of Property is Intellectual Property?' (2014) 52 *Houston Law Review* 691; P. Chapdelaine, 'The Property Attributes of Copyright' (2014) 10 *Buffalo Intellectual Property Law Journal* 34.

[4] See E. Hudson, 'Copyright and Invisible Authors: A Property Perspective' in A. Johnston and L. Talbot (eds), *Great Debates in Critical Commercial and Corporate Law* (Basingstoke: Palgrave, forthcoming).

[5] See generally P. Brannon, 'Reforming Copyright to Foster Innovation: Providing Access to Orphaned Works' (2006) 14 *Journal of Intellectual Property Law* 145; United States Copyright Office, *Report on Orphan Works: A Report of the Register of Copyrights* (Washington DC: Library of Congress, 2006); M. Pallante, 'Orphan Works & Mass Digitization: Obstacles & Opportunities' (2012) 27 *Berkeley Technology Law Journal* 1251; Australian Law Reform Commission (ALRC), *Copyright in the Digital Economy: Final Report*, Report No. 122 (November 2013), ch. 13.

[6] Whether such evidence should be relevant to the *legal* question of whether an exception is available is more controversial: see, e.g., M. Africa, 'The Misuse of Licensing Evidence in Fair Use Analysis: New Technologies, New Markets, and the Courts' (2000) 88 *California Law Review* 1145. This is discussed further in the analysis of the *Georgia State* litigation in Chapter 5.

II The Empirical Work

A *Why Cultural Institutions*

The empirical work described in this book centres on museums, galleries, libraries and archives in Australia, Canada, the United Kingdom and the United States. There are many other sectors and creator groups that could be studied; however, cultural institutions are an attractive target for a number of reasons. One is the breadth of their activities, which range from internal collection management and preservation through to facilitating researcher requests, hosting online content and developing their own products and merchandise. This means that cultural institutions engage in a mix of inward-looking and public-facing activity, in both commercial and non-commercial contexts – although the dividing line between these different spheres can be controversial. Second, institutions collect many different types of copyright work, being items made in a range of creative conditions.[7] Third, given this backdrop, institutions must consider the needs of a diverse constituency when managing collection items, including authors and creators, publishers and distributors, donors, teachers and scholars, and (through funding and patronage) the general public. Cultural institutions are therefore sites at which a broad range of interests intersect. A fourth reason is the disruptive effect of digital technologies. Such technologies have expanded the potential accessibility of institution holdings and have changed expectations of how such items will be made available, with a series of increasingly ambitious projects seeking to harness the potential that digitisation brings.[8] One famous example is the Google Books project, to which a

---

[7] The significance of different collection genres was mentioned by 318X, who observed that 'although I can logically see that libraries, archives and museums are very similar types of entities and share many goals, the way in which they interact with copyright is very different', in that 'libraries are in the business of acquiring content-based materials ... whereas museums and archives very often collect objects for which copyright is a tangential issue'. For 318X, this meant that the copyright issues around a museum cataloguing an object and a library acquiring and developing content are 'of a different order and magnitude'.

[8] For analysis of copyright and other legal issues surrounding digitisation (including large-scale or mass digitisation), see, e.g., M. Malaro and I. DeAngelis, *A Legal Primer on Managing Museum Collections*, 3rd edition (Washington: Smithsonian Books, 2012), pp. 188–203; M. Borghi and S. Karapapa, *Copyright and Mass Digitization* (Oxford: Oxford University Press, 2013); United States Copyright Office, *Orphan Works and Mass Digitization: A Report of the Register of Copyrights* (United States Copyright Office, June 2015).

number of leading cultural institutions have contributed, and which has been controversial due to questions about copyright.[9] Fifth, cultural institutions are the beneficiaries of privileges under copyright law, with the legislation in each of the four countries studied containing sector-specific exceptions. As discussed in Chapter 4, the enactment of these exceptions reflects the view that cultural institutions carry out important tasks in preserving content and facilitating research and learning, with the result that they deserve accommodations to help them pursue these missions.[10] Finally, the relevance of these exceptions and others – notably fair dealing and fair use – enables comparisons to be made between how institutions operate within rule-like and standard-like drafting.

B   Methodology

The Appendix sets out in greater detail the methodology used for the fieldwork, including ethical matters, justifications for the target institutions and interviewees, and the strength of the conclusions that can be drawn from the fieldwork data. This section instead provides an overview of the key points.

As noted earlier, the interviews described in this book date back to 2004, when in-depth case studies were undertaken at six leading cultural institutions in Australia. Since that time, the fieldwork methodology has remained largely the same, revolving around semi-structured interviews with staff of institutions and other peak bodies, the latter including copyright collectives, creator representatives and other sector and industry bodies. Interviews have generally lasted around 60 to 120 minutes, been audio-recorded (if consent is granted) and been

---

[9] This led to litigation: *The Authors Guild, Inc* v. *Google Inc*, 770 F Supp 2d 666 (SDNY 2011) (District Court rejecting amended settlement agreement); 954 F Supp 2d 282 (SDNY 2013) (District Court granting Google's motion for summary judgment); 804 F 3d 202 (2nd circuit, 2015) (affirming the decision in the District Court). For discussion, see, e.g., M. Sag, 'The Google Book Settlement and the Fair Use Counterfactual' (2010/11) 55 *New York Law School Law Review* 19. Chapter 5 of this book discusses related litigation against the HathiTrust Digital Library.

[10] As discussed by Burrell and Coleman, one might ask whether cultural institutions are the *only* locations at which these activities take place; however, granting wide-ranging rights to other entities may be 'to go too far – indeed, it is difficult to see what scope would be left for copyright under such a system': R. Burrell and A. Coleman, *Copyright Exceptions: The Digital Impact* (Cambridge: Cambridge University Press, 2005), pp. 136–137; see also pp. 138–142 (describing the roles of libraries, archives, museums and galleries, and how their collections and functions overlap).

supplemented with analysis of internal copyright documentation (where supplied by the interviewee) and publicly available information. In order to encourage full and frank disclosure, the interviews have been conducted on the basis that responses are anonymous, meaning that interviewees are referred to with a pseudonym in this book, and other personal and identifying information has been removed.[11] The use of semi-structured interviews permitted each interview to elicit responses to a set of common questions about institutional practices, but to also probe additional matters to gain a deeper understanding of particular activities, experiences and opinions. This was seen as superior to the use of quantitative methods or a questionnaire because of the nature and volume of information that could be gathered from an interview relative to that which could be written on a survey in a similar timeframe. This ability to generate particularised data has proven to be very important given the focus of this book on the law in action and its relationship with the law in books.

Although the conduct and ethical framework of the interviews has remained largely constant over the years, there has been a shift in the focus of the interview questions, with the fieldwork able to be classified into three broad phases. The first phase took place in Australia in 2004 and 2005 as part of a research project conducted at the University of Melbourne. This phase had two stages, with the first batch of interviews comprising in-depth case studies at six major public cultural institutions in relation to legal and non-legal aspects of digitisation. The next year, further interviews were conducted at a range of institutions – larger and smaller, metropolitan and regional – to get a sense of experiences across the sector. As seen in Table 1, whilst fewer staff were interviewed at any given body, this second stage involved fieldwork at 32 cultural institutions and peak bodies. Various trends and common experiences

---

[11] In this book, interviewees from the United States have been randomly assigned a number between 1 and 55; Canadian participants a number between 101 and 164; Australian participants in the phase three fieldwork a number between 201 and 280; and UK participants a number between 301 and 329. The body from which they come is designated as follows: A (archives); G (gallery or art museum); L (library, including academic libraries attached to universities); M (museum not being a designated art museum); and X (industry peak bodies and other non-institutional respondents). This means that, for example, a person who works with the picture or art collection at a library would be given the designation 'L', even though they are working with photographs or fine art. Interviewees who were interviewed on more than one occasion have retained the same interviewee number. In addition, there were some institution staff who also answered some questions in a different capacity (e.g., as member of a peak body) – for those responses, their pseudonym letter (but not number) has been changed to reflect this.

Table 1: *Statistics about fieldwork participants*

Phase	Period	Country	Number of bodies visited	Number of interviewees	Pseudonym numbers
I.	2004–2005	Australia	Case studies: 6 Sector-wide: 32	Case studies: 94 Sector-wide: 40	N/A*
II.	2007–2009	United States	CI: 22 Other: 7	CI: 48 Other: 7	1–55
		Canada	CI: 22 Other: 10	CI: 48 Other: 11	101–159
III.	2012–present	Australia	CI: 21 Other: 4	CI: 77 Other: 5	201–280**
		Canada	CI: 5 Other: 1	CI: 5 Other: 1	101–164**
		United Kingdom	CI: 18 Other: 5	CI: 27 Other: 5	301–329**

'CI' = cultural institutions; 'Other' = industry and peak bodies; *Results of this empirical research cited by reference to earlier published outputs by Emily Hudson and Andrew Kenyon; ** Where a person was re-interviewed in a later tranche of fieldwork, or participated in different capacities, they retained the same interview number.

were discerned from this fieldwork, albeit in the context of research which was intended to be qualitative in nature.[12]

The second phase of fieldwork took place between 2007 and 2009 in the United States and Canada, as part of doctoral research conducted at the University of Melbourne.[13] These interviews covered similar ground to those undertaken during the stage two fieldwork in Australia, although the questions were structured slightly differently from the earlier fieldwork, being explicitly organised around five categories of institution

---

[12] See especially E. Hudson and A. Kenyon, 'Digital Access: The Impact of Copyright on Digitisation Practices in Australian Museums, Galleries, Libraries and Archives' (2007) 30 *University of New South Wales Law Journal* 12; E. Hudson and A. Kenyon, 'Without Walls: Copyright Law and Digital Collections in Australian Cultural Institutions' (2007) 4 *SCRIPTed* 197. To the extent that results from this fieldwork are discussed in this book, citations will be to these published outputs, rather than the pseudonyms adopted in those outputs for the interviewees. Fresh pseudonym codes have been generated for the later Australian interviews in phase three (i.e., the fieldwork conducted from 2012 to the present), although some interviewees participated in both the first and third phases of research.

[13] E. Hudson, 'Copyright Exceptions: The Experiences of Cultural Institutions in the United States, Canada and Australia' (PhD thesis, University of Melbourne, November 2011).

activity: collection management, preservation, user requests, onsite public access and offsite public access. Interviewees were asked to identify each category for which their institution reproduced or digitised collection items, and then describe those activities and explain their institution's strategies for complying with copyright. This allowed a picture to be developed of each institution's digitisation and copyright practices, including licensing, reliance on exceptions, and experiences with orphaned works.

There were two other key differences in the methodology utilised in the Australian and North American work. Whilst the target participants for the Australian fieldwork included institutions of varying sizes and locations, the US and Canadian fieldwork focused mainly on large institutions in major cities. These institutions were of interest for a number of reasons, including that they were believed to have greater resources and expertise to engage with questions about copyright, and would likely be at the forefront of copyright trends and practices across the sector. A further difference was that the North American cohort included institutions that form part of universities. Those interviews were therefore able to elicit information about activities undertaken primarily for the benefit of staff and students, such as the creation of electronic reserves and virtual learning environments – although it was not intended that the fieldwork cover educational copying more generally.

Perhaps the strongest lesson to come from the first two phases of fieldwork was the different experiences of cultural institutions in Australia, Canada and the United States in relation to free exceptions. Whilst many similar observations were made about the use of public domain materials and the benefits and challenges of licensing and dealing with collectives, there was far greater divergence in the reported relevance of exceptions. The third phase of fieldwork from 2012 onwards, whilst using the same basic questions as those developed for the United States and Canada, retained a focus on exceptions. Key aspects of that research included a fresh suite of interviews in Australia to ascertain developments in that country, especially as regards new section 200AB of the Copyright Act; some follow-up interviews in Canada, especially with academic librarians in relation to new licensing strategies and the *Access Copyright v. York* litigation;[14] and the introduction of the United Kingdom as a jurisdiction for empirical study, with some preliminary work around the time of the 2014 amendments to the CDPA, and further study from 2017 onwards to explore the reception of those reforms. An overview of

---

[14] *Canadian Copyright Licensing Agency ("Access Copyright") v. York University* [2018] 2 FCR 43.

the timing of each phase of the fieldwork and the number of participants is set out in Table 1.

III Compliance Options

Doctrinal research suggests that copyright law has had a significant and growing impact on cultural institutions.[15] Copyright issues can arise at a number of junctures, with the main focus of this research being institutional use of collection items.[16] The reason for copyright's relevance is straightforward: institutions often do not own copyright in these items but wish to undertake acts that fall within the copyright owner's exclusive rights, such as copying, public performance and online communication. This raises doctrinal and logistical questions about copyright compliance, including the role of licensing and exceptions. These issues have only grown in the last few decades with the increasing power and ubiquity of digital technologies. This has led to a re-appraisal of how institutions should present their collections and facilitate public access, with an expectation that such technologies should be used and that a virtual institution should operate alongside the physical space. Importantly for the research in this book, the use of digital technologies implicates copyright in ways that traditional methods of collection presentation (e.g., items in glass display cabinets and books on shelves) do not.[17]

---

[15] See, e.g., S. Appel, 'Copyright, Digitization of Images, and Art Museums: Cyberspace and Other New Frontiers' (1999) 6 *UCLA Entertainment Law Review* 149; L. Gasaway, 'Values Conflict in the Digital Environment: Libraries versus Copyright Holders' (2000) 24 *Columbia-VLA Journal of Law and the Arts* 115; A. Kenyon and E. Hudson, 'Copyright, Digitisation and Cultural Institutions' (2004) 31 *Australian Journal of Communication* 89; M. Mumford, 'Copyright in Canadian Archives: An Evolving Challenge' (2006) 31 *Canadian Law Library Review* 238; Hudson and Kenyon, 'Digital Access', n. 12 above; G. Pessach, 'Museums, Digitization and Copyright Law: Taking Stock and Looking Ahead' (2007) 1 *Journal of International Media & Entertainment Law* 253; D. Leenheer Zimmerman, 'Can Our Culture Be Saved? The Future of Digital Archiving' (2007) 91 *Minnesota Law Review* 989; J. Besek and P. Loengard, 'Maintaining the Integrity of Digital Archives' (2008) 31 *Columbia Journal of Law and the Arts* 267; L. Gasaway, 'Libraries, Digital Content, and Copyright' (2010) 12 *Vanderbilt Journal of Entertainment and Technology Law* 755.

[16] Institutions may also be exposed to copyright liability for infringing copies made by researchers and patrons, for instance where they are said to have authorised such acts by installing self-serve copying equipment: see, e.g., *University of New South Wales v. Moorhouse* (1975) 133 CLR 1; *CCH Canadian Ltd v. Law Society of Upper Canada*, [2004] 1 SCR 339. This was discussed at various points in the fieldwork, including whether institutions might have any liability in relation to copies made by patrons on self-supplied equipment such as smartphones.

[17] The degree to which analogue viewing and consultation implicates copying will depend on the scope of the relevant rights, including any display right: e.g., Canadian Copyright Act s. 3(1)(g) (public exhibition right for certain artistic works); US Copyright Act s. 106

That said, the underlying phenomena of technological disruption is not of itself unprecedented,[18] including in the cultural institution sector. For instance, the photocopying revolution of the mid-twentieth century generated debates about how libraries should use such technologies; in Australia, the United Kingdom and the United States, one response was the introduction of sector-specific exceptions for libraries and archives.[19]

This section describes four options for dealing with the copyright issues of institutional use. These are: (1) selecting works that avoid copyright issues; (2) acquiring a licence or assignment of rights; (3) reliance on an exception or compulsory licence; and (4) adopting a 'pure' risk management position.

A Selection-Based Approaches

Perhaps the easiest strategy to deal with copyright is via avoidance, and in particular by the targeting of items that have fallen into the public domain.[20] This was seen in the first phase of empirical work in Australia, where it was observed that

> with tight institution budgets and timelines, selecting works for public digitisation is often based, in whole or part, on the ease of copyright compliance. This creates a preference for works outside the term of copyright, or works for which negotiating with copyright owners will be relatively straightforward.[21]

Similarly, interviewees participating in the second and third phases of fieldwork reported frequently that copyright status was an important consideration when selecting material to digitise, and that public domain materials were particularly attractive for mass digitisation and projects involving public access.[22]

---

(5) (public display right for certain works, but with display defined in s. 101 to mean the showing of a copy either directly or through a device or process). In Europe, the broad definition of the communication right given by the CJEU means that this right is implicated where there is no transmission in the usual sense: see discussion in L. Bently, B. Sherman, D. Gangjee and P. Johnson, *Intellectual Property Law*, 5th edition (Oxford: Oxford University Press, 2018), pp. 162–163.

[18] See generally A. Johns, *Piracy: The Intellectual Property Wars from Gutenberg to Gates* (Chicago: University of Chicago Press, 2009).
[19] See Chapter 4.
[20] See, e.g., Leenheer Zimmerman, n. 15 above, 996; United States Copyright Office, n. 8 above, 74.
[21] Hudson and Kenyon, 'Digital Access', n. 12 above, 42.
[22] E.g., 1G, 2L, 3X, 4L, 7G, 9M, 10L, 14G, 18G, 19L, 20G, 25X, 26G, 27M, 28G, 29L, 30G, 32M, 43M, 47X, 51G, 53G, 55L, 102L, 103G, 105G, 115A, 117L, 120G, 123L, 124A, 128L, 130M, 135G, 136L, 139L, 146L, 147L, 153M, 206G, 214G, 218M,

The use of public domain materials does not eschew intellectual property issues entirely. One question that has been of interest to cultural institutions is whether reproductions of public domain works are protected by a new copyright.[23] The copyright status of such 'literal' copies turns on whether these reproductions meet the originality requirements of the relevant law.[24] This question has been particularly difficult for high-end photographs of fine art, as such images require considerable effort and technical expertise to create but are intended to reproduce faithfully the underlying work.[25] A second question has a more normative orientation:

221L, 225G, 228M, 230A, 232L, 245A, 249L, 250L, 257L, 301L, 303G, 306L, 307M, 313M, 315A, 319L, 320L, 325M, 327L.

[23] See generally K. Garnett, 'Copyright in Photographs' (2000) 22 *European Intellectual Property Review* 229; R. Matz, '*Bridgeman Art Library, Ltd v Corel Corp*' (2000) 15 *Berkeley Technology Law Journal* 3; S. Stokes, '*Graves' Case* and Copyright in Photographs: *Bridgeman v. Corel (USA)*' in D. McClean and K. Schubert (eds), *Dear Images: Art, Copyright and Culture* (London: Ridinghouse and Institute of Contemporary Arts, 2002); T. Kogan, 'Photographic Reproductions, Copyright and the Slavish Copy' (2012) 35 *Columbia Journal of Law and the Arts* 445; J. Hughes, 'The Photographer's Copyright – Photograph as Art, Photograph as Database' (2012) 25 *Harvard Journal of Law & Technology* 339.

[24] There is authority that where a photograph is taken of a three-dimensional object or a contrived scene, originality can arise through elements such as lighting, composition and camera angle: see, e.g., *Rogers v. Koons*, 960 F 2d 301 (2nd circuit, 1992); *Antiquesportfolio.com v. Rodney Fitch & Co* [2001] FSR 348; *Painer v. Standard Verlags GmbH* (C-145/10) [2012] ECDR 6 (Third Chamber); *Temple Island Collections Ltd v. New English Teas Ltd* [2012] EWPCC 1. In contrast, the reproduction of a two-dimensional item using automated equipment may fail to meet even a sweat of the brow standard: *Reject Shop v. Manners* [1995] FSR 870; see also *Hyperion Records Limited v. Sawkins* [2005] EWCA Civ 565, paras. 83–86 (Jacob LJ suggesting that performing easy mechanical tasks such as photocopying will not be enough to make a work original).

[25] See especially *The Bridgeman Art Library v. Corel Corp*, 25 F Supp 2d 421 (SDNY, 1998), 36 F Supp 2d 191 (SDNY, 1999) (Judge Kaplan concluding that under US and UK law, such reproductions are *not* original). Judge Kaplan later elaborated on his reasoning in *Mannion v. Coors Brewing Company* 377 F Supp 2d 444, 451–452 (SDNY, 2005). In 2009, the National Portrait Gallery (NPG) was involved in a dispute with the Wikimedia Foundation in relation to the uploading, onto Wikimedia Commons, of high-resolution images derived from images on its website: see G. Petri, 'Copyright and Reproductions of Two-Dimensional Works of Art' (2014) 12 *Journal of Conservation and Museum Studies* Art.8. In 2015, the Reiss Engelhorn Museum in Germany commenced proceedings against a Wikimedia user in relation to the uploading of images derived from museum photographs of works in its collection. The German Federal Court of Justice held in December 2018 that those photographs were protected under s. 72 of the German Copyright Act 1965: see B. Beck and K. von Werder, 'German Federal Court of Justice Confirms Copyright in Photographs of Public Domain Paintings', *All About IP* (21 March 2019), www.allaboutipblog.com/2019/03/german-federal-court-of-justice-confirms-copyright-in-photographs-of-public-domain-paintings/. Whilst Art. 6 of the Term Directive countenances that Member States may protect 'other' photographs that are not original (for instance via a snapshot right), this would seem to have been foreclosed for photographs of public domain artworks by Art. 14 of the DSM Directive,

when *should* cultural institutions seek to limit the availability and use of public domain materials?[26] Even if no protection arises in copyright, institutions can still rely on other rights (notably from contract and property) to set conditions for access and re-use, including the provision of copies.[27] At one level, access limitations are implicit in day-to-day decisions about public-facing activities, for instance in selecting what to exhibit. However, restrictions on access are particularly significant for unique and rare works where the cultural institution is the only site at which access to the original or a copy is possible.[28] Furthermore, whilst some restrictions may respond to pragmatic or logistical concerns – for example, that there are only so many paintings that can be hung on the wall – a number of these considerations do not apply to digital content.

Perhaps the bigger policy issue is what custodianship means for cultural institutions, including whether they should attempt to oversee or profit from the reproduction, explanation and recasting of collection items.[29] Where items are out of copyright, these questions can carry greater weight, as reference to a work being in the 'public domain' may suggest that use is essentially unrestricted. Given the diversity of collection content and the importance of authenticity, one can think of a number of circumstances in which completely unmediated access is not a desirable goal. Collections with indigenous content provide one example, as it is not uncommon that the nature of these items and the circumstances of their acquisition mean that care is required in the way they are managed.[30]

---

the effect of which is that such photographs may only be protected if they are the author's own intellectual creation.

[26] See generally P. Menell, 'Knowledge Accessibility and Preservation Policy for the Digital Age' (2007) 44 *Houston Law Review* 1013; J. Purday, 'Intellectual Property Issues and Europeana, Europe's Digital Library, Museum and Archive' (2010) 10 *Legal Information Management* 174; H. Sun, 'Copyright and Responsibility' (2013) 4 *Harvard Journal of Sports & Entertainment Law* 263.

[27] See, e.g., A. Reese, 'Photographs of Public Domain Paintings: How, if at All, Should We Protect Them' (2009) 34 *Journal of Corporation Law* 1033.

[28] Ibid., 1036–1039.

[29] For similar themes, see, e.g., R. Allan, 'After *Bridgeman*: Copyright, Museums, and Public Domain Works of Art' (2007) 155 *University of Pennsylvania Law Review* 961, 982–984; Pessach, n. 15 above, 254–256; K. Crews, 'Museum Policies and Art Images: Conflicting Objectives and Copyright Overreaching' (2012) 22 *Fordham Intellectual Property, Media & Entertainment Law Journal* 795.

[30] See, e.g., K. Bowrey and J. Anderson, 'The Politics of Global Information Sharing: Whose Cultural Agendas Are Being Advanced?' (2009) 18 *Social & Legal Studies* 479; S. Singh, M. Blake and J. O'Donnell, 'Digitizing Pacific Cultural Collections: The Australian Experience' (2013) 20 *International Journal of Cultural Property* 77; S. Corbett, 'Copyright Norms and Flexibilities and the Digitisation Practices of New Zealand Museums' (2013) 29 *Law in Context: A Socio-Legal Journal* 55, 62–64; L. Amineddoleh, 'The Role of Museums in the Trade of Black Market Cultural Heritage Property' (2013) 18 *Art Antiquity and Law* 227.

It is not the aim of this book to develop an argument regarding how institutions should manage, or whether they should commercialise, any given collection item. Nor should the focus on exceptions be taken as supporting the view that certain approaches to collection management are invariably desirable. Whilst this book supports a strong role for exceptions, this should not be taken as implying that our goal should be to maximise access in all circumstances. Nonetheless, questions of custodianship clearly inform the themes raised in this work, as views on how collection items should be used will inform decision-making regarding the rights institutions require, and what forms of downstream re-use should be permissible.

B   *Negotiation-Based Solutions*

1 Background A second strategy for copyright compliance is to negotiate for a licence or assignment of rights. Many of the reported benefits and challenges of right clearance recurred across the interviews, and there were similarities in experiences. This raised an interesting observation from the fieldwork: whilst differences in local understandings of copyright seemed to have led to marked differences in the interpretation of free exceptions, these views had not translated to significantly different strategies for rights clearance. This was somewhat surprising, as one might expect that a narrower understanding of exceptions might trigger (or reflect) the development of measures to make licensing more efficient. Such a phenomenon was not observed in this research, and if anything, those with more forward-leaning attitudes to exceptions had the more sophisticated licensing practices. As will be seen, this would seem to relate to knowledge and resources: that those with the time and expertise to understand the operation of exceptions will generally focus similar levels of attention on licensing.

2 Individual Negotiation From the earliest research in Australia through to the third phase of fieldwork, interviewees reported workable systems for one-on-one rights negotiation, especially for fine art, published print works and other materials that had been produced by well-known creators or distributed using traditional channels.[31]

[31] E.g., 2L, 3X, 7G, 17G, 23X, 26G, 28G, 30G, 36M, 43M, 46G, 48G, 53G, 102L, 103G, 106A, 113X, 120G, 135G, 137G, 141L, 155M, 202G, 207L, 208G, 210A, 215G, 218M, 221L, 225G, 255G, 303G, 305M, 308G, 311M, 314G, 315A, 317G, 323X, 325M, 329M; see also Hudson and Kenyon, 'Digital Access', n. 12 above, 37–38.

A common goal of those overseeing licensing was to find ways to reduce transaction costs and promote efficiency.[32] Some interviewees reported that to reduce repeat negotiations with the same individual, they requested general licences covering a range of activities rather than project-specific rights.[33] There were also reports of forward-looking copyright procedures at acquisition, such as obtaining thorough rights information from the donor or seller, or including copyright licensing as part of the acquisition workflow.[34] As discussed in the next sub-section, collective administration was another mechanism to streamline rights negotiation, although experiences varied. Finally, a number of interviewees spoke about issues with securing access to large electronic databases.[35] This remains a contentious issue, with concerns relating not only to the expense of licences but the role of academic publishing in a world where scholarly outputs are increasingly expected to be distributed in open access form.[36]

Although licensing experiences were often positive, the interviews also revealed common issues with such processes. These included the costs of securing large numbers of separate licences; incomplete rights management information; the presence of non-attributed works in the collection; difficulties in tracking down copyright owners; the level of retrospective

---

[32] See Hudson and Kenyon, 'Digital Access', n. 12 above, 23–27.
[33] E.g., 2L, 7G, 9M, 26G, 28G, 29L, 30G, 35L, 43M, 46G, 48G, 53G, 55L, 113X, 135G, 136L, 137G, 322G, 155M, 158M, 202G, 214M, 215G, 225G, 228M, 250L, 255A, 267G, 303G, 307M, 317G, 322G, 323X, 325M. Asking for additional rights can lead to an increase in licence fees, particularly where the requested uses are seen as profit-making. As such, many broader licences were unremunerated and applied only to what may loosely be called non-commercial uses.
[34] E.g., 2L, 4L, 16G, 20G, 26G, 28G, 30G, 36M, 43M, 45M, 46G, 53G, 55L, 103G, 106A, 116M, 126A, 130M, 135G, 136L, 137G, 150G, 155M, 214M, 215G, 218M, 225G, 228M, 267G, 250L, 254L, 255A, 303G, 313M, 314G, 317G, 325M, 329M.
[35] Reported experiences varied. Whilst some participants described positive dealings with 'library-friendly' distributors (152L; similar 52M, 101L, 117L, 119L, 156L, 237L, 312L), others pointed to challenges in negotiating access, including that some licences sought to limit reliance on statutory exceptions: e.g., 15L, 19L, 35L, 101L, 128L, 146L, 152L, 201X, 224X, 238L, 301L. See generally A. Bartow, 'Electrifying Copyright Norms and Making Cyberspace More Like a Book' (2003) 48 *Villanova Law Review* 13; Gasaway, 'Libraries, Digital Content, and Copyright', n. 15 above; G. Laughlin, 'Digitization and Democracy: The Conflict between the Amazon Kindle License Agreement and the Role of Libraries in a Free Society' (2010) 40 *University of Baltimore Law Review* 3. Following the 2014 reforms to the CDPA, a number of exceptions have a prohibition on contracting out, i.e., that any contractual term that purports to prevent or restrict reliance on that exception is unenforceable: e.g., ss. 29A (5), 30(4), 41(5), 42(7).
[36] A prominent example at the time of writing is the boycott of Elsevier products by universities in the United States and Europe: see, e.g., S. Zhang, 'The Real Cost of Knowledge', *The Atlantic* (4 March 2019) www.theatlantic.com/science/archive/2019/03/uc-elsevier-publisher/583909/.

licensing that may be required for older works in the collection; and the challenges of future-proofing licences for new technologies and platforms.[37] Resourcing was perhaps the key internal impediment to licensing, both in terms of being able to dedicate staff time to rights and having budgets to spend on licence fees. However, there were also market failures that no amount of resourcing could correct. The paradigmatic example was orphaned works, but interviewees also reported difficulties with nonresponsive copyright owners.[38] Whilst in some cases this might reflect a positive desire to reject licence terms, one can imagine other reasons for inaction, including that the copyright owner is not aware of their status or does not have the inclination or resources to manage rights (especially for uses perceived as low value).[39] This would seem to be a predictable by-product of a system in which protection is automatic rather than tied to some formality such as registration or assertion of rights; and in which copyright owners are not under any meaningful obligation to maintain an ongoing connection to their works.[40]

Whilst issues with licensing occurred in all collections, they were more prevalent for materials that often end up in archival, social history and special collections: unpublished manuscripts, letters and diaries, posters, amateur and personal photography, raw footage, and so on.[41] For instance, one interviewee described an externally funded project to create

---

[37] E.g., 3X, 4L, 13M, 17G, 19L, 20G, 22L, 26G, 29L, 30G, 35L, 43M, 45M, 105G, 117L, 123L, 124A, 126A, 135G, 136L, 139L, 142M, 158M, 202G, 203M, 207L, 210A, 219M, 221L, 246A, 250L, 251M, 305X, 307M, 308M, 317G, 320L, 325M, 327L.

[38] Especially 13M, 27M, 41G, 48G, 106A, 135G, 155M, 260M, 314G.

[39] In the United States, 3X, 16G and 19L hinted that failure to respond to requests encouraged institutions to consider fair use arguments; whilst in Australia and the United Kingdom, 260M and 314G suggested that the lack of a response may, in some instances, be relevant for risk management: see further Chapter 8.

[40] See Hudson, n. 4 above. The linking of copyright subsistence to formalities such as registration is precluded by Art. 5(2) of the Berne Convention: see S. van Gompel, 'Formalities in the Digital Era: An Obstacle or Opportunity?' in L. Bently, U. Suthersanen and P. Torremans (eds), *Global Copyright: Three Hundred Years Since the Statute of Anne, from 1709 to Cyberspace* (Cheltenham: Edward Elgar, 2010). In addition, it seems to be accepted that copyright owners can be inactive for many years but still bring a claim *to* copyright, as illustrated by *Fisher* v. *Brooker* [2009] UKHL 41 (Fisher recognised as joint author and co-owner of the musical copyright in the song 'A Whiter Shade of Pale', despite having been inactive for thirty-eight years). For consideration of whether limiting doctrines such as abandonment should apply to copyright, see, e.g., E. Hudson and R. Burrell, 'Abandonment, Copyright and Orphaned Works: What Does it Mean to Take the Proprietary Nature of Intellectual Property Rights Seriously?' (2011) 35 *Melbourne University Law Review* 971.

[41] E.g., 2L, 4L, 9M, 10L, 13M, 22L, 39L, 43M, 45M, 106A, 116M, 117L, 123L, 124A, 136L, 139L, 210A, 221L, 235L, 246A, 248L, 307M, 313M, 320L, 326L, 328G. See also Hudson and Kenyon, 'Digital Access', n. 12 above, 39–41.

Compliance Options   77

a digital repository about a major creative industry.[42] Relevant items – many of which were historical – had been identified from the institution's collection, including photographs, promotional materials, archival documents and a range of ephemera. Significantly, this selection process was undertaken solely by reference to each item's relevance to the themes of the project. Whilst the project was intended to progress through multiple stages, it was terminated early because of copyright issues. This was an important lesson for the institution regarding the role of copyright in project design. 'In retrospect', the interviewee observed, 'I would not do it that way again: I would go where I can clear copyright.'

When asked to expand upon the issues encountered, the interviewee explained that, even though the institution had many years' experience with rights clearance and copyright management:

> We didn't really fully understand the implications of trying to do this large-scale copyright clearance project. It was very difficult; to be honest, it brought us to our knees. We had to assign an additional person full time to help to manage the process. We generated reams of paper, all of which had to be tracked. We established a very rigorous process, I did a lot of liaison with our [legal advisors] about what we could ask people for, how we should ask it, trying to ensure that we were meeting the legislation.

The success of these efforts varied. Whilst the best-case scenario was to locate a copyright owner who was able to grant rights in relation to an entire tranche of works, some owners were only willing to give permissions for a subset of materials, whilst others doubted whether they held any rights at all. The 'even worse' scenario was orphaned material, which was not used due to requirements of the external funder and legal advice about the risks of copyright infringement. In the end, the project website hosted several thousand reproductions, all of which were cleared.

This was not an isolated example, with similar issues reported by other interviewees. For instance, one interviewee described a project for the creation of an online database where works had been selected by 'intrinsic quality' rather than the presence of a living artist or readily identifiable copyright owner. The interviewee described the rights clearance process as 'too complicated' and hampered by numerous logistical challenges, with the result that the institution decided to limit future digitisation initiatives to public domain material. The resource-intensiveness of licensing was also emphasised by another interviewee, who said:

> Just to put an exhibit together is almost a full-time employee working for a series of months just to get the pictures in the exhibit. And we're not talking about a

---

[42] To further protect anonymity, pseudonyms will not be used for some examples.

large exhibit ... You end up filling boxes of thousands of images and paperwork and rights. You need to hire someone full-time to get the rights, and then after that, if you decide that this exhibit will go on tour, then all of this needs to be renegotiated.

The sheer time and costs of clearance were not the only challenges reported by interviewees. For instance, one interviewee referred to difficulties in clearing rights with other institutions, noting the lack of consistency in request procedures and the existence of 'archaic' and uncooperative practices by some entities. Still another described issues in implementing standardised documentation and processes within their own institution, where 'our forms are being used to collect everything from a set of cups and saucers to somebody's family photos'. This presented challenges given the different types and layers of rights, and exposed failures in integrating the work of different departments:

We have collection managers [and] our database team ... and then on the other side we have our image management team [who handle rights], and they seem to get pushed in between the two. So the collection manager has not necessarily got the information or asked the right questions [about copyright]; the database team may not have explained what the standard [copyright] fields are [in the collection database], or worked with anyone to standardise the fields, and express frustration that the database doesn't integrate because people describe things differently; and the rights management guys are trying to make sure we don't infringe [copyright] later on ... without having access to [the primary documents].

Given this backdrop, it was not surprising that many larger-scale, public-facing projects were designed to minimise copyright issues, for instance by prioritising public domain works or those for which rights had been cleared or could be obtained relatively easily.[43] This meant that copyright was not merely procedural but influenced, at times strongly, the content of websites and other public outputs. This reflects an ongoing challenge for copyright lawmakers: that the economic rights of copyright are best classified as 'property rules';[44] but that licensing is often impaired where transaction costs and/or the value of the prospective use mean the game is not worth the candle.[45] If no exceptions are

---

[43] See also the discussion of public domain works at n. 20 to n. 22 above and surrounding text.
[44] Being entitlements that may be bought by a third party in a voluntary transaction at a price agreed by the seller: see G. Calabresi and A. Melamed, 'Property Rules, Liability Rules, and Inalienability: One View of the Cathedral' (1972) 85 *Harvard Law Review* 1089. Such rights are often explained in economic terms, for instance, in relation to incentivisation and concerns about free riding: see generally W. Landes and R. Posner, 'An Economic Analysis of Copyright Law' (1989) 18 *Journal of Legal Studies* 325.
[45] Discussed in Hudson, n. 4 above.

relevant, and risk management is precluded (for instance due to reputational concerns or the requirements of funders), then institutions may simply avoid certain content. Importantly, it was not obvious from the fieldwork that these self-imposed restrictions necessarily supported the interests of creators and copyright owners, or reflected the preferences of such individuals.[46] Many interviewees reported that creators were often willing to grant unremunerated licences that included some public activities,[47] and that for archival and social history content, copyright owners and their heirs were often excited to see their works being made available.[48] In fact, there seemed to be a shift in creator attitudes over the course of the fieldwork, with increasing numbers of people not only comfortable with some online uses (especially informational and non-commercial ones) but *expecting* their works to be visible on the institution's website.[49]

One way to help overcome some of these issues is to continue efforts to lower the transaction costs of licensing. This does not necessarily require statutory reform; for instance, improvements could be made through better internal workflows, new measures to facilitate communication between rightsholders and institutions,[50] and improvements to the voluntary licences offered by collective management organisations (discussed next). As will be seen later in this chapter and in Chapter 8, changed institutional attitudes to risk may also alter the degree to which licensing issues are perceived as immutable roadblocks. However, part of the answer may also be found in expanding the role of exceptions.

---

[46] Especially for works with no obvious commercial value or quality of 'auteurship': see also Hudson and Kenyon, 'Digital Access', n. 12 above, 42–43; Hudson and Kenyon, 'Without Walls', n. 12 above, 209–210.

[47] E.g., 7G, 20G, 31G, 36M, 46G, 48G, 53G, 102L, 103G, 105G, 120G, 139L, 154L, 202G, 215G, 218M, 221L, 225G, 228M, 250L, 267G, 303G, 307M, 314G, 317G, 323X, 325M, 327L, 328G, 329M. See also A. Kenyon and R. Wright, 'Whose Conflict? Copyright, Creators and Cultural Institutions' (2010) 33 *University of New South Wales Law Journal* 286, 296–300 (empirical study with Australian creators; whilst there were criticisms of some institutional practices and a desire to be paid for commercial uses, there were also activities for which participants were willing to forego licensing fees).

[48] E.g., 228M, 248L, 255A.

[49] E.g., 42G, 102L, 105G, 208G, 215G, 225G, 273L, 314G, 321X, 322G; see also Kenyon and Wright, n. 47 above, 298. This shift seemed to coincide with cultural institutions also retreating from earlier predictions regarding the income that could be generated from digitisation; as explained by 317G, although some institutions generate healthy proceeds from such practices, 'picture libraries have evolved from where they were originally – a financial saviour – to where they are now, often a philanthropic exercise to get the collections out'.

[50] See also I. Hargreaves, *Digital Opportunity: A Review of Intellectual Property and Growth* (May 2011) ch. 4 (recommending measures including development of a 'cross sectoral Digital Copyright Exchange' to streamline licensing arrangements).

3 Collective Management Collective management (sometimes referred to as collective administration) refers to the joint management of the rights of multiple individuals, often by a collecting society.[51] There are a number of different mechanisms by which this can take place, there being voluntary, extended and mandatory forms.[52] In addition, the collective can mediate transactions with third parties in a number of ways. One approach is for individual members to set their own terms and royalties, with the collective acting as an administrative clearing house; in others, the collective decides the terms and royalties that will apply across the repertoire, subject to approval or review by a tribunal or court.[53] One of the main rationales for collective management is to reduce problems associated with licensing by lowering the costs of locating and negotiating with rightsholders.[54] That said, concerns have been raised that practices can be monopolistic and anti-competitive, with potential adverse effects for members and users.[55]

Whilst collective administration has been utilised for many years in all four countries studied, a review of the literature suggests its role and prominence might differ between each jurisdiction. In Canada, for example, the Copyright Board currently identifies more than 30 organisations that it classifies as 'copyright collective societies'.[56] The existence of such a large number of collectives can be traced back to copyright reforms of the 1980s. These reforms included expansion of the regulation of collectives through the supervisory functions of the Copyright Board,[57] thereby confirming the legality and legitimacy of collective

---

[51] See generally M. Ficsor, *Collective Management of Copyright and Related Rights* (Geneva: World Intellectual Property Organization, 2002), pp. 17–18, 22–23.

[52] For voluntary collective licensing, copyright owners decide whether to authorise representation by the collective. For extended collective licensing, the repertoire extends automatically to all rightsholders in a class, but owners can opt out of representation. Finally, mandatory collective licensing makes the management of a particular right by a collective compulsory. See D. Gervais, 'Collective Management of Copyright and Neighbouring Rights in Canada: An International Perspective' (2002) 1 *Canadian Journal of Law and Technology* 21, 22, 27–31.

[53] See, e.g., G. Lunney, 'Copyright Collectives and Collecting Societies: The United States Experience' in D. Gervais (ed), *Collective Management of Copyright and Related Rights*, 3rd edition (Alphen aan den Rijn: Wolters Kluwer, 2015), pp. 319–320.

[54] See, generally, Bently, Sherman, Gangjee and Johnson, n. 17 above, pp. 320–321; D. Gervais, 'Collective Management of Copyright: Theory and Practice in the Digital Age' in D. Gervais (ed), *Collective Management of Copyright and Related Rights*, 3rd edition (Alphen aan den Rijn: Wolters Kluwer, 2015).

[55] See, e.g., J. Band and B. Butler, 'Some Cautionary Tales About Collective Licensing' (2013) 21 *Michigan State International Law Review* 687.

[56] Copyright Board of Canada, *Copyright Collective Societies* (last modified 8 March 2018), www.cb-cda.gc.ca/societies-societes/index-e.html.

[57] See generally R. Pantalony, *Illustrating Options: Collective Administration of Intellectual Property for Canadian Cultural Heritage Institutions* (Canadian Heritage Information

management. In further reforms in 1997, the reach of collective administration was extended further, and a number of statutory licences introduced that are administered by collectives.[58] In the United States, on the other hand, attitudes towards collectives have been less charitable. For instance, it has been said that entities that set licence terms and fees across their portfolio may violate antitrust laws by not permitting competition between members. According to Glynn Lunney, the three organisations that adopt this model – all of which administer rights in music – are 'viewed as something of a necessary evil' because they enable music producers and their licensees to avoid prohibitive transaction costs.[59] Other US collectives instead use a clearing house model, such as the Copyright Clearance Center.[60]

Collective administration has had a less fractious history in the United Kingdom and Australia. In both countries, the first collectives appeared in the early part of the twentieth century,[61] and recent law reform efforts suggest that collective management will have continued relevance.[62] Nevertheless, when compared with the fast-paced growth of collectives in Canada, one might ask whether collective management plays a more prominent role in that country or is otherwise experienced differently. For instance, Mario Bouchard, writing in 2006, offered the tentative view that 'Australian rightsholders appear to be less likely than Canadians to resort to collectives as a means of obtaining compensation for the use of their protected works and other copyright subject matters'.[63]

Network, 1999); Monique Hébert, *Background Paper: Copyright Reform* (Library of Parliament, March 1996), pp. 10–12.

[58] See generally D. Gervais, 'A Uniquely Canadian Institution: The Copyright Board of Canada' in Y. Gendreau, *An Emerging Intellectual Property Paradigm: Perspectives from Canada* (Cheltenham: Edward Elgar, 2008), p. 209.

[59] Lunney, n. 53 above, p. 320.

[60] Copyright Clearance Center, 'Rightsholder Products & Solutions', www.copyright.com/rightsholders/.

[61] The first collective in the United Kingdom was the Performing Right Society, formed in 1914, whilst in Australia it was the Australasian Performing Right Association Limited, formed in 1926: see Bently, Sherman, Gangjee and Johnson, n. 17 above, p. 318; S. Simpson, *Review of Australian Collecting Societies: A Report to the Minister for Communications and the Arts and the Minister for Justice* (July 1995), para. 3.2.

[62] See Copyright and Rights in Performances (Extended Collective Licensing) Regulations 2014 (SI 2014/2588) (implicitly affirming collective management); Copyright Amendment (Disability Access and other Measures) Act 2017 (Cth) (simplification of the compulsory licences for educational copying in the backdrop of calls for such schemes to be repealed).

[63] M. Bouchard, 'Collective Management in Commonwealth Jurisdictions: Comparing Canada with Australia' in D. Gervais (ed), *Collective Management of Copyright and Related Rights* (Alphen aan den Rijn: Kluwer Law International, 2006), p. 308.

In this research, interviewees reported mixed experiences with collectives, although these did not divide according to jurisdiction, as might have been suggested by the foregoing analysis. There was perhaps something in the proposition that Canadian interviewees were more accepting of the legitimacy of collectives, especially when compared with their US counterparts.[64] As one US interviewee said, 'there must be something that's too free enterprise about us' for collective models to flourish.[65] Despite this, reported day-to day practices shared much in common, and Canadian interviews did not reveal innovative or more efficient models.

There are a number of explanations for this observation. One is that voluntary collective administration is particularly well suited to some collections – notably art and published print-based works – but has limited relevance to others, especially those containing large quantities of archival and social history material.[66] Indeed, certain proposals to help improve the reach of collective management, such as extended collective licensing (ECL), may be inapt if there is no collective that can plausibly claim to represent a critical mass of rightsholders.[67] It is therefore significant that the ECL scheme in Article 8 of the Directive on Copyright in the Digital Single Market (DSM Directive), which will apply to non-commercial use of out-of-commerce works by cultural heritage institutions, has been paired with an exception which applies where there is no collective management organisation that is sufficiently representative of the relevant rightholders.[68]

A second reason is that the advantages and disadvantages of collective licensing have a universal quality that transcends national boundaries. For instance, when asked about the benefits of collective management, responses were fairly consistent: collectives are well known and easy to contact;[69] will respond to requests (often speedily for time-sensitive matters);[70] and can help streamline rights management, for example where a single organisation represents a large number of rightsholders

---

[64] E.g., 3X, 6X, 19L, 28G, 29L, 36M, 37M, 47X, 53G (all stating that they preferred dealing direct with individual authors, publishers or artists); and note 1G, 3X, 36M, 43M (questioning the efficiency of collective administration in the institutional context). Some Canadian interviewees also criticised the power and practices of collectives: e.g., 115A, 120G, 124A, 127L, 128L, 144X.

[65] 53G.   [66] As noted explicitly by 35L, 104M, 106A, 115A; similar 325M.

[67] See, e.g., L. Guibault and S. Schroff, 'Extended Collective Licensing for the Use of Out-of-Commerce Works in Europe: A Matter of Legitimacy vis-à-vis Rights Holders' (2018) 49 *IIC* 916.

[68] See Directive (EU) 2019/790 of the European Parliament and of the Council of 17 April 2019 on copyright and related rights in the Digital Single Market and amending Directives 96/9/EC and 2001/29/EC, Art. 8(2).

[69] E.g., 42G, 49G, 51G, 104M, 137G, 329M.

[70] E.g., 33G, 135G, 137G, 314G, 329M.

Compliance Options 83

or can offer blanket licences.[71] Similarly, interviewees gave fairly consistent responses about the drawbacks of collective administration. The price-point for licences was of particular concern, notably for larger-scale projects where even a low 'per work' fee could be high in the aggregate.[72] There was also a concern that copyright collectives could be inflexible in their licence terms and did not give due regard to the parameters in which cultural institutions operate.[73] In some cases this appeared to be contrary to the approaches often adopted by individual rightsholders. For example, a number of interviewees reported that many artists were willing to grant unremunerated licences for uses for which collectives would demand a fee, such as the inclusion of images in online collection databases.[74] Finally, some interviewees expressed concern about proposals that collectives be allowed to administer ECL schemes for orphaned works, viewing such a move as unnecessary and unjustified.[75] It may be that the scheme for out-of-commerce works in the DSM Directive has gone some way to allay these concerns, as a number of UK interviewees suggested that the scheme may provide a useful release valve for some works.[76] In contrast, one Australian interviewee said:

I've been hearing rumours that some of the collecting agencies are keen to licence orphan works, and I think that is absolutely reprehensible – that some body would take it upon themselves to insert themselves into the process, to say we don't know who the rightsholder is either, but we'll charge you money to put it online or in a book, [and] we'll hang onto that money in case the rightsholder ever shows up ... [I]t's morally wrong.[77]

It is important to bear in mind that experiences with collective management were not static. For instance, a new compliance paradigm was seen in Canadian academic libraries from 2010 onwards, including the

---

[71] E.g., 7G, 49G, 113X, 125L, 132X, 141L, 309L, 312L, 314G, 316L, 321X. Interviewees 113X, 125L and 155M noted that efficiency advantages can be curtailed by a limited repertoire.
[72] E.g., 36M, 41G, 46G, 53G, 120G, 125L, 135G, 155M, 225G, 314G.
[73] E.g., 7G, 21M, 36M, 127L, 135G, 144X, 208G, 229X, 303G.
[74] E.g., 3X, 7G, 20G, 36M, 41G, 46G, 53G, 113X, 154L, 208G, 225G, 303G.
[75] E.g., 210X (concerns amongst institutions include whether those who administered rights could claim to have any legitimate basis to do so; and whether cultural institutions are, in fact, better placed to track down rightsholders), 238L, 248L, 324X (there is an 'ethical question' of whether money should be collected and redistributed for personal letters, photos and films, leaflets, posters, and so forth, that were never created for remuneration); note too 301L (querying whether collectives are sufficiently accountable in relation to the distribution of funds).
[76] E.g., 313M, 320L (ECL may have a role for certain content that does not suit a risk-based approach), 325M, 326L, 327L.
[77] 225G; similar 228M ('horrified' at the suggestion), 324X (has heard ECL described as a 'protection racket').

rejection of blanket licences offered by Access Copyright.[78] In contrast, other interviewees described improved relations with collectives, reflecting better communication and compromise on both sides and efforts by collectives to improve the value-add of their products, especially in relation to digital uses.[79] There was no suggestion in the United Kingdom that universities were seriously contemplating withdrawing from the educational copying licence offered by the Copyright Licensing Agency (CLA).[80] At least amongst interviewees, it was said that the relationship between universities and CLA was good, although concerns were raised about aspects of the licence, including whether it represented value for money across the sector.[81] Similarly, although Australian interviewees were not predicting the imminent demise of the copyright collective, questions were raised by some interviewees about the need for collective licensing given primary licences with content producers, moves to open access, and so forth.[82]

In sum, at least for now, collective management remains a significant part of the copyright landscape for many cultural institutions.

C   Compulsory Licences and Free Exceptions

1 Background The third main strategy for copyright compliance is to invoke a statutory provision that alleviates the need for consent, i.e., an exception or compulsory licence. Where such a provision applies, an institution may proceed with conduct without permission, so long as all requirements are met, and, for remunerated exceptions and compulsory licences, any fees paid.

A number of justifications have been put forward for these provisions.[83] One explanation is that they respond to market failure, for

---

[78] See Chapter 8. Seeds of change were discussed by some Canadian interviewees in the 2008/2009 research: e.g., 101L, 117L, 128L, 144X, 146L, 156L.

[79] E.g., 103G, 141L, 225G, 309L, 310X, 312L, 314G, 316L.

[80] Information about the CLA UUK/GuildHE Higher Education Licence is available at www.cla.co.uk/higher-education-licence.

[81] E.g., 301L, 309L, 312L. These interviewees all noted variation in levels of use of the CLA licence, with much activity under the licence being undertaken by a small group of institutions. In contrast 316L was of the view that the licence may change in the future, but was of 'considerable value' for now.

[82] Especially 248L, 265L; similar 272L (noting the benefits of making the Australian compulsory licence for education more flexible and less administratively burdensome); note 237L (leaving a collective requires the right infrastructure and institutional support, as it is still necessary to comply with the law).

[83] For a recent discussion, see P. Samuelson, 'Justifications for Copyright Limitations and Exceptions' in R. Okediji, *Copyright Law in an Age of Limitations and Exceptions* (New York: Cambridge University Press, 2017).

instance where structural barriers or other circumstances prevent voluntary transactions from occurring.[84] Prohibitive transaction costs are one such example.[85] Thus, in the copyright context, an exception might be appropriate where the costs of identifying and negotiating with copyright owners outweigh the value of the resulting licences. In addition, exceptions and compulsory licences have been justified where broader social interests are said to demand them, for instance to promote free speech or public access to copyright works, or to rein in the anti-competitive characteristics of copyright. On some views, this is an iteration of market failure, in that transactions do not take place because positive externalities cannot be internalised by the copyist (such as the benefit to society of certain transformative uses), or because one party is swayed by interests that are difficult to monetise and hence 'purchase' under a licence (such as the interest in reputation that may prevent an author permitting someone else to make a parody of his or her work).[86]

This section provides a brief overview of the compulsory licences and exceptions that are most relevant to the practices of cultural institutions.

2 Compulsory Licences Under a compulsory licence, an otherwise infringing act can be performed without the permission of the copyright owner, but that person remains entitled to remuneration.[87] Although compulsory licences preserve the right to be paid, they are controversial for a number of reasons: they change the nature of the owner's interest from a property rule to a liability rule by removing his or her capacity to withhold consent for acts covered by the licence;[88] they require some sort of bureaucracy for their administration; and they take the determination of the licence fee outside usual voluntary negotiations, a matter that sits particularly awkwardly with neoliberal conceptions of the supremacy of the market.

---

[84] See, e.g., W. Gordon, 'Fair Use as Market Failure: A Structural and Economic Analysis of the Betamax Case and its Predecessors' (1982) 82 *Columbia Law Review* 1600; W. Gordon, 'Excuse and Justification in the Law of Fair Use: Commodification and Market Perspectives' in N. Elkin-Koren and N. Netanel (eds), *The Commodification of Information* (The Hague: Kluwer Law International, 2002).
[85] See, e.g., Landes and Posner, n. 44 above, 357–358; M. Spence, *Intellectual Property* (Oxford: Oxford University Press, 2007), p. 18.
[86] See, e.g., R. Merges, 'Are You Making Fun of Me?: Notes on Market Failure and the Parody Defense in Copyright' (1993) 21 *AIPLA Quarterly Journal* 305; L. Pallas Loren, 'Redefining the Market Failure Approach to Fair Use in an Era of Copyright Permission Systems' (1997) 5 *Journal of Intellectual Property Law* 1, 5–6.
[87] See generally Bently, Sherman, Gangjee and Johnson, n. 17 above, pp. 314–315.
[88] Applying the analysis of Calabresi and Melamed, n. 44 above.

A number of compulsory licences apply to educational use and hence some activities of academic libraries. The most prominent examples in this research were the Australian schemes formerly contained in Part VA and Part VB of the Copyright Act.[89] These were repealed in 2017 and replaced by a simplified version.[90] There is also an educational statutory licence in Canada, but it is of limited reach.[91] As such, voluntary blanket licences with reprography collectives were of far greater relevance to academic libraries in that country. As discussed in Chapter 8, there has been considerable movement in the utilisation of these licences over the course of this research.

3 Exceptions Ahead of the fieldwork, doctrinal analysis identified the provisions that seemed to have the greatest relevance to the activities of cultural institutions.

First, some copyright statutes contain exceptions that are tailored to, and may only be invoked by, cultural institutions. As discussed in Chapter 4, such provisions can be found in the legislation of Australia, the United Kingdom, the United States and Canada, being introduced by the first three in the middle of the twentieth century, and in Canada in the late 1990s. A number of questions arise in relation to these provisions, including policy questions about their coverage, and drafting questions about whether their form – which often, but not always, adopts rule-like language[92] – is fit-for-purpose.

Second, some activities of cultural institutions and their patrons may fall within the fair dealing exceptions of Australian, Canadian and UK law. These provide that there will be no infringement of copyright where a use is fair and undertaken for a prescribed purpose. These purposes vary between different jurisdictions, but can include research and private study, education, criticism and review, parody and satire, and news reporting. As noted in Chapter 2, the fair dealing exceptions are less restrictive than the sector-specific libraries and archives provisions, and would appear to have a more standard-like coverage. That said, there are limits on their application, including through the exhaustive list of

---

[89] These applied to the use of radio and television broadcasts (administered by Screenrights) and textual material and images (administered by Copyright Agency Limited).

[90] See new Division 4 of Part IVA; this reform was effected by the Copyright Amendment (Disability Access and other Measures) Act 2017 (Cth).

[91] Canadian Copyright Act s 29.7 (reproduction and performance of broadcasts).

[92] See, e.g., D. Nimmer, *Nimmer on Copyright*, Volume 2 (LexisNexis, online resource, accessed 15 January 2019), para. 8.03 (describing the US provisions as comprising 'complex and highly technical rules').

purposes. Experiences with fair dealing are discussed in detail in Chapters 7 and 8.

Third, section 107 of the US Copyright Act provides that a fair use of a copyrighted work is not an infringement of copyright. As discussed in Chapter 2, section 107 includes a non-exhaustive list of purposes to which fair use might apply, and sets out four factors that 'shall' be considered in determining whether 'any particular case is a fair use'. One of the key differences between the drafting of fair dealing and fair use is that the latter is open-ended. This raises empirical questions about whether fair use functions differently from fair dealing. Fair use is considered in detail in Chapter 5.

Fourth, in Australia there is an autochthonous exception for cultural and educational institutions and (until 2017[93]) those assisting users with a disability: section 200AB. This exception was introduced in 2006 with the stated aim of capturing some of the benefits of fair use.[94] Despite this, it uses language very different from section 107 – as seen in the confined list of users that may rely on the provision, and the inclusion of three-step test language rather than fairness factors.[95] As will be discussed in Chapter 6, empirical work with Australian cultural institutions suggested that section 200AB has been of very limited relevance, and that this is unlikely to change. One of the questions for this book is why this exception has failed to achieve its stated goals, and what this means for the use of 'flexible' drafting in copyright exceptions.

Finally, the copyright statutes of Australia, Canada and the United Kingdom contain exceptions permitting certain dealings with artistic works located in public places.[96] These provisions have similar content, applying to sculptures and works of artistic craftsmanship situated 'permanently' (Canada and the United Kingdom) or 'otherwise than temporarily' (Australia) in a public place, building or premises. Where applicable, there is no infringement by the performance of specified acts, such as making a painting or drawing of the work, photographing it, or including it in a broadcast or cinematographic work. These exceptions

---

[93] See Copyright Amendment (Disability Access and other Measures) Act 2017 (Cth), repealing elements of s. 200AB that related to disabled users.
[94] See the second reading speech of the Attorney-General: Commonwealth, *Parliamentary Debates*, House of Representatives, 19 October 2006 (Philip Ruddock).
[95] Australian Copyright Act ss. 200AB(1), (7).
[96] See CDPA s.62; Australian Copyright Act s. 65; Canadian Copyright Act s. 32.2(1)(b)(ii). For discussion of s. 62, see M. Iljadica, 'Copyright and the Right to the City' (2017) 68 *Northern Island Legal Quarterly* 59.

have been controversial because there is no requirement that the use be fair.[97] That said, there are limits to their relevance; for instance, depending on the wording they may not permit the resulting copies to be published in hard copy form or distributed online. Given that these provisions were not mentioned by any interviewees during the fieldwork, this book does not include any empirical analysis of their operation.

IV Risk Management

A Overview

As discussed in Chapter 2, any consideration of the law in action must consider risk preferences: the degree of comfort that users have with uncertainty regarding the legal consequences of their actions. There is, after all, only so much we can do to eliminate risk from the copyright system. Leaving aside issues with the operation of exceptions, other copyright doctrines also have varying degrees of uncertainty;[98] plus there are evidentiary challenges in assembling information to determine copyright status and ownership; plus there are works that are orphaned, and for which no amount of research or legal analysis will enable voluntary negotiations to take place. Decision-making about copyright is therefore influenced strongly by attitudes to risk.

Risk management is one manifestation of risk-informed decision-making, and can be contrasted with analysis that takes place 'within' the copyright system. In the latter case, risk preferences are relevant to the degree of certainty demanded from legal and factual inquiry into the content and application of the law. To illustrate, one interviewee described using a risk-informed approach to help assess whether old scientific and technical papers had fallen into the public domain (there being difficulties in assessing duration on a work-by-work basis),[99] whilst another described the challenges in determining whether attractive but utilitarian objects were protected artistic works for the purposes of copyright law.[100] As will be seen in this book, risk preferences can also be highly relevant to interpretations of exceptions.

But in addition to risk-informed decision-making, in all four countries there were repeated reports of institutions 'risk managing' uses, i.e.,

---

[97] See, e.g., E. Hudson, 'Copyright and Publicly Located Artistic Works: The End of an Exception?' (2006) 19 *Intellectual Property Law Bulletin* 106.
[98] See, e.g., M. Spence and T. Endicott, 'Vagueness in the Scope of Copyright' (2005) 121 *Law Quarterly Review* 657 (discussing substantial part).
[99] 313M. Rules of thumb included that authors would be at least twenty years of age before they could write such a paper, and that they lived to be eighty.
[100] 317G.

deciding to proceed with conduct despite awareness that it would, or might, infringe copyright.[101] Such decision-making was largely 'outside' the copyright system, in terms of not generally being supported by defences or remedies limitations. It could therefore be contrasted with risk-informed decision-making as there was not necessarily any meaningful *ex ante* belief that the use was non-infringing. Interestingly, the term 'risk management' was typically used by interviewees only for public-facing activities. This suggests that the concept was considered inappropiate for administrative and preservation uses, perhaps reflecting the (often limited) degree that copyright was perceived as relevant to such activities.[102]

Risk management was not a collection-wide copyright management strategy but tended to be used in cases where some constellation of the following applied: (1) the institution's use was non-commercial, would not generate a profit, and supported core institution missions; (2) the work to be dealt with was orphaned or of such an age that it might be, or soon would be, in the public domain; (3) the work had no current or likely commercial market, and was not made by a professional creator who generated a living from their craft; (4) reasonable efforts had been made to locate a rightsholder, or were planned to occur in the future; and (5) the likelihood of an adverse outcome from the use was perceived to be low, given the chances of an owner resurfacing, the limited harm thought to arise from the institution's use, or the predicted ease with which any complaint could be dealt.

Examples of risk management will appear throughout this book, but three are given now to illustrate the different circumstances in which such reasoning has been applied.[103] The first exemplifies the use of risk management for old, unpublished collections, and relates to the digitisation of World War I diaries. Despite uncertainty regarding the rights status of those items (in particular ownership), the institution decided to proceed with the project, given the social importance of those works. Efforts were made to encourage copyright owners and heirs to come forward, and consideration was given to the likelihood that anyone would complain. A similar approach had also been taken to material from other special collections, where 'materials have been assessed, we haven't

---

[101] E.g., 1G, 2L, 4L, 7G, 15L, 16G, 23X, 28G, 29L, 30G, 33G, 45M, 52M, 54M, 106A, 135G, 139L, 204A, 207L, 208G, 210X, 214M, 218M, 221L, 225G, 228M, 229X, 234A, 237L, 246A, 248L, 255A, 257L, 259L, 262M, 264L, 303G, 304M, 305M, 314G, 315A, 316L, 317G, 319L, 320L, 322G, 325M, 327L, 328G, 329M. A number of Canadian interviewees who reported using risk management also emphasised that it was on the periphery of copyright management, being used sparingly: e.g., 102L, 103G, 108G, 124A, 130M, 137G, 153M.

[102] Discussed further in Chapter 4. As seen there, these internal uses were often driven by institutional and ethical views regarding best practices in collection management.

[103] To further protect anonymity, pseudonyms will not be used for some examples.

wilfully violated any clear rights, but where there are orphaned works, or works where rights persist [such as] manuscripts, that hasn't really inhibited us – we've made an assessment there that the purpose of providing open access is sufficient justification.'

The second example involved an exhibition that was to contain a couple of thousand copyright works. The decision was made that some unlicensed content would be included, as it would not be possible to obtain all the necessary permissions prior to opening. The proposed content was triaged from high to low risk, so that licensing efforts could focus on high and medium risk items. Factors relevant to that assessment included the age and nature of the content (moving image being particularly risky due to multiple rightsholders and underlying rights) and ownership of the content (e.g., rightsholders with strong preferences about their works). In making this decision, it was thought that potential remedies would be limited as there was no charge for entry, and that any potential relationship damage could be dealt with through having a take-down system. Later reports were that this procedure had never been invoked.

The final example draws from interviews with a number of people managing collections of fine art, in which it was reported that institutions were seeking to increase the number of works represented visually online – including in the absence of a licence. Institutions were experimenting with different approaches, but interviewees referred to similar reasons for hosting some unlicensed content on their own websites, such as the educational or informational context of the use, the resolution of images (i.e., lower rather than higher), difficulties in identifying and locating rightsholders, that the institution maintained a dialogue with artists about its activities, and that artists could opt out of online representation.[104]

The interviews suggested that over the course of the fieldwork, numerous institutions became more risk tolerant, with flow-on effects for compliance strategies.[105] To put this in context, the cultural institution sector has tended to describe itself as conservative, as seen in the comments of numerous interviewees in this research.[106] Various reasons have

---

[104] Such a use might also fall within copyright exceptions (e.g., fair dealing for the purpose of quotation), illustrating that the line between risk-informed and risk-managed activity can be blurred; see also Chapter 5 (US interviewees reporting using thumbnail images by reference to fair use).

[105] Discussed further in later chapters, especially Chapter 8. This conclusion was derived primarily from the fieldwork in Australia and the United Kingdom, and is not intended to imply a universal trend. Indeed, 324X described risk management as an 'Anglo' concept, and particularly well-developed in the United States due to fair use.

[106] E.g., 7G, 22L, 28G, 53G, 105G, 106A, 107L, 108G, 123L, 124A, 126A, 128L, 130M, 139L, 144X, 151A, 153M, 201X, 202G, 206G, 208G, 215G, 223A, 224X, 234A, 238L, 247A, 249L, 264L, 279A, 301L, 302M, 306L, 308M, 309L, 310X, 312L, 315A, 319L, 322G, 324X, 326L.

Risk Management 91

been given for this, with many grounded in reputational and relationship management concerns and a desire to protect creator rights,[107] and staff preferences to operationalise clear rules rather than vague principles.[108] There were therefore reports that institutions did not want to be seen as playing fast and loose with copyright,[109] and of staff being concerned about their own contribution to a bad outcome; as one interviewee said, people 'don't want to be seen to be the person who started a court case'.[110]

But it would also seem that some institutions have become more comfortable with risk, even if still self-describing as preferring a conservative approach.[111] For instance, when asked to compare experiences between institutions, one UK interviewee observed that 'ten years ago, I'd say we were quite bullish with our risk taking. However, more recently it seems a lot of peer institutions are comfortable taking some element of risk. I don't see much difference anymore – it feels quite par for the course now.'[112] This may reflect the lesson that the worst-case scenarios – the front-page headline alleging egregious behaviour, or an aggrieved copyright owner making a significant financial claim – have not materialised and are unlikely to do so in the future. Interviewees whose institutions had engaged in risk management noted that complaints were few and far between; and amongst those who had received complaints, it appeared there were effective measures to deal with them.[113] More broadly, those with greater tolerance of risk had generally dedicated time and resources to developing procedures for risk assessment and dealing with complaints, and some had also rolled out other measures such as self-insurance. As one interviewee said, people who were risk-averse tended not to have the 'tools and the confidence' to make decisions.[114]

---

[107] E.g., 7G, 16G, 28G, 33G, 105G, 124A, 201X, 206G, 230A, 234A, 306L, 308M, 309L, 315A, 323X, 326L.
[108] E.g., 148L, 201X, 301L, 312L, 319L.
[109] E.g., 106A, 115A, 119L, 203M, 234A, 264L, 306L, 308M, 309L, 322G.
[110] 308M; similar 211X, 309L. This is one iteration of the litigation aversion reported across the sector: e.g., 7G, 108G, 119L, 141L, 146L, 203M, 225G, 250L, 308M, 322G, 324X.
[111] Although numerous interviewees described their institution as comfortable or somewhat comfortable with risk (at least for some uses): e.g., 1G, 7G, 9M, 16G, 30G, 43M, 53G, 106A, 117L, 147L, 207L, 208G, 218M, 221L, 225G, 228M, 237L, 248L, 250L, 265L, 257L, 303G, 305M, 312L, 313M, 314G, 315A, 317G, 322G, 323X, 325M, 328G, 329M. In addition, some interviewees said that they were personally disposed to a more risk tolerant approach than that of their institution: e.g., 208G, 301L, 302M, 304M, 308M, 319L.
[112] 325M.
[113] E.g., 4L, 14G, 30G, 43M, 49G, 204A, 207L, 214M, 215G, 225G, 249L, 255A, 310A, 314G, 323X, 328G.
[114] 305M. Although a number of interviewees noted concerns that staff might sometimes use risk management in the absence of proper, documented analysis: e.g., 220M, 327L.

At the moment, risk management is largely outside the copyright system. If we believe that this is a problem, one way to give it a more formalised standing is through remedies limitations and safe harbours: provisions that limit relief, especially monetary claims, where users have acted reasonably in their attempts to locate a copyright owner or have implemented processes to address complaints of copyright infringement.[115] However, other mechanisms have also been developed to deal with the sort of market failures to which risk management often responds, these mechanisms seeking to uphold the appearance of property rules by ensuring that permission is supplied for the use of the work – just not from the copyright owner.[116] These include ECL (the mechanism of choice for out-of-commerce works in the DSM Directive)[117] and centralised licensing (in which licences are granted by a state body or tribunal). Experiences in Canada and the United Kindom in relation to the latter are discussed in Section IV.B, next.

B *Legislative Schemes for Orphaned Works*

This section discusses three legislative schemes directed to orphaned works: the centralised licensing schemes of Canada and the United Kingdom, and the EU exception covering certain uses by cultural institutions and other specified users. It will be observed that Canadian and UK cultural institutions have not used these schemes in any meaningful way, although it must be remembered that the UK reforms are relatively new, and that the European position is in a state of flux due to the DSM Directive and uncertainty regarding Brexit.

The Canadian scheme for unlocatable copyright owners is set out in section 77 of the Copyright Act. It applies to published works and sound recordings, and fixations of performances and communication signals, and permits the Copyright Board to issue a non-exclusive licence where it is satisfied that 'the applicant has made reasonable efforts to locate the

---

[115] See, e.g., G. Austin and E. Hudson, 'Why the Not-for-Profit Cultural Sector Needs Tailor-Made Copyright Safe Harbours', *The Conversation* (13 February 2018), http://theconversation.com/why-the-not-for-profit-cultural-sector-needs-tailor-made-copyright-safe-harbours-89564.

[116] See Hudson, n. 4 above.

[117] DSM Directive, Art. 8; see also n. 68 above and surrounding text. Under the Directive, an out-of commerce work is one that is 'not available to the public through customary channels of commerce': Art. 8(5). Whilst this may suggest that Art. 8 is directed towards out-of-print works, Recitals 30 and 37 suggest a far broader definition that includes unpublished works and those never intended for commerce. For discussion of ECL generally, see Australian Law Reform Commission, *Copyright in the Digital Economy: Final Report*, Report No. 122 (November 2013), paras. 13.35–13.54.

Risk Management 93

owner of the copyright and that the owner cannot be located'.[118] The copyright owner has five years from expiration of a section 77 licence to either collect royalties or issue proceedings for their recovery.[119] Where royalties are required to be paid upfront, it is common that the licensee will pay these to a nominated copyright collective, who will then conduct a search for the owner.[120] In the meantime, the collective may apply the money as it wishes, subject to an obligation to compensate the owner under the terms of the licence should he or she be found. If that individual is not located within the prescribed timeframe, the money does not need to be returned.[121] For some uses, the licence fee is nominal, or only becomes payable if the owner comes forward.[122]

Interviews in 2008 and 2009 suggested that the number of applications by cultural institutions had been low,[123] a matter confirmed by analysis of the licences granted by the Copyright Board, both contemporaneously and more recently. These statistics show that from August 1990 (when the first licence was issued) to December 2018, the Board has issued approximately 298 licences[124] and denied 22 applications.[125] Of the licences granted, around 32 (or 10.7%) were issued to cultural institutions,[126] divided as follows: 26 were granted to six institutions in the

---

[118] Canadian Copyright Act s. 77(1).   [119] Ibid., s. 77(3).
[120] Under the Copyright Act, 'a licence issued under subsection (1) is non-exclusive and is subject to such terms and conditions as the Board may establish': s. 77(2). For further information about the setting and payment of royalties, see Copyright Board of Canada, *Unlocatable Copyright Owners: Brochure*, https://cb-cda.gc.ca/unlocatable-introuvables/brochure2-e.html; J. de Beer and M. Bouchard, *Canada's "Orphan Works" Regime: Unlocatable Copyright Owners and the Copyright Board* (1 December 2009), pp. 24–29.
[121] Vaver describes this as 'questionable' on the basis that it constitutes authorisation of the confiscation of money by collectives: D. Vaver, *Copyright Law* (Toronto: Irwin Law, 2000), p. 226.
[122] See de Beer and Bouchard, n. 120 above, pp. 24–25.
[123] E.g., 106A, 107L, 113X, 123L, 124A, 127L, 157M.
[124] Copyright Board of Canada, *Unlocatable Copyright Owners: Decisions/Licences Issued*, www.cb-cda.gc.ca/unlocatable-introuvables/licences-e.html As at 13 January 2019 that website listed 303 sets of reasons, but at least five were in relation to the same licence or application.
[125] Copyright Board of Canada, *Unlocatable Copyright Owners: Applications Denied (Reasons)*, www.cb-cda.gc.ca/unlocatable-introuvables/denied-refusees-e.html.
[126] See n. 124 above, decision numbers 4[a], 10[b] & 11[b] (same application), 15[c], 27[d], 32[b], 33[d], 39[d], 47[d], 52[d], 55[e], 60[d], 62[d], 68[d], 72[d], 75[d], 81[f], 83[f], 89[d], 90[g], 128[h], 131[i], 164[j], 185[k], 203[l], 225[m], 231[n], 246[o], 263[p], 271[p], 272[q], 273[p], 293[p]. The notations in superscript were added by the author and are a pseudonym for each applicant. Thus, applicants b, d, f and p made two, eleven, two and four successful applications, respectively. The remaining applicants made one successful application. In making this list, libraries that formed part of educational institutions were included, but not educational institutions generally, or applicants who appeared to be historical societies or community organisations.

period August 1990 to August 2000;[127] ten were granted to ten institutions from August 2000 to August 2010; and five were granted to two institutions since August 2010.

There are a number of explanations for the relatively low utilisation of the section 77 scheme. The requirement that the work must have been published excludes a lot of items that are found in institution collections.[128] The Board's practice of limiting its licences to activity within Canada is problematic for online publication unless access from other countries is blocked.[129] Finally, there are the costs involved in using the scheme, including the need to demonstrate that 'reasonable efforts' were used in searching for the copyright owner.[130] Whilst the Board has sought to leave this requirement flexible and assess it on a case-by-case basis, in their 2009 study, Jeremy de Beer and Mario Bouchard noted that the Board 'generally expects an applicant to have consulted most of the repertoires of copyright licensing agencies and collective societies, as well as national libraries' indices, copyright offices' registration records, publishing houses and corporate records'.[131] Depending on the project, this may render the cost of making an application disproportionate to the value of the use.

As noted above, the United Kingdom currently has a two-pronged approach to orphaned works, with Schedule ZA1 of the CDPA containing the EU-mandated exception for digitisation by cultural institutions and other bodies, and the Intellectual Property Office (IPO) overseeing a centralised licensing scheme for uses of orphaned works. Dealing first with the exception in Schedule ZA1, this reform implements obligations

---

[127] One applicant was responsible for a particularly high number of applications: the Canadian Institute for Historical Microreproductions (applicant d in the list in n. 126, above). Its applications related to preservation copying of works on microfiche and CD-ROM formats.

[128] E.g., 106A ('the great mass of material in archives is unpublished material, so the great mass is not covered by that provision'). In 2017, the Royal Canadian Mint applied for a licence to reproduce, on collector coins, the image of the sculpture *Angel of Victory* by Cœur de Lion McCarthy. This was denied on the basis that the work had not been published, despite three castings being erected in 1921 at train stations in Vancouver, Winnipeg and Montreal, these having been seen by thousands of people: Copyright Board of Canada, *Application by the Royal Canadian Mint for the reproduction of the image of the Angel of Victory sculpture created by Cœur de Lion McCarthy* (17 January 2018).

[129] E.g., 124A; see also de Beer and Bouchard, n. 120 above, p. 22.

[130] For instance, the application process was described by interviewees as 'rather daunting' (123L) and 'a royal pain to navigate' (106A), whilst 124A said the scheme was 'a last resort, it's not very practical' and 113X observed that 'no-one' was very excited about the Canadian scheme, which is 'too regulatory'. For analysis of costs, see de Beer and Bouchard, n. 120 above, pp. 16–19.

[131] de Beer and Bouchard, n. 120 above, p. 18; see also information from the Copyright Board at n. 120 above.

Risk Management 95

under the 2012 Orphan Works Directive, and therefore follows the detailed guidance in that instrument.[132] It provides that a 'relevant body'[133] does not infringe copyright in an orphaned 'relevant work'[134] in its collection by '(a) making the orphan work available to the public; or (b) reproducing the orphan work for the purposes of digitisation, making available, indexing, cataloguing, preservation or restoration'.[135] There are numerous limitations and administrative requirements in Schedule ZA1. A significant exclusion is that the exception does not apply to photographs and other artistic works unless they are embedded in a relevant work.[136] It is also necessary that the work was first published or broadcast in a Member State,[137] or has been 'made publicly accessible by a relevant body with the consent of the rightholders'.[138] The relevant body must have undertaken in good faith a 'diligent search' for the rightsholders,[139] maintain records of that search and report to the European Union Intellectual Property Office (EUIPO) information about the orphaned work and its use.[140] Whilst it is possible to generate revenue from uses under the exception, such income can pertain only to the costs of digitisation and making available.[141] If a rightsholder comes forward, the relevant body 'must within a reasonable period provide the rightholder with fair compensation for that body's use of the relevant work'. If agreement cannot be reached on the amount to be paid, either party may apply to the Copyright Tribunal for a determination.[142]

The Schedule ZA1 exception has been used by UK bodies, albeit with three entities responsible for the vast majority of notifications to the

---

[132] Directive 2012/28/EU of the European Parliament and of the Council of 25 October 2012 on certain permitted uses of orphan works. As noted below at n. 178, Schedule ZA1 may be repealed when the United Kingdom exits the European Union.

[133] CDPA Sch. ZA1, para. 2(1) (exhaustive definition that includes publicly accessible libraries, educational establishments and museums, archives, and film and audio heritage institutions).

[134] Ibid., para. 2(2) (exhaustive definition that covers books, journals, newspapers, magazines and other writings, and cinematographic, audiovisual works and sound recordings).

[135] Ibid., para. 1(1); see also para. 1(2) (equivalent provision for economic rights of performers).

[136] Ibid., paras. 2(2), (5).   [137] Ibid., para 2(3).

[138] Ibid., para. 2(6) (defined to mean 'an owner of the copyright in the work, a licensee under an exclusive licence in relation to the work, a person with [performers' economic rights] in relation to a performance recorded by the work, or a licensee under an exclusive licence in relation to those rights'). For these works to be covered by the exception, it must be 'reasonable to assume that the rightholders would not oppose the use of the work' by the relevant body.

[139] Ibid., paras. 3, 5, Part 2.

[140] Ibid., para. 5(9). The EUIPO was formerly known as the Office for Harmonisiation in the Internal Market (OHIM).

[141] Ibid., para. 6(a).   [142] Ibid., paras 7(3), (4).

EUIPO. Information provided by the EUIPO to the author in June 2019 revealed that at that date, UK organisations had registered 723 main works and 10,648 embedded or incorporated works.[143] The fourteen organisations that were responsible for these notifications were the British Library; British Film Institute; Wellcome Trust; University of Kent; King's College, Cambridge; LSE Library; CREATe; Jaguar Daimler Heritage Trust; Northern Ireland Screen; Stirling Council Archives; Humanist Library and Archives; Imperial War Museum; Museum of the Order of St John; and Roman Roads Research Association.[144]

Turning to the Directive's implementation across Europe, analysis of the EUIPO statistics for 31 organisation countries (a total of 6,106 entries) revealed that use of the scheme was patchy but generally low, and that amongst countries that were higher utilisers, it was common that most of the notifications came from one or two bodies. Thus, judged in terms of number of files, the highest use was seen in Poland (3,250 entries, mostly from one entity[145]), the Netherlands (802 entries, mostly from one entity[146]), the United Kingdom (723 entries, mostly from three entities) and Hungary (548 entries, divided between two entities[147]). For fifteen countries there were no notifications on the database,[148] whilst for a further five countries there were fewer than ten files each.[149]

As noted above, in addition to Schedule ZA1, the United Kingdom has implemented a scheme in which bodies may apply to the IPO for a licence to make use of orphaned works.[150] This scheme covers copyright works and performances,[151] and allows the IPO to grant a non-exclusive licence in the United Kingdom for a term not exceeding seven years,[152] with renewal for a further seven years possible.[153] A licence is available only where a diligent search has been carried out, defined as 'a

---

[143] Email from the EUIPO to the author dated 19 June 2019. Statistics on the number of registrations differ between the 'front office' (the orphaned works database as accessible to the general public) and the 'back office' (accessible only to the EUIPO and registered users, and which includes additional works, for instance those whose entries are being edited). The statistics in this book are from the 'back office'.

[144] The number of main works registered by each of these entities was 282, 279, 99, 17, 14, 9, 6, 5, 3, 3, 2, 2, 1 and 1 respectively.

[145] Wydzial Polonistyki Uniwersytet Warszawski (3,188 entries).

[146] Eye Film Institute (781 entries).

[147] Magyar Nemzeti Digitális és Filmintézet (345 entries) and National Széchényi Library (198 entries).

[148] Bulgaria, Cyprus, Czech Republic, Finland, France, Greece, Iceland, Italy, Liechtenstein, Luxembourg, Malta, Norway, Romania, Slovenia and Spain.

[149] Austria, Croatia, Ireland, Latvia and Slovakia.

[150] Copyright and Rights in Performances (Licensing of Orphan Works) Regulations 2014 (SI 2014/2863), made pursuant to powers in CDPA s. 116A.

[151] Ibid., reg. 3(1).   [152] Ibid., reg. 6(2).   [153] Ibid., reg. 8.

Risk Management

reasonable search of the relevant sources',[154] including the EUIPO register and other sources set out in Part 2 of Schedule ZA1.[155] The IPO will impose a 'reasonable licence fee',[156] which must be retained by it in a separate ring-fenced bank account for no less than eight years from the grant of the licence.[157] If no rightsholder comes forward during that time, the licence fee may be put towards the reasonable costs of running the orphaned works scheme, or, if there is a surplus, for 'social, cultural and educational activities'.[158]

There has been some uptake of the licences offered by the IPO, but like the Schedule ZA1 exception, use has been patchy and dominated by a small group of particularly active entities. From launch of the licensing scheme in 2014 through to January 2019, the IPO received a total of 160 applications in relation to 892 works.[159] The vast majority of these works were still visual art (647 works) and written works (212 works). At least fourteen cultural institutions were granted licences by the IPO,[160] with particular utilisation by the Museum of the Order of St John,[161] the Humanist Library and Archives,[162] Impressions Gallery,[163] Linen Hall Library[164] and the University of Reading Art Collection.[165] Other applicants included Leeds Museums and Galleries, Museums Sheffield, Glasgow Museums, the British Library and King's College, Cambridge. As at early 2019, application fees ranged from £20 (for an application relating to a single work) to £80 (for an application in relation to 30 works).[166] Licence fees varied, with the IPO reporting that it charged a nominal fee

---

[154] Ibid., reg. 4(2).   [155] Ibid., reg. 4(3).   [156] Ibid., reg. 10(1)(a).
[157] Ibid., reg. 10(2).   [158] Ibid., regs. 13(1), (2).
[159] IPO, *Orphan Works Register*, www.orphanworkslicensing.service.gov.uk/view-register (accessed 13 January 2019). As of January 2019, licences had been granted for 801 works (including five works for which the licence has already expired); the application had been withdrawn for 80 works; and there were eleven pending applications. The IPO stated in early 2018 that since launching the scheme in 2014, no applications had been refused: IPO, *FOI release: Information released under the Freedom of Information Act: Orphan works registered in the UK* (9 March 2018).
[160] It may be that other applications that appear to be from (say) an educational institution were in fact made by a library or archives within that institution.
[161] Eight applications in 2014–2015 in relation to 179 works, all being still visual art.
[162] Two applications in 2016 in relation to 60 works, being a mix of written works and still visual art.
[163] Three applications in 2017 in relation to 42 works, all being still visual art.
[164] Four applications in 2017–2018 in relation to 104 works, all being still visual art.
[165] Two applications in 2018 in relation to 38 works, all being still visual art.
[166] IPO, *Costs: Application and Licence Fees*, www.gov.uk/guidance/copyright-orphan-works#costs-application-and-licence-fees (accessed 13 January 2019).

of £0.10 per work for non-commercial uses and a higher fee (based on market rates) for commercial uses.[167]

A number of UK interviewees could speak to the European exception and the IPO scheme. Their comments were consistent with other reports that the main stumbling blocks for both initiatives were the administrative and financial burdens of a diligent search and reporting to, or applying for a licence from, the EUIPO or IPO.[168] The IPO's scheme was the target of particular criticism due to its administrative demands, lack of scalability and narrow licences.[169] One interviewee observed that when they commenced work in the sector, 'orphan works were like, "yay, it's an orphan - let's use it!" Then the government came up with this [scheme], and at the beginning I thought it was great [and that] I would be able to licence everything – until the day when I tried.'[170] For this interviewee, the issue was not just the application and licence fees but the staff time in undertaking and documenting diligent searches that would satisfy the IPO, and then completing IPO paperwork and awaiting an answer. More broadly, the empirical work suggested that whilst the IPO scheme may be useful for some discrete uses, it was not fit-for-purpose for the larger-scale and mass digitisation projects that many cultural institutions undertake.

One answer may be that institutions should – at least for now – use the European exception, as embodied in Schedule ZA1, for these projects. One matter to bear in mind is that the exception does not cover artistic works, which is a significant exclusion given the large numbers of photographs and images that cultural institutions wish to digitise. However, even for works within its ambit, it would seem that there are logistical issues with the EU scheme. For instance, one interviewee who was familiar with the EUIPO notification process described it as 'horrible':

There are usability issues in getting onto the database and trying to register things. You need to be a copyright specialist to understand what you're entering. The language used is the language of EU Directives, in defining what the work is [and other fields], and you need to understand how the Directives are written.

---

[167] IPO, *Orphan Works: Review of the First Twelve Months* (2015), p. 4. To give a sense of the numbers, this report stated that during the period October 2014 to October 2015 the IPO received £1,492 in application fees and collected just over £8,000 in licence fees: pp. 6–7. A response to a Freedom of Information request revealed that from April 2015 to March 2016 the IPO received £730 in application fees and just over £5,000 in licence fees, and from April 2016 to March 2017, it received £812 in application fees and just over £2,000 in licence fees: IPO, *FOI Release*, n. 159 above. Figures for licence fees exclude VAT.
[168] E.g., EUIPO, *Orphan Works Survey 2017 – Summary Report* (November 2017), pp. 19–22.
[169] E.g., 305M, 314G, 315A, 316L, 319L, 320L, 322G, 325M, 327L, 328G, 329M.
[170] To further protect anonymity, pseudonyms will not be used for some examples.

Another interviewee had a more positive experience but nevertheless concluded that resourcing was the major impediment to using the exception again in the future. That interviewee described a fairly involved process of assessing the copyright status of many thousands of works, and then performing diligent searches for those that were assessed as potentially orphaned. Whilst this process was undertaken with pragmatism – that 'you as a rights researcher will know and will have a gut instinct' about whether a rightsholder is locatable, and hence 'I would never go down [a list] dutifully ticking every thing off' – this took up a lot of time and resources.

We might ask whether the benefits of these administrative requirements outweigh their costs. In theory the databases run by the EUIPO and IPO help ensure transparency and accountability in the use of orphaned works, and include information that may be valuable to other users (to check the status of particular works) and rightsholders (to search for their own works). Providing a definition of a 'diligent search' may be said to give cultural institutions confidence in what is expected of them, and help alleviate concerns that institutional uses might encroach unduly on the rights of copyright owners. But to generate these benefits, the definition of a diligent search must accord with institution workflows. Databases must contain clear, up-to-date information and be readily searchable, all of which requires administrative and technical support. Furthermore, for a centralised licensing scheme, there must be a bureaucracy to assess applications and set licence fees – a process that could quickly spiral out of control if UK cultural institutions were to use the IPO's scheme with any vigour. With so many funding imperatives for cultural institutions and governments, it is open to question whether models that prescribe search requirements (even if loosely) or incorporate notification and licensing limbs are the best use of scarce resources.

We also need to think about the policy underlying these legislative interventions. For instance, one argument in favour of remedies limitations is to signal that the thinking behind risk management is legitimate: that there are limits to the availability and feasibility of voluntary negotiation, and that strict compliance with the law is not a desirable goal. In contrast, licensing schemes reinforce the need for a property-style transaction, seemingly revolving around the idea that everything is okay so long as *someone* grants permission and is paid, irrespective of whether that person has any direct connection to the author. The European exception is perhaps more similar to remedies limitations in its intellectual foundations, as there is no upfront licensing fee. That said, the requirement that a resurfacing rightsholder must be provided with 'fair compensation'[171] might be at odds with the remainder of the scheme unless 'reasonable' includes no payment or a minimal sum.

In thinking about how we got into this situation, it may be that orphaned works policymaking represents another example of difficulties in the legislative process as it relates to copyright.[172] For instance, one interviewee described the UK schemes as like 'milk chocolate and dark chocolate teapots: they're alternatives and they're both pretty useless', and saw this as a product of the intense lobbying around orphaned works: 'it's the inevitable outcome of that sort of political process that you'll end up with a dog's dinner'.[173] Another interviewee made a similar point, describing the IPO scheme as 'rubbish, it's too limited', and arguing that the only solution was the exception: 'none of the other solutions, apart from risk management, are acceptable'.[174] There seemed to be issues with orphaned works schemes duplicating the sort of internal risk assessments that museum staff have been undertaking for many years,[175] but in a more laborious and bureaucratised environment; as one interviewee said in relation to their experience of using the exception, it would be 'a "shoot me now" experience if we were using it all the time'. Those interviewees were aware that their views may not be shared across the sector, especially at institutions whose risk management practices were not as well developed; and indeed some interviewees spoke of the exception in positive terms.

With debates continuing in relation to orphaned works,[176] the Canadian and UK experiences may provide a cautionary tale about over-regulated and bureaucratised responses.[177] However, as explored further in Chapter 8, with many cultural institutions becoming increasingly comfortable with risk management, it may be that the time for legislative intervention has passed – or at least intervention that adopts a licensing answer to the orphaned works problem.[178] Institutional utilisation of

---

[171] CDPA Schedule ZA1, para. 7(3).   [172] See Chapter 2, Section IIIA.   [173] 319L.
[174] 305M. Even then the benefits were low, as the exception mainly operated to give 'slightly more reassurances to more risk averse organisations'.
[175] A point made by 317G.
[176] E.g., the 2018 Copyright Modernisation Consultation of the Department of Communications and the Arts in Australia: www.communications.gov.au/have-your-say/copyright-modernisation-consultation.
[177] As argued in E. Hudson, T. Aplin and R. Burrell, 'Submission to the Copyright Consultation: Department of Communications and the Arts' (4 July 2018).
[178] This also leads to questions about the use of ECL for out-of-commerce works, as set out in Art. 8 of the DSM Directive. As noted at n. 76 and surrounding text, some UK interviewees spoke positively about the scheme, although there are numerous questions about how it will operate in practice, for instance in relation to the definition of an out-of-commerce work (see Art. 8(5); Recitals 30 and 37 suggest that the term can include works that were never intended for commercial use); given this definition, whether some works will only ever fall within the exception in Art. 8(2), as there will never be a sufficiently representative collective; the publicity measures in Art. 10 (which require notification to the EUIPO at least six months before a work is made available

orphaned works therefore illustrates the significance of changes to ethical and other norms, and the emergence of organisational rules to fill a perceived hiatus in the law in books.

V   Conclusion

This chapter has explored the reasons for selecting cultural institutions as a cohort for empirical analysis, and has considered the main ways that such entities can deal with the copyright implications of digitising collection items. The first of these was to use public domain works. Whilst such materials are attractive because of the avoidance of copyright issues, there are a number of other reasons why they make excellent targets for digitisation, including that they are often old, fragile, rare and not the subject of any privately based digitisation efforts. That said, focusing on public domain materials is not satisfactory as the main long-term strategy for dealing with copyright. The duration of copyright is such that much time must transpire before works fall into the public domain. If, in the meantime, the strategy is to focus energies on works for which copyright has expired, this will exclude vast quantities of material from digitisation efforts. As one US interviewee observed, 'there's only so long we can avoid the issue'.[179]

Negotiation-based strategies appeared to offer a partial solution for works within the copyright term, however their efficacy varied considerably. For instance, interviewees managing collections of contemporary, high-value works frequently reported that licensing practices were relatively successful, which would seem to be a related to an active or readily locatable copyright owner who is interested in exploiting the rights granted to him or her by law. In contrast, for those working with other collections, finding a copyright owner was sometimes difficult or

---

pursuant to a licence or the exception); and the steps that count as the rightsholder opting out for the purposes of Art. 8(4), if we take seriously the indications of the CJEU in *Soulier* v. *Premier Ministre* (C-301/15) [2017] ECDR 23 (Third Chamber). The future, in the United Kingdom, of this and other European initiatives will depend on how the United Kingdom exits the European Union. For instance, the Intellectual Property (Copyright and Related Rights) (Amendment) (EU Exit) Regulations 2019 (SI 2019/605) anticipate in reg. 23 the removal of Schedule ZA1 from the CDPA. The Explanatory Memorandum explains that this is due to the lack of mutual recognition by the European Union: that the European Union will not recognise the status of works declared orphaned by UK institutions; and that UK institutions will not have access to the EUIPO database. The IPO licensing scheme will continue. See Explanatory Memorandum, The Intellectual Property (Copyright and Related Rights) (Amendment) (EU Exit) Regulations 2019, para. 7.10.

[179]   117L.

impossible. Negotiation-based models were also challenged by the administrative burdens and other costs of clearance, the lack of collectives for certain classes of work, inadequacies in the repertoire for collectives that do exist, and difficulties in undertaking retrospective licensing for existing collections. These issues impaired voluntary negotiation as a solution to the management of third-party content. Indeed, the clear political decision in Australia, Canada, the United Kingdom and the United States is that these issues are *not* simply left to private transactions, but that there is intervention through the use of free exceptions and (to a lesser degree) compulsory and centralised licensing.

This book focuses on cultural institution experiences in relation to free exceptions. In the next four chapters, it examines the law in action as it relates to sector-specific exceptions, fair use, section 200AB and fair dealing. This analysis will be synthesised in the final two chapters to draw lessons about the decision-making processes of institutional uses, how attitudes and processes change, and what this means for the drafting of copyright exceptions.

Part II

The Law in Action

4   Sector-Specific Exceptions

I   Introduction

This first chapter on institutional practices focuses on sector-specific exceptions: provisions that are directed at certain activities of cultural institutions, and which by and large may be invoked only by such entities.[1] The aims of this chapter are to describe the history and content of these provisions and to consider the role they have played in institutional practices. As will be seen, there is overlap in the classes of activity to which the sector-specific exceptions of different jurisdictions relate, reflecting a degree of international consensus regarding the areas where cultural institutions should be afforded special privileges.[2] That said, each statute adopts its own form of drafting, which at times particularise these areas with considerable specificity. Whether institutional practices correspond with the statutory language, and whether that language is clear, are further questions this chapter will address. The chapter therefore draws from the fieldwork to understand how institutional users engage with the law in books.

---

[1] At the time of writing: Australian Copyright Act ss. 48–53, 110A, 113G–113M (and note s. 200AB, discussed Chapter 6); Canadian Copyright Act ss. 30.1, 30.2, 30.21; CDPA ss. 40A–44B; and US Copyright Act s. 108. Some of these provisions were reformed during the course of the fieldwork, with amendments in Australia (2006, 2017) and the United Kingdom (2014) being of particular significance.

[2] One observation from standards and rules analysis (see Chapter 2) is that the legislative process in drafting rules can be streamlined through copying the approach of other jurisdictions. Amongst countries in the Commonwealth it is common for copyright legislation to be based on British statutes, as illustrated by the original libraries and archives provisions in Australia, which were influenced greatly by British legislation and law reform activity: see section II.A(2) of this chapter. More recently, there has been greater harmonisation of sector-specific exceptions through supranational instruments such as the Marrakesh Treaty to Facilitate Access to Published Works for Persons Who Are Blind, Visually Impaired or Otherwise Print Disabled (adopted 27 June 2013) and Directive (EU) 2019/790 of the European Parliament and of the Council of 17 April 2019 on copyright and related rights in the Digital Single Market and amending Directives 96/9/EC and 2001/29/EC (DSM Directive), especially Arts. 6 (preservation of cultural heritage), 8 (use of out-of-commerce works).

In order to set the scene for later analysis, Section II describes key aspects of the history of sector-specific exceptions, including the technological developments and legal debates that prompted their introduction in the United Kingdom, Australia and the United States in the 1950s to 1970s. Although similar debates also occurred in Canada during this period, the introduction of sector-specific exceptions did not occur until legislation passed in 1997. As will be seen, the argument developed in this book is that the 'late' arrival of these provisions was significant because it reflected and served to entrench certain ideas about copyright and the (limited) role of exceptions. Section III then considers the content and operation of the sector-specific exceptions in all four countries, dealing with eligibility requirements and then the uses covered by such provisions, the latter analysis being structured around preservation and replacement copying, collection management, user request services and interlibrary supply, and onsite consultation.

At a broad level the aim of sector-specific provisions is twofold, and mirrors those of exceptions generally: to permit activities that are so fundamental to the missions of cultural institutions that an exception is appropriate; and to facilitate conduct where licencing is unlikely because of the high risk of market failure.[3] There are situations in which sector-specific exceptions seem to have functioned as intended, helping cultural institutions meet their objectives. In other instances, however, the picture is less clear cut. First, whilst detailed rule-like regulation is often credited with bringing certainty to the law, this research identifies ways in which existing provisions have not embodied this quality, for instance due to ambiguous language. Second, because many provisions contain restrictions and utilise specialised language, the scope of the exception and the practice it aims to facilitate do not always correspond. Finally, there is much institutional activity that falls outside the reach of sector-specific exceptions, especially in relation to public-facing and online uses.[4]

Lest these observations suggest manifold problems for cultural institutions, the empirical research also revealed that ethical beliefs and other norms can inform and even override copyright considerations. This means that whilst a doctrinal analysis may point to gaps and drafting

---

[3] See, e.g., Section 108 Study Group, *The Section 108 Study Group Report: An Independent Report sponsored by the United States Copyright Office and the National Digital Information Infrastructure and Preservation Program of the Library of Congress* (March 2008), pp. 8–16.

[4] See, e.g., E. Hudson and A. Kenyon, 'Without Walls: Copyright Law and Digital Collections in Australian Cultural Institutions' (2007) 4 *SCRIPTed* 197, 205–206; L. Gasaway, 'Libraries, Digital Content, and Copyright' (2010) 12 *Vanderbilt Journal of Entertainment and Technology Law* 755, 761–763.

issues with sector-specific exceptions, these did not necessarily translate to issues for institutional users. This chapter therefore illustrates the capacity of best practice norms to inform decision-making, whether through the application of intuitive understandings of what the law 'must' provide, the use of standard-like interpretations of rule-like language, or copyright being ousted as a relevant consideration. The desirability of this state of affairs depends on a number of factors, including one's view on the substantive decisions being made by institutions. But it highlights the problems with assessing the law by reference to a purely doctrinal analysis, and raises questions about how to operationalise lessons drawn from empirical study. For instance, do the strong ethical imperatives around certain areas of cultural institution activity suggest that law reform is not required, or that law reform is essential? Does drafting even matter? These questions will be explored in this and later chapters.

II   History of Sector-Specific Exceptions

A   Early Adopters: The United Kingdom, Australia and the United States

1 Background The introduction of exceptions directed at libraries and archives was one of the products of copyright reform efforts in the middle part of the twentieth century. In a twenty-year period, such exceptions appeared in new copyright statutes in a number of jurisdictions, including the United Kingdom, Australia and the United States.[5]

The Anglo-Australian and US experiences were prompted by the same question: how copyright law should treat the use of photocopiers to maintain library collections and provide services to users. Throughout the twentieth century, advances in mechanical reproductive technologies had made such equipment increasingly powerful and affordable, and by the 1950s and 1960s photocopiers were widespread in libraries.[6] In the United States, the absence of any statutory exceptions in the Copyright Act of 1909 meant that the status of duplications depended in large part

---

[5] Enacted as UK Copyright Act 1956, s. 7; Australian Copyright Act ss. 49–52; US Copyright Act s. 108.

[6] See, e.g., Copyright Law Review Committee, *Report of the Committee Appointed by the Attorney-General of the Commonwealth to Consider what Alterations are Desirable in The Copyright Law of the Commonwealth* (CGP, 1959), para. 130 ('Spicer Committee'); L. Gasaway, 'Libraries and Copyright at the Dawn of the Twentieth Century: The 1909 Copyright Act' (2010) 11 *North Carolina Journal of Law & Technology* 419, 457–458.

on the (then) judicial doctrine of fair use.[7] Similarly, in the United Kingdom and Australia, if a copy was an infringement under the Copyright Act 1911 then in the absence of permission, fair dealing was the main avenue for a library to defend its making.[8] This led to tensions between librarians and publishers, with the former concerned about their potential exposure to liability for what they perceived as important services, and the latter of the view that those services might encroach unfairly on their markets.[9]

There had been attempts to find a way forward using industry guidelines and agreements. For instance, library and publisher representatives in the United States had come to a 'Gentleman's Agreement' in 1935 regarding the making and supply to scholars of reproductions from published works.[10] At that time, the development of smaller and cheaper photostatic equipment had resulted in reprographic services being offered at more and more libraries,[11] although Peter Hirtle argues that the need for a negotiated agreement was originally pressed by research scholars rather than librarians.[12] In the United Kingdom, the Royal Society issued a Fair Copying Declaration in 1950 regarding the application of fair dealing to the making and supply of single copies from scientific and technical journals.[13] Not unlike the Gentleman's Agreement, the impetus for the Declaration came from consideration of how access to scientific information could be improved, including through use of reprographic technologies. Brad Sherman and Leanne Wiseman observe that the Royal Society had to deal with the copyright implications

---

[7] See, e.g., M. Rasenberger and C. Weston, 'Overview of the Libraries and Archives Exception in the Copyright Act: Background, History, and Meaning', attached as Appendix K to the Section 108 Study Group, n. 3 above.

[8] See, e.g., Spicer Committee, n. 6 above, para. 129. The 1911 Act was incorporated wholesale into Australian law by the Copyright Act 1912 (Cth).

[9] See, e.g., Copyright Committee, *Report of the Copyright Committee*, Cmd 8662 (1952) para. 43 ('Gregory Committee'); Spicer Committee, ibid., para. 131; Copyright Law Committee on Reprographic Reproduction, *Report of the Copyright Law Committee on Reprographic Reproduction* (AGPS, 1976), paras. 1.01–1.23 ('Franki Committee').

[10] See, e.g., P. Hirtle, 'Research, Libraries, and Fair Use: The Gentlemen's Agreement of 1935' (2006) 53 *Journal of the Copyright Society of the USA* 545.

[11] See, e.g., Gasaway, n. 6 above, 457.

[12] Hirtle, n. 10 above. Hirtle says that the Agreement had its origins in the work of the Joint Committee on Materials for Research which had been formed in 1929 by the American Council of Learned Societies and the American Social Science Research Council, these bodies being concerned to increase access to research materials. The Agreement was brokered by Harry Lydenberg, a Member of the Joint Committee who had strong ties to New York publishing houses. Hirtle argues that Lydenberg's background as an employee of the New York Public Library caused him to focus on the interests of libraries.

[13] See B. Sherman and L. Wiseman, 'Fair Copy: Protecting Access to Scientific Information in Post-War Britain' (2010) 73 *Modern Law Review* 240, 242–252.

of their call for improved access, including uncertainty in relation to fair dealing.[14] The Declaration was therefore a pragmatic way of sidestepping arguments that fair dealing did not or might not apply.

Library photocopying was therefore already an issue by the time of copyright law reform debates from the 1950s onwards. Although there was much interest in getting further clarity on the limits of permissible activity, finding a compromise that was satisfactory for diverse stakeholders proved to be challenging, and sector-specific exceptions have been the focus of ongoing interest to the present day.[15]

2 Anglo-Australian Response The solution recommended by the United Kingdom's Gregory Committee in a report published in 1952 was the introduction of a cluster of free exceptions permitting specific instances of library photocopying.[16] These recommendations were predicated on the assumption that whilst fair dealing might apply to dealings by a student for research or private study, it 'would not necessarily' apply if those acts were performed by a librarian.[17] Although the premise of the proposed reforms was to create symmetry between student and librarian copying – i.e., that 'any action which would come within the description of "fair dealing" if done by the student himself, should be so regarded if done by a librarian acting on his behalf'[18] – this was not achieved via fair dealing, perhaps reflecting concern that reforms not unduly erode the rights of authors and publishers.[19] Instead the Committee made a series of recommendations regarding the permissible copying by libraries of periodicals, books and manuscripts.[20] When the Copyright Act 1956 was passed, it followed the Gregory Committee's recommendations and included special exceptions in section 7.[21]

---

[14] Sherman and Wiseman, ibid., 245–246, citing the 9th edition of Copinger where it was said that fair dealing 'would no doubt protect the student who, himself, copied out passages from a book in a library for his own private use, but would not, it was thought, protect a librarian who produced such copies by photographic means': F. Skone James and E. Skone James (eds), *Copinger and Skone James on the Law of Copyright*, 9th edition (London: Sweet & Maxwell, 1958), p. 230.

[15] See, e.g., United States Copyright Office, *Section 108 of Title 17: A Discussion Document of the Register of Copyrights* (United States Copyright Office, September 2017).

[16] Gregory Committee, n. 9 above, paras. 43–54.   [17] Ibid., para. 43.   [18] Ibid.

[19] Ibid., paras. 43, 46, 51, 53.

[20] The suggestions for periodicals were influenced by the Royal Society's Fair Copying Declaration: ibid., paras. 45–46; see also Sherman and Wiseman, n. 13 above, 252–253. The Committee also discussed the publication of posthumous manuscripts: paras. 29–35. This included an approach for facilitating the publication of old manuscripts held at public archives, if specified procedures were followed.

[21] Whilst most of the provisions were directed only at libraries, s. 7(6) covered manuscripts in the collections of libraries, museums and other institutions.

In Australia, the Gregory Report influenced the analysis of the Spicer Committee, which in 1959 recommended that the new Australian statute include provisions modelled on section 7 of the 1956 Act.[22] These recommendations were acted upon, and libraries provisions included in the legislation passed in 1968. In explaining its approach to reform, the Spicer Committee emphasised not only the position of authors but the need to ensure that the exclusive rights were not overbroad:

> In arriving at our recommendations our task has essentially been one of balancing the interests of the copyright owner with those of copyright users and the general public. The primary end of the law on this subject is to give to the author of a creative work his just reward for the benefit he has bestowed on the community and also to encourage the making of further creative works. On the other hand, as copyright is in the nature of a monopoly, the law should ensure, as far as possible, that the rights conferred are not abused and that study, research and education are not unduly hampered.[23]

In considering the position of libraries, the Spicer Committee seemed to proceed from the assumption – which it never developed or explained – that the appropriate way to deal with photocopying was via free exceptions, with activity outside these provisions presumably dealt with through voluntary licensing. A similar position seems to have underpinned the Gregory Report. This was revisited in both countries in reviews in the 1970s. In Australia, this was via the Franki Committee, which was appointed in 1974 to examine whether further developments in reprographic reproduction necessitated additional reform to the Copyright Act.[24] That Committee observed that the key question surrounding library photocopying was not whether institutions should offer services to patrons but whether they should be required to pay remuneration to copyright owners.[25] This was not just a philosophical matter but required engagement with logistical aspects about how payments would be effected.[26] For instance, the Australian Copyright Council had proposed a scheme under which royalties for photocopying would be paid to a collecting society for distribution to individual authors,[27] but the Franki Committee formed the view that it would be impractical and undesirable to overlay this on the existing exceptions, in part because of the prohibitive costs of administration and the lack of any 'benefit of any substantial

---

[22] Spicer Committee, n. 6 above, Part XI. [23] Ibid., para. 13.
[24] Franki Committee, n. 9 above, para. I.01.
[25] Ibid., para. 3.04 (discussing user request services). [26] Ibid., para. 1.20.
[27] Ibid., paras. 1.38, 2.26–2.30. For discussion of some of the Australian Copyright Council's activities during the 1970s to help establish 'photocopying rights', see J. Lahore, 'Photocopying in Australian Libraries: Developments in Copyright Law' (1976) 4 *International Journal of Law Libraries* 32.

consequence on copyright owners'.[28] This was not indicative of the outright rejection of collective administration, as the Committee was supportive of a compulsory licensing scheme for multiple copying by educational institutions.[29] Rather, the Committee's view seemed to be based on the assessment that libraries exceptions were directed to acts of smaller-scale, one-off copying, which was very important for research and access to information, but for which any royalties would be dwarfed by the administrative costs of collection and distribution.

In the United Kingdom, on the other hand, the Whitford Committee recommended in 1977 that the libraries provisions in section 7 be abolished.[30] This recommendation formed one limb of the Committee's conclusions regarding the legal challenges posed by reprographic technologies, namely that negotiated blanket licences 'are seen as the only practicable solution by the majority of interested parties'.[31] In reaching this conclusion, the Committee was clearly of the view that authors and publishers ought to be remunerated for copying by libraries, educational institutions and other users; as they observed, '[n]obody suggests that the makers of note books, compasses and rulers should supply these products to educational establishments free of charge'.[32] Although it was possible for such a scheme to be developed alongside the existing legal framework, the Committee was concerned that there would be no meaningful incentive for libraries to join whilst section 7 was in existence.[33] They therefore made a number of suggestions to encourage all sides to act, including repeal of section 7, a winding back of fair dealing to apply only to notes transcribed by hand or typewriter, and a timeframe within which owners must put voluntary licensing schemes in place.[34] If such schemes were not rolled out by this date, a free-for-all would be

---

[28] Ibid., para. 1.39. The Committee also rejected an alternate scheme under which such royalties were paid to a collective for the general benefit of its members or authors generally: para. 1.42.

[29] Ibid., Section 6. Such a scheme was subsequently introduced as Part VB of the Australian Copyright Act: for an overview, see A. Stewart, P. Griffith, J. Bannister and A. Liberman, *Intellectual Property in Australia*, 5th edition (Chatswood, NSW: LexisNexis Butterworths, 2014), para. 7.22. In 2017, Part VB was repealed and replaced with a new, simpler, scheme by the Copyright Amendment (Disability Access and Other Measures) Act 2017 (Cth).

[30] Committee to Consider the Law on Copyright and Designs, *Report on Copyright and Designs Law*, Cmnd 6732 (1977) [274]–[291] ('Whitford Committee'). For discussion, see G. Dworkin, 'Reports of Committees: The Whitford Committee Report on Copyright and Designs Law' (1977) 40 *Modern Law Review* 685, 696–698.

[31] Whitford Committee, ibid., para. 273.   [32] Ibid., para. 268.   [33] Ibid., para. 276.

[34] Ibid., para. 280.

permitted until they were operational.[35] In contrast with the Franki Committee's questioning of the economics of blanket licensing for library photocopying, the Whitford Committee was confident that measures such as simplified administration and differential pricing would result in such a scheme being viable.[36] Interestingly, the Whitford Committee also made a separate recommendation for what has been described as fair use: a 'general exception in respect of "fair dealing" which does not conflict with a normal exploitation of the work or subject matter and does not unreasonably prejudice the legitimate interests of copyright owners'.[37] This was explained by the need to provide greater clarity and uniformity in the law. In the end, neither of these proposals were acted upon, and libraries provisions were retained when the CDPA was passed in 1988, including a new exception dealing with preservation and replacement.[38]

Further amendments have been made to the libraries and archives provisions since the passage of the CDPA. This included some minor changes in 2003 as part of regulations to bring British law into line with the Information Society Directive (ISD).[39] Writing in 2005, Robert Burrell and Allison Coleman criticised the libraries and archives provisions as 'complex and old-fashioned', and drawing 'unnecessary and inappropriate distinctions between institutions in a sector that has changed rapidly over recent years'.[40] They argued that this was not necessitated by the ISD, and in fact that Article 5 countenanced broader accommodations for cultural institutions than those in the CDPA.[41] More extensive reform took place in 2014 following lengthy consultation into copyright, including as part of the Gowers and Hargreaves Reviews.[42] As discussed later in this chapter, the 2014 reforms reworded some existing exceptions, expanded others to cover archives and museums (including galleries), added prohibitions on contracting out,

---

[35] Ibid., para. 279. The Committee envisaged that users would have 'the right to make copies free of payment, otherwise than for issue to the public at large'.
[36] Ibid., in particular paras. 281–288.   [37] Ibid., para. 677.
[38] CDPA ss. 37–44A; discussed in G. Cornish, 'The New United Kingdom Copyright Act and Its Implications for Libraries and Archives' (1991) 83 *Law Library Journal* 51, 54–57; R. Burrell and A. Coleman, *Copyright Exceptions: The Digital Impact* (Cambridge: Cambridge University Press, 2005), ch. 5.
[39] Copyright and Related Rights Regulations 2003 (SI 2003/2498), reg. 14 (amending ss. 38(2)(a), 39(2)(a) and 43(3)(a) so that the reference to 'research' became 'research for a non-commercial purpose').
[40] Burrell and Coleman, n. 38 above, p. 136.   [41] Ibid., pp. 143–145.
[42] A. Gowers, *Gowers Review of Intellectual Property* (HM Treasury, 2006); I. Hargreaves, *Digital Opportunity: A Review of Intellectual Property and Growth* (May 2011).

History of Sector-Specific Exceptions 113

and introduced a new exception covering onsite browsing via dedicated terminals.[43] On paper these reforms might go some way to addressing the concerns of Burrell and Coleman, although empirical analysis is required to determine how far these amendments have translated to new practices. Looking to the future, should UK copyright law remain tied to that of the European Union, then further reform may be required by virtue of the new Directive on Copyright in the Digital Single Market (DSM Directive), which Member States must transpose into their domestic laws by June 2021.[44]

In Australia, the Copyright Amendment Act 1980 (Cth) effected other recommendations of the Franki Committee. One amendment responded to the proposal that the libraries provisions be extended to include preservation copying, about which the Committee commented that 'no reason exists why a library or archives should not be able to reproduce an unpublished work solely for the purpose of preservation or security'.[45] The 1980 Act also extended the libraries provisions to archives, a matter for which the Franki Committee did not provide any express justification.[46] Since then there have been three further occasions in which the libraries and archives provisions have undergone significant reform: first, under the Copyright Amendment (Digital Agenda) Act 2000 (Cth), which added a new exception covering administrative copying;[47] second, by the Copyright Amendment Act 2006 (Cth), whose reforms included special preservation copying provisions for key cultural institutions,[48] and the introduction of section 200AB;[49] and most recently under the Copyright Amendment (Disability Access and Other Measures) Act 2017 (Cth), which sought to consolidate and streamline exceptions in relation to preservation and administration.[50]

---

[43] Copyright and Rights in Performances (Research, Education, Libraries and Archives) Regulations 2014 (SI 2014/1372), regs. 5, 6. The exceptions directed to libraries and archives are now contained in CDPA ss. 40A–44B.
[44] DSM Directive, n. 2 above.   [45] Franki Committee, n. 9 above, para. 5.04.
[46] Ibid., paras. 3.34, 4.21, section 5.
[47] Australian Copyright Act ss. 51A (2), (3). The overarching goal of the Digital Agenda Act was to make the Copyright Act more 'technology neutral'; for discussion, see, e.g., T. Aplin, 'Contemplating Australia's Digital Future: The *Copyright Amendment (Digital Agenda) Act*' (2001) 23 *European Intellectual Property Review* 565; L. Wiseman, 'Beyond the Photocopier: Copyright and Publishing in Australia' (2002) 7 *Media and Arts Law Review* 299.
[48] Ibid., ss. 51B, 110BA, 112AA.
[49] See E. Hudson, 'The Copyright Amendment Act 2006: The Scope and Likely Impact of New Library Exceptions' (2006) 14 *Australian Law Librarian* 25.
[50] Explanatory Memorandum, Copyright Amendment (Disability and other Measures) Bill 2017, p. 2.

3 US Response Legislative activity in relation to a new copyright statute began in earnest in the United States in 1955, when the Copyright Office was asked by Congress to produce a series of reports to help guide the development of what was to become the Copyright Act of 1976.[51] One such report was Borge Varmer's study of copying by libraries,[52] which identified various ways the United States could deal with the copyright implications of such activities, including through a general exception, the introduction of specific provisions, and greater utilisation of voluntary licensing.[53] Much of this report focused on researcher requests, which Varmer saw as revolving around the question of how researchers could be 'supplied with the materials they need for study, without undercutting the publisher's market'.[54] The Study did not come to any conclusions regarding which option would best deal with library photocopying, instead identifying questions that might help guide the legislature in its thinking on this matter. It also avoided a sustained analysis of fair use, which was the focus of another study.[55] Like the Varmer report, this study discussed key matters to inform the decision whether to introduce a statutory fair use provision.

In 1961 the Register of Copyrights recommended that the new statute contain a free exception permitting non-profit libraries to supply single photocopies in response to certain user requests.[56] This elicited a range of responses, some of which argued that such an exception would unduly curtail the rights of authors, and others of which said that it did not reflect what libraries considered allowable under fair use and may prevent such bodies from utilising new technology.[57] Although the draft copyright bill of 1963 included a section reflecting the Register of Copyrights' recommendation,[58] ongoing debate and disagreement prompted its removal

---

[51] See, e.g., National Commission on New Technological Uses of Copyright Works, *Final Report* (Library of Congress, 1979), p. 3 ('CONTU Report'); Library of Congress, US Copyright Office, *Library Reproduction of Copyrighted Works (17 U.S.C. 108): Report of the Register of Copyrights* (Library of Congress, 1983), pp. 15–17 ('1983 Report'); Rasenberger and Weston, n. 7 above, p. 11.

[52] B. Varmer, *Study No 15: Photoduplication of Copyrighted Material by Libraries* (May 1959), reproduced in Committee Print, 86th Congress, 2nd Session, Studies 14–16 (United States Government Printing Service, 1960), pp. 45–76.

[53] Ibid., pp. 64–66; see also summary in Rasenberger and Weston, n. 7 above, pp. 11–12.

[54] Ibid., p. 63.

[55] A. Latman, *Study No 14: Fair Use of Copyrighted Works* (March 1958), reproduced in Committee Print, 86th Congress, 2nd Session, Studies 14–16 (United States Government Printing Service, 1960), pp. 1–44.

[56] *Report of the Register of Copyrights on the General Revision of the US Copyright Law*, 87th Congress, 1st Session (Comm Print, 1961), pp. 25–26.

[57] See Rasenberger and Weston, n. 7 above, p. 13.

[58] Set out in W. Patry, *The Fair Use Privilege in Copyright Law*, 2nd edition (Washington, DC: BNA Books, 1995), pp. 270–271.

from revisions in 1964 and 1965–1966.[59] Behind-the-scenes discussions at the time

revealed a widening schism among librarians, educators, and proprietors on the general question of library photocopying and the more specific question of whether fair use covered it. Some commentators felt that photocopying could be treated under fair use; others urged that the two were separate. ...

Publishers argued that there were no judicial decisions concerning the application of fair use to library photocopying, and that any statute should be drawn narrowly since technology was changing. Users wanted either a generous photocopying provision which legitimized existing practices (and confirmed their legal basis), or a general fair use provision with specific reference to library photocopying.[60]

Following a House Judiciary Committee Report of 1966, a sector-specific exception was re-introduced into the draft bill,[61] but this was directed towards preservation copying of archival collections. This was uncontroversial for the key stakeholders, and attention remained on researcher photocopying services, about which disagreement still reigned.[62] In 1967, the Joint Libraries Committee on Copyright, a consortium of library associations, gave its support to a library photocopying provision;[63] however, the new iteration of sector-specific provisions in the 1969 revision bill still revolved around preservation and replacement copying.[64] Over the next few years interest in library-related issues seemed to take a back-seat to other debates.

This changed with the *Williams & Wilkins* litigation. The plaintiff, a medical publisher, had instituted proceedings in the Court of Claims in relation to activities by libraries attached to the National Institutes of Health and the National Library of Medicine. These libraries copied journal articles for use by physicians and researchers in their professional duties and for background reading. The plaintiff was initially successful. In a decision handed down in 1972, Commissioner Davis observed that '[w]hatever may be the bounds of "fair use" as defined and applied by the courts, defendant is clearly outside those bounds'.[65] In subsequent debates on the 1973 revision bill, there was a push from library representatives to include provisions to preserve royalty-free copying services by

---

[59] See Rasenberger and Weston, n. 7 above, pp. 13–14.
[60] 1983 Report, n. 51 above, pp. 20–21.   [61] HR Report No 89-2237 (1966), p. 5.
[62] See, e.g., Rasenberger and Weston, n. 7 above, pp. 15–16; 1983 Report, n. 51 above, pp. 24–25.
[63] Rasenberger and Weston, ibid., p. 16.
[64] Ibid., 17–18; see also 1983 Report, n. 51 above, pp. 42–43.
[65] *Williams & Wilkins Company* v. *The United States*, 172 USPQ 670, 679 (Court of Claims, 1972).

libraries. Publishers and authors, on the other hand, resisted these and reiterated their concerns about the market impact of library photocopying.[66]

In 1973, however, the initial result in *Williams & Wilkins* was overturned on appeal in a four–three decision.[67] The majority focused on the lack of evidence of actual harm to the plaintiff, and contrasted this with what they saw to be obvious damage to medical science if the libraries' practices were prohibited.[68] While the publisher had argued that photocopying had an effect on its business because photocopies supplanted the demand for original articles, the majority considered that in the absence of library-made copies, most researchers would go without rather than subscribing personally to infrequently used journals or purchasing back-issues or individual articles.[69] In contrast, the dissenting judges viewed the case as involving the 'wholesale, machine copying, and distribution of copyrighted material by defendant's libraries on a scale so vast that it dwarfs the output of many small publishing companies'.[70] Because many journals had limited markets, they concluded that even slightly reduced subscription rates could make a journal uncommercial.[71] Although the dissenting judges accepted that reduced availability of articles would harm medical science, they noted that the plaintiff did not seek to completely prohibit such copying but merely benefit through receiving royalties.[72]

While the defendant's fair use arguments prevailed on appeal, the *Williams & Wilkins* litigation demonstrated the divergent and strongly held attitudes in relation to library photocopying. The opinions of the judges hearing the appeal were far apart. In fact, the only matter on which they all agreed was that the issue was more suitable for the legislature.[73] On further appeal to the Supreme Court, the decision of the majority was affirmed by an equally divided Court.[74] Although this resulted in victory for the defendant, when the decisions at all three levels are aggregated, the judges who heard the litigation were evenly split on which party should prevail.

The eventual approach of Congress was to include in the new statute provisions allowing single copies to be made for user request

---

[66] See, e.g., 1983 Report, n. 51 above, pp. 30–31, 43–47; Rasenberger and Weston, n. 7 above, pp. 18–19.
[67] *Williams & Wilkins Company* v. *The United States*, 487 F 2d 1345 (Court of Claims, 1973).
[68] Ibid., 1354–1359.   [69] Ibid., 1356–1358.   [70] Ibid., 1364.
[71] Ibid., 1369–1379.   [72] Ibid., 1371.   [73] Ibid., 1363, 1383.
[74] *Williams & Wilkins Company* v. *The United States*, 420 US 376 (1975).

and interlibrary supply, subject to a prohibition on systematic copying.[75] Together with provisions on preservation and replacement, these became the kernel of section 108. There was subsequently some minor revision of section 108 by the Digital Millennium Copyright Act of 1998, but more extensive reform has not yet been made.[76]

B   Late Adopter: Canada

Exceptions for libraries, museums and archives – often referred to as the LAM provisions – were first introduced into the Canadian Copyright Act by legislation passed in 1997. Their history is particularly significant given the observation in this book that Canadian interviewees were relatively reluctant to invoke free exceptions, especially when compared with US counterparts. It will be argued that the long path to introducing the LAM provisions provides part of the explanation for this state of affairs.

Despite being a late adopter, the introduction of sector-specific exceptions had been contemplated in Canada as early as the 1950s. In 1954, for example, a Royal Commission was appointed to consider the adequacy of legislation in relation to copyright and other intellectual property regimes.[77] The statute in force at that time was the Copyright Act 1952, which followed the content of the 1921 Act, including its fair dealing exception.[78] In its report published in 1957, one question considered by the Commission was whether existing exceptions should be supplemented by special exemptions for libraries.[79] The recommendations on this matter were influenced greatly by the Gregory Report, with the Commission supportive of provisions based on those in the United Kingdom. In coming to this recommendation, the Commission considered whether library photocopying services should fall within fair dealing, but ultimately decided against this on the basis that such services needed to be 'carefully restricted' because of their potential to harm the interests of authors.[80]

---

[75] Rasenberger and Weston, n. 7 above, pp. 19–22.
[76] Although such reform has been recommended by the Section 108 Study Group, n. 3 above, and the United States Copyright Office, n. 15 above. These are discussed further in Chapter 9, Section III.
[77] Royal Commission on Patents, Copyright, Trade Marks and Industrial Designs, *Report on Copyright* (Queen's Printer, 1957) ('Ilsley Report'), p. 7.
[78] Copyright Act (R.S.C. 1952, c. 55), s. 17(2)(a); see also Burroughs & Co, *Canadian Encyclopedic Digest Western, Second edition, Volume 5* (Calgary: Burroughs & Co 1958), paras. 3, 51.
[79] Ilsley Report, n. 77 above, pp. 57–60.   [80] Ibid., p. 58.

After the Commission's report, the treatment of library activities remained an area of debate, although many later reports focused not on free exceptions but the development of collective licensing as a means to deal with reprographic reproduction.[81] As will be discussed further in Chapter 9, the reasoning in these reports often reflected a particular property-based understanding of copyright that was more absolutist and saw a narrow role for exceptions.[82] For instance, whilst the Keyes and Brunet Report of 1977 was willing to countenance a preservation copying exception,[83] it was also clear that the report's authors were wary of affording special privileges to cultural institutions, observing that '[c]opyright deals with the rights of authors first and not with the cultural objectives of society as manifested in any policy concerning the preservation and archival storage of copyright works'.[84] During this time there was instead much focus on the establishment of a collective to administer rights in print materials, with oversight being exercised by the Copyright Appeal Board.[85] When reforms were introduced in Bill C-60 of 1987, these calls were followed, and one of the key aspects of the legislation eventually passed by Parliament was the inclusion of provisions designed to stimulate the formation of collectives.[86] In taking this step, it was not the intention to reject the possibility of exceptions; rather, it was proposed that the reform process be divided in two, with a first stage of amendments in Bill C-60 (including in relation to collective

---

[81] See, e.g., Economic Council of Canada, *Report on Intellectual and Industrial Property* (Information Canada, January 1971), p. 164; A. Keyes and C. Brunet, *Copyright in Canada: Proposals for a Revision of the Law* (Consumer and Corporate Affairs Canada, April 1977), pp. 162–165; J. Erola and F. Fox, *From Gutenberg to Telidon: A White Paper on Copyright: Proposals for the Revision of the Canadian Copyright Act* (Department of Consumer and Corporate Affairs and Department of Communications, 1984), pp. 40–41; House of Commons Standing Committee on Communications and Culture, Sub-Committee on the Revision of Copyright, *A Charter of Rights for Creators* (Minister of Supply and Services Canada, October 1985), pp. 21–22.
[82] See Chapter 9, Section II.D.
[83] Keyes and Brunet, n. 81 above, p. 175 (recommending that the only exception for libraries and archives should be a provision allowing a preservation copy to be made of deteriorating or damaged material); see also *A Charter of Rights for Creators*, n. 81 above, pp. 68–70 (recommending two exceptions for archival institutions in relation to preservation copying and research being undertaken at another institution).
[84] Keyes and Brunet, n. 81 above, p. 173. For a response that archivists 'cannot accept a situation in which a large percentage of its daily work is technically illegal', see G. Maurice Hyam, 'The Working Paper on Copyright: A Preliminary Response' (Summer 1977) 4 *Archivaria* 188, 190.
[85] See summary in M. Hébert, *Copyright Act Reform* (Library of Parliament, 25 October 1982 revised 9 January 1990), pp. 6–10.
[86] Ibid., pp. 15–16.

History of Sector-Specific Exceptions 119

administration), and other matters such as exceptions deferred to a second round.[87] This two-stage approach was controversial, and amongst the library sector there was a perception that Bill C-60 excessively favoured owner interests,[88] and that libraries would be disadvantaged in their negotiations with any new reprographic collective if they did not know the scope of new exceptions.[89]

Although it had been anticipated that the second-stage reforms would be turned around relatively quickly, it was not until 1996 that Bill C-32 was tabled in federal parliament.[90] In addition to advocating for provisions in relation to copying services, the legislative treatment of other activities was also pressed by cultural institution representatives. The possibility that user groups would be disappointed with the stage two reforms was anticipated in a Library of Parliament report written by Monique Hébert. Based on her observation of the reluctance in Canada to embrace free exceptions, she wrote:

While requests for special consideration are likely to be made, it is questionable whether phase two will be as accommodating as some user groups might like. The trend in recent years has been to grant exemptions only where there are compelling reasons to do so, and not because particular user groups might be deserving of preferential treatment because of who they are or what they do.

In terms of balancing the interests of creators and users, collectives are increasingly being viewed as the option of choice. The Sub-Committee [in *A Charter of Rights for Creators*] favoured the use collectives over the grant of exemptions.[91]

As with the first-stage reforms that preceded it, there was controversy surrounding the second-stage amendments. In their submissions to the Standing Committee on Canadian heritage, cultural institutions and peak bodies were relatively supportive of the initial drafting of new sector-specific exceptions, although often arguing that the reforms did not go far enough.[92] In contrast, a number of publishers and creator

---

[87] M. Hébert, *Background Paper: Copyright Reform* (Library of Parliament, March 1996), pp. 18–19.
[88] L. Murray and S. Trosow, *Canadian Copyright: A Citizen's Guide* (Toronto: Between the Lines, 2007), p. 143.
[89] Hébert, n. 87 above, pp. 18–19, 50.
[90] The Bill eventually received royal assent on 25 April 1997; see summary in M. Hébert, *Bill C-32: An Act to Amend the Copyright Act* (Library of Parliament, 17 May 1996 revised 21 March 1997) ('Hébert Bill C-32').
[91] Ibid., p. 53.
[92] See, e.g., Canadian Library Association, *Brief to the Standing Committee on Canadian Heritage Respecting Bill C-32* (August 1996), p. 1; British Columbia Library Association, *Brief Regarding Bill C-32 An Act to Amend the Copyright Act* (13 August 1996), p. 2; Association of Canadian Archivists, L'association des archivistes du Québec and the Canadian Council of Archives, *Brief to the Standing Committee on Canadian Heritage*

representatives argued that the provisions needed to be scaled back or deleted, with particular concern focused on exceptions relating to request-based services and the provision of self-serve copying equipment.[93] Certain themes recurred in the reasoning adopted in the owner submissions, including the need for creators to be fully compensated for use of their works, and the lack of any need for free exceptions where collective licensing practices were working efficiently.[94] Many of these concerns were accommodated in the version of the bill eventually passed by Parliament; for instance, a number of provisions, including those permitting preservation and replacement copying, excluded works that were 'commercially available', a term defined to include available under a licence from a collective.[95] In their book on Canadian copyright law, Laura Murray and Samuel Trosow described the new exceptions as therefore being a 'messy compromise measure' due to the insertion of limitations and qualifications at the behest of owner representatives,[96] whilst David Vaver also pointed to the 'uneasy' compromises in provisions dealing with the copying of articles upon request.[97] A number of interviewees in the Canadian fieldwork also described the challenges of the reform process; for instance, one described it as a

rough ride, in terms of how the exceptions were treated. They were scaled back considerably, especially through the use of a restriction for commercial availability. That restriction was quite explicit in including not just books available for sale, but also licensing.[98]

Regarding Bill C-32, an Act to Amend the Copyright Act (August 1996), p. 2; letter from Dr Shirley L Thomson, National Gallery of Canada, to the Standing Committee on Canadian Heritage, 30 August 1996, p. 1; Ontario Library Association, *Position Statement by the Ontario Library Association respecting Bill C-32 An Act to Amend the Copyright Act* (30 August 1996), p. 1; Canadian Museums Association, *Brief on Bill C-32 Amendments to the Copyright Act to the Standing Committee on Canadian Heritage from the Canadian Museums Association* (undated), p. 2.

[93] See, e.g., Canadian Publishers' Council, *Submission of the Canadian Publishers' Council to the Standing Committee on Canadian Heritage Regarding Bill C-32* (August 1996), pp. 13–15; The Writers' Union of Canada and the League of Canadian Poets, *Submission to Bill C-32, An Act to Amend the Copyright Act* (under cover letter dated 28 August 1996), pp. 7–12; Canadian Copyright Licensing Agency, *Submission of the Canadian Copyright Licensing Agency to the Standing Committee on Canadian Heritage Regarding Bill C-32, An Act to Amend the Copyright Act* (29 August 1996), pp. 14–24; Association of Canadian Publishers, *Submission to the Standing Committee on Canadian Heritage Regarding Bill C-32 "An Act to Amend the Copyright Act"* (1 September 1996), pp. 10–12.

[94] See, e.g., Canadian Conference of the Arts, *A Brief to the Standing Committee on Canadian Heritage on Bill C-32* (30 August 1996), pp. 8–9; Association of Canadian Publishers, ibid., p. 7; Canadian Publishers' Council, ibid., p. 11.

[95] Canadian Copyright Act ss. 30.1(1)(a)–(c), (2).

[96] Murray and Trosow, n. 88 above, p. 143.

[97] D. Vaver, *Copyright Law* (Toronto: Irwin Law, 2000), p. 206.   [98] 144X.

Another stated:

> It was a long struggle to get [the second phase] through. ... The outcome was certainly not what we wished, and in fact, the bill was better when it was initially tabled in the House than it ended up being. It was amended during the process of debate in the House, there was a very strong lobby against the exceptions, and that lobby resulted in some narrowing of those exceptions. So, both in the lead up to the tabling of the bill, and the actual process of working through the House, it was a real struggle.[99]

In 2012, the LAM provisions underwent limited reform by the Copyright Modernization Act, a statute which also expanded the fair dealing purposes and added new closed exceptions.[100] The fair dealing aspects of these reforms are discussed in detail in Chapter 7.

C Concluding Remarks

One observation that can be drawn from the history in Section II is the contested ground occupied by libraries and archives provisions. Although the copyright statutes of Australia, Canada, the United Kingdom and the United States all contain unremunerated sector-specific exceptions, there has been ongoing debate about their content. A preliminary question is whether there should be a statutory response to copying by cultural institutions or whether such activities should be left to voluntary licensing.[101] In the United Kingdom, Australia and the United States, law reform efforts resulted in some dealings being mediated by free exceptions, with Australia also adopting a compulsory licensing scheme for educational copying. The existence of libraries and archives provisions has been reconsidered at a number of junctures; however, current discussions seem to proceed on the basis that cultural institutions should be afforded *some* privileges in copyright law,[102] with attention turned to the scope of those privileges and the form they should take.[103]

---

[99] 107L.
[100] An Act to amend the Copyright Act (S.C. 2012, c. 20), in particular ss. 21 (expansion of fair dealing to include education, parody and satire), 28–30 (amendments to LAM provisions).
[101] See, e.g., Varmer, n. 52 above, pp. 66–67.
[102] Such a position being bolstered by new mandatory exceptions for cultural institutions (and other users) in the DSM Directive, n. 2 above.
[103] This includes discussion of whether some exceptions should be subject to a requirement to pay remuneration. In Europe, for example, the cases in Arts. 5(2)(a), (b) and (e) of the Information Society Directive refer to the payment of fair compensation: for analysis, see, e.g., A. Dias Pereira, 'Levies in EU Copyright Law: An Overview of the CJEU's Judgments on the Fair Compensation of Private Copying

122   Sector-Specific Exceptions

In contrast, despite early recommendations that sector-specific exceptions be developed in Canada, subsequent efforts in that country focused on collective licensing as the key way to facilitate library activities. This is significant. Although LAM provisions were eventually inserted in the Copyright Act in the late 1990s, this was in the context of blanket licensing schemes having been in operation for a number of years. It will be argued in this book that this history has had a significant impact on copyright experiences in Canada. In addition to influencing the drafting of sector-specific exceptions, it encouraged the development of institutional management norms that de-emphasised reliance on exceptions. That said, it will also be seen that such norms are not immutable, and that aspects of the more recent history reveal that some Canadian practices, especially those in academic libraries, are in flux.[104]

III Content and Operation

This chapter now examines the content of sector-specific exceptions in the four jurisdictions studied. It does this using doctrinal analysis of the language of these provisions and empirical analysis of reported practices of institutional users. As noted earlier, the fieldwork is not intended to present a fixed picture of what cultural institutions 'do', as this may change over time, including in response to legislative reform. Rather, the goal is to get a sense of the decision-making practices of cultural institutions, and what this means for the drafting of sector-specific exceptions and whether they are fit-for-purpose. Section III starts with a summary of eligibility requirements before addressing the substantive provisions, these being grouped around: preservation, replacement and obsolete technology; collection management; user request, researcher use and interlibrary supply; and onsite consultation.

---

and Reprography' (2017) 12 *Journal of Intellectual Property Law & Practice* 591. The CJEU has also discussed the relevance of remuneration to other exceptions, citing Art. 5(5): see, in particular, *Technische Universität Darmstadt v. Eugen Ulmer KG* (C-117/13) [2014] ECDR 23 (Fourth Chamber), paras. 43–49 (consideration of whether libraries may digitise analogue works so those digitised versions can be made available publicly on dedicated terminals; the applicable German law 'takes due account' of Art. 5(5) because, *inter alia*, it requires the payment of adequate remuneration to rightsholders when those works are made available). Finally, the mandatory exception for teaching in Art. 5 of the DSM Directive, n. 2 above, countenances that Member States 'may' provide that the exception is subject to the payment of fair remuneration.
[104] See Chapter 8.

Content and Operation

A   Eligibility

1   United Kingdom Following reforms in 2014, there has been some extension of the reach of the UK libraries and archives provisions. Whilst the provisions in relation to interlibrary supply and researcher requests are available only to librarians,[105] a similar provision dealing with unpublished works covers librarians and archivists,[106] whilst exceptions for dedicated terminals, preservation copying and orphaned works may be invoked by libraries, archives, museums (defined to include galleries)[107] and, in some cases, other bodies.[108] These amendments therefore represent a shift from previous arrangements where no mention was made of museums and galleries.[109]

The CDPA does not define the term 'library', although it does provide that for the purposes of sections 40A to 43, a library must be publicly accessible or form part of an educational establishment.[110] We must therefore look to general understandings of the term.[111] Historically, libraries acquired books, journals, newspapers and other print-based materials for reference and circulating collections, along with other matter – such as maps and drawings – for special collections. The development of digital technologies has changed the ways in which libraries acquire materials, with an increasing amount of born-digital content entering their collections, and subscriptions to electronic databases supplementing and replacing the purchase of hardcopy titles. The boundaries between libraries and other cultural institutions are not always clear cut, especially given convergence in the roles of, and subject matter collected by, different types of institution.[112] That said, one

---

[105] CDPA ss. 41 (interlibrary supply), 42A (researcher requests). Interlibrary supply is sometimes referred to as interlibrary loan, although such usage must be clarified; the exception in s. 41 countenances the supply of a copy of a work by a library where it would not be feasible for the that library to lend its own copy to another library: see Gregory Committee, n. 9 above, para. 49.

[106] Ibid., s. 43. Section 40A, dealing with the lending of books and other works, also applies to libraries and archives.

[107] Ibid., s. 43A(3).

[108] Ibid., ss. 40B (dedicated terminals; may also be claimed by educational establishments), 42 (preservation and replacement copying), 44B (orphaned works; under Schedule ZA1, educational establishments, film or audio heritage institutions and public service broadcasting organisations may also rely on this exception).

[109] For discussion of previous arrangements, see, e.g., T. Padfield, *Copyright for Archivists and Users of Archives*, 2nd edition (London: Facet Publishing, 2004), pp. 118–119; L. Bently and B. Sherman, *Intellectual Property Law*, 3rd edition (Oxford: OUP, 2009), pp. 221–222.

[110] CDPA s. 43A(2). The orphaned works provisions in Schedule ZA1 apply to 'relevant bodies'; this includes 'a publicly accessible library, educational establishment or museum' and 'an archive'.

[111] Burrell and Coleman, n. 38 above, pp. 138–139.   [112] Ibid., p. 138.

interviewee emphasised that whilst 'I can logically see that libraries, archives and museums are very similar types of entities and share many goals, the way in which they interact with copyright is very different', in particular that

> libraries are in the business of acquiring content-based materials ... whereas museums and archives very often collect objects for which copyright is a tangential issue. The copyright issue in cataloguing an object might come across as part of what they're doing, whereas the copyright question with a library acquiring and developing content, which is central to its purposes and what it's trying to do – they're of a different order and magnitude.[113]

In terms of other eligibility requirements, at a number of points the UK provisions exclude institutions that are 'conducted for profit'.[114] This is defined to mean a body 'which is established or conducted for profit or which forms part of, or is administered by, a body established or conducted for profit'.[115] Although corporate libraries and other private bodies are not, therefore, excluded from the libraries and archives provisions, their ability to operate under those provisions is limited, and at times they can invoke them only when supplying copies to other, non-profit, institutions.

2 Australia As with the United Kingdom, eligibility for the sector-specific exceptions has been widened from the original enactment. Not only were the Australian provisions extended in 1980 to apply to archival collections,[116] but the definition of that term was amended in 2000 with a notation that '[m]useums and galleries are examples of bodies that could have collections covered by ... the definition of archives'.[117] The intention, here, was to confirm the reach of the sector-specific exceptions to public institutions but not private entities

---

[113] 318X.
[114] CDPA ss. 41(2) (interlibrary supply; requesting institution must not be conducted for profit), 42(4) (supply of replacement copy to another library, archives or museum; requesting institution must not be conducted for profit), 42A(1) (researcher requests for copies of published works; exception only available to libraries not conducted for profit).
[115] CDPA s. 43A(4).
[116] Copyright Amendment Act 1980 (Cth), ss. 5 (adding a definition of archives into ss. 10 (1) and (4) of the Australian Copyright Act), 10–12 (extending the substantive provisions of the Act). The definition of archives covered four named institutions as well as the collections of other bodies where they contain material 'of historical significance or public interest', are held 'for the purpose of conserving or preserving' those items, and are not maintained 'for the purpose of deriving a profit'.
[117] Copyright Amendment (Digital Agenda) Act 2000 (Cth), Schedule 1, item 21, adding a notation to Australian Copyright Act, s. 10(4).

such as commercial art galleries.[118] In contrast, and again like the United Kingdom, 'library' is not given a separate definition in the Copyright Act, and we must turn to usual understandings.[119]

There have been debates in Australia regarding the application of the sector-specific exceptions to libraries in profit-making enterprises, for which there is no general exclusion in the Act.[120] However, two of the key exceptions – for user requests (section 49) and supply of other libraries (section 50) – apply only to libraries whose collections are, in whole or part, 'accessible to members of the public directly or through interlibrary loans'.[121] This would seem to prevent corporate libraries from relying on these sections unless their collections are sufficiently open, although they may still invoke other sector-specific exceptions should they be relevant.

3   *United States* The exceptions in section 108 are subject to a number of general limitations,[122] one of which is that they apply only to libraries and archives whose collections are either open to the public or available to external researchers doing work in a specialised field.[123] Neither library nor archives is defined in the Copyright Act; however, these terms have been interpreted strictly, and it is generally accepted

---

[118] Explanatory Memorandum, Copyright Amendment (Digital Agenda) Bill 1999, para. 21.

[119] Discussed in E. Hudson and A. Kenyon, 'Digital Access: The Impact of Copyright on Digitisation Practices in Australian Museums, Galleries, Libraries and Archives' (2007) 30 *University of New South Wales Law Journal* 12, 31.

[120] See, e.g., Phillips Fox, *Digital Agenda Review: Report and recommendations* (January 2004), paras. 9.1–9.4, 14.1–14.15, Recommendation Four. At the time of this report, ss. 49 and 50 did not apply to a library conducted for profit. However, in s. 18, the Act stated that 'a library shall not be taken to be established or conducted for profit by reason only that the library is owned by a person carrying on business for profit'. Given that internal libraries in commercial organisations tend to be loss-making, this led to the concern that the exclusions in ss. 49 and 50 were illusory, and that clusters of corporate libraries were running interlibrary loan schemes with one another: see submissions made to Phillips Fox, especially at para 14.5. Sections 49 and 50 have since been amended as per n. 121, next.

[121] Australian Copyright Act ss. 49(9), 50(10). The same requirement exists for archives seeking to rely on these provisions. As noted at n. 105 above, the term interlibrary *loan* might be replaced with interlibrary *supply*, which more accurately captures the process being described.

[122] US Copyright Act s. 108(a).

[123] Ibid., s. 108(a)(2). This has the potential to limit their relevance to corporate libraries and similar entities: see D. Nimmer, *Nimmer on Copyright*, Volume 2 (LexisNexis, online resource, accessed 15 January 2019), para. 8.03[A][2].

that museums and galleries cannot invoke section 108.[124] The Section 108 Study Group observed that the legislative record does not contain any explanation as to why museums were not included, although it can be hypothesised that when these provisions were being developed, museum practices were not thought to implicate copyright to the same degree as those of libraries.[125]

Whatever may have been the case when the Copyright Act was passed, it is clear that in the present day, copyright is of great significance to museums and galleries.[126] For such institutions, the eligibility requirements of section 108 mean that fair use is often the sole exception that can be invoked to justify otherwise infringing activity. Both the Section 108 Study Group and the Copyright Office have recommended that the sector-specific provisions in the Copyright Act be extended to include museums (presumably used in the broader sense to include galleries). Whilst this may seem an uncontroversial step, the research in this book raises questions regarding the need for such a reform, and whether it may have the unintended consequence of casting doubt on the existing fair use practices of US institutions.[127]

Section 108 contains some other general limits on when its provisions apply. This includes that section 108 may only be used for reproductions and distributions made 'without any purpose of direct or indirect commercial advantage'.[128] The Copyright Act does not elaborate on when such 'commercial advantage' occurs. In *American Geophysical Union v. Texaco, Inc*, it was held that a library photocopying service for research scientists at Texaco fell outside of section 108, in part because articles were copied to help those scientists 'in their profit-motivated research'.[129] That analysis has been described by *Nimmer on Copyright* as 'unconvincing' on the basis that it considered 'indirect commercial benefit', when the better reading of section 108 is that commercial advantage refers to the copy itself.[130]

---

[124] See Section 108 Study Group, n. 3 above, pp. 17–18, 31–33; United States Copyright Office, n. 15 above, pp. 17–18.
[125] Section 108 Study Group, ibid., pp. 31–32.
[126] Ibid., p. 32; see also United States Copyright Office, n. 15 above, pp. 17–18.
[127] See Chapter 9, Section III. [128] US Copyright Act s. 108(a)(1).
[129] 802 F Supp 1, 28–29 (SDNY, 1992). This aspect was not appealed, with the District Court decision affirmed on other grounds in 60 F 3d 913 (2nd circuit, 1993).
[130] Nimmer, n. 123 above, para. 8.03[A][1]. The legislative history contains inconsistent statements in relation to the application of s. 108 to libraries in commercial organisations; see, e.g., L. Gasaway, 'Values Conflict in the Digital Environment: Librarians Versus Copyright Holders' (2000) 24 *Columbia-VLA Journal of Law and the Arts* 115, 135; M. Minow and T. Lipinski, *The Library's Legal Answer Book* (Chicago: American Library Association, 2003), pp. 42–43.

4 Canada The LAM provisions cover libraries, archives and museums, the latter of which would seem to include galleries. In section 2 of the Canadian Copyright Act it is stated that

library, archive or museum means

(a) an institution, whether or not incorporated, that is not established or conducted for profit or that does not form a part of, or is not administered or directly or indirectly controlled by, a body that is established or conducted for profit, in which is held and maintained a collection of documents and other materials that is open to the public or to researchers, or
(b) any other non-profit institution prescribed by regulation.

As Vaver explains:

The world of institutional information is thus divided into the public and private sectors. The public sector is intended to benefit from the special exemptions; the private sector is not. The public sector is, moreover, treated as part of an information network. One non-profit LAM can copy material for another non-profit LAM in the same way as it can for its own use or for its own patrons. Private sector LAMs fall outside this network. Copies they request from one another or from a non-profit LAM are not exempt. Such copies may fall under a collective reprographic agreement.[131]

Examined in isolation, the definition in section 2 may seem to be stricter than those in the UK, Australian and US statutes because of the exclusion of for-profit bodies. But as seen above, other limitations in those statutes will in many instances lead to the same result.

The definition in section 2 was considered by the Supreme Court in *CCH Canadian Ltd* v. *Law Society of Upper Canada*, where the Law Society pleaded a defence under the LAM provisions in addition to its fair dealing arguments.[132] The publishers argued that this defence was unavailable as the Law Society, who operated the Great Library at Osgoode Hall, was indirectly controlled by lawyers who practised law for profit. Given the success of the fair dealing arguments, it was unnecessary for the Law Society to rely on its LAM submissions. However, the Supreme Court said that had it been necessary to consider this defence, the Library would have fallen within the definition in section 2: it was not operated for profit, and it was irrelevant that some of the benchers who helped in its administration were separately involved in

---

[131] Vaver, n. 97 above, p. 202.
[132] [2004] 1 SCR 339. The Law Society cited s. 30.2(1), under which a library may do on behalf of a patron anything that person may themselves do under fair dealing.

128   Sector-Specific Exceptions

the business of law, as their Law Society work was performed in a separate capacity.

B   *Preservation, Replacement and Obsolete Technology*

1 The Provisions All four statutes contain exceptions which permit the making of preservation and replacement copies, with provisions in the United States and Canada also dealing explicitly with technological obsolescence.[133] In copyright law, exceptions directed to preservation are concerned with the creation of new copies, whether to act as surrogates for collection items (thereby reducing the handling of fragile or high demand works) or to substitute for those items should they physically disintegrate or can no longer be opened or played.[134] Preservation copying provisions sometimes appear alongside exceptions for replacement copying, which in copyright legislation are typically directed to instances where damage or loss has already occurred. There are questions over the degree to which these copyright concepts map onto institutional understandings of preservation, conservation and restoration.[135] For instance, preservation as a term of art would seem to include activities that seek to conserve the original media or manifestation of a work, and which do not involve the making of copies (except, perhaps, to record those efforts).[136] In fact, there are those who question whether copying the information content of a work onto new media is truly an instance of preservation.

On their face, some of the preservation copying exceptions contain language and restrictions that seem difficult to square with their legislative purpose. For instance, some exceptions contain, or have in the past

---

[133] US Copyright Act s. 108(c); Canadian Copyright Act s. 30.1(1)(c). In Australia, the legislative intent in relation to s. 113H(1) of the Copyright Act, introduced by the Copyright Amendment (Disability Access and Other Measures) Act 2017 (Cth), was that new preservation copies may be made if best practices change regarding, e.g., the format that such copies should take: Explanatory Memorandum (Disability Access and Other Measures) Bill, n. 50 above, p. 18. To the extent this may not cover certain forms of copying for technological change, it may be possible to rely on s. 200AB. Similarly, it may be possible to argue that the language of the UK provisions in s. 42 of the CDPA is sufficiently broad to permit preservation copying due to technological obsolescence.

[134] See, e.g., Franki Committee, n. 9 above, paras. 5.01–5.03.

[135] For discussion of meanings of those terms, see, e.g., M. Cloonan, 'W(h)ither Preservation?' (2001) 71 *The Library Quarterly: Information, Community, Policy* 231.

[136] See, e.g., R. Oakley, 'Preservation and Copyright' in L. Gasaway (ed), *Growing Pains: Adapting Copyright for Libraries, Education, and Society* (Littleton, Colorado: Fred B. Rothman & Co., 1997); P. Hirtle 'The History and Current State of Digital Preservation in the United States' in *Metadata And Digital Collections: A Festschrift in Honor of Thomas P. Turner* (Cornell University Library, online resource), http://cip.cornell.edu/cul.pub/1238609304.

contained, subject-matter limitations which restrict preservation copying to unpublished or original works, and replacement copying to published materials.[137] As stated by the Section 108 Study Group, this division may reflect the assumption that unpublished works tend to be unique and not available on the market, whereas for published works, the opposite is the case.[138] Assuming that market availability should be relevant to determining whether an exception is available, it is questionable whether publication status operates as a satisfactory proxy for such a consideration. For instance, for rare and out-of-print published material there may be no readily available copy, and the event that necessitates the making of a replacement may mean that an institution is unable to use its own copy to generate it.[139] In the United States, the Copyright Office has recommended that preservation and replacement copying provisions abandon the concept of 'published' versus 'unpublished' works, and instead differentiate between works that have been 'lawfully disseminated to the public' and those that have not.[140]

Other preservation copying provisions have already moved away from this dichotomy, especially those passed in more recent times. Thus the CDPA permits the copying of items in the permanent collection of a library, archives or museum 'in order to preserve or replace that item in that collection'.[141] No distinction is made between published and

---

[137] US Copyright Act ss. 108(b) (copying of unpublished works for 'preservation and security' purposes), 108(c) (replacement copying of published works). Such a distinction was also made until 2017 in preservation copying provisions in the Australian Copyright Act: see n. 147 to n. 152 below.
[138] Section 108 Study Group, n. 3 above, pp. 18–19.   [139] Ibid., p. 49.
[140] United States Copyright Office, n. 15 above, pp. 24–25. This Report envisaged an expansion to the preservation copying provisions, which would apply to both categories of work, although there would be different rules in relation to the availability of the resulting copies: pp. 26–29, and see below n. 269 and surrounding text. The recommendation to replace 'publication' with 'dissemination to the public' reflected the concern that the internet had rendered inapt certain analogue understandings of publication. The Office emphasised that this distinction would apply only to s. 108: at p. 24. However, as seen in the discussion of quotation in Chapter 8, Section II.B, we need to be careful in writing different rules for works not publicly disseminated, lest we unduly tie up unpublished cultural heritage collections. For instance, the Office used the example of a draft manuscript posted to a blog without the permission of the author: this would *not* be a dissemination to the public for the purposes of s. 108: p. 25. Logic would suggest that this conclusion would also apply to a manuscript donated to a library without the author's permission, should such an act even be seen as public dissemination.
[141] CDPA s. 42(1)(a). As enacted, this provision could be invoked only by libraries and archives, and applied only to literary, dramatic and musical copyright (including illustrations) and to copyright in the typographical arrangement. Reforms in 2014 broadened the scope of the exception.

unpublished works, although other restrictions, notably in relation to commercial availability, limit the provision's reach.[142] The mandatory preservation copying exception in the DSM Directive likewise has a broad sweep, applying to 'any works or other subject-matter that are permanently in [the collection]'.[143] In Canada, the Copyright Act permits items in the permanent collection to be copied 'if the original is rare or unpublished' and is 'deteriorating, damaged or lost' or at risk of one of these.[144] As with the United Kingdom, it does not apply where an appropriate copy is 'commercially available',[145] although this term is defined more broadly as it includes not just copies on the Canadian market but works 'for which a licence to reproduce ... is available from a collective society'.[146]

The position in Australia has undergone some change. The earliest suite of preservation copying provisions, first introduced in 1980, distinguished between manuscript and other original material (which could be copied for preservation purposes) and works held in 'published form' (which could be copied for replacement purposes).[147] In 2006, these provisions were supplemented with new exceptions directed to key cultural institutions.[148] These provisions had the stated aim of enabling those institutions 'to more effectively deal with items of historical and

---

[142] Ibid., s. 42(3) (for s. 42 to apply, it must not be 'reasonably practicable [for the institution] to purchase a copy of the item' to achieve either the purpose or preservation or replacement).

[143] DSM Directive, n. 2 above, Art. 6. The exception applies to acts done 'for purposes of preservation of such works or other subject-matter and to the extent necessary for such preservation'. Recital 29 states that a work or subject matter is held permanently in the collection if it is 'owned or permanently held by that institution, for example as a result of a transfer of ownership or a licence agreement, legal deposit obligations or permanent custody arrangements'. As discussed by 324X, much will turn on how this provision is implemented into domestic law. Although the Recital refers to content acquired via licence agreements, the emphasis on permanent arrangements could exclude materials where the licence does not provide for perpetual access or a right to archive. That said, it was also emphasised by 318X that there is far greater awareness amongst publishers of their archiving responsibilities, including through work with libraries and other third parties. 318X expressed concern about the polarised debate that can surround preservation copying, and that 'when you stop talking about institutions, companies and sectors and start talking about people, there's a huge amount of alignment [regarding what most] people are motivated by and what they're in it for'.

[144] Canadian Copyright Act s. 30.1(1)(a). [145] Ibid., s. 30.1(2).

[146] Ibid., s. 2 (definition of 'commercially available').

[147] Australian Copyright Act ss. 51A(1)(a) (preservation copying of manuscripts and original artistic works), 51A(1)(b), (c) (replacement copying of works held in a published form), 110B(1)(a), (2)(a) (preservation copying of sound recordings held 'in the form of a first record' and cinematograph films held 'in the form of a first copy'), 110B(1)(b), (c), 2(b), (c) (replacement copying of sound recordings and cinematograph films held in published form).

[148] Australian Copyright Act ss. 51B, 110BA, 112AA.

cultural significance to Australia that are in their collections',[149] and extended preservation copying privileges to material not held in its original form, but only where an authorised officer was 'satisfied that a copy of the work cannot be obtained within a reasonable time at an ordinary commercial price'.[150] All of these provisions were repealed by the Copyright Amendment (Disability Access and Other Measures) Act 2017 (Cth) and replaced with new sections 113H (preservation generally) and 113M (key cultural institutions). Both sets of provision may be invoked for works material held 'in original form'[151] and/or where 'a copy of the material cannot be obtained in a version or format that is required for [preservation], consistent with best practice for preserving such collections'.[152]

Subject-matter limitations are not the only way that preservation and replacement copying exceptions are restricted. Some statutes contain statements regarding the public accessibility of preservation copies; this will be discussed later in the analysis of onsite consultation. A further limitation relates to the number of copies that may be made under the exception. In Australia, the preservation copying provisions for key cultural institutions originally contained a three-copy limitation, and such a restriction is still found in sections 108(b) and (c) of the US Copyright Act.[153] It could be argued that there are implicit quantitative limits in other provisions. For instance, the preservation copying provisions of the CDPA and the Canadian Copyright Act both use the language of 'a copy' being able to be made,[154] which could be said to permit only the making of single copies.[155] Such a reading would, however, require a particular

---

[149] Explanatory Memorandum, Copyright Amendment Bill 2006 (Cth), p. 3.
[150] Australian Copyright Act s. 51B(4)(a); similar ss. 110BA(3), (5), 112AA(2). This was further defined to include electronic copies.
[151] Defined in ibid., s. 10(1) as 'a form that embodies the material as initially prepared by the author or maker of the material. Example: A manuscript of a literary, dramatic or musical work'.
[152] Ibid., ss. 113H(1)(b), 113M(1)(d).
[153] Section 404 of the Digital Millennium Copyright Act, 112 Stat. 2860 (DMCA) amended s. 108 to provide that these copies can be made in digital format. For discussion, see Gasaway, n. 130 above, 138–139.
[154] CDPA s. 42(1); Canadian Copyright Act s. 30.1(1)(a).
[155] Similar language was used previously in ss. 51A(1), 110B(1), (3) of the Australian Copyright Act (allowing the making of 'a reproduction' of a manuscript or original artistic work, and 'a copy' of a sound recording or cinematograph film). These provisions were in force when fieldwork was undertaken in Australia in 2012/2013 and 2016, and a number of interviewees discussed the proposition that they covered only a single copy: e.g., 201X, 210A, 218M. See also S. Ricketson and C. Creswell, *Law of Intellectual Property: Copyright, Design and Confidential Information* (Legal Online, electronic resource at April 2011), para. 11.320 (suggesting that a single reproduction 'would be all that would be necessary' to satisfy the preservation limb of these provisions).

literalist interpretation that sits awkwardly with the legislative intent behind these provisions, and would render them unworkable in a digital environment. It is therefore not surprising that in 2014 guidance to cultural institutions, the UK Intellectual Property Office stated that a work 'can be copied as many times as necessary for the work to be preserved'.[156]

Drawing together the preceding analysis, it would appear that preservation copying provisions often utilise rule-like language and are limited in various ways. This raises a number of questions for which empirical analysis is crucial. Are institutional staff aware of the copyright implications of preservation copying and of the existence and content of exceptions that cover such activities? Has copyright impeded preservation efforts? In addition, the legislative history raises questions about the efficiency of rule-based drafting in this space. For instance, the Australian experience has been of preservation copying provisions being introduced in 1980,[157] expanded in 1986 to cover sound recordings and films,[158] revised in 2000 as part of digital agenda reforms,[159] supplemented in 2006 by new provisions for key cultural institutions,[160] and finally consolidated and revised in 2017.[161] One may question the desirability of Parliament having amended the preservation copying exceptions so many times, both in terms of the resources expended and the potentially destabilising effect on users.

2 The Practices Although the interviews focused particular attention on the use of digital technologies to fulfil institutional missions, questions about preservation were less oriented towards digitisation,

---

[156] Intellectual Property Office, *Exceptions to copyright: Libraries, archives and museums* (May 2014), p. 4. Recital 27 of the DSM Directive, n. 2 above, in relation to the new mandatory preservation copying exception in Art. 6, likewise states that the exception 'should allow the making of copies by the appropriate preservation tool, means or technology, in any format or medium, in the required number, at any point in the life of a work or other subject matter and to the extent required for preservation purposes'.
[157] Copyright Amendment Act 1980 (Cth), s. 12, inserting s. 51A into the Australian Copyright Act.
[158] Copyright Amendment Act 1986 (Cth), s. 12, inserting s. 110B.
[159] Copyright Amendment (Digital Agenda) Act 2000 (Cth), Schedule 1, items 73–78.
[160] Copyright Amendment Act 2006 (Cth), Schedule 6, items 26–29, inserting ss. 51B, 110BA and 112AA.
[161] Copyright Amendment (Disability Access and Other Measures) Act 2017 (Cth), Schedule 1, items 1–2 (inserting ss. 113G–113M, covering preservation copying by libraries and archives and by key cultural institutions), 22, 30, 35 (repealing ss. 51A, 51B, 110B, 110BA, 112AA).

given the changing and contested status of digitisation as a preservation technique.[162] As observed in the literature on preservation, analogue methods often involve well-honed practices that have been built into institution workflows and which produce copies of known physical stability. In contrast, there has been widespread concern that digital preservation is expensive and experimental, and that the resulting digital assets are at far greater risk of technological obsolescence and catastrophic loss when compared with analogue equivalents. These concerns have been especially pronounced for moving image, where the traditional preservation method of 'film in a cold room' has been particularly resistant to change.[163] Despite this, digital preservation has grown from the 1990s onwards, and it has been observed that digitisation has certain advantages over analogue reformatting. For instance, it has been said that digital copies not only 'protect' and 'represent' originals but can 'transcend' them, because of the level of detail revealed in photographic reproductions, the overlay of indexing and search functions, etc.[164] More generally, digital preservation has close synergies with access, given the ease with which digital assets can be repurposed.[165]

This relationship between preservation and access is particularly significant for mass digitisation, where access is not a mere by-product of digitisation but is usually the driver behind such projects. Amongst participants in the fieldwork, it was observed that most digitisation was undertaken with access in mind, meaning that truly stand-alone preservation work made up a lower proportion of practices.[166] Interviewees gave two reasons for this: first, that the creation of a 'dark' archive was anathema to the reasons for maintaining collections, which demand that

---

[162] See, e.g., M. Hedstrom, 'Digital Preservation: A Time Bomb for Digital Libraries' (1998) 31 *Computers and the Humanities* 189; L. Capell, 'Digitization as a Preservation Method for Damaged Acetate Negatives: A Case Study' (2010) 73 *The American Archivist* 235; K. Matusiak and T. Johnston, 'Digitization for Preservation and Access: Restoring the Usefulness of the Nitrate Negative Collections at the American Geographical Society Library' (2014) 77 *The American Archivist* 241.

[163] See, e.g., S. Conrad, 'Analog, the Sequel: An Analysis of Current Film Archiving Practice and Hesitance to Embrace Digital Preservation' (2012) 34 *Archival Issues* 27; K. Gracy, 'Ambition and Ambivalence: A Study of Professional Attitudes towards Digital Distribution of Archival Moving Images' (2013) 76 *The American Archivist* 346.

[164] See, e.g., P. Conway, 'Overview: Rationale for Digitization and Preservation' in M. Sitts (ed), *Handbook for Digital Projects: A Management Tool for Preservation and Access* (Andover, Massachusetts: Northeast Document Conservation Center, 2000).

[165] See, e.g., O. Rieger, *Preservation in the Age of Large-Scale Digitization: A White Paper* (February 2008), pp. 1–2. Traditional understandings of archival copying included that an access copy is made: see, e.g., Oakley, above n. 136, p. 112.

[166] Especially 1G, 2L, 9M, 14G, 20G, 33G, 53G, 102L, 105G, 127L, 135G, 249L, 261M, 302M, 326L.

134 Sector-Specific Exceptions

access be given, even if on a limited basis; and second, that the resource-intensiveness of digitisation and the requirements of funding bodies meant that, especially for larger projects, it was often essential that outputs be publicly accessible.[167] This is extremely significant for copyright, as reliance on exceptions will only get an institution so far if those exceptions permit the making of preservation copies but not public-facing uses. Thus, whilst some institutions could, in theory, digitise great swathes of the collection by reference to preservation copying exceptions, the fieldwork suggested that, by and large, they only committed resources to large-scale projects when they were confident that public access could be given. As seen in Chapter 3, this often involved the selection of materials in the public domain.

How, then, have cultural institutions dealt with copyright when making copies of in-copyright items for preservation purposes? The headline message from the fieldwork was that copyright has not operated as a particular constraint on these practices, although the reasons have varied. Amongst US interviewees, for example, preservation copying was facilitated not only by section 108 but by fair use, licensing and institutional norms. Fair use is dealt with in detail in Chapter 5, but for now it can be observed that amongst those who said their institutions undertook preservation activity pursuant to an exception, slightly more reported reliance on fair use[168] than section 108.[169] Those invoking fair use included participants from the library sector, indicating that librarians did not see the presence of sector-specific exceptions as foreclosing reliance on section 107. For instance, one library interviewee noted that fair use can be used to justify the preservation copying of film, observing that a committee report during the 1976 Act reform process referred specifically to this.[170] Another said that the wording of section 108 was problematic for some media, and that when there were ambiguities the institution looked instead to section 107.[171] These experiences illustrate

---

[167] Especially 9M, 10L, 107L, 113X, 117L, 124A, 126A, 151A. For instance, 151A observed that 'none of the formal funding programs would support preservation-only digitisation – they all require some level of access'.
[168] E.g., 1G, 7G, 9M, 12L, 13M, 19L, 28G, 29L.
[169] E.g., 4L (but referring to these as 'fair use copies'), 10L, 15L, 19L, 35L, 45M (in relation to archival collection).
[170] 12L. This interviewee appeared to be referring to HR Report No 94-1476, 94th Congress, 2nd Session (1976), p. 73 which, in reference to efforts at a number of institutions to preserve older motion pictures, commented that 'the making of duplicate copies for purposes of archival preservation certainly falls within the scope of "fair use"'.
[171] 19L.

the potential for fair use to be used when section 108 is inapplicable or perceived as unworkable.

As noted above, US interviewees also reported that the right to make preservation copies had been included in licences with copyright owners, even if such acts could be undertaken pursuant to an exception.[172] Such an approach was not peculiar to the United States, with interviewees from Australia, Canada and the United Kingdom likewise reporting that their institutions undertook preservation copying by reference to rights under licences.[173] This was particularly so for digital and audiovisual works, where it was common for content to be acquired pursuant to comprehensive licence agreements. It was reported that licences were used not only due to the complexity of rights in such items but in order to maintain good relations with artists, films studios, distributors, etc.

The fieldwork in the United States also suggested that some interviewees had internalised ideas about collection management that overrode copyright considerations to varying degrees. For instance, it would seem that best practice norms had led to disregard of the three-copy limitation in sections 108(b) and (c); not only was this restriction *not* mentioned by interviewees as raising a problem, but it was described as 'honoured in the breach'[174] and seen by 'most people ... as very low risk'.[175] This is not surprising given that a quantitative limit is incompatible with digital preservation standards, which require the making of a considerably greater number of copies.[176] At its strongest, however, management norms resulted in collection items being preservation copied without *any* meaningful engagement with the law.[177] It was therefore said that although licences and exceptions might be relevant to these acts, preservation is 'so inherent and fundamental to our missions' that copying was undertaken without a detailed copyright analysis.[178] For instance, one interviewee, discussing the preservation of oral history and other archival recordings, commented:

I think [staff] think about it the same way as you would send a book that was published in 1962 down to the conservation lab to have it repaired. And if you

---

[172] E.g., 4L, 7G, 13M, 16G, 21M, 28G, 33G, 45M, 53G.
[173] E.g., 107L, 115A, 124A, 126A, 128L, 210A, 215G, 219M, 225G, 255A, 267G, 305M, 314G, 323X.
[174] 12L.
[175] 55L. Compare Nimmer, n. 123 above, para. 8.03[E][1][a] (applying the language of the provision to note that, 'presumably', any additional copy would be 'related' and not exempt).
[176] See, e.g., Section 108 Study Group, n. 3 above, p. 44; United States Copyright Office, n. 15 above, p. 25. Both reports recommended abolition of this requirement.
[177] E.g., 4L, 5M, 14G, 20G, 30G, 43M, 52M, 53G.   [178] 43M; similar 4L, 12L, 53G.

have to repair a tear and you had to replace part of the page you probably wouldn't think twice about it. ... If the real issue is ... making a copy for the purposes of distribution ... then [copyright issues surrounding preservation] don't really come up because [the copy] wasn't meant for the purposes of distribution.[179]

To emphasise, the US fieldwork did not suggest that institutions were systematically digitising their collections by reference to preservation norms. These reflections typically related to specific items or substrates that were particularly fragile or at immediate risk.

In the three other countries, reported experiences also revealed how ethical views and best practice norms had influenced preservation copying practices. Starting with Canada, it was less common for participants to report that preservation copying had been undertaken without *any* preceding copyright analysis,[180] and interviewees were generally able to point to the legal basis for digitisation, whether this was a work's public domain status,[181] the receipt of rights under a licence or assignment,[182] or reliance on privileges in the Copyright Act.[183] As discussed above, section 30.1(1)(a) of the Canadian Copyright Act permits rare or unpublished collection items to be copied for preservation purposes so long as an 'appropriate copy' is not 'commercially available'. Despite concerns that the reach of this section might be limited, in particular by the definition of 'commercially available', no interviewees suggested that the language of s. 30.1(1)(a) had caused difficulties.[184] The indications from the fieldwork were therefore that the Canadian preservation copying provision was applied in a manner that was workable and relevant to institutional practices, even if aspects of its language might potentially be limiting. This may reflect the influence of longstanding management norms. For instance, whilst section 30.1(1)(a) only came into effect in 1999, there were reports from a number of interviewees that this did not result in a 'turning of the page' in relation to preservation.[185] Rather, the

---

[179] 4L. See also C. Russell, *Complete Copyright: An Everyday Guide for Librarians* (Chicago: American Library Association, 2004), p. 36 (the act of copying articles or pages that have been ripped out of a publication 'is common practice among libraries and in general has been considered a clear fair use').
[180] E.g., 142M, 146L (but observation made in relation to librarians generally).
[181] E.g., 130M, 136L, 151A. [182] E.g., 107L, 115A, 124A, 126A, 128L.
[183] E.g., 103G, 106A, 113X, 115A, 117L, 120G, 124A, 125L, 126A, 130M, 135G, 136L, 146L, 156L.
[184] 113X observed that this requirement 'has sat in the law for ten years, and we've never heard any issues about it, we've never heard that it's not working. I think that for the purposes of audiovisual collections, there could be a greater angst, because this is a medium where so much is now available in the marketplace.'
[185] 106A. Similar: 113X, 120G, 124A, 125L, 144X.

introduction of this exception created greater parity between existing institutional practices and the operation of the Copyright Act. As stated by one interviewee:

> I'm not sure that we ever did anything that would have been problematic before 1997 [the year the second-stage reforms were passed]. Many of the things that we do preservation on, the copyright has run out, or there's been a clear intention on the part of the donor that we preserve the materials. So some of that may have been tacit ... which it certainly is better to have very clear now.[186]

It therefore seemed that any question marks over the legal status of existing preservation copying norms were seen as dealt with by the second-stage reforms – i.e., that which was tacit had been made explicit.

In Australia, the first tranche of fieldwork pre-dated the 2006 reforms. At that stage, the only preservation copying exceptions differentiated between original manifestations of works (which could be preservation copied) and published forms (which could only be copied for replacement purposes).[187] This distinction was significant for some interviewees. For instance, there were reports from people managing collections of published films that licences were sought for all acts of copying, including internal uses.[188] This could lead to old films not being copied for preservation purposes, despite those prints being rare and recorded on formats prone to rapid deterioration.[189] The stated reasoning was that there might be some films that were, unbeknownst to the institution, controlled by an active rightsholder. Although this may seem to be an extremely risk-averse position to adopt, it reflected accurately the restrictions and ambiguities of the statutory language at the time.[190]

---

[186] 106A.   [187] Australian Copyright Act ss. 51A(1), 110B(1), (2).

[188] Hudson and Kenyon, above n. 119, 38–39, 44–45; E. Hudson and A. Kenyon, 'Communication in the Digital Environment: An Empirical Study into Copyright Law and Digitisation Practices in Public Museums, Galleries and Libraries' (Working Paper No 15/05, Intellectual Property Research Institute of Australia, July 2005), p. 15

[189] For a discussion of the history of film preservation, including the stability of different film formats, see, e.g., K. Gracy, 'The Evolution and Integration of Moving Image Preservation Work into Cultural Heritage Institutions' (2013) 48 *Information & Culture* 368.

[190] Sections 110B(2)(b) and (c) of the Copyright Act, dealing with replacement copying of films held 'in a published form', were only applicable where the film 'has been damaged or has deteriorated' or 'has been lost or stolen': see E. Hudson and A. Kenyon, *Copyright and Cultural Institutions: Guidelines for Digitisation* (Melbourne: University of Melbourne, 2005), p. 83. Copying of published films would either require a relaxed interpretation of 'has deteriorated' under s. 110B(2)(b), or an even more creative interpretation of s. 110B(2)(a) (preservation copying of films held 'in the form of a first copy') to say that this included the institution's *own* master recording. This issue was not dealt with by the Franki Committee, who merely recommended a replacement copying provision without noting the source from which this would come for lost, stolen and severely damaged works: see n. 9 above, paras. 5.09–5.11.

By the time of the second round of Australian fieldwork, which commenced in 2012, the legislative environment had changed as the existing suite of exceptions had been supplemented with section 200AB and the new preservation copying provisions for key cultural institutions.[191] Again, there were concerns about the statutory language. Section 200AB will be discussed in Chapter 6. In relation to the exceptions for key cultural institutions, a recurring observation was that the three-copy limitation was entirely unsuited to preservation activity.[192] Leaving aside the question of what counts as a copy,[193] the overarching concern was that it was impossible to operationalise any requirement to monitor and limit the number of copies made as part of preservation activities. Some interviewees also discussed the lack of clarity around the identity of 'key cultural institutions'.

Importantly, though, criticisms of the drafting of the Australian provisions did not translate to widespread reports that preservation activity was being curtailed due to copyright. In some instances, this was because of licences that facilitated a range of institutional activity, including preservation copying.[194] In other instances, however, it appeared that like their US counterparts, Australian staff had internalised norms of management that caused them to overlook or reimagine aspects of the statutory language (such as the three-copy limit) or to disregard copyright completely. Thus, there were repeated reports that those undertaking preservation focused on the immediate need to protect or conserve the object (or its information content), with copyright concerns either taking a back seat or not perceived to have any relevance at all.[195] One interviewee therefore described preservation as an 'operational' rather than a copyright issue,[196] whilst another said that when it came to conserving works, 'the copyright consideration would be so far down the list that it does not factor'.[197] Decision-making was imbued with the strong ethical and institutional norm that

---

[191] Described above n. 147 to n. 150 and surrounding text.
[192] E.g., 201X, 209L (describing the limit as 'patently stupid', with the result that 'the rule is too technically specific to be of any value'), 221L, 229X, 230A, 259L.
[193] E.g., 230A described the steps in making a preservation copy of nitrate film, including the number of intermediate copies generated, and the need to permit access in a variety of formats, these formats changing over time (and at times quite rapidly) due to technological obsolescence; and 250L noted that in addition to making an archival quality TIFF file (which might be stored on more than one server), there will be lower-resolution access copies.
[194] E.g., 210A, 215G, 219M, 225G, 255A, 267G.
[195] E.g., 201X, 203M, 204A, 206G, 214M, 215G, 220M, 225G, 228M, 229X, 249L, 250L; note also 210A (although some institutions take a more cavalier approach, others have to be cautious, especially to maintain good relations with content creators).
[196] 249L.   [197] 203M.

Content and Operation 139

[t]he main concern is with the object. If that object is deteriorating and we need to produce several files for different reasons, then the preservation of that physical object is the most important thing, not whether we've done more copies under the preservation copying [provisions]. [The focus is] access to that object in the future, not that we've committed a sin in producing more copies.[198]

Although some interviewees raised concerns about statutory drafting, others spoke of themselves or other staff having limited knowledge of the specific text of the preservation copying provisions, as captured by this exchange:

Interviewer: What is the thinking in relation to copyright and preservation activities?
239L: My take on it is that we're not infringing, because of one of the things under the Act.
Interviewer: You're right that there's something in the Act. Do you have any familiarity with it?
239L: No.

One further thing to bear in mind is that items earmarked for preservation copying – e.g., old unpublished manuscripts, glass slides and rare films printed on fragile substrates – often had qualities that made it more likely that they were out of copyright or otherwise lacked an active rightsholder.[199] When seen in the backdrop of the strong institutional norms around care for the collection, it is not surprising that for many Australian interviewees the copyright implications of preservation copying did not occupy any meaningful intellectual bandwidth, although this is not to suggest that legislative reform was not unwelcome.[200]

Turning lastly to the United Kingdom, a similar picture emerged in relation to decision-making around preservation copying. An exception for preservation and replacement first appeared in the UK with the passage of the CDPA, and for many years this provision contained some significant limits.[201] It was expanded as part of the 2014 reforms such that its reach extended to museums and to preservation copying of all types of copyright work.[202] That said – and at least amongst participating

---

[198] 228M.
[199] In fact, 239L also stated that 'we're [digitising] the out of copyright stuff first because it is easy. Or if it's in danger of disintegration, we do it for preservation.'
[200] E.g., 210A, 221L, 230A and 259L spoke particularly strongly of drafting problems with the previous suite of provisions, which were said to make them unworkable.
[201] CDPA s. 42; see n. 38 above and surrounding text. Two significant limits were that s. 42 could only be invoked by libraries and archives, and applied only to copyright in literary, dramatic and musical works, accompanying illustrations and (for published editions) the typographical arrangement.
[202] Copyright and Rights in Performances (Research, Education, Libraries and Archives) Regulations 2014 (SI 2014/1372), reg. 5.

140 Sector-Specific Exceptions

institutions – it seems that this significant change to the wording of section 42 did not lead to any significant change in practices. As one interviewee said during the first batch of UK fieldwork in 2014:

> No-one in their right mind would not make a preservation copy of one-off items. They would have to as part of their insurance. It's their duty of care. So what do you do? Your duty of care, your contractual insurance provisions and your accreditation status is bound by the fact that you have a back-up copy, but the copyright law says no – so what do you do? As I've said for many years, we might as well shut up shop and go home. This is not going to change practices; we're just removing bad laws. ... I think that what's going to change is ... that [museums are] going to be able to do many of the things they were already doing anyway, legally; but also they're going to have a greater respect for copyright law, because they understand it works.[203]

These comments aligned with reports from other museum interviewees in 2014, where it was said that there was an awareness that the need to undertake preservation copying may produce 'tensions'[204] with copyright law, but also that institutional duties 'trumped'[205] copyright. Fast forwarding to 2017 and beyond, and the clear message was that institutions were confident in their ability to make preservation copies, and that copyright problems related to the accessibility and use of those reproductions rather than their making.[206] Whilst it appears that licensing was relevant to practices,[207] as was the exception,[208] there was also a sense that copyright was not at the front of people's minds: as one interviewee said of their experiences of that and other organisations, 'I don't understand that people are ever worried about copyright. The images are never good enough [for other uses].'[209] Another said:

---

[203] 305X.   [204] 302M.
[205] 311M; similar 303G (it would be 'against the gallery's remit' not to make preservation copies of fragile, one-off items, such as negatives).
[206] E.g., 319L, 321X, 322G.
[207] E.g., 305M, 314G, 323X, 328G. It was noted by 323X that the reason for including conservation in the licence for time-based media works (but not other artworks) was that it was not clear that s. 42 covered the back-up copying and format shifting they might need to undertake. Similarly, 314G spoke of the complicated protocols that can surround such works (including in relation to preservation and archival use), which tended to be recorded in a comprehensive agreement.
[208] Mentioned explicitly by 305M, 313M, 314G, 319L, 320L, 322G, 325M, 326L, 328G. Reliance on the exception appeared to be implicit in the reasoning of other interviewees.
[209] 305M; similar 317G, 320L, 321X, 322G.

Content and Operation 141

I think the preservation exception – because everyone had been doing it anyway, you were just like 'ok, great, we'll just carry on then'. I don't think anything's been written to say that anything's officially changed.[210]

This also meant that certain drafting limitations did not seem to be a problem in practice. For instance, whilst on a strict reading it is open to argue that section 42 permits the making of only a single copy, this interpretation did not seem to have any traction amongst those participating in this research.[211] Similarly, there were reports that preservation was given a liberal interpretation,[212] and that the commercial availability qualification – that section 42 did not apply where it was 'reasonably practicable to purchase a copy of the item'[213] – was not a problem as it dovetailed with existing preservation practices, which were typically directed to 'things that only come around once' such as unique items and those with a small print run.[214]

In sum, copyright had a relatively limited impact on standalone preservation copying. Sector-specific exceptions were only part of the reason for this state of affairs, with interviewees also pointing to licences and other exceptions (notably fair use) to justify copying. Furthermore, this comfort with preservation appeared to have been facilitated by best practice norms in the care of the collection, either because those norms permitted more workable interpretations of the statutory language, or – more radically – served to oust copyright from decision-making. The influence of norms varied amongst those who participated in the research, with Canadian interviewees perhaps less likely to report practices taking place without *any* consideration of copyright, and also seeming to derive comfort from pointing to the legality of such acts,

---

[210] 315A; similar 313M, 314G, 325M (also noting that the exception might give greater confidence to those undertaking pre-emptive digitisation of older, in-copyright works), 328G (also noting that the exception may be helpful to give a firmer sense of permissble uses, which may be useful for some externally-funded projects).
[211] Discussed by 319L, 326L; see above n. 154 to n. 156 and surrounding text. 326L described making multiple copies as 'within the feeling of what the law is meant to cover', and observed that this was an instance where the CDPA was not 'as modern in its writing', a critique that was all the more damning given s. 42 was last amended in 2014. Under Art. 6 of the DSM Directive, n. 2 above, the mandatory preservation copying exception refers to cultural heritage institutions being able to 'make copies'. If CDPA s. 42 is amended in light of this provision, it may be another example of the law following existing practice, at least in the United Kingdom. As noted by 324X, there is variation in the legal regimes and preservation practices across the European Union.
[212] Especially 305M, 314G, 320L.   [213] CDPA s. 42(3).
[214] 320L; similar 312L and 326L, both noting that if a damaged or high-demand item is available on the market, it will be purchased rather than copied under s. 42.

whether under an exception, a licence, or through the selection of public domain works.[215]

One question is how preservation copying will change in the coming years, in particular for content acquired in digital form. Such content requires earlier and more drastic intervention to maintain the integrity and accessibility of data, given the potential for failures in both the physical media and the availability of technology to open or play digital files. As stated by Hirtle:

> To preserve analog information resources, it is often sufficient to house them in a benign, monitored, environment. In particularly bad cases, it might be necessary to make a microfilm or xerographic copy of the original, but copying is the exception rather than the rule. Digital preservation requires much more. Successful digital preservation encompasses a broad range of activities designed to extend the usable life of machine-readable computer files and protect them from media failure, physical loss, and obsolescence.[216]

With copyright implicated to a far greater degree in these practices, and digital material often acquired subject to technological protection measures (TPMs) and/or contractual restrictions on archival copying, it might be doubted whether analogue norms will simply transpose to a digital setting. Indeed, the use of TPMs and contract raises questions about the role of public cultural institutions in ensuring the continued availability of content. In a world where rightsholders attempt to erect technological and contractual walls around content – and indeed where certain content is not actually bought, as exemplified by licences by subscription databases – where ought responsibility for preserving those works to reside?[217]

---

[215] E.g., 103G ('we take copyright very seriously; the law is not always clear cut, and we are trying to be fair to the copyright holder'); 117L ('Canadians follow rules – we're very law abiding'), 124A ('we think a lot about copyright – it's a very big issue'), 128L ('this is a law-abiding culture'). But compare 141L (preservation copying exceptions are not really needed because copyright law is not applied as diligently in Canada as elsewhere), 146L (many librarians are not familiar with exceptions).

[216] Hirtle, n. 136 above.

[217] The 2014 reforms in the United Kingdom prohibited contracting out for a number of exceptions, including preservation copying (see CDPA s. 42(7)); and Art. 7(1) of the DSM Directive likewise renders unenforceable any contractual provision contrary to the mandatory preservation copying exception in Art. 6. The Australian Law Reform Commission has recommended the introduction of a similar prohibition in relation to the Australian libraries and archives provisions: Australian Law Reform Commission, *Copyright in the Digital Economy: Final Report*, Report No. 122 (November 2013), recommendation 20-1. Preservation copying provisions are often limited to items in the permanent collection, meaning that such exceptions may be inapplicable for content that is accessed on subscription databases. Furthermore, questions arise regarding the relationship between copyright exceptions and TPMs, including whether it should be lawful to circumvent TPMs in order to enjoy the benefits of an exception. In the United

C   *Collection Management*

1 The Provisions Exceptions directed to internal administrative activities are found in the Australian and Canadian statutes but not the libraries and archives provisions of the CDPA or section 108 of the US Copyright Act.[218] In Canada, the 1997 reforms included a provision that allows a work or other subject-matter from the permanent collection to be copied for the purposes of internal recording-keeping and cataloguing, insurance purposes and police investigations, and if necessary for restoration.[219] In Australia, the relevant exception, introduced in 2000,[220] originally allowed libraries and archives to reproduce Part III works – i.e., literary, dramatic, musical and artistic works[221] – held in their collection for administrative purposes.[222] This reproduction could also be communicated to officers of the library or archives using onsite intranet facilities.[223] Although not originally defined, following amendments in 2006 it was clarified that 'administrative purposes' meant 'purposes directly related to the care or control of the collection'.[224] In 2017, the existing administrative purposes exception in Part III was replaced with new section 113K, covering use of copyright material 'if the use is for purposes directly related to the care or control of the collection comprising the library or archives'. This provision removed one limitation in the administrative copying exception that had been the subject of criticism, namely that there was no provision for Part IV

States, for example, there is an enforcement regime in relation to the circumvention of TPMs in s. 1201 of the Copyright Act, but there are also permanent exemptions plus a scheme that enables the Librarian of Congress to grant temporary exemptions: see J. Ginsburg, 'Legal Protection of Technological Measures Protecting Works of Authorship: International Obligations and the US Experience' (2005) 29 *Columbia Journal of Law and the Arts* 11; United States Copyright Office, *Section 1201 of Title 17: A Report of the Register of Copyrights* (United States Copyright Office, June 2017). In Europe, Art. 6(4) of the ISD contains what is described by Bently *et al.* as a 'strange, barely comprehensible, compromise' in relation to TPMs and exceptions: L. Bently, B. Sherman, D. Gangjee and P. Johnson, *Intellectual Property Law*, 5th edition (Oxford: Oxford University Press, 2018), p. 379.

[218] Section 108(b) permits three copies of an unpublished work to be made for 'preservation and security', however these terms tend to be read as a single unit, rather than the latter embodying some free-standing, management-related purpose. For instance, neither the Section 108 Study Group, n. 3 above, pp. 18–19 nor Nimmer, n. 123 above, para. 8.03[E][1][a], provide a separate definition of 'security'. Even if it does perform some additional function, it may be stretching its ordinary interpretation to attempt to apply it to administrative uses generally.

[219] Canadian Copyright Act s. 30.1(1)(d)–(f).
[220] Copyright Amendment (Digital Agenda) Act 2000 (Cth) Schedule 1, item 75.
[221] Australian Copyright Act s. 10(1).   [222] Ibid., s. 51A(2).
[223] Ibid., s 51A(3). Officers is defined to include volunteers: s 51A(6).
[224] Ibid., s. 51A(6), added by Copyright Amendment Act 2006 (Cth) Schedule 6, item 24.

144   Sector-Specific Exceptions

subject-matter such as sound recordings and cinematograph films.[225] In the Explanatory Memorandum to the 2017 reforms, it was stated that section 113K might extend to 'for example, back up copying, reporting (for example, to government) and record keeping, training and use for the purpose of exhibitions'.[226]

  2 The Practices At the time of the fieldwork the Canadian and Australian statutes utilised different drafting styles, with the former spelling out particular classes of collection management activity that are permitted (seemingly more rule-like) and the latter using the overarching criterion of administrative purposes (possibly more standard-like).[227] Reported practices were, nevertheless, fairly similar, in that interviewees from both countries reported that copyright did not generally constrain copying for internal management purposes.[228] Although some Canadian interviewees were able to point to the relevant provisions from the copyright statute,[229] others did not volunteer this information. This was not dissimilar to the fieldwork in Australia, where many interviewees could not identify the legal basis for administrative copying.[230] Similar to preservation copying, it would seem that practices were influenced strongly by best practice norms in relation to care of the collection. For instance, in both Canada and Australia, the introduction of an exception directed at collection management seemed to codify existing norms of copying rather than prompt the development of new ones.[231] As one Canadian interviewee said, 'there has always been documentation of the collection, and ... the law could have said what it wanted to, but the simple managing of the collection requires us [to take photographs for management purposes]'.[232] Similar comments were made by an Australian interviewee, who noted that collection management photography has been going on for years, originally film based and now digital, and that

---

[225] See, e.g., Hudson and Kenyon, n. 119 above, 34–35.
[226] Explanatory Memorandum (Disability Access and Other Measures) Bill, n. 50 above, p. 19.
[227] As discussed in Chapter 2, this question turns on when 'information processing and acquisition takes place': L. Kaplow, 'Rules versus Standards: An Economic Analysis' (1992) 42 *Duke Law Journal* 557, 601. If everyone already knows what is meant by 'administrative purposes' then it can be viewed as a rule.
[228] E.g., 103G, 105G, 108G, 110M, 130M, 135G, 142M, 208G, 215G, 225G, 228M. See also Hudson and Kenyon, above n. 119, 34–35.
[229] They were referred to by, e.g., 105G, 108G, 135G.
[230] E.g., 203M, 218M, 219M, 220M, 228M, 229X, 225G, 262M, 267G. See also Hudson and Kenyon, n. 190 above, 15.
[231] E.g., 105G, 113X, 142M, 225G, 228M. See also Hudson and Kenyon, n. 4 above, 208.
[232] 142M.

'[t]hat practice of archiving your collection is inherent in what you do as part of the acquisition process'.[233] Another said:

> We have an internal database for the collection, and [for] every work in the collection, we aim to put an image of it on the database, just for reference purposes. It could be a pretty good image, or a really crap image that the curator shot on their smartphone in the storage room. So that whoever's looking at that record knows what the work is. We cannot function – if there was some copyright law saying that we couldn't do that, then we couldn't function. It's just common sense: for internal, administrative stuff, we have to use images of the work for our administrative purposes.[234]

Thus, whilst some of the comprehensive licences sought by cultural institutions covered management activity, interviewees in Canada and Australia did not generally suggest that receipt of a licence was viewed as a precondition for these administrative acts.

The strength of internal management norms would also seem to explain the reported experiences of interviewees in the United States and the United Kingdom, where it was also said that copyright had minimal impact on internal management activities.[235] In the United States, this might be put down to fair use. Some of the doctrinal indications in relation to fair use are discussed in Chapter 5. For now, it can be said that the arguments in favour of its application to administrative uses are strong, particularly given the purpose of the use (caring for and managing a collection) and the lack of public distribution (although there may be occasions when reproductions are sent externally, for instance when arranging loans). Interestingly, however, US interviewees repeatedly described processes in which decision-making about administrative activities took place without any meaningful – or indeed any – analysis of the law. It therefore appeared that interviewees either: (1) believed that copyright was irrelevant to these activities; (2) assumed that fair use *must* apply, even if their reasoning had never been fully particularised; or (3) had not given the question a second thought. They did not report seeking legal advice or producing formal policies on this question; as one interviewee observed, 'it's not an issue, so why make it an issue?'[236] Nor were they concerned about possible legal repercussions as best practice demanded that proper records be kept of collection items.[237] This lack

---

[233] 228M.   [234] 225G.
[235] E.g., 1G, 7G, 9M, 14G, 16G, 20G, 28G, 29L, 30G, 33G, 43M, 45M, 48G, 53G, 303G, 305M, 307M, 314G, 320L, 322G, 323X, 328G, 329M.
[236] 26G.
[237] Such practices may be crucial to accreditation and other forms of official overview: 9M (referring to requirements of the American Association of Museums, now the American Alliance of Museums).

of appetite to revisit longstanding practices was summed up by one interviewee who said:

> It's a standard practice in museums to document using imagery, and this was true before digital images, people were pulling out Polaroid cameras and taking pictures. So I think the assumption has been that it's been okay. But if you scrutinise the exclusive rights that an artist enjoys, and one of them is to make a copy ... it really calls into question the things that are standard museum practice. [But] we have not, to any great extent, seriously questioned our assumption.[238]

Turning to the United Kingdom, the situation was even more stark, there being no fair use and no sector-specific exception that referred explicitly to administrative copying. And yet there was no concern about the legality of copying for collection management purposes, or any suggestion that licences were essential for such activity.[239] As one interviewee said,

> I see it as being good practice, it is in controlled circumstances for use by the museum, as opposed to something that can be used for other reasons. When I started it was about analogue cameras making prints that were stuck on the side of boxes, so in my head there's a very clear distinction between that kind of making of images, and those used elsewhere.[240]

Although practices seemed to be influenced strongly by best practice norms, some interviewees had given consideration to the legal basis for record photography and other administrative acts, with a number of people suggesting that this might fall within the preservation copying exception in section 42 of the CDPA.[241] Although this might seem like a forward-leaning interpretation, it could be argued that it reflects the broad range of activities that are all directed to caring for collection items, only some of which involve the making of surrogate and

---

[238] 33G. [239] E.g., 303G, 305M, 307M, 314G, 320L, 322G, 323X, 325M; c.f. 317G.
[240] 307M.
[241] E.g., 314G, 326L; similar 305M (the sector is taking a very generous definition of preservation), 320L (if pressed might point to preservation, but 'the reason why I don't have an answer is because, bluntly, it's never come up as an issue'). No interviewees suggested quotation in CDPA s. 30(1ZA), although this may be open for some works: see Chapter 8, Section II.B(1). Briefly, there is acceptance that quotations can be made from non-text works, and that a quotation can comprise the entire surface of a two-dimensional work: e.g., *Painer* v. *Standard Verlags GmbH* (C-145/10) [2012] ECDR 6 (Third Chamber), paras. 122–123. The CDPA does not specify the particular purposes for which the quotation is made, stating instead that it must be 'for criticism or review or otherwise', although 2019 case law from the CJEU suggests that some sort illustration of a point, defence of an opinion or intellectual comparison is required: *Pelham GmbH* v. *Hütter* (C-476/17) [2019] Bus LR 2159 (Grand Chamber), para. 71. A further question is whether s. 30(1ZA) applies to unpublished works given the requirement that the source work has been made available to the public.

Content and Operation   147

access copies. Recital 27 of the DSM Directive might also support this interpretation through its statement that preservation copying can be undertaken 'to address technological obsolescence or the degradation of original supports or to insure such works and other subject matter'.

Drawing this analysis together, the fieldwork suggested that in the four jurisdictions studied, many institution staff had internalised ideas about collection management that did not contemplate copyright in any detailed or systematic way. In its most extreme form, they did not believe that administrative copying even implicated copyright, whilst in milder versions they had an awareness of copyright but operated under the assumption – never properly tested or explored – that such acts are or should be privileged under the law. A question for further consideration, and explored in Chapters 8 and 9, is whether this means that the form of drafting of administrative copying exceptions – or even their existence – is therefore irrelevant.

D   *User Request, Researcher Use and Interlibrary Supply*

   1   The Provisions This third group of exceptions pertain to copying services and other instances where reproductions are made for external requestors. These provisions are often detailed and must therefore be read closely to discern their scope, for instance in relation to the purpose of requests, their subject-matter, whether they may be fulfilled using electronic delivery, any documentation required, etc. It is common that these provisions apply only to research-oriented requests, both from an institution's own patrons and, through interlibrary supply, those of other institutions.[242]

From a drafting standpoint, request-based copying provisions often have many rule-like indications, and can be striking in their specificity and complexity. Starting with specificity, the current Canadian statute seems to have the most extensive subject-matter limitations: only articles from newspapers and periodicals may be copied under section 30.2(2), and only unpublished works held by archives (but not libraries or museums) copied under section 30.21. In the United States, section 108(d) applies to requests for an article or a 'small part of any other copyrighted work', whilst section 108(e) relates to requests for entire works or a substantial part thereof. Despite the breadth of this language, the reach of these provisions is narrowed by section 108(i), which excludes from their ambit musical, pictorial, graphic and sculptural

---

[242] Especially CDPA ss. 41, 42A, 43; Australian Copyright Act ss. 49, 50, 51, 110A; US Copyright Act ss. 108(d) and (e); Canadian Copyright Act ss. 30.2, 30.21.

148   Sector-Specific Exceptions

works, motion pictures and audiovisual recordings (other than recordings 'dealing with news').[243] In the United Kingdom, in contrast, reforms in 2014 streamlined and expanded provisions dealing with researcher requests, including via replacing sections 38 and 39 with section 42A (permitting libraries to supply a copy of an article or 'a reasonable proportion of any other published work'), and extending the reach of section 43 (permitting libraries and archives to supply a copy of the whole or part of an unpublished work).[244] In both cases, these provision now include all copyright works, and not just literary, dramatic and musical works, as was the case previously.

Complexity can manifest in a number of ways. For instance, the Australian provisions have a complicated presentation, with copying for researcher request scattered across numerous provisions, located in multiple divisions, in the Copyright Act. Thus, copying of articles and published works is covered by sections 49 and 50 (Part III); certain old unpublished works, recordings and films may be copied by and for people who require them for research or study under sections 51(1) (Part III) and 110A (Part IV);[245] section 113J (Part IVA) permits the making of research copies of collection material held 'in original form' and required 'for the purpose of research carried out at that or another library or archives'; and finally, it is possible that requests that fall outside these provisions might be caught by section 200AB (Part X). Looking within each provision, there is further complexity through the number of sub-limbs and requirements. To illustrate, section 49, which covers user requests, requires that such requests be made in writing and accompanied by a signed declaration covering certain matters (although the need for writing may be dispensed with for urgent requests), and sets out rules in relation to the charging of fees, the making of commercial availability declarations for certain requests, electronic delivery of copies and so forth.

---

[243] The United States Copyright Office has recommended that s. 108(i) be removed, and restrictions instead placed on the way works are made available to users: United States Copyright Office, n. 15 above, pp. 38–39.

[244] Introduced by the Copyright and Rights in Performances (Research, Education, Libraries and Archives) Regulations 2014 (SI 2014/1372). As discussed in the Explanatory Note, the reforms introduced by this instrument expanded the types of copyright works the subject of the researcher request provisions. The existing provisions were directed to articles (s. 38), a 'reasonable proportion' from a 'published edition' of a literary, dramatic or musical work (s. 39), and unpublished literary, dramatic and musical works (s. 43).

[245] These provisions apply only where 50 years has passed since the author of the work died (s. 51) or the sound recording or cinematograph film was made (s. 110A).

Content and Operation 149

A crucial lesson from the standards and rules literature is that specificity and complexity are not inherently problematic. For instance, whilst the structural complexity of the Australian statute may be criticised for reducing ease-of-use, such complexity might be justified if it reflects important policy or doctrinal distinctions.[246] One such argument is that the division between Part III works and Part IV subject-matter reflects the distinction between authorial works and neighbouring rights, which require different rules in relation to authorship, duration, rights and so on.[247] However, if we agree that libraries and archives exceptions should not distinguish unnecessarily between Part III and Part IV matter, one might question whether the 2017 reforms, which shifted provisions in relation to preservation and administration to new Part IVA, should not have moved all libraries and archives provisions to a single home.

2   *The Practices*   The overarching message from the empirical work in Australia, the United Kingdom and the United States was that staff relied on these longstanding exceptions and had a relatively good understanding of their content, such that instances of drafting complexity did not necessarily translate to day-to-day problems with applying the law.[248] This seems to be because copying services, of their nature, lend themselves to a bureaucratised system in which staff decision-making is guided by routinised workflows. This means that the pertinent question for frontline staff was not what the Copyright Act requires or what the court held, but what it says in the manual. For instance, Australian interviewees noted that the rules in sections 49 and 50 had been embodied in institutional systems for processing requests, and in fact some interviewees who oversaw document supply had never even read

---

[246] See generally the project of the Copyright Law Review Committee (CLRC), *Simplification of the Copyright Act 1968 Part 1: Exceptions to the Exclusive Rights of Copyright Owners* (September 1998).

[247] See, e.g., M. Davison, A. Monotti and L. Wiseman, *Australian Intellectual Property Law*, 3rd edition (Melbourne: Cambridge University Press, 2016), p. 213. The division in the Australian Act is tested by certain genre that could be authorial or surface works, such as photographs and films: see, e.g., M. Handler, 'Continuing Problems with Film Copyright' in F. Macmillan (ed), *New Directions in Copyright Law, Volume 6* (Cheltenham: Edward Elgar, 2007).

[248] E.g., 10L, 15L, 19L, 29L, 35L, 44X, 226L, 237L, 245A, 248L, 250L, 253L (although noting some challenges, for instance regarding the application of exceptions to licensed content), 263L, 265L, 301L, 312L, 313M, 316L, 319L, 320L, 326L, 328G; but note 230A (for moving image, the layers of rights and interplay of different exceptions can make the law very difficult to understand), 242L (discussing instances where publishers had been concerned about the supply of scientific articles to requestors, although for that institution the number of copies in that category was low, and related mostly to old material outside of any current market). See also Hudson and Kenyon, n. 119 above, 38.

150   Sector-Specific Exceptions

the relevant provisions in the Copyright Act.[249] Copying of unpublished works under sections 51 and 110A was more challenging because of the work involved in determining authorship and life dates, and checking any donor-imposed limits in relation to the file.[250] However, interviewees also noted that much copying of unpublished collections (and indeed other content) was done by users themselves in reading rooms, often with their own devices rather than institution-supplied equipment.[251]

In addition to efforts within institutions to translate statutory rules to internal procedures, there were some sector-wide attempts to provide clarity to language that might be ambiguous. Perhaps the strongest example was the 'CONTU rule of 5', a US protocol developed in the late 1970s in relation to the repeat copying of articles from the same journal title for interlibrary supply, this copying having the potential to contravene the prohibition against systematic reproduction in section 108(g) of the Copyright Act.[252] The CONTU guidelines are incomplete as they deal only with journal articles, and even then only those published recently.[253] More generally, concerns have been expressed that these sort of guidelines can come to be understood as ceilings on the scope of permissible copying, thus exerting an inhibiting force on practices.[254]

As well as relying on sector-specific exceptions for external requests and interlibrary supply, it was also common for those running copying services to point to licences granted by copyright owners.[255] There was variation in the mechanics of these processes, for instance in relation to

---

[249] 256L, 258L; similar 226L, 237L, 253L, 312L, 319L (all describing automated or standardised procedures for staff to handle requests).
[250] E.g., 207L, 213L, 257L.
[251] E.g., 204A, 257L; also 311M, 326L. This raises a further issue: whether the use of such equipment could expose institutions to liability for infringement by authorisation.
[252] CONTU Report, n. 51 above. The CONTU guidelines state that in a single calendar year, a requesting institution may, within the boundaries of s. 108, receive up to five articles from issues of a periodical title published in the last five years.
[253] See, e.g., K. Crews, *Copyright Law for Librarians and Educators: Creative Strategies and Practical Solutions* (Chicago: American Library Association, 2nd edition, 2006), pp. 77–78.
[254] For instance, one argument made by the plaintiffs in the *Georgia State* litigation (discussed in detail in Chapter 5) was that assessment of the amount copied by the University should be undertaken by reference to the quantitative thresholds in the Classroom Guidelines, HR Rep No 94-1467, 94th Congress, 2nd Session (1976). These Guidelines were an industry-negotiated attempt to develop a safe harbour for educational copying, and the thresholds were therefore restrictive. This argument was rejected for various reasons, including because it would transform the Guidelines from a safe harbour to a limit: *Cambridge University Press* v. *Becker*, 863 F. Supp. 2d 1190, 1227–1229 (ND Georgia, 2012); this aspect affirmed in *Cambridge University Press* v. *Patton*, 769 F 3d 1232, 1274 (11th circuit, 2014).
[255] E.g., 202G, 204A, 206G, 213L, 218M, 225G, 228M, 229X, 230A, 237L, 240L, 248L, 246A, 250L, 255A, 257L, 263L, 303G, 305M, 311M, 313M, 314G, 317G, 319L.

Content and Operation 151

whether the requestor was responsible for clearing rights; whether evidence of a permission was required before the copy would be supplied; and whether fees were charged. These variations applied not just between institutions but for different types of request.[256] Furthermore, interviewees also reported some reliance on fair use, section 200AB and fair dealing for their request services. This book will therefore return to request-based copying in the coming chapters, to ascertain the degree to which other exceptions have been viewed as relevant to these practices. This question is particularly significant for Canada, where the LAM provisions for user requests are fairly narrow; and where the leading Supreme authority on fair dealing, *CCH Canadian Ltd* v. *Law Society of Upper Canada*,[257] pertained to copying services of a law library.

E   Onsite Consultation

1   The Provisions This final section considers exceptions that allow institution-made copies to be made available for onsite consultation by individual patrons. This might be said to be implicit in some provisions. Consider preservation copying. Reproductions made during these processes are intended to be used instead of the fragile work, whether to reduce handling or to replace the item if it later falls apart. In the analogue era, acts of onsite consultation – reading newspaper articles via microfilm, examining a facsimile of a map or listening to an audio recording in a booth – often did not implicate copyright, there being no exclusive right to read or view, and acts of auditioning not taking place in public. With the emergence of digital technologies, however, far more acts of onsite consultation might be caught by copyright, leading to an asymmetry between analogue and digital browsing.

In some statutes, there are now provisions dealing explicitly with onsite consultation. In Canada, for example, section 30.1(1)(b) the Copyright

---

[256] To illustrate, a number of interviewees distinguished between requests for high-resolution images for use in commercial publications and merchandise, and requests for other uses, such as scholarly publications or use in a thesis: e.g., 202G, 206G, 218M, 225G, 228M, 311M. There also seemed to be a practice of supplying lower resolution images for research-oriented use, without the need for clearance and with fees waived or discounted heavily. Interviewees were vague about the precise legal basis for this activity, with fair dealing for research being the most likely explanation for items not covered by sector-specific exceptions: e.g., 225G, 229X; c.f. 259X (observing that doctrinal analysis of the Australian case law suggests that agency arguments are not available for fair dealing). Some interviewees also reported that the inclusion of lower resolution images on the website satisfied a fair amount of public demand: e.g., 228M, 305M, 313M, 322G; similar 249L (contemplating making better use of open access models).
[257] [2004] 1 SCR 339.

152   Sector-Specific Exceptions

Act permits copying 'for the purpose of on-site consultation if the original cannot be viewed, handled or listened to because of its condition or because of the atmospheric conditions in which it must be kept'.[258] Similarly, the Australian Copyright Act allows preservation copies in electronic form to be made available 'at the library or archives' so long as 'reasonable steps [are taken] to ensure that a person who accesses the preservation copy ... does not infringe copyright in the preservation copy'.[259] With no equivalent provision for physical copies, it can be surmised that an exception covering such copies was considered unnecessary for the reasons given above.

A different form of words is used in the United Kingdom, where section 40B of the CDPA allows libraries, archives, museums and educational establishments to make works available on dedicated terminals so that they may be consulted for research or private study.[260] This provision was introduced in 2014, and follows the wording of Article 5 (3)(n) of the Information Society Directive. Although it refers only to communicating and making available (which might suggest that it applies only to works already in electronic form), the CJEU has said in *Technische Universität Darmstadt* v. *Eugen Ulmer KG* that Article 5(3)(n) 'would risk being rendered largely meaningless, or indeed ineffective, if those establishments did not have an ancillary right to digitise the works in question'.[261] The CJEU located this right in Article 5(2)(c) of the Directive,[262] which permits Member States to recognise exceptions and limitations to the reproduction right 'in respect of specific acts of reproduction [by institutions] which are not for direct or indirect economic or commercial advantage'. In the United Kingdom, the CDPA does not contain a provision that follows the language of Article 5(2)(c), nor an exception directed to digitisation for the purposes of section 40B. Applying the doctrinal indications in *Ulmer*, it would seem that preservation copies made under section 42 can be made available on dedicated terminals so long as the conditions of section 40B are also satisfied. A more important question is whether institutions can digitise other works for onsite consultation, perhaps because section 40B *itself* carries

---

[258] This exception does not apply if an appropriate copy is available commercially: Canadian Copyright Act s. 30.1(2).
[259] Australian Copyright Act s. 113H(2); see also ss. 113J(2) (equivalent provision for research copies), 113M(2) (equivalent provision for key cultural institutions). There is a note to each provision stating that '[o]ther uses of the preservation copy might not infringe copyright because of other provisions of this Act, such as section 49'.
[260] CDPA s. 40B. That exception is available only for works that have 'been lawfully acquired by the institution', and is subject to any purchase or licensing terms.
[261] (C-117/13) [2014] ECDR 23 (Fourth Chamber), para. 43.   [262] Ibid., para. 44.

the right to digitise. This argument is not without problems,[263] and it may be that institutions will rely on a broad reading of the preservation copying exception instead.

In addition to questions regarding the right to digitise, a further question about section 40B pertains to its requirement that copies are used for the purposes of research or private study. Does this mean that only *obviously* scholarly works or resources can be made available, such as copies of reference works or a collection database containing images and great quantities of metadata? Or does Article 5(3)(n), from which the language of section 40B is derived, have in mind other acts of browsing and consultation? In *Ulmer*, the CJEU observed that this Article 'aims to promote the public interest in promoting research and private study, through the dissemination of knowledge, which constitutes, moreover, the core mission of publicly accessible libraries'.[264] This statement is not particularly helpful in answering this question.

In contrast with Australia, Canada and the United Kingdom, the US statute takes a proscriptive approach, stating that any digital copies made under sections 108(b) and (c) – preservation and replacement copying, respectively – may not be 'made available to the public in that format outside the premises of the library or archives'.[265] This language, which was introduced by the Digital Millennium Copyright Act,[266] was intended to allow libraries and archives to make use of digital technologies when taking advantage of sections 108(b) and (c), but not in a way that might lead to 'uncontrolled public access' and thus harm the interests of copyright owners.[267] Although not expressly permitted, it would seem that onsite access – for instance browsing on copy-disabled terminals – would not contravene the proviso.[268] In its discussion paper on section 108, the Copyright Office recommended a more intricate set of provisions dealing with the making and accessibility of preservation copies, these provisions distinguishing between works that had been lawfully disseminated to the public and those that had not.[269] The necessity and impact of any such change needs to be assessed in light

---

[263] See, also, E. Rosati, 'CJEU says that Member States may grant public libraries the right to digitize works in their collections' (2015) 10 *Journal of Intellectual Property Law & Practice* 6, 7.
[264] *Ulmer*, n. 261 above, para 27.   [265] US Copyright Act ss. 108(b)(2), (c)(2).
[266] DMCA, n. 153 above, s. 404.
[267] Senate Report 105–109, *The Digital Millennium Copyright Act of 1998* (11 May 1998), p. 61.
[268] The version of the DMCA that passed the Senate included language that allowed use on the premises: Bill S. 2037, 105th Congress, s. 403 (passed 14 May 1998).
[269] United States Copyright Office, n. 15 above, pp. 24–25. For the latter, the proposed revisions would allow public consultation of copies on the institution's 'premises', lending

of fair use, which would seem to be invoked by US cultural institutions for a range of onsite activity.[270]

2 The Practices This section focuses on UK experiences in relation to section 40B of the CDPA, as Australian and Canadian interviewees said very little about their equivalent provisions. In fact, given this backdrop, the level of take-up of section 40B was initially a surprise. One reason for the difference may relate to the reach of the respective provisions, which at the time of the fieldwork were directed towards a subset of preservation copies in Australia and Canada,[271] but applied to all works that have been 'lawfully acquired by the institution' in the United Kingdom.[272] One could therefore speculate that either (1) the Australian and Canadian provisions were narrow and of limited relevance to institutions, or (2) they covered the sort of preservation activity for which decision-making was influenced by best practice norms rather than close doctrinal analysis.

Whatever the position in Australia and Canada, it was clear that in the United Kingdom, a number of interviewees had directed a significant amount of attention to the reach of section 40B, and that they were considering liberal – but not unavailable – interpretations of the statutory language.[273] For example, interviewees indicated that 'dedicated terminals' could extend beyond computers to include touchscreens, iPads and other hand-held devices, sound and media booths, and headphones.[274] There was no suggestion that the requirement that the copy be communicated or made available 'for the purposes of research or private study' effected a significant narrowing of the provision, for

---

of physical copies and single-user, time-limited online consultation. For the former, preservation copies would not be accessible by members of the public at all, these being intended to serve as a source of replacement copies in the future: pp. 26–29. Under this model, 'premises' would be given a broad interpretation, and could include an entire campus (for university libraries) or password-protected digital network: p. 27.

[270] See Chapter 5, Section III.C(2) and Chapter 9, Section III.

[271] At the time of the fieldwork in 2012/2013 and 2016, the relevant Australian provision was found in s. 51(3A) of the Copyright Act, and permitted preservation copies of unstable artistic works to be made available onsite on copy-disabled terminals.

[272] CDPA s. 40B(3)(a). A further condition is that the work must only be communicated or made available 'in compliance with any purchase or licensing terms to which the work is subject': s. 40B(3)(c).

[273] Those who had applied the exception, or who were actively considering its use, included 303G, 305M, 314G, 315A, 320L, 322G, 326L. Other interviewees also reported having given consideration to the exception: e.g., 312L, 313M, 317G, 323X.

[274] E.g., 303G, 305M, 314G, 315A, 326L.

instance by meaning that only designated researchers could access content.[275] Thus interviewees described the use of section 40B to allow patrons to audition content or to browse image-rich collection databases,[276] as well as the use of dedicated terminals in exhibitions as a further way to present information.[277] Finally, interviewees discussed strategies to limit the accessibility of content, for instance by prohibiting multi-user access, or by locking content on a tablet device.[278]

Given the focus of this book on decision-making practices, it was noteworthy that these interpretations had developed without legislative definition of key phrases (e.g., 'dedicated terminal'), and in the absence of any UK case law. One interviewee whose institution had used fixed terminals and was considering expanding to mobile terminals connected interpretative practices to comfort with risk, stating:

Staff are encouraged by me to think as generously and broadly about dedicated terminals as possible. And I'm clear to them that the terminology – from 1999, if not before, when all you had was a fixed dedicated terminal that was a computer screen on a PC, and I'm encouraging staff to think of devices like iPads as dedicated terminals. Dedicated towards that particular usage at that time. ... I'm saying, 'be brave, because the use of exceptions is also about appetite for risk'. And ultimately, what are rightsholders worried about? They are worried about the fact that [people might] take the images away ... If we can demonstrate that people don't, that it's transient, then there's a better chance we won't be challenged.[279]

Other interviewees remarked positively about the drafting of section 40B. For example, one interviewee described section 40B as 'very sparse on detail', but also made the observation that the CDPA was often 'quite good' in '[leaving] things a little bit vague [as] it allows you to do what's sensible'.[280] Interestingly, in the case of the dedicated terminals exception, this interviewee saw vagueness as allowing the institution – whose risk preferences tended to be conservative – to develop what might be viewed as forward-leaning interpretations. The interviewee explained that where there were limited doctrinal cues, staff had to work from scratch to determine the scope of a provision. In contrast, in areas where there was case law and detailed commentary, 'to shift against some of that takes a bit more institutional risk or want. It's one thing to know that [a provision is] badly defined and we have to come up with our own

---

[275] Although 315A asked whether mere curiosity was enough.
[276] E.g., 303G, 305M, 314G, 315A, 320L, 326L.
[277] E.g., 303G, 322G (although querying whether the exception applied if the exhibition was income-generating), 326L; possible future use for 323X.
[278] CDPA s. 40B(1).   [279] 305M.   [280] 326L.

definition; [it's] another to know it's defined and to go against that.'[281] Not dissimilar views were expressed by another interviewee, who in talking about legislative drafting, risk management and institutional use of exceptions remarked:

> I would always prefer if there was an exception that was pragmatically used. Things like section 40B is very short and light on words, and that leaves room for interpretation rather than being highly prescriptive – that is really valuable. Once there is an exception that is too prescriptive to be useful ... [It can] push us back to a risk-managed approach, and while it's good that there's an indication from the policy makers that they want us to be doing those activities, if we don't use the exceptions that are provided it is harder to ask for future exceptions, and justify what we've done, and it adds risk.[282]

In sum, the fieldwork suggested that section 40B was emerging as a meaningful part of copyright management practices at UK institutions. Although key phrases were not defined in the statute and could be understood in different ways, this did not seem to be an impediment to institutions making use of the provision. In fact, the malleability of certain language – including the central concept of a 'dedicated terminal' – enabled staff to upload interpretations that were consistent with the statutory wording and views on how institutions should be making their collections available. It could therefore be said that section 40B was experienced as a (reasonably) well-drafted rule, with users able to discern some *ex ante* content from the text, but not in a way that was unduly prescriptive.

IV Conclusion

This chapter has discussed the history and content of sector-specific exceptions in Australia, Canada, the United Kingdom and the United States, with particular focus on their reported relevance to preservation, collection administration, copying requests and onsite consultation. Its doctrinal analysis at times painted a bleak picture of the operation of these provisions, for instance in relation to their apparent verbosity, uncertainty and under-inclusiveness. However, the fieldwork suggested that day-to-day experiences within cultural institutions were not as negative as this analysis might imply. This section draws together some explanations for this observation, and what it means for the drafting of copyright exceptions.

One explanation is that institutions have developed workflows that operationalise the privileges in copyright legislation. This was

[281] Ibid.   [282] 320L.

Conclusion

exemplified by user request, an area that seems particularly well-adapted to complex rules due to the volume of requests that institutions (particularly libraries) receive, and the amenability of those requests to structured workflows based on the requestor's identity and purpose, the type and amount of material being sought, etc. For requests that fall within specific exceptions – and it must be remembered that many requests will fall outside these provisions – institutions can implement systems that embody the statutory requirements. Although the development and refinement of these systems may require the input of people with specialist legal knowledge, many frontline staff will never have to acquaint themselves with the wording of the legislation, instead being guided by institution-produced forms and manuals. User request might therefore reinforce observations from the standards and rules literature regarding the suitability of complex rules to respond to instances of recurring, homogenous behaviours. Whilst the initial outlay in understanding the law and developing procedures may be high, once set up, ongoing compliance costs relate not so much to legal knowledge but day-to-day administration.

Another explanation for the experiences of cultural institutions – and one that is an important qualification on the first – arises where staff have internalised ideas about best practice that inform, qualify or even oust copyright considerations. Collection management was arguably the strongest example of copyright being excluded by ethical and management norms, with staff seeing record photography and other administrative acts as fundamental to institution processes and 'before'[283] the law. Similarly, although numerous interviewees were aware of the copyright implications of preservation copying, it was often the case that practices were not constrained by the statutory language. One explanation related to the nature of the target works: that standalone preservation was often undertaken on older works that were likely to be in the public domain. However, attitudes towards preservation as a mission often had the practical effect of ameliorating both uncertainty and specificity in legislative drafting. This meant that, for example, the rule-like and much pilloried three-copy limit in the United States and (formerly) Australia seemed to be applied in the standard-like way of meaning a reasonable number of copies.

Importantly, it appeared that these interpretations accorded not only with personal ethics and institutional norms but with accepted views on why we have cultural institutions, i.e., that institutions exist to take care

---

[283] To follow the language of 7G.

of collection items and to preserve them and/or their contents for generations to come. The lack of legal challenge by authors and copyright owners suggests that those individuals have not, by and large, been concerned about preservation copying and record photography.[284] This can be contrasted with copying services and onsite consultation, which have occupied contested territory because they are public-facing and have more obvious overlaps with the commercial activities of content producers. For these uses, institutional decision-making would seem to involve greater engagement with copyright law and the language of any exception.

As noted by Burrell and Coleman in their critique of the 'fair use panacea', concerns about the drafting of sector-specific exceptions are often met with calls for the introduction of flexible exceptions.[285] This chapter raises questions about the desirability and efficacy of such a move for cultural institutions. In relation to desirability, it suggests that some institutional activities are well suited to complex rules (e.g., request-based copying), and that well-drafted rules will be embraced by institutions (e.g., the dedicated terminals exception of UK law). Whilst such rules may need to be revised on policy grounds or to remove unnecessary administrative burdens, the research does not suggest that their drafting style is fundamentally inappropriate for the behaviour to be regulated.

Turning to the efficacy of the fair use panacea, this chapter raises questions about how much such a reform would lead to changed institutional practices. For administration and preservation copying, for example, there are strong best practices norms, raising the possibility that amendment to the law – whether to add or reword specific exceptions, or to introduce new fair dealing purposes or a fair use provision – may simply reinforce the acceptability of existing practices rather than lead to new ones. This does not mean that legal amendment is unnecessary, as some interviewees nevertheless expressed concern about unduly

---

[284] c.f., the complaint about the mass digitisation of full-text works in *Authors Guild, Inc v. HathiTrust*, 902 F Supp 2d 445 (SDNY, 2012); 755 F 3d 87 (2nd circuit, 2014). The defendant libraries had three main goals when digitising in-copyright texts: creating a searchable database for researchers; providing access for people with print disabilities; and making preservation copies that could, in future, be used to generate replacement copies for member libraries. At first instance, digitisation was held to be within fair use, but on appeal it was doubted whether the plaintiffs had standing to complain about the preservation aspect, this being speculative. The Court of Appeals for the Second Circuit therefore vacated that aspect of the District Court judgment, and remanded it for fresh consideration. The case settled on the basis that the defendants had, and would continue to, limit any replacement activity to the requirements in s. 108(c) of the US Copyright Act: see K. Cox, '*Authors Guild* v. *HathiTrust* Litigation Ends in Victory for Fair Use', *ARL Policy Notes Blog* (8 January 2015), http://policynotes.arl.org/?p=837.

[285] Burrell and Coleman, n. 38 above, pp. 250–251.

Conclusion

narrow language; plus legislative reform may be useful to foreclose any legal challenge. But the benefits may relate to legitimising copyright law and giving greater confidence to institutions, rather than effecting some 'turning of the page'[286] in relation to practices.

In contrast, it may be that for public uses – and especially online access – the arguments in favour of fair use are stronger. Whilst drafting failures for specific exceptions might be corrected by internal norms, it is not obvious that we can rely on such considerations once we are in the public sphere. And from an efficiency standpoint, the standards and rules literature suggests significant drawbacks in using rule-based drafting for public-facing activities, particularly given the diversity of institutional practices and the pace of technological change. In the coming chapters, this book turns to consider experiences in relation to general exceptions, dealing with fair use, section 200AB and fair dealing in turn.

---

[286] To follow the language of 106A.

5 Functional Fair Use

I Introduction

Doctrinal analysis suggests that the US copyright exceptions most relevant to cultural institutions are fair use in section 107 and the libraries and archives provisions in section 108. The latter were analysed in detail in Chapter 4, where it was observed that they are limited in various ways, most notably by their exclusion of museums and galleries and their focus on preservation, replacement and fulfilling some external requests. But as will be discussed in this chapter, the US fieldwork also revealed how cultural institutions have used section 107 in ways that overlap with, and extend far beyond, the activities contemplated in section 108. Indeed, fair use was the predominant exception amongst participants in this study, and was used more often and in a broader range of circumstances than the fair dealing exceptions of Australian, Canadian and UK law.

This chapter has a number of goals. One is to describe the circumstances in which fair use was relied upon by US institutions. Here it will be seen that interviewees reported using fair use for collection management, preservation, exhibition, onsite digital access, promotional activities, fulfilling external requests and providing offsite access via the internet. This is not to suggest that interviewees saw fair use as inevitably available for these activities, and in some instances fair use was applied only in limited circumstances. However, this list illustrates the malleability of fair use reasoning and the legal awareness of participating interviewees.

A second goal is to explore fair use decision-making at participating institutions, bearing in mind that interpretative practices are crucial not only for classifying a legal command as a standard or rule,[1] but to assess how that command is understood and whether it is perceived as relevant

---

[1] Especially C. Sunstein, 'Problems with Rules' (1995) 83 *California Law Review* 953, 959–960. The standards and rules literature is discussed in detail in Chapter 2 of this book.

Introduction

to user practices. This empirical work needs to be seen in light of a large body of academic commentary on fair use, some of which has concluded that the doctrine is unpredictable and is applied by the courts in unprincipled ways.[2] However, at least in this study, there appeared to be a good deal of activity for which participants were confident that fair use applied.

A number of factors influenced the degree to which institutions relied on fair use. Some appeared to relate to the language of section 107 and its judicial interpretations. For instance, when asked to explain why fair use was being relied upon for a particular activity or project, interviewees often answered by reference to the statute and indications in the case law. However, this book will argue that doctrinal considerations alone do not explain why the US experience differed so markedly from the other countries in this research. Comparing experiences across the four jurisdictions studied, it will be argued that other matters contributed to the divergence in experiences, such as institutional resourcing of copyright, risk preferences, and prevailing understandings of the justifications for copyright and exceptions.

This chapter is structured as follows. Section II sets out an overview of doctrinal cues from section 107 and some of the associated case law, thus focusing on the law in books. Section III then describes how participating interviewees reported using fair use in different scenarios, i.e., the law in action. Finally, Section IV discusses two important developments that post-dated the main US fieldwork, being the litigation against HathiTrust[3] and Georgia State University.[4] One of the overarching observations to

---

[2] E.g., W. Fisher III, 'Reconstructing the Fair Use Doctrine' (1988) 101 *Harvard Law Review* 1659 (criticising the fair use analysis of the US Supreme Court in the 1980s as uncertain and not resting on a coherent foundation); M. Madison, 'Rewriting Fair Use and the Future of Copyright Reform' (2005) 23 *Cardozo Arts & Entertainment Law Journal* 391, 393 ('[b]oth abstractly and concretely, however, fair use has been spectacularly unsuccessful as a substantive player in copyright theory and practice'); M. Carroll, 'Fixing Fair Use' (2007) 85 *North Carolina Law Review* 1087, 1092 (fair use is 'sufficiently uncertain that [it] is not effectively fulfilling its important functions'); D. Nimmer, *Nimmer on Copyright*, Volume 4 (LexisNexis, online resource, accessed 15 January 2019), para. 13.05[A][5] ('the four factors of Section 107 purport merely to aid analysis of whether a given use is "fair," not to offer a comprehensive framework from which that answer may be mechanically determined. It is open to question, however, whether even that modest goal is achieved by the amorphous language of the statute.').

[3] *Authors Guild, Inc v. HathiTrust*, 902 F Supp 2d 445 (SDNY, 2012) ('*HathiTrust District Court*'), 755 F 3d 87 (2nd circuit, 2014) ('*HathiTrust Appeal*').

[4] *Cambridge University Press v. Becker*, 863 F Supp 2d 1190 (ND Georgia, 2012) ('*GS District Court I*'), appealed as *Cambridge University Press v. Patton*, 769 F 3d 1232 (11th circuit, 2014) ('*GS Appeal I*'), remanded as *Cambridge University Press v. Becker*, 2016 WL 3098397 (ND Georgia, 31 March 2016) ('*GS District Court II*'), further appealed as *Cambridge University Press v. Albert*, 906 F 3d 1290 (11th circuit, 2018) ('*GS Appeal II*').

emerge from this chapter will be the workability of fair use, which would seem to illustrate the benefits of standard-like drafting and in turn lend support to the fair use panacea.[5] However, with the success of fair use attributable to far more than the statutory language, it will be necessary to identify the range of factors that contribute to the functioning of the doctrine, and to ask whether they can be transplanted elsewhere.

II Doctrinal Indications

A The Statutory Language

As discussed in Chapter 2, any assessment of the operation of a legal command must start with its language. The full text of section 107 states:

Limitations on exclusive rights: Fair use

Notwithstanding the provisions of sections 106 and 106A, *the fair use of a copyrighted work*, including such use by reproduction in copies or phonorecords or by any other means specified by that section, for purposes such as criticism, comment, news reporting, teaching (including multiple copies for classroom use), scholarship, or research, *is not an infringement of copyright*. In determining whether the use made of a work in any particular case is a fair use the factors to be considered shall include —

(1) the purpose and character of the use, including whether such use is of a commercial nature or is for nonprofit educational purposes;
(2) the nature of the copyrighted work;
(3) the amount and substantiality of the portion used in relation to the copyrighted work as a whole; and
(4) the effect of the use upon the potential market for or value of the copyrighted work.

The fact that a work is unpublished shall not itself bar a finding of fair use if such finding is made upon consideration of all the above factors. (emphasis supplied)

The italicised words identify the kernel of section 107: that it is not an infringement of copyright to make a fair use of a protected work. The remainder of the provision helps guide when this might be the case through the four fairness factors, the indicative list of purposes and the clarification that section 107 can apply to unpublished works.

Much has been written about the history of fair use, including its origins in eighteenth- and nineteenth-century case law and the process

---

[5] This language is taken from R. Burrell and A. Coleman, *Copyright Exceptions: The Digital Impact* (Cambridge: Cambridge University Press, 2005), ch. 9.

of introducing what became section 107 into the Copyright Act of 1976.[6] For the purposes of this book, key insights from that literature include that: (1) the legislative intent was to codify the existing judicial doctrine, meaning that section 107 was not a blank slate; and (2) the general ideas underpinning the provision, in particular that it would operate as an *ex post* balancing test, were well appreciated when the 1976 Act came into force.[7] This is relevant for a number of reasons, including that other jurisdictions that may be attracted to fair use would not be starting from the same historical backdrop, raising questions about the operation of an equivalent provision without the same foundations.[8]

B   Fair Use in the Courts

The language and structure of section 107, being non-prescriptive and open-ended, show all the hallmarks of a standard. Given that standards suggest a preference for judicial rather than legislative rulemaking,[9] analysis of any case law is also necessary to understand judicial interpretations, including whether the accumulation of judicial precedent has led to judge-made rules emerging beneath the overarching standard. If such trends can be discerned, the next question – and the focus of Section III – is whether judicial interpretations have been relevant to the decision-making of users. In the case of fair use, there is already a great deal of scholarly analysis of the extensive case law, including in relation to the doctrine's coherence and predictability. Whilst some commentary has argued that this case law is characterised by much uncertainty,[10] other contributions have identified trends in the ways that judges interpret and apply fair use.[11] Rather than seeking to recreate this work, this section

---

[6] Especially W. Patry, *The Fair Use Privilege in Copyright Law*, 2nd edition (Washington DC: BNA Books, 1995); L. Patterson, '*Folsom v Marsh* and its Legacy' (1998) 5 *Journal of Intellectual Property Law* 431; Burrell and Coleman, ibid.; R. Reese, 'The Story of *Folsom v. Marsh*: Distinguishing Between Infringing and Legitimate Uses' in R. Dreyfuss and J. Ginsburg (eds), *Intellectual Property Stories* (New York: Foundation Press, 2006).

[7] See, e.g., M. Sag, 'God in the Machine: A New Structural Analysis of Copyright's Fair Use Doctrine' (2005) 11 *Michigan Telecommunications and Technology Law Review* 381; N. Elkin-Koren and O. Fischman-Afori, 'Rulifying Fair Use' (2017) 59 *Arizona Law Review* 161.

[8] See, e.g., Burrell and Coleman, n. 5 above, pp. 267–269.

[9] See I. Ehrlich and R. Posner, 'An Economic Analysis of Legal Rulemaking' (1974) 3 *The Journal of Legal Studies* 257, 261.

[10] See n. 2 above.

[11] See, especially, B Beebe, 'An Empirical Study of U.S. Copyright Fair Use Opinions' (2008) 156 *University of Pennsylvania Law Review* 549; P. Samuelson, 'Unbundling Fair Uses' (2009) 77 *Fordham Law Review* 2537; N. Netanel, 'Making Sense of Fair Use' (2011) 15 *Lewis & Clark Law Review* 715; M. Sag, 'Predicting Fair Use' (2012) 73 *Ohio State Law Journal* 47.

focuses on the cases and doctrinal principles that had the most relevance to the research with cultural institutions. It starts from the observation that in the US fieldwork in 2008 and 2009, institutions with forward-leaning approaches to fair use were commonly reasoning by analogy to the case law, especially for new online uses. Whilst interviewees cited numerous decisions, three cases (all in relation to thumbnail images) recurred in discussions: *Kelly* v. *Arriba Soft*,[12] *Bill Graham Archives*[13] and *Perfect 10*.[14] Of these cases, only one concerned a cultural collection (*Bill Graham Archives*), and even then, the collection was not managed by a public institution but by a private entity. However, it seemed that institutions saw analogies between their own activities and those in these cases, and were able to reason from first principles.[15]

This section begins by describing the three thumbnails cases, above. It will be seen that in each decision, transformativeness was a central element of the court's fair use analysis, and so the section then turns to the meaning of transformative use and its role in the case law. Finally, this section discusses market harm, this being a particularly contentious and difficult consideration for literal copying.

1 The Thumbnails Cases Decisions on the appeals in *Kelly*, *Bill Graham Archives* and *Perfect 10* were handed down in 2003, 2006 and 2007, respectively, and seemed to influence strongly the fair use analysis of interviewees participating in the fieldwork in 2008 and 2009. In all three cases, the defendants successfully argued that their thumbnail images fell within fair use. In *Kelly* and *Perfect 10*, this was in the context of search engines that presented results as low-resolution images rather than text, it being alleged that the plaintiffs' copyrights had been

---

[12] *Kelly v. Arriba Soft Corporation*, 77 F Supp 2d 1116 (CD Cal, 1999); 336 F 3d 811 (9th circuit, 2003) ('*Kelly Appeal*').
[13] *Bill Graham Archives v. Dorling Kindersley Limited*, 386 F Supp 2d 324 (SDNY, 2005); 448 F 3d 605 (2nd circuit, 2006) ('*Bill Graham Archives Appeal*').
[14] *Perfect 10 v. Google*, 416 F Supp 2d 828 (CD Cal, 2006); appealed as *Perfect 10 v. Amazon.com*, 487 F 3d 701 (9th circuit, 2007) ('*Perfect 10 Appeal*').
[15] Despite fair use being a regular subject of judicial analysis (see, e.g., Beebe, n. 11 above, 564–565), very few cases have directly concerned cultural institutions: see, e.g., K. Crews, *Copyright Law for Librarians and Educators: Creative Strategies and Practical Solutions*, 2nd edition (Chicago: American Library Association, 2006), p. 40. At the time of the main fieldwork, two of the more prominent cases both related to photocopying services provided by libraries for employee researchers: *Williams & Wilkins Company v. The United States*, 487 F 2d 1345 (Court of Claims, 1973), affirmed by an equally divided Court in 420 US 376 (1975) (discussed in Chapter 4) and *American Geophysical Union v. Texaco, Inc*, 60 F 3d 913 (2nd circuit, 1994; amended 1995). Since the main fieldwork, there has been litigation in relation to the HathiTrust Digital Library and the library at Georgia State University: see Section IV of this chapter.

infringed in the making of those images. *Bill Graham Archives*, on the other hand, concerned the publication of seven small-scale images of concert posters and tickets in the 480-page biography, *Grateful Dead: The Illustrated Trip*. These reproductions were considerably smaller than the original items, and appeared with explanatory captions regarding the concerts for which they were produced. The defendant publisher had originally sought to clear rights with Bill Graham Archives (BGA), but negotiations stalled when the parties could not agree on a licence fee. The publisher then proceeded to use the images without permission.

There were numerous similarities in the fair use analysis of each case, including in relation to the structure of the analysis – in which the four fairness factors were each considered in turn – and the significant attention given to the first factor: the purpose and character of the use.

In *Kelly*, for example, the Court of Appeals for the Ninth Circuit held that while the search engine had been developed for commercial purposes, this consideration weighed only 'slightly against' fair use as Arriba's reproduction of Kelly's images was 'more incidental and less exploitative in nature than more traditional types of commercial use'.[16] In contrast, the Court held that transformativeness favoured Arriba because the thumbnails 'served an entirely different function than Kelly's original images', namely 'a tool to help index and improve access to images on the internet'.[17] The use of low-resolution images was important to this conclusion because it reflected the placeholder function that the images served, and meant that they would not generally be amenable to artistic re-use because of the loss of clarity upon enlargement.

Similarly, in *Bill Graham Archives*, the Court of Appeals for the Second Circuit stated that '[m]ost important to the court's analysis of the first factor is the "transformative" nature of the [defendant's] work'.[18] This consideration weighed in favour of the publisher because of the nature of its work (biographical and historical scholarship) and because this use was said to be very different to the purposes of the original works (which were produced for artistic expression and promotion). These conclusions were fortified by the size and context of the images: they were too small for any meaningful expressive value to be conveyed, were presented with other textual and graphic information, and formed only a tiny percentage of the defendant's work. Although the book was produced

---

[16] *Kelly Appeal*, n. 12 above, 818, citing *A&M Records, Inc v. Napster, Inc*, 239 F 3d 1004 (9th circuit, 2001).
[17] Ibid., 818.   [18] *Bill Graham Archives Appeal*, n. 13 above, 608.

commercially, this did not alter the Court's conclusion, in part because many of the indicative purposes in section 107 are commonly undertaken in profit-making circumstances.[19]

By the time of *Perfect 10*, it was possible for certain propositions to be dispatched by the Court of Appeals for the Ninth Circuit as apparently uncontroversial: that the 'central purpose of [first factor] inquiry is to determine whether and to what extent a new work is "transformative"';[20] and that Google's use was 'highly transformative' because an image originally created 'to serve an entertainment, aesthetic or informative function' had become 'a pointer directing a user to a source of information'.[21] The analysis instead focused on arguments that sought to distinguish the character of Google's use from that in *Kelly*, including the potential for Google images to supersede the plaintiff's market for mobile phone images.

The thumbnails cases also exhibited similarities in their treatment of the remaining fairness factors. In all three cases, the copied works were creative and hence 'closer to the core of intended copyright protection than are more fact-based works',[22] although this consideration (relevant to the second factor) did not seem to receive a great deal of weight. In *Kelly* and *Perfect 10*, the third factor (the amount taken) favoured neither party, because it was essential for a search engine to reproduce entire images to facilitate user recognition and selection. Similarly, in *Bill Graham Archives*, the Court held that although the entire image was reproduced, the small reproductions had only limited 'visual impact' and had been 'tailored' (in terms of size and quality) to 'further [the defendants'] transformative purpose'.[23] This meant the third factor did not favour BGA, although the Court did not go so far to say that it favoured the defendants.

Finally, in none of the three thumbnails cases was it held that the fourth factor, market harm, favoured the plaintiffs. In *Kelly*, the plaintiff was a professional photographer, and the Court identified two markets for his images: as part of his own website (where he sold books and travel packages); and on other websites and image banks by way of licence. However, Arriba's thumbnails did not adversely affect either market because they helped users locate Kelly's website and could not (due to resolution) substitute for authorised images on third-party websites. This possibility of market substitution loomed larger in *Perfect 10*, where the

---

[19] Ibid., 612, quoting *Campbell* v. *Acuff-Rose Music, Inc*, 510 US 569, 584 (1994).
[20] *Perfect 10 Appeal*, n. 14 above, 720 citing *Campbell* v. *Acuff-Rose*, n. 19 above, 579.
[21] Ibid., 721.
[22] *Kelly Appeal*, n. 12 above, 820, quoting *A&M Records, Inc* v. *Napster, Inc*, n. 16 above.
[23] *Bill Graham Archives Appeal*, n. 13 above, 613.

Doctrinal Indications 167

plaintiff's works were photographs of nude models, for which it was said there was a market for small-size, mobile telephone images. While not disputing the actual or potential existence of such a market, the Court considered that in the absence of evidence that users were actually downloading Google thumbnails for mobile phone use, the harm was 'hypothetical' and the factor was therefore neutral.[24]

In *Bill Graham Archives*, the analysis of market harm focused on derivative markets, as both sides accepted that the defendants' use did not usurp the primary market: sale of poster images. BGA argued that it had an established market for licensing images for publication in books, however the Court held that where a use is transformative, 'a copyright holder cannot prevent others from entering fair use markets merely "by developing or licensing a market for parody, news reporting, educational or other transformative uses of its own creative work"'.[25] The evidence suggested that BGA's licensing revenues related to projects very different from that of the defendants, such as full-page reproductions without meaningful commentary. Furthermore, it was not determinative that the defendants had originally requested a licence, as fair use could still be available as an option to lawfully proceed with a use.[26]

   2   *Transformativeness* A key reason why the defendants succeeded in *Kelly*, *Bill Graham Archives* and *Perfect 10* was that their uses were viewed as transformative. This consideration has long been a part of fair use analysis, through the concept of productive use.[27] However, in the early 1990s, after a period in which the commerciality of the use had been at the forefront of first factor analysis, two contributions revitalised the role of transformative use in US copyright law: Pierre Leval's article in the *Harvard Law Review*,[28] and the Supreme Court decision in

---

[24] *Perfect 10 Appeal*, n. 14 above, 725.
[25] *Bill Graham Archives Appeal*, n. 13 above, 614–615, quoting *Castle Rock Entertainment, Inc* v. *Carol Publishing Group, Inc*, 150 F 3d 132, 146, FN11 (2nd circuit, 1998).
[26] Ibid., 615, citing *Campbell* v. *Acuff-Rose*, n. 19 above, 585, FN18.
[27] In early US cases, judges were more likely to find a work to be non-infringing if it served a new purpose, was publicly beneficial, and did not not act as a surrogate for the earlier work or usurp its market: e.g., *Folsom* v. *Marsh*, 9 F Cas 342 (CCD Mass, 1841). See also *Nimmer on Copyright*, n. 2 above, para. 13.05[A][1][b]; L. Lape, 'Transforming Fair Use: The Productive Use Factor in Fair Use Doctrine' (1995) 58 *Albany Law Review* 677.
[28] P. Leval, 'Towards a Fair Use Standard' (1990) 103 *Harvard Law Review* 1105.

Campbell v. *Acuff-Rose*.[29] In the latter, the Supreme Court saw transformativeness as aligned closely with the very purpose of copyright:

> The goal of copyright, to promote science and the arts, is generally furthered by the creation of transformative works. Such works thus lie at the heart of the fair use doctrine's guarantee of breathing space within the confines of copyright ... and the more transformative the new work, the less will be the significance of other factors, like commercialism, that may weigh against a finding of fair use.[30]

The facts of *Campbell* involved a 'parodic' version of Roy Orbison's 'Oh, Pretty Woman' by musical act, 2 Live Crew.[31] The Supreme Court stated that a transformative work 'adds something new, with a further purpose or different character, altering the first with new expression, meaning, or message'.[32] Similarly, in *HathiTrust*, discussed later in this chapter, the Court of Appeals for the Second Circuit observed that a use is transformative 'if it does something more than repackage or republish the original copyrighted work'.[33] The mere adding of value or utility is not enough; a transformative work 'is one that serves a new and different function from the original work and is not a substitute for it'.[34]

The classification of a use as 'transformative' can be controversial.[35] To illustrate, consider *Cariou* v. *Prince*, in which the defendant created a series of artworks that incorporated a range of source materials, including the plaintiff's photographs. Those materials were altered to varying

---

[29] As demonstrated by Beebe's quantitative study, not all post-*Campbell* decisions discussed transformativeness: Beebe, n. 11 above, 604. Within his dataset, 41.2 per cent of 119 district court decisions, and 18.6 per cent of 43 circuit court opinions, did not refer to transformativeness. Charting these figures chronologically revealed that while there was a steady increase in the proportion of opinions referring to transformativeness from 1994 to 2000, peaking at around 80 per cent, not long after that, these figures started to track downwards towards 50 per cent: at 603, Figure 7.

[30] *Campbell* v. *Acuff-Rose*, n. 19 above, 579 (footnotes omitted).

[31] Views may differ as to the artistic merit of 2 Live Crew's creation.

[32] *Campbell* v. *Acuff-Rose*, n. 19 above, 579. The Supreme Court did not find that 2 Live Crew's fair use arguments were successful. Rather, it held that the case needed to be remanded 'for further proceedings consistent with this opinion'.

[33] *HathiTrust Appeal*, n. 3 above, 96. For similar, see *Blanch* v. *Koons*, 467 F 3d 244, 252 (2nd circuit, 2006), observing that courts have declined to find there was transformative use 'when the defendant has done no more than find a new way to exploit the creative values of the original work'. One such example was the Seinfeld aptitude test in *Castle Rock Entertainment, Inc* v. *Carol Publishing Group, Inc*, n. 25 above, as the quiz book merely 'repackaged' entertaining aspects of the television series.

[34] Ibid.

[35] See, e.g., M. Madison, 'A Pattern-Oriented Approach of Fair Use' (2004) 45 *William and Mary Law Review* 1525; L. Heymann, 'Everything Is Transformative: Fair Use and Reader Response' (2008) 31 *Columbia Journal of Law and the Arts* 445.

degrees through techniques such as collage, cropping and overprinting.[36] The District Court rejected the argument that the defendant's images fell within fair use, partly on the basis that the defendant's work must 'comment on, relate to the historical context of, or critically refer back to the original works'.[37] Here, the defendant's own testimony was that he did not have any real interest in the source artist's intent because his goal was to 'change [the source works] into something that's completely different'.[38] However, the Court of Appeals for the Second Circuit held that the District Court had been wrong to impose any requirement for commenting back. It held that twenty-five of the defendant's artworks were transformative, as judged by viewer perception: that in those works, 'Prince's composition, presentation, scale, color palette, and media are fundamentally different and new compared to the photographs, as is the expressive nature of Prince's work'.[39] It has been said by Christine Haight Farley that as a matter of aesthetics, *Cariou* emphasised form (i.e., visual qualities such as line, colour, composition, and so forth) over content (e.g., story, message, information).[40] For Haight Farley, '[t]he major significance of *Cariou* ... is that [it] frees courts from the activity of assigning interpretations to works of art in order to determine whether or not they offer a new comment'.[41] However, the case has been criticised for being '[e]mblematic of the almost limitless expansion of cases holding uses transformative'.[42] In a later case, the Second Circuit emphasised that the images held to be transformative in *Cariou* involved significant modification to the plaintiff's photographs.[43]

---

[36] The plaintiff's works were black-and-white photographs of the Rastafarians in Jamaica, and were published in the book *Yes Rasta*. The defendant used photographs from the book in a series of works entitled *Canal Zone*.
[37] *Cariou* v. *Prince*, 784 F Supp 2d 337, 348 (SDNY, 2011).
[38] Deposition quoted in *Cariou* v. *Prince*, 714 F 3d 694, 706–707 (2nd circuit, 2013). The defendant described his vision in this project as to 'make a kind of fantastic, absolutely hip, up to date, contemporary take on the music scene'.
[39] Ibid., 706. There were also five works whose modification had been less extensive, and which the Court of Appeal was unwilling to characterise as transformative as a matter of law. It remanded to the District Court for those works: at 710–711.
[40] C. Haight Farley, 'No Comment: Will *Cariou v. Prince* Alter Copyright Judges' Taste in Art?' (2015) 5 *IP Theory* 19, 31.
[41] Ibid., 33.
[42] *Nimmer on Copyright*, n. 2 above, para. 13.05[B][6]. See also D. Brooks, 'Rectifying Fair Use After *Cariou v. Prince*: Reviving the Forgotten Statutory Text and Requiring that Unauthorized Copying Be Justified, rather than Merely "Transformative"' (2016) 15 *Chicago-Kent Journal of Intellectual Property Law* 93; B. Sites, 'Fair Use and the New Transformative' (2016) 39 *Columbia Journal of Law and the Arts* 513. The Court of Appeals for the Seventh Circuit expressed skepticism about *Cariou* in *Kienitz* v. *Sconnie Nation LLC*, 766 F 3d 756 (7th circuit, 2014).
[43] *TCA Television Corp* v. *McCollum*, 839 F 3d 168, 181 (2nd circuit, 2016). In *Graham* v. *Prince*, No. 15-CV-10160 (SDNY, 18 July 2017), Judge Stein applied the reasoning in

The decisions in *Kelly*, *Bill Graham Archives* and *Perfect 10* were also controversial due to their treatment of transformativeness. In each case, the change of context was crucial, with comparison being made between the original purpose (e.g., artistic expression) and the new one (e.g., biographical scholarship or facilitating online research). But it has been asked whether these cases truly involved transformative scenarios.[44] In all three cases, the only change *within* the work was to reduce the size and resolution – a change that was not, of itself, able to ground an argument that the use was transformative.[45] As such, changes *outside* the work were crucial to the defendants' successful fair use arguments. This led Paul Goldstein to argue that in cases like *Bill Graham Archives* and *Perfect 10*, transformativeness was 'a triumph of mindless sound bite over principled analysis', representing a mere asportation of a work 'from one medium to another'.[46] For example, Goldstein said that unlike the parody in *Campbell*, the defendant's reproductions in *Bill Graham Archives* 'did no more to "transform" the copyrighted images than to reduce their scale to fit the format of its coffee table book'.[47] Bill Patry (who was counsel for the appellant in *Bill Graham Archives*) was also damning of the result. He described the defendant's work as a 'coffee table, eye candy' book containing 'thousands of visual works and precious little text'.[48] In his view, the outcome 'badly misconstrued' the concept of transformative use, as the commentary was rudimentary and the timeline format used 'precisely to avoid engaging in any intellectual effort'.[49]

As seen in the foregoing analysis, one difficulty with transformative use relates to disagreement regarding the meaning and limits of the term. However, in the cultural institution context, a further issue is whether emphasis on transformativeness might cause us to forget that it is not the

---

Cariou in another case involving Prince. The plaintiff's work was a black-and-white portrait titled *Rastafarian Smoking a Joint*. Prince's work was a large inkjet print of an Instagram post of the plaintiff's photograph, this post having been made by another Instagram user. Judge Stein held that there was minimal alteration to the plaintiff's work, and that Prince's work was not transformative as a matter of law.

[44] See, e.g., P. Goldstein, 'Copyright's Commons' (2005) 29 *Columbia Journal of Law and the Arts* 1, 5–6; M. Williams, 'Recent Second Circuit Opinions Indicate that Google's Library Project is Not Transformative' (2007) 25 *Cardozo Arts & Entertainment Law Journal* 303, 306.

[45] Just like the change in medium from photograph to painting was not what made the use transformative in *Blanch v. Koons*, n. 33 above, 252.

[46] P. Goldstein, 'Fair Use in Context' (2008) 31 *Columbia Journal of Law and the Arts* 433, 442.

[47] P. Goldstein, *Goldstein on Copyright Volume II* (New York: Aspen Publishers, 2008), para. 12.1.

[48] W. Patry, *Patry on Copyright*, Volume 4 (Thomson Reuters, online resource, updated to March 2018), para. 10:16.50.

[49] Ibid., para 10:21.

sine qua non of fair use. The concern here is that many educational and research uses are not transformative,[50] unless we adopt a very loose definition of that term. Rebecca Tushnet wrote about similar themes when she argued that transformative use has the potential to limit the circumstances in which fair use is found, insofar as it emphasises certain paradigmatic instances of transformation (e.g., criticism, review and parody), with the result that 'nontransformative copying, including plain old photocopying even in educational or scientific contexts, begins to look unfair'.[51] Tushnet's focus was free speech, and she identified instances of 'pure' copying that she saw as important for speech-related reasons.[52] However, she also stated:

> The condemnation of pure copying that is a natural consequence of the elevation of transformative uses obviously helps content owners against file-trading services and their enemies of long standing, the university and the library. Thus, courts increasingly find copiers liable even when their aims were educational or research oriented. If re-visioning fair use as being about transformation is what it takes to keep rights over every pure copy, that's an acceptable price for content owners to pay.[53]

As an empirical matter, it would seem that transformativeness has not become a quasi-compulsory element of fair use, at least as applied in the courts. In Barton Beebe's review of fair use case law, for example, the data indicated that when transformativeness was found, it was associated strongly with a successful fair use defence.[54] The data did not, however, suggest that transformative use was *necessary* for a finding of fair use.[55] Although providing some comfort, this does not provide a complete answer to Tushnet's concerns; plus there remains the question of how

---

[50] For consideration of ways in which teaching might be said to involve transformative activity, see B. Butler, 'Transformative Teaching and Educational Fair Use After Georgia State' (2015) 48 *Connecticut Law Review* 475.

[51] R. Tushnet, 'Copy This Essay: How Fair Use Doctrine Harms Free Speech and How Copying Serves It' (2004) 114 *Yale Law Journal* 535, 556. See also P. Samuelson, 'The Relative Virtues of Bottom-Up and Top-Down Theories of Fair Use' (2017) 83 *University of Chicago Law Review Online* 206, responding to A. Bell and G. Parchomovsky, 'The Dual-Grant Theory of Fair Use' (2016) 83 *University of Chicago Law Review* 1051.

[52] Ibid., 565–581.   [53] Ibid., 559.

[54] Beebe, n. 11 above, 605–606. In 42 district and circuit court opinions that found that a defendant's use was transformative, 40 concluded that section 107 applied – and of the two district court decisions to come to the opposite result, one was reversed on appeal.

[55] Ibid. Beebe observed that 36.8 per cent of the 68 post-*Campbell* decisions that did not discuss transformativeness nevertheless concluded that fair use applied.

172   Functional Fair Use

users apply fair use to literal copying. Some of the ideas are explored further in the analysis of market harm, next.

3 The Market Effect of the Use In each of *Kelly*, *Bill Graham Archives* and *Perfect 10*, the courts were unwilling to entertain what they saw as inadequate, unsubstantiated and unsound claims about market effect. In *Kelly*, it was held that the relevant markets were only for full-sized images, none of which were impacted by the creation of thumbnails by the defendant.[56] In contrast, it was accepted that Perfect 10 might have a market for the download of small-scale images for use on mobile telephones; however, in the absence of evidence of people using Google-produced thumbnails for this purpose, it was concluded that 'the potential harm ... remains hypothetical'.[57] Finally, even in *Bill Graham Archives*, where there were established industry practices for licensing images for book publication, it was found that there was no market harm.[58] The Court considered arguments regarding actual and potential licensing practices, but held that where a use is transformative, a defendant cannot seek to circumvent fair use arguments by offering licences for those uses.

Market harm is tricky,[59] and raises questions about what matters should be relevant to analysis under this factor.[60] This has been a particular issue in the *Georgia State* litigation, discussed later in this chapter. However, it is worth signposting some matters now. Reference to market effect sounds empirical, and might convey the idea that courts should look to actual practices as part of their assessment of whether a use is fair.[61] This proposition is not uncontroversial, due to its capacity to invite self-serving arguments and rest on circular reasoning, especially as this relates to licensing.[62] For instance, in Canada, 'alternatives to the dealing' and 'the effect of the dealing' were two of the six fairness factors

---

[56] *Kelly Appeal*, n. 12 above, 821.   [57] *Perfect 10 Appeal*, n. 14 above, 725.
[58] *Bill Graham Archives Appeal*, n. 13 above, 612–615.
[59] See, e.g., Patry, n. 48 above, para. 10:145 (describing the fourth factor as the 'least understood, and, as a consequence, most misapplied').
[60] See, e.g., *Nimmer on Copyright*, n. 2 above, para. 13.05[A][4]; E. Hudson, 'The *Georgia State* Litigation: Literal Copying in Education' (2019) 82 *Modern Law Review* 508.
[61] See World Trade Organization, *United States – Section 110(5) of the US Copyright Act: Report of the Panel* (15 June 2000, WT/DS160/R), para. 6.178 (the meaning of 'normal exploitation' of a work encompasses empirical and normative elements).
[62] For discussion, see *American Geophysical v. Texaco*, n. 15 above; *Princeton University Press v. Michigan Document Services*, 99 F 3d 1381, 1386–1388 (6th circuit, 1996); M. Sag, 'God in the Machine: A New Structural Analysis of Copyright's Fair Use Doctrine' (2005) 11 *Michigan Telecommunications and Technology Law Review* 381, 391–395.

Doctrinal Indications 173

approved by the Supreme Court in *CCH Canadian Ltd* v. *Law Society of Upper Canada*.[63] However, the Court also said that the availability of a licence was *not* a relevant alternative: '[i]f a copyright owner were allowed to license people to use its work and then point to a person's decision not to obtain a licence as proof that his or her dealings were not fair, this would extend the scope of the owner's monopoly over the use of his or her work in a manner that would not be consistent with the Copyright Act's balance between owner's rights and user's interests.'[64]

In the United States, courts have considered licensing practices when analysing fair use, raising the question of when a 'right' to licence should arise.[65] Consider the litigation in *Basic Books* v. *Kinko's*.[66] The defendant was a photocopy shop that sold course packs to university students in New York. These packs contained unauthorised photocopies of extracts from books produced by the consortium of publishers who brought the action. Kinko's raised a fair use defence but this was unsuccessful, with the fourth factor weighing 'heavily'[67] against the defendant. In part this was due to the Court's finding of market substitution: that the course packs would reduce student demand for textbooks. However, the Court also considered the diversion of licensing revenue from the publishers, which was said to be particularly important for out-of-print works.

This consideration of licensing markets has proven to be significant, especially in contexts such as academic publishing, where content is increasingly being distributed in electronic, disaggregated forms and on an 'all you can eat' basis. As stated by Mary Minow and Tomas Lipinski, 'as commercial vendors either express an interest or move into a market that makes smaller and smaller pieces of information available for purchase or license, there will be ample evidence for copyright owners to demonstrate secondary market harm'.[68] If judges 'reason backwards from the fact of marketability to the construct of property',[69] the case law

---

[63] [2004] 1 SCR 339, paras. 57, 59.
[64] Ibid., para. 70. As discussed in Chapter 8, in a 2017 decision of the Federal Court of Canada where the copying practices at York University were held to be outside fair dealing, diminution in licensing incoming was relevant to the effect of the dealing: *The Canadian Copyright Licensing Agency ("Access Copyright")* v. *York University* [2018] 2 FCR 43, para. 351.
[65] See, e.g., M. Africa, 'The Misuse of Licensing Evidence in Fair Use Analysis: New Technologies, New Markets, and the Courts' (2000) 88 *California Law Review* 1145, 1156–1160; L. Pallas Loren, 'Redefining the Market Failure Approach to Fair Use in an Era of Copyright Permission Systems' (1997) 5 *Journal of Intellectual Property Law* 1.
[66] *Basic Books, Inc* v. *Kinko's Graphics Corporation*, 758 F Supp 1522 (SDNY, 1991).
[67] Ibid., 1534.
[68] M. Minow and T. Lipinski, *The Library's Legal Answer Book* (Chicago: American Library Association, 2003), p. 33.
[69] Sag, n. 62 above, 394.

174   Functional Fair Use

may serve to entrench these 'markets', thus narrowing fair use arguments. On the other hand, there are dangers in judges impairing or foreclosing (reasonable) secondary markets through their approach to fair use.[70]

Beebe considered the role of the fourth factor in his systematic analysis of fair use case law. One of the key points to come from his data was the degree to which the outcomes of the fourth factor and overall section 107 analysis went hand-in-hand.[71] However, Beebe did not interpret this as meaning market harm is the 'most influential' factor;[72] rather, he concluded that '[t]he fourth factor essentially constitutes a metafactor under which the courts integrate their analyses of the other three factors and, in doing so, arrive at the outcome not simply of the fourth factor, but the overall test'.[73] Normatively, then, it is 'no factor, no independent variable, at all'.[74] Instead,

> judges appear to apply section 107 in the form of a cognitively more familiar two-sided balancing test in which they weigh the strength of the defendant's justification for its use, as that justification has been developed in the first three factors, against the impact of that use on the incentives of the plaintiff. Factor four provides the analytical space for this balancing test to occur, and the various doctrinal propositions under factor four are merely there to tilt the scales one way or the other.[75]

The 'metafactor' understanding goes some way to explain the reasoning in the thumbnails cases, and in particular *Bill Graham Archives* and *Perfect 10*, where there were stronger arguments that there was an existing or likely market for licensing small-scale images. In all three cases, the conclusion regarding market harm was influenced strongly by the analysis of the other factors. Beebe's regression analysis suggests this is also consistent with broader trends: that factors one and four not only correlate strongly with the overall conclusion regarding fair use, but also with one another.[76]

---

[70] This also raises questions about the relationship between fair use and the right, in US law, to prepare derivative works: see, e.g., R. Reese, 'Transformativeness and the Derivative Work Right' (2008) 31 *Columbia Journal of Law and the Arts* 467.
[71] Beebe, n. 11 above, 617. Of 116 opinions in which the court held that the fourth factor favoured fair use, the result favoured the defendant in 110 of these; of the 141 opinions in which the final factor tended against fair use, 140 found in favour of the plaintiff.
[72] On this, see *Harper & Row Publishers, Inc v. Nation Enterprises*, 471 US 539, 566 (1985) ('[t]his last factor is undoubtedly the single most important element of fair use').
[73] Beebe, n. 11 above, 617.   [74] Ibid., 621.   [75] Ibid.
[76] Ibid., 584. On the relatively rare occasions that opposite findings were reached on factors one and four, the overall conclusion tended to follow the fourth factor (14 times compared with six).

However, it is also noteworthy that in all three cases there was a finding that the defendant's use was transformative. Such a finding may render the analysis of the fourth factor more straightforward, especially if it allows the court to conclude that there was neither market substitution nor a reasonable licensing market.[77] That is, it is often said that factor four is not concerned with market damage per se (as a pointed criticism might reduce demand for a work) but market usurpation.[78] For many transformative uses, it may be easier to rationalise the lack of relevant economic harm on the basis that the plaintiff and defendant have different purposes, are targeting different audiences and hence operating in different markets. How, then, should we consider the fourth factor in cases where such arguments are not as clear-cut? This chapter will return to this question in its analysis of *Georgia State*, which is interesting because of the different approaches to the fourth factor that have emerged over the course of the litigation.

III   Fair Use Practices

Having examined doctrinal indications in relation to fair use in Section II, this section now provides an empirical account of how users understand the doctrine, and in particular how US interviewees reported using fair use as part of their copyright management practices. After some general observations, it discusses fair use experiences in a range of scenarios, starting with those that are largely internal to the institution (collection management and preservation), before turning to activities that involve copies being distributed to, and accessible by, members of the public. Although institutional practices are often motivated by multiple goals and do not necessarily reflect a compartmentalised model, presenting the fieldwork according to activity is useful as it illustrates common themes in the reasoning between different institutions and different collection genre, and highlights divergences in approach where they arise.

A   *General Observations*

A number of preliminary observations can be made about how US interviewees described their understandings and utilisation of fair use. First, the fieldwork suggested that at least in participating institutions, fair use was flexible and responsive, as suggested by its open-ended

---

[77] See, e.g., Hudson, n. 60 above.
[78] E.g., *Campbell* v. *Acuff Rose*, n. 19 above, 590–594.

drafting style. Fair use was relied upon in a fairly broad range of circumstances, these circumstances having changed – and continuing to change – over time. The degree of comfort with fair use varied, and while many interviewees described forward-leaning interpretations of the doctrine, especially for public activities,[79] others described a more cautious approach.[80] That said, even amongst institutions with more limited fair use practices, the fieldwork suggested that fair use can and does play a meaningful role in copyright management, including in relation to the gamut of public activities that cultural institutions undertake.

Second, many interviewees demonstrated considerable familiarity with the fair use doctrine and the law in books.[81] They were able to list the four fairness factors and explain what they considered to be their content. Some also referred to the guidance they received from specific fair use opinions; as noted above, prominent examples were *Kelly*, *Bill Graham Archives* and *Perfect 10*,[82] with other cases also mentioned.[83] While a number of interviewees said that fair use can be uncertain or must be considered on a case-by-case basis,[84] there also seemed to be widespread acceptance that the four factors had some prospectively ascertainable meaning, resulting in the ability to make predictions about how the doctrine would likely be applied by a judge. This is also not surprising given the standards and rules literature, which observes that case law and user protocols can cause a body of rules to emerge from legal regulation drafted as a standard. In the case of fair use, it appears that judicial precedent has been particularly important in giving institutions confidence in their interpretations of section 107.

---

[79] E.g., 1G, 7G, 9M, 16G, 22L, 29L, 30G, 35L, 39L, 43M, 45M, 53G; also 3X, 6X, 23X, 47X.

[80] E.g., 4L, 10L, 14G, 15L, 20G, 28G, 30G, 33G.

[81] E.g., 1G, 7G, 9M, 12L, 14G, 15L, 16G, 19L, 22L, 26G, 27M, 28G, 29L, 30G, 33G, 35L, 38G, 39L, 43M, 45M, 46G, 53G, 54M, 55L. Also 3X, 6X, 23X, 25X, 44X, 47X.

[82] E.g., 1G, 9M, 16G, 23X, 39L, 43M, 47X and 53G (citing *Kelly v. Arriba*, n. 12 above); 6X, 7G, 16G, 39L, 43M and 47X (*Bill Graham Archives*, n. 13 above); and 1G, 7G, 9M, 26G, 33G, 43M, 47X and 53G (citing *Perfect 10*, n. 14 above);.

[83] E.g., *Campbell v. Acuff-Rose*, n. 19 above (47X); *Sundeman v. Seajay Society, Inc* 142 F 3d 194, (4th circuit, 1998) (39L); *The Bridgeman Art Library, Ltd v. Corel Corporation*, 36 F Supp 2d 191 (SDNY, 1999) (12L, 39L, 53G); *New York Times v. Tasini*, 533 US 483 (2001) (52M, 53G, 54M); *Suntrust v. Houghton Mifflin Co*, 268 F 3d 1257 (11th circuit, 2001) (39L); *Field v. Google, Inc*, 412 F Supp 2d 1106 (D Nev, 2006) (47X). Interviewees were not asked to identify cases from which they drew guidance, so this list only represents interviewees who volunteered case names when answering questions. Other interviewees described principles that may have been derived from these cases, but in the absence of citing a particular case name or parties, are not included.

[84] E.g., 2L, 7G, 11M, 14G, 36M, 39L, 41G and 47X (the ambit of fair use can be uncertain); 6X, 14G, 16G, 23X, 28G and 35L (fair use analysis must proceed on a case-by-case basis).

Third, the interviewees that described the more forward-leaning approaches to fair use came from institutions with one or more of: (1) a centralised unit for managing copyright; (2) what we might term 'copyright experts' on staff, including but not limited to attorneys and rights officers; (3) a willingness to dedicate resources to copyright management and policy development; (4) a more 'commercial' perspective regarding fair use arguments, for instance through risk-assessed reasoning or through using the doctrine to negotiate more favourable terms in licences; and (5) a management structure in which copyright experts either had the authority to direct institutional decision-making or whose recommendations were acted upon by decision-makers. Again, this would seem to correlate with predictions in the literature about how risk preferences, information costs and access to legal advice all impact on the operation of standards.

Finally, although the bulk of the empirical data was generated in interviews in 2008 and 2009, there have also been follow-up conversations with US interviewees over the years, plus examination of other publicly available information about fair use interpretations and practices. This work does not suggest any significant winding back of the applications described in this chapter; on the contrary, it would seem that certain uses (for instance, in relation to online use) have become more common and less contentious. As with all the fieldwork in this book, the precise applications are not fixed but are intended to give a sense of the ways in which individuals engage with the law.

B   *Internal Activities*

   1   *Collection Management* As seen in Chapter 4, section 108 of the US Copyright Act does very little to facilitate the administrative work of cultural institutions, being directed towards preservation, replacement and request-based copying services. There is therefore no provision equivalent to Canadian and Australian exceptions for collection management, and while three copies of an unpublished work may be made for preservation and security, this phrase has not been understood as relating to administration generally.[85] For instance, in the Section 108 Study Group report, it was said that inclusion of the word 'security' meant that 'a library or archives could make a copy of a one-of-a-kind unpublished

---

[85] US Copyright Act s. 108(b). No such meaning was ascribed to this phrase in United States Copyright Office, *Section 108 of Title 17: A Discussion Document of the Register of Copyrights* (United States Copyright Office, September 2017).

work available to users under this exception in order to safeguard and secure the integrity of its original copy'.[86]

Given this backdrop, it appeared that for US cultural institutions, the exception most relevant to administrative activities was fair use. In the absence of directly relevant case law, the application of section 107 must be considered as a matter of first principles. As stated in Chapter 4, there are strong reasons to believe that fair use covers many examples of internal administration, particularly given the non-commercial nature of such acts, their importance to collection administration and the lack of public distribution. For instance, one US text on law and museum management states that 'most experts would agree that reproducing or photographing a work for internal registrarial or archival purposes is permissible [under fair use], including digital copies for internal museum databases, certainly if the images were limited to thumbnail size';[87] and later that '[d]igital reproduction, display and adaptation for purely in-house needs, for preservation, and for administrative purposes are within the fair use arena. This is especially the case if the size and image quality is restricted in line with the needs of the intended in-house user.'[88]

Most of the interviewees who could comment directly on the role of fair use in administration came from institutions overseeing collections of art, photographs and/or three-dimensional objects, which is not surprising as management of those items – cataloguing, seeking insurance, etc. – will often require a visual record in addition to any written description. These interviewees reported that, by and large, there were no major copyright issues in relation to collection management.[89] That said, decision-making about these activities often seemed to take place without any meaningful, or indeed any, analysis of the law. The imperative to make these copies was reported by numerous interviewees:

> This is even before we get to fair use, from our perspective it's just something we have to have ... we're just making an image because we know we need to for our administrative purposes.[90]

> [Accepting that the institution would rely on fair use, but adding:] Maybe I think [it's] something beyond fair use, and I would say that it gets back to that standard practice.[91]

---

[86] Section 108 Study Group, *The Section 108 Study Group Report: An Independent Report sponsored by the United States Copyright Office and the National Digital Information Infrastructure and Preservation Program of the Library of Congress* (March 2008), p. 62.
[87] M. Malaro and I. DeAngelis, *A Legal Primer on Managing Museum Collections*, 3rd edition (Washington, DC: Smithsonian Books, 2012), p. 187.
[88] Ibid., p. 197.
[89] E.g., 1G, 7G, 9M, 14G, 16G, 20G, 28G, 29L, 30G, 33G, 43M, 45M, 48G, 53G.
[90] 53G.   [91] 33G.

Fair Use Practices 179

It's either such a clear-cut case of fair use that we're going with it, or it's so critical to our function that we're going to do it and deal with any issues that come up along the way.[92]

[Stating that digitisation for administrative purposes was probably a fair use but that no-one has turned their mind to it.] We're just doing it.[93]

Another undertook a fair use analysis on the spot:

I think we would probably argue fair use: it is very small reproduction; it's a very limited group of people who have access to it; it's not available to the general public; it's free; it's a transformative use, in the sense that it is used to create an internal collection management database, so we can track where the art is. I don't think anyone every bothered to do that, I'm just doing it now for the first time; I don't really think it's hard. ... It also ties into other uses, such as condition reports, so it has to do with conservation as well. The risk of somebody coming in and saying that they're losing a market because [the Museum] has reproduced these images in an intranet, that is only available to password-protected people, is so remote that no-one would think twice about it. So those internal uses are not problematic: conservation, collection management, registration.[94]

As stated in Chapter 4, the overarching sense to come from the fieldwork was that interviewees did not experience copyright problems in relation to internal administration because they: (1) believed that copyright was irrelevant to these activities; (2) assumed that fair use *must* apply, even if the reason why had never been fully particularised; or (3) had not given the question a second thought. This did not reflect a general attitude towards copyright; as one interviewee noted, the absence of any meaningful copyright research for collection management could be contrasted with the extensive work done for images on the public websites.[95] It did mean, however, that certain criticisms of fair use, for instance that it lacks certainty, did not seem to arise, albeit not because staff had already undertaken a detailed fair use analysis but because of a largely intuitive sense that collection management was squarely within the sorts of uses that are privileged by section 107. That is, whilst no interviewees disagreed with the proposition that fair use was applicable to collection management, nor had they thought carefully about this question until prompted. This might be seen to align with one of the stated benefits of standards: that many have a 'large intuitive element which makes them comprehensible without special training'.[96]

---

[92] 7G.   [93] 14G.   [94] 16G.   [95] 20G.
[96] I. Ehrlich and R. Posner, 'An Economic Analysis of Legal Rulemaking' (1974) 3 *Journal of Legal Studies* 257, 270–271.

180   Functional Fair Use

2 Preservation In Chapter 4 it was seen that preservation is one of the special privileges in section 108, but that those provisions were limited in various ways: by reference to subject-matter and the number of copies that may be made, and through the exclusion of museums and galleries. As discussed in that chapter, to the extent that US interviewees reported relying on an exception for preservation copying, slightly more indicated that they were using fair use[97] than section 108.[98] In addition, it was common for non-exclusive licences to cover preservation and archival activity,[99] especially for digital art and audiovisual items.[100] Discussing the relationship between fair use, licences and norms of best practice, it was observed:

So, where we are making a archival record, it's nice to have a licence, but fair use is our primary justification – it's something we do as a museum.[101]

Generally speaking, the litany of rights we ask for [include] rights to reproduce the work for things that probably you don't need to ask for, like internal archival purposes, conservation purposes.[102]

Rights are a concern, and money. We are concerned about the content of the distribution agreements that we haven't seen. However, if the film is really important, we will make the preservation copy; if the film is going, and we're pretty sure we haven't been able to make another print, we'll do it. If there is video available, we won't. If anyone ever challenged, we would invoke fair use. But as some point, we won't even think about it.[103]

It would therefore appear that fair use was one reason for the reports, from numerous US interviewees, that copyright's impact on preservation was often low.[104] Although institutions could obtain licences for such conduct or (in some cases) rely on sector-specific exceptions, fair use supplemented these strategies and served to counteract some of the drafting limitations in section 108. As seen in Chapter 4, staff were also driven by strong ethical norms about the importance of preservation to institutional missions, meaning that copying sometimes proceeded without any detailed copyright analysis. With suggestions that section 108 be broadened to cover additional institutions and works,[105] this fieldwork raised questions about the necessity and desirability of such a change. This is discussed further in Chapter 9.

---

[97] E.g., 1G, 7G, 9M, 12L, 13M, 19L, 28G, 29L.
[98] E.g., 4L, 10L, 15L, 19L, 35L, 45M (in relation to archival collection).
[99] E.g., 4L, 16G, 28G, 45M.   [100] E.g., 7G, 13M, 21M, 33G, 53G.   [101] 7G.
[102] 16G.   [103] 13M.
[104] E.g., 1G, 4L, 5M, 7G, 9M, 10L, 14G, 15L, 29L, 30G, 35L, 43M, 52M, 53G.
[105] See, e.g., Section 108 Study Group, n. 86 above; United States Copyright Office, n. 87 above.

C   *Fair Use and Public Activities*

1 Request-Based Services Amongst US participants there was a clear trend in procedures for copying services falling outside of section 108, with requestors generally given responsibility for clearing rights, and institutions disclaiming that they had any authority to grant permissions.[106] In terms of the legal basis for the institution *itself* making a copy, some interviewees reported that reproductions were supplied within the parameters of fair use and that anything beyond this required permission.[107] In other cases, it appeared that institutions were relying on rights having been cleared by the requestor, with their disclaimer about copyright often being coupled with an indemnity. That said, it was not uncommon for institutions to supply reproductions without seeing evidence of the requestor's licence, although this depended on the circumstances, meaning that institutions might have different procedures for particular copyright owners (e.g., an artist with known preferences regarding re-use) or requests (e.g., where high-quality content was requested for commercial use).[108] Although it may be questioned whether a disclaimer provides any meaningful protection against a lawsuit directed at the institution,[109] the absence of complaints by copyright owners suggested that this approach has been tolerated, and might even be welcomed. For instance, one interviewee observed that 'we are aware that rightsholders may ultimately disagree with our right to [supply copies], but it's been our experience that they appreciate the function, in terms of delivering images to clients that they can collect royalties for'.[110] Given that commercial requests often came from repeat players in the industry (e.g., publishers, media organisations and filmmakers), it might be hypothesised that there are strong social norms under which such entities clear and pay for rights. In sum, it appeared that institutions

---

[106] E.g., 4L, 5M, 7G, 10L, 13M, 14G, 24G, 26G, 28G, 32M, 37M, 42G, 46G, 53G.
[107] Especially 10L, 29L, 32M, 53G. It was also common that the terms and conditions of public websites expressly permitted online content to be re-used in accordance with fair use: e.g., 1G, 4L, 7G, 14G, 24G, 26G, 28G, 37M, 42G, 43M, 45M, 53G. This was said to reduce the workload for request services, as many people who required content for non-commercial purposes would be satisfied with the reproduction that appeared online.
[108] E.g., 4L, 5M, 7G, 13M, 14G, 26G, 28G, 32M.
[109] Asking for an indemnity does not absolve an institution from liability but enables it to be compensated by the requestor for expenses such as costs and the payment of damages. This will be of no practical use if the requestor is impecunious or unlocatable.
[110] 7G.

182   Functional Fair Use

used a mix of approaches – including fair use – in their handling of external requests.[111]

    2   *Onsite Uses* The fieldwork suggested that amongst participating US institutions, fair use was invoked regularly for onsite activities. For instance, interviewees described a range of different exhibition uses for which they had relied on fair use, such as presenting digitised text and images on copy-disabled computer terminals, playing short extracts of films, and using images in explanatory panels or signage.[112] As one interviewee whose institution utilised interactive kiosks in some exhibitions explained:

> Anything that happens in the museum with an educational purpose, that's not just decoration, we'll usually take the position that it's fair use. So I don't think we would clear rights ... unless we had a sensitive relationship with a contemporary, living artist.[113]

Another described their institution's reasoning in relation to kiosks in more detail:

> It's non-commercial; there's no copying ability; it's in the context of the museum, in an exhibition, with commentary. It does include the whole work, which weighs against [fair use], but it's not a substitution for the original work, nobody can make a copy of it or take it away. We take the position that an exhibition brochure, onsite ephemera and exhibition design is all fair use. Living artists are always treated differently, we always talk to them – even if we tell them we're doing this under fair use. ... There's no real opportunity for further copying, which is all, I think, the rights holders are concerned about. We've never been called [to account].[114]

The fact that some onsite uses were being undertaken by reference to fair use needs to be subject to the caveat that there were also interviewees who made no mention of any such perspective and who were routinely clearing rights, including for things like signage and way-finding materials. Furthermore, even amongst interviewees who relied on fair use, this was often project specific rather than reflecting a universal or default approach. As with other examples given in this chapter, the responses are

---

[111] See also Minow and Lipinski, n. 68 above, 34 (stating that 'sometimes library copying [for a patron who requires a copy for research use only] will fall into fair use, after a careful analysis of the factors').
[112] E.g., 1G, 4L, 7G, 9M, 16G, 23X, 43M, 45M, 54M. Lack of clearance for onsite uses was also reported by 14G, 20G, 27M, although they did not expressly situate this within a fair use analysis.
[113] 7G. [114] 1G.

intended to illustrate the range of applications of fair use and factors relevant to decision-making practices.

The invocation of fair use for onsite use seemed to reflect two important ideas, going to institutional missions and the purpose of copyright. In relation to missions, interviewees appeared to have internalised an understanding of 'providing access' that was not just about making objects available but also educating patrons, providing contextual information about collection items, and even assisting people in moving about the exhibition space. In relation to the purpose of copyright, many interviewee responses were consistent with a philosophy of copyright in which the key owner interest was not the ability to control the creation of copies per se but to authorise and/or receive income from commercialisation and distribution.[115] For onsite uses, the fact that access was restricted to the physical premises was therefore important for decision-making;[116] as one interviewee said, 'we draw a strong line between things we do in the museum and things that take place outside'.[117] Similarly, another interviewee described an exhibition of books in which an interactive terminal was installed so that patrons could view different pages from the books without having to physically handle them. When asked why copyright had not been considered, the answer was that the reproductions were on a kiosk in the exhibition space and people do not walk away with them.[118]

It can be asked whether it has ever been possible to deliver *purely* onsite access, given the ability of patrons to make copies of collection items and take those copies off the premises. It may be that such activity was of little concern when it was undertaken by hand. However, the power and ubiquity of cameras in laptops, tablets and smartphones is such that patrons are now able to produce excellent reproductions without institution supplied or high-end equipment. In addition to challenging the notion of onsite use descriptively (because patrons can readily make their own images), there is also a normative element, in terms of public expectations about how they – and institutions – will use digital technologies. This raises questions about how technological developments will influence decision-making, and whether the breakdown between onsite and offsite will lead to freer or more restrictive norms in how collections are presented.

---

[115] See also J. Litman, 'Revising Copyright Law for the Digital Age' (1996) 75 *Oregon Law Review* 19 (arguing that, in the digital age, 'reproduction is no longer an appropriate way to measure infringement' (at 37) and that an alternative approach – and one that would accord with the perspectives of non-lawyers – would be for copyright to be an exclusive right of commercial exploitation).
[116] Especially 1G, 4L, 9M, 14G, 45M.   [117] 9M.   [118] 14G.

3 Offsite Uses The headline message from the US fieldwork was that fair use played a more limited role for public activities in which copies were distributed or could be taken off the institution's premises, but certainly not a meaningless role, and indeed the interviews in 2008 and 2009 pointed to an emerging norm of online fair use that seems to have continued in the intervening years.

Although this section focuses on public websites, it is worth making a few remarks on the reported relevance of fair use for publications and marketing. Here it was common for institutions to obtain permissions for the reproduction of material not in the public domain,[119] and there were often well-established procedures for clearance. However, reliance on licences was not inevitable, and the fieldwork revealed that in certain cases, institutions relied on fair use. For example, a number of interviewees reported making images available to the media under a fair use analysis,[120] while others noted the possible application of fair use to comparative and smaller-scale images appearing in scholarly publications and catalogues.[121] It was also observed that fair use may be relevant for some brochures and exhibition flyers,[122] with one interviewee identifying relevant factors that had supported such an analysis in their institution as including the nature of the proposed reproductions (small, black and white images), the fact that these materials were being given away for free, and synergies with news reporting (as the flyers notified recipients of upcoming exhibitions).

Turning to online uses, amongst participants in the 2007–2009 research, the usual starting point was that copies of collection items would only be included on public websites where there was permission from the copyright owner, the institution owned copyright or the underlying work was in the public domain.[123] This approach was informed by a number of matters, including the scale and reach of distribution (including to countries that may not have equivalent exceptions to the United States) and concerns about relationship management. However, the fieldwork also revealed ways in which fair use was reported to be relevant to online uses, with many participating institutions having released content online under a fair use justification and others considering such a move. These behaviours therefore constituted an important qualification

---

[119] E.g., 7G, 11M, 14G, 16G, 23X, 26G, 31G, 41G, 46G, 48G, 49G, 50G, 51G.
[120] E.g., 33G, 48G.
[121] E.g., 7G, 16G, 23X, 54M. Interviewees 8M and 28G reported that fair use was relied upon for images that were used in lectures.
[122] E.g., 16G, 41G.
[123] E.g., 2L, 4L, 14G, 19L, 20G, 26G, 28G, 29L, 46G, 52M, 54M.

to the default position of permissions-based compliance, and demonstrated the relevance of fair use and risk management considerations.

To expand on the above, interviewees from more than half of the participating institutions reported that copies of collection items had been included on websites and online resources without obtaining permissions.[124] Indications suggested that the size of this group and the reach of these arguments might continue to grow, with interviewees noting ongoing review and revision of copyright management policies in this space.[125] Three matters about these practices should be clarified at the outset. First, these approaches did not represent a renunciation of licensing or a fair use free-for-all; as with other forms of public use, justifications based on fair use were limited to particular projects and classes of use.

Second, the uses described in this section often occurred when licensing was possible but institutions elected to instead adopt an exceptions-based approach. They did not, therefore, limit their fair use arguments to orphaned works. That said, market failure (in terms of impediments to licensing) played a role in the decision to rely on fair use. Clearing rights can be costly, protracted and resource intensive, meaning it may be logistically impossible for institutions to obtain licences for all uses, particularly for mass digitisation.[126] This led institutions to ask whether other approaches may be available, with some forming the view that, at least in some circumstances, they could justify online distribution under fair use. As one interviewee observed:

Granted, we do have works that are worth quite a lot, but ... we are a not-for-profit ... and we have a mission that is based on providing these works to the public, and as technology moves on, we see it, philosophically, as providing access as a research tool. [Websites like Flickr] have whetted the appetite of the public to say, 'what is involved in this museum, what is available?' And they come to expect to see a lot more online, in a way that fits our mission and fair use quite well.[127]

---

[124] E.g., 2L, 7G, 9M, 10L, 12L, 16G, 29L, 30G, 39L, 43M, 45M, 53G; also 1G (occasional use of thumbnail images under fair use). Reasoning supported by 6X, 23X, 47X.
[125] E.g., 9M, 16G, 26G, 33G, 35L.
[126] For discussion of market failure arguments, see, e.g., W. Landes and R. Posner, 'An Economic Analysis of Copyright Law' (1989) 18 *Journal of Legal Studies* 325; W. Gordon, 'Excuse and Justification in the Law of Fair Use: Commodification and Market Perspectives' in N. Elkin-Koren and N. Netanel, *The Commodification of Information* (The Hague: Kluwer Law International, 2002).
[127] 36M.

Third, although in other areas copyright analysis seemed largely intuitive or influenced by institutional norms, when it came to online uses, interviewees appeared to have thought deeply about how and when fair use might apply. This is not to say that normative considerations were absent, as interviewees often had strong views on the importance of institutions providing access to content.[128] However, the section 107 reasoning described in interviews often involved fairly sophisticated legal analysis: participants referred to the fairness factors and indicative purposes, used terms of art from copyright jurisprudence, and cited the most analogous case law.[129] The fact that low-resolution, small-scale images were a particularly common class of works being made available under fair use would seem to have been influenced, at least in part, by the subject matter of some key cases to which interviewees referred.[130] That said, institutions applied similar reasoning to other collection genre, showing that they were willing to reason from first principles.

Given its prominence in the fieldwork, it is useful to focus particular attention on the treatment of images of artistic works. All interviewees from institutions using fair use for public websites reported making available online, without permission, reproductions of things like photographs, fine art and ephemera, albeit often at reduced size or in thumbnail form. This was generally in the context of a collection database or research-oriented tool, and the purpose of the use was a key factor in decision-making – in fact, some interviewees described it as the most important consideration.[131] Outputs for which fair use was claimed were therefore said to: (1) act as reference aid to document the content of the collection; and/or (2) facilitate research and educational activities by users.[132] These discussions were clearly informed by fair use jurisprudence, with some interviewees expressly using the language of transformativeness to explain their practices.[133] Finally, they also classified their activities as non-commercial and not deriving any income, which was said to further a fair use approach.[134]

In addition to the nature and purpose of the use, another key consideration related to the size and resolution of images, with institutions often restricting fair use arguments to smaller images and clearing rights for

---

[128] E.g., 9M, 19L, 29L, 30G, 35L, 36M, 39L, 43M, 53G.
[129] E.g., 7G, 9M, 12L, 16G, 29L, 30G, 33G, 35L, 36M, 39L, 43M, 53G, 54M; also 3X, 6X, 23X, 47X.
[130] See *Kelly*, *Bill Graham Archives* and *Perfect 10*, discussed in Section II.B above.
[131] E.g., 16G, 30G; similar 3X.
[132] E.g., 2L, 3X, 7G, 9M, 10L, 16G, 29L, 30G, 36M, 53G, 54M. Also: 26G.
[133] E.g., 7G, 16G, 29L, 30G, 39L, 54M. [134] E.g., 2L, 7G, 9M, 10L, 16G, 29L, 53G.

high-resolution versions.[135] While it was necessary to copy the entire surface of the underlying work in order to create a visual reference, interviewees reported that they restricted the amount taken by using lower quality images. As explained by one interviewee:

> If we are trying to comply with a fair use exception, we need to consciously limit the ability of others to make a different use of it. If it's meant to be a scholarly or research tool, then people don't need to download [the image] or blow it up at all. ... Even in a research context, they're not using it to get a detailed look at the work itself; they're using it as a point of reference. You couldn't get the same point of reference by listing these works without a picture of them. You can justify the need to show an image of the work in that fair use context, but not a high-resolution, large-scale picture of the work.[136]

Another stated:

> In a way, it comes back to the balance that fair use tries to strike between the rights of the copyright holder and the rights of the public to a robust discussion about music, art, literature and all kinds of things. A low-resolution – regardless of size – reproduction of a work of art posted on a website in the context of an online exhibition, article or something scholarly, to me, in striking that balance, should weigh in favour of the public's right to have access to that.[137]

These quotes hint at a further consideration: the market effect of the institution's use. Interviewees who spoke to this factor argued that there is not and should not be any market for licensing thumbnails to cultural institutions, and/or that their use did not adversely impact on any market for the work.[138] Their reasoning – and indeed the fact that others did not explicitly address the fourth factor – was in many ways consistent with Beebe's interpretation of how judges understand this factor, namely as a metafactor which synthesises and tests the reasoning in the previous three factors.[139] In many instances, the analysis described by interviewees did not seem to generate new and independent considerations but to rest on normative conclusions regarding the scope of the copyright owner's market, this being tied to factors such as the nature of the institution's use. For instance, pointing to diversion of revenue was not considered enough to establish market harm as this could potentially be asserted for every use, meaning that without more it was not probative as a stand-alone factor.[140] As one interviewee explained:

---

[135] E.g., 3X, 7G, 12L, 16G, 30G, 35L, 36M, 53G.   [136] 16G.   [137] 43M.
[138] E.g., 3X, 7G, 10L, 16G, 29L, 53G; also 26G.   [139] Discussed in Section II.B above.
[140] E.g., 1G, 7G, 53G. Interviewee 53G stated 'other than museums who are paying [for all online uses of images], there is not a market impact to what we're doing'.

My sense ... is that [the fourth factor] has more to do with the overall larger market for a work, or the value of copyright in a work, and we don't think a museum that owns an original of a work, making some limited use of the fact that it has that work, is really something that can be replicated time and time again by others to undermine the value. If anything, we think we're enhancing value, because we're promoting the work and making it available. Perhaps a licensee will want to use the image, and they'll pay royalties for use of that image.[141]

The fairness factor that was least prominent in discussions about thumbnails was the second: the nature of the copyright work. Those who discussed this factor accepted that the works being copied were often creative but did not see that as insurmountable in fair use analysis.[142] Furthermore, a range of visual works were being digitised, and while some were pieces of fine art, others seemed to be significant for historical rather than aesthetic reasons. Finally, institutional practice in this space seemed to have a snowball effect, as interviewees commented that they were aware of and influenced by the interpretations of other cultural institutions.[143] Thus, their research included not just indications from traditional legal sources but those from others within the sector.

In addition to visual works, some interviewees reported applying fair use to other types of copyright subject matter, including print, sound and audiovisual items.[144] The fair use analysis described by interviewees was generally linked to a particular project or collection, or part of one of these, consistent with a case-by-case analysis. Nevertheless, many of the reported considerations dovetailed with those discussed above in relation to thumbnails. For instance, these projects were often seen as educationally driven and non-commercial. If an institution was concerned about the substantiality of copying, it might only make part of a work available. Similarly, if there were concerns that widespread access might be contrary to fair use, then gradations of access might be developed in which some content was only available onsite or to discrete online groups. Finally, the works being digitised often came from archival and social history collections in which the transaction costs of licensing were high, and poorly attributed and orphaned material common. Orphaned works are discussed further below.

Some of these themes are illustrated by a project in which an institution streamed short audio clips to authenticated users of its website.[145] The underlying works were sound recordings of musical performances, many of which were produced by local record labels in the first half of the

---

[141] 7G. [142] E.g., 7G, 29L, 30G. [143] E.g., 1G, 7G, 33G, 35L, 36M.
[144] E.g., 2L, 9M, 12L, 29L, 39L, 43M, 45M.
[145] This individual's pseudonym is not used, so as to maintain anonymity.

twentieth century. A solely clearance-based approach would have greatly restricted the public release of content for two main reasons: first, the nature of the recordings made it very difficult to assess their copyright status (given their age and the layers of rights);[146] and second, there were many recordings for which the composer and/or record label were not listed, or for which no current rights holder could be identified. Given that there was significant interest in the collection and many works were believed to be the sole surviving copy of these recordings, it was decided that fair use would be part of the copyright management strategy. There were still efforts to clear rights, but fair use was seen to facilitate some online public access even in the absence of permissions.

The preceding discussion has focused on instances in which fair use has been used to justify activities without permission. However, a number of interviewees also discussed using fair use as a bargaining tool in licensing and other negotiations.[147] For example, if an art museum required permission for a particular use – say, including a high-quality image in a book accompanying an exhibition – then it may be efficient to bundle other uses into the same licence, including some which may arguably fall under section 107. The museum could then point to fair use when negotiating the licence price. As one interviewee explained, this style of thinking approached copyright in a more business-like way, for instance by identifying reasonable compromises that can be made, or benefits given, to reach a commercial deal.[148] That said, other interviewees criticised this approach, both on philosophical grounds and because of the concern that licensing fair uses, even if on the basis that section 107 rights are reserved, had the potential to slowly erode the application of the doctrine.[149]

4 Orphaned Works Institutional comfort with fair use, even if only within conservative parameters, appeared to have also lessened the impact of orphaned works in the United States. For instance, it was

---

[146] Including the complex rules regarding protection of pre-1972 sound recordings: for a full analysis, see J. Besek, *Copyright and Related Issues Relevant to Digital Preservation and Dissemination of Unpublished Pre-1972 Sound Recordings by Libraries and Archives* (Council on Library and Information Resources and Library of Congress, March 2009).
[147] Especially 16G, 23X, 28G, 46G.   [148] 23X.
[149] Especially 35L, 53G. See also J. Gibson, 'Risk Aversion and Rights Accretion in Intellectual Property Law' (2007) 116 *Yale Law Journal* 882.

common for US participants to use orphaned works on institution websites[150] and other public outputs,[151] even amongst those who otherwise adopted a permissions-based approach to online use. Practices were often moderated, for instance by limiting the size and resolution of digital images, by releasing textual works and recordings in extract form or by restricting access to certain user groups. In determining the uses to be made of orphaned material, the nature of the use was significant, with reports that institutions were willing to use such works in what they saw as non-commercial and educational contexts, but much less so for profit-making enterprises.[152] One interviewee observed:

> I'm pretty bullish on orphan works, though ... as long as we're providing as much information as we have about the work, in connection with the picture – so whatever kind of metadata we have. What was it called, when was it taken, do we know who the creator was. You don't have to provide everything, but if you couple an image with metadata, and you're claiming it's an orphan work, I think you have a very strong case. At least, a case I'm willing to consider.[153]

When asked to explain their decision-making in relation to orphaned works, the interviews disclosed two parallel but overlapping streams of reasoning. Some interviewees reported that they justified using orphaned works under fair use.[154] Much of this reasoning echoed the interpretations of fair use described throughout this chapter, but with greater emphasis on the nature of the work and circumstances of creation, and the resulting diminution in likelihood of any adverse market effect.

In addition, many institutions seemed to engage in a free-standing assessment of risk in which they decided to proceed with a use despite the possibility that it might be infringing:[155] what was termed 'pure' risk management in Chapter 3. The reasoning here revolved around the prediction that the likelihood of receiving complaints would be low and the likelihood of resolving any disputes high. An institution might therefore reason that its internal procedures to declare a work orphaned made it unlikely that there was any active copyright holder. Even if such a person did appear, if the institution had appropriately limited its uses, it could be confident that any complaint could be resolved without any significant consequences. Interviewees also reported keeping a paper trail of licensing attempts, and making efforts to demonstrate their good faith

---

[150] E.g., 1G, 4L, 7G, 9M, 10L, 13M, 16G, 19L, 26G, 28G, 29L, 30G, 35L, 43M, 45M, 53G.
[151] Especially in catalogues and publications: e.g., 1G, 16G, 20G, 26G, 28G, 41G, 49G, 50G, 53G.
[152] E.g., 1G, 7G, 26G, 37M, 43M, 53G.   [153] 1G.
[154] E.g., 1G, 9M, 10L, 16G, 23X, 29L, 35L, 39L, 45M, 54M.
[155] E.g., 1G, 2L, 4L, 7G, 16G, 23X, 28G, 29L, 30G, 33G, 45M, 54M.

in relation to copyright compliance, for instance through copyright warnings and take-down notices.

The preceding analysis should not be taken as suggesting that orphaned works were not a problem for US institutions.[156] Rather, it is included to demonstrate that fair use had an impact on US practices in a number of ways. First, an institution might apply fair use reasoning across a group of items (for instance by making images available in an exhibition), including orphaned and non-orphaned material. Second, fair use might be used specifically for orphaned items, with the lack of a readily identifiable copyright owner relevant to fair use reasoning. Finally, given that there were significant overlaps in the reasoning that sits behind fair use and pure risk management, it is possible that an institution challenged about its use of orphaned works might point to fair use as a defence.

The limitations in fair use analysis must also be emphasised: the doctrine only permits so much activity, may not cover the re-use of material by other users, and may not produce a satisfactory answer for institutions with large numbers of orphaned works or a greater aversion to risk. While it may be easy for an institution to remove online content or pay a retrospective licensing fee for an image in a scholarly journal, such options may not be readily available for other projects. However, the fact that US interviewees regularly reported that they were willing to make public uses of orphaned works may suggest that this dual fair use and risk management strategy has been fairly successful and may provide useful lessons for other countries.

IV   Later Developments

The fieldwork described Section III occurred in 2008 and 2009. Since that time, a number of follow-up interviews have been conducted with US interviewees, plus there has been monitoring of legislative and judicial developments. As noted earlier, post-fieldwork developments do not suggest any major unwinding of trends observed in the interview data, and certain developments have fortified arguments about the relevance of fair use to institutional activity. For instance, one interviewee participating in a follow-up interview said:

---

[156] For instance, a number of interviewees reported that orphaned works were a significant challenge for copyright management practices: e.g., 3X (a 'very significant issue' for the sector), 7G (a 'big problem'), 17G, 19L (a 'big deal'), 23X, 35L, 36M ('one of my biggest concerns'), 45M. See also United States Copyright Office, *Orphan Works and Mass Digitization: A Report of the Register of Copyrights* (United States Copyright Office, June 2015).

There has been continued growing interest in applying fair use in the US. ... If anything, I think people are doing more. And we're more open to the idea of putting up a collection and having a transformative purpose. ... The language of *Bill Graham Archives* has been very influential ... with the argument being that this is to illustrate history and a timeline, and this is not the same reason as why the poster was created, which was to advertise a concert. We're still nervous about the rights of first publication of an unpublished work, or reproducing an entire visual work not at lower resolution. We're pushing it further, but we're still not sure how far it can push.[157]

This section discusses two cases that were described as 'tremendously important' by this interviewee: *HathiTrust* in relation to library digitisation practices, and *Georgia State* in relation to electronic reserves and virtual learning environments (VLEs). As with all the material in this book, the analysis here is not intended to suggest a fixed trend in fair use practices or that some arguments are now immutable, but to give a sense of the way arguments have played out. Indeed, at the time of writing, the *Georgia State* litigation is yet to come to a conclusion, and could still have a significant impact on how fair use is relied on by academic libraries.

A   HathiTrust

The *HathiTrust* litigation pertained to a project to make available the digitised collections of a number of universities, this being undertaken through a venture known as the HathiTrust Digital Library ('HDL').[158] Content in the HDL has been created mostly by virtue of the Google Books project, pursuant to which universities had allowed Google access to books in their collections, and Google, having digitised those volumes, retained a digital copy of each book and also provided a copy to the university.[159] Content in the HDL was used in a various ways.[160] For instance, technical functionality permitted full-text searching across all books in the HDL, with the results for unlicensed copyright works referring only to the page number on which the term was found and

---

[157] 29L.   [158] For information, see www.hathitrust.org.
[159] This project has also been the subject of litigation, including in relation to the creation and use of Google's own copies: *Authors Guild, Inc* v. *Google Inc*, 954 F Supp 2d 282 (SDNY, 2013), 804 F 3d 202 (2nd circuit, 2015). For discussion of the fate of the Google Books project, see J. Somers, 'Torching the Modern-Day Library of Alexandria', *The Atlantic* (20 April 2017), www.theatlantic.com/technology/archive/2017/04/the-tragedy-of-google-books/523320/.
[160] Described in *HathiTrust Appeal*, n. 3 above, 91–92. The litigation also touched on an Orphan Works Project headed by the University of Michigan, however it was held at trial and on appeal that claims in relation to this project were 'not ripe for adjudication', the project having been indefinitely suspended by the University after proceedings were launched (but before any content was hosted online).

the number of occurrences. Second, users with certified print disabilities were able to access all digitised books in full, these texts being able to be listened to or viewed via adaptive technologies. Finally, the HDL was said to have a preservation function, as it was planned that digitised books could be accessed by participating universities to generate replacement copies if their own copy was lost, destroyed or stolen and they could not obtain a replacement at a fair price.

A group of authors and authors associations claimed that these activities infringed copyright. At first instance, Judge Parker concluded that each of the three uses above fell within fair use.[161] On appeal to the Court of Appeals for the Second Circuit, this decision was vacated and remanded in relation to preservation copying on the basis that the trial judge had not considered whether the plaintiffs had standing to sue, the claims being speculative. On the other two uses, the Court agreed that fair use was applicable.

For the full-text searchable database of books, a key matter contributing to the success of the section 107 arguments was that the use was 'quintessentially transformative',[162] being of an entirely different purpose to the constituent books. This conclusion was bolstered by a comparison with other cases, including *Kelly*, *Bill Graham Archives* and *Perfect 10*,[163] on the basis that full-text search added 'a great deal more to the copyright works at issue than did the transformative uses' in those cases.[164] It was not fatal that entire books were copied; on the contrary, this was essential for *full-text* searching; and the storage of copies on a number of different servers was reasonably necessary to ensure ongoing public access and as a back-up in the event of data loss. On market effect, the Court said that this factor 'is concerned with only one type of economic injury to a copyright holder: the harm that results because the secondary use serves as a substitute for the original work'.[165] Because the Court considered that transformative uses 'by definition' did not substitute for original works, any 'harm' they caused did not count for the purpose of the fourth factor.[166] The plaintiffs sought to identify other harms, including the risk of widespread distribution of digitised books following a data breach. However, with the defendants showing evidence of extensive security measures, these arguments were not accepted, and the fair use arguments of the defendants prevailed.[167]

---

[161] *HathiTrust District Court*, n. 3 above. [162] *HathiTrust Appeal*, n. 3 above 97.
[163] Discussed in Section II.B above. [164] *HathiTrust Appeal*, n. 3 above 97.
[165] Ibid., 99. [166] Ibid.
[167] The Court dealt briefly with the second factor as the creative nature of the copied works was not dispositive in cases involving transformative use: ibid., 98.

The creation of versions for print-disabled users was also held to be within fair use, but for different reasons to the searchable database. In particular, the provision of accessible copies was held *not* to be transformative as it replicated the purpose of the original authors, albeit to a wider audience.[168] However, the first factor still favoured fair use because of legislative and judicial cues regarding the need to make accommodations for print-disabled users. In relation to the third factor, it was agreed that it was reasonable for the libraries to retain text and image versions of the digitised books, given variation in the needs of print-disabled users. Finally, the fourth factor was said to weigh in favour of fair use because of the small size of the market for accessible books.

The *HathiTrust* decision was significant because it 'was another clear voice'[169] that many online research tools are transformative and likely to fall within fair use. In addition, it is notable that, in relation to disabled users, the case turned not on transformativeness but that copyright law must make accommodations for such users. This is significant, as a focus on transformative use might devalue the speech and other benefits of 'pure' copying,[170] and may (wrongly) suggest that such uses do not fall within fair use.

B Georgia State

The *Georgia State* litigation related to the posting of book extracts on electronic reserves and VLEs by library staff and members of faculty at Georgia State University. Before analysing the litigation itself, this section describes the reserve collection in library practice, the historical relevance of fair use to the creation of such collections, and indications from the empirical work in 2007–2009.

The term 'reserve collection' traditionally referred to a set of high-demand volumes from the general collection with no or only short-term borrowing rights.[171] The need for a reserve arose as libraries developed more extensive circulating collections, it being necessary to maximise the availability of popular reference works and those set as prescribed readings. With the development of reprography equipment, reserves also started to include institution-made photocopies of individual chapters and articles.[172] Digital technologies gave rise to further possibilities, with

---

[168] Ibid., 101.   [169] 29L.   [170] A point made by Tushnet, n. 51 above.
[171] See, e.g., L. Gasaway, 'Library Reserve Collections: From Paper to Electronic Collections' in L. Gasaway (ed), *Growing Pains: Adapting Copyright for Libraries, Education, and Society* (Littleton: Fred B Rothman & Co, 1997), pp. 127–129.
[172] Ibid., pp. 129–130.

libraries attracted to electronic reserves as a way to enhance the access-related benefits of reserves but to remove some of limitations and logistical challenges of analogue collections.[173] In the university setting, it is also common for readings and other course materials to be hosted on VLEs such as Blackboard and Moodle.

The inclusion of copy material in reserve collections and VLEs raises copyright issues, including whether such copies can be made available under exceptions.[174] In his ground-breaking study of fair use and universities in the early 1990s, Kenneth Crews noted the absence of express indications about this question in the legislative history of the US Copyright Act, and asked whether copying for analogue reserves might fall within section 107 and how fair use reasoning might be applied.[175] To help understand practices in the sector, Crews examined the reserves policies of some eighty universities. On the number of copies that could be made under fair use, the cohort divided approximately into thirds, with twenty-eight limiting this to single copies, twenty-two allowing multiple copies but under relatively narrow parameters modelled on the Congress-approved Classroom Guidelines for multiple copying by teachers, and thirty adopting a more lenient approach, often based on guidelines produced by the American Library Association.[176] Given that some two-thirds of his sample leant towards more restrictive interpretations of fair use, Crews concluded that librarians tended 'to implement the strictest legal interpretations, despite the potential constraints on library service, and despite their professed concerns about the law's inhibiting force'.[177]

Although on one view Crews's empirical observations suggested that institutions were not fully embracing fair use arguments, it is noteworthy that his data revealed widespread acceptance of fair use, i.e., that librarians had rejected an even stricter interpretation of the statute that would have foregone *any* reliance on section 107 in favour of obtaining

---

[173] Ibid., pp. 141–142; see also S. Melamut, 'Pursuing Fair Use, Law Libraries, and Electronic Reserves' (2000) 92 *Law Library Journal* 157, 158–162.
[174] K. Crews, *Copyright, Fair Use, and the Challenge for Universities: Promoting the Progress of Higher Education* (Chicago: University of Chicago Press, 1993), pp. 83–92.
[175] Ibid., pp. 84–85.
[176] Ibid., p. 89. The policies were the Classroom Guidelines, HR Rep No 94-1467, 94th Congress, 2nd Session (1976) and the American Library Association, *Model Policy Concerning College and University Photocopying for Classroom, Research and Library Reserve Use* (1982). See Crews at pp. 85–86; see also Gasaway, above n. 171, pp. 134–140.
[177] Ibid., p. 89. For similar concerns regarding the conservatism of librarians in relation to reserves and their attraction to rule-like guidance, see C. Loring, 'Library Reserves and Copyright: Thirty Years on and Still Changing' (1997) 21 *Library Acquisitions: Practice & Theory* 29.

196 Functional Fair Use

permissions in all cases. One might also observe that this state of affairs arose despite rejection of fair use in cases such as *Marcus* v. *Rowley*[178] and the *Kinko's* litigation.[179]

Fast-forwarding to the fieldwork in 2008 and 2009, although there had been disagreements about the parameters of such arguments,[180] it seemed that US institutions had transplanted fair use reasoning to electronic reserves.[181] For instance, at all four academic libraries that participated in that fieldwork, the electronic reserves policy included a fair use analysis.[182] Examination of a further thirty publicly available copyright policies from academic libraries[183] likewise revealed that twenty-six stated explicitly that materials could be scanned and made available in electronic reserves by virtue of fair use,[184] while another two had general statements about fair use and library activities.[185] Only two did not mention fair use, although it is possible that internal documents referred to such arguments.[186] Use of section 107 for electronic reserves was also

---

[178] 695 F 2d 1171 (9th circuit, 1983) (fair use held not to apply to the defendant's twenty-four-page learning guide on cake decorating, this work copying eleven pages of the plaintiff's booklet on the same topic).

[179] *Basic Books* v. *Kinko's*, n. 66 above. For a similar conclusion that post-dated Crews's study, see *Princeton University Press* v. *Michigan Document Services*, n. 62 above.

[180] See especially the failed attempts to negotiate electronic reserves guidelines at the Conference on Fair Use (CONFU), which was attended by representatives of user and owner stakeholders: K. Crews, 'Electronic Reserves and Fair Use: The Outer Limits of CONFU' (1999) 50(14) *Journal of the American Society for Information Science* 1342.

[181] For a 2003 study on the approach of libraries to reserves, see T. Gould, T. Lipinski and E. Buchanan, 'Copyright Policies and the Deciphering of Fair Use in the Creation of Reserves at University Libraries' (2005) 31 *Journal of Academic Librarianship* 182.

[182] 2L, 10L, 19L, 29L; also 44X.

[183] This analysis was performed via internet search of publicly available websites on 30 November 2010. In order to help maintain the anonymity of the participants in the fieldwork, libraries were selected on the basis that they were not located in the same state as participating institutions. Institutions whose websites did not disclose any copyright information for electronic or course reserves were not included in this analysis. Copies of the relevant policies are on file with the author.

[184] These were libraries the following universities and colleges: Brown University, RI; Dartmouth College, NH; Duke University, NC; Emory University, GA; Georgia Institute of Technology, GA; Indiana University, IN; Marquette University, WI; Rutgers University, NJ; University of Alaska Fairbanks, AK; University of Delaware, DE; University of Denver, CO; University of Florida, FL; University of Georgia, GA; University of Idaho, ID; University of Kansas, KS; University of Miami, FL; University of Minnesota, MN; University of North Carolina, NC; University of Oklahoma, OK; University of Oregon, OR; University of Pennsylvania, PA; University of Richmond, VA; University of Texas, TX; University of Utah, UT; University of Washington, WA; and University of Wisconsin-Madison, WI.

[185] These were: Princeton University, NJ; University of Iowa, IA.

[186] These were: University of Rhode Island, RI; Vanderbilt University, TN.

Later Developments 197

contemplated in leading library law texts by Carrie Russell,[187] Crews,[188] and Minow and Lipinski.[189]

Turning now to the *Georgia State* litigation,[190] these proceedings were instituted in 2008 by three academic publishers: Cambridge University Press, Oxford University Press and Sage Publications.[191] The plaintiffs' case was built around instances where extracts from their publications had been posted to ERES, the University's electronic reserves, and to its VLE.[192] The plaintiffs eventually pressed seventy-four acts of alleged infringement in relation to sixty-four books.[193] These excerpts had been selected by members of faculty, with the act of uploading undertaken either by library staff or faculty. The extracts came from monographs, edited collections and the like. On average they comprised 10.1 per cent of the pages in each book. In most cases, the extract comprised up to one chapter, but in fifteen cases more than one chapter was copied.[194]

The defendants were not the professors or librarians who selected or posted the extracts but various Georgia State officials: the President, Dean of Libraries, members of the Board of Regents, etc. The essence of the plaintiffs' case was that the defendants had infringed copyright by 'maintaining a policy which allows GSU professors to make digital copies of excerpts of Plaintiffs' books available to students without paying Plaintiffs'.[195] The policy that was the focus of the case came into effect in 2009 and revised earlier guidance in relation to electronic readings, including by making it explicit that professors were responsible for any fair use assessment and that this assessment was to be undertaken by reference to a fair use checklist.[196] This revised policy was said by the trial judge to have 'significantly reduced the unlicensed copying of Plaintiffs' works (and, by inference, the works of other publishers) at Georgia State'.[197]

Although the policy was central to the plaintiffs' complaint, Judge Evans's opinion was structured around a case-by-case examination of

---

[187] C. Russell, *Complete Copyright: An Everyday Guide for Librarians* (Chicago: American Library Association, 2004), pp. 77–84.
[188] Crews, n. 15 above, pp. 62–63.   [189] Minow and Lipinski, n. 68 above, p. 48.
[190] The proceeding analysis draws from arguments presented in Hudson, n. 60 above.
[191] It appears that the Copyright Clearance Center and the Association of American Publishers were the moving spirits behind this litigation, and at least at the time of the first trial were each paying half of the plaintiffs' litigation expenses: *GS District Court I*, n. 4 above, 1213.
[192] Ibid., 1220–1221.
[193] Ibid., 1201–1205, 1218–1219. Judge Evans referred at 1204 to 75 acts of alleged infringement, but her case-by-case analysis pertained to only 74 instances.
[194] Ibid., 1218–1219.   [195] *GS Appeal I*, n. 4 above, 1237.
[196] For discussion of the drafting of the earlier policy, see Butler, n. 50 above, 509–510.
[197] *GS District Court I*, n. 4 above, 1219.

198   Functional Fair Use

each alleged act of infringement. In twenty-six instances she held that there was no case,[198] a conclusion not challenged on appeal. For the forty-eight extracts where a prima facie case was established, she held that forty-three were within fair use and therefore non-infringing. In reaching this conclusion, Judge Evans adopted an approach that is typical of US judges, in which each of the fairness factors is analysed one by one.[199] She held that for all forty-eight extracts the first factor strongly favoured the defendants as the copies were made by a non-profit educational institution for the purposes of teaching and scholarship.[200] The second factor was also held to point universally towards fair use, on the grounds that the works were informational.[201]

The application of the third factor required individualised assessment because of the variation in the quantity of material copied. Judge Evans's overarching observation was that '[t]he fact that the excerpts were mirror-image copies favors market substitution (thus leaning against fair use), but this tendency is reduced when the excerpt is small'.[202] She applied a benchmark to assist her analysis: for books not divided into chapters or with fewer than ten chapters, factor three favoured fair use where no more than 10 per cent of the pages were copied; for books with ten or more chapters, this amount was a single chapter.[203] In undertaking her factor three analysis, Judge Evans rejected the plaintiffs' submission that she should apply the quantitative limits in the Classroom Guidelines of 1976, noting that these were an industry-negotiated, narrow safe harbour rather than an accepted statement of the maximum parameters of fair use.[204]

---

[198] There were a number of different reasons for reaching this conclusion. For instance, a number of extracts uploaded to the electronic reserves were not on the syllabus and did not appear to have been accessed by any students. In those cases, Judge Evans held that any use that arose was *de minimis* and did not give rise to an infringement. Another reason related to standing to sue, e.g., where the plaintiffs failed to show an assignment of rights from the author that enabled an infringement action to be brought. The plaintiffs did not seek to challenge this aspect of the case in their appeal to the Court of Appeals.

[199] As observed by, e.g., Beebe, n. 11 above.

[200] *GS District Court I*, n. 4 above, 1224–1225.   [201] Ibid., 1225–1227.

[202] Ibid., 1227.

[203] Ibid., 1232–1235, 1243. In calculating these figures, Judge Evans cited the course packs cases (*Basic Books* v. *Kinko's*, n. 66 above, and *Princeton University Press* v. *Michigan Document Services*, n. 62 above) which suggested that copying 5 per cent of a work would tend against fair use. However, she also observed that a more liberal approach was appropriate in the present case because it involved nonprofit educational copying by a nonprofit educational institution.

[204] Ibid., 1227–1229. The Classroom Guidelines, n. 176 above, were negotiated by representatives of publishers and educators, and stated that certain educational uses would be fair if they met certain requirements. This included quantitative limits, for

On the fourth factor, Judge Evans held that the key question was whether there was market substitution, and that in this case it was appropriate to look to the market for licensing copies.[205] The defendants had sought to argue that such activity was irrelevant, but this was rejected by Judge Evans on the basis that permission fees contribute to the value of the work – a matter squarely within factor four.[206] That said, Judge Evans required the plaintiffs to show that in 2009 (when the allegedly infringing acts took place) there was available 'reasonably efficient, reasonably priced, convenient access to the particular excerpts which are in question in this case'.[207] The valence of factor four depended on whether such digital permissions were available. If not, this factor weighed in favour of the defendants. But if they were, it favoured the plaintiffs, and 'heavily' so, on the basis that the court was required to consider not just the copying at Georgia State (for which any damage would be 'extremely small') but what would happen if this conduct was widespread.[208] If the initial assessment of four factors was closely balanced, Judge Evans undertook further analysis to determine whether the fair use defence was made out.[209]

Applying this reasoning to the forty-eight instances where a prima facie case had been made out, liability was established in five instances and the remaining forty-three were held to fall within fair use. For those five cases, Judge Evans accepted that the 2009 copyright policy caused the infringements, as

---

instance that the copy may only be of 'a complete article, story or essay of less than 2,500 words' or 'an excerpt from any prose work of not more than 1,000 words or 10% of the work, whichever is less'.

[205] Ibid., 1236–1237, citing *American Geophysical* v. *Texaco*, n. 15 above.
[206] Ibid., 1237.
[207] Ibid. The plaintiffs argued that such licences were available from the Copyright Clearance Center (CCC), so much of the evidence on this point related to CCC's activities.
[208] Ibid., 1239, citing *Campbell* v. *Acuff-Rose*, n. 19 above, 590.
[209] To illustrate, in relation to the copying of two chapters (or 12.5 per cent) from C. Wright Mills, *The Power Elite*, new edition (Oxford University Press, 2000), Judge Evans held that factor one strongly favoured the defendants, factor two favoured the defendants, factor three favoured the plaintiffs and factor four strongly favoured the plaintiffs (as digital permissions were available). But on examining the situation further, she concluded that the third factor weighed even more heavily for the plaintiffs as these two chapters were the 'heart' of the original work: ibid. 1358–1359. In another example, where the factors were closely balanced for the copying of two chapters (or 8.28 per cent) from M. Patton, *Utilization-Focused Evaluation*, 3rd edition (Sage, 1996), Judge Evans's further analysis of sales data and permission fees was said to demonstrate that permissions were an important part of the value of the copyright in that title, thus strengthening the degree to which the fourth factor favoured the plaintiffs: ibid., 1362–1363.

the policy did not limit copying in those instances to decidedly small excerpts ... Nor did it proscribe the use of multiple chapters from the same book. Also, the fair use policy did not provide sufficient guidance in determining the 'actual or potential effect on the market or the value of the copyrighted work,' a task which would likely be futile for prospective determinations (in advance of litigation). The only practical way to deal with factor four in advance likely is to assume that it strongly favors the plaintiff-publisher (if licensed digital excerpts are available).[210]

That said, the sense that the University was, nevertheless, the ultimate winner was bolstered by the award of attorneys' fees and costs in their favour, on the basis that the plaintiffs prevailed in only five of the ninety-nine claims they identified at the start of trial.

The plaintiffs appealed on a number of grounds, including that Judge Evans had wrongly applied the fairness factors and had utilised reasoning that failed to appreciate the scale of infringement brought about by the 2009 policy. The Court of Appeals for the Eleventh Circuit identified a number of issues with Judge Evans's analysis, although much of the reasoning was affirmed. For instance, the appellate court agreed with the case-by-case assessment of individual infringements, stating that if the analysis instead pertained to copying generally, 'the District Court would have no principled method of determining whether a nebulous cloud of infringements purportedly caused by GSU's "ongoing practices" should be excused by the defense of fair use'.[211] In contrast, the Court of Appeals disapproved of what it described as the District Court's 'arithmetic' approach to fairness.[212] It stated that Judge Evans should have 'undertaken a holistic analysis' and given the fourth factor 'more significant weight in the overall fair use analysis'.[213] Finally, some discrete aspects of Judge Evans's decision-making were criticised, such as her use of a 10 per cent or one chapter benchmark when analysing the third factor.[214] The case was remanded back to the District Court for further consideration.

---

[210] Ibid., 1363.   [211] *GS Appeal I*, n. 4 above, 1259.   [212] Ibid., 1260.
[213] Ibid., 1283.
[214] Ibid., 1271–1272. The Eleventh Circuit's complaint was that this was contrary to the case-by-case analysis demanded by fair use, which meant that 'hard evidentiary presumptions' are inapt: at 1272, citing *Campbell* v. *Acuff-Rose*, n. 19 above. In reaching this conclusion, the Court rejected the defendants' argument that Judge Evans's benchmark was a mere starting point, stating that in practice it was decisive of the valence of the third factor, and that even if it were truly a starting point, it was inappropriate to use the same benchmark across all acts of infringement. For a criticism of this conclusion as being unduly resistant to the 'rulification' of fair use, see Elkin-Koren and Fischman-Afori, n. 7 above. The defendants also sought to buttress a 10 per cent or one-chapter benchmark by reference to best practice guidelines released by the CCC, which suggested that extracts on electronic reserves be limited to 'small excerpts',

With the appeal successful but much of the District Court's reasoning affirmed, the question arose as to whether the Court of Appeals' decision was a win for the plaintiffs. For instance, one interviewee reported that although the result initially seemed bad, the judgment was in many respects a victory to Georgia State as the heart of the District Court decision had been upheld.[215] That said, this interviewee also observed that the emphasis by the Court of Appeals on a non-mechanical, case-by-case fair use analysis might be difficult for universities to implement in practice. A similar criticism was made by Brandon Butler, who described the Court of Appeals' opinion as 'a half-measure in the right direction' that 'marks the end of the Guideline-coursepack paradigm' but without 'offer[ing] a useful substitute'.[216]

The course of the litigation took an interesting turn with the remanded District Court opinion. The genesis seems to have been a statement of the Court of Appeals that may have been intended as a trite observation in relation to fair use. Having noted the utilitarian understanding of copyright that characterises US law,[217] and the need to ensure that copyright does not overreach (including through limiting doctrines such as fair use), the Court of Appeals said that

> the proper scope of the fair use doctrine in a given case boils down to an evidentiary question. As a conceptual matter, in making fair use determinations, we must conjure up a hypothetical perfect market for the work in question, consisting of the whole universe of those who might buy it, in which everyone involved has perfect knowledge of the value of the work to its author and to potential buyers, and excluding for the moment any potential fair uses of the

---

being a single article or chapter. But at first instance and on appeal, the judges seemed concerned not to substitute industry practices or guidelines for their own assessment of the third factor: at 1272; and also *GS District Court I*, n. 4 above, 1232 (rejecting evidence regarding fair use policies at other universities). In addition to concerns about the third factor analysis, the Court of Appeals were concerned that: (1) there were some instances where the second factor ought to have been viewed as neutral or tending against fair use; and (2) the District Court applied two 'non-statutory' considerations that should have been considered under the analysis of the first and fourth factors.

[215] 219L.

[216] Butler, n. 50 above, 479. See also 477 in relation to the call for a more flexible application of fair use: '[w]hat this application will look like is anyone's guess'.

[217] For instance, the Intellectual Property Clause of the US Constitution gives Congress the power '[t]o promote the Progress of Science and useful Arts, by securing for limited Times to Authors and Inventors the exclusive Right to their respective Writings and Discoveries': Art. I, s. 8, cl. 8. This has been read as capturing a consequentialist justification for intellectual property rights, although it has also been argued that some developments in US law have (inappropriately) tended towards more maximalist protection: see M. Lemley, 'Property, Intellectual Property, and Free Riding' (2005) 83 *Texas Law Review* 1031.

work. Then, keeping in mind the purposes animating copyright law – the fostering of learning and the creation of new works – we must determine how much of that value [fair users] can capture before the value of the remaining market is so diminished that it no longer makes economic sense for the author – or a subsequent holder of the copyright – to propagate the work in the first place.[218]

This analysis captures an economic understanding of free riding. Such an understanding emphasises that the problem with free riding is not the mere existence of uncompensated positive externalities, as such externalities are ubiquitous in a competitive market and do not, without more, warrant legal intervention.[219] Rather, as an economic concept, free riding is problematic when it destroys the incentives to invest in the relevant product or activity.[220] But if we take seriously the idea that fair use 'boils down to an evidentiary question',[221] it may seem logical to conclude that our analysis should demonstrate, as an empirical matter, that the plaintiff was incentivised by copyright's bounty, and that the actions of free riders changed (or would change) his or her calculus of whether to dedicate resources to that endeavour.

On remand in *Georgia State*, Judge Evans adjusted her fair use analysis in response to the Court of Appeals' decision, including by placing factor three at the 'vortex'[222] of the holistic analysis (i.e., that assessment of that factor took into account the analysis of purpose and market substitution in factors one and four), and through a revised methodology for the

---

[218] *GS Appeal I*, n. 4 above, 1258.
[219] For further discussion, see Lemley, n. 217 above, 1037–1050; D. Gangjee and R. Burrell, 'Because You're Worth It: *L'Oréal* and the Prohibition on Free Riding' (2010) 73 *Modern Law Review* 282, 288–292.
[220] For an illustration, consider *National Basketball Association* v. *Motorola, Inc*, 105 F 3d 841 (2nd circuit, 1997). In that case, the NBA complained about a service in which real-time information about NBA basketball games was communicated through the defendants' SportsTrax pager. This information was generated by reporters watching matches on television or listening to them on the radio. In rejecting the argument that this service fell afoul of a limited, 'hot news' misappropriation doctrine in US law, the Court of Appeals for the Second Circuit held that an action would succeed only where there was, *inter alia*, free riding on the plaintiff's efforts, direct competition with a product or service offered by the plaintiff, and that such free riding 'would so reduce the incentive to produce the product or service that its existence or quality would be substantially threatened': at 845, repeated 852. However, the NBA 'failed to show any competitive effect whatsoever from SportsTrax on its main business (running NBA leagues and selling broadcasting rights). To the extent there might be a market for real-time transmission of factual information, there was no free ride, as those running the SportsTrax service generated their own data and bore the costs of that process. Nor was the Court willing to engage in a hypothetical in which some future, enhanced information service of the NBA was used to populate the fields on the SportsTrax pager.
[221] *GS Appeal I*, n. 4 above, 1258.   [222] *GS District Court II*, n. 4 above, 7.

fourth factor. Judge Evans held that if digital permissions were available in 2009, that factor 'initially' favoured the plaintiffs.[223] However, she drew from the Court of Appeals' decision the proposition that the defendants could change this conclusion through evidence regarding the market for, and value of, the copyright work. Judge Evans seemed to countenance a number of possibilities, for instance that this evidence might show that demand for a work was extremely low, or that 'the portion of the market captured by unpaid use is so slight that it would have had no effect on the author's or the Plaintiffs' decision to propagate the work in the first place'.[224] Her analysis therefore sought to operationalise the Court of Appeals' emphasis on fair use as an 'evidentiary question'.[225] If such a description had been intended as uncontroversial backgrounding, then *Georgia State* demonstrates the perils of ill-considered rhetorical flourishes.

Applying this revised approach, of the forty-eight instances of alleged infringement, the plaintiffs prevailed in seven instances. With so many of the extracts being held to be within fair use, Georgia State was again seen as the winning party, not only by the judge in her award of costs but amongst the parties and those commenting on the case.[226] Nonetheless, some of the commentary raised concerns about whether such a fact-intensive approach could be performed by libraries and educational institutions. For instance, Kevin Smith stated that whilst the ruling was a 'disaster for the plaintiff publishers' as it showed the 'significant space for fair use in higher education', it was also 'a difficult victory for libraries, in the sense that the analysis it uses is not one we can replicate; we simply do not have access to the extensive data about revenue, of which Judge Evans makes such complex use'.[227] That is, Judge Evans's fourth-factor analysis made extensive use of data in relation to book and permission sales, much of it not publicly accessible. Whether it was realistic

---

[223] Ibid. The plaintiffs sought to introduce evidence showing that seventeen excerpts from Cambridge and Oxford titles could have been licensed from CCC in 2009. In sixteen cases this departed from the trial evidence (where no such availability was demonstrated), and for various reasons this evidence was not allowed: at 8–9.

[224] Ibid., 7.   [225] *GS Appeal I*, n. 4 above, 1258.

[226] E.g., A. Albanese, 'GSU Prevails (Again) in Key Copyright Case', *Publishers Weekly* (1 April 2016), www.publishersweekly.com/pw/by-topic/digital/copyright/article/69830-gsu-prevails-again-in-key-copyright-case.html; K. Courtney, 'GSU e-Reserves Decision | Peer to Peer Review', *Library Journal* (12 May 2016), https://lj.libraryjournal.com/2016/05/opinion/peer-to-peer-review/gsu-e-reserves-decision-peer-to-peer-review/.

[227] K. Smith, 'Here we go again: latest GSU ruling an odd victory for libraries' (1 April 2016), https://blogs.library.duke.edu/scholcomm/2016/04/01/fgo-latest-gsuruling-odd-victory-libraries/; see also B. Butler, 'My GSU Hot Take' (1 April 2016), http://brandonbutler.info/post/142052963020/my-gsu-hot-take.

or even possible for a librarian to undertake a similar assessment was open to question.

The take-home messages pressed by pro-library commentators following the remanded District Court opinion were therefore at a higher level of generality: that the case confirmed the relevance of fair use to electronic reserves; that a mere reduction in licensing revenue was not enough to demonstrate market harm under the fourth factor; and that it was important that universities continue with fair use arguments, given the degree to which evidence of actual market behaviour drove analysis of non-transformative uses. For instance, Kyle Courtney recommended that

> we stay the fair use course. If anything, this decision has led me to conclude that *licensing is for the birds*. How can I say this? Well, in the analysis, the greater the chapter licensing revenue was for the publisher, the lesser the scope for fair use. So, by analogy, the less we license, the more room for fair use. Therefore, let's continue to make the best fair use decisions possible instead of licensing: let's make our e-reserves more fair use-friendly, and focus on fair use and other alternatives to licensing fees. The moment we start paying licenses, we will actually be hurting our own cause.[228]

However, the revised approach of the District Court was rejected in a second decision of the Court of Appeals. Following a further appeal by the plaintiffs, it was held in October 2018 that the District Court had erred in the way it had implemented the first appeal judgment.[229] One problem related to the overarching analytical techniques. If the first decision of the Court of Appeals cautions us against rhetorical flourishes, the second opinion of the District Court warns us against cheeky asides. Having discussed guidance from the Court of Appeals regarding the different fair use factors, and bearing in mind the concern regarding the arithmetic approach said to bedevil the first opinion, Judge Evans inserted an entirely unnecessary statement, estimating 'the initial, approximate respective weights of the four factors as … 25% for factor one, 5% for factor two, 30% for factor three, and 40% for factor four'.[230] This may have eased the way for the Court of Appeals to conclude that the District Court had 'failed to break free' of its earlier mathematical approach.[231]

More significantly, the Court of Appeals sought to recast its comments regarding economic harm and incentives, which it described as 'merely echo[ing] longstanding precedent' and intended to explain why Judge Evans's initial analysis of the fourth factor was correct. 'On remand', the

---

[228] Courtney, n. 226 above (emphasis in the original). [229] *GS Appeal II*, n. 4 above.
[230] *GS District Court II*, n. 4 above, 7. [231] *GS Court of Appeals II*, n. 4 above, 1300.

Court of Appeals wrote, 'the district court must reinstate its original finding that the fourth factor strongly disfavors fair use for the 31 excerpts for which the publishers proved the availability of digital licences'.[232] This would seem to be a very different sort of evidentiary analysis from that suggested in the Court of Appeals' original opinion. As discussed earlier in this chapter, for many transformative uses it may be easier to rationalise the lack of relevant economic harm on the basis that the plaintiff and defendant have different purposes, are targeting different audiences, and hence operating in different markets.[233] But for literal, non-transformative copying, such divisions are far more difficult to draw. An attraction of economic free riding and incentives may therefore relate to the recognition that some directly competing, substitutive copying is acceptable *so long as this does not destroy the incentives of the authors and publishers*.[234] But by its direction that the mere availability of a licence tolls strongly against fair use, the Court of Appeals seemed to reject such an approach, instead adopting one grounded in other moral precepts.

It remains to be seen how the District Court will respond, assuming that the parties do not settle in the interim. But it can be said that *Georgia State* illustrates ongoing challenges in relation to the fourth factor, especially for 'pure' copying.

V Conclusion

This chapter has used doctrinal and empirical techniques to explore the relevance of fair use to US cultural institutions. It began by discussing doctrinal indications in relation to fair use, drawing from the legislative drafting and the case law. It then considered the reported fair use practices of participating institutions: the law in action. This fieldwork suggested that despite concerns about the uncertainty of fair use, the doctrine offered a meaningful alternative to other options for copyright compliance, such as licensing and targeting public domain works. There was variation in decision-making around fair use, with some instances being more intuitive and influenced by ethics and institutional norms, and others grounded in close legal analysis. Furthermore, comfort with fair use varied amongst institutions, and applications were dynamic, with the fieldwork suggesting emerging norms in relation to online use. However, even amongst those who preferred a more restricted interpretation, fair use played a role in copyright management, helped ameliorate the

---

[232] Ibid.   [233] See discussion above n. 65 to n. 76 and surrounding text.
[234] See Hudson, n. 60 above.

effect of limitations in section 108 and provided a release valve in relation to orphaned works.

A number of questions arise in relation to fair use. Some of these relate to the future of the doctrine in US law, including the meaning of transformativeness and how empirical and normative matters should inform market harm in factor four. Other questions are externally focused, asking whether the US experience suggests that other countries should make greater use of standard-like language in their copyright exceptions, perhaps even through the introduction of a fair use provision. A key question for this book is whether the benefits of fair use are capable of replication elsewhere. It will be argued that the success of fair use can be attributed only partly to its drafting, and that other factors, including in relation to the characteristics and decision-making processes of users, have played an extremely important role. In making out these arguments, this book now turns in Chapter 6 to another example of standard-liked drafting: section 200AB of the Australian Copyright Act. As will be seen, the experiences of Australian interviewees stood in marked contrast to their US counterparts.

6 Australian Section 200AB

I Introduction

Chapter 5 of this book discussed the fair use experiences of US cultural institutions, observing that section 107 of the US Copyright Act was relied upon in a range of circumstances and that interviewees were comfortable with the reasoning demanded by a standard. Its analysis therefore rejected a view of fair use as uncertain and unworkable, and could be seen to support the greater utilisation of standard-like concepts in copyright exceptions, including fair use itself. This chapter continues this discussion by considering experiences in relation to section 200AB, an autochthonous exception introduced into Australian copyright law in 2006 with the stated intention of capturing, for cultural institutions and other specified users, some of the benefits of fair use.[1] This chapter asks whether section 200AB has met its stated aims, and what this means for the drafting of copyright exceptions.

Despite the legislative goals of section 200AB, one matter that is immediately apparent is that the Australian government drafted section 200AB in terms very different to section 107 of the US Copyright Act. Instead of being structured around fairness factors, section 200AB utilises language from the three-step test in TRIPS.[2] Under its current wording, a use will fall within section 200AB where:

(a) the circumstances of the use (including those described in paragraphs (b), (c) and (d)) amount to a special case;

---

[1] See the second reading speech of the Attorney-General: Commonwealth, *Parliamentary Debates*, House of Representatives, 19 October 2006 (Philip Ruddock). In its original form, s. 200AB could be invoked by cultural and educational institutions and those assisting users with a disability. This latter application was repealed in 2017: Copyright Amendment (Disability Access and other Measures) Act 2017 (Cth) (repealing elements from s. 200AB that referred to assisting those with a disability, and introducing a new fair dealing exception for such uses).

[2] Australian Copyright Act s. 200AB(7) (the phrases 'conflict with a normal exploitation', 'special case' and 'unreasonably prejudice the legitimate interests' all have the 'same meaning as in Article 13 of the TRIPS Agreement').

(b) the use is covered by subsection (2) or (3);
(c) the use does not conflict with a normal exploitation of the work or other subject-matter;
(d) the use does not unreasonably prejudice the legitimate interests of the owner of the copyright.[3]

Subsection (2) relates to cultural institutions. In order for a use to fall within section 200AB it must be:

(a) ... made by or on behalf of the body administering a library or archives; and
(b) ... made for the purpose of maintaining or operating the library or archives (including operating the library or archives to provide services of a kind usually provided by a library or archives); and
(c) ... not made partly for the purpose of the body obtaining a commercial advantage or profit.[4]

Section 200AB does not apply 'if, because of another provision of this Act: (a) the use is not an infringement of copyright; or (b) the use would not be an infringement of copyright assuming the conditions or requirements of that other provision were met'.[5]

Viewing section 200AB through the lens of standards and rules, it can be said that whilst the provision is verbose and contains numerous sub-elements, the core limbs are open-ended and give section 200AB the appearance of a complex standard. Section II of this chapter discusses the developments that led to the introduction of section 200AB, including the US–Australia Free Trade Agreement and the Fair Use Review of 2005. A key message is that amongst respondents to the Review – which ranged from those who did not see the need for any significant reform through to those pressing for new exceptions, new fair dealing purposes and in some cases fair use – no-one suggested anything that resembled section 200AB. It would therefore appear that section 200AB was an attempt to find a legislative compromise between divergent positions, with Article 13 language being included to meet the concern that the provision might not comply with the three-step test. Section III discusses experiences in relation to section 200AB as reported by Australian interviewees in 2012 and 2013 and, in follow-up interviews, 2016. This fieldwork revealed the extremely limited circumstances in which

---

[3] Ibid., s. 200AB(1).
[4] Ibid., s. 200AB(2). The prohibition on commercial advantage or profit is not activated purely because of the imposition of a cost-recovery fee in connection with the use: s. 200AB(6A).
[5] Ibid., s. 200AB(6).

interviewees reported using section 200AB, with many of those uses – highly constrained as they were – relating to orphaned works. Australian experiences therefore shared little with US practices in relation to fair use, and did not appear to be amenable to change without a significant rethinking of the meaning of section 200AB.

Given the foregoing, it may be asked whether this chapter lends support to the view that fair use requires US-specific conditions to be meaningful, for instance in terms of the wording of the provision, the volume and history of case law, the First Amendment environment and so forth.[6] The thesis developed in this book is that (1) the US experiences provide indications of legal and non-legal factors that help make fair use functional (at least in the cultural institution sector), and that (2) the Australian experiences illustrate *not* that fair use cannot operate outside the United States but that section 200AB is a poorly drafted standard that has mostly been experienced as unknown and unknowable. Section 200AB should not, therefore, caution us against fair use but cause us to think about the crafting of standards and the desirability of downloading three-step concepts into domestic provisions.[7]

II Fair Use in Australia: The 2006 Reforms

A History

In May 2005, the Attorney-General's Department of the Australian federal government released an Issues Paper for its latest inquiry: the Fair Use Review.[8] The immediate impetus for the Review was the implementation of copyright-related aspects of the US–Australia Free

---

[6] For discussion, see, e.g., B. Fitzgerald, 'Underlying Rationales of Fair Use: Simplifying the Copyright Act' (1998) 2 *Southern Cross University Law Review* 153; D. Hunter, 'American Lessons: Implementing Fair Use in Australia' (2014) 24 *Australian Intellectual Property Journal* 192; M. Senftleben, 'The Perfect Match: Civil Law Judges and Open-Ended Fair Use Provisions' (2017) 33 *American University International Law Review* 231.

[7] The three-step test was analysed in Chapter 1, Section III.A. As discussed in that chapter, there are historical, doctrinal and normative reasons why a broader and more flexible interpretation of the test is to be preferred, i.e., one which supports the development of new exceptions. Some commentators have also suggested that when transposed into domestic legislation, the three-step test can have a further enabling function, by allowing judges to expand the scope of exceptions: e.g., C. Geiger, D. Gervais and M. Senftleben, 'The Three-Step Test Revisited: How to Use the Test's Flexibility in National Copyright Law' (2014) 29 *American University International Law Review* 581, especially 616–625.

[8] Attorney-General's Department, Parliament of Australia, *Fair Use and Other Copyright Exceptions: An Examination of Fair Use, Fair Dealing and Other Exceptions in the Digital Age* (May 2005).

Trade Agreement (FTA), which had been concluded on 8 February 2004.[9] These aspects focused on strengthening and expanding rights and enforcement mechanisms, and harmonising aspects of Australian copyright law with that in the United States. FTA-related amendments included a twenty-year extension to the term of protection for published works, granting new economic and moral rights to performers, and revising provisions relating to technological protection measures.[10] But as Parliament was considering the reforms necessary to implement the FTA, concern began to grow that the Agreement had not taken adequate account of the legal and economic framework of Australian copyright law and its differences with US law.[11] One difference that became the focus of considerable attention was the latter's open-ended fair use exception, which was said to give US users, consumers and creators an ability to utilise and transform copyright works that was more extensive than their Australian counterparts. It was perceived that there was a lack of 'balance'[12] in the FTA because it had cherry-picked elements from US law that strengthened rights without giving corresponding benefits to Australian users. This led to fresh calls for Australia to adopt a fair use-style exception,[13] which was supported by the parliamentary committees that had been charged with scrutinising the FTA.[14]

With a federal election on the horizon, the government was keen to defer the fair use debate so that the US Free Trade Agreement Implementation Bill 2004 could be passed before Parliament was prorogued. As part of its re-election policy, the government therefore committed to

---

[9] Australia–US Free Trade Agreement (Washington, 18 May 2004) [2005] ATS 1. The articles in relation to copyright were set out in chapter 17, as supplemented by three side letters to that chapter.

[10] For discussion, see, e.g., R. Burrell and K. Weatherall, 'Exporting Controversy? Reactions to the Copyright Provisions of the U.S.–Australia Free Trade Agreement: Lessons for U.S. Trade Policy' [2008] 2 *University of Illinois Journal of Law, Technology and Policy* 259, 264–270, 272–274, 276.

[11] See, e.g., Joint Standing Committee on Treaties (JSCOT), Parliament of Australia, *Report 61: Australia-United States Free Trade Agreement* (23 June 2004) paras. 16.35–16.50; Senate Select Committee on the Free Trade Agreement between Australia and the United States of America, Parliament of Australia, *Final Report on the Free Trade Agreement between Australia and the United States of America* (5 August 2004) paras. 3.93–3.126. See also Burrell and Weatherall, ibid., 276–278.

[12] JSCOT, n. 11 above, para. 16.39; Senate Select Committee, n. 11 above, para. 3.93; see also Burrell and Weatherall, n. 10 above, 277.

[13] See responses described in JSCOT, above n. 11, paras. 16.38–16.40; see also Senate Select Committee, n. 11 above, paras. 3.104–3.116. For an earlier recommendation that fair dealing be reformed to be an open-ended provision, see Copyright Law Review Committee, *Simplification of the Copyright Act 1968 Part 1: Exceptions to the Exclusive Rights of Copyright Owners* (September 1998) paras. 6.33–6.34, recommendation 6.35.

[14] JSCOT, n. 11 above, Recommendation 17; Senate Select Committee, n. 11 above, para. 3.117.

holding a review asking whether a new exception based on fair use should be introduced into the Copyright Act.[15] The government was re-elected in October 2004, and the Fair Use Review commenced the following May. Respondents were invited to address two key questions. The first was whether existing exceptions were adequate in the digital age, that is, whether the Copyright Act needed to be reformed to permit additional acts of consumption and re-use of copyright material.[16] The second asked how any new exceptions should be drafted, including whether Australia should introduce a flexible, open-ended provision similar to fair use.[17] The responses to the Review repeated many arguments that have long featured in debates about the drafting of copyright exceptions, such as the respective merits of flexibility and certainty, the risks of unpredictability and obsolescence, and the association of these qualities with general and specific exceptions, respectively.[18]

For instance, complaints that Australia's existing suite of exceptions were inflexible and outdated underpinned many of the submissions that called for open-ended drafting, either through reform to fair dealing and/ or a new fair use provision.[19] The Australian Digital Alliance described the fair dealing provisions as 'technical, complex, inflexible and not well suited to the rapidly changing technological environment in which we all live and work',[20] whilst the Australian Vice-Chancellors' Committee said they 'are not broad or flexible enough to effectively keep up with technological progress'.[21] Similar observations were made by the Internet Industry Association, which viewed copyright law in Australia as 'archaic and out of step with the realities of the digital age',[22] and Electronic Frontiers Australia, which described the fair dealing defences as 'fundamentally flawed in their construction and legal interpretation'.[23] In relation to the libraries and archives provisions, the Copyright in Cultural

---

[15] Liberal Party of Australia, *Strengthening Australian Arts* (2004), p. 22.
[16] Attorney-General's Department, n. 8 above, paras. 11.1–11.21.
[17] Ibid., paras. 1.1–1.7, 14.1–14.14.
[18] See M. Handler and E. Hudson, 'Fair Use as an Advance on Fair Dealing? Depolarising the Debate' in H. Sun, S. Balganesh and W. Ng-Loy (eds), *Comparative Aspects of Limitations and Exceptions in Copyright Law* (New York: Cambridge University Press, forthcoming).
[19] Submissions to the Review were previously available at Attorney-General's Department, *Copyright – Review of Fair Use Exception – May 2005*, www.ag.gov.au. Copies are on file with the author. They are referred to below as '[Respondent Name] Submission'. Pinpoint references are to the page number on the version on the Attorney-General's website.
[20] Australian Digital Alliance (ADA) Submission, p. 2.
[21] Australian Vice-Chancellors' Committee Submission, p. 10.
[22] Internet Industry Association Submission, p. 2.
[23] Electronic Frontiers Australia Submission, p. 6.

Institutions Group articulated numerous concerns, including that such exceptions are 'highly complex, ambiguous and therefore uncertain', 'outdated and restrictive' and 'do not allow institutions to make the best use of digital technologies available to them'.[24] Similarly, the Australian Film Commission, which at the time oversaw the National Film and Sound Archive, argued that the relevant provisions 'are complex, contain a multitude of anomalies, and are unclear, making the AFC's ability to fulfil its statutory mandate difficult'.[25] More generally, the need for new exceptions to be technologically neutral and responsive to new practices was pressed by a number of respondents.[26]

On the other hand, another group of submissions articulated concerns in relation to fair use. One concern was whether fair use complies with the three-step test,[27] a matter discussed in Chapter 1 of this book. A further complaint was that fair use would be too uncertain.[28] Many of the submissions that raised this complaint came from entities that represent creators and copyright owners. For example, Copyright Agency Limited (CAL) highlighted the importance of predictability to the successful commercialisation of copyright works, observing that 'CAL and our members want a system which provides for market security and development – and believes this is an outcome desirable for both owners and consumers'.[29] The central role of courts in the interpretation of fair use was also of concern, for instance on the basis that an Australian exception would not, as with the US version, codify a well-established doctrine,[30] and because many Australian creators would be unable to finance litigation to challenge the fair use claims of better resourced users.[31]

Importantly, legal certainty was also attractive to contributors to the Review who were critical of the status quo, with some recommending fair use *and* retention of fair dealing and other closed-ended exceptions, perhaps with some expansion of those provisions. For instance, the

---

[24] Copyright in Cultural Institutions Group (CICI) Submission, pp. 21–22.
[25] Australian Film Commission Submission, p. 8.
[26] See, e.g., Apple Computer Inc and Apple Computer Australia Pty Ltd Submission, p. 19; Australian Consumers' Association Submission, pp. 10–11; Australian War Memorial Submission, pp. 5–6.
[27] See, e.g., Arts Law Centre of Australia Submission, p. 4; Australian Copyright Council Submission, p. 4. See also Copyright Agency Limited (CAL) Submission, p. 12; Intellectual Property Committee of the Law Council of Australia, Business Law Section, Submission, p. 12.
[28] See, e.g., Music Council of Australia Submission, paras. 1.1–1.8; National Association for the Visual Arts Submission, p. 2; Australian Copyright Council Submission, p. 4.
[29] CAL Submission, p. 12.
[30] See, e.g., Australian Copyright Council Submission, p. 4.
[31] See, e.g., Viscopy Submission, p. 4; Music Council of Australia Submission, para. 1.3.

Australian Digital Alliance recommended a hybrid model involving retention of fair dealing, the introduction of new exceptions for such things as orphaned works, format shifting, preservation copying and transformative uses, and 'a technologically neutral flexible provision which allows for the development of new exceptions in accordance with principles of fairness'.[32] Whilst they recognised that the certainty of the existing provisions could be problematic and at times illusory, they saw a fair use-style provision as 'not detract[ing] from the certainty that currently exists' and able to provide 'an additional workable mechanism to assist users in ascertaining the fairness of uses which are currently not permitted'.[33] Amongst cultural institution respondents, the submission of the National Archives of Australia emphasised the importance of sector-specific exceptions in 'provid[ing] certainty for public archives and their users',[34] whilst the Australian War Memorial observed that retaining specific exceptions would help ensure cultural institutions 'feel secure when providing access to orphaned works in their respective collections, or creating copies for the purpose of preservation, storage or access, knowing that there were provisions in the Act outlining the circumstances in which they could do so'.[35] Thus, whilst the pro-reform camp raised issues with the existing closed exceptions, there was acceptance – implicit and explicit – that they provided or could provide certainty, and that it was important that any reform not sacrifice this quality.

The Attorney-General's Department never issued a formal response to the Review. However, a bill was introduced into Parliament the following year whose comprehensive reforms included amendment to exceptions.[36] In his Second Reading Speech for the 2006 Bill, the Attorney-General referred to new section 200AB, stating:

There are also new exceptions to provide flexibility to allow copyright material to be used for certain socially useful purposes, where this does not significantly harm the interests of copyright owners. The Bill provides for a new exception to allow cultural and educational institutions and certain individuals to make a use of copyright where that use does not undermine the copyright owner's normal market. The flexibility of this new exception will provide, in these specified areas, some of the benefits that the fair use doctrine provides in US law.[37]

---

[32] ADA Submission, pp. 2–3.
[33] Ibid., p. 18; see also p. 20 (description of hybrid model as 'Retain some Certainty with Added Flexibility').
[34] National Archives of Australia Submission, p. 11.
[35] Australian War Memorial Submission, p. 6.
[36] Copyright Amendment Bill 2006 ('2006 Bill').
[37] Ruddock, n. 1 above.

In a press release, the Attorney-General's Department stated that reform had been guided by a number of principles, including that:

> Australia has a unique regime that should be maintained. In particular, stakeholders support the fair dealing regime and do not want to replace it with a US style fair use regime.[38]

This goes some way to explain the drafting of section 200AB. As seen in the Explanatory Memorandum to the 2006 Bill,[39] the government accepted concerns that existing exceptions were too restrictive and had failed to keep pace with digital technologies.[40] But a further message it took from the Review was that respondents did not unambiguously support fair use – a conclusion that was not surprising given that the pro-reform camp did not speak with a unified voice in relation to fair use, and often emphasised the need for any changes to retain favourable qualities of the existing system, including its certainty.[41] In drafting section 200AB, the government therefore appeared to straddle the positions communicated to the Review by devising an exception that had open-ended qualities but was not an identikit of fair use. First, it targeted section 200AB to three groups who seemed particularly hamstrung by the rigidity and arbitrariness of the existing exceptions: cultural and educational institutions, and users assisting those with a disability.[42] Second, it placed broad limits on permissible uses for which section 200AB may be claimed. In the case of cultural institutions, the use needed to be 'for the purpose of maintaining or operating the library or archives' and not 'made partly for the purpose of ... obtaining a commercial advantage or profit'.[43] Finally, by incorporating three-step test language into section 200AB, the government sought to respond to concerns that introducing fair use would place Australia in contravention of its obligations under international copyright law.[44]

---

[38] Attorney-General's Department, 'Major Copyright Reforms Strike Balance', Media Release 088/2006 (14 May 2006); see also House of Representatives (circulated by authority of the Attorney-General), Copyright Amendment Bill 2006: Explanatory Memorandum, p. 10 ('[i]n the public consultation phase of the Fair Use review, no significant interest supported fully adopting the US approach') ('2006 EM').
[39] 2006 EM, n. 38 above, pp. 7–13 (discussing an 'extended use exception').
[40] Ibid., p. 7.   [41] Also discussed in Handler and Hudson, n. 18 above.
[42] 2006 EM, n. 38 above, p. 10, paras. 6.55–6.60. In its original form in the Copyright Amendment Bill 2006, s. 200AB(5) covered parody and satire. In the legislation passed, parody and satire were instead included as new fair dealing purposes in ss. 41A and 103AA.
[43] Ibid., para. 6.55; and see Australian Copyright Act s. 200AB(2).
[44] Ibid., pp. 7–8, 10, para. 6.54.

In short, section 200AB was a legislative compromise between different viewpoints addressed to Fair Use Review. No-one who contributed to the Review asked for this provision.

B   *Competing Interpretations*

Given this backdrop, an immediate question in the wake of the 2006 reforms was the meaning of section 200AB. This led a number of peak bodies to release interpretative guides, including the Australian Copyright Council (ACC),[45] the Australian Libraries Copyright Committee (ALCC) and Australian Digital Alliance (ADA),[46] and the Copyright in Cultural Institutions Group (CICI).[47] The overarching philosophy behind these texts was different. The ALCC/ADA, for example, emphasised the flexibility of section 200AB,[48] which they considered would be 'particularly helpful' where specific exceptions did not apply.[49] They stated that section 200AB would help with format-shifting, use of orphaned works, digitisation and the production of accessible copies.[50] Similar sentiments were presented by CICI, which described section 200AB as 'an important new exception'[51] that was introduced to '[broaden] the ways in which copyright material can be used for purposes that benefit the wider public interest', thus helping institutions fulfil their mandates.[52] In contrast the ACC was more guarded;[53] indeed, in an overview of the 2006 reforms, it described section 200AB as 'drafted as a "gap-filler"'[54] and a 'last resort provision'.[55] The ACC guide also had a quite doctrinal flavour, identifying numerous technical issues with the

---

[45] Australian Copyright Council (ACC), *Special Case Exception: Educations, Libraries, Collections: A Practical Guide*, B130v01 (December 2007) (text attributed to Ian McDonald).
[46] Australian Libraries Copyright Committee (ALCC) and the Australian Digital Alliance (ADA), *A User's Guide to the Flexible Dealing Provision for Libraries, Educational Institutions and Cultural Institutions: Section 200AB of the Copyright Act 1968 (Cth)* (2008) (text attributed to Laura Simes).
[47] Copyright in Cultural Institutions (CICI), *Flexible dealing and cultural institutions: Statement of Principles regarding the use of section 200AB of the Copyright Act (1968): An Industry Standard and User Guide for the Cultural Sector* (September 2010) (text attributed to Sarah Waladan).
[48] ALCC/ADA, n. 46 above, pp. 4–5.
[49] Ibid., p. 4. In making this statement they identified fair dealing as a specific exception.
[50] Ibid., p. 5.   [51] CICI, n. 47 above, p. 3.   [52] Ibid., p. 4.
[53] ACC, n. 45 above, pp. 1–3 (noting the complexity and uncertainty of section 200AB).
[54] Australian Copyright Council, *2006 Copyright Amendments: A Practical Guide* (December 2007), p. 14.
[55] Ibid., p. 15.

drafting of, and legislative guidance in relation to, section 200AB,[56] and construing the three-step test language as meaning that section 200AB only covered uses that were quantitatively limited.[57] The ACC was not alone in such an approach; for instance, one of the leading academic commentaries on Australian copyright law described section 200AB as a 'residual exception',[58] and stated, in relation to libraries and archives, that given the provisions for administrative and preservation use, 'it is not easy to envisage a situation in which s 200AB(1) and (2) would apply – bearing in mind that it cannot be relied on where another exception would apply'.[59]

That said, the three guides also contained some similar messages in relation to section 200AB. One was that even copyright experts could not state with confidence the application of the provision.[60] This was also foreshadowed by the government in its Explanatory Memorandum to the 2006 Bill, which noted the benefits of an extended exception (flexibility and responsiveness) but also that

> this approach may add to the complexity of the Act. There would be some uncertainty for copyright owners until case law developed. Until the scope was interpreted by the courts, there may be disruption to existing licensing arrangements. Similarly, a user considering relying on this exception would need to weigh the legal risk of possible litigation.[61]

Similar observations were made in the academic commentary on section 200AB, especially as regards the utilisation of three-step test language.[62] For instance, an article written by the author of this book observed that:

---

[56] For instance, the ACC described the drafting as 'hard to follow' and generating 'uncertainties about how [s. 200AB] should be interpreted and applied': ACC, n. 45 above, p. 8.

[57] For instance, the ACC interpreted the 'special case' limb as requiring that 'the use must be narrow or limited; and the need for the use must be specific and identified (rather than speculative)' (ibid., p. 13), and stated that factors that rendered s. 200AB more likely to apply included that 'the number of people the use is for is small; the time-frame of the use is short; [and] the proportion of the work you are using is small' (p. 14).

[58] S. Ricketson and C. Creswell, *Law of Intellectual Property: Copyright, Design and Confidential Information* (Legal Online, electronic resource at 31 December 2011), paras. 11.109, 11.109A, 11.469.

[59] Ibid., para 11.336.

[60] For instance, each guide noted the existence of alternative interpretations and the lack of case law: see ACC, n. 45 above, p. 3; ALCC/ADA, n. 46 above, p. 1; CICI, n. 47 above, pp. 3–4.

[61] 2006 EM, n. 38 above, p. 10.

[62] See, e.g., M. de Zwart, 'The Copyright Amendment Act 2006: The New Copyright Exceptions' (2007) 25 *Copyright Reporter* 4, 13–15; Ricketson and Creswell, n. 58 above, para. 11.109.

The incorporation of terminology from TRIPS into domestic law is controversial. In particular, such a step has been criticised for generating uncertainty regarding the ambit of [section 200AB]. There is validity in these concerns. ... [The three-step test] is to be applied by copyright interpreters (e.g., judges and lawyers) and stakeholders (e.g., copyright owners and cultural institutions) in relation to whether particular *activity* is permitted within Australian law. This is not only a very different function from that which the three-step test was [originally] designed to fulfil, but may suggest that those terms have accepted, readily ascertainable and *easy to apply* meanings. This does not appear to be the case.[63]

Despite uncertainty about the meaning of the three-step test language, the industry guides all communicated a second message: that these sub-limbs, and indeed the other elements of section 200AB, all performed meaningful work. The ACC identified seven steps that needed to be satisfied for section 200AB to apply: (1) user is of a prescribed type; (2) use is for a permissible purpose; (3) no commercial advantage or profit; (4) no other statutory exception or scheme available; (5) no conflict with a normal exploitation of the work; (6) no unreasonable prejudice to the legitimate interests of the copyright owner; and (7) the circumstances of the use amount to a special case.[64] CICI also described a seven-part test but presented its steps in a different order, merged items (1) and (2) into a single limb, and added a further requirement: that users must not circumvent a technological protection measure to make the use.[65] In the ALCC/ADA guide only six steps were mentioned, these mirroring the same matters as the ACC but again using a different order and with items (1) and (2) fused as one limb.[66] Each guide then used this six- or seven-step framework to discuss instances where section 200AB might apply, with the analysis of CICI and the ALCC/ADA displaying a particularly mechanical, factor-by-factor application of the provision.

To conclude, the drafting of section 200AB raised a number of possibilities in relation to its future utilisation by cultural institutions. One was that institutions would not be willing and/or able to glean any meaningful guidance from the standard-like language, i.e., that section 200AB would be considered an 'unknown quantity' on which it would be 'too risky to rely'.[67] Another possibility, however, was that 'a flexible exception, using phrases like "normal exploitation" and "legitimate interests", may be more readily understandable by lay people (without extensive legal

---

[63] E. Hudson, 'The *Copyright Amendment Act 2006*: The Scope and Likely Impact of New Library Exceptions' (2006) 14 *Australian Law Librarian* 25, 31.
[64] ACC, n. 45 above, pp. 4–14.
[65] CICI, n. 47 above, p. 5. This matter was addressed in ACC, n. 45 above, p. 16, and ALCC/ADA, n. 46 above, pp. 8–9.
[66] ALCC/ADA, n. 46 above, p. 7. [67] Hudson, n. 63 above, 32.

advice), because they accord with intuitive notions of what is fair and reasonable'.[68] As will be seen in Section III, empirical work with Australian cultural institutions in 2012/2013 and 2016 revealed not only that institutions saw section 200AB as having an extremely narrow application but that prospects for renewed interpretations were bleak.

III   Experiences

A   2012/2013

With the initial Australian fieldwork having predated the 2006 reforms, and a fairly significant period of time having elapsed since those changes, a fresh tranche of fieldwork was conducted in Australia in 2012 and 2013, including interviews at many of the same institutions – and sometimes with the same interviewees – as the earlier fieldwork.[69] A total of twenty-one institutions participated in this fieldwork, along with four industry bodies. The content of these interviews differed to a degree from the earlier fieldwork, with less discussion of descriptive matters in relation to the use of digitisation and greater focus on copyright management and the role of exceptions. This included questions in relation to knowledge and utilisation of section 200AB.[70]

Despite some five and a half years having elapsed between the introduction of section 200AB and the commencement of this fieldwork, interviewees reported that reliance on section 200AB had been sporadic and often limited to uses of orphaned works.[71] Of the twenty-one participating institutions, ten indicated that they had not yet relied on section 200AB, although some had discussed this possibility.[72] Of the

---

[68] Ibid., 32–33.
[69] As noted in the description of the methodology in Chapter 3, any interviewee who participated in more than one tranche of fieldwork retained the same pseudonym. Interviewees who participated in more than one capacity (e.g., in some aspects as staff member of an institution, but in others as representative of a peak body) retained the same interview number but were given a different designation depending on the role in which they were speaking (e.g., 500L and 500X).
[70] Some findings from this fieldwork were discussed in E. Hudson, 'Implementing Fair Use in Copyright Law: Lessons from Australia' (2013) 25 *Intellectual Property Journal* 201.
[71] E.g., 201X, 207L, 213L, 229X, 237L.
[72] E.g., 203M, 204A, 208G, 215G, 225G, 228M, 249L, 238L, 255A 262M. To avoid duplication, this list includes only one representative of each institution.

Experiences   219

remaining eleven, section 200AB practices included digitising materials recorded in VHS and other old formats in response to technological obsolescence;[73] digitising other old materials such as glass slides, ephemera and archival records for preservation and access purposes;[74] inclusion of orphaned works in exhibition materials, online or in a publication;[75] and narrow examples of section 200AB being used to justify the supply of material to external requestors.[76] Amongst those who had made use of section 200AB, such utilisation was not widespread and usually arose at the end of an involved process in which items were assessed individually and records kept of the institution's decision-making. For instance, one interviewee described the use of approximately 50 orphaned works in a forthcoming exhibition:

> They want digital copies [of various items] to put onto a poster board in the exhibition area ... Some of the material – ephemera, posters, little news sheets – it was extremely difficult to identify the copyright owner or the copyright status. So we have relied heavily on 200AB to do this, because to me, you go through that three-step test, it's an in-house thing, the risk is extremely low and the benefit is extremely high. And it's the sort of activity that would ordinarily be undertaken by a [library or archives]. So we're increasingly relying on section 200AB for that type of purpose. But that would probably make us one of the less risk averse institutions, and probably one that is applying section 200AB more.[77]

Another described using section 200AB for the reformatting of VHS tapes:

> When we go to apply section 200AB, what we first do is – we don't bother to [consider section 200AB] if there's a statutory licence in place, because we know [the use is] already falling outside – we'll look to see if there's a purchasable DVD, so whether [that work] has already been transferred, and if we can purchase a DVD we'll go ahead and do that. If not, then we'll try to track down a rightsholder. We'll start with a production company; if we can't find a production company then we'll go to one of the producers to figure out who owns what. And if at that point we're getting nowhere, and it's been a month or two, then we'll proceed with section 200AB.

Finally, one interviewee described the use of section 200AB in relation to public uses of images of an iconic artwork in the collection:

---

[73] E.g., 237L, 259L; 263L, 265L; similar 224X (most advice given by 224X in relation to s. 200AB pertained to orphaned works and technological obsolescence).
[74] E.g., 213L, 223A, 245A.
[75] E.g., 202G, 218M, 230A, 250L, 263L; also 237L (planned).
[76] E.g., 226L, 230A; also 245A (planned).
[77] Some examples in this chapter will not be attributed to an interviewee pseudonym in order to preserve anonymity.

In that particular case, [with] all the work that had been done with the object and trying to find the copyright holder, we felt that we had ticked all the boxes for 200AB. We had documentary evidence of the work that had gone on, it was all in an official file and not in somebody's head. In that instance we could comfortably say that, and we were prepared to do that because it is a beautiful object and a major component of our collection.

In considering the reasons for the unenthusiastic reception of section 200AB, one matter that can be eliminated at the outset is lack of awareness of the *existence* of the provision. In fact, whilst familiarity with the precise language of section 200AB varied, many interviewees were able to describe the limbs of the provision and discuss internal and sector interpretations, industry guidelines, and so forth.[78] Even amongst those whose recollection was less detailed, there was still awareness of the broad goals of the provision. Whilst this may seem unsurprising given the participants in this fieldwork (staff from major institutions who manage or oversee copyright as part of their duties), the baseline knowledge of copyright seemed to have lifted from the fieldwork in 2004 and 2005.[79] This shift was not a by-product of the greater employment of lawyers and their ilk – there were just as few people with law degrees in the cohort in 2012–2013 as there were in 2004–2005.[80] Instead, it would seem to reflect a heightened interest in copyright law across the sector, and better cross-institutional communication and cooperation.

A second plausible reason for the failure of section 200AB might be risk aversion: that cultural institutions are not the sort of users who readily embrace the uncertainty that surrounds standard-like drafting.[81] It is often said that cultural institutions have a cautious attitude to risk, and a conservative risk profile was reported by numerous participants in this tranche of fieldwork,[82] with some interviewees linking this to a reluctance to rely on section 200AB.[83] But the fieldwork also suggested that despite self-describing as cautious, many participating institutions were becoming more comfortable with risk, perhaps reflecting the lived

---

[78] E.g., 201X, 202G, 204A, 206G, 207L, 210A, 211X, 212M, 215G, 217L, 223A, 224X, 225G, 226L, 227X, 228L, 230A, 237L, 242L, 245A, 246A, 249L, 250L, 251M, 255A, 259L, 263L, 264L, 266A. The interviews were not intended to be a test of interviewee knowledge and did not, for instance, ask participants to recite the text of s. 200AB.

[79] See E. Hudson and A. Kenyon, 'Digital Access: The Impact of Copyright on Digitisation Practices in Australian Museums, Galleries, Libraries and Archives' (2007) 30 *UNSW Law Journal* 12, 36–37.

[80] Ibid., 37, noting that 'few' staff had a law degree. Of the 62 cultural institution interviewees in 2012–2013, only three had formal legal training (having been admitted to practice).

[81] For discussion of the characteristics of standards and how they might be received by different target audiences, see Chapter 2.

[82] See Chapter 3, Section IV.A.   [83] E.g., 203M, 210X.

Experiences

experience that they had not been inundated with lawsuits as they experimented with new iterations of risk-informed decision-making, and on the contrary had received few complaints and much positive feedback.[84]

For instance, at almost all participating institutions, interviewees reported that pure risk management had been used in the creation of public outputs, i.e., a decision to proceed with a use based on commercial reasoning about harm and the likelihood of complaint rather than legal reasoning that suggested a viable defence.[85] This was not a general strategy for copyright management but was cited as a mechanism for dealing with copyright in problematic scenarios such as digitisation of orphaned works; or digitising mixed collections where the bulk of items were public domain or cleared, and removing the odd in-copyright work would be difficult and detrimental to the presentation of the collection as a single entity; or where deadlines and the quantity of clearances led to some licences being sought retrospectively. Interviewees described some quite detailed policies to assess the risk status of proposed uses, and spoke of strategies to prevent downstream commercial re-use (such as releasing online content at low resolution).[86] A number of interviewees also described the benefits of having take-down systems and other mechanisms to respond to complaints.[87] This was perceived to be desirable not only because it supported the economic and moral interests of creators but because it made institution staff more comfortable in embracing risk management.

This raised the question of why the matters that informed risk management were not seen as relevant to section 200AB, given that both required an open-textured analysis considering many of the same matters. The answer to come from the fieldwork was that the failure of section 200AB could be attributed largely to its drafting: that many interviewees saw the provision as blighted by manifold interpretative challenges. As one interviewee said in relation to training institution staff, 'as soon as somebody in a library who isn't a copyright expert has to look at section 200AB, it's almost [as if] a wall goes up. It's a long provision; they say it has too many steps, or that it looks too hard to apply.'[88] Another also referred to lack of confidence and knowledge around section 200AB, describing themselves and colleagues as 'the bush lawyers of it, but we're only experts in our own little domain … you take

---

[84] See Chapter 3, Section IV.A and Chapter 8, Section III.B.
[85] E.g., 204A, 207L, 208G, 210X, 214M, 218M, 221L, 225G, 228M, 229X, 234A, 237L, 246A, 248L, 255A, 257L, 259L, 262M, 264L.
[86] E.g., 228M, 229X, 239L, 250L, 255A. [87] E.g., 229X, 255A. [88] 201X.

the safe way out, which is not to use it'.[89] Section 200AB was seen as convoluted and technical:

> We weren't trained as legal people. We find it too legalise to read; we go round in circles when we question does it meet the three-step test, is it a special case – what makes it a special case? We feel more comfortable approaching it from a fair and logical analysis of the potential rightsholder and the intended use. It's what we're all arguing for: an educational fair use approach to the Copyright Act.[90]
>
> I've had to have a degree of familiarity with parts of the Copyright Act over my working life, and have done a reasonable degree of copyright advocacy – and it's one of the most complex exceptions, in its expression. If you pointed a gun at my head and said, 'describe section 200AB in plain English, what does it mean and what can you do with it', you'd be gasping for air and thoughts. It's so circuitous. If people at the [names their institution] cannot work it out, how some person in a tiny institution ... might think about it, I do not know.[91]
>
> My opinion of section 200AB is that it's useless. ... And it's ridiculous to jump through so many hoops before you can even think about using it. ... It's not broad enough; it's not clearly worded in the legislation. The fact that we're copyright professionals, this is our job, and even we couldn't work out - it took us two years to get some sort of handle on it. Heaven help anyone else. And even at the end of all of that, we were still a bit unsure. I know the [names institution] has used section 200AB for a couple of projects, but the amount of rigmarole that they went through in documenting things and presenting that to management ... it was just crazy that they should have to do that, just for the institution to be able to perform its mandated function. ... I had great hopes for section 200AB when I first came across it. It looked promising. I thought, maybe it will allow us to put thumbnails on the website. But the more we looked at the legislation and the hoops we had to go through, the less joy it was giving us. So in the end we had to concede that it does not allow us to do that.[92]

Complaints and problems with section 200AB recurred across the interviews. For instance, numerous interviewees referred to the number of limbs in section 200AB and the lack of consensus regarding the meaning of those elements.[93] With no case law to consider section 200AB and disagreement between copyright experts on its application,[94] interviewees lacked what they considered to be authoritative guidance on the ambit of the provision. It was therefore said that 'we get lots of feedback that the criteria under section 200AB are concepts that mean nothing to institutions',[95] and that 'one of the issues is a lot of people don't really

---

[89] 232L. [90] 228M. [91] 242L. [92] 225G.
[93] E.g., 201X, 204A, 219M, 225G, 229X, 249L, 255A, 259L.
[94] E.g., 208G (noting narrower views of s. 200AB pressed by copyright collectives), 229X (views on s. 200AB often split between owners' and users' interests), 250L (noting divergence between the analysis of the ACA and ALCC/ADA guidelines), 259L (s. 200AB cannot even be applied by people with a good copyright knowledge).
[95] 201X.

know what it means, and there are varying interpretations about it'.[96] Seeking the advice of external lawyers did not necessarily help; for example, one interviewee said that their lawyers had found section 200AB to be 'problematic' and that this 'really put us off, because we thought that if they couldn't really analyse section 200AB, then we've pretty much got Buckley's of trying to apply it'.[97] Interestingly, the manuals produced by peak bodies[98] appeared to have had limited traction, not only because of the different analysis in each publication but because their doctrinal analysis, even if accompanied by strong philosophical statements regarding the goals behind section 200AB, sent a message of rigidity rather than flexibility.

Two further matters to emerge from the fieldwork were the impact of the special case requirement[99] and the exclusion of 200AB where another exception or a statutory licensing scheme applies.[100] Dealing with each in turn, there was uncertainty as to what the special case limb added,[101] but whatever this was, it was roundly accepted as requiring work-by-work analysis, making section 200AB impossible to apply to mass digitisation and other large-scale projects due to the administrative burdens that such granular analysis would create.[102] For instance, it was observed that 'ultimately it's asking you to go through so many hoops. You might be able to do it if you're doing 50 works, but if you're trying to do 1,000 books or 40,000 books, it just wouldn't work.'[103] On the exclusion of section 200AB, it appears the legislative intent in making section 200AB secondary to other provisions was to prevent the subversion of those provisions, and in particular compulsory licensing schemes (for which remuneration is payable).[104] However, it appeared to add further complexity to section 200AB,[105] and some interviewees reported uncertainty as to whether reliance on section 200AB was curtailed by section 183 of the Act covering Crown use of copyright material.[106]

---

[96] 204A. Similarly, 202G described external lawyers as 'risk averse and conservative; they often act like there's no room for interpretation'.
[97] 228M. 'Buckley's chance' is an Australian expression meaning an extremely low or no chance.
[98] Described above n. 45 to n. 66 and surrounding text.
[99] Australian Copyright Act s. 200AB(1)(a).   [100] Ibid., s. 200AB(6).
[101] E.g., 201X, 217L, 224X, 225G, 249L, 250L, 259L, 264L. Interviewee 264L also noted that the direct incorporation of three-step test language 'encourages an enormous conservatism'.
[102] E.g., 201X, 210X, 211X, 218M, 228M, 249L.   [103] 249L.
[104] 2006 EM, n. 38 above, para. 6.62.
[105] E.g., 203M, 230A, 255A, 259L, 264L, 265L, 266A.
[106] Section 183 provides that acts performed by the Commonwealth or State are not infringing if undertaken 'for the services of the Commonwealth or State'. For national and state institutions, this raises two questions: are they the Crown, and if so, to what

Importantly, these interpretative issues were not just a problem because interviewees *themselves* struggled with section 200AB. A number of interviewees said they had a sense of how they would like to use the provision but hit a roadblock when trying to convince colleagues and senior management to incorporate section 200AB into workflows because of the challenges in presenting a clear and particularised case for change, especially given the lack of authoritative guidance regarding things like the three-step test language.[107] For instance, interviewees remarked:

Even for me, it's really difficult to understand section 200AB. It's difficult to interpret with any sense of certainty. I think, personally, my keenness dropped away because there was no support within the institution. It was difficult to understand, and I talked a lot about us getting some sort of risk management strategy, so that 200AB could be encompassed in that – but it never went anywhere.[108]

In a sense, because there's so much doubt about what it means, you might as well just use a risk management approach. Relying on a provision of the Copyright Act that no-one is quite sure what it covers, you might as well just do risk management and say, well, we'll put it up anyway, regardless of whether it's covered by a particular exception or not, if we don't really understand what it is.[109]

A number of interviewees spoke of the possibility of using section 200AB as a fallback in the event a risk-managed use was challenged,[110] and it may be that section 200AB had some signalling effects:

You asked us before, are you more or less risk averse? And we answered that we're less risk averse than we used to be. I think that is the case because section 200AB came in. It's like it legitimised us to take a bit more risk, but we don't look at the specific provisions of section 200AB and say why. It's psychological.[111]

Finally, the interviews also revealed other issues with section 200AB, for instance a lack of joined-up policy thinking by government (e.g., some public funding of digitisation was conditional on permissions in all cases[112]), and the challenges in generating industry standards in relation to section 200AB when people lacked the confidence in making public

---

extent are their activities 'for the services of' the Crown? One significant difference between section 183 and section 200AB is that remuneration can be payable under the former whereas the latter is a free exception. For further discussion of the Crown copying provisions and their relevance to Australian cultural institutions, see E. Hudson and A. Kenyon, *Copyright and Cultural Institutions: Guidelines for Digitisation* (Melbourne: University of Melbourne, 2005), pp. 36–37.

[107] E.g., 203M, 220M, 229L, 255A, 263L.   [108] 220M.   [109] 204A.
[110] E.g., 207L, 209L, 210A, 242L.   [111] 207L.   [112] E.g., 229X.

pronouncements about their interpretation and utilisation of the provision.[113]

In sum, although the stated aim of section 200AB was to capture some of the benefits of fair use, the 2012/2013 fieldwork suggested that it operated on the margins, mostly as a de facto orphaned works provision. Without more consideration, this evidence might be said to militate against the introduction in Australia of an open-ended exception such as fair use. But when one examines the reported practices closely, it can be said that section 200AB failed not because it is a standard but because it is an overly complex and ambiguous standard. As such, Australian experiences with section 200AB not only provide important lessons for the drafting of exceptions but may lend support to fair use.

B   2016

In August 2016, follow-up interviews were conducted at seven Australian cultural institutions. All of the institutions that participated in this fieldwork had taken part in the 2012/2013 study, and in some cases it was possible to speak with the same interviewees as previously. The headline message to come from the follow-up interviews was that the trends observed in the 2012/2013 fieldwork had continued. Interviewees spoke of the continued utilisation of risk management processes, with some having developed new policies to facilitate public-facing uses of low risk materials, especially unpublished materials and ephemera.[114] Section 200AB continued to be viewed as mainly an orphaned works provision, with some interviewees reporting no utilisation,[115] some noting discrete use in relation to format-shifting due to technological obsolescence,[116] and others indicating that section 200AB was fast being overtaken by risk management processes.[117] The problem of scaling up was again mentioned as being a problem for section 200AB. For instance, one interviewee said:

When section 200AB first became available, we all got very excited, and thought, yes this is the thing that will help us make more material available. I'm [now] less excited about section 200AB, and more going down the path of risk management which says we're unlikely to be sued, because you have to do a quite bit of work just to invoke section 200AB ... [*The interviewee was asked to elaborate. They referred to limbs from section 200AB and continued:*] To test those things means that you have to look at each item. ... In a way, it requires a bit more analysis, and also it's making a call which sometimes it is easier to say [for a big swathe of

---

[113] E.g. 227X, 228M, 250L.   [114] E.g., 215G, 235L, 255A, 269L.
[115] E.g., 215G, 255A, 270L.   [116] E.g., 265L, 272L.   [117] E.g., 229L, 248L.

material]: we've decided that it's low risk, and we're going to make it accessible online, and hope that that call is a good call, but if anyone disagrees then we'll deal with it on a case-by-case basis. Whereas if we were to do section 200AB, we would have to go into assessing each thing.[118]

Similarly, another interviewee said that section 200AB 'is not part of the discourse; it is perceived to be bureaucratic and time-consuming'.[119] That institution had digitised and made available a great deal of manuscript material by reference to risk management, and had received 'no pushback' but only 'great delight' at this new digital content. For this interviewee, the issue with section 200AB was not just the language but that 'it's seen as part of the old regime where you need permissions for everything and everything needs to be documented. It's an overly-formalised approach.'[120]

Although the emergence of robust iterations of risk management were described for old and unpublished collections, the growth in such practices was not limited to those spheres. For instance, an interviewee from an art museum described some fairly dramatic changes to copyright management at their institution, which centred on forward-looking licensing practices but also included a greater role for risk-managed decision-making:

The perceived risk is lower because we're doing more and we haven't had infringement [actions against us]. We always try to clear first before we use something. ... We used to say, if we can't clear it we can't use it, whereas now we might say, we've tried three times, we've also contacted a subscriber group of 200 people from museums around the world and no-one has details for this person, we've gone through the provenance – we have a bit of risk management, due diligence stuff in place that we're more comfortable with.[121]

This interviewee described a collection of artistic works that were contemporary but in many cases orphaned. Much time had been spent attempting to identify copyright holders, but to no avail. The institution was prepared to negotiate licences and pay fees if owners were found, but in the meantime was comfortable to

publish [images] on our collection online; use them on social media with captions and a little bit about the work; put [the works] on display and take installation photos of them; have them featured in news articles about that collection area; put them in our gallery mag; they've been on digital screens. We've not done merchandise, that's where we've drawn a line. And we've not done a television commercial. ... I guess we've always said for that particular group of works that

---

[118] 221L. [119] 248L. [120] 248L. [121] 215G.

Conclusion

we need context ... In the past we wouldn't have done that, we would have just said you can't use it.[122]

This interviewee described their approach as largely independent of exceptions. When pressed further, it was acknowledged that some uses may be coterminous with activities for which exceptions are used across the collection, most notably fair dealing for criticism, review and news reporting (which were agreed to be of considerable relevance), although not section 200AB. The interviewee continued:

We have made a call, when discussing this with senior curators and senior management, that the greatest risk for those artists was falling into obscurity. They're incredible contemporary works in a nationally-regarded collection, it was more of a risk that they'd never see the light of day, because that's not why you acquire works for a public collection. We've been thinking a lot about access, and balancing access with artist rights, that's been part of the risk management approach. And also we don't do things that we're not comfortable with – I know that's a broad sweeping statement, but we don't heavily overprint an entire work without showing a copyright holder ... it's still about the work as a central point and about preserving the integrity of that work. ... We're not doing things that are too aggressive.[123]

In sum, the fieldwork in 2016 did not reveal any divergence from the trends observed in 2012 and 2013. Whilst this research was conducted with a smaller group of participants, they were well connected and able to speak to experiences elsewhere. As such, it can be said with some confidence that ten years after its introduction, section 200AB had not yet emerged as a meaningful part of cultural institution practices.

IV   Conclusion

This chapter has considered Australian experiences in relation to section 200AB, an autochthonous exception introduced into the Copyright Act in 2006. Despite the legislative aim that this exception capture some of the benefits of fair use, the empirical work at Australian institutions suggested that section 200AB shared little in common with its US counterpart. Whilst there was variation in practices, the US fieldwork suggested that fair use was seen as relevant to a range of internal and public-facing activities; was used for many different types of copyright subject-matter; and that some interviewees were comfortable in pressing new interpretations. In contrast, section 200AB was understood as an orphaned works provision that required work-by-work analysis. If anything, its place in

---

[122] 215G.   [123] 215G.

copyright decision-making appeared to be diminishing as institutions decided that they could undertake more activity with orphaned and low-risk works, with fewer administrative burdens, via risk management.

Can it be concluded that section 200AB has been a failure? To the extent that the government intended a provision with fair use characteristics, the answer would appear to be yes. Despite cultural institutions growing in knowledge and confidence in relation to other copyright matters, these qualities did not translate to them being willing to make greater use of section 200AB. Reported reliance was sporadic, and to the extent section 200AB had been used, this was largely for orphaned works. This can be compared with US reports of, for example, using fair use for small-scale images in online collection databases, or playing extracts from films or other recordings in exhibitions. It would appear that section 200AB had, at most, signalled that institutions should not feel wedded to permissions for all public uses. This idea had traction at many institutions, but it was operationalised largely via risk management.

In terms of lessons for the future, the fieldwork suggested that the single biggest impediment to utilisation of section 200AB was its lack of comprehensibility to institutional users and their legal advisors. Standards and rules analysis teaches us that comprehensibility can arise in a number of ways. In the case of a fair use-style exception, interpretations might be informed by common-sense understandings of the scope of reasonable markets and the policy goals of copyright; by principles developed in the case law; through indications in the statute and its explanatory materials; and in industry guidelines and codes of practice. One way or another, none of these had cut-through for section 200AB. There has been no case law, and at least for cultural institutions it is unlikely that a judgment will ever be handed down given the litigation aversion of the sector. Rather than the three-step test language providing useful guidance via academic opinion and foreign case law, those concepts were viewed as uncertain and deeply contested. This also served to oust intuitive understandings and industry norms. To the extent some meaning was given to section 200AB, it was that analysis should be individualised and recorded, producing administrative burdens that were seen as impractical for institutions managing thousands or even millions of items.

Despite or perhaps because of their experiences with section 200AB, a number of Australian interviewees were supportive of fair use.[124] This would seem to indicate that for those people, problems with section 200AB

---

[124] E.g., 201X, 208G, 213L, 225G, 228M, 229L, 247A, 250L (but needs to apply to entities other than libraries), 255A, 259L, 263L, 264L, 265L (also supportive of expanding fair dealing).

reflected 'an administration issue rather than a philosophical disagreement with [its] concept'.[125] As one interviewee said in relation to the growing use of risk management practices, 'you've made your judgment based on your knowledge of what's acceptable and reasonable, on what's fair. We're already making a decision on what's fair.'[126] Another said that a further benefit to fair use 'is that people know about it; the number of times you have to say that there's no fair use [in Australia]'.[127] Although said jokingly, this comment touched on the idea that fair use was familiar, would be a natural extension of existing approaches, and would therefore be more workable than section 200AB. Support for fair use was not universal, with some pro-reform interviewees instead supportive of the liberalisation of exceptions through other mechanisms such as new fair dealing purposes[128] and broader exceptions for cultural institutions.[129] Somewhat ironically, the only reform question on which there was consensus was that section 200AB did not work.

---

[125] 221L.
[126] 229L. Similar 259L (fair use would match the way that institutions already operate).
[127] 263L.
[128] E.g., 210X, 248L ('I think [fair use is] quite a big step for the Australian copyright tradition to take, and I doubt that it would be successful. It's better to rethink the fair dealing approach, and broaden that ... Overall, I think it's a matter of clarifying than stepping out of our tradition, which I think is likely to produce a lot of unanticipated consequences.'). Some similar concerns were expressed by 237L, who was 'not against' fair use, but questioned the benefits to the educational sector given the breadth of uses that are currently covered by the statutory licence scheme.
[129] E.g., 204A, 246A (supporting some clearer rules for items in cultural collections).

7 Fair Dealing's Failures?

I Introduction

The previous chapter discussed Australia's experiment with homegrown 'flexible' drafting in section 200AB. But Australia, like other countries whose copyright laws derive from the Imperial Copyright Act 1911, also recognises fair dealing exceptions.[1] In its original statutory form in the 1911 Act, the relevant text stated that there was no infringement by any 'fair dealing with any work for the purposes of private study, research, criticism, review, or newspaper summary'.[2] In the intervening years, fair dealing provisions have become more complex. In Australia, Canada and the United Kingdom, for example, they are longer, split across multiple provisions in the copyright statute and are more particularised.[3] That said, the central requirement of fairness is suggestive of a standard, and this open-ended concept, combined with the introduction of new fair dealing purposes,[4] raises the question of how much day-to-day fair dealing practices overlap with fair use activity in the United States.

This chapter focuses on Canadian experience in the five years following *CCH Canadian Ltd* v. *Law Society of Upper Canada*.[5] It has been suggested that this case effected a significant expansion of Canadian

---

[1] At the time of writing, the relevant provisions are found in: Australian Act ss. 40–42, 43 (2), 103A–103C, 113E; Canadian Copyright Act ss. 29, 29.1, 29.2; and CDPA ss. 29, 30, 30A, 32. Over the course of this research, new fair dealing purposes have been added in all three fair dealing jurisdictions studied.

[2] Copyright Act 1911, s. 2(1)(i). It appears that this provision was intended to codify the existing fair use defences that had developed at common law: see R. Burrell and A. Coleman, *Copyright Exceptions: The Digital Impact* (Cambridge: Cambridge University Press, 2005), pp. 256–259. The use of the plural 'defences' is used to indicate that fair use arguments had not coalesced into a single doctrine by the time of codification.

[3] For instance via requirements for a sufficient acknowledgement, or that criticism and review relate to 'that or another work'.

[4] Since 2006, for parody (Australia, Canada, UK), satire (Australia, Canada), caricature and pastiche (UK), education (Canada, UK), quotation (UK) and assisting users with a disability (Australia).

[5] [2004] 1 SCR 339 ('*CCH*').

Introduction

fair dealing due to the Supreme Court's explicit affirmation that exceptions are users' rights, such that terms like research 'must be given a large and liberal interpretation'.[6] For instance, Michael Geist, writing at the time of decision's release, said that *CCH* 'instantly ranks as one of the strongest pro-users' rights decisions from any high court in the world, showing what it means to do more than pay mere lip service to balance in copyright'.[7] Similarly, Teresa Scassa described the case as likely to have 'far-ranging' effect,[8] 'breath[ing] significant life into the [fair dealing] defence'.[9] That said, whilst there was consensus that *CCH* was a 'landmark' case,[10] there were some who questioned its reasoning and future, including whether it would constitute a temporary high-water mark in fair dealing analysis. For example, it was observed that *CCH* marked an abrupt shift in the Canadian approach to copyright exceptions,[11] and possibly placed Canada outside its obligations under Article 13 of TRIPS.[12] On the other hand, it was also suggested that without legislative transformation of fair dealing into a fully open-ended fair use exception, the vision of the Supreme Court would not be realised.[13]

It is not the purpose of this chapter to engage with the normative aspects of this analysis. Instead, it asks two rather different questions. The first is to consider what impact *CCH* had on cultural institution practices, bearing in mind that the facts concerned a library photocopying service, which suggests that the case might be of direct relevance to institutional decision-making. Second, it asks how doctrinal analysis of *CCH* – the law in books – compared with the law in action. In order to set the scene for this discussion, Section II describes the *CCH* decision, including why it was of interest for the empirical work in this book. Section III then explores judicial and academic responses to the case, and Section IV sets out the reported response of cultural institution

---

[6] Ibid., para. 51.
[7] M. Geist, 'Low-tech Case has High-tech Impact', *The Toronto Star* (22 March 2004), www.michaelgeist.ca/resc/html_bkup/mar222004.html.
[8] T. Scassa, 'Recalibrating Copyright Law?: A Comment on the Supreme Court of Canada's Decision in *CCH Canadian Limited et al v Law Society of Upper Canada*' (2004) 3 *Canadian Journal of Law & Technology* 89.
[9] Ibid., 94.
[10] P. Esmail, '*CCH Canadian Ltd v Law Society of Upper Canada: Case Comment on a Landmark Copyright Case*' (2005) 10 *Appeal* 13.
[11] R. Hughes, 'Evolution of the Concept of Fair Dealing in Canadian Copyright Law' (2008) 26 *Copyright Reporter* 44.
[12] D. Gervais, 'Canadian Copyright Law Post-*CCH*' (2004) 18 *Intellectual Property Journal* 131, 163–167. The three-step test was discussed in Chapter 1, Section III.A.
[13] C. Craig, 'The Changing Face of Fair Dealing in Canadian Copyright Law: A Proposal for Legislative Reform' in M. Geist (ed), *In the Public Interest: The Future of Canadian Copyright Law* (Toronto: Irwin Law, 2005).

users. Here it will be seen that despite the extremely positive reaction from scholars and *CCH* being applied in later cases, in the five years following *CCH*, the response amongst institutions was extremely muted.

The fieldwork described in this chapter therefore tends against the suggestion that *CCH* recalibrated Canadian fair dealing so that it was much closer to US fair use; in fact, at least for participating cultural institutions, it casts doubts on whether *CCH* did much to shift practices at all. This raises questions about reform options for copyright exceptions. For instance, for those supportive of the liberalisation of exceptions, it might be argued that fair dealing contains under-exploited flexibilities, and that changing the interpretative milieu around the doctrine – as the Supreme Court sought to do in *CCH* – may serve to expand fair dealing without statutory intervention. So why did cultural institutions not embrace the Supreme Court's vision? One possibility might be that the fieldwork highlights the difficulties in reframing fair dealing, such that more radical interventions, such as fair use, are superior reform options. But another is that they illustrate that the Canadian copyright environment is unsuited to exceptions drafted as standards.

This chapter is the first of two to consider Canadian fair dealing. Although it describes a muted response to *CCH*, the changeability of seemingly entrenched norms was illustrated by the subsequent fair dealing experiences of academic libraries, discussed in Chapter 8. As such, it might be said that the Canadian experience also shows that practices that seem immutable can undergo significant change. More generally, the Canadian fieldwork puts into focus the range of factors that influence the law in action. And as we will see in the next two chapters, the law in books is but one of these.

II The Supreme Court's Vision

A Background

When the *CCH* decision was handed down, preparations were underway for the first tranche of fieldwork with Australian cultural institutions.[14] This section starts with a brief overview of the fair dealing experiences as reported in those interviews, as they prompted the question of whether

---

[14] Discussed in E. Hudson and A. Kenyon, 'Digital Access: The Impact of Copyright on Digitisation Practices in Australian Museums, Galleries, Libraries and Archives' (2007) 30 *University of New South Wales Law Journal* 12; E. Hudson and A. Kenyon, 'Without Walls: Copyright Law and Digital Collections in Australian Cultural Institutions' (2007) 4 *SCRIPTed* 197.

new and more forward-leaning interpretations of fair dealing might have arisen post-*CCH* in Canada.

A statutory fair dealing exception first appeared in Australia when the federal parliament adopted wholesale, in 1912, the Copyright Act 1911.[15] Fair dealing was retained with some modification when the Copyright Act 1968 (Cth) came into force. At the time of the Australian fieldwork in 2004 and 2005, fair dealing covered research, study, criticism, review, news reporting and giving legal advice.[16] Amongst interviewees, knowledge of fair dealing was mixed, with some people familiar with a '10 per cent rule' or the existence of an exception for research and study, but others not aware of the provisions or only able to describe their contents in vague terms.[17] Those with greater knowledge described fair dealing as being of relatively limited assistance to cultural institutions. In so far as it was perceived to be helpful, it was reported to be invoked in two main scenarios: 'research and study being undertaken by patrons and staff' (which seemed to relate to an individual's *own* research, not the institution providing assistance or support to others); and 'some institutional lectures, public programs and publications', where the criticism and review limb was understood to permit some uses without clearing rights.[18]

Interviewees able to discuss fair dealing in detail made statements that seemed to accord with existing doctrinal indications. Although based on a small body of Australian case law, the tenor of these indications had often been to apply fair dealing in narrower terms than its language might require. For example, although it was only a decision of a single judge of the Federal Court of Australia, *De Garis v. Neville Jeffress Pidler Pty Ltd*[19] was and remains a leading case in Australian understandings of fair dealing.[20] The defendant ran a media monitoring business in which it supplied copies of newspaper articles to its clients for a fee. It did not

---

[15] Between 1905 and 1912, Australian copyright legislation contained a protean statutory fair use defence in s. 28 of the Copyright Act 1905 (Cth). For discussion, see Burrell and Coleman, n. 2 above, pp. 257–258.

[16] Hudson and Kenyon, 'Digital Access', n. 14 above, 27. These provisions were found in the Australian Copyright Act ss. 40–42, 43(2), 103A–103C.

[17] Ibid., 28. The notion of a '10 per cent rule' comes from s. 40 of the Australian Copyright Act (fair dealing for the purpose of research or study), in which the reproduction of not more than a 'reasonable portion' is deemed to be a fair dealing. A reasonable portion has long been defined to mean, inter alia, 10 per cent of the number of pages. There is no general 10 per cent rule in the Australian fair dealing provisions; and nor do the deeming provisions mean that reproduction of greater than 10 per cent of the work can never be fair.

[18] Ibid.   [19] (1990) 18 IPR 292 (Beaumont J).

[20] To illustrate, it is extracted three times in the discussion of copyright exceptions in K. Bowrey, M. Handler, D. Nicol and K. Weatherall, *Australian Intellectual Property Law:*

have any licensing arrangements in place to make these reproductions. In copyright infringement proceedings, one argument run by the defendant was that its activities fell within fair dealing. This defence failed, a result that may seem reasonable given the scale of copying and the possibility of market substitution. But the case was decided not on the basis of fairness but by reference to purpose. For instance, Beaumont J held that the intended use of the client was irrelevant (the relevant purpose being that of the person or entity making the copy),[21] and that the defendant's activities were not research but locating articles for a fee. An alternative approach, i.e., to hold that the activities were research-based but not fair, was not taken.

This focus on the defendant's purpose also characterised another leading case in Australian fair dealing jurisprudence: *TCN Channel Nine Pty Ltd* v. *Network Ten Pty Ltd*,[22] in relation to the use of extracts from Channel Nine programmes in satirical talk show, The Panel. Relevantly, in discussing whether any particular extract fell within fair dealing, a great deal of judicial energy was spent determining whether there was sufficient commentary for 'criticism or review', or whether any 'news' was being 'reported'. In contrast, there was very little analysis of fairness, giving the appearance that classification of the defendant's purpose was determinative of whether fair dealing applied. With the judges often split on this classification exercise, *The Panel* has been criticised for resting on ad hoc and impressionist reasoning.[23]

Returning to cultural institutions, the 'law in books' in Australia therefore seemed to reject both agency-style arguments and an interpretation of research that included the broader research process. The *CCH* case was therefore of interest because, on both these matters, the Supreme Court of Canada came to a very different set of conclusions. This raised the question of whether a new vision of fair dealing might

---

Commentary, Law and Practice, 2nd edition (South Melbourne: Oxford University Press, 2015), pp. 269–270, 272–273, 290–291.

[21] For similar reasoning, see *Sillitoe* v. *McGraw-Hill Book Co (UK) Ltd* [1983] FSR 545, 558. But c.f. *Telstra Corporation Pty Ltd* v. *Premier Media Group Pty Ltd* (2007) 72 IPR 89, 98 (Allsop J, in denying Telstra's motion for interlocutory relief, refusing to rule out an argument that the provision of content to third parties by Premier was not a fair dealing associated with the reporting of news by those recipients). For analysis of the agency reasoning in *De Garis* and later cases, see J. McCutcheon and S. Holloway, 'Whose Fair Dealing? Third-Party Reliance on the Fair Dealing Exception for Parody or Satire' (2016) 27 *Australian Intellectual Property Journal* 54.

[22] Fair dealing discussed in (2001) 50 IPR 335 (Federal Court per Conti J); (2002) 190 ALR 468 (Full Court).

[23] M. Handler and D. Rolph, '"A Real Pea Souper": The Panel Case and the Development of the Fair Dealing Defences to Copyright Infringement in Australia' (2003) 27 *Melbourne University Law Review* 381.

The Supreme Court's Vision   235

help change the doctrine's relevance not just to Canadian users but elsewhere.

B   The CCH Litigation

Although the Supreme Court decision in *CCH* was delivered in March 2004, it was almost eleven years earlier, in July 1993, that the plaintiffs – all publishers of legal materials – commenced proceedings against the Law Society of Upper Canada.[24] The publishers' complaints related to copyright infringement said to be occurring at the Great Library at Osgoode Hall (run by the Law Society) through its request-based copying service and its installation of self-serve photocopiers. These types of practices, although longstanding in libraries throughout the world, were still under a legal question mark in Canada. As seen in Chapter 4, some four years were to elapse before the passage of a reform bill that introduced libraries, archives and museums exceptions into the Copyright Act, including provisions relevant to researcher services.[25] There was little Canadian case law interpreting the existing exception most relevant to library photocopying: fair dealing.[26] Blanket photocopying licences from the recently established Canadian Copyright Licensing Agency were being negotiated with libraries,[27] but at that time were of little use to the Great Library as it was not until late 1996 that the major legal publishers became members.[28] The existence of these licences underscored the uncertainty over fair dealing and the possibility of routine infringement by libraries through their own acts of copying, and/or by authorisation.

The patrons of the Great Library were members of the Law Society and judiciary as well as other authorised researchers. From 1996, the request-based service – called the 'custom photocopying service' – was administered under an Access to the Law Policy which explicitly invoked

---

[24] The three publishers were CCH Canadian Limited, Carswell Thomson Professional Publishing and Canada Law Book Inc.
[25] An Act to amend the Copyright Act (S.C. 1997, c. 24) (assented to 25 April 1997).
[26] As discussed in Chapter 9, Section II.D, to the extent indications could be found, these preferred narrower interpretations. For instance, in the 1992 edition of Tamaro's *Annotated Copyright Act*, the discussion on exceptions commenced with the statement that '[j]urisprudence has established that these exceptions should be interpreted restrictively and the courts will not take the role of legislator in order to create any': N. Tamaro, *The Annotated Copyright Act 1992* (Toronto: Carswell, 1992), p. 271.
[27] See, e.g., K. Adams, 'The Library Exceptions' in H. Knopf (ed), *The New Copyright Act: Managing the Impact* (Toronto: Insight Press, 1997), p. 351.
[28] See, e.g., D. Marshall, 'Access to the Law: Should Copyright Play a Role?' in H. Knopf (ed), *The New Copyright Act: Managing the Impact* (Toronto: Insight Press, 1997), p. 378.

fair dealing as the basis for making and supplying reproductions.[29] The Policy had five limbs: (1) only single copies would be provided; (2) copies would only be supplied where required for the purpose of research, review, private study, criticism or use in court; (3) this purpose, and the identity of the requestor, had to be disclosed on a request form; (4) requests for a copy of one case, article or statutory reference would usually be fulfilled, however larger requests, for instance for greater than 5 per cent of a work, would be reviewed and could be refused; and (5) the fee charged was for cost-recovery only. Copies could either be collected from the Library, mailed to requestors or sent to them by facsimile transmission. The self-serve machines were not monitored closely by the Library but had posted near them a notice which read:

The copyright law of Canada governs the making of photocopies or other reproductions of copyright material. Certain copying may be an infringement of the copyright law. This library is not responsible for infringing copies made by users of these machines.[30]

The publishers alleged that the Library had made and distributed unauthorised copies of legal materials and that this infringed copyright in two ways: first, under section 27(1), by infringing their exclusive rights of reproduction and communication to the public by telecommunication; and second, under section 27(2), by running afoul of the prohibition against sale or distribution of infringing copies. They also claimed the Law Society authorised infringement of copyright through the provision of the self-serve machines. The publishers sought a number of remedies, including declarations and a permanent injunction restraining the library from reproducing works they had published. Three key issues emerged by the time the case reached the Supreme Court: (1) whether the publishers' works were original and hence capable of copyright protection; (2) the meaning of authorisation for the purposes of infringement; and (3) in relation to the custom photocopying service, whether such reproductions – if they were prima facie infringing – were fair dealings. This book focuses on the last of these.

The matter was first heard in the Federal Court in late 1998 and a decision handed down on 9 November 1999, just after the libraries,

---

[29] The Access to the Law Policy is reproduced in full in *CCH*, n. 5 above, para. 61. The preamble stated that the service 'supports users of the Great Library who require access to legal materials while respecting the copyright of the publishers of such materials, in keeping with the fair dealing provisions in Section 27 of the Canadian *Copyright Act*'. The Library stated that introduction of the Policy did not change its existing practices in relation to its photocopying service.

[30] Ibid., para. 39.

archives and museums provisions had come into force.[31] Justice Gibson held that copies made by the custom photocopying service infringed copyright in some but not all of the publishers' works, there being some works that were not original and hence outside of copyright protection.[32] Because of this, Gibson J refused to grant the permanent injunction sought by the publishers, instead making some narrowly worded declarations.[33] On the self-serve photocopiers, Gibson J declined to reach a view, in part due to the lack of evidence and in part due to the possible relevance of the new sector-specific provisions.[34]

The Law Society ran a number of defences to the claims regarding its custom photocopying service, including that its activities were fair dealings. However, Gibson J rejected these arguments:

> The copying by the defendant in the course of its custom photocopy service was done in response to requests received, directly or indirectly, from members of the defendant; it was not done for the defendant's own use in research, private study, criticism or review.[35] ...
>
> The copying by the defendant in the course of its custom photocopy service was not for a purpose within the ambit of fair dealing notwithstanding that the ultimate use by the requester of the photocopying might itself be within the ambit of fair dealing. The conclusion in *Sillitoe* quoted above has been followed in both Australia and New Zealand. I am satisfied that the fair dealing exception should be strictly construed.[36]

Given that the Law Society had failed to establish that its activities were within the listed purposes, no consideration of the fairness of the photocopying service was necessary. Nor did Gibson J undertake any detailed analysis of the statutory purposes, suffice to say that fair dealing 'should be strictly construed'.[37] The introduction of the libraries, archives and museums provisions bolstered this conclusion, as it demonstrated that library photocopying was 'a matter of public policy concern that

---

[31] *CCH Canadian Ltd* v. *Law Society of Upper Canada* [2000] 2 FC 451 (Federal Court of Canada) ('*CCH Federal Court*'). The libraries, archives and museums provisions came into force on 1 September 1999.

[32] Ibid., 466–477, citing cases including *Tele-Direct (Publications) Inc* v. *American Business Information, Inc* [1998] 2 FC 22 and *Edutile Inc* v. *Automobile Protection Assn* (1997) 81 CPR (3d) 338. The items held *not* to be original were reported judicial decisions, headnotes, a case summary and a topical case index. The protected works were an annotated statutory instrument, a textbook and a monograph.

[33] Ibid., 496. Justice Gibson made two declarations, one recognising that copyright subsists in the annotated statutory instrument, textbook and monograph, and another stating that copyright had been infringed in the textbook and monograph.

[34] Ibid., 494–496.   [35] Ibid., 488.

[36] Ibid., 489, citing *Sillitoe*, n. 21 above, *De Garis*, n. 19 above and *Longman Group Ltd* v. *Carrington Technical Institute Board of Governors* [1991] 2 NZLR 574, 584.

[37] Ibid.

warranted special attention by Parliament' and that any exception-based defence should be argued within the parameters of those provisions.[38] Justice Gibson was therefore unsympathetic to the view that passage of the sector-specific exceptions left fair dealing arguments intact – even though one of those provisions expressly permitted libraries to do on behalf of a patron any act they themselves could do as a fair dealing.[39]

The case was appealed by both the publishers and the Law Society to the Federal Court of Appeal.[40] The Court of Appeal concluded that certain works that had been held to be unprotected by Gibson J were in fact original,[41] a matter affirmed by the Supreme Court. On the alleged authorisation of infringement, the Court of Appeal found in favour of the publishers but the Supreme Court held no such authorisation was made out. Finally, the Court of Appeal and the Supreme Court took a very different approach to fair dealing than that of Gibson J at first instance. The majority in the Court of Appeal stated that Gibson J had been in error in construing fair dealing so narrowly, but ultimately declined to make broad declarations in relation to the Library's Access to the Law Policy, concluding that determinations of fairness are 'enormously complex' and 'uniquely fact-specific', and must be undertaken 'each time an infringement is alleged'.[42] In contrast, the Supreme Court was prepared to reach such a blanket conclusion, holding that as the Law Society could establish that its Access to the Law Policy was research-based and fair, it could take the benefit of the fair dealing exception in section 29.

The first step towards understanding the reason for these different perspectives is to compare the justifications for copyright protection advanced in each judgment. Whilst Gibson J saw copyright as existing primarily for the benefit of authors, with a possible flow-on benefit to the public,[43] Linden JA in the Court of Appeal construed copyright as having dual purposes: it both rewarded the author with exclusive rights *and* encouraged the dissemination of works 'for the benefit of society at large'.[44] His Honour observed that 'the person who sows must be

---

[38] Ibid., 490.   [39] Canadian Copyright Act s. 30.2(1).
[40] *CCH Canadian Ltd* v. *Law Society of Upper Canada* (2002) 212 DLR (4th) 385 ('*CCH Court of Appeal*'). The majority decision was written by Linden JA with whom Sharlow JA concurred. A separate opinion was delivered by Rothstein JA.
[41] These being reported judicial decisions, headnotes, a case summary and a topical case index.
[42] *CCH Court of Appeal*, n. 40 above, 452.
[43] *CCH Federal Court*, n. 31 above, 464 ('[t]he object and purpose of the *Copyright Act* ... is to benefit authors, albeit that in benefiting authors, it is capable of having a substantially broader-based public benefit through the encouragement of disclosure of works for the advancement of learning or, as in this case, the wider dissemination of law').
[44] *CCH Court of Appeal*, n. 40 above, 407

allowed to reap what is sown, but the harvest must ensure that society is not denied some benefit from the crops'.[45] In Linden JA's view, the 'challenge facing this Court, and copyright law generally, is to find a fair and appropriate equilibrium that achieves both goals'.[46] Similar views were presented by McLachlin CJC writing the opinion of the Supreme Court. She referred with approval to the statement of Binnie J in *Théberge v. Galerie d'Art du Petit Champlain* that:

> The *Copyright Act* is usually presented as a balance between promoting the public interest in the encouragement and dissemination of works of the arts and intellect and obtaining a just reward for the creator ...
>
> The proper balance among these and other public policy objectives lies not only in recognising the creator's rights but in giving due weight to their limited nature.[47]

These understandings of copyright seem to have influenced the approach to fair dealing taken by both appellate courts. For instance, Linden JA commented that fair dealing 'is one of the provisions that grants users' rights',[48] and took the view that there was 'no basis in law or in policy' for the trial judge's narrow reading.[49] In the Supreme Court, McLachlin CJC stated:

> The fair dealing exception, like other exceptions in the *Copyright Act*, is a user's right. In order to maintain the proper balance between the rights of a copyright owner and users' interests, it must not be interpreted restrictively. As Professor Vaver ... has explained ...: 'User rights are not just loopholes. Both owner rights and user rights should therefore be given the fair and balanced reading that befits remedial legislation.'[50]

Against this backdrop, the Supreme Court's first important doctrinal conclusion was that fair dealing 'is always available': that a library could argue fair dealing and, if these arguments failed, then invoke a sector-specific exception.[51] This was in contrast to the approach of Gibson J at

---

[45] Ibid. The words used by Linden JA might be said to invoke concepts typically associated with Lockean justifications for property protection. The statement that society must 'not [be] denied some benefit from the crops' may align with the enough and as good proviso. For discussion of these concepts, see, e.g., W. Gordon, 'A Property Right in Self-Expression: Equality and Individualism in the Natural Law of Intellectual Property' (1993) 102 *Yale Law Journal* 1533; H. Breakey, 'Natural Intellectual Property Rights and the Public Domain' (2010) 73 *Modern Law Review* 208.

[46] Ibid.

[47] *CCH*, n. 5 above, para. 10, quoting *Théberge* v. *Galerie d'Art du Petit Champlain* [2002] 2 SCR 336, paras. 30–31.

[48] *CCH Court of Appeal*, n. 40 above, 440.   [49] Ibid., 441.

[50] *CCH*, n. 5 above, para. 48 citing D. Vaver, *Copyright Law* (Toronto: Irwin Law, 2000), p. 171.

[51] Ibid., para. 49.

first instance, who used the introduction of such provisions as a reason for reading down the ambit of fair dealing.

Second, the Supreme Court held that research should be defined expansively: that the term 'must be given a large and liberal interpretation in order to ensure that users' rights are not unduly constrained', and that research could include activity in commercial contexts such as lawyers 'carrying on the business of law for profit'.[52] A similar conclusion was reached in the Court of Appeal, albeit with somewhat different reasoning. There, Linden JA noted that Parliament had elected to qualify the exemption for study (i.e., it must be 'private' study) but not research. This was said to evidence an intention that *all* research – including commercial research – could fall within fair dealing, with the commerciality of research possibly relevant to the question of whether such activity was fair.[53]

Third, the Law Society was able to take the protection of fair dealing even though its activities were not undertaken in pursuit of its own research but that of its patrons. Chief Justice McLachlan wrote:

> Although the retrieval and photocopying of legal works are not research in and of themselves, they are necessary conditions of research and thus part of the research process. The reproduction of legal works is for the purpose of research in that it is an essential element of the legal research process.[54]

It was also relevant to the Supreme Court's conclusions that the Library had no other purpose in providing the custom photocopying service. For instance, the fees charged to patrons were calculated on a cost-recovery basis, meaning that the service was not being provided to generate a profit.

Although the Supreme Court did not use the language of agency, its findings clearly accepted that the research endeavours of one person could be relied upon by those who assist in the research process. In coming to this view, the Court did not refer to overseas case law cited by the trial judge, such as *Sillitoe* and *De Garis*.[55] These cases were dealt with by Linden JA in the Court of Appeal, who reached a similar conclusion to the Supreme Court: that the Library had no purpose other than assisting the research needs of its patrons, and could 'be said to have adopted that purpose as its own'.[56] Justice Linden held that the overseas decisions could be distinguished from the facts before the court, first, because the defendants in those cases 'had ulterior motives and simply

---

[52] Ibid., para. 51.   [53] *CCH Court of Appeal*, n. 40 above, 442.
[54] *CCH*, n. 5 above, para. 64.   [55] *Sillitoe*, n. 21 above and *De Garis*, n. 19 above.
[56] *CCH Court of Appeal*, n. 40 above, 443.

tried to adopt customers' or students' purposes as their own in order to escape liability', and second (and less convincingly), because 'the otherwise infringing activity was initiated by the alleged infringer, rather than the end user'.[57]

Fourth, the Supreme Court approved the non-exhaustive list of factors identified by Linden JA as relevant to the inquiry of whether a particular dealing was fair:[58]

(1) *The purpose of the dealing.* The Supreme Court acknowledged that whilst only dealings within the closed-ended list of purposes would be fair, 'these allowable purposes should not be given a restrictive interpretation or this could result in the undue restriction of users' rights'.[59] This was not a binary test; some allowable purposes might be more fair than others (e.g., research done for charitable purposes compared with research undertaken for commercial use).

(2) *The character of the dealing ('how the works were dealt with'[60]).* The Supreme Court gave the example of the quantity and availability of copies made, noting that '[i]f multiple copies of works are being widely distributed, this will tend to be unfair', but that a 'single copy of a work ... used for a specific legitimate purpose' will be 'easier' to characterise as a fair dealing.[61] Industry practices may be relevant in assessing the character of the dealing.

(3) *The amount of the dealing.* The Supreme Court held that this factor should be judged by reference to the quantity taken and its importance. Taking an entire work was not fatal to a fair dealing defence if this was necessary having regard to the work and the purpose of use.

(4) *Alternatives to the dealing (including 'whether the dealing was reasonably necessary to achieve the ultimate purpose'[62]).* It was observed that analysis of fairness should consider whether a non-infringing work could have been substituted and whether it was necessary to copy the underlying work at all.

(5) *The nature of the work.* Although not determinative, the Supreme Court accepted that dealing with published works might be fairer,

---

[57] Ibid. This argument is less persuasive as the activities challenged by the copyright owners in *De Garis* and *CCH* were broadly similar: the reproduction of materials in response to a client request. Although the service in *De Garis* was broader (as it also included identification of relevant material using criteria set by the client), it is difficult to see how the *CCH* activities could be construed as initiated by the end user but not those in *De Garis*. The services in *CCH* and *De Garis* did, however, differ in other crucial respects, e.g., the fee structure and ongoing supply of materials.

[58] See *CCH* (Court of Appeal), n. 40 above, 446–451; *CCH*, n. 5 above, paras. 53–60.

[59] *CCH*, n. 5 above, para. 54. [60] Ibid., para. 55. [61] Ibid. [62] Ibid., para. 57.

in particular when compared with use of a work that was confidential.

(6) *The effect of the dealing on the work*. The Supreme Court did not attempt a detailed analysis of this factor, noting only that it included consideration of any competition with the market for the original work and that although 'an important factor, it is neither the only factor nor the most important factor that a court must consider in deciding if the dealing is fair'.[63] As noted in Chapter 5, there are challenges in determining what considerations should be relevant to any market-focused factor, including the operation of normative and empirical considerations.

Applying these factors, the Supreme Court held that the Law Society's activities were fair, as assessed by the Access to the Law Policy. For instance, the Policy placed limits on when requests would be filled, based on the user's purpose and the amount of material requested. It stated that only single copies would be provided. The nature of the copied items – legal materials – also supported fair dealing. Further, the Supreme Court concluded that there were not any *reasonable* alternatives to the dealing, noting that it would not be realistic to expect researchers to perform all their research onsite. Nor was it relevant to this factor that a licence could be obtained from the copyright owners: '[i]f a copyright owner were allowed to licence people to use its work and then point to a person's decision not to obtain a licence as proof that his or her dealings were not fair, this would extend the scope of the owner's monopoly over the use of his or her work in a manner that would not be consistent with the *Copyright Act*'s balance between owner's rights and user's interests.'[64] Finally, the publishers did not introduce any evidence that the market for their works was impacted by the Great Library's photocopying service.

III   The Response from Lawyers

A   *Later Cases*

By the time of the Canadian fieldwork, a number of cases had cited or applied *CCH*, in particular its dicta on originality and infringement by authorisation.[65] However, two cases stood out as being of particular

---

[63] Ibid., para. 59, citing *Pro Sieben Media AG* v. *Carlton UK Television Ltd* [1999] FSR 610.
[64] Ibid., para. 70.
[65] See, e.g., *BMG Canada Inc* v. *John Doe* [2004] 3 FCR 241; *Society of Composers, Authors and Music Publishers of Canada* v. *Canadian Association of Internet Providers* [2004] 2 SCR 427; *Robertson* v. *Thomson Corporation* [2006] 2 SCR 363; *Canadian*

relevance to the empirical work as they analysed elements of the Supreme Court's decision that are relevant to exceptions. The first was the decision of Bastarache J in *Euro-Excellence Inc* v. *Kraft Canada Inc*, in relation to the philosophy of copyright.[66] The second was the Copyright Board's *Tariff No. 22A* decision in relation to fair dealing.[67] The facts of *Euro-Excellence* and *Tariff No. 22A* were both removed from *CCH*, demonstrating the decision's potential to influence outcomes in a variety of cases. Furthermore, the reasons delivered by Bastarache J in *Euro-Excellence* evidenced a clear intention to adopt a robust if not extended approach to the reasoning in *CCH*.[68] These cases, in the way they treated *CCH*, seemed to confirm its status as the most important fair dealing decision to have been handed down by a Canadian court.

1 Euro-Excellence After *CCH* it was common for courts to refer to the 'dual purposes' of and 'balance' in copyright law.[69] However, one judgment was particularly significant because of its depth of analysis regarding the philosophy of copyright: the decision of Bastarache J in *Euro-Excellence*. This case related to the parallel importation into Canada, by Euro, of Côte d'Or and Toblerone chocolate bars. Kraft had contractual arrangements with the European makers, under which it was the exclusive distributor of each product. In an attempt to stop Euro's activity, the European makers registered as artistic works various logos associated with the chocolate bars, and then executed an exclusive licence in favour of Kraft in relation to use of those works in Canada. Kraft sought to use its rights under this licence to bring proceedings for secondary infringement against Euro,[70] on the basis that Euro had contravened section 27(2)(e) of the Copyright Act:

> It is an infringement of copyright for any person to ... import into Canada for the purpose of doing anything referred to in paragraphs (a) to (c) [namely, sale and other commercial dealings] ... a copy of a work ... that the

---

Wireless Telecommunications Association v. *Society of Composers, Authors and Music Publishers of Canada* [2008] 3 FCR 539.

[66] [2007] 3 SCR 20.

[67] *Statement of Royalties to be Collected by SOCAN for the Communication to the Public by Telecommunication, in Canada, of Musical or Dramatico-Musical Works*, Tariff No 22A (Internet – Online Music Services) 1996–2006, Copyright Board of Canada, 18 October 2007.

[68] See, e.g., Hughes, n. 11 above, 58–60.

[69] See, e.g., *Society of Composers, Authors and Music Publishers of Canada* v. *Canadian Association of Internet Providers*, n. 65 above, 448–449; *Robertson* v. *Thomson Corporation*, n. 65 above, para. 69 (Abella J).

[70] Kraft was the Canadian owner of 'Côte d'Or' and 'Toblerone' trade marks but it did not rely on those rights in the proceedings.

person knows or should have known infringes copyright or would infringe copyright if it had been made in Canada by the person who made it.

Kraft were successful at first instance and in the Court of Appeal,[71] but in the Supreme Court a split bench held in favour of Euro.[72] Of the judges in the majority, four decided the case by reference to the words of section 27,[73] whilst three others, in reasons delivered by Bastarache J, grounded their decision in a purposive understanding of copyright law informed by *CCH* and *Théberge*.[74] Justice Bastarache referred to statements in both cases regarding the dual purposes of copyright law,[75] and observed that fair dealing was an 'essential part of copyright protection' because it recognises 'the limited nature of the rights of a copyright holder' and that '[n]ot every substantial reproduction of a copyrighted work counts as an infringement of copyright'.[76]

Justice Bastarche went further, however, by drawing from *Théberge* the proposition that to achieve balance, copyright protection should be limited to the 'legitimate economic interests' of rightsholders.[77] In his opinion, given copyright exists to protect 'the economic gains resulting from an exercise of skill and judgment', such protection 'cannot be leveraged to include protection of economic interests that are only tangentially related to the copyrighted work'.[78] In this case, the relevant copyright work was incidental to the consumer good being sold – it was a logo on the packaging of a chocolate bar. Justice Bastarache stated that paragraph (e) dealt with importation of infringing copies of 'works which are the result of skill and judgment' and not merely consumer goods that have a 'copyrighted work affixed to their wrapper'.[79]

---

[71] *Kraft Canada Inc* v. *Euro Excellence Inc* [2004] 4 FCR 410 (Federal Court per Harrington J); *Euro Excellence Inc* v. *Kraft Canada Inc et al* [2006] 3 FCR 91 (Federal Court of Appeal).

[72] Although seven judges held for Euro and two dissented (McLachlan CJ and Abella J), three of the majority judges noted that if, contrary to their opinion, section 27 was applicable, they would have agreed with the dissenting judges that its infringement had been established by Kraft (which would have generated a 5–4 decision in favour of Kraft).

[73] Binnie, Deschamps and Rothstein JJ, with whom Fish J agreed. They held that Euro's conduct did not contravene s. 27(2)(e) because Kraft could not establish that Euro had imported a copy of a work that 'would infringe copyright if it had been made in Canada by the person who made it'. The 'person who made it' was the European makers, and Kraft, as exclusive licensee, could not maintain an action against them.

[74] *Théberge*, n. 47 above.   [75] *Euro-Excellence*, n. 66 above, 60.

[76] Ibid., 59, referring to A. Drassinower, 'Taking User Rights Seriously' in M. Geist (ed), *In the Public Interest: The Future of Canadian Copyright Law* (Toronto: Irwin Law, 2005).

[77] Ibid., 58.   [78] Ibid., 62.

[79] Ibid., 63. Similar statements were made in relation to infringement by sale in paragraph (a).

Justice Bastarache's use of the language of 'legitimate economic interests' was a (controversial[80]) extension of the *Théberge* reasoning. In that case a number of commercial galleries created canvass posters of works by artist Claude Théberge via an ink-transfer process that lifted the image from authorised paper products. This resulted in a different type of product but did not change the number of products. Mr Théberge obtained pre-judgment seizure of canvasses, but the legality of that act depended on whether the items were infringing copies under the Copyright Act. Writing for the majority in a 4–3 decision in favour of the galleries, Binnie J held that the ink-transfer process did not infringe any 'legitimate economic interest'[81] as the substrate in which the intellectual property manifested (i.e., the ink) remained unaltered – it was only the backing that had changed. To hold differently would be to insert a new meaning for reproduction, because no new works (whether directly copied or otherwise) had been created.[82] The phrase 'legitimate economic interest' was therefore used to highlight that the applicable cause of action for modification without reproduction was under moral rights,[83] and to argue that extension of copyright to facts such as those in *Théberge* would create uncertainty regarding the permissible exploitation of tangible property rights in copies of artistic works.[84]

Justice Bastarache's decision in *Euro-Excellence* can thus be seen as an amalgam of the reasoning in *Théberge* and *CCH*. Justice Bastarache took seriously the idea of balance, using the language of 'legitimate economic interest' to act as a limit on copyright owner rights, in this case in relation to the interpretation of the secondary infringement provisions. The approach of Justice Bastarache could therefore be seen as invoking balance as an explicit 'meta-standard' by which to judge the content of copyright. Although the facts of *Euro-Excellence* were not directly relevant to cultural institutions, the case illustrated how the reasoning of *CCH* had the potential to influence judges in other cases – even those not involving exceptions or fair dealing. It therefore helped affirm the status

---

[80] For instance, Rothstein J stated that a purposive approach to statutory interpretation did not 'give judges licence to substitute their policy preferences for those of Parliament' (ibid. at 28), and considered that Bastarache J's interpretation went well beyond a permissible reading of the Copyright Act. Similarly, Abella J was critical of an approach to section 27 that, in her opinion, would be intolerably uncertain, 'inviting case-by-case judicial explorations into the uncharted area of what is "merely" incidental, "somewhat" incidental, or not incidental at all': at 73.

[81] *Théberge*, n. 47 above, para. 38.   [82] Ibid., paras. 42–50.

[83] Ibid., paras. 59–61. Because seizure was not possible where the complaint related to moral rights, it was necessary to show infringement of the reproduction right.

[84] Ibid., para. 40.

of *CCH* as an extremely important case in Canadian copyright jurisprudence.

2   *Tariff No. 22A* More relevant to cultural institutions was the reasoning of the Copyright Board of Canada in its *Tariff No. 22A* decision, handed down in October 2007. The Society of Authors, Composers and Music Publishers of Canada (SOCAN) had been involved in longstanding litigation to set tariffs for the online communication of music for the period 1996 to 2006. There had already been a series of proceedings in relation to the tariff, including appeals to the Federal Court of Appeal and Supreme Court.[85] The matter was then returned to the Board so it could deal with some discrete questions and determine whether SOCAN's tariff should be certified. At this point, fair dealing was not amongst the issues being presented to the Board. Instead, the question of whether it was a fair dealing for the purpose of research for online music sellers to offer previews of works – i.e., short excerpts to help consumers identify and select music they wished to purchase – was undertaken on the initiative of the Board and without submissions from the parties. To the extent that fair dealing was applicable, it would bring those excerpts outside the parameters of the tariff.

The Board concluded that fair dealing applied to previews. In a decision that quoted extensively from *CCH*, it noted that 'research' is not limited to non-commercial and private activities, and that if copying legal materials for the purpose of giving legal advice is 'research', 'so is streaming a preview with a view to deciding whether or not to purchase a download or CD'.[86] As in *CCH*, it was not fatal that music sites were not themselves conducting research, so long as they were facilitating the research of others.[87] The Board then turned to the question of fairness and, applying all six fairness factors recognised in *CCH*, held that each one supported the application of fair dealing to the practices before it.[88] For instance, the length of extracts and their availability through streaming but not download helped ensure that an excerpt only satisfied research purposes rather than substituting for the original work. The amount of the dealing was also modest when compared with ordinary consumption of musical works (which are listened to repeatedly and *in toto*). The Board could not think of a better or even viable alternative to ensure consumers selected the correct work, the availability of a licence

---

[85] See *Society of Composers, Authors and Music Publishers of Canada* v. *Canadian Association of Internet Providers* [2002] FCA 166; [2004] SCC 45.
[86] *Tariff No. 22A*, n. 67 above, para. 109.   [87] Ibid., para. 108.
[88] Ibid., paras. 111–115.

being irrelevant to determinations of fairness. Finally, the Board considered that any market impact would be positive, as facilitating consumer search activity for what it characterised as 'objects of commerce' would support sales, to the benefit of copyright owners.

A number of observations can be made about the *Tariff No. 22A* decision. First, it detached 'research' from the concept of 'private study', at least in so far as it accepted a definition of research that included investigation that would not fall within ordinary understandings of study. As noted by the Board in its comparison between the facts before it and those in *CCH*, '[t]he object of the investigation [here] is different, as are the level of expertise required and the consequences of performing an inadequate search. Those are differences in degree, not differences in nature'.[89] Thus the Board emphasised a process of research that consumers were required to undertake to identify music they wished to purchase and held that auditioning previews was part of that investigation.

Second, by adopting this reasoning, the Board gave effect to the *CCH* directive that research be given a liberal interpretation. Not only was it accepted that 'research' could be connected with ordinary consumer transactions (and not just high-brow activities involving thick books with big words), but the Board's fair dealing assessment was done by reference to the fairness and research orientation of the policies and practices of the music providers.[90]

Third, the *Tariff No. 22A* decision applied to audio works rather than textual materials. This was significant because much existing case law on the research limb has considered uses of literary works – examination papers, study guides, newspaper articles and the like[91] – leading to possible difficulties in applying dicta to other copyright works, or even to a perception that fair dealing does not apply to non-print items.

Finally, the Board held that fair dealing was applicable, even though the relevant works were being transmitted to an effectively unlimited audience of internet users, as other factors – such as the amount extracted and its lack of competition with full copies purchased for repeat listening – favoured fair dealing. Thus, even though *CCH* applied to the analogue world of library photocopying and dealt with a service dispatching point-to-point single copies, the Copyright Board did not consider fair dealing as inapplicable where copies were more broadly available. The *Tariff No. 22A* decision therefore confirmed and built on the

---

[89] Ibid., para. 109.   [90] Ibid., para. 116.
[91] See *University of London Press* v. *University Tutorial Press* [1916] 2 Ch 601, *Sillitoe*, n. 21 above and *De Garis*, n. 19 above.

precedent of *CCH*, sending a clear message that fair dealing can play a role in the online environment.

B   Academic Commentary

As noted at the outset of this chapter, the decision in *CCH* elicited a great deal of commentary: much laudatory, some equivocal, but all acknowledging its significance for understandings of copyright and the role of exceptions. Particularly for those who supported the decision's explicit users' rights language, *CCH* represented a welcome shift away from narrow, pro-owner interpretations of fair dealing. For instance, Abraham Drassinower encapsulated the views of many academics when he wrote that *CCH* 'is rightly and widely regarded as bringing forth a truly fundamental shift in the way Canadian copyright law is to be understood and practised'.[92] Commentary that was openly hostile to *CCH* is more difficult to come by, although some writing hinted that the Supreme Court's rejection of fair dealing orthodoxy was unprincipled and unlikely to persevere.[93]

This section explores four propositions that recurred in the academic response to *CCH*. There were that: (1) the case 'changed the copyright landscape' through its users' rights language;[94] (2) the elucidation of the six fairness factors, and the liberal interpretation of 'research', injected much-needed flexibility and responsiveness into fair dealing; (3) *CCH* could have a significant influence on user practices, including in the cultural institution sector; and (4) Canadian fair dealing now shared much common ground with fair use from US law. Each of these is discussed in turn.

Starting with the users' rights language, a number of different terms have been used to describe statutory provisions that permit activity that would otherwise infringe copyright,[95] such as exceptions (the language

---

[92] Drassinower, n. 76 above, p. 462.
[93] For example, Justice Hughes, writing extra-judicially, described the degree to which *CCH* departed from the restrictive interpretations of fair dealing in the prevailing case law. He attributed this shift to the lack of legislative appetite to undertake a wholesale review of Canadian copyright law: Hughes, n. 11 above, 60. Although not commenting on the merits of the *CCH* approach, his analysis might cause the reader to doubt the longevity of the decision.
[94] L. Murray and S. Trosow, *Canadian Copyright: A Citizen's Guide* (Toronto: Between the Lines, 2007), p. 74.
[95] See, e.g., D. Vaver, 'Canada's Intellectual Property Framework: A Comparative Overview' (2004) 17 *Intellectual Property Journal* 125, 148–149; A. Sims, 'Abundant Pest or Endangered Species? The Future of Fair Dealing in Copyright Law' (2008) 14 *New Zealand Business Law Quarterly* 231, 239–240.

used in the Canadian statute),[96] limitations and defences.[97] However, in David Vaver's book on copyright law published in 2000, these provisions were addressed under the heading 'Users' Rights'.[98] This text was highly influential on the decisions handed down by the Federal Court of Appeal and Supreme Court in *CCH*, both of which quoted with approval from Vaver's work.[99] In their guide to copyright published in 2007, Laura Murray and Samuel Trosow also used the terminology of users' rights, noting that had their book 'been written even just a few years earlier', they would have referred to 'exceptions to infringement'.[100]

This raises the question of the analytical significance of the phrase 'users' rights'. For instance, it might be argued that in the absence of some Hohfeldian-style significance to the term 'rights', in which copyright owners have corresponding duties,[101] there is no meaningful difference in styling fair dealing as a users' right as opposed to a defence, exception, limitation and so forth.[102] Similarly, one might speculate whether the Supreme Court's reference to users' rights was nothing more than a judicial shorthand to reiterate existing mantras on balance in copyright law.[103] For many commentators, however, the users' rights terminology of *CCH* was highly significant as it explained or even reconceptualised the role of exceptions in copyright law. For instance, Matthew Rimmer argued that the Supreme Court decision affirmed the

---

[96] Canadian Copyright Act ss. 29–32.2 (headed 'Exceptions').
[97] See, e.g., L. Harris, *Canadian Copyright Law*, 3rd edition (Toronto: McGraw Hill, 2001), pp. 126–150 (discussing 'limitations on, or exceptions from' rights of authors and copyright holders in a chapter titled 'limitations on rights'); E. Judge and D. Gervais, *Intellectual Property: The Law in Canada* (Toronto: Thomson Carswell, 2005), pp. 80–98 (using the terminology of 'exceptions' in their analysis of 'Statutory Defences').
[98] Vaver, n. 50. above, pp. 169–227. Vaver was not the first scholar to use the language of users' rights in relation to copyright: see, e.g., L. Patterson and S. Lindberg, *The Nature of Copyright: A Law of Users' Rights* (Athens: University of Georgia Press, 1991). For a recent contribution that presents a broader picture of users' rights by bringing together analysis of copyright, tangible property and contract, see P. Chapdelaine, *Copyright User Rights: Contracts and the Erosion of Property* (Oxford: Oxford University Press, 2017).
[99] *CCH Court of Appeal*, n. 40 above 441; *CCH*, n. 5 above, para. 48.
[100] Murray and Trosow, n. 94 above, p. 74.
[101] W. Hohfeld, 'Some Fundamental Legal Conceptions as Applied in Legal Reasoning' (1913) 23 *Yale Law Journal* 16. For discussion, see, e.g., H. Breakey, 'User's Rights and the Public Domain' [2010] *Intellectual Property Quarterly* 312; Chapdelaine, n. 98 above, pp. 45–54.
[102] Others have argued that there is or should be a qualitative difference between, for instance, what we label as 'exceptions' and 'limitations': e.g., A. Drassinower, 'Exceptions Properly So-Called' in A. Drassinower and Y. Gendreau (eds), *Language and Copyright* (Montréal: Carswell, 2010); A. Christie, 'Maximising Permissible Exceptions to Intellectual Property Rights' in A. Kur and V. Mizaras (eds), *The Structure of Intellectual Property Law: Can One Size Fit All?* (Cheltenham: Edward Elgar, 2011).
[103] For a consideration (and rejection) of this view, see Gervais, n. 12 above, 155–156.

importance of exceptions for cultural institutions: that they are not 'historical accidents and contingencies' but are 'essential and necessary to promote ... education, learning and research'.[104] Carys Craig noted the potential for 'conflicts between owners and users to be fought on equal footing' because rights-based language legitimises and elevates the user interest.[105] Similarly, Daniel Gervais noted that '[w]hen reading *CCH*, one is drawn to the conclusion that the court weighted the authors' exclusive rights and the users' "right" to use the work on level plates of the proverbial scale'.[106] He suggested that the Supreme Court was saying that '[u]sers have a "right" to deal fairly with a protected work' in furtherance of the broader 'equilibrium' the Act is trying to achieve.[107] Even Normand Tamaro, who was sceptical of *CCH* if his *Annotated Copyright Act* is anything to go by,[108] amended the introductory remarks from previous editions to add that the 'modern' rule is that exceptions must be 'construed to their fullest extent'.[109]

Second, one of the recurring themes in the commentary was that *CCH* created, for the first time in Canada, an explicit but flexible framework for fair dealing analysis.[110] Gervais saw this as 'perhaps the area where the Court's decision, in confirming with some clarifications the Court of Appeal's approach, may have a significant impact'.[111] Murray and Trosow noted that in the absence of legislative reform, 'the test in *CCH* constitutes the most authoritative guide to the question of fair dealing'.[112] It therefore became standard for copyright treatises to include extensive discussion on the meaning of fairness following the six-factor analysis in *CCH*.[113]

A third theme in the academic commentary was that *CCH* may have a significant influence on the development of fair dealing practices and industry norms. Precisely how this impact would manifest was not

---

[104] M. Rimmer, 'Canadian Rhapsody: Copyright Law and Research Libraries' (2004) 35 *Australian Academic & Research Libraries* 193.
[105] Craig, n. 13 above, p. 454. Craig has also argued that there are risks associated with users' rights language, notably that it may be to accept that authors are granted strong, individual rights: C. Craig, 'Globalizing User Rights-Talk: On Copyright Limits and Rhetorical Risks' (2017) 33 *American University International Law Review* 1.
[106] Gervais, n. 12 above, 156.   [107] Ibid., 157.
[108] The analysis of *CCH* being, in comparison with other topics, particularly heavy on editorialising.
[109] E.g., Normand Tamaro, *2009 Annotated Copyright Act* (Toronto: Carswell, 2008), p. 525.
[110] See, e.g., Scassa, n. 8 above, 96.   [111] Gervais, n. 12 above, 157.
[112] Murray and Trosow, n. 94 above, p. 81.
[113] See, e.g., Judge and Gervais, n. 97 above, pp. 84–85; Murray and Trosow, n. 94 above, pp. 81–85; see also *The Canadian Encyclopedic Digest (Western)*, Fourth Edition, Volume 8, Title 35, 'Copyright' (title current to November 2008), para. 279.

necessarily explored in detail, but scholars saw much promise for the decision. For instance, Drassinower's words were ripe with *CCH*'s potential: the case 'is rightly and widely regarded as bringing forth a truly fundamental shift in the way Canadian copyright law is to be understood and practiced'.[114] There was also the suggestion from Scassa that cultural institutions may benefit from a liberalised fair dealing provision:

> The impact of *CCH Canadian* is likely to be far-ranging. ... Individual and institutional users of works are given broader latitude to make use of the works without payment to the creators. The implications of the decision may be particularly important for those who assist users in accessing works; such as libraries, schools and other public institutions.[115]

In Scassa's view, acceptance that fair dealing could apply to a fair and research-based copying policy was particularly significant for institutional users with document delivery services, as it alleviated the need for each individual request to be monitored closely.[116] Pina D'Agostino made a similar point, noting that *CCH* might open the way to other industry- or sector-specific guidelines being given judicial approval, with attendant benefits in discouraging litigation and encouraging permissible re-use of protected material.[117]

Finally, the perceived liberalisation of fair dealing by *CCH* led to comparative analysis,[118] in particular with the position in the United States. Pre-*CCH* analysis observed what Vaver termed a 'striking' contrast between US and Canadian law,[119] particularly by virtue of the open-ended fair use exception in the former. Following 2004, there was said to be a greater synergy between the two systems, not only in the relevant fairness factors, but the types of activities to which fair dealing and fair use might apply. This is encapsulated in the following statement of Gervais, who wrote in 2004 that there is

> little doubt that with respect to fair dealing Canada's copyright legislation is now closely aligned with the United States' fair use doctrine. Canadian courts do, however, have significantly more flexibility in that, first, they do not have to apply all criteria in each case; and, second, criteria (1) and (6) are defined in a more open fashion than the corresponding US criteria. An important distinction between the two systems is that for the dealing to be fair in Canada, it must be

---

[114] Drassinower, n. 76 above, 462.   [115] Scassa, n. 8 above, 89.   [116] Ibid., 94.
[117] G. D'Agostino, 'Healing Fair Dealing? A Comparative Analysis of Canada's Fair Dealing to UK Fair Dealing and US Fair Use' (2008) 53 *McGill Law Journal* 309, 357.
[118] See, e.g., D'Agostino, ibid.; B. Ong, 'Fissures in the Façade of Fair Dealing: Users' Rights in Works Protected by Copyright' [2004] *Singapore Journal of Legal Studies* 150 (drawing some comparisons with fair dealing law in Singapore).
[119] Vaver, n. 95 above, 149.

for a designated purpose. Yet, even on this point the two systems are fairly close.[120]

D'Agostino's work echoed these sentiments. In her comparison of Canadian and UK fair dealing and US fair use, she concluded that in contrast with the United Kingdom, the enumerated purposes in Canadian law 'are no longer rigid', and when compared with the United States, the fairness factors were more flexible, as they provide a 'future guiding framework' for analysis and may be supplemented by other considerations.[121] Overall, D'Agostino considered Canada's regime 'the most user-centred'.[122]

IV The Response from Cultural Institutions

A Introduction

The analysis in Section III suggested that far-ranging effects might arise from the *CCH* decision. The Supreme Court's acceptance that copyright furthers dual purposes was repeated in subsequent case law, and in Bastarache J's judgment in *Euro-Excellence*, there was a particularly strong post-*CCH* statement of the policy considerations said to drive interpretation of the Canadian Copyright Act. The Supreme Court's decision was also viewed as significant because of its insistence that terms such as 'research' be read broadly, raising the possibility that fair dealing could arise in circumstances beyond those seen traditionally in the case law. An example of this occurred with the Copyright Board's *Tariff No. 22A* decision of October 2007, which applied fair dealing to consumer search activity in an online environment – circumstances very different from the world of library photocopying in *CCH*. Finally, the academic reception given to *CCH* was overwhelmingly positive, emphasising the desirability of the Supreme Court's articulation of the philosophical framework underpinning copyright, and foreseeing shifts in the way exceptions were utilised by Canadian users.

However, the institutional responses to *CCH* as described by participants in fieldwork conducted in 2008 and 2009 made it clear that the decision's reception had been extremely muted. As discussed in Section IV.B, the main reported shift in practice related to user request services at academic libraries, where fair dealing arguments were used to justify new digital delivery platforms. In public libraries already relying on fair dealing, there was additional comfort that this analysis was correct. The

---

[120] Gervais, n. 12 above, 159. [121] D'Agostino, n. 117 above, 356. [122] Ibid., 358.

CCH decision also appeared to influence some universities to incorporate fair dealing into policies on electronic reserves, although at the time of the fieldwork this was only the case for a handful of institutions and was said to be highly controversial. For other public activities, including mass digitisation and online publication, reported practices were relatively consistent: fair dealing arguments were not being considered; public-domain works were preferred; and when third-party copyright works were used, this was with the permission of the copyright owner.

Section IV.B describes the reported responses to *CCH*. Its analysis is grouped around three categories of practice: (1) user request services; (2) electronic reserves; and (3) online activities.

B Reported Impact

1 User Request Services In terms of numbers, the largest reported shift in practice following *CCH* occurred in academic libraries, where a significant number of institutions rolled out desktop delivery as part of their user request services. Prior to *CCH*, standard practice was for recipients to receive requested material in hardcopy form. Under new systems, copies were supplied electronically, for instance using a password-protected central server from which the copy could be printed, or (for the 'wild and crazy types'[123]) sending the material by email. One interviewee estimated that, as at May 2008, approximately 20 to 30 per cent of university libraries had moved to desktop delivery. Amongst institutions participating in this project, a number of interviewees confirmed that digital delivery was being (or was planned to be) provided under a fair dealing analysis.[124] One explained:

> We used to really rely on [sector-specific] exceptions ... that's where we hooked the right for us to do something. But we've actually really pulled back from that, and we're saying that [specific] exceptions [are] not the way to go, because really, anything that we're doing should be able to be done under fair dealing. And so much more now, when we look at our strategy, it's fair dealing.[125]

Another stated *CCH* was

> definitely having an impact in terms of giving people a little bit more confidence that they can do some things – probably most in the document delivery theme than anything else. ... More and more institutions here, as part of pilot projects [for new interlibrary loan procedures] are now receiving digitally and passing copies along digitally, to a point where an individual can pick them up, and then our intermediary copy will disappear after a period of time. Prior to *CCH*, we had

[123] 117L.   [124] E.g., 101L, 117L, 127L, 146L, 156L. Also: 144X.   [125] 117L.

all talked about doing that ... but there wasn't anyone who was willing to make that leap.[126]

It appeared that the prevailing view in Canada was that the applicable specific exceptions did not extend to the supply of copies electronically.[127] This analysis was clearly right for the interlibrary supply provision in section 30.2(5), which allowed institutions to do certain acts for patrons of other institutions, 'but the copy given to the patron must not be in digital form'. In contrast, section 30.2(2) provided that a library, archives or museum may make 'by reprographic reproduction' a copy of certain scholarly and newspaper articles for a user who requires that copy for research or private study. Whether digital distribution was permitted depended on the meaning of 'reprographic reproduction', a term not defined in the Act, but suggested by other sources to exclude electronic reproductions.[128] This was consistent with reported industry attitudes, meaning that, in general, it was not until *CCH* that academic libraries became confident that they could justify digital delivery by reference to fair dealing.

In contrast with academic libraries, copying services in public libraries seemed to be less well utilised. At the time of the fieldwork, many public libraries had self-serve photocopiers for public use and offered interlibrary loan services[129] (these relating to original rather than copy material).[130] Some libraries also maintained special collections,[131] some

---

[126] 127L.   [127] E.g., 127L, 146L.
[128] See, e.g., J. Erola and F. Fox, *From Gutenberg to Telidon: A White Paper on Copyright* (Consumer and Corporate Affairs Canada and Department of Communications, Government of Canada, 1984), p. 40 (defining the term 'reprography' as 'the making of visually perceptible copies by any means'); Harris, n. 97 above, p. 144 (reprographic reproduction 'is generally photocopying and does not include, for example, scanning the article into a computer'); Vaver, n. 50, p. 207 (user request provisions would not apply to 'downloading [a] work from the Internet or an electronic database' as '[t]his copying is clearly not "reprographic reproduction"').
[129] Examples of libraries that (as at July 2009) referred to self-serve photocopiers and interlibrary loan services on their public websites: Edmonton Public Library, Alberta; Greater Victoria Public Library, British Columbia; Halifax Public Libraries, Nova Scotia; Montréal Public Libraries Network, Quebec; Newfoundland & Labrador Public Libraries; Regina Public Library, Saskatchewan; Saskatoon Public Library, Saskatchewan; Vancouver Island Regional Library, British Columbia; Waterloo Public Library, Ontario; Winnipeg Public Library, Manitoba; and Yukon Public Libraries.
[130] E.g., as explained by 107L.
[131] These were commonly collections of genealogical and local history material. Examples of libraries that (as at July 2009) referred to special collections on their public websites: Central Library branch, Regina Public Library (Prairie History Collection); Central Library branch, Greater Victoria Public Library (Local History Room); Frances Morrison Library, Saskatoon Public Library (Local History Room); Main Library branch, Waterloo Public Library (Ellis Little Local History Room); Nanaimo

of which were described as having associated copying services.[132] Public websites tended not to discuss the copyright aspects of these services in detail. One might speculate that blanket licences with Access Copyright and Copibec might be relevant to published print materials, and that the sector-specific exceptions would be of very limited relevance to special collections given restrictions in their application.[133] The fact that some websites referred to non-commercial and research-based requests being filled raised the possibility that fair dealing might be relevant.

Amongst the public library participants in the fieldwork, it was reported that materials from special collections were often copied for researchers without regard to copyright status.[134] This was linked with fair dealing; as one interviewee said, 'it's a little bit like allowing people to photocopy from books or any other medium'.[135] It was only when some form of redistribution or commercial use was anticipated that permission was required. In some instances, requestors were asked to produce evidence of clearance before the request was fulfilled, whilst in others, copies were provided subject to a disclaimer that use was at the recipient's own risk and may require a licence. Importantly for this discussion, fair dealing arguments were not reported to have changed following *CCH*. One interviewee said that the 'very conservative' practices of their institution had remained and 'I don't see it changing rapidly soon'.[136] For another, there was greater confidence that existing interpretations of the law were defensible:

In the few instances where situations have arisen, we're probably a little more comfortable about some of the things that we're doing, than we might have been in the past. But I certainly cannot point to any significant policy change arising from it.[137]

The position of the libraries that participated in this research can be contrasted with that of the museums and archives, who implemented disparate practices for their user request services. Some interviewees described procedures in which licences were more or less mandatory, even for research use.[138] For instance, one archivist commented that 'in

---

Harbourfront Library, Vancouver Island Regional Library (British Columbia North West Collection).

[132] Examples from the list, ibid: Local History Room Saskatoon Public Library; Ellis Little Local History Room, Waterloo Public Library, Ontario.

[133] E.g., Canadian Copyright Act s. 30.2 applies only to articles, whilst s. 30.21 relates to the copying of unpublished works deposited in archives, which under ordinary usage would seem to exclude library collections even if they have an archival quality.

[134] 102L, 136L, 147L.   [135] 147L.   [136] 125L.   [137] 107L.

[138] E.g., 106A, 108G, 124A.

my experience here, fair dealing is just not used in audiovisual and visual works'.[139] Another archivist explained that a much more restrictive policy had been adopted for audiovisual works than print collections, because many of the former items were made by commercially active creators and were often being requested for profit-making activities, 'so the risk is higher, right off the bat'.[140] One of the art museums also noted that permissions were always essential; that institution had not considered that fair dealing might be available as an alternative for some requests.[141]

For other museums and archives, there was a degree of comfort in fulfilling researcher requests without requiring permission,[142] including using electronic delivery. Whilst some interviewees situated their treatment of researcher requests within the prism of fair dealing,[143] others did not mention these arguments.[144] It did not appear that *CCH* had done much to encourage recourse to fair dealing, except (for those aware of the decision) to provide greater comfort that such arguments were defensible.[145] Finally, certain norms did not seem to be coterminous with the law. For instance, some institutions treated similarly things such as 'research', 'private', 'personal' and 'non-commercial' use, as distinguished from 'commercial use' or 'publication', even though there was no such delineation in the Copyright Act.

Where material was requested for purposes outside research and personal use, the non-library participants either required evidence that permission had been obtained before supplying the reproduction, or fulfilled the request on the basis that the requestor was responsible for clearing any rights.[146] This was not dissimilar to their colleagues in libraries.

In sum, there was some common ground in US and Canadian experiences in relation to external requests outside of sector-specific exceptions. Leaving aside academic libraries, there were interviewees from both countries who reported that responsibility for clearing rights was generally placed on the requestor, but that they would fulfil requests without any evidence of clearance. For some requests, it seemed that the institution was *itself* invoking fair dealing (or for US interviewees, fair use) for their act. In others, it seemed that institutions were relying primarily on the disclaimer of copyright responsibility. Significantly for

---

[139] 124A.   [140] 106A.   [141] 108G.
[142] E.g., 103G, 104M, 106A, 115A, 126A, 130M, 135G, 137G.
[143] E.g., 106A, 115A, 126A, 135G.   [144] E.g., 103G, 104M, 130M, 137G.
[145] For instance, 106A observed that 'there was probably not dramatic change in the activities, but from a legal perspective, I think we had more foundation for what the content is'.
[146] E.g., 103G, 104M, 108G, 126A, 130M, 135G, 137G, 138M.

this discussion, however, whilst some fair dealing practices overlapped with those under fair use, *CCH* did not seem to have had a significant impact on this position. The only Canadian interviewees who reported any significant change to external request practices in response to *CCH* came from academic libraries – institutions whose collections, services and patrons are arguably closest to those of the Great Library of Osgoode Hall.

2 Electronic Reserves and Virtual Learning Environments (VLEs)

As discussed in Chapter 5, many universities now use electronic reserves and VLEs rather than supplying course readings and other materials in hardcopy form. At the time of the fieldwork in 2008 and 2009, only a handful of academic libraries had amended their electronic reserves policies to refer to fair dealing. Although quantitatively small in terms numbers, this application of fair dealing was perhaps the most analytically significant post-*CCH* shift, because such a practice is a number of steps removed from a request-based copying service: it applies fair dealing in an environment in which copies are made available to multiple people; and it tests the capacity of research and private study (as understood in copyright law) to apply to aspects of teaching and instruction.

Prior to the fieldwork there were reports that whilst many Canadian universities were moving to electronic reserves, their contents were frequently limited, and 'the single most inhibiting factor to the widespread adoption of electronic reserves in Canada is copyright clearance'.[147] For instance, in an email survey of universities undertaken by Joan Dalton in June 2004,[148] although 20 out of 28 respondents had electronic reserves, only half included links to scanned copyright materials. These were cleared under permissions negotiated individually or through Access Copyright.[149] For those not hosting scanned materials, the costs of licensing was cited most frequently as the reason.[150]

To put these findings in context, Dalton described an electronic reserves pilot study at her own institution, the Leddy Library at the University of Windsor, covering four semesters from the second half of 2002 to the first half of 2004.[151] Whilst the Library experienced a reasonably good clearance rate (with 84 per cent of the 189 permissions

---

[147] P. Warner, 'Reserves, Electronic Reserves and Copyright in Canada' (2006) 1 *Canadian Online Library and Archives Journal*.
[148] J. Dalton, 'Electronic Reserves and the Copyright Challenge in Canada' (2007) 17 *Journal of Interlibrary Loan, Document Delivery & Electronic Reserve* 97. The email was sent to 36 libraries, thus eliciting a 77 per cent response rate: at 99.
[149] Ibid., 99–100.   [150] Ibid., 100.   [151] Ibid., 105–109.

sought being granted[152]), it was also noted that during peak clearance time (which started a few weeks prior to semester, and then continued well into it), the time and resources required for clearance accounted for 70 per cent of a full time library position. By the end of these four semesters, reserves had only been constructed for twenty-nine courses, a long way from the 240 offered on average.[153] 'This quickly convinced us', wrote Dalton, 'that a long-term sustainable electronic reserves service could not be accomplished at this rate'.[154] This experience was similar to that of an institution that participated in this research, which ran its own pilot study at around the same time.[155] Like the Leddy Library, it sought to clear content for electronic reserves for a small number of courses. The result was that this institution decided not to roll out this approach across all courses as the costs – in terms of licence fees and the time involved in clearing rights – would have been prohibitive. The *CCH* decision did not alter this position, largely due to risk aversion: the university was not comfortable with the possibility that reliance on fair dealing might result in a lawsuit, a position it has retained over the years.

Other experiences from this research were also consistent with the study by Dalton. Interviewees reported that instead of uploading copies of articles to subject web pages, many reserves simply provided links to records in subscription databases, should that be permitted by the relevant licence. Material included in full was generally authored by faculty members, such as lecture slides and course materials. For third-party copyright, the usual approach was to insist that permission be obtained, and as noted above, only a few universities were reported to have introduced an explicit fair dealing analysis in their electronic reserves policies. Interviewees who were familiar with these policies pointed to a number of aspects that were said to keep copying within the exception. Where the desired material was available electronically, such policies would advise that a persistent URL be used instead of making a fresh copy. There were also limits on the accessibility of reserves, typically being confined to the instructor and students of a given course. One contentious matter was whether the use was for 'research', 'private study' or another recognised purpose. Some interviewees argued that the expansive interpretation of fair dealing urged by the Supreme Court was such that reserves could be seen as facilitating the research and private study of students. Nevertheless, amongst the majority of institutions, understandings of the law had not coalesced to the stage where they were comfortable in applying fair

---

[152] Ibid., 107 (Table 1).   [153] Ibid., 106.   [154] Ibid., 108.
[155] As an added measure to preserve the anonymity of research participants, pseudonyms will not be used for certain elements of this analysis.

dealing to electronic reserves.[156] As such, to the extent that other universities had considered following suit, decision-makers were said to frightened that their institution might become 'the test case'[157] for an activity considered the 'hot button'[158] in Canada.

As will be seen in the Chapter 8, the hints of change in 2008 and 2009 crystallised into a significant departure from existing practices from about 2012 onwards, with many universities withdrawing from the Access Copyright blanket licence. This raised the question – addressed in further interviews and examination of publicly available sources – as to what happened to cause such a marked shift, including the role of fair dealing arguments. As will be seen in Chapter 8, these developments did not involve a renunciation of licensing as institutions still relied heavily on permissions. At the time of the first round of fieldwork, however, universities had largely continued their existing arrangements rather than roll out new, *CCH*-inspired practices.

3 *Online Activities* For online activities such as the creation of virtual exhibitions and collection databases, the practices across participating institutions were similar: exceptions were not considered relevant, and the copyright management strategy was to only use public domain materials or items for which they had rights, meaning that third-party copyright material was cleared.[159] There were a handful of reports of institutions hosting uncleared content,[160] but these were exceptional amongst participants.

Given the academic and judicial response to *CCH*, it was striking that no institutions in this study had considered the possibility of fair dealing arguments applying to public uses beyond request services and electronic reserves. Interviewees did not, for example, situate the creation of online collection databases as possibly within fair dealing. The capacity of an institution to adopt such a position would obviously depend on the extent to which the database was research-based and fair. But even here, the Copyright Board's decision in *Tariff No. 22A* illustrated that fair dealing can apply for non-traditional forms of research undertaken in

---

[156] 127L noted that '[*CCH*] was a huge step forward, but when you look at where the yardsticks are for fair dealing and fair use for US ... that yardstick is way down the road, still. ... The legislation is the biggest hold back, because the interpretation is not as open as it is in the US.'
[157] 119L.   [158] 117L.
[159] E.g., 102L, 103G, 105G, 106A, 108G, 110M, 124A, 126A, 125L, 128L, 130M, 136L, 141L, 146L, 147L, 153M.
[160] One example was a collection of historical ephemera that was largely orphaned. Another related to works that were in the public domain in Canada but not in the United States.

an online environment. When other fairness factors are considered, such as the nature of the underlying work, the resolution of digital reproductions and any limitations on access or re-use, there would seem to be a defensible argument that fair dealing can be applicable, using arguments modelled after US cases such as *Kelly v. Arriba Soft*,[161] *Bill Graham Archives*[162] and *Perfect 10*.[163]

It seemed, therefore, that existing understandings of fair dealing had only moved so far after *CCH*. There seemed to be apprehension regarding the longevity of the decision, for instance by interviewees who questioned whether exceptions may be narrowed in the future or dicta from *CCH* overturned.[164] Some interviewees also observed that the conservatism of their institution stood in the way of developing fair dealing arguments for broader public uses.[165] Institutions were said to be fearful of being sued and wanted assurance that their practices were lawful, even if individual staff were attracted to forward-leaning interpretations of exceptions. For instance, one interviewee said:

Personally, I [prefer] a more liberal interpretation of the law [where you] risk getting sued, just so you can establish the case law. But there's a great risk aversion, at the moment, both within the federal government and this institution, towards any sort of liberalisation of access through the web. Everything's got to be cut and dried, and it's quite incredible.[166]

Another stated:

I would say most libraries have no idea what to do with that *CCH* case. ... Most people don't want to deal with copyright at all; they want a prescriptive [answer] because they don't know. ... So we need to give people the tools to be able to make some really good decisions, and to help our users. My idea is that librarians,

---

[161] *Kelly v. Arriba Soft Corporation*, 77 F Supp 2d 1116 (CD Cal, 1999); 336 F 3d 811 (9th circuit, 2003).
[162] *Bill Graham Archives v. Dorling Kindersley Limited*, 386 F Supp 2d 324 (SDNY, 2005); 448 F 3d 605 (2nd circuit, 2006).
[163] *Perfect 10 v. Google*, 416 F Supp 2d 828 (CD Cal, 2006); appealed as *Perfect 10 v. Amazon.com*, 487 F 3d 701 (9th circuit, 2007).
[164] E.g., 106A ('my concern is that the creators want no exceptions anymore; so my concern is to at least maintain what we have'), 113X ('there's always the chance that [*CCH*] will be reinterpreted [or] legislation will override it, so the ultimate tool is the legislative tool, so we have a better understanding of what the exceptions are'), 141L (predicting reform of the Copyright Act to deal with *CCH*), 144X (once exceptions are opened up for legislative consideration, there is a risk they will be narrowed), 146L (people do not consider a Supreme Court decision as proper law and will only revise practices in response to legislative change).
[165] E.g., 107L, 108G, 119L, 123L, 125L, 136L, 144X, 146L, 148L. Interviewee 148L said that their institution was unlikely to 'push the envelope' without clarity regarding the content of the law.
[166] 102L.

for instance, need to take up as much room in user rights as we can. [...] And it is our right to be able to do this, so it's not threatening the creator community, it's not threatening the publishers, it's a right of a Canadian citizen, to make use of fair dealing. And that's our role: to permit that.[167]

Others also indicated that lack of expert knowledge was a problem:

If we had a lawyer around, if we knew more, we'd take more risks. We would be able to go a little further. There's probably things we're not doing, but we don't know about, and we don't have time to [find out ourselves].[168]

[Copyright is] big, it's very big. And it covers many areas and many different angles, with the exhibition, publication, library, archives, other related laws: privacy, access to information. And the reality is we're just overwhelmed with keeping up.[169]

In sum, when licensing was not possible, for instance because of prohibitive transaction costs or because material was orphaned, it was often the case that participating institutions simply avoided using those items on websites and other online outputs. Whilst there were some exceptions to this general trend, they were rare and seemed to be grounded primarily in pure risk management rather than fair dealing.

V   Conclusion

In Chapter 5 it was observed that fair use played a meaningful role in the reported practices of US cultural institutions. Although drafted as a standard, a number of factors appeared to give institutions comfort in relying on section 107, including interpretations in the case law. Whilst the volume of fair dealing case law in Canada was considerably lower, the Supreme Court decision in *CCH* appeared to match and even surpass many of the US decisions because it was a unanimous decision from Canada's highest court; it related directly to cultural institutions; and it contained statements urging an expansive interpretation of fair dealing. The Supreme Court's sentiments were repeated in other decisions and, in the Copyright Board's *Tariff No. 22A* decision, were applied to preview facilities used by online music sellers. It might therefore be hypothesised that *CCH* would encourage greater reliance on fair dealing by cultural institutions, thus unlocking the flexibility of a provision centred on fairness.

However, the 2008 and 2009 fieldwork suggested that the institutional response to *CCH* had been extremely muted. Academic analysis that lauded the decision sat in stark contrast to the actual practices of the

[167] 101L.   [168] 104M.   [169] 116M.

sector, which had not, by and large, been influenced by the Supreme Court's vision of fair dealing as a user's right. This raised the question of why: what had happened in Canadian cultural institutions to make their response to *CCH* so different from their US counterparts? Was this a product of the purpose-based limitations of fair dealing? Did institutions require further judicial or legislative reassurance that *CCH* was not a temporary aberration? Were there other non-legal factors that limited Canadian reliance on fair dealing even though, on a purely doctrinal analysis, it may extend much further?

The thesis of this book is that drafting, alone, does not explain the difference between US and Canadian experiences. Instead, the fieldwork also revealed numerous historical, cultural and institutional factors that influenced the decision-making of cultural institutions, with the result that fair use was a far more significant component of copyright management practices than fair dealing. If the fieldwork had stopped there, we might conclude that expanded fair dealing would be unlikely to have traction in Canada, let alone fair use. However, another lesson from the empirical work is that norms and interpretative practices are susceptible to change – and sometimes at a pace and magnitude that is highly surprising. As discussed in Chapter 8, such a change was to occur in academic libraries in Canada in the years following the main tranche of fieldwork. These developments showed the capacity for decision-making practices to change, with ramifications for the fair use panacea and the drafting of copyright exceptions.

Part III

The Future

8 New Norms and Practices

I Introduction

The previous three chapters focused on reported institutional practices in relation to three standard-like exceptions: fair use in US law; section 200AB in Australian law; and fair dealing in Canada in the five years following *CCH Canadian Ltd* v. *Law Society of Upper Canada*.[1] The differences in practices were stark. Despite all three provisions adopting open-ended language, US interviewees reported that fair use was invoked for a range of internal and public-facing uses,[2] whilst Australian interviewees treated section 200AB as an extremely narrow orphaned works provision,[3] and Canadian institutions had not, with one minor exception, shifted their practices in response to *CCH*.[4] If the narrative stopped there it might leave questions about the fair use panacea, including the capacity of other forms of drafting to capture the benefits of fair use, but also the ability of fair use (or equivalent standards) to flourish outside of US conditions.

This chapter is about changing norms, and how later developments in Australia, Canada and the United Kingdom add to our understandings of exceptions. One of the key ideas in this book is the importance of interpretative practices for the day-to-day operation of the law, and for the choice between different drafting options. But those interpretative norms are not fixed in time. This chapter starts in Section II by discussing changes in the reported utilisation of fair dealing arguments in Canada and the United Kingdom. Here we will see that a variety of matters have encouraged greater use of fair dealing, these extending beyond the law in books to a range of internal and external influences. In Section III the analysis then shifts to the effect of new approaches to copyright management, including repeated reports that institutions were

---

[1] [2004] 1 SCR 339 ('*CCH*'). [2] Chapter 5. [3] Chapter 6.
[4] Chapter 7. This exception was some academic libraries moving to digital delivery for user requests.

265

becoming more comfortable with risk. One manifestation of this change was the increased utilisation of pure risk management: the use of content in ways that are or might be infringing on the basis of a risk assessment, rather than a belief that a viable defence would be available in the event of challenge.

The experiences described in Section II lend support to expanded fair dealing – i.e., the addition of new fair dealing purposes – as a worthwhile reform option.[5] This is significant, as it has been suggested that such a move would be 'a pragmatic second-best option' because expanded fair dealing, whilst having 'many of the same benefits of fair use' (due to fairness infrastructure), would be 'considerably confined by its pre-scribed purposes'.[6] There may be something in the argument that unless the statutory language is disregarded, fair dealing – with its in-built limits in relation to permissible purposes, sufficient acknowledgement, and so forth – will never be coterminous with fair use. But even if this is correct, it leaves the question of whether judges and users will, or would, apply fair use considerably more frequently and/or in a much broader range of situations than expanded fair dealing. Doctrinal analysis of fair dealing's legislative history and case law,[7] and indeed this book's analysis of post-*CCH* practices in Canada, highlights the challenges of displacing longstanding understandings and creating new workflows in which fair dealing plays a meaningful role. This chapter paints a more optimistic picture of the potential for change, although the post-script in Section IV about the ongoing litigation between Access Copyright and York University must be noted.[8]

The analysis of risk management in Section III leads to a more fundamental question, given the focus of this book: if, at least amongst

---

[5] See, also, M. Handler and E. Hudson, 'Fair Use as an Advance on Fair Dealing? Depolarising the Debate' in H. Sun, S. Balganesh and W. Ng-Loy (eds), *Comparative Aspects of Limitations and Exceptions in Copyright Law* (New York: Cambridge University Press, forthcoming).

[6] Australian Law Reform Commission (ALRC), *Copyright in the Digital Economy: Discussion Paper*, DP 79 (May 2013), para. 6.40.

[7] See especially R. Burrell and A. Coleman, *Copyright Exceptions: The Digital Impact* (Cambridge: Cambridge University Press, 2005). This monograph questioned whether fair use would liberalise exceptions in jurisdictions such as the United Kingdom, given prevailing judicial attitudes. For instance, in the analysis of twentieth-century experiences, it was observed that 'by the early 1950s the dominant view had become that the fair dealing exceptions were confined to the list of approved purposes and that the purposes themselves were to be construed relatively narrowly': p. 259. It was further argued that this reluctance to protect user interests in large part came from the judges themselves, and had continued in more recent times with the treatment of parodies: pp. 264–267.

[8] *Canadian Copyright Licensing Agency ("Access Copyright") v. York University* [2018] 2 FCR 43 ('*Access Copyright v. York*').

participating institutions, staff were increasingly comfortable with 'risk managing' uses, are the niceties of legal regulation – including the respective merits of different drafting options for copyright exceptions – becoming obsolete? The fieldwork suggested that some problems are, to a degree, yesterday's news. The treatment of orphaned works is the clearest example of an area that was a hot topic for many years but which a number of interviewees said was no longer a major concern due to risk management. The fieldwork also revealed changes in the principles that informed copyright management at participating institutions, including the rejection of strict legal compliance as a goal, and the use of decision-making frameworks that emphasised pragmatism and ethics. This shift was not universal, and nor was it a rejection of copyright. Rather, it seemed to recognise that attempts to adhere precisely to the law can be contrary to institutional missions and, indeed, the interests of creators and copyright owners. Exceptions remained relevant, and perhaps more than ever given their ability to provide a release valve in instances of market failure and copyright overreach. With many institutions displaying greater levels of legal knowledge and sophistication in copyright management, the question raised by Section III and explored in Chapter 9 is how these changes impact on the choice between rules and standards in the drafting of copyright exceptions.

II   The Revival of Fair Dealing?

A   *CCH and Academic Libraries: The Gap Narrows*

This section focuses on Canada, and in particular on the withdrawal of universities from arrangements with Access Copyright ('Access').[9] Until 2010, Access's blanket licence covered the creation of physical course packs and reserves, and allowed copying on self-serve photocopiers. Following *CCH*, questions had arisen in relation to the continued relevance of this licence, a matter that related not only to the expanded role for fair dealing envisaged by the Supreme Court but other changes, such as the replacement of physical learning materials with electronic reserves and virtual learning environments (VLEs), and the execution of licences

---

[9] The term 'arrangements' is used as Access changed its approach from concluding blanket licences between itself and the Association of Universities and Colleges of Canada (these licences being rolled over from time-to-time) to applying, in March 2010, to the Copyright Board for a tariff that would cover copying across the post-secondary sector: see, e.g., S. Trosow, S. Armstrong and B. Harasym, 'Objections to the Proposed Access Copyright Post-Secondary Tariff and its Progeny Licenses: A Working Paper' (14 August 2012), https://ir.lib.uwo.ca/fimspub/24/.

268   New Norms and Practices

with large subscription databases. Despite this, the Access licence was rolled over in the years following *CCH*, a matter that was criticised by participants in the research.[10] To the extent that some institutions had experimented with clearing rights for electronic reserves, it was concluded that that the cost of obtaining all the necessary licences was prohibitive.[11]

Seeds of change were observed during the main Canadian fieldwork, as there were reports that a handful of universities had introduced a fair dealing analysis into their electronic reserves policies.[12] This was described as a highly contested application of fair dealing, and to the extent that other universities had considered following suit, decision-makers were said to be frightened that their institution might become 'the test case'[13] for an activity considered the 'hot button' in Canada.[14] As such, it was difficult to predict whether this small group of universities were ahead of their time or engaged in an experiment that would sooner or later be abandoned. Subsequent developments revealed that the first possibility was closest to the truth but did not capture the pace and scale of change: not only did other universities start to embrace fair dealing for VLEs but by 2012 many were turning away from arrangements with Access. Whilst this coincided with the Supreme Court 'Pentalogy'[15] and the expansion of fair dealing to education by the Copyright Modernization Act,[16] the consistent message from follow-up fieldwork in Canada was that the tariff proposed by Access was a crucial instigator for new copyright management practices.

---

[10] A number of interviewees were critical of the negotiation of the blanket licences for academic libraries and queried their relevance to current practices, e.g.: 101L, 117L, 119L, 128L, 144X. See also V. Owen, 'The Librarian's Perspective on Collecting Societies' (Paper presented at the World Library and Information Congress: 73rd IFLA General Conference and Council, Durban, South Africa, 19–23 August 2007); S. Trosow, 'Bill C-32 and the Educational Sector: Overcoming Impediments to Fair Dealing' in M. Geist (ed), *From "Radical Extremism" to "Balanced Copyright": Canadian Copyright and the Digital Agenda* (Toronto: Irwin Law, 2010).
[11] See Chapter 7, Section IV.B(2).   [12] Ibid.   [13] 119L.   [14] 117L.
[15] This was a set of five cases all handed down by the Canadian Supreme Court on 12 July 2012: *Entertainment Software Association v. Society of Composers, Authors and Music Publishers of Canada* [2012] 2 SCR 231; *Rogers Communications Inc v. Society of Composers, Authors and Music Publishers of Canada* [2012] 2 SCR 283; *Society of Composers, Authors and Music Publishers of Canada v. Bell Canada* [2012] 2 SCR 326; *Alberta (Education) v. Canadian Copyright Licensing Agency (Access Copyright)* [2012] 2 SCR 345 ('*Alberta v. Access Copyright*'); and *Re:Sound v. Motion Picture Theatre Associations of Canada* [2012] 2 SCR 376. For discussion, see M. Geist (ed), *The Copyright Pentalogy: How the Supreme Court of Canada Shook the Foundations of Canadian Copyright Law* (Ottawa: University of Ottawa Press, 2013).
[16] Copyright Modernization Act (S.C. 2012, c. 12) (assented to 29 June 2012).

The Revival of Fair Dealing? 269

As noted above, there were already concerns that the Access licence no longer reflected good value for money given changes in the ways institutions were acquiring and using content. On 31 March 2010, Access indicated that it intended to change tack from the blanket licences negotiated with the Association of Universities and Colleges of Canada (AUCC) by filing with the Copyright Board a proposed tariff pursuant to section 70.14 of the Copyright Act.[17] Significantly, the royalty rate proposed in that tariff was a flat rate of $45 per full time equivalent (FTE) student, the rate under the existing licence having been $3.38 per FTE student plus a payment of $0.10 per page for course packs.[18] Although the new tariff included digital uses, this change to the remuneration structure was seen as unrealistic and excessive, especially given the sums being spent on new acquisitions and licences to subscription databases. For this and other reasons, the proposed tariff was met with criticism from universities, libraries and other observers.[19] With the existing licence due to expire at the end of December, Access applied for an interim tariff to take effect from 1 January 2011 on the same terms as that licence. The Board granted this application on 23 December 2010.[20]

Debate about Access's proposed tariff continued throughout 2011. With concerns about the cost and value proposition of the tariff, and questions over Access's digital repertoire, universities started exploring other approaches to copyright management, and in particular whether the Access tariff was needed given primary and transactional licensing, use of open access materials, reliance on fair dealing and so forth. The conclusion reached at numerous universities was that it would be more cost effective to increase the resources directed to in-house management,

---

[17] *Statement of Proposed Royalties to Be Collected by Access Copyright for the Reprographic Reproduction, in Canada, of Works in its Repertoire: Post-Secondary Educational Institutions (2011–2013)*, Supplement, Canada Gazette, Part I (12 June 2010), https://cb-cda.gc.ca/tariffs-tarifs/proposed-proposes/2010/2009-06-11-1.pdf.

[18] Ibid., section 7(1)(a); see, also, J. Lorinc, 'Universities in dispute with copyright collective over fees', *University Affairs* (16 August 2010), www.universityaffairs.ca/news/news-article/universities-in-dispute-with-copyright-collective/.

[19] These criticisms included queries about Access's digital repertoire, lack of value, the application of the proposed tariff to activities not covered by copyright (e.g., linking to a digital copy), and audit and monitoring requirements. For examples, see, e.g., Canadian Library Association, *CLA objection to the Access Copyright Post Secondary Tariff* (27 July 2010), http://cla.ca/wp-content/uploads/CLA_Tariff_objections_jul2010_final.pdf; H. Knopf, 'Access Copyright's excessive $45 per university student proposed tariff – August 11, 2010 deadline', *Excess Copyright* (8 August 2010), http://excesscopyright.blogspot.com/2010/08/access-copyrights-excessive-45-per.html; Trosow, Armstrong and Harasym, n. 9 above.

[20] Copyright Board, *Post-Secondary Educational Institutions – 2011–2013: Decisions of the Board*, 16 March 2011; amendments in reasons dated 7 April 2011.

including by establishing or expanding copyright offices.[21] The result was that university after university announced it was 'opting out' of the interim tariff in favour of a new management approach.[22] This move away from Access was not universal. For instance, in late January 2012, the University of Toronto and Western University announced that they had concluded separate deals with Access, these utilising a lower royalty rate of $27.50 per FTE and expiring in December 2013.[23] Not long after, AUCC announced that it had negotiated a model licence with Access for a slightly lower price ($26 per FTE) and with a discount on retroactive payments for universities that took up this agreement by 30 June 2012.[24] For those who signed, this agreement would exclude them from Access's proposed tariff (once certified). But with the model licence seen as including many problematic elements of the proposed tariff, for a price that was still a significant increase from existing fees, the AUCC also became a target of criticism. For instance, Ariel Katz said that by withdrawing its objection to Access's proposed tariff, the AUCC '[forced] universities who feel that they still need a license from Access Copyright to choose between a bad agreement [i.e., the model licence] and a combination of an even worse Tariff and continued litigation before the Board'.[25] Howard Knopf's critique was even more pointed, saying that 'those three dozen or so brave institutions' that had opted out

---

[21] See also L. Di Valentino, 'Laying the Foundation for Copyright Policy and Practice in Canadian Universities' (PhD Thesis, The University of Western Ontario, 2016), section 5.5.9, https://ir.lib.uwo.ca/etd/4312. As part of her analysis of fair dealing policies at forty-one Canadian universities, Di Valentino examined whether those policies supplied contact details for an internal copyright person, should staff have questions or require assistance. In 2013, 31 universities had a copyright-specific contact (compared with six having another internal contact, and four having no internal contact person). By 2016, forty universities had a copyright specific contact, and one had no internal contact.

[22] For a list of 26 universities that had announced that they had or planned to opt out, see M. Geist, 'The Access Copyright Interim Tariff Opt-Out List', *Michael Geist* (29 July 2011), www.michaelgeist.ca/2011/07/access-copyright-opt-out-list/. By the end of August that list extended to 34 institutions: see J. Brown, 'Copyright Board warns universities they can't dodge copying tariff', *Canadian Lawyer* (29 August 2011), www.canadianlawyermag.com/author/jennifer-brown/copyright-board-warns-universities-they-cant-dodge-copying-tariff-1311/.

[23] See, e.g., H. Knopf, 'U. of T. and Western Capitulate to Access Copyright', *Excess Copyright* (31 January 2012), http://excesscopyright.blogspot.com/2012/01/u-of-t-and-western-capitulate-to-access.html.

[24] See, e.g., M. Geist, 'Access Copyright and AUCC Strike a Deal: What It Means for Innovation in Education', *Michael Geist* (17 April 2011), www.michaelgeist.ca/2012/04/access-copyright-and-aucc-deal/.

[25] A. Katz, 'The Voice of Canadian Universities?', *Arial Katz* (24 April 2012), https://arielkatz.org/the-voice-of-canadian-universities/.

of the interim tariff had 'now effectively been thrown under the AC bus by AUCC itself'.[26]

With the 30 June deadline for discounted rates looming, universities began to execute the model licence,[27] although there was also a sizeable group that announced that they would not be signing on.[28] For those in the latter group – and those who were prevaricating – further reason to reject the model licence came on 12 July 2012 when the Pentalogy was handed down by the Canadian Supreme Court. One decision had particular relevance to academic libraries: that in *Alberta* v. *Access Copyright*.[29] This case concerned Access's proposed tariff for copying by elementary and secondary schools, and specifically whether material intended for student use but copied at the initiative of the teacher came within the scope of fair dealing. It had been held by the Copyright Board and Federal Court of Appeal that such copying was subject to a royalty,[30] but the Supreme Court held that the Board's finding was unreasonable and remitted the case for reconsideration.[31] The key issue was whether the dealings were fair, as it was agreed at all three levels that the copying fell within the allowable purpose of research or private study.[32]

---

[26] H. Knopf, 'AUCC Follows UofT & Western and Capitulates to Access Copyright's Copyright Bullying – And It Still "Ain't Over"', *Excess Copyright* (19 April 2012), http://excesscopyright.blogspot.com/2012/04/aucc-follows-uoft-western-and.html.

[27] It was reported by Access in July 2012 that 65 per cent of eligible institutions outside Quebec had signed a licence: see P. Berkowitz, 'Majority of Canadian universities sign licence with Access Copyright', *University Affairs* (9 July 2012), www.universityaffairs.ca/news/news-article/majority-of-canadian-universities-sign-licence-with-access-copyright/.

[28] For a list of some institutions who opted out, see, e.g., S. Trosow, 'Compilation of Announcements for Institutions Opting-Out of Model Licence', *Sam Trosow* (29 June 2012), https://samtrosow.wordpress.com/2012/06/29/compilation-of-annoucements-for-institutions-opting-out-of-model-license/.

[29] *Alberta* v. *Access Copyright*, n. 15 above.

[30] Copyright Board, *Educational Institutions – 2005–2009: Decision of the Board* (26 June 2009); *Alberta (Education)* v. *Access Copyright* [2011] 3 FCR 223. The conclusion of the Federal Court of Appeal (FCA) was that there was 'no reviewable error', i.e., that the finding that the copying was unfair was 'a legitimate conclusion that was open to the Board based on the evidence before it': para. 48.

[31] The Board subsequently ruled that the 'decision of the Supreme Court is clear and leaves no room for interpretations: based on the record before the Board and the findings of fact of the Supreme Court, Category 4 copies constitute fair dealing for an allowable purpose and as such, are non-compensable': see Copyright Board, *Educational Institutions – 2005–2009: Decision of the Board (Redetermination)* (18 January 2013), para. 5.

[32] Earlier in the tariff renewal process, the parties had agreed to a volume study to help calculate the royalty, i.e., a study in which records were kept of the maker, use and purpose of photocopies made at schools. One of those purposes was 'research or private study'.

For instance, the Board and Federal Court held that when the purpose of the dealing was considered at the fairness stage, this disfavoured fair dealing as the predominant purpose of the teacher was instruction or non-private study.[33] Writing for the majority in the Supreme Court,[34] Abella J held that the relevant principle was that a copier could not use the recipient's allowable purpose to mask their own separate (unfair) purpose,[35] but that here there were no ulterior motive on the part of the teachers, and nor could

> teachers be characterized as having the completely separate purpose of "instruction"; they are there to facilitate the students' research and private study. It seems to me to be axiomatic that most students lack the expertise to find or request the materials required for their own research and private study, and rely on the guidance of their teachers. They study what they are told to study, and the teacher's purpose in providing copies is to enable the students to have the material they need for the purpose of studying. The teacher/copier therefore shares a symbiotic purpose with the student/user who is engaging in research or private study.[36]

Justice Abella stated that this 'skewed characterization of the teacher's role' also led to problems in the analysis of the amount of the dealing. The Board stated that teachers tended to limit their copying to short extracts (which pointed towards fairness), but that these would often be copied multiple times (which weighed against fairness).[37] Justice Abella identified a number of problems with this analysis, including that it conflated the 'amount' factor (which asks how much was taken from source works) with the 'character' factor (which includes the number of copies made),[38] meaning that the quantification of teacher copying was counted twice.[39] Furthermore, in relation to the 'alternatives to the dealing', Abella J disagreed with the Board's proposition that buying class sets was a reasonable alternative to copying extracts: under this approach, 'schools would be required to buy sufficient copies for every student of every text, magazine and newspaper in Access Copyright's repertoire that is relied on by a teacher. This is a demonstrably unrealistic outcome.'[40]

---

[33] Board, n. 30 above, para. 98; FCA, n. 30 above, paras. 37–46.
[34] The Supreme Court was split 5–4, with the majority comprising McLachlin CJ and LeBel, Abella, Moldaver and Karakatsanis JJ.
[35] *Alberta v. Access Copyright*, n. 15 above, para. 22. [36] Ibid., para. 23.
[37] Board, n. 30 above, para. 98. This matter was not dealt with in detail by the FCA, it merely being said that the Board's findings on the other factors were reasonable: FCA, n. 30 above, para. 47.
[38] *Alberta v. Access Copyright*, n. 15 above, para. 29. [39] Ibid., para. 30.
[40] Ibid., para. 32, referring to Board, n. 30 above, para. 107.

The final problem identified by Abella J related to analysis of the effect of the dealing. The Board had placed weight on evidence from publishers that over the last twenty years textbook sales had decreased by over 30 per cent.[41] Although the Board was 'not able to determine precisely' the contributions of various possible causes of this decline, it concluded that the impact of photocopies, 'while impossible to quantify, is sufficiently important to compete with the original to an extent that makes the dealing unfair'.[42] In the Supreme Court, Abella J discussed a number of problems with this reasoning, including the lack of evidence of a link between reduced textbook sales and the photocopying under consideration,[43] and the lack of credible evidence for market substitution. Justice Abella was therefore of the view that if 'such photocopying did not take place, it is more likely that students would simply go without the supplementary information, or be forced to consult the single copy already owned by the school'.[44]

The decision in *Alberta v. Access Copyright* came at a crucial time in debates about the Access-AUCC model licence as it reinforced the central message of *CCH* that exceptions should be given a robust interpretation and demonstrated the application of fair dealing to multiple copying for student use. The outcome was therefore seen to support broader interpretations of fair dealing (for instance in relation to VLEs and electronic reserves), and to fortify the views of those who had not yet signed the model licence; for instance, one interviewee said that those who *did* sign felt like they had 'egg on their face' following the Supreme Court decision.[45] The relevance of fair dealing was also bolstered by the Copyright Modernization Act, which received assent on 29 June 2012 and which amended fair dealing so that it applied to three new purposes, one of which was education.[46] But as noted above, it appears that a crucial instigator for change was the view that arrangements with Access were no longer commercially viable.[47] Although many of the objections to the new Access tariff were grounded in longstanding doctrinal and policy concerns, the ultimate problem was that the tariff was too expensive for what it was perceived to deliver, thus piquing the

---

[41] Board, n. 30 above, para. 110.   [42] Ibid., para 111.
[43] In the Board it seemed significant that the schools admitted to copying more than a quarter of a billion textbook pages every year. But Abella J noted that the vast majority of this copying was paid for, and that the dispute related only to 7 per cent of those copies: *Alberta v. Access Copyright*, n. 15 above, para. 34.
[44] Ibid., para 36.   [45] 160L.
[46] Copyright Modernization Act 2012 (S.C. 2012, c. 20) s. 21. The other two were parody and satire.
[47] Discussed by 146L, 160L, 161L, 163L, 164X.

interest of senior management. To put it another way, had the Access proposal *not* involved such a high headline figure, senior administrators may have (again) made the pragmatic decision to retain arrangements with Access. Instead, many universities committed substantial resources to reconfiguring their copyright management, a move that has proven difficult to reverse.

This became particularly evident in 2015. With the AUCC-negotiated model licence due to expire on 31 December 2015, Access offered universities two replacement options: a 'premium' version that included course packs, digital copying and transactional licences, and whose fees ranged from $18 per FTE for a single year agreement through to $12 per FTE per year for a five-year term; and a less extensive licence that was $6 per FTE for a single-year agreement and $5 per year for a three-year deal.[48] This did not stem the tide. Analysis of publicly available information by Lisa Di Valentino suggested that in 2015, thirty-eight out of sixty-five AUCC-member universities had a licence with Access, twenty-four did not have a licence and the status of two institutions was unknown. By February 2016 three universities had signed onto a new licence, thirty-six had announced they would not be using Access licences and twenty-five were unknown.[49] A further update in May 2019 revealed that despite the litigation between Access and York University (discussed in Section IV, below), universities had continued to move away from Access licences, with forty-eight universities having no such arrangements.[50] Only twelve were using an Access licence, and the status of the remaining three universities was unknown.

As noted above, this move away from blanket licensing with Access was not a renunciation of licensing itself. On the contrary, it seems that licensing remained a central strategy for copyright compliance, albeit achieved through agreements with large subscription databases and through transactional licences. But the additional confidence that fair dealing could apply to multiple copying in an educational context – this being an approach that took seriously the vision of the Supreme Court in *CCH* – was a factor in encouraging new workflow models, even if (as

---

[48] See, e.g., L. Di Valentino, 'Access Copyright's new offerings and the collective's future with universities', *Fair Dealing in Education* (5 January 2016), https://fairdealingineducation.com/2016/01/05/access-copyrights-new-offerings-and-the-collectives-future-with-universities/.

[49] L. Di Valentino, 'Access Copyright renewals update', *Fair Dealing in Education* (updated 8 February 2016), https://fairdealingineducation.com/2015/10/15/access-copyright-renewals-update/.

[50] L. Di Valentino, 'Access Copyright renewals update 2019', *Fair Dealing in Education* (updated 21 February 2019), https://fairdealingineducation.com/2019/05/21/access-copyright-renewals-update-2019/#more-790.

interviewees reported) fair dealing only covered a limited subset of copying.[51] It can therefore be said that after a period in which there was a gap between the views of academics in relation to *CCH* and the day-to-day practices of their universities, from 2010 onwards that gap narrowed considerably.

Throughout that time, the approach of Canadian universities was questioned, including through litigation by Access against York University seeking to enforce the interim tariff granted by the Copyright Board in December 2010. On 12 July 2017 – five years to the day after the Supreme Court Pentalogy was handed down – Phelan J of the Federal Court held that the interim tariff was mandatory and that York's Fair Dealing Guidelines did *not* satisfy the fairness limb of fair dealing.[52] An appeal from this decision is ongoing.[53] Some comments are made in Section IV about Phelan J's decision, and what this might mean for the revival of fair dealing.

B   *UK 2014 Reforms*

In 2014, UK fair dealing was expanded to include quotation; caricature, parody and pastiche; and illustration for instruction.[54] In considering options for reform, the United Kingdom had rejected fair use due to its incompatibility with the list of permitted cases in Article 5 of the Information Society Directive (ISD).[55] But there is evidence that reform of

---

[51] 146L, 160L, 161L, 163L. See also Di Valentino, n. 21 above, sections 5.53 and 5.54. Di Valentino tracked the number of universities with up-to-date fair dealing policies, and the content of those policies. In 2013, twenty-seven out of forty-one universities had such a policy, whilst in 2016, this had grown to thirty-six universities. Her analysis suggested that universities that had opted out of Access's blanket licence were significantly more likely to have an up-to-date policy. She also asked whether the policy countenanced that fair dealing might apply to course packs, and observed a growth in such a position from twenty-six universities in 2013 to thirty-four universities in 2016.

[52] *Access Copyright* v. *York*, n. 8 above.

[53] Arguments were heard by the Federal Court of Appeal on 5 and 6 March 2019: see H. Knopf, 'Access Copyright v. York U – The Federal Court of Appeal Hearing Is March 5 and 6, 2019', *Excess Copyright* (4 March 2019), http://excesscopyright.blogspot.com/2019/03/access-copyright-v-york-u-federal-court.html.

[54] See CDPA 1988 ss. 30(1ZA) (quotation), 30A (caricature, parody or pastiche), 32 (illustration for instruction). These were introduced by the Copyright and Rights in Performances (Quotation and Parody) Regulations 2014 (SI 2014/2356), regs. 3, 5 and the Copyright and Rights in Performances (Research, Education, Libraries and Archives) Regulations 2014 (SI 2014/1372), reg. 4. Other reforms introduced in 2014 included new and revised specific exceptions (see Chapter 4), regimes directed to orphaned works (see Chapter 3) and limits on contracting out.

[55] See I. Hargreaves, *Digital Opportunity: A Review of Intellectual Property and Growth* (May 2011), para. 5.19: see discussion in Chapter 1, Section III.B.

fair dealing has been perceived as significant, not only by academics pressing forward-leaning interpretations of the new purposes, but by UK cultural institutions that have used fair dealing in new situations. This sub-section will address each of the three new provisions in turn.

1 *Quotation* Section 30(1ZA) of the CDPA provides that:

Copyright in a work is not infringed by the use of a quotation from the work (whether for criticism or review or otherwise) provided that—

(a) the work has been made available to the public,
(b) the use of the quotation is fair dealing with the work,
(c) the extent of the quotation is no more than is required by the specific purpose for which it is used, and
(d) the quotation is accompanied by a sufficient acknowledgement (unless this would be impossible for reasons of practicality or otherwise).

As with all the 2014 fair dealing reforms, the introduction of section 30 (1ZA) was tied to Article 5 of the ISD, in this instance Article 5(3)(d) permitting exceptions directed to 'quotations for purposes such as criticism or review'.[56] Aspects of Article 5(3)(d) were incorporated expressly into section 30(1ZA), namely that the work has been made available to the public, that the use is proportionate (i.e., that 'the extent of the quotation is no more than is required by the specific purpose for which it is used') and that the quotation is accompanied by a sufficient acknowledgement. In contrast, the requirement that the use be in accordance with fair practice seems to be respected implicitly through the fairness infrastructure of fair dealing.

Quotation has attracted some scholarly attention over the years, albeit often in the context of analysis of the Berne Convention.[57] Of particular

---

[56] The full text of Art. 5(3)(d) states that exceptions and limitations are permitted for 'quotations for purposes such as criticism or review, provided that they relate to a work or other subject-matter which has already been lawfully made available to the public, that, unless this turns out to be impossible, the source, including the author's name, is indicated, and that their use is in accordance with fair practice, and to the extent required by the specific purpose'.

[57] See especially S. Ricketson and J. Ginsburg, *International Copyright and Neighbouring Rights: The Berne Convention and Beyond*, vol. 1, 2nd edition (Oxford: Oxford University Press, 2006), paras. 13.38–13.42. Article 10(1) of Berne states that: 'It shall be permissible to make quotations from a work which has already been lawfully made available to the public, provided that their making is compatible with fair practice, and their extent does not exceed that justified by the purpose, including quotations from newspaper articles and periodicals in the form of press summaries.' Article 10(3) then provides that: 'Where use is made of works in accordance with the preceding paragraphs of this Article, mention shall be made of the source, and of the name of the author if it appears thereon.'

interest to this book is the work of Tanya Aplin and Lionel Bently.[58] They argue that Article 10(1) of the Berne Convention requires Member States to implement a quotation exception,[59] and that this exception is of broad reach being applicable to: (1) all Berne Convention works and not just literary or dramatic works; (2) all Berne Convention rights *and* rights in later treaties; (3) longer takings (including entire works) and uses in which the source material is altered, and not merely short, literal excerpts; and (4) uses undertaken for a variety of purposes, there being no set limits on the circumstances in which quotation may be used (save that the defendant has *a* purpose). For these reasons, they describe quotation as 'global, mandatory fair use'. This is an explicitly forward-leaning designation and has been described as a 'provocation'.[60] In speculating about the reasons for this response, it may be that the term 'fair use' invites certain expectations about the reach of an exception, but that these expectations sit uncomfortably with the words of Article 10(1), some of which would seem to encompass a far more complex standard than US fair use, and others of which may not be standard-like at all.[61] Much will therefore turn on interpretative practices.

To illustrate, consider what is meant by the term 'quotation'. Starting with the law in books, analysis of the history of the Berne Convention suggests that the drafters of Article 10(1) had an expansive definition in mind. The immediate precursor to the current provision appeared in the 1948 Brussels text, and stated that '[i]t shall be permissible in all countries of the Union to make short quotations from newspaper articles and periodicals, as well as to include them in press summaries'.[62] This Article was reformed to the present text at the 1967 Stockholm conference, such a move having been motivated by a desire that Article 10(1) reflect and

---

[58] T. Aplin and L. Bently, 'Displacing the Dominance of the Three-Step Test: The Role of Global, Mandatory Fair Use' in W. Ng, H. Sun and S. Balganesh (eds), *Comparative Aspects of Limitations and Exceptions in Copyright Law* (New York: Cambridge University Press, forthcoming); L. Bently and T. Aplin, 'Whatever Became of Global Mandatory Fair Use? A Case Study in Dysfunctional Pluralism' in S. Frankel (ed), *Is Intellectual Property Pluralism Functional* (Cheltenham: Edward Elgar, 2019).

[59] Other scholars to reach the same conclusion include Ricketson and Ginsburg, n. 57 above, para. 13.38; J. Sterling, *World Copyright Law*, 3rd edition (London: Sweet & Maxwell, 2008), para. 18.10.

[60] Bently and Aplin, n. 58 above.

[61] Aplin and Bently in fact recognise that Art. 10(1) is not as broad as US fair use, given the limiting conditions and the application of fair use in situations that would not be included by the broadest notion of 'quotation' such as copying as part of text or data mining, and time-shifting: ibid.

[62] For analysis of the current and earlier iterations, see S. Stewart, *International Copyright and Neighbouring Rights*, 2nd edition (London: Butterworths, 1989), ch. 5; T. Aplin and L. Bently, 'Global, Mandatory, Fair Use: The Nature and Scope of the Right to Quote Copyright Works' (unpublished manuscript; copy on file with the author).

encompass the use of quotation in other circumstances and disciplines.[63] As argued by Aplin and Bently, this aligns with the plain meaning of the term 'quotation', which has been used to describe borrowings in art, film, music and so forth.[64] They therefore push back against a meaning of quotation that relates to only short, unmodified extracts of text.

The CJEU has accepted that quotation can apply to a range of works, and not merely literary content.[65] However, a more contentious question is whether the term 'quotation' incorporates other requirements, for instance that the quoted content is reproduced without modification; is identifiable; and refers back to the source work.[66] The quotation exception was considered in a number of CJEU judgments in 2019, with the definition of quotation a particular focus of *Pelham v. Hütter*, in relation to the unauthorised use of a looped, two-second sample from Kraftwerk's 'Metall auf Metall' in the song 'Nur Mir' by Sabrina Setlur.[67] In his opinion, Advocate General Szpunar suggested that a lawful quotation 'must enter into some kind of dialogue with the work quoted'.[68] The Grand Chamber agreed that an intention to enter into such a dialogue was necessary, observing that the 'essential characteristics' of quotation, as drawn from the term's 'usual meaning ... in everyday language', are the use of a work or more usually an extract 'for the purposes of illustrating an assertion, of defending an opinion or of

---

[63] See, e.g., BIRPI, *General Report of the Swedish/BIRPI Study Group Established at July 1, 1964* (BIRPI: DA/22/2, 1965), pp. 52–54; BIRPI, 'Proposals for Revising the Substantive Copyright Provisions (Articles 1 to 20)', Document S/1, pp. 46–47 in WIPO, *Records of the Intellectual Property Conference of Stockholm*, Volume 1 (Geneva: WIPO, 1971), pp. 116–117.

[64] See *Oxford English Dictionary* (OUP online edition, 2018) ('OED'), definition 5a ('A passage quoted from a book, speech, or other source; (in modern use esp.) a frequently quoted passage of this nature') and definition 5b: 'A short musical passage or visual image taken from one piece of music or work of art and used in another'.

[65] E.g., *Painer v. Standard Verlags GmbH* (C-145/10) [2012] ECDR 6 (Third Chamber), paras. 122–123 (judgment assuming that Art. 5(3)(d) can apply to entire photographs, although not forming a concluded view); *Pelham GmbH v. Hütter* (C-476/17) [2019] Bus LR 2159, para. 68 (Grand Chamber) (Art. 5(3)(d) can apply to uses of protected musical works).

[66] These requirements were identified in AG Trstenjak's opinion in *Painer*, n. 65 above, para. AG210.

[67] *Pelham v. Hütter*, n. 65 above; see also *Funke Medien NRW GmbH v. Germany* (C-469/17) [2019] All ER (D) 48 (Aug) (Grand Chamber) (publication of confidential military reports on a news website); *Spiegel Online GMBH v. Volker Beck* (C-516/17) [2019] Bus LR 2787 (Grand Chamber) (hyperlinks to the manuscript and published versions of a book chapter, these being made available by a media outlet to counter a suggestion that the published text had been modified by the publisher). The Advocate General's opinion in *Spiegel Online* was not released in English; for a summary, see T. Rendas, 'Advocate General Szpunar in *Spiegel Online* (or Why We Need Fair Use in the EU)' (2019) 14 *Journal of Intellectual Property Law & Practice* 265.

[68] *Pelham v. Hütter* (C-476/17) [2019] ECDR 3, para. AG64 (AG Opinion).

allowing an intellectual comparison between that work and the assertions of that user'.[69] The Grand Chamber countenanced that sampling could be quotation, but only if the sampled sounds were 'recognisable to the ear': 'there can be no such dialogue where it is not possible to identify the work concerned by the quotation at issue'.[70]

At the time of writing it remains to be seen how the German courts will respond to the CJEU's guidance. It has been suggested that the sample from 'Metall auf Metall' is a 'very recognisable' part of 'Nur Mir' and forms a key element of the percussion track,[71] which if right means that much will turn on what is meant by a 'dialogue'. If we take seriously the Grand Chamber's definition of quotation, it might be difficult to point to any intellectual illustration, defence or comparison being made in the defendant's work.[72] In other sampling cases, the requirement for recognisability may also be significant. Advocate General Szpunar in *Pelham* identified this as a general requirement for Article 5(3)(d): that a quotation must be 'unaltered and distinguishable'.[73] Although not adopting these words, in the Grand Chamber it was concluded that quotation 'does not extend to a situation in which it is not possible to identify the work concerned by the quotation in question'.[74] If this limits the

---

[69] *Pelham* v. *Hütter* (Grand Chamber), n. 65 above, para. 71.   [70] Ibid., paras. 72–73.
[71] R. Smirke, 'European Court Rules in Favor of Kraftwerk in 20 Year-Long Copyright Dispute', *Billboard* (29 July 2019), www.billboard.com/articles/business/8524267/kraftwerk-european-court-justice-ruling-metall-auf-metall.
[72] Note also the comments of Advocate General Szpunar that 'sampling in general' does not satisfy the conditions for a lawful quotation, being an act of 'appropriation' rather than 'interaction', and being 'modified and mixed in such a way that all original integrity is lost': *Pelham* v. *Hütter* (AG Opinion), n. 68 above, para. AG67.
[73] Ibid., para. AG65, also stating that the source work should be unmodified (but for changes that are 'traditionally permitted, particularly translation') and be 'easily distinguished as a foreign element'.
[74] *Pelham* v. *Hütter* (Grand Chamber), n. 65 above, para. 74. This must be read in light of other conclusions in the judgment, in particular that there is no reproduction of a phonogram for the purposes of Art. 2(c) of the ISD where 'a user, in exercising the freedom of the arts, takes a sound sample from a phonogram to use it, in a modified form unrecognizable to the ear, in a new work': para. 31. The Grand Chamber explained this by reference to the need to achieve a fair balance between the interests of rightsholders and users: paras. 32–38. The Grand Chamber's conclusion could be said to align with the traditional Anglo-Australian approach, in which copyright protection of sound recordings is thin and is only infringed by exact copying of the recording, such that making a sound-alike of a song does not infringe the mechanical copyright: e.g., *CBS Records Australia Ltd* v. *Telmak Teleproducts (Aust) Pty Ltd* (1987) 9 IPR 440; similar *Norowzian* v. *Arks Ltd (No. 1)* [1998] FSR 394 (films). Applying this logic, one could say that if significant changes are made to the sample, it is no longer a copy. But the Grand Chamber used 'fair balance' to reach its conclusion; and it must be asked whether this approach would also apply to musical works, which under traditional Anglo-Australian law can be infringed, under the reproduction right, through non-literal and not just exact copying: e.g., *Norowzian* v. *Arks Ltd (No. 2)* [2000] FSR 363.

circumstances in which modified material falls within Article 5(3)(d), this may make it harder to argue that quotation operates as a de facto fair use exception.

In the fieldwork with UK cultural institutions, numerous interviewees described reliance on section 30(1ZA) of the CDPA, with the provision being used for reproductions from a range of works – e.g., literary, artistic and audio items – in such things as publications, onsite exhibitions, educational materials, and information-oriented aspects of public websites.[75] Amongst those examples, there was variation in the reasoning and frequency of reliance. For instance, one interviewee reported using quotation for small pieces of music used in exhibitions, but was not inclined to use quotation for entire works – including the entire surface of an artistic work – as this would not be in the 'spirit of getting the balance right'.[76] In contrast, another described the decision-making behind making images of artistic works available online under a quotation analysis, there being contextual information along with the photograph of the item.[77] A number of interviewees mentioned that the quotation needed to help make a point,[78] although 'you don't necessarily need to have reams of commentary'.[79] One interviewee also said that an attraction of quotation was that other countries have similar provisions, which made it attractive for outputs that were accessible outside the UK.[80]

It should be emphasised that institutions were still finding their way in relation to quotation, including how to incorporate it into workflows and whether its use might sometimes be antithetical to the maintenance of good relations with artists and other creators.[81] However, interviewees did not view section 30(1ZA) as technical and unknowable, or as limited to the paradigmatic example of short snippets of literary content in quotation marks.[82] Nor did it seem to be fatal that there had, at the time of most of the interviews, been little case law in relation to quotation, or that other institutions might take a different view on when the exception applied. The breadth of the drafting was praised by a number of people. For instance one interviewee said:

---

[75] These reports came in the second batch of UK fieldwork, from 2018 onwards: especially 305M, 313M, 314G, 315A, 316L, 319L, 320L, 322G, 323X, 325M, 327L, 328G.
[76] 305M.   [77] 322G.   [78] E.g., 305M, 314G, 320L, 322G.   [79] 314G.
[80] 323X.
[81] E.g., 313M (asking whether the institution could rely on quotation to a far greater extent), 323X (noting quotation had not been used for artistic works), 328G (there is much potential to use quotation in a broader range of circumstances).
[82] Although this appeared to be a prominent use of the exception, with such quotations having been used in publications, explanatory panels in exhibitions, in online databases, and in learning materials: e.g., 305M, 316L, 319L, 320L, 323X, 325M, 328G.

It's very useful to have a straightforward quotation exception. It does say quotation 'whether for criticism or review or otherwise', which arguably they didn't need to put in, but it's broad, and that's really useful. Similarly, the amount of content is very broad: the extent of the quotation is no more than is required for the specific purpose for which it is used. Things like that are great, because it's about the situation itself, rather than an arbitrary amount. ... I know there were earlier discussions in 2014 – how would quotation work for an artwork? We've always come at a view if it were necessary, for the specific purpose, to quote from the entire work, then that would be defendable. So things like that are really good.[83]

Another said:

Quotation is nicely nondescript, isn't it? We were discussing this with [names sector copyright group], amongst people who know reasonable amounts about copyright. And looking at how [the quotation exception] would be interpreted, we concluded that it was loose enough to not exclude using an entire work if that were appropriate, and it's not specific to a type of work either, so that's nice as well.[84]

It was striking how quickly participating institutions had embraced section 30(1ZA), especially when compared with the reception afforded section 200AB in Australian copyright law.[85] Indeed, of all the non-US exceptions considered in this research, quotation had the most in common with how US interviewees described fair use, as judged by (1) the confidence with which interviewees described the language of the provision, and (2) the range of circumstances – including public and online uses – in which it had been used. The discussion of quotation therefore illustrated the dynamism of decision-making practices, and reinforced the proposition that cultural institutions can respond positively to standards.

A number of questions remain about the future of quotation, especially given the judgments handed down by the CJEU in July 2019. These cases would seem to have placed doctrinal limits on the circumstances in which quotation can plausibly be argued. This sub-section has already discussed the definition of quotation; another question relates to the requirement that the source work 'has been made available to the public'.[86] This was identified as a problem by some interviewees, on the basis that it suggests that fair dealing for quotation (and indeed criticism and review) cannot be used for unpublished collections.[87] This

---

[83] 320L. [84] 313M.
[85] Discussed Chapter 6; and see E. Hudson, 'Implementing Fair Use in Copyright Law: Lessons from Australia' (2013) 25 *Intellectual Property Journal* 201.
[86] CDPA s. 30(1ZA)(a). [87] Especially 320L, 326L, 327L.

book argues that there are good reasons for concluding that the term 'lawfully made available to the public' in Article 10(1) of Berne is not as limited as may first appear, but that a more restrictive approach seems to have been taken by the CJEU in relation to Article 5(3)(d) of the ISD.

Looking at the UK implementation, according to the CDPA, the making available of a work can be effected 'by any means', this including such things as issuing copies to the public, making the work available by means of an electronic retrieval system, and the exhibition or showing of the work in public, but 'no account shall be taken of any unauthorised act'.[88] 'Unauthorised' is defined in section 178, and in essence refers to 'anything' done without the licence of the copyright owner or, if copyright does not subsist in the work, author. The principal relevance of this definition is to qualification of a work for copyright protection via publication, i.e., that when considering subsistence, a work is not published by an unauthorised act.[89] But when applied to section 30(1ZA), it might suggest that fair dealing only applies where the copyright owner has consented to the work being made available publicly, *even if* that act does not implicate copyright. This would mean that, for instance, neither a museum exhibiting a painting nor the inclusion of unpublished private correspondence in a publicly accessible archives would count to make the work publicly available for the purpose of section 30(1ZA) unless the institution had the permission of the copyright owner.[90]

One counter-argument is that the words 'licence of the copyright owner' refer only to acts that are within the restricted rights in section 16 of the CDPA, and that these acts of accession and exhibition could be relied upon to permit fair dealing arguments as they are outside those rights. This approach would accord with Sam Ricketson and Jane Ginsburg's analysis of the equivalent language in Article 10(1) of Berne, where they say that (1) 'made available' was intended to have a broad reach and include not only publication but other forms of presentation such as performance in public and broadcast,[91] and (2) these words were

---

[88] CDPA s. 30(1A).
[89] Ibid., s. 175(6); for discussion see L. Bently, B. Sherman, D. Gangjee and P. Johnson, *Intellectual Property Law*, 5th edition (Oxford: Oxford University Press, 2018), pp. 121–122.
[90] Public exhibition is one of the illustrative examples of how a work can be made available to the public by 'any means': CDPA s. 30(1A)(d). Inclusion of a work in a publicly accessible collection is not on this list, but there are good arguments that there are synergies between this form of availability (even if onsite only) and acts that are on the illustrative list, especially making the work available by means of an electronic retrieval system: CDPA ss. 30(1A)(b). As such, the key question is the meaning of the exclusion for 'any unauthorised act'.
[91] Ricketson and Ginsburg, n. 57 above, para. 13.41.

The Revival of Fair Dealing? 283

not qualified by authorial consent, in contrast with other provisions in Berne, such as the definition of published works in Article 3(3).[92]

The Ricketson and Ginsburg reading is not shared by other commentaries on Article 10(1), which instead suggest that the quotation right does not generally apply to unpublished works.[93] Looking to the *travaux*, the pre-Stockholm Study Group expressed the concern that liberalised Article 10(1) not allow third parties to place in the public sphere extracts of manuscripts and works of closed circulation, seemingly reflecting the view that the right to quote should exist only for works intended for public consumption.[94] The concerns underlying this perspective are not unfounded. Consider, for example, an academic who sends the draft of an article to colleagues for comment. Allowing recipients to quote from the draft might enable them to gazump the author's work or attribute to the author a perspective he or she did not end up taking. But there are also circumstances in which the right to quote from an unpublished work is important, for instance where a scholar uses archival documents to trace the development of a work of fiction from manuscript to published form, or where a newspaper wishes to use leaked documents to comment on the views or processes of a political party.[95] It is therefore suggested

---

[92] Ibid., also citing Berne Art. 7(2) (referring to cinematographic works that have 'been made available to the public with the consent of the author'). In the report of the Main Committee I at the Stockholm Convention, at which current Art. 10(1) was drafted, it was stated that 'it was felt that the reasons for replacing the word "lawfully" in connection with condition (i) by the words "with the consent of the author" were not valid here, and the word "lawfully" was therefore retained': S. Bergström, 'Report on the Work of Main Committee I (Substantive Provisions of the Berne Convention: Articles 1 to 20), para. 90, in WIPO, *Records of the Intellectual Property Conference of Stockholm*, Volume II (Geneva: WIPO, 1971), p. 1147.

[93] See, e.g., Stewart, n. 62 above, para. 5.56; W. Nordemann, K. Vinck, P. Hertin and G. Meyer, *International Copyright and Neighbouring Rights Law* (Weinheim: VCH, 1990), p. 111 (the phrase lawfully made available to the public 'is the continental European concept of publication' and that 'we consider a publication without proof of consent of the author to be permissible only in cases of anonymous and pseudonymous works').

[94] Summarised in BIRPI, 'Proposals', n. 63 above, p. 47. The proposed text taken to the Stockholm Conference referred to 'lawfully made available to the public' not 'lawfully made accessible to the public'.

[95] There are questions about how legality of access should be analysed in copyright cases given the existence of other laws (privacy, breach of confidence, conversion, etc.) that can apply to documents obtained surreptitiously. Such a question arose in *HRH Prince of Wales* v. *Associated Newspapers Ltd* [2006] EWHC 522 (Ch), affirmed [2006] EWCA Civ 1776. This case pertained to the publication by the *Mail on Sunday* of extracts from a journal written by Prince Charles, a photocopy of the journal having been supplied to the newspaper surreptitiously by a member of Prince Charles's staff. One claim related to infringement of copyright. It was held that the journal had not been 'made available to the public' for the purpose of a fair dealing defence under CDPA s. 30(1) (criticism or review) as there was no issuing of copies to the public by Prince Charles (even though copies had been distributed at his behest to a select group of recipients) and no lawful

that the Ricketson and Ginsburg reading is not only open doctrinally but is superior from a normative perspective, and that the Berne language of 'already been lawfully made available' should be given a broader conception in which 'lawfully' means 'not unlawfully' rather than 'with authorial permission'.

Applying this reasoning to the language of the CDPA, this would mean that the reference to ignoring 'unauthorised' acts in section 30(1A) would apply only to acts requiring the copyright owner's permission. Thus, rightsholder consent would be required for, say, online publication, but not placing that work in a publicly accessible collection. However, this argument may have been weakened considerably by the CJEU judgment in *Spiegel Online* v. *Beck*, which considered whether the manuscript for a book chapter had been 'lawfully made available to the public' by the chapter's publication, allegedly with editorial amendments, in the book itself.[96] The Grand Chamber held that a work 'must' satisfy this limb 'if it has been made available to the public with the authorisation of the copyright holder or in accordance with a non-contractual licence or a statutory authorisation'.[97] On the facts, if the publisher did not have the right to make the (alleged) revisions, then absent the author's consent, the book's publication would not lawfully make the work available to the public.[98] The key question for the future is whether the Grand Chamber's guidance is exhaustive of the circumstances in which a work has been lawfully made available to the public.

2 Illustration for Instruction In 2014, the existing text of section 32 was replaced with a new version, this being a less verbose and, it would seem, less restrictive exception permitting fair dealing for the sole purpose of illustration for instruction. To invoke this exception, the dealing must be undertaken for a non-commercial purpose by a person giving or receiving instruction (including preparatory work, and setting and answering examination questions). A sufficient acknowledgment is required unless this would be impossible. In its previous iteration, section 32 could also be invoked for preparation, teaching and examination, but there were significant restrictions: subsection (1) applied to dealings with literary, dramatic, musical and artistic works, but not when carried out 'by means of a reprographic process', whilst subsection (2) only permitted sounds recordings and films to be copied as part of instruction on 'the

---

publication by the newspaper under another exception or by virtue of a public interest defence: para. 176 (Ch), paras. 81–82 (CA).
[96] *Spiegel Online* v. *Beck*, n. 67 above, paras. 85–95.   [97] Ibid., para. 89.
[98] Ibid., para. 92.

making of films or film sound-tracks'.[99] Old section 32 therefore allowed a lecturer to write text by hand on a blackboard or whiteboard (so-called chalk and talk uses), but not to cut-and-paste the same text into electronic slides, or distribute photocopies to students, or for that matter print the work onto acetate for display on an overhead projector.[100]

According to the 2014 Explanatory Memorandum, the overarching goal of reform to the education exceptions was to 'bring these exceptions up-to-date, reflecting advances in digital technology'.[101] Bearing this in mind, an important question regarding new section 32 is the meaning of 'illustration for instruction'.[102] Statements in the Explanatory Memorandum suggest that section 32 is qualitatively and quantitatively limited, it being emphasised that the exception permits small takings that are used to illustrate a teaching point.[103] As discussed by the authors of *Intellectual Property Law*, there are doctrinal and policy reasons for questioning this statement.[104] One reason is that such an interpretation belies the very examples in section 32, which cover preparatory acts, examinations and acts undertaken by students. Furthermore, given the legislative aim of enhancing the use of digital technologies in the education experience, it would be odd to then read section 32 in a way that only covers a narrow range of in-classroom acts by teachers.

Although the fieldwork in this book did not extend to education generally, there was some discussion of section 32 as cultural institutions – and in particular academic libraries – are involved in education in

---

[99] CDPA ss. 32(1)(b), (2A)(c).
[100] See Burrell and Coleman, n. 7 above, p. 122; C. Morrison, 'Illustration for Instruction and the UK Higher Education Sector' (MA Dissertation, King's College London, 2018) pp. 10–12, https://kar.kent.ac.uk/73310/. This state of affairs arose due to the definition of reprographic process in CDPA s. 178, which means a process '(a) for making facsimile copies, or (b) involving the use of an appliance for making multiple copies; and includes, in relation to a work held in electronic form, any copying by electronic means, but does not include the making of a film or sound recording.' Copying text onto acetate would fall within this definition if undertaken using 'an appliance for making multiple copies' such as a photocopier.
[101] Intellectual Property Office, Explanatory Memorandum to The Copyright and Rights in Performances (Research, Education, Libraries and Archives) Regulations 2014 (2014 No 1372), The Copyright and Rights in Performances (Disability) Regulations 2014 (2014 No 1384), The Copyright and Rights in Performances (Public Administration) Regulations 2014 (2014 No 1385) ('EM Education'), para 7.10.1.
[102] This phrase includes language from ISD Art. 5(3)(a) (covering uses 'for the sole purpose of illustration for teaching ...') and Berne Art. 10(2) (under which Member States may 'permit the utilization ... of literary or artistic works by way of illustration in publications, broadcasts or sound or visual recordings for teaching').
[103] EM Education, n. 101 above, paras. 7.10.2 ('teachers will be able to copy a small amount of material where necessary to illustrate a point'), 7.10.3 (for s. 32 to apply, it is necessary that the use is 'to illustrate a teaching point').
[104] Bently, Sherman, Gangjee and Johnson, n. 89 above, p. 264.

various ways. First, non-university interviewees reported that they had used the exception for their own in-house education programmes,[105] there being no requirement that section 32 applies only to instruction in schools, universities and equivalent bodies.[106] Whilst this did not necessarily involve teaching in a traditional classroom-style setup, interviewees seemed to give weight to the need for 'instruction' and did not, for example, report using section 32 to justify making digitised content available online on general websites because of its potential use as an educational resource.

Amongst interviewees from academic libraries, it appeared that a quite complex set of considerations influenced decision-marking around section 32.[107] As noted above, some questions related to the scope of section 32, including whether it could be invoked for uses outside the physical classroom, including for lecture capture and materials hosted on VLEs. In addition, interviewees noted challenges brought about by the interaction between section 32 and the many other ways that universities may lawfully re-use content, e.g., under licences with publishers of subscription databases; under blanket licences offered by copyright collectives such as the Copyright Licensing Agency (CLA); under Creative Commons and open access initiatives; and by reference to exceptions in sections 33 to 36A of the CDPA.[108] Finally, challenges arose in promoting institution-wide compliance with the law, but without acting like the copyright police,[109] or inadvertently encouraging a 'complete free-for-all' in relation to copying.[110]

The complexity of the copyright environment meant that, at the time of the interviews, utilisation of section 32 was very much a work in progress. Amongst interviewees, the least contentious application of section 32 was similar to that noted in the Explanatory Memorandum: a lecturer displaying or playing copyright works in the classroom to help explain the learning activity or content being taught. Interviewees emphasised that there needed to be a direct connection to teaching and not, say, the use of images for mere decorative purposes. They also noted the need for acknowledgement, and explained how this might be effected. When asked about the implications of lectures being recorded, there was some confidence that section 32 could still apply, especially if recordings were accessible only to enrolled students via the VLE

---

[105] E.g., 303G, 305M, 313M, 323X.   [106] Cf. CDPA ss. 34–36A.
[107] E.g., 309L, 312L, 316L, 319L; similar 310X. See also Morrison, n. 100 above.
[108] For discussion of the educational copying exceptions, see Bently, Sherman, Gangjee and Johnson, n. 89 above, pp. 262–267.
[109] 319L; similar 316.   [110] 309L.

or another password-protected platform. This conclusion reflected pedagogical views about the use of digital technologies in teaching and logistical challenges in editing recordings to remove third-party content. But interviewees also described some reticence around pressing certain interpretations of section 32, given uncertainties in the scope of the provision and the desire not to be the 'test case' in relation to its operation.[111]

To conclude, the fieldwork suggested that cultural institutions were relying on section 32, and that copyright specialists in academic libraries were focusing particular attention on the reach of that exception. Whilst the Canadian experience was of universities shifting away from blanket licences offered by Access Copyright, in the UK there was no discernible appetite to abandon the CLA UUK/GuildHE Higher Education Licence, although questions about the value proposition of the licence were raised.[112] One consequence was that UK experiences with educational fair dealing were quite different from their Canadian counterparts, and indeed from universities in the United States, where fair use has been relied upon for acts of digitisation that in the UK would be covered by the CLA licence. It remains to be seen whether practices will change in the future, including due to the direct or indirect effect of the new Directive on Copyright in the Digital Single Market, which mandates an exception for the digital use of works for the sole purpose of illustration for teaching.[113]

3 Caricature, Parody or Pastiche Of the three new fair dealing exceptions, participants in the UK fieldwork made least reference to section 30A, which provides that fair dealing for the purposes of

---

[111] 309L, 312L. See, also, the empirical study of Morrison, n. 100 above, in relation to the reported utilisation of s. 32 at ten UK universities. Morrison concluded that practices were 'not consistently aligned across the sector' (p. 49). He identified a number of reasons for this, including the complexity of the copyright environment in relation to education, and unhelpful guidance from government in relation to the role and coverage of s. 32.

[112] For information on the licence, see www.cla.co.uk/higher-education-licence; and for analysis of its content and operation, see J. Secker, E. Gadd and C. Morrison, *Understanding the Value of the CLA Licence to UK Higher Education* (Universities UK / GuildHE Copyright Negotiation and Advisory Committee, July 2019).

[113] Directive (EU) 2019/790 of the European Parliament and of the Council of 17 April 2019 on copyright and related rights in the Digital Single Market and amending Directives 96/9/EC and 2001/29/EC, Art. 5. The exception mandated in Art. 5 applies only to uses by educational establishments, and may be subject to a qualification that it does not apply to certain works and uses where 'suitable licences' are 'easily available on the market': Art. 5(2). The exception may also be subject to a requirement that fair compensation be paid to rightsholders: Art. 5(4).

caricature, parody or pastiche does not infringe copyright.[114] This is not surprising, as institutions would not usually consider *themselves* to be engaged in any of these acts. The analysis in this sub-section is therefore more doctrinal in its orientation, and focuses on two matters: can institutions point to section 30A for their own acts even if they do not share the creator's purpose; and might institutions (and indeed legislators and other stakeholders) have overlooked the significance of the pastiche limb of section 30A?

This first question arises because a strict reading of the CDPA might suggest that section 30A only applies where the copyist's purpose is parody, caricature or pastiche.[115] This argument is an application of cases such as *Sillitoe* v. *McGraw-Hill Book Company (UK) Ltd*,[116] where it was stated that the relevant purpose, in relation to fair dealing, is that of the defendant and not any downstream recipient. In *Sillitoe* this meant that authors of study notes for literature students could not invoke fair dealing in relation to passages quoted in those notes, as the authors were not, when writing the notes, engaged in private study or research.[117] Applying this to section 30A, one can imagine the argument that the purpose of a commercial radio station that plays a parodic song is to provide a broadcasting service and raise revenue through advertising, and that the purpose of a public gallery that plays a pastiche film is to present that work to the public.

The difficulty with this approach is that if taken seriously – i.e., if we required the radio station and gallery to clear rights – it would effect a significant restriction on the public presentation of works to which section 30A applies, thereby undermining the operation of that provision. One way to avoid this outcome would be via a purposive approach in which fair dealing can extend to those involved in the dissemination of section 30A works, on the basis that dissemination is an essential part of the artistic process.[118] This approach would not only be consistent with

---

[114] Two interviews included meaningful discussion of s. 30A: 320L reported having used the exception in an exhibition on a major political event, the exhibition including some items of a satirical nature; and 314G discussed whether s. 30A might apply to the public presentation of certain items in the institution's collection.

[115] See also J. McCutcheon and S. Holloway, 'Whose Fair Dealing? Third-Party Reliance on the Fair Dealing Exception for Parody or Satire' (2016) 27 *Australian Intellectual Property Journal* 54.

[116] [1983] FSR 545 (Ch); see also *De Garis* v. *Neville Jeffress Pidler Pty Ltd* (1990) 18 IPR 292, 298.

[117] Ibid., 558.

[118] Such an approach has parallels to *CCH*, n. 1 above, para. 64, where it was held that a library making copies of legal texts for supply to patrons had the purpose of research, these acts being 'necessary conditions of research and thus part of the research process'.

the legislative goals of section 30A but is open on the statutory text as section 30A is not qualified by any restrictions on the distribution or sale of works within its ambit.[119] It is also noteworthy that *Sillitoe* pre-dates the CDPA, and that the current statute countenances the use of agency arguments by those making copies for students and researchers.[120] This suggests that the comments in *Sillitoe* must be approached with caution.[121]

The second question relates to the additional work performed by the pastiche limb of section 30A.[122] The language of that section was modelled on Article 5(3)(k) of the ISD, which permits Member States to enact exceptions in relation to 'caricature, parody or pastiche'. There has been a great deal of attention given to the justifications for, and operation of, exceptions directed to parody.[123] However, it seems that the significance of pastiche as a separate fair dealing purpose has been less appreciated.[124] This is not because of ignorance of the meaning of that term.

---

[119] Cf. CDPA s. 31A (the making of accessible copies for the use of persons with a disability; provision contains restrictions on distributing and selling those copies).

[120] CDPA s. 29(3)(b), discussed in Bently, Sherman, Gangjee and Johnson, n. 89 above, p. 243.

[121] Similarly, it has been observed by McCutcheon and Holloway, n. 115 above, that in Australia, later cases have questioned *De Garis*. This was explicit in *Telstra Corporation Pty Ltd* v. *Premier Media Group Ptd Ltd* (2007) 72 IPR 89, para. 51 (application for interlocutory injunction; Allsop J not convinced that the defendants, who had created sports news content, were outside fair dealing for the purpose of news reporting by providing that content to third parties, as it could be 'associated with' reporting by those parties). They argue that this was implicit in *TCN Channel Nine Pty Ltd* v. *Network Ten Pty Ltd* (2001) 108 FCR 235; (2002) 118 FCR 417, on the basis that no distinction was made between Network Ten (the defendant, and the party that commissioned and broadcast the content) and Working Dog (the production company that actually produced the television programme at the heart of the dispute).

[122] The material that follows is a summary of the key ideas in E. Hudson, 'The Pastiche Exception in Copyright Law: A Case of Mashed-Up Drafting?' [2017] *Intellectual Property Quarterly* 346.

[123] See, e.g., R. Posner, 'When Is Parody Fair Use?' (1992) 21 *Journal of Legal Studies* 67; M. Spence, 'Intellectual Property and the Problem of Parody' (1998) 114 *Law Quarterly Review* 594; D. Brennan, 'Copyright and Parody in Australia: Some Thoughts on *Suntrust Bank* v *Houghton Mifflin Company*' (2002) 13 *Australian Intellectual Property Journal* 161; R. Deazley, 'Copyright and Parody: Taking Backward the Gowers Review?' (2010) 73 *Modern Law Review* 785; J. Griffiths, 'Fair Dealing after *Deckmyn* – The United Kingdom's Defence for Caricature, Parody or Pastiche' in M. Richardson and S. Ricketson (eds), *Research Handbook on Intellectual Property in Media and Entertainment* (Cheltenham: Edward Elgar, 2017).

[124] Whilst there was a lot of discussion of a new parody exception, such analysis did not tend to include any meaningful consideration of pastiche: e.g., *Gowers Review of Intellectual Property* (HM Treasury, 2006), pp. 67–68 (discussing music sampling and transformative use but without any suggestion that such practices may fall within pastiche); Deazley, n. 123 above, 786 (describing parody as 'multivalent' and including practices such as pastiche); Hargreaves, n. 55 above (only including the word pastiche on a single occasion).

For instance, advice on section 30A released by the Intellectual Property Office (IPO) stated:

> In broad terms: parody imitates a work for humorous or satirical effect. It evokes an existing work while being noticeably different from it. Pastiche is musical or other composition made up of selections from various sources or one that imitates the style of another artist or period. A caricature portrays its subject in a simplified or exaggerated way, which may be insulting or complimentary and may serve a political purpose or be solely for entertainment.[125]

This accords with the meaning of pastiche given in the *Oxford English Dictionary*, where the entry for pastiche as a noun reads:

> 1.a. A novel, poem, painting, etc., incorporating several different styles, or made up of parts drawn from a variety of sources. b. A musical composition incorporating different styles; a medley.
>
> 2.a. A work, esp. of literature, created in the style *of* someone or something else; a work that humorously exaggerates or parodies a particular style. b. The technique of incorporating distinctive elements of other works or styles in a literary composition, design, etc.[126]

Although the OED cannot capture all the nuance that comes from a detailed examination of the history and meaning of pastiche, its entry accords with descriptions in specialist texts.[127] These texts indicate that pastiche covers laudatory and non-critical imitation, and that it has two main forms: creating a new work in the style of another artist or genre, and making a new work from a compilation or assembly of pre-existing works. Pastiche therefore covers 'non-twist' and 'anti-twist' uses, i.e., those where there is no attempt to ridicule or satirise the source work, or comment critically on that work or other themes. This can be contrasted with the 'expectation-defying alterations'[128] of parody and the exaggeration of caricature, and raises doubts about assertions that caricature, parody and pastiche are 'too similar for it to be possible to distinguish between them'.[129]

---

[125] Intellectual Property Office, *Exceptions to Copyright: Guidance for Creators and Copyright Owners* (IPO, 2014), p. 6.

[126] OED, n. 64 above. [127] Hudson, n. 122 above, 348–351 and references therein.

[128] Brennan, n. 123 above, 166.

[129] Description of the oral argument of Belgium by AG Villalón in *Deckmyn* v. *Vandersteen* (C-201/13) [2014] ECDR 21, para. AG42. The Grand Chamber did not include any comment on this matter: c.f. S. Jacques, 'Are National Courts Required to have an (Exceptional) European Sense of Humour?' (2015) 37 *European Intellectual Property Review* 134, 136 (suggesting that the Grand Chamber 'implicitly indicates that "parody", "pastiche" and "caricature" are overlapping, rather than impervious terms', but not explaining from where this conclusion is drawn, or just how much overlap is

There has not yet been a decision from the CJEU in relation to the meaning of pastiche. Some guidance can be drawn from the analysis of parody in *Deckmyn* v. *Vandersteen*, as logic dictates that the ideas underpinning that judgment should apply to all three legislative bunkmates.[130] In that case it was held that parody should be given its 'usual meaning in everyday language, while also taking into account the context in which it occurs and the purposes of the rules of which it is part'.[131] Applying this approach, the Grand Chamber located two essential characteristics of parody – that it evokes, but is noticeably different from, an existing work; and that it involves humour or mockery[132] – and rejected certain additional limbs that may have narrowed this definition.[133] This was seen to accord with the relevant legal context, namely the CJEU interpretative canons that exceptions be interpreted strictly but in a way that enables their effectiveness,[134] and the objectives of Article 5(3)(k), notably support of free speech and the public interest.[135]

Applying this approach to pastiche, the starting point is the ordinary meaning of the term, which as discussed above has two subtypes: imitation and incorporation. Consistent with this definition, it should not be necessary to include any humour, critical commentary or element of surprise, as these are inapt for a 'non-twist' or 'anti-twist' genre, and nor should acknowledgement or evident recombination be essential, although these might be relevant to whether there has been a *fair* dealing.[136] If right, this means that section 30A has the potential to apply to mash-ups, fan fiction, music sampling, collage, appropriation art,

---

suggested). The Belgian submissions might accord with some descriptions of the French approach: see description in Hudson, n. 122 above, 353–354.

[130] Discussed in Hudson, n. 122 above, 354–361. In *Deckmyn* v. *Vandersteen*, a far-right political party produced and distributed calendars that included an image based on a drawing from the comic strip *Suske en Wiske*. The Court of Appeal of Brussels referred to the CJEU questions in relation to the meaning of parody. For analysis of *Deckmyn*, see, e.g., Griffiths, n. 123 above; Jacques, n. 129 above.

[131] *Deckmyn* v. *Vandersteen*, n. 129 above, para. 19. For a similar approach to the definition of quotation, see *Pelham* v. *Hütter* (Grand Chamber), n. 65 above, para. 71.

[132] Ibid., para. 20.

[133] Ibid., para. 21 (these being that 'that the parody should display an original character of its own, other than that of displaying noticeable differences with respect to the original parodied work; could reasonably be attributed to a person other than the author of the original work itself; should relate to the original work itself or mention the source of the parodied work').

[134] Ibid., paras. 22–24.

[135] Ibid., para. 25. The Grand Chamber also stated that in applying the parody exception in Art. 5(3)(k), a 'fair balance' must be maintained between the rights and interests of rightholders and the freedom of expression of users: paras. 26–27.

[136] See Hudson, n. 122 above, 361–364.

medleys, and many other forms of homage and compilation.[137] Lest this definition seem broad, it must be remembered, first, that many instances of pastiche will not implicate copyright (there being no reproduction of protectable expression but new works in the style of earlier works and artists), and second, that this act of classification is not the end of the story because of the requirement for fairness.[138] Applying this analysis to cultural institutions, whilst it is open to question whether they regularly create pastiche works, they will likely collect many items that fall within this designation.

In conclusion, given doctrinal and empirical indications, it is open to argue that between quotation, parody, pastiche and illustration for instruction, there is potential for the reach of fair dealing to expand significantly. This is particularly so given the emergence of new attitudes to copyright at UK institutions, a matter to which this chapter now turns in Section III.

III   New Institutional Attitudes

So far, this chapter has focused on two sets of experiences in relation to fair dealing: the sea change in copyright management at Canadian universities that included a more significant role for fair dealing; and the responses of UK cultural institutions to new fair dealing exceptions introduced as part of the 2014 reforms. These experiences give support to the proposition that, if existing exceptions are inadequate, meaningful change can be effected within a fair dealing framework.[139] But they are also part of a broader narrative regarding the changing attitudes of cultural institutions towards copyright, and in particular increased

---

[137] Cf. *Pelham* v. *Hütter* (AG Opinion), n. 68 above, para. AG70, where AG Szpunar stated *en passant* that Art. 5(3)(k) would not apply to music sampling, because that exception, like quotation, 'presupposes interaction with the work used, or at least with its author, which is lacking in the case of sampling, such as that at issue in the main proceedings'. *Deckmyn* was cited as authority for this proposition, however this would seem to be contrary to *Deckmyn's* definition of parody, which does not require that the defendant's work relate to the source work. In FN30, AG Szpunar also rejected the proposition that the defendant's phonogram was a pastiche, as pastiche 'consists in the imitation of the style of a work or an author without necessarily taking any elements of that work'. However, this would seem to misunderstand the definition of pastiche.

[138] As stated in n. 135 above, the Grand Chamber also spoke of the need for fair balance in the application of the parody exception. This raises the question of whether this human rights balancing exercise merely *informs* the traditional British analysis of fairness, or must *supplant* that case law, at least so long as UK copyright law remains tied to that in the European Union: see *England and Wales Cricket Board* v. *Tixdaq* [2016] EWHC 575 (Ch); Griffiths, n. 123 above.

[139] See also Handler and Hudson, n. 5 above.

New Institutional Attitudes

knowledge of copyright law, changes in the resources dedicated to copyright, and – perhaps most importantly – the emergence of a less risk averse mindset in relation to copyright. Greater utilisation of fair dealing is just one manifestation of these changes. This section discusses the increasing use of risk management, i.e., that institutions have responded to perceived difficulties and failures in the copyright system by grounding certain copyright decision-making in pragmatism and ethics rather than strict legal compliance.

This section begins by providing an overview of reported attitudes to copyright amongst interviewees in Australia in 2004 and 2005, and Canada in 2008 and 2009. This is contrasted with experiences in the United States, where interviewees had a more commercial approach to copyright. It then discusses subsequent experiences, including in the United Kingdom, where it was seen that in numerous institutions, staff had become more knowledgeable, less risk averse and had adjusted the principles that underlie copyright management.[140] In presenting this aspect of the fieldwork, it is not suggested that the observations apply across the entire sector or are universal, or that changes are unidirectional. For instance, the follow-up interviews in Canada suggested that the broader understanding of fair dealing in academic libraries was not necessarily shared by public libraries, archives and museums.[141] But the analysis supports the propositions that: (1) there has been a notable shift in attitude amongst many participating institutions; and (2) these shifts seem to be connected to, and are perhaps even a precondition for, a more robust utilisation of copyright exceptions (and especially general provisions like fair dealing). The key question to arise from this discussion, and one addressed in Chapter 9, is what this means for the drafting of copyright exceptions.

A Looking Back

When the first tranche of fieldwork took place in Australia in 2004 and 2005, it quickly became apparent that even at major collecting institutions, staff struggled with what they saw as the complexity of copyright law,[142] and reported a preference for conservative risk management

---

[140] Although the United Kingdom was not the subject of pre-2014 fieldwork, the interviewees were able to speak to changes in resourcing and risk management over time.

[141] E.g., 146L, 162L, 163L.

[142] E. Hudson and A. Kenyon, 'Digital Access: The Impact of Copyright on Digitisation Practices in Australian Museums, Galleries, Libraries and Archives' (2007) 30 *University of New South Wales Law Journal* 12, 36–37.

positions, especially for public-facing activities.[143] This was 'not an image of users that has great prominence in debates about digital copyright, where pirates and parasites have taken centre stage',[144] but 'was a prominent feature in the fieldwork carried out in Australia, and deserves careful consideration in relation to copyright exceptions and licensing practices'.[145] One manifestation of this risk aversion related to orphaned works, where many interviewees reported that it was often easier to delete or omit such content than to proceed.[146] This was not universal, and there were instances when a more relaxed approach was taken, especially for social history collections.[147] But the overarching impression was that interviewees were very concerned about the ramifications of non-compliance. Knowledge of the law was mixed,[148] and although some larger institutions had dedicated copyright officers, very few of these individuals had a law degree.[149] Concern was expressed that copyright was under-resourced, with the result that institutions often gave excessive deference to cost and ease of compliance when determining the targets of digitisation and other projects.[150]

A similar picture emerged in the Canadian fieldwork in 2008 and 2009; in fact, if anything interviewees in that country described an approach that was even more cautious than Australia. This has already been seen at a number of points in this book, for instance in the greater comfort that Canadian interviewees seemed to derive from sector-specific exceptions for management and preservation,[151] and in the extremely muted response to *CCH*.[152] Interestingly, this concern to comply with the law was not generally matched by a well-resourced copyright office, and it was common that interviewees did not have any formal legal training and self-reported that their copyright knowledge was not high. The level of engagement with the law was greater amongst library participants, and in particular those working in academic institutions. But even here there were repeated instances where librarians were, say, pressing for broader roles for fair dealing, but this was not accepted by university counsel and those in senior management positions.

---

[143] Ibid., 40–41.
[144] E. Hudson and A. Kenyon, 'Without Walls: Copyright Law and Digital Collections in Australian Cultural Institutions' (2007) 4 *SCRIPT-ed* 197, 207.
[145] Ibid., 207–208. [146] Hudson and Kenyon, n. 142 above, 40. [147] Ibid., 41.
[148] Ibid., 28 ('Most interviewees who were directly asked about their familiarity with the fair dealing exceptions reported limited knowledge of their scope and application in the sector').
[149] Ibid., 37. [150] Ibid., 42–43. [151] See Chapter 4. [152] See Chapter 7.

New Institutional Attitudes 295

The difference in the US experience was palpable.[153] Although there was variation in practices, many interviewees reported such things as: (1) a centralised unit for managing copyright; (2) the employment of copyright experts, including legal attorneys and rights officers; (3) a willingness to dedicate resources to copyright management and policy development; (4) a more commercial posture, including a degree of comfort with risk; and (5) a management structure in which copyright experts either had the authority to direct institutional decision-making or whose recommendations were acted upon by the executive team. The interviewees who described this sort of copyright environment also described the more forward-leaning applications of fair use and had greater sophistication in their copyright management more generally, including in relation to licensing.[154] The experiences in this project therefore suggested that institutions with greater copyright resourcing were better placed to undertake the legal analysis necessary to develop and defend new fair use positions. For institutions that had them, in-house counsel seemed to play a particularly significant role, being 'more prepared to take an adversarial role' where required.[155] For instance, one interviewee observed that when it came to negotiation, 'you sort of want someone who's savvy and can really manage this with some sense of expertise'.[156]

In contrast with the majority of the cohort, some US institutions had less centralised copyright management models, and this was reported to be a hindrance to the development of new and efficient practices. For instance, one interviewee observed:

The headaches here can relate to the lack of centralisation – for instance, curators may end up separately clearing rights for the same images. There's not the knowledge of who to go to, or when we have to clear rights and when we do not need to worry. We don't have internal counsel to advise us that way. We'd have to go to [names external counsel]. This can be a very time-intensive procedure. ... The joke here is that our contract with [names entity] took a year and a half to be approved ... and people said 'wow, you're lucky – that was fast.' Maybe we're not their highest focus.[157]

In sum, following the first phases of empirical research in Australia, Canada and the United States, there seemed to be some correlation between the resources directed to copyright and the degree to which institutions relied on general exceptions. Canadian interviewees, arguably the least well resourced, appeared more comfortable operating

---

[153] See Chapter 5.
[154] Eg, 1G, 3X, 7G, 12L, 16G, 23X, 26G, 29L, 30G, 35L, 36M, 39L, 43M, 45M, 53G.
[155] 7G.   [156] 4L.   [157] 20G.

within the paradigm of closed-ended exceptions, whilst numerous US interviewees were comfortable with life in a fair use system. This was consistent with the literature on legal rulemaking. As discussed in Chapter 2, this literature predicts that it will often be cheaper to learn about the content of a rule than a standard because the former has been imbued with content by the legislature but the latter needs to be predicted.[158] If cultural institutions place a high value on complying with the law, then it might be expected that institutions with fewer resources will be more comfortable in relying on rules than multifactor standards. This level of comfort will depend on the legislative drafting, as complex rules or those with technical language may require expertise to understand. However, it seemed that Canadian exceptions for collection management and preservation were not experienced in this way, and formed a meaningful part of institutional practices even in cultural institutions whose engagement with copyright was lower and who were cautious about expanding fair dealing arguments.

The empirical work was also consistent with ideas from the standards and rules literature regarding risk preferences, where it is predicted that individuals with conservative mindsets will tend to place higher weight on *ex ante* certainty than those who are more comfortable with risk.[159] Although interviewees in all three jurisdictions often emphasised the conservatism of their institutions, some were less cautious than others, and it appeared that numerous US institutions were willing to take what they considered to be 'reasonable' risks in copyright management, including in emerging understandings of fair use.[160] For instance, one interviewee said that their institution was trying to 'provide as much access as we can, while being responsible and being moderately careful about risk but not crazy about it'.[161] Another said that 'our mission is to provide access to the public, so after we've done our research, and after we're confident that we've exhausted all means of trying to find rightsholders, we'll let it out there'.[162] This did not result in unrestricted use by the institution; as noted by another interviewee, 'in some things, I'm pretty aggressive, in other things, I'm pretty conservative', meaning that the institution may proceed with certain non-commercial activities under fair use but not use uncleared material in profit-making enterprises.[163] A forward-leaning approach to fair use was also described by an

---

[158] See, e.g., L. Kaplow, 'Rules versus Standards: An Economic Analysis' (1992) 42 *Duke Law Journal* 557, 596–599.
[159] Ibid., 605. [160] Especially 1G, 4L, 7G, 9M, 16G, 29L, 30G, 35L, 43G, 53G.
[161] 9M. [162] 30G. [163] 43G.

interviewee who said that the institution would not resile from certain fair use understandings until there was a defining lawsuit in the sector.[164]

At this point in the fieldwork, it was proposed that if countries such as Australia and Canada wished to encourage greater use of flexible standards, consideration needed to be given to the broader environment in which these new or rebooted exceptions were intended to operate, including levels of copyright knowledge, prevailing attitudes to risk and so forth.[165] It was also questioned whether some norms would be amenable to change, being grounded in legal history and cultural understandings of copyright, and cemented in internal workflows and policies. But as discussed in Section III.B, the later fieldwork revealed the dynamism of norms and practices, not only through incremental development but through some abrupt changes in approach.

B   New Attitudes

This chapter has discussed new applications of fair dealing in Canadian and UK cultural institutions. In each case, this enlarged role for fair dealing can be connected, at least in part, to changes in the legal environment, i.e., new fair dealing purposes or statements in the case law. But this is not the complete story, as the fieldwork also revealed changes in the ways that cultural institutions approached copyright management. These changes were not universal, either in their uptake across or within countries, or in their manifestation from one institution to the next. Nevertheless, when comparing interview data spanning over fourteen years, there was a trend towards a more confident and sophisticated approach to copyright. This seemed to be the product of a number of factors, such as: (1) better knowledge of copyright law; (2) increases in the resourcing of copyright within institutions; (3) the employment of copyright specialists to provide in-house advice; (4) cooperation between institutions in relation to policies, practices and law reform activities; and (5) greater comfort with risk and uncertainty. This is consistent with the observations in Chapters 6 and 7 that change to the law in books will not necessarily generate new norms if users do not know about or understand these changes; or are not willing or able to dedicate resources to developing new workflows; or see the law as excessively uncertain, contrary to relationship management imperatives, etc.

[164] 53G.
[165] E. Hudson, 'Copyright Exceptions: The Experiences of Cultural Institutions in the United States, Canada and Australia' (PhD thesis, University of Melbourne, November 2011).

For instance, we have already seen in this chapter that the rollout of new fair dealing policies at Canadian universities involved a significant redeployment of resources to open or expand copyright offices. It was not enough that some academic librarians had been keen, in the years following *CCH*, to re-imagine the role of fair dealing in the sector; to operationalise such a vision, it was necessary that this position be translated into new practices that had the imprimatur of senior staff. What is particularly interesting about the Canadian experience is the magnitude and pace of change, involving not just heightened reliance on fair dealing but a fundamental reappraisal of the role of blanket licences from Access Copyright. The Canadian experiences illustrate that apparently sticky norms can change, and dramatically so, when the right set of factors converge.

In the United Kingdom, it seemed that the 2014 reforms coincided with growth in the view – at least in larger institutions – that copyright needs to be approached with a less nervous and more pragmatic mindset.[166] This approach starts from the premise that the aim of copyright management should not be strict legal compliance, as such a goal is impossible and does not necessarily further the interests of creators and copyright owners. Instead, greater consideration should be given to the principles that underpin the law, with the result that institutions should be open to risk management and more generally to applying the law in a risk aware rather than risk averse fashion. As mentioned in Chapter 3, such an approach may be appropriate in numerous different scenarios, for example where there is uncertainty regarding the content of the law, or gaps in the evidence of authorship or ownership, or where it is not possible for reasons of time and expense to undertake a full copyright analysis for every item appearing in an exhibition, publication or internet resource. To illustrate, one interviewee said:

> We do bring the risk framework in for early twentieth century and late nineteenth century material, that may or may not be in copyright, where there's a huge swathe of copyright owners, [and] they're all called John Smith and we have no idea who they are. ... [These materials are] not by famous people [and] not by people who've made anything else, there's no real information in that sense. We needed an approach for that. We have a risk-based approach that's all about identifying relevant factors [to help decide whether to publish or not]. We look at whether authorship is known, the age of the content, whether it was likely to be produced with commercial intent, and depending on the outcomes of those factors, whether some specified level of research into the right status is

---

[166] E.g., 305M, 312L, 313M, 314G, 315A, 317G, 322G, 323X, 325M, 328G, 329M; although in the earlier UK fieldwork, there were still reports of significant conservatism: e.g., 301L, 302M, 306L, 309L; cf. 303G (expressing comfort with even medium risk).

undertaken or not. And we are implementing procedures to record the doing of that.[167]

Another said:

I think because they've got someone here who they can ask – me – that gives you confidence to take risks [when] you might otherwise have said, 'we don't know, so let's not'. ... I understand that if people are spending museum money, they want to be cautious. The library and archives [in the institution] are becoming less risk averse, because we're more confident in what legal options are available to us that don't involve clearance, and also because ... I work quite closely with them, and they want to do it right, but not more than they have to because they don't have the resources.[168]

Importantly, these changes to internal resourcing and mindset meant that new copyright management norms arose that seemed to be *independent of the prevailing legal environment*. The use of orphaned works was one such example. Although they are not a new phenomenon, over the last twenty years orphaned works have occupied a prominent spot in debates about copyright, with a great deal of scholarly and law reform attention directed towards measures to reduce their incidence and impact.[169] Such possibilities have included alternatives to negotiation (e.g., centralised licensing, extended collective licensing and free exceptions), remedies limitations for good faith users, and special privileges for cultural institutions as bodies particularly impeded by orphaned works problems.[170]

Of the four countries studied, the United Kingdom was the only jurisdiction that saw the passage of specific orphaned works legislation during the course of this project.[171] In Australia, section 200AB was intended to

---

[167] 320L. [168] 313M.
[169] See, e.g., P. Brannon, 'Reforming Copyright to Foster Innovation: Providing Access to Orphaned Works' (2006) 14 *Journal of Intellectual Property Law* 145; United States Copyright Office, *Report on Orphan Works: A Report of the Register of Copyrights* (United States Copyright Office, 2006); *Gowers Review*, n. 124 above, paras. 4.91–4.101; Hargreaves, n. 55 above, paras. 4.52–4.60; M. Pallante, 'Orphan Works & Mass Digitization: Obstacles & Opportunities' (2012) 27 *Berkeley Technology Law Journal* 1251; M. Favale, F. Homberg, M. Kretschmer, D. Mendis and D. Secchi, *Copyright, and the Regulation of Orphan Works: A Comparative Review of Seven Jurisdictions and a Rights Clearance Simulation* (IPO, 2013); ALRC, n. 6 above, ch. 13; United States Copyright Office, *Orphan Works and Mass Digitization: A Report of the Register of Copyrights* (United States Copyright Office, 2015).
[170] See Chapter 3, Section IV. See also E. Hudson, 'Copyright and Invisible Authors: A Property Perspective' in A. Johnston and L. Talbot (eds), *Critical Corporate and Commercial Law* (London: Palgrave, forthcoming).
[171] CDPA Sch. ZA1 (EU-mandated orphaned works exception for cultural and educational institutions) and Copyright and Rights in Performances (Licensing of Orphan Works) Regulations 2014 (SI 2014/2863) (licensing scheme operated by the IPO). In the United States, the Shawn Bentley Orphan Works Act of 2008 (S 2913 [110th]) was passed by the Senate but was never passed in the House of Representatives.

have relevance to various acts by cultural institutions, including in relation to orphaned works. As has already been discussed, neither the UK orphaned works initiatives nor section 200AB were embraced with gusto by participating cultural institutions.[172] And yet in both Australia and the United Kingdom, it seemed that orphaned works were not necessarily experienced as such a big issue, as captured by one interviewee who said that 'to be honest, I know that there's a lot of academic interest in orphan works, but it doesn't trouble us a great deal'.[173] Rather than being a product of legal intervention, this appeared to reflect a growing comfort in using risk management in decision-making about copyright.

As discussed in Chapter 3, 'risk managing' a use involves a decision to proceed with conduct despite awareness that it will, or might, infringe copyright. The line between a risk-informed and risk-managed decision can be difficult to draw, but it can be said that in the latter case, there is no meaningful *ex ante* belief that any infringement would fall within an exception or could be defended in another way. The fieldwork suggested that each time an institution used risk management and experienced no adverse consequences, it led to greater confidence that the risk calculus had not overlooked an important matter and could be used for other works and projects. This did not result in a free-for-all, with risk management serving as a supplement for other copyright compliance options. Furthermore, we must remember that the factors that permitted risk management in larger institutions – especially copyright expertise – might not necessarily be found in smaller institutions.[174] But amongst participants in this project, orphaned works seemed to be retreating as an issue, and indeed interviewees volunteered concerns about other problems, including misplaced certainty (e.g., institutions relying on rights that were granted by someone without the power to do so) and non-responsive copyright owners.[175] For the latter, some interviewees reported using risk management to undertake some public-facing acts that were consistent with their public interest missions.

The empirical research in this book focused on larger cultural institutions, and different experiences may emerge from smaller institutions and from other copyright constituencies. But if there is consensus that risk management is an appropriate way for users to respond to problems such as orphaned works, there may be an argument in favour of statutory reforms that support such processes. For instance, remedies limitations for good faith users, or safe harbours for institutions with reasonable internal copyright processes, might reinforce and guide the risk

---

[172] See Chapters 3 and 6, respectively.   [173] 317G.
[174] A point made by, e.g., 312L, 319L, 322G.   [175] E.g., 210A, 255A, 305M, 314G.

management calculus, send a signal regarding the legitimacy of risk-informed decision-making, and encourage those who are strongly risk averse to adopt a less cautious posture.[176] On the other hand, the empirical work cast doubt on the utility of schemes with registration or licensing requirements, at least in the cultural institution sector. Such approaches might be said to help address confirmation bias (i.e., that institution decision-making might be influenced by self-interest), support transparency, and provide a central database for owners and users. However, the fieldwork highlighted issues with such schemes, for instance their administrative and bureaucratic costs, the limits of the licences offered by the IPO, and whether databases and registries in fact help copyright owners to resurface or provide a hub in which cultural institutions can share information with one another.[177]

In sum, the fieldwork not only accorded with insights from the standards and rules literature in relation to the relevance of user characteristics to interpretations of legal commands, but also demonstrated how decision-making can at times transcend the law in books.

IV The Canadian Post-Script

On 12 July 2017, Phelan J of the Federal Court of Canada released his decision in *Access Copyright* v. *York*.[178] There were two main aspects to the case: whether the Access Copyright interim tariff approved by the Copyright Board in 2010[179] was binding on York; and whether copies made in accordance with York's Fair Dealing Guidelines were fair dealings. On the first question, Phelan J answered in the affirmative that the interim tariff was 'mandatory and enforceable against York'.[180] On the second question, he held that whilst the dealings pursuant to the Guidelines were for educational purposes within section 29 of the Copyright Act, they were not fair.[181] This raised the question of whether this litigation might precipitate a reversal of the fair dealing practices of Canadian universities.

---

[176] On safe harbours, see G. Austin and E. Hudson, 'Why the Not-for-Profit Cultural Sector Needs Tailor-Made Copyright Safe Harbours', *The Conversation*, 13 February 2018, http://theconversation.com/why-the-not-for-profit-cultural-sector-needs-tailor-made-copyright-safe-harbours-89564.
[177] See Chapter 3, Section IV.B.   [178] See n. 8 above.   [179] See n. 20 above.
[180] Phelan J said that to 'hold otherwise would be to frustrate the purpose of the tariff scheme of the Act and the broad powers given to the Board to make an interim decision ... and to choose form over substance': n. 8 above, para. 7. The full reasoning was set out at paras. 188–248.
[181] Ibid., full reasoning at paras. 249–357.

In considering this question, it is worth noting a few matters about the litigation and Phelan J's judgment. The claim brought by Access did not include a challenge to York's Fair Dealing Guidelines. Instead, fair dealing was in issue because of a counter-claim by York which sought declarations that copies made pursuant to its Guidelines fell within fair dealing. This strategy has been criticised on the basis that York should have focused on denying the proposition that tariffs approved by the Board are mandatory, or at least split the issues so that fair dealing was considered only if York lost on this point.[182] It also meant that Phelan J was asked to consider York's copying practices generally, rather than any specific acts of alleged infringement.[183]

The substantive elements of York's Guidelines applied to 'Short Excerpts',[184] and permitted staff to make a single copy of a Short Excerpt for each student enrolled in a class or course, such copies being able to be distributed as handouts, made as part of a course pack or hosted on a password-protected learning management system. The Guidelines stated that the extract 'in each case must contain no more of the work than is required in order to achieve the fair dealing purpose', these purposes matching those in the Copyright Act. The Guidelines noted that 'other sources of permission' would be required for copies falling outside its parameters and provided contact details of York's Copyright Office.

Implementation of the Guidelines occurred on 22 December 2010.[185] At that point York had a blanket licence with Access (this licence expiring on 31 December 2010), and for the first half of 2011, York operated

---

[182] See especially A. Katz, 'Access Copyright v. York University: An Anatomy of a Predictable But Avoidable Loss', *Ariel Katz* (26 July 2017), https://arielkatz.org/access-copyright-v-york-university-predictable-avoidable-loss/. Part of Katz's argument was that approval of a tariff by the Board serves only to render that tariff 'mandatory on the collective', i.e., that the collective 'cannot legally withhold a licence or refuse to issue one' to a user who wishes to operate under the approved scheme': e.g., A. Katz, 'Spectre: Canadian Copyright and the Mandatory Tariff – Part I' (2015) 27 *Intellectual Property Journal* 151; A. Katz, 'Spectre: Canadian Copyright and the Mandatory Tariff – Part II' (2015) 28 *Intellectual Property Journal* 39. York instead argued that an *interim* tariff was not mandatory as it was not an 'approved tariff', or that this tariff was not binding as it was not published in the *Canada Gazette*: *Access Copyright v. York*, n. 8 above at para. 189.

[183] Cf. *Cambridge University Press v. Patton*, 769 F 3d 1232, 1259 (11th circuit, 2014) (the District Court was correct to assess the fair use status of each alleged act of infringement, as to focus instead on copying practices generally would leave 'no principled method' to analysing fair use).

[184] Defined to mean the greater of: (1) 10 per cent or less of a work; or (2) no more than one chapter from a book, a single article from a periodical, an entire entry from an encyclopaedia or similar reference work, or an entire artistic work, poem or musical score from a work containing other artistic works, poems or musical scores: ibid., Guidelines summarised at para. 3 and reproduced in full at Schedule A.

[185] Ibid. at para. 173.

The Canadian Post-Script 303

under the interim tariff. On 4 July 2011, York notified Access that it had decided to opt out of the tariff effective 31 August 2011.[186] From that point, and similar to other universities that had adopted this course, York relied on other strategies to manage copyright, including licensing. Significantly, a number of evidentiary difficulties arose in the Federal Court in relation to the level of copying at York and the coverage of licences, and the evidence of Access's witnesses tended to be preferred.[187]

Although Phelan J cited dicta from cases such as *CCH* and *Alberta v. Access Copyright*, he saw the facts as very different from those cases. For instance, he stated that '[t]here is an objectivity in *CCH* which is absent in York's case',[188] and drew contrasts between the practices of York and the library in *CCH*, including in the number of copies made,[189] the amount taken from copied works,[190] and the level of supervision and monitoring of copying, especially for resources uploaded to virtual learning environments.[191] In relation to *Alberta v. Access Copyright*, he said that there was 'no parallel' to the 'limited copying of excerpts' in that case, the York Guidelines permitting 'significant copying' and forming part of a 'mass and massive enterprise' for the distribution of material to students:[192] it 'is one thing for a teacher to have the school librarian run off some copies of a book or article in order to supplement school texts' but 'quite another for York to produce coursepacks and materials for distribution through [learning management systems] which stand in place of course textbooks, through copying on a massive scale'.[193]

Importantly, Phelan J not only suggested that York's practices lacked proper intellectualisation and oversight but questioned the motivations behind those practices. For example, he emphasised on a number of occasions what he saw as the self-interest behind York's actions, as illustrated by his comment that it was 'evident that York created the Guidelines and operated under them primarily to obtain for free that which they had previously paid for'.[194] Similarly, Phelan J stated that there were alternatives to making fair dealing copies (e.g., production of custom books, or purchasing more articles or books from publishers) but that there was 'just no reasonable free alternative to copying'.[195] This conception of York's goal as being oriented towards its financial bottom line not only weakened arguments in relation to the first fairness factor (the purpose of the dealing) but seemed to set the tone for Phelan J's

---

[186] Ibid. at paras. 168–172. [187] Ibid. at paras. 83–143. [188] Ibid. at para. 260.
[189] Ibid. at paras. 276–289 (character of the dealing), 339–355 (effect of the dealing).
[190] Ibid. at paras. 290–318. [191] Ibid. at paras. 58–62, 266, 314.
[192] Ibid. at para. 344. [193] Ibid. at para. 324. [194] Ibid. at para. 272.
[195] Ibid. at para. 330. Emphasis in original.

reception of all of York's arguments.[196] York's position was not helped by its response to a raid on a copy shop in January 2012, which revealed that 10–15 members of faculty had used this (unauthorised) shop to produce course packs.[197] York's lack of disciplinary or other 'effective remedial'[198] action was said to be 'consistent with its wilfully blind approach to ensuring compliance with copyright obligations, whether under the Interim Tariff or under the Fair Dealing Guidelines'.[199]

As noted above, the reasoning and outcome of *Access Copyright* v. *York* raised the question of whether universities would rethink their approach to fair dealing. Amongst those who participated in interviews after delivery of the judgment, it was reported that universities were not making any significant changes to their practices.[200] Thus, one interviewee said that we need to 'dust off the copyright apparatus and re-ignite outreach and education',[201] whilst another stated that after some initial panic about how 'far-reaching' the decision was, people have 'sobered up and are a little calmer now'.[202] In that interviewee's institution it was not quite business as normal, as frontline staff were more cautious, but the response was pragmatic and geared towards lessons that might be learned from the decision, for instance regarding the use of quantitative benchmarks such as ten per cent rules,[203] and the need for better internal monitoring.[204] Interviewees therefore seemed to view *York* as a reminder

---

[196] Ibid. at para. 275 (observing that the mixed goals of York meant the first factor was 'not a strong factor in the fairness analysis').
[197] Ibid. at paras. 153–161.   [198] Ibid. at para. 244.   [199] Ibid. at para. 245.
[200] 146L, 161L, 163L, 164X. See also Di Valentino, n. 50 above, noting that the number of universities that had opted out of licences with Access Copyright increased between 2016 and 2019.
[201] 161L.   [202] 146L.
[203] This referred to Phelan J's criticism of the lack of a clear rationale for the copying thresholds used in York's Fair Dealing Guidelines: *Access Copyright* v. *York*, n. 8 above, paras. 305–309.
[204] Phelan J seemed to observe at York a set and forget attitude to copyright management: that '[s]afeguards were virtually non-existent in the York system' to ensure that copying took place within the Guidelines: ibid. para. 266. The degree to which this captures accurately the practices at York is open to question. York pointed to measures it had taken in relation to educating staff, requiring them to agree to comply with copyright policies etc., but these were discounted by Phelan J as being ineffective and not involving any active monitoring or enforcement process: paras. 58–62. This aspect of the case highlights the challenges in scaling up fair dealing arguments in the university environment: whilst it may be relatively easy to implement compliance and monitoring strategies for a self-contained library photocopying service, difficulties can arise when a policy is to be applied by a large group of disparate staff. The degree to which such monitoring is required has been challenged: see M. Geist, 'Ignoring the Supreme Court: Federal Court Judge Hands Access Copyright Fair Dealing Victory', *Michael Geist* (13 July 2017), www.michaelgeist.ca/2017/07/ignoring-supreme-court-trial-judge-hands-access-copyright-fair-dealing-victory/, suggesting that the Supreme Court

not to be complacent with fair dealing practices but did not want to preempt the ultimate outcome of the litigation, which they also described as out of step with Supreme Court precedent and unlikely to survive an appeal intact.

There are reasons to agree with the view that Phelan J did not apply correctly dicta from *CCH, Alberta v. Access Copyright* and other Supreme Court cases. To illustrate, whilst *Alberta* would suggest that the first factor (the purpose of the dealing) favoured fair dealing, as it was held in that case that the teachers had no motivation other than facilitating the research and private study of students,[205] Phelan J held that the 'history of the dispute is a relevant consideration'[206] and characterised York's motivation in relying on its Fair Dealing Guidelines as reducing its financial bottom line.[207] In addition to overlooking the significant money still spent by York on licensing, this statement rests on the assumption that not paying is wrong, thus pre-empting the conclusion on fair dealing. A further error can be seen in the analysis of the amount of the dealing: despite stating that this relates to the quantitative and qualitative importance of the part taken to the source work,[208] Phelan J went on to apply this factor by reference to the volume of copying by York and, indeed, all post-secondary institutions if they implemented the same policy.[209] This is contrary to statements in *Alberta*, where a similar mistake had been made by the Copyright Board.[210] Finally, there were difficulties in how Phelan J considered market harm and licensing. In the analysis of alternatives to the dealing, it was said that the strength of this factor was diminished as 'York has not actively engaged in the consideration or use of alternatives which exist or are in development',[211] but all the suggested alternatives involved purchasing more books, articles or chapters. There was no explanation of how students would access this content, including whether they would consult physical copies or whether electronic access would be purchased. If the latter, this would sit uncomfortably with the statement from *CCH*, cited by Phelan J, that the availability of a *licence* is not a relevant alternative.[212] Later, in

---

in *CCH* 'never injected a control or monitoring requirement in order to qualify for fair dealing'. Although true, in accepting that a defendant could rely on its practices and policies to establish fair dealing (*CCH*, n. 1 above, para. 63), it would seem logical that a significant discrepancy between the written policy and actual practices would be relevant.

[205] *Alberta v. Access Copyright*, n. 15 above, para. 26.
[206] *Access Copyright v. York*, n. 8 above, para. 271.   [207] Ibid., para. 272.
[208] Ibid., paras. 277, 290.   [209] Ibid., paras. 296–304.
[210] *Alberta v. Access Copyright*, n. 15 above, paras. 29–30.
[211] *Access Copyright v. York*, n. 8 above, para. 329.
[212] Ibid., para. 320, citing *CCH*, n. 1 above, para. 70.

reflecting on the effect of the dealing, Phelan J considered loss of licensing income as a relevant matter.[213]

With an appeal ongoing it is too soon to judge whether this litigation will produce a further shift in the practices of academic libraries. Even if Access is successful again in relation to fair dealing, it may be that universities will not make any significant changes to their practices, for instance because they see the case as turning on its own facts. But the *Access Copyright* v. *York* litigation is not the only challenge to educational copying in Canada. In May 2019, and as part of a review of copyright law being undertaken by the Canadian government, the House of Commons Standing Committee on Canadian Heritage suggested that the Copyright Act be amended 'to clarify that fair dealing should not apply to educational institutions when the work is commercially available'.[214] This recommendation was based primarily on concerns about a decrease in the royalties flowing to authors and publishers.[215] If implemented, it could effect a considerable narrowing of the 'education' limb of fair dealing, and would raise doctrinal questions about the operation of fair dealing in Canada. With pushback against this approach having already occured,[216] the Canadian situation remains a work in progress.

V   Conclusion

In Chapters 6 and 7, this book described empirical data that cast doubt on the capacity of fair use to perform meaningful work at cultural institutions outside the United States, and for fair dealing to function more significantly in institutional copyright management practices. This generated the question of what legal and non-legal steps might be taken to support the utilisation of standard-like exceptions, and indeed whether any deficiencies in the reach of copyright exceptions might be best rectified through drafting new and better rules rather than adding new fair dealing purposes or a fair use-style exception. However, one of the benefits of a long-term study of cultural institution practices has been

---

[213] Ibid., para. 351.
[214] House of Commons Standing Committee on Canadian Heritage, *Shifting Paradigms: Report of the Standing Committee on Canadian Heritage*, 42nd Parliament, 1st Session (May 2019), recommendation 18. Note too recommendation 19: that 'the Government of Canada promote a return to licensing through collective societies.
[215] Ibid., pp. 38–40; similar p. 48 (visual artists).
[216] House of Commons Standing Committee on Industry, Science and Technology, *Statutory Review of the Copyright Act: Report of the Standing Committee on Industry, Science and Technology*, 42nd Parliament, 1st Session (June 2019), especially pp. 55–69 (including a recommendation that fair dealing be reformed so that the purposes are illustrative rather than exhaustive).

to observe how practices change over time. This has helped qualify and add further nuance to the conclusions from the initial fieldwork in Australia, Canada and the United States.

First, this chapter has shown how certain changes to the law in books have led to changes to the law in action, in particular as illustrated by the expansion of fair dealing in the CDPA, but also as seen by the influence of the Pentalogy and the Copyright Modernization Act on the copyright management strategies of academic libraries in Canada. This went some way to qualify the narrative of Chapters 6 and 7 in relation to the lack of traction that statutory reform and case law has had in the sector.

Second, this chapter has shown how new interpretations and norms can be generated by changes to the knowledge, risk preferences and decision-making practices of users. For instance, whilst many academic librarians in Canada had for years been keen for their institutions to make greater use of *CCH*-inspired fair dealing arguments, it seems that a turning point was a change in the economics of licensing, which encouraged greater resourcing of copyright offices and a change in the utilisation of different compliance strategies, including fair dealing. In Australia and the United Kingdom, on the other hand, numerous interviewees reported that their institutions were becoming more tolerant of risk, with this change in attitude reflected in a number of ways, including in the increased use of pure risk management in decision-making.

Chapter 9 now brings together the material in the foregoing chapters, asking what that material means for the drafting of copyright exceptions and the fair use panacea.

9 Drafting Copyright Exceptions

I Introduction

In the previous five chapters, it has been observed that there are significant differences in the ways that cultural institutions in Australia, Canada, the United Kingdom and the United States utilise copyright exceptions. The aim of this final chapter is to analyse why these differences have arisen and what this means for the drafting of copyright exceptions, in particular the respective merits of open- and closed-ended drafting. As discussed in detail by Robert Burrell and Allison Coleman, concerns about the operation of specific exceptions have led to repeated calls for legislatures to enact fair use, which is often seen as offering a 'panacea' to the ills commonly associated with closed-ended drafting.[1] There is undoubtedly truth in the proposition that certain characteristics tend to be associated with certain forms of drafting, for instance that general exceptions have the advantage of flexibility but can lack predictability, whilst specific exceptions have greater certainty but can be rigid and non-responsive. However, as noted by Burrell and Coleman, this understanding of exceptions can reflect an oversimplified view of the law.

Burrell and Coleman offered three important contributions to what one might term orthodox thinking about exceptions. First, they questioned whether certainty is an inevitable feature of specific exceptions, and suggested that because this is often not the case, 'to a large extent the strongest argument for the current approach rests on an illusory

---

[1] R. Burrell and A. Coleman, *Copyright Exceptions: The Digital Impact* (Cambridge: Cambridge University Press, 2005), ch. 9; see also R. Burrell, 'Reining in Copyright Law: Is Fair Use the Answer?' [2001] *Intellectual Property Quarterly* 361. For a summary of recent calls for fair use (including in Australia), see M. Handler and E. Hudson, 'Fair Use as an Advance on Fair Dealing? Depolarising the Debate' in H. Sun, S. Balganesh and W. Ng-Loy (eds), *Comparative Aspects of Limitations and Exceptions in Copyright Law* (New York: Cambridge University Press, forthcoming).

Introduction

foundation'.[2] But would fair use produce a noticeably different result? On this question, Burrell and Coleman's second contribution was to question whether such a doctrine would effect any meaningful change in the United Kingdom given prevailing judicial attitudes. Here, Burrell and Coleman traced the development of 'fair use' defences in the common law from the eighteenth century onwards, and judicial attitudes towards fair dealing under the 1911 Act.[3] They concluded that judges tended to construe fair dealing narrowly, an approach that was not demanded by the statutory text; and that these interpretative practices paved the way for fair dealing to be described in increasingly prescriptive terms in later copyright statutes.[4] With this reluctance to protect user interests being said to come in large part from judges themselves, Burrell and Coleman concluded that this did not bode well for fair use being applied in the United Kingdom in anything other than a restrictive manner. Finally, Burrell and Coleman argued that if US fair use were to be used as a model for reform, any analysis would need to look beyond the words of section 107 and pay due regard to the broader environment in which the US doctrine operates, including local case law, user guidelines and First Amendment jurisprudence.[5] Their aim was not to undertake this analysis themselves, but to point out that anyone advocating for fair use would need to ask whether an

---

[2] Ibid., p. 252. By 'current approach', Burrell and Coleman were referring to the drafting preferred in the United Kingdom and other jurisdictions whose copyright statutes contain a large number of closed-ended exceptions.

[3] To summarise, Burrell and Coleman rejected a romantic vision of the early case law in which judges were champions of the rights of users, observing that if anything many of the cases applying fair use principles served to expand the rights of copyright owners, because they read those rights more broadly than that suggested by the plain words of the relevant legislation: ibid., pp. 253–256; see also L. Patterson, '*Folsom v Marsh* and Its Legacy' (1998) 5 *Journal of Intellectual Property Law* 431; M. de Zwart, 'A Historical Analysis of the Birth of Fair Dealing and Fair Use: Lessons for the Digital Age' [2007] 1 *Intellectual Property Quarterly* 60. To the extent that fair dealing was intended to codify understandings developed in the pre-twentieth century jurisprudence, it was further read down in the post-1911 Act case law: pp. 256–263 discussing *University of London Press* v. *University Tutorial Press* [1916] 2 Ch 601, *British Oxygen* v. *Liquid Air* [1925] 1 Ch 383 and *Hawkes and Sons* v. *Paramount Film Service* [1934] 1 Ch 593.

[4] E.g., compare the Copyright Act 1911, s. 2(1)(i) (copyright is not infringed by any 'fair dealing with any work for the purposes of private study, research, criticism, review, or newspaper summary') with the fair dealing provisions enacted in the Copyright Act 1956, ss. 6(1)–(3), 9(1)–(2) (fair dealing spread across five subsections; no equivalent provisions for sound recordings, films, broadcasts and published editions; the criticism or review exception qualified by the need for a sufficient acknowledgement, and that the criticism or review is 'of that or of another work'; and so forth).

[5] Burrell and Coleman, n. 1 above, pp. 267–274.

excised doctrine would retain the qualities that it enjoys in the United States when transplanted to a new jurisdiction.[6]

This book has sought to respond to the thesis presented by Burrell and Coleman. It agrees with the first contention regarding oversimplified thinking, and through its use of standards and rules literature has sought to deploy a more nuanced assessment of the drafting options for copyright exceptions.[7] This involved acceptance of the general proposition underlying their second claim, i.e., the degree to which interpretative practices bear upon the operation of exceptions. This book has sought to present an empirically informed analysis by examining the reported experiences of one subset of copyright users (cultural institutions), across four jurisdictions and over time, thereby observing the law in action. This chapter draws this analysis together, and in doing so responds to Burrell and Coleman's third challenge: what does this research mean for the fair use panacea? It is hoped that this analysis will be of interest not only to copyright scholarship but to broader debates about legal drafting, behavioural law and economics, and social norms.

This chapter is divided into two parts. Section II discusses the factors that were observed to be relevant to copyright decision-making at participating cultural institutions, only some of which pertained directly to the statutory text. Section III assesses fair use and other reform options, with a particular focus on the ramifications of the changeability of user norms. Standards and rules scholarship makes a number of suggestions regarding how legislators should choose between standards and rules, some of which relate to user characteristics (knowledge, risk aversion, and so forth). But this book also demonstrates how those characteristics can undergo significant change. This raises the question of how much weight should be given to current practices, and whether legislative drafting might be one driver of new approaches, for instance through signalling effects. This chapter argues that in some jurisdictions, the ultimate argument in favour of fair use may be to 'future proof' the statute, i.e., that in the long-term, fair use is the best exception to deal with changes to technology and user practices. That said, this chapter does not go so far as to suggest that this argument has universal applicability, and therefore discusses other reform options.

---

[6] For discussion of similar concerns, see, e.g., B. Fitzgerald, 'Underlying Rationales of Fair Use: Simplifying the Copyright Act' (1998) 2 *Southern Cross University Law Review* 153; D. Hunter, 'American Lessons: Implementing Fair Use in Australia' (2014) 24 *Australian Intellectual Property Journal* 192.

[7] See Chapter 2 for a description of the standards and rules literature, and the key lessons to come out of that scholarship.

II   Decision-Making Factors

A   *Statutory Language and Interpretations*

An obvious starting point for any analysis of the operation of exceptions is their language, statutory context and interpretations in the case law and commentary. This sort of doctrinal analysis – the law in books – is the bread-and-butter of those with legal training, and characterises much academic scholarship in relation to the adequacy of exceptions and options for reform. It is based on the idea that language matters: that even for standards, the statutory text channels and sets limits on decision-making.

In addition to analysing exceptions themselves, it may also be necessary to consider the effect of other provisions. For instance, it has been argued in this book that the Canadian copyright reforms of the 1980s emphasised licensing and collective administration, setting the tone for understandings of copyright for years to come.[8] In the United States, a number of interviewees discussed the significance of limitations on the availability and quantum of statutory damages, including for libraries and archives relying reasonably on fair use.[9] These provisions were said to reinforce good faith behaviour; for instance, one interviewee noted that the remedies limitation for fair use served as a 'clear reminder of what fair use is: a reasoned application of the four fair use factors'.[10]

In emphasising the significance of the statutory language, it is not difficult to find examples where judges have located meanings that might be said to be problematic or contrary to the text being considered.[11] The question for this book is not whether judicial interpretations sometimes stray from or disregard the statutory language (which is clearly true), but whether the different audiences of a legal command – judges, lawyers,

---

[8] See especially Chapter 4, Section II.B. Aspects of the Canadian history are also discussed in this chapter: see Section II.D.
[9] Eg, 3X, 6X, 7G, 23X, 29L, 39L, 47X. See US Copyright Act ss. 412 (registration requirement), 504(c)(2) (reduction of award of statutory damages for innocent defendants; and statutory damages to be remitted where the infringer 'believed and had reasonable grounds for believing that his or her use of the copyrighted work was a fair use under section 107', and the infringer was, *inter alia*, a nonprofit library or archives or its employee or agent).
[10] 39L. Interviewee 47X argued that good faith is important in fair use litigation – that judges will respond favourably to people who act reasonably.
[11] Although not a copyright case, for a particularly strong example, see *Davidoff & Cie SA v. Gofkid Ltd* (C-292/00) [2003] 1 WLR 1714 (Sixth Chamber) (interpreting the words 'in relation to goods or services which are not similar to those for which the trade mark is registered' to include circumstances where the defendant's sign is registered for or used in relation to identical or similar goods or services).

users, etc. – engage with the law in a similar way. In this research there were instances where the analytical techniques of cultural institution staff showed significant parallels to those of lawyers. For instance, numerous US interviewees cited the text of section 107 and indications in the case law when explaining their copyright management approaches for online uses.[12] Similarly, many Australian interviewees attempted a doctrinal analysis of section 200AB, albeit one that was frustrated by the view that the three-step test language had a meaning that was international, contested and difficult to pin down.[13] On the other hand, the fieldwork revealed instances where institution staff disregarded the detail of copyright law or did not even consider copyright to be relevant to certain practices. This produced a gap between the academic question of, say, the existence and scope of privileges in relation to collection management, and the real-world perspective that this question was not even on the radar. Finally, there were instances where the gap between lawyers and staff manifested in different ways, for instance in the evidence that academics and judges took seriously the statements of the Canadian Supreme Court in *CCH Canadian Ltd* v. *Law Society of Upper Canada*,[14] but that the response of Canadian cultural institutions was for many years extremely muted.

It is therefore necessary to consider other factors that influence the decision-making of cultural institutions. The following are discussed in turn: institutional and ethical norms; copyright management techniques; and the historical and philosophical context in which copyright operates.

B   Institutional and Ethical Norms

Whilst there were some areas in which cultural institution practices seemed to be guided heavily by doctrinal analysis, in others the link between the law in books and the law in action was more tenuous. In many instances, these practices appeared to be influenced heavily by views on the attributes and duties of a 'good' cultural institution. Placing this in the context of Robert Ellickson's five 'controllers' that may be a source of 'rules of behavior', these examples seemed to involve 'personal ethics' (being ideas of desirable conduct that emanate from the staff themselves) and 'organization rules' (being ideas that derive from the institution), perhaps with the backing of social norms.[15]

---

[12] See Chapter 5, Section III.C.3.   [13] See Chapter 6, Section III.
[14] [2004] 1 SCR 339 ('*CCH*').
[15] R. Ellickson, *Order Without Law: How Neighbors Settle Disputes* (Cambridge, MA: Harvard University Press, 1991), p. 127.

Decision-Making Factors 313

The most extreme example – at least in terms of the *process* of decision-making – was where institutions had internalised ethical considerations and norms of best practice that left no room for copyright considerations. This was particularly apparent for collection management.[16] In the United States, numerous interviewees treated such activities as 'before' fair use and not subject to a copyright analysis. Similarly, there were repeated instances in Australia and Canada of interviewees who were confident that administrative activities raised no copyright issues but who could not point to any principle or provision from the law that supported this assertion. In each of these three countries, a doctrinal analysis suggested that much collection management would be caught by exceptions in the copyright statute (under fair use or sector-specific exceptions), meaning that norms and law coincided to some degree. But there was no evidence that collection management changed when sector-specific exceptions were introduced; and for the United Kingdom, where there existed exactly the same ideas about collection management, one could not be so confident that the law aligned with standard institutional practices, given the lack of an exception directed explicitly to administration.[17] It therefore appeared that interviewees saw collection management as involving numerous non-negotiable duties in the proper care of the collection.[18]

It was also observed that institutional norms could override limitations and ambiguities in closed-ended exceptions. For instance, Australian and US interviewees did not report problems with the three-copy limit in preservation and replacement copying exceptions, and indeed there were repeated suggestions that this restriction was nonsensical in a digital environment and was not treated as a literal command.[19] Given the familiarity of interviewees with these provisions, non-compliance with the words of the statute could not be put down to lack of knowledge. Instead, this example reflected the phenomenon of rule-like provisions being read in standard-like ways, i.e., that interviewees interpreted the

---

[16] See Chapter 4, Section III.B.2 and Chapter 5, Section III.B.1.
[17] As discussed in Chapter 4, if such activity was challenged, the two strongest arguments would be based on: (1) a broad definition of the preservation copying exception in CDPA s. 42 as encompassing acts that care for the collection; or (2) fair dealing for the purpose of quotation in CDPA s. 30(1ZA).
[18] Indeed, as discussed by 9M, accreditation of institutions is often linked to maintaining high standards in management of the collection: e.g., American Alliance of Museums, 'Accreditation', www.aam-us.org/programs/accreditation-excellence-programs/accreditation/; see also International Council of Museums, *ICOM Code of Ethics for Museums* (Paris: ICOM, 2017), pp. 14–15 (regarding care of collections, including in relation to documenting and conservation of the collection).
[19] See Chapter 4, Section III.B.1.

three-copy limit as indicating that institutions should only make a reasonable number of copies. Thus, the words were not ignored but given a reading that was seen to better reflect the legislative intent and the logistical realities of preservation copying.

Whilst institutional norms sometimes operated to oust copyright considerations or re-imagine the words of an exception, such disregard of the statute was less likely in cases where new practices or interpretations were emerging, especially for public-facing activity. Nevertheless, the influence of ethical considerations could still be seen. For instance, the 2014 reforms in the United Kingdom included the insertion of a new exception that allows cultural institutions to make works available to the public, for research or private study purposes, 'by means of a dedicated terminal on its premises'.[20] Interviews with UK staff revealed that some were engaging closely with this provision, which they saw as going beyond an intranet-connected computer in the corner to include electronic devices that were carried around by patrons (such as a tablet) and large, interactive screens installed in exhibition spaces.[21] Such an interpretation was not to overlook the words of the statute but to give it an interpretation that accorded with the way digital technologies are being used to help patrons understand the collection.

Similarly, the US fieldwork saw the emergence of new practices for the online presentation of collection content, with those practices also involving close engagement with copyright law and the parameters of fair use.[22] Again, ethical and normative ideas about institution missions seemed to inform interpretations of fair use. For instance, one interviewee said:

It's like a moral code, an act of conscience, to say fair use. The fact that everyone … has this view 'of course', the fact we're not-for-profit, have educational missions, are not circumventing the rights of artists to have their works put on a cup – lots of these come into our understanding of fair use. The fair use guidelines as they stand … really speak to what we've come to understand. Which one is the chicken and which one is the egg? It makes me think that fair use is used as an extension of cultural institutions' understanding of their missions.[23]

There was, however, only so far institutional norms could go. For instance, ethical views about institution missions and the interests of creators did little to inform understandings of section 200AB in Australia, despite such views sitting behind the greater utilisation of

---

[20] CDPA s. 40B.   [21] See Chapter 4, Section III.B.4.
[22] See Chapter 5, Section III.C.3.   [23] 36M.

risk management.[24] It appears that in that case, interviewees saw section 200AB as having a meaning that was in many ways unknowable, but which seemed to be narrow and covering ad hoc rather than larger-scale acts.

In sum, there was variation in the degree to which cultural institutions engaged with the details of copyright law. It seemed that the form of wording adopted by the copyright statute bore least upon collection management activities due to well-established norms of practice. That said, even when institutions were engaging in a close doctrinal analysis of the statutory text, ethical understandings were still relevant, to varying degrees, to inform decision-making. The fieldwork did not, however, suggest that institutions dismissed copyright simply because they did not like or agree with the law's outcomes. As one interviewee said, 'we are a national institution and cannot be seen to take accepted law as something which we can pick and choose as to whether we stick to it'.[25] Despite sometimes expressing frustration with copyright, interviewees accepted the legitimacy of the law, and spoke repeatedly about the importance, both legal and ethical, in supporting the interests of creators and copyright owners.[26] Whilst the research encountered interpretations that were forward-leaning, there was no evidence of a fair use free-for-all, or that interviewees were developing understandings of exceptions that were outside any reasonable interpretation of copyright law.

C   Copyright Management Techniques

The third suite of factors that influenced the law in action related to how copyright was managed by institutions. There seemed to be a broad correlation between the level of resources directed to copyright management and the degree to which institutions relied on general exceptions. The employment of copyright specialists; measures to support copyright awareness amongst staff; the development of policies and procedures in relation to copyright workflows; some level of centralisation, for instance through a copyright office and/or copyright managers; and senior staff who dedicated sufficient bandwidth to copyright all contributed to a more proactive approach to copyright. This observation was borne out amongst US institutions that adopted forward-leaning interpretations of fair use;[27] UK institutions that made use of new fair dealing arguments

---

[24] See Chapter 3, Section IV, Chapter 6, Section III and Chapter 8, Section III.
[25] 304M.   [26] E.g., 304M, 305X, 308M, 314G, 317G, 322G, 326L.
[27] See Chapter 5, Section III.A.

following the 2014 reforms;[28] and Canadian academic libraries that had withdrawn from Access Copyright licences.[29] These institutions seemed to be more comfortable with the sort of reasoning demanded by a standard, and the uncertainty that inevitably surrounds reliance on an exception whose application in any given case is only known for sure once determined by a judge. This was consistent with predictions from the standards and rules literature considered in Chapter 2, for example in relation to the influence of legal knowledge and risk tolerance on the decision-making of users. It suggests that if we are of the view that institutions ought to make greater use of free exceptions, it may be that *no further legal reform is required* but that institutions need to be given the resources to allow proper engagement with copyright law, including locating pockets of under-exploited flexibility. This was particularly so in the UK given the expansion of fair dealing in 2014, which according to a doctrinal analysis could result in much common ground with US fair use.[30]

Two caveats are important. First, amongst institutions with higher levels of copyright knowledge and resourcing, the sophistication of their management applied not just to exceptions but to all areas: licensing, risk analysis, etc.[31] Second, not all institutions with high levels of copyright resourcing made greater use of exceptions. For instance, interviewees managing audiovisual collections noted the complexity of rights in relation to such materials and the need to maintain close relationships with content producers and distributors, especially for film, television and other commercial content. As such, they made use of comprehensive licences when acquiring and using content, and those licences often covered ground that might be occupied by exceptions.[32] This is not to suggest that exceptions were irrelevant but that there were strong licensing norms from which institutions, for reasons of pragmatism and social norms, were disinclined to deviate.

---

[28] See Chapter 8, Section II.B. Some interviewees expressed concern that exceptions were underutilised due to resourcing: e.g., 304M, 308M.
[29] See Chapter 8, Section II.A.
[30] See Chapter 8, Section II.B. As noted there, much will turn on CJEU case law (at least while the United Kingdom is subject to EU copyright law).
[31] Especially 305X ('one of the benefits of a copyright officer is better systems, but there's also a better and more informed perspective on risk').
[32] Especially 255A, 308M.

D Historical and Philosophical Context

The final set of factors to affect institutional decision-making were historical and philosophical influences on understandings of copyright. One must be cautious when making these sorts of assessments. As noted by Paul Goldstein and Bernt Hugenholtz, writing in relation to common law and civil law approaches to copyright, whilst 'in principle' there may be deep and fundamental differences in the premises underlying each system (utilitarianism versus natural rights), 'on almost every point of consequence, the traditions ... are far more alike than they are unlike.'[33] However, in this research, there emerged some strong national divisions in attitudes to exceptions, particularly in North America. There, the approach of numerous US interviewees to fair use could be said to align with the utilitarian underpinnings of copyright law in that country.[34] In Canada, on the other hand, it appeared that one reason for the muted reaction to *CCH* was that institution staff – even if they personally agreed with the outcome and reasoning – perceived the decision as out of step with prevailing views about copyright, leading them to question its legitimacy and longevity.[35]

It is worth pausing to consider the Canadian history in further detail, given its influence on reported practices. Recall that in *CCH*, legal proceedings were instituted against the Law Society in 1993. At this point, it was accepted by many copyright stakeholders that exceptions should be given a narrow interpretation. This seems to have been one result of law reform activities of the 1970s and 1980s. The view that emerged during that period was that licensing should be the main approach for complying with copyright obligations, with exceptions playing a limited and subsidiary role. As discussed in Chapter 4, reform of the Copyright Act to facilitate the establishment of collective management organisations (via Bill C-60 of 1987) pre-dated reforms that introduced Canada's first exceptions for libraries, archives and museums

---

[33] P. Goldstein and B. Hugenholtz, *International Copyright: Principles, Law, and Practice*, 3rd edition (Oxford: Oxford University Press, 2013), p. 14.

[34] For instance, the Intellectual Property Clause of the US Constitution gives Congress the power '[t]o promote the Progress of Science and useful Arts, by securing for limited Times to Authors and Inventors the exclusive Right to their respective Writings and Discoveries': Art. I, s. 8, cl. 8. In *Campbell v. Acuff-Rose Music, Inc.*, 510 US 569, 577 (1994), the consequentialist underpinnings of US copyright law can be seen in the Supreme Court quoting from *Stewart v. Abend*, 495 US 207, 236 (1990) that the fair use doctrine 'permits [and requires] courts to avoid rigid application of the copyright statute when, on occasion, it would stifle the very creativity which that law is designed to foster'.

[35] See Chapter 7.

(via Bill C-32 of 1996).[36] This meant that there was a period during which collective management was being expanded, but cultural institutions did not know the form that the coming sector-specific exceptions would take.

This downplaying of the role of exceptions also reflected a particular property-based conception of author's rights preferred by some of the leading law reform reports. For instance, the Keyes and Brunet Report of 1977 stated repeatedly that the rights of copyright owners should be maintained wherever possible and that the legislature should support mechanisms to facilitate voluntary licensing.[37] Keyes and Brunet made only modest recommendations for sector-specific exceptions for cultural institutions,[38] stating that it 'is clear that libraries engaged in supplying copies of copyright material without consent of the owners are in effect using someone else's property without paying for that property'.[39] Similarly, the Federal Cultural Policy Review Committee stated that authors should be able to control and receive remuneration for public uses of their works,[40] and that any limitations on such rights 'should be applied with caution and sensitivity'.[41] Although it did not make any detailed recommendations, the Committee observed that this attitude 'would tend to remove many of the exemptions from infringement now found in the Copyright Act'.[42] Finally, in the 1985 report *A Charter of Rights for Creators*, the House of Commons' Sub-Committee on the Revision of Copyright recommended that fair dealing be retained with some modification, including that only *private* research qualify and that fair dealing be unavailable for unpublished

---

[36] For an outline of this process, see M. Hébert, *Background Paper: Copyright Reform* (Library of Parliament, March 1996), pp. 18–19.

[37] A. Keyes and C. Brunet, *Copyright in Canada: Proposals for a Revision of the Law* (Consumer and Corporate Affairs Canada, April 1977). One example was their recommendation that there be no specific exception for photocopying, but that any new legislation 'encourage the formation of collectives ... under the supervision of a government tribunal': p. 165. The authors also observed that 'the primary purpose of the copyright law is to enumerate and protect the rights of creators': p. 164.

[38] Ibid., pp. 162–165 (photocopying generally), 166 (libraries), 173–175 (archival activities).

[39] Ibid., p. 146.

[40] Federal Cultural Policy Review Committee, *Report of the Federal Cultural Policy Review Committee* (Information Services, Department of Communications, Government of Canada, 1982), p. 98.

[41] Ibid., p. 99.

[42] Ibid. The Committee may have had in mind certain specific exceptions, it being said that there is 'no reason why authors should be asked to provide special subsidies to agricultural fairs, juke-box operators and religious institutions'.

works.⁴³ The Sub-Committee resisted the suggestion, made in some reform contributions, that Canada introduce a fair use exception.⁴⁴ It said that 'fair use implies that rights in intellectual property are definitely second class rights, very different from rights in personal property' but that

'ownership is ownership is ownership.' The copyright owner owns the intellectual works in the same sense as a landowner owns land. Infringement of copyright is analogous to trespass and the owner in real estate does not have to prove damages before asserting his rights against a trespasser; that does not mean to say that there are no differences at all between ownership in works of the mind and ownership of physical objects, as we shall presently see. However, those differences that do exist are adequately reflected in the fair dealing concept.⁴⁵

A proprietary explanation of copyright does not, in fact, demand this sort of reasoning.⁴⁶ But that is beside the point, as whatever the rights or wrongs of this statement, property rhetoric was being used to support a copyright system with strong rights and narrow exceptions.

Similar ideas also informed a number of judicial pronouncements on copyright made during this era. Following the passage of Canada's first comprehensive copyright statute, the Copyright Act 1921, there was a lengthy period when there was little analysis of fair dealing in the case law. Thus, for many decades, the only relevant Canadian case was *Zamacoïs* v. *Douville and Marchand*,⁴⁷ a decision of a single judge of the Exchequer Court.⁴⁸ Fair dealing was mentioned in a number of cases in

---

⁴³ House of Commons Standing Committee on Communications and Culture, Sub-Committee on the Revision of Copyright, *A Charter of Rights for Creators: Report of the Sub-Committee on the Revision of Copyright* (October 1985), pp. 63–66.

⁴⁴ See B. Torno, *Fair Dealing: The Need for Conceptual Clarity on the Road to Copyright Revision* (Consumer and Corporate Affairs, 1981); J. Erola and F. Fox, *From Gutenberg to Telidon: A White Paper on Copyright* (Consumer and Corporate Affairs Canada and Department of Communications, Government of Canada, 1984).

⁴⁵ *A Charter of Rights for Creators*, n. 43 above, p. 9.

⁴⁶ For discussion of the question of whether intellectual property rights are proprietary and the consequences of such a characterisation, see, e.g., M. Carrier, 'Cabining Intellectual Property Through a Property Paradigm' (2004) 54 *Duke Law Journal* 1; H. Dagan, 'Property and the Public Domain' (2006) 18 Supplement *Yale Journal of Law and the Humanities* 84; T. Aplin 'Confidential Information as Property?' (2013) 24 *King's Law Journal* 172; L. Bently, 'Trade Secrets: "Intellectual Property" but not "Property"?' in H. Howe and J. Griffiths (eds), *Concepts of Property in Intellectual Property Law* (Cambridge: Cambridge University Press, 2013); E. Hudson, '*Phillips v Mulcaire*: A Property Paradox' in S. Douglas, R. Hickey and E. Waring (eds), *Landmark Cases in Property Law* (Oxford: Hart, 2015).

⁴⁷ (1943) 2 CPR 270.

⁴⁸ That case made fairly fleeting reference to fair dealing, but was nevertheless used as authority for a number of propositions, including that 'quotation of a work in its entirety is not fair dealing': H. Fox, *The Canadian Law of Copyright* (The University of Toronto Press, 1944), p. 426. In that text, Fox also drew from the British case law in discussing

the 1980s, albeit without any sustained consideration.[49] Case law in the 1990s made more significant contributions, but mainly to emphasise the *limits* of exceptions.

The first case of significance was the Supreme Court decision in *Bishop v. Stevens*.[50] Fair dealing was not in issue in this case, which asked whether the making of a pre-broadcast recording of a performance infringed copyright, the television station having a licence to broadcast the performance but not make the recording. However, this case is interesting because the Court analysed certain copyright questions in ways that were very different to its later decision in *CCH*. First, the Court quoted with approval the proposition that the Copyright Act 'was passed with a single object, namely, the benefit of authors of all kinds, whether the works were literary, dramatic or musical'.[51] Second, the Court adopted a literal reading of the Act in which the reproduction and broadcast rights are wholly separate, and clearance of broadcast rights should not be taken to impliedly include the making of ephemeral copies. This was despite the practice of making such recordings being common and 'highly useful' for broadcasters;[52] this practice not being prejudicial to copyright owners; and the low risk that recordings would be the subject of unauthorised copying and distribution. It appears that the Court considered itself ill-equipped to assess the policy and economic ramifications of implying even a limited right to make ephemeral copies, this being a step that would raise 'policy issues ... beyond the proper purview of the courts' and which should be left for the legislature.[53] Finally, the Court observed that the presence of 'detailed and explicit' exceptions rendered the existence of any implied exemption for ephemeral copies 'all the more unlikely'.[54] Although the Court did not expand on this statement, it appears to rest on the assumption that the legislature

---

the ambit of fair dealing, and made a number of statements that might be said to have read down the exception. The second edition of Fox's book, published in 1967, largely followed the contents of the first edition: H. Fox, *The Canadian Law of Copyright and Industrial Designs*, 2nd edition (Carswell Company Limited, 1967), pp. 419–425. Fox did not cite the Ilsley Report which had been published in 1957 and which suggested that any new Canadian copyright statute include provisions adopting the form of words of the revised fair dealing exceptions in the UK Copyright Act 1956: Royal Commission on Patents, Copyright, Trade Marks and Industrial Designs, *Report on Copyright* (Queen's Printer, 1957).

[49] E.g., *The Queen* v. *James Lorimer and Co Ltd* [1984] 1 FC 1065; *Breen* v. *Hancock House Publishers Ltd* (1985) 6 CPR (3d) 433.
[50] (1990) 72 DLR (4th) 97. Certain propositions from *Bishop* v. *Stevens* were followed in *Canadian Broadcasting Corporation* v. *SODRAC 2003 Inc.* [2015] 3 SCR 615.
[51] Ibid., 105, citing *Performing Right Society, Ltd* v. *Hammond's Bradford Brewery Co, Ltd* [1934] Ch 121, 127 (per Maugham J).
[52] Ibid., 109.   [53] Ibid.   [54] Ibid., 107.

had intended to cover the field with the list of exceptions in section 27(2) of the Copyright Act.

On all three of these matters – the object of copyright, the role of the courts in setting copyright policy, and the impact of detailed exceptions on the reading of other provisions – the Supreme Court took the opposite approach in *CCH*. In a further twist, McLachlin J delivered the opinion of the Court in both cases. However, in the years between the two decisions, a number of fair dealing decisions were handed down whose analysis either expressly endorsed, or was implicitly aligned with, a narrow interpretation of fair dealing. For instance, in the *Michelin* case of 1996, the defendant union sought to rely on fair dealing in relation to its reproduction of the corporate logo of Michelin ('Bibendum', the Michelin Man) on campaign materials to encourage unionisation of the plaintiff's workforce.[55] Teitelbaum J held that fair dealing should be 'restrictively interpreted' and that criticism did not extend to parodic use.[56] Later in *Hager* v. *ECW Press Ltd*,[57] the plaintiff claimed that the biography *Shania Twain: On My Way* infringed copyright in a book chapter she wrote on the singer, the biography having included quotes attributed to Twain (and which came from interviews conducted by the plaintiff) and having otherwise paraphrased material from the chapter. The defendants sought to rely on fair dealing but failed as their purpose was neither research nor criticism. In coming to this conclusion, Reed J held that the absence of a requirement to acknowledge the source work indicated 'that the use contemplated by private study and research is not one in which the copied work is communicated to the public',[58] a statement that was arguably unnecessary to decide the case,[59] but which was consistent with the view that fair dealing occupied a limited space in copyright law. Finally, fair dealing failed in the trial decision in *CCH*, where Gibson J held that 'the fair dealing exception should be strictly construed'.[60]

Statements in leading copyright texts likewise supported the contention that fair dealing should be read narrowly and that the cases 'have not been generous to users'.[61] In the third edition of *Fox*, the chapter on

---

[55] *Cie Générale des Etablissements Michelin-Michelin & Cie* v. *CAW-Canada* (1996) 71 CPR (3d) 348 (Federal Court).
[56] Ibid., 379.   [57] [1999] 2 FC 287.   [58] Ibid., 315.
[59] It is likely that the same result could have been reached by, e.g., finding that the conduct was unfair or pressing the defendants to particularise the research which their book furthered or facilitated.
[60] *CCH Canadian Ltd* v. *Law Society of Upper Canada* [2000] 2 FC 451, 489.
[61] H. Knopf, 'Limits on the Nature and Scope of Copyright' in G. Henderson (ed), *Copyright and Confidential Information Law of Canada* (Toronto: Carswell, 1994), p. 259.

copyright exceptions drew from the case law the proposition that 'the provisions of an exception should be applied strictly against the party seeking to take advantage of them'.[62] Similarly, Lesley Ellen Harris concluded that given confusion about its scope, a 'common sense approach' to fair dealing 'might be that if a "very small" portion of a copyright work is being used and the use is clearly for the purposes of research, private study, criticism, review or news reporting, then it is probably acceptable to use that work'.[63] Whilst there was a steady increase in the quantity of text directed to fair dealing in successive editions of Normand Tamaro's *Annotated Copyright Act*, this analysis remained subject to the initial proposition that 'jurisprudence has established that these exceptions should be interpreted restrictively', for which *Bishop v. Stevens* was cited as authority.[64] In 1992, Tamaro's work contained a little over a page of fair dealing analysis, which for a text spanning more than 500 pages would seem to reflect the marginal status of the defence. By the 1997 edition this had grown to a little under five pages, although much of this came from the addition of a comparative treatment of overseas cases. With new Canadian case law, analysis of fair dealing in the 1999 edition expanded to almost 11 pages, most of which was taken up with the criticism and review limbs. Tamaro drew extensively from *Michelin* and quoted (apparently with approval) from statements in that case contrasting the structure of section 107 of the US Copyright Act with the Canadian system.[65] In comparison, analysis of the research-oriented defence in 1999 was relatively short and stated that it permitted consultation but not publication. Similar text on research and private study appeared in the 2002 edition, which did not cite the trial decision that had been handed down in *CCH*.

The Canadian history has been described in detail to illustrate the degree to which the Supreme Court's decision in *CCH* was neither an incremental change to the law nor a recalibration to reflect prevailing views. Rather, the Court sought to effect a major reconceptualisation of both the philosophical basis of copyright and the doctrinal content of fair

---

[62] J. McKeown, *Fox Canadian Law of Copyright and Industrial Designs*, 3rd edition (Toronto: Carswell, 2000), p. 547.
[63] L. Harris, *Canadian Copyright Law*, 3rd edition (Toronto: McGraw-Hill, 2001), p. 129.
[64] See N. Tamaro, *The Annotated Copyright Act 1992* (Toronto: Carswell, 1992), p. 271; N. Tamaro, *The 1997 Annotated Copyright Act* (Toronto: Carswell, 1996), p. 330; N. Tamaro, *The 1999 Annotated Copyright Act* (Toronto: Carswell, 1999), p. 379; N. Tamaro, *The 2002 Annotated Copyright Act* (Toronto: Carswell, 2002), p. 428.
[65] See also Knopf, above n. 61, pp. 258–259 (stating that in comparison with fair use, fair dealing is 'statutorily restrictive and not easily capable of a remedial, flexible, or evolutionary interpretation').

dealing. It is therefore not surprising that cultural institutions did not rush to embrace this new vision, and that a number of Canadian interviewees still placed significant emphasis on the idea that exceptions should occupy a narrow space. Even for those who agreed with the Supreme Court's perspective on fair dealing, it appeared that entrenched workflows and risk averse tendencies were such that it remained attractive to 'buy' certainty through licensing arrangements. With *CCH* representing such a departure from prevailing understandings, there was concern that it might reflect a high-water mark in exceptions analysis, to be undone by legislative intervention or a subsequent Supreme Court decision.

Seen in this context, the later developments in the university sector are all the more significant, illustrating that even in the face of sticky norms, attitudes and practices can change. This raises a question: is long-term change more likely to be produced where exceptions are reformed incrementally and largely within the existing drafting framework, or does the fieldwork suggest that legislators should bite the bullet and adopt more radical interventions such as fair use? This question will be considered in Section III, which makes some proposals regarding the drafting of copyright exceptions.

III   Drafting Copyright Exceptions

In Section II it was seen that a number of factors bear on the ways that exceptions operate, many of which may not be readily apparent from their language alone. In the cultural institution sector these factors include case law and other statutory provisions, views on the ethical duties and best practices of a 'good' institution, internal copyright arrangements (e.g., the resources devoted to copyright, and attitudes towards risk, reputation and relationship management) and historical and philosophical matters. The impact of changes to the law in books may depend on the degree to which those changes align with existing attitudes and practices. For instance, the *CCH* case study illustrates that if a court presses interpretations that are perceived as out of step with historical trends or the way things are done, then it may have limited impact *even if* users agree with its reasoning. This section asks what these lessons mean for the drafting of copyright exceptions, including the merits of fair use.

An initial lesson is the importance, when considering the drafting of new exceptions, to give full consideration not just to the policy goals of reform but the full legal and non-legal environment in which those reforms are intended to operate. The statutory text is obviously part of this. For instance, despite the legislative intention that section 200AB capture some of the benefits of fair use,[66] the Australian fieldwork suggested it has a bleak future, in large part due to drafting that institution staff and their advisors struggled to interpret.[67] This was not due to lack of knowledge, as interviewees were generally familiar with section 200AB; and nor could it be put down to risk aversion, as the fieldwork suggested that institutions had become increasingly comfortable with risk in the years following the introduction of the provision.[68] Rather, it seemed that staff felt unable to apply to section 200AB the decision-making processes used for other copyright analysis. For instance, whilst pure risk management might incorporate consideration of the interests of the copyright owner and whether the institution's proposed use would harm those interests, institution staff seemed to think that section 200AB countenanced a different balancing exercise. Despite being intended to operate as a flexible standard, the complexity of section 200AB (through its multiple limbs) and the use of three-step test language was interpreted by staff as indicative of a narrow field of application.

It might be asked what this means for the use of three-step test language in domestic copyright exceptions.[69] Some academic commentary has suggested that the three-step test might be usefully deployed in such legislation on the basis that it has an enabling function, i.e., that it could provide judges with a flexible instrument to find that conduct is non-infringing.[70] Leaving aside the lack of consensus as to whether the three-step test has this quality, the Australian fieldwork raised questions about whether copyright stakeholders (let alone judges and lawyers) would interpret the law in this way. To be fair, issues with section 200AB might also have been connected to its particular formulation, such as having qualifying requirements in addition to the three-step test. It may also be that staff were unable to shake off their initial perceptions of section 200AB as complex, uncertain and unknowable, despite subsequent changes to their own decision-making practices. But the use of

---

[66] See the second reading speech of the Attorney-General: Commonwealth, *Parliamentary Debates*, House of Representatives, 19 October 2006 (Philip Ruddock).
[67] See Chapter 6, Section III; see also E. Hudson, 'Implementing Fair Use in Copyright Law: Lessons from Australia' (2013) 25 *Intellectual Property Journal* 201.
[68] See Chapter 3, Section IV and Chapter 8, Section III.
[69] This possibility was foreshadowed in the analysis of the three-step test in Chapter 1, Section III.A.
[70] See especially M. Senftleben, *Copyright, Limitations and the Three-Step Test: An Analysis of the Three-Step Test in International and EC Copyright Law* (The Hague: Kluwer, 2004), pp. 280–281; C. Geiger, D. Gervais and M. Senftleben, 'The Three-Step Test Revisited: How to Use the Test's Flexibility in National Copyright Law' (2014) 29 *American University International Law Review* 581; M. Senftleben, 'The Perfect Match: Civil Law Judges and Open-Ended Fair Use Provisions' (2017) 33 *American University International Law Review* 231.

TRIPS language was clearly problematic, first, because it suggested that the three-step test had some agreed meaning at the international level (albeit one not accessible to institution staff), second, because the 'special case' limb suggested that section 200AB applied only in exceptional circumstances and required item-by-item decision-making, and finally, because Australian interviewees had no experience with three-step test reasoning. Anyone arguing that the three-step test should be used as some sort of domestic fair use exception would therefore need to consider the likely interpretations of those subject to the law (and not just judges), and whether ongoing debate about the test's content have rendered it so fraught and contested that there would be significant impediments to it being embraced as a meaningful and flexible standard.[71]

As noted above, the interviews also illustrated the need for those drafting exceptions to give consideration to the characteristics of users, existing copyright workflows, and the broader social and cultural milieu in which exceptions operate. For instance, whilst section 107 of the US Copyright Act seemed to be an important part of the copyright management landscape in US cultural institutions,[72] in the five years following *CCH*, the response amongst Canadian cultural institutions was extremely muted.[73] Viewed through the lens of the law in books, this seemed contrary to various doctrinal indications that post-*CCH* fair dealing shared much with fair use due to its fairness factors,[74] broad reading of the permissible purposes,[75] forward-leaning judicial interpretations,[76] and philosophical underpinnings.[77] However, by analysing

---

[71] For similar concerns, see J. Griffiths, 'The "Three-Step Test" in European Copyright Law: Problems and Solutions' [2009] *Intellectual Property Quarterly* 428, 447–448, observing that to the extent the three-step test had been considered by national courts in Europe, the resulting decisions were highly inconsistent and made it 'difficult to escape the impression that the "test" had been employed simply as a legitimising cloak for pre-formulated judicial preferences'.

[72] See Chapter 5. [73] See Chapter 7.

[74] *CCH*, n. 14 above, paras. 52–60; in the United States, s. 107 sets out four factors that shall be considered.

[75] Ibid., para. 51 (giving research 'a large and liberal interpretation'); in the US, s. 107 sets out illustrative purposes.

[76] Following *CCH*, the Supreme Court's reasoning was applied by the Copyright Board in *Tariff No 22A (Statement of Royalties to be Collected by SOCAN for the Communication to the Public by Telecommunication, in Canada, of Musical or Dramatico-Musical Works*, Tariff No 22A (Internet – Online Music Services) 1996–2006, Copyright Board of Canada, 18 October 2007), and informed the decision of Bastarache J in *Euro-Excellence Inc v. Kraft Canada Inc* [2007] 3 SCR 20.

[77] *CCH*, n. 14 above, paras. 10, 12, 48 (emphasising the need to maintain a 'proper balance' between owner and user interests, and stating that fair dealing, like other exceptions, is 'a user's right').

decision-making of participating institutions it was possible to gain an understanding of why experiences were so different. For instance, the knowledge of individual interviewees was variable, but tended to be higher amongst those from the United States than those from Canada. Institutions in the former jurisdiction also seemed to dedicate greater resources to copyright, for instance as seen in centralised copyright offices and/or specialist staff; in Canada, such units and expertise were far less common. In terms of risk preferences, interviewees from the United States, whilst noting their conservatism, seemed to approach copyright with a more commercial attitude, whereas those from Canada described practices that were very conservative and expressed fear of being the test case. Finally, the legal history in Canada emphasised licensing models and relegated exceptions to a marginal role, helping to generate workflows and understandings about copyright that were very different to the vision of the Supreme Court.

The Canadian experience raised the possibility that, at least amongst participating cultural institutions, fair use would be a mistake or be ineffective. It would be a mistake if reform involved a comprehensive revision of the Canadian copyright statute so that fair use replaced fair dealing and some specific exceptions. Although such an approach might be principled (in terms of positioning fair use as the predominant exception), it would risk departing too much from the status quo. On the other hand, a change to fair use might be ineffective if the doctrine were added alongside existing exceptions, perhaps as a safety net, this being contrary to how section 107 operates in the United States and potentially generating such a blank slate that users might find it impossible to predict, with any confidence, the operation of the Canadian version.[78] Indeed, the Canadian fieldwork of 2008 and 2009 suggested that if there was desire to increase the utilisation of free exceptions by cultural institutions in that country, a better approach might be through well-drafted closed exceptions, this being an incremental shift that better reflected existing norms and decision-making practices.[79]

But another message from the empirical work was that user practices are not fixed, raising the question of whether this conclusion about Canadian law reform paid adequate attention to the changeability of norms and, perhaps, the capacity of legislative reform to prompt such

---

[78] For instance, this approach might generate confusion about the hierarchy of arguments and applicable interpretative principles in a regime in which fair use sits alongside fair dealing and other exceptions.

[79] This point was made in E. Hudson, 'Copyright Exceptions: The Experiences of Cultural Institutions in the United States, Canada and Australia' (PhD thesis, University of Melbourne, November 2011).

changes. Amongst those supporting the liberalisation of exceptions this might even suggest that fair use should be introduced immediately, on the basis that (1) it is the best mechanism to future-proof the copyright statute against inevitable changes to technology and practices and (2) it would send the strongest signal to users to update their practices. In order to assess this proposition, let us return to ideas from the standards and rules literature in relation to some of the factors that inform the relative efficiency of different forms of legal drafting,[80] and consider how they might apply to the cultural institution sector.

We might start by identifying factors that we predict will be relatively stable over time. One such example is promulgation costs, these costs being influenced heavily by the frequency and homogeneity of the conduct to be regulated. Here it might be observed that cultural institutions collect a variety of copyright works produced in range of creative conditions and use them in myriad ways, leading to fact patterns that are sufficiently variable that it would be inefficient for the legislature to write a comprehensive list of precise legal commands in advance. We might also observe that this variability in conduct is only compounded by 'chronological heterogeneity',[81] i.e., changes to uses over time. Promulgation costs will therefore tend to support the introduction of standards, including fair use.

On the other hand, the costs of learning about the law would seem to point consistently towards rules. As seen in the analysis of sector-specific exceptions for user requests,[82] detailed copyright exceptions can involve a high initial outlay to operationalise, but once understood do not require significant ongoing legal input. This can be contrasted with reported experiences in relation to fair use and fair dealing, where interviewees noted the level of legal knowledge required to understand these provisions and concerns about staff elsewhere in the institution uploading their own homespun interpretations. Indeed, one reason for the trial decision going against the university in *Access Copyright* v. *York* related to the finding that there was a lack of oversight of staff implementation of the fair dealing policy.[83] Thus, although it has been said that standards often 'have a large intuitive element which makes them comprehensible

---

[80] See Chapter 2, Section III. That section considered: promulgation costs; costs of learning about the law; user characteristics; and costs of enforcement.
[81] R. Korobkin, 'Behavioral Analysis and Legal Form: Rules vs. Standards Revisited' (2000) 79 *Oregon Law Review* 2334.
[82] See Chapter 4.
[83] *Canadian Copyright Licensing Agency ("Access Copyright")* v. *York University* [2017] FC 669, discussed in Chapter 8, Section IV.

without special training',[84] it appeared that for fair use and fair dealing, continued engagement with the law by a copyright expert was still important, these provisions requiring fact-dependent analysis and therefore being less amenable to being analysed once and transposed into a staff manual.[85]

Other factors that bear upon the efficiency of different forms of drafting would seem to be more amenable to change. For example, this research observed a shift in the reported risk preferences of participating cultural institutions, especially in the latter tranches of fieldwork in Australia and the United Kingdom. The standards and rules literature predicts that greater risk tolerance may lead to greater comfort with the uncertainty that inheres in standards, and in fact there seemed to be a correlation between a more commercial attitude to risk and reported reliance on fair use (in the United States) and fair dealing (especially in the United Kingdom). In Australia, these more robust attitudes did not translate to utilisation of section 200AB, a matter which, as discussed earlier, seemed to relate to drafting matters. That is, the experience with section 200AB cautions us not against the use of standards but the use of poorly written complex ones.

Reputational concerns would also seem to have changed over the years, not in terms of the *relevance* of those relationships (which remain extremely important) but the *expectations* of those who interact with cultural institutions. Early in this research, the use of digitisation seemed to spark fear amongst cultural institutions and their stakeholders, for instance that works presented online might be the objects of significant unauthorised re-use. In later fieldwork, it appeared that more and more creators believed that an 'all rights reserved' model was unsuited to the internet and may be contrary to their own interests. At art museums, for example, this resulted in a change in the nature of complaints from artists, with less concern about images appearing on the institution website and more concern about the *absence* of any such images.[86] More

---

[84] I. Ehrlich and R. Posner, 'An Economic Analysis of Legal Rulemaking' (1974) 3 *The Journal of Legal Studies* 257, 270–271; see also Korobkin, n. 81 above, 35.

[85] See also L. Di Valentino, 'Laying the Foundation for Copyright Policy and Practice in Canadian Universities' (PhD thesis, The University of Western Ontario, 2016), ch. 5 (suggesting that, as part of their move away from Access Copyright blanket licences, Canadian universities had increased their internal resourcing of copyright).

[86] E.g., 225G, 314G, 322G; similar 208G (noting generational change in the attitudes of artists), 317G (noting the strong relationships developed with artists and the role of institutions in promoting public awareness of their works). 225G said: 'Artists hardly ever get concerned about our licences. I have artists emailing me and ringing me up, and asking, "you've got some works of mine in the collection; why are there no images online?" [The interviewee gives an example of an artist complaining last week that it was

broadly, there was only growth in the expectation amongst stakeholders and the public that institutions should use digital and online technologies to present their collections. In terms of legal interpretations, whilst cultural institutions still believed it was very important to respect copyright law, they were also keen to find ways to meet stakeholder expectations – these expectations dovetailing with their own ethical views about institutional missions and the need to provide access. Reputational and ethical concerns might therefore support not just a robust role for exceptions but the use of standards such as fair use as one mechanism to help institutions in their practices.

On the other hand, enforcement costs may favour rules, and all the more so given the litigation aversion that characterises the sector, such that many institutions would rather discontinue a use than defend their fair use interpretations in court. However, this observation needs to be qualified by lessons from the United States. First, the fieldwork suggested that many applications of fair use were incremental and relatively uncontentious. Second, it could not be said that cultural institutions inevitably avoided litigation, especially where important matters of principle were at stake.[87] Finally, cultural institutions' lack of appetite for litigation is hardly unique, being shared by many copyright stakeholders, including creators.[88] It appeared that fair use worked in the United States not because institutions participated regularly in litigation but because there was an extensive body of case law from which guidance could be drawn. Thus, focusing on cultural institutions, whilst enforcement costs and litigation aversion would seem to disfavour fair use, it may be that this can be afforded lower weight. In contrast, if general conditions are such that there is little if any case law (for instance,

---

"a great dishonour" not to be on the website.] I get more demands for greater access, rather than complaints that the gallery is exploiting works.' 317G said: 'the prospect of an artist complaining that we're letting the public know that we have something of theirs in our collection – the chance of them complaining that we have a low-resolution image on our website – is remote'.

[87] See especially the litigation against the HathiTrust Digital Library in *Authors Guild, Inc v. HathiTrust*, 755 F 3d 87 (2nd circuit, 2014) and the litigation against Georgia State University in *Cambridge University Press v. Albert*, 906 F 3d 1290 (11th circuit, 2018), both discussed in detail in Chapter 5, Section IV, and pertaining to data mining, preservation copying and the production of accessible copies for disabled users (*HathiTrust*) and multiple copying for educational use (*Georgia State*).

[88] Indeed, enforcements costs have been identified in arguments against fair use, not because of concerns that *users* would not have the resources or expertise to defend their position, but on the basis that *creators and copyright owners* would not be able to afford to litigate: see discussion in Australian Law Reform Commission (ALRC), *Copyright and the Digital Economy: Final Report*, Report No. 122 (November 2013), para. 4.118.

because there are few well-resourced entities to litigate, or procedural matters – such as the award of costs – disfavour litigation), then this may serve as a more compelling argument against fair use.[89]

Taken together, it would appear that for the cultural institution sector, promulgation costs strongly favour fair use; the costs of learning about the law disfavour it; decision-making factors can go either way; and enforcement costs lie somewhere between supporting rules and being neutral. Thus, if there is change to internal management at cultural institutions (for instance through greater resourcing of copyright and lower levels of risk aversion), and social norms do not require rigid adherence to the law, the case for fair use also firms. In addition, we might ask how much the costs of learning about the law should weigh against fair use, given that cultural institutions must already acquire knowledge about copyright for licensing and management of their own rights. That is, concerns about the costs of understanding fair use may in fact reflect a problem with the under-resourcing of copyright per se, especially at smaller institutions. As seen in the US fieldwork, those institutions relying on fair use had good copyright knowledge and sophisticated practices across the board, not just in relation to exceptions.

The foregoing analysis therefore lends support to the proposition that the fair use panacea is a viable approach to exceptions reform. When we also consider other copyright stakeholders, it may be that fair use becomes even more attractive on the basis that: (1) there is even greater variation in practices once we consider stakeholder practices generally; (2) these practices are hugely susceptible to chronological heterogeneity; (3) a critical mass of users would already have the legal knowledge and decision-making practices to embrace fair use; (4) other users can develop these capabilities, even if this takes time; and therefore (5) as an efficiency matter, fair use is the best long-term solution to address stakeholder practices in an ever-changing technological and creative landscape. Whether this conclusion is compelling will depend on a number of matters, including the accuracy of the empirical claims that are implicit in items (3) and (4).

To expand on this last point, one possible benefit of fair use is to effect a complete reboot of copyright exceptions. Fair use is open-ended. This difference from the existing drafting infrastructure in countries such as Australia, Canada and the United Kingdom, especially if accompanied by repeal of fair dealing and the streamlining of specific exceptions, might send a strong signal that new interpretations are required and that

---

[89] Discussed in Hunter, n. 6 above.

users should change their practices. But questions also arise in relation to the sources that users would initially use when analysing fair use.[90] As seen with Australian experiences in relation to section 200AB, problems arise if users feel bereft of authoritative guidance. One attraction of a fair use provision modelled on section 107 of the US Copyright Act is that many users are already familiar with the term 'fair use' (given the dominance of the United States as an intellectual property exporter) and could look to the extensive US case law for assistance. Fair use would not, as such, be an entirely unknown concept. Of course, each legislature would need to consider the risks of linking that country's own law to that in the United States, especially if some US considerations are specific to US social and economic conditions.[91] More generally, there may be benefits in emphasising the value of forms of guidance other than case law and legislative indications, such as industry-led interpretations.[92] As one UK interviewee said:

> I'm increasingly thinking that the real benefit comes in engaging communities to do things themselves, autonomously. Whilst it is important to keep lobbying for the best policy environment in which to work, when you get into the detail of it, the government can only spend so much time trying to understand how cultural institutions work. The cultural institutions themselves know what is the best thing to do, and they all want to do the right thing. If they got together and worked out what that was, they could save themselves a lot of time and effort in trying to re-invent the wheel every time they do it.[93]

A second concern relates to the possibility that fair use would sit for too long, unused, on the statute books, leading to the stultification seen in relation to section 200AB. The problem here is that if there are anxieties about a new exception, such that a large number of users adopt a wait-and-see approach, the sheer passage of time can cement the view that the exception is marginal. The empirical work in this book showed that norms and practices can change, and sometimes abruptly and comprehensively. However, even if the legislature is playing the long game in its copyright reforms, it may be desirable that there be some early uptake (even if patchy and conservative) in order to lay the foundations for later practices.

---

[90] Discussed in ALRC, n. 88 above, paras. 4.117–4.130, 5.133–5.160.
[91] Discussed in Handler and Hudson, n. 1 above.
[92] See especially P. Aufderheide and P. Jaszi, *Reclaiming Fair Use: How to Put Balance Back in Copyright* (Chicago: University of Chicago Press, 2011), chs. 7–8. For analysis of the challenges in cross-sector guidelines, see, e.g., K. Crews, 'Electronic Reserves and Fair Use: The Outer Limits of CONFU' (1999) 50 *Journal of the American Society for Information Science* 1342.
[93] 319L.

One way to assess willingness to embrace fair use (or indeed other reforms) would be to ask whether a sufficient number of users already *want* such a provision. For instance, during the Fair Use Review of 2005 in Australia, the reforms called for by cultural institution respondents lacked consensus, there being a concern that the injection of flexibility not come at the expense of certainty. Submissions therefore included requests for new specific exceptions, the expansion of fair dealing, fair use, and sometimes all three.[94] The government responded by introducing a reform no-one asked for: section 200AB. Whilst the failure of section 200AB can in large part be put down to its drafting, a further issue is whether, at the time of its introduction, cultural institutions had fears and confusions about open-ended exceptions that made it difficult for any new provision to get off the ground. In contrast, numerous UK interviewees spoke of having 'fought for' the 2014 reforms and the importance of not squandering the benefits of new exceptions by failing to invoke them.[95] This seemed to feed naturally into a desire to consider bolder interpretations, especially of fair dealing, and to encourage patrons to also make use of the rights granted to them by law. Similarly, the Copyright Modernization Act of 2012 was passed in Canada at a point when copyright practices at academic libraries were in a state of flux, with that statute's expansion of fair dealing to education serving to fortify views that greater reliance should be placed on fair dealing arguments.[96]

In addition to demonstrating the importance of user traction when reform is introduced, the UK and Canadian experiences lend support for expanded fair dealing (i.e., the addition of new fair dealing purposes) as an attractive alternative to fair use.[97] In the United Kingdom, for

---

[94] See Chapter 6, Section II.A.

[95] Especially 305M, 306L, 309L, 313M, 314G, 319L, 320L, 322G. For instance, 309L described a more expansive interpretation of one of the new fair dealing purposes, and said: 'This comes down to, because we're now in 2018 and people are feeling a bit more like "we've got these new exceptions, and we need to use them" – people are feeling a bit more confident, and want to push back a bit. I don't think anyone felt that way in 2015. People were nervous; they didn't want to be the test case or the first ones. ... I definitely would say that as time's gone on, I've got less cautious and more "we've got these exceptions, why are we not making the most of them"? The sky hasn't fallen in.' Similarly, 322G said: 'There's also a feeling that we got new exceptions into law, and if we don't use them, what's the point? If people are not using them because they're too worried about the wording, then why did we get them? We should be making the argument for using them.'

[96] Copyright Modernization Act (S.C. 2012, c. 20) s. 21 (amending s. 29 of the Canadian Copyright Act); see Chapter 8, Section II.A.

[97] See Handler and Hudson, n. 1 above; M. Geist, 'Fairness Found: How Canada Quietly Shifted from Fair Dealing to Fair Use' in M. Geist (ed), *The Copyright Pentalogy: How the Supreme Court of Canada Shook the Foundations of Canadian Copyright Law* (Ottawa:

Drafting Copyright Exceptions 333

example, it has been accepted that fair use is off the table as a reform option due to Article 5 of the Information Society Directive.[98] However, a doctrinal analysis of the new fair dealing purposes – quotation, caricature, parody and pastiche, and illustration for instruction – suggests that they cover a lot of similar ground to section 107 of the US statute.[99] It may be that fair use would represent a cleaner break from past practices and would have stronger signalling effects, but this should not be to dismiss expanded fair dealing as an option, particularly if there are political impediments to introducing fair use, or concerns about fair use being tied too closely to US copyright law. It should also be observed that in countries such as Australia and Canada, there are strong arguments that introduction of a quotation exception is necessary to comply with obligations under Article 10(1) of the Berne Convention.[100]

The experiences in this book therefore lend weight to the fair use panacea, and to alternative models such as expanded fair dealing. But as noted above, this does not mean that, for the cultural institution sector, rule-like drafting should be abandoned. On the contrary, a key lesson from the theoretical and empirical inquiry in this book is that whether exceptions are better drafted as standards, rules or some combination of the two can only be addressed in context-dependent ways, and that general exceptions should not be viewed as inevitably superior to specific ones. Thus, one part of law reform may relate to improving the drafting of sector-specific exceptions to remove ambiguous or unnecessarily restrictive language. For instance, in 2017 the Australian preservation copying provisions were consolidated and some limitations removed,[101] making those rules less complex and confined.[102]

University of Ottawa Press, 2013). Another possible reform to fair dealing is to make the purposes illustrative. In June 2019, this was recommended for Canada by the House of Commons Standing Committee on Industry, Science and Technology, *Statutory Review of the Copyright Act: Report of the Standing Committee on Industry, Science and Technology*, 42nd Parliament, 1st Session (June 2019), recommendation 18.

[98] See Chapter 1, Section III.B. [99] See Chapter 8, Section II.B.
[100] See Chapter 8, Section II.B.1.
[101] Copyright Amendment (Disability Access and other Measures) Act 2017 (Cth), Schedule 1, items 1–2 (inserting ss. 113G–113M, covering preservation copying by libraries and archives and by key cultural institutions), 22, 30, 35 (repealing ss. 51A, 51B, 110B, 110BA, 112AA). The Australian fieldwork did not suggest that the additional exception for key cultural institutions added anything to the general preservation copying exception, making it somewhat curious that a provision for key cultural institutions was retained.
[102] The term 'preservation' seems to be rule-like, because of the widespread institutional understanding of that term. That said, the UK experiences with administrative copying raise the question of whether 'preservation' could be interpreted as referring to care of the collection more generally: see Chapter 4, Section III.A.2.

In the United States, there has also been discussion of the perceived inadequacies of section 108, including through a Study Group that reported in 2008 and a discussion paper of the Copyright Office in 2017.[103] Both reports made numerous recommendations for reform, for instance that museums be covered by section 108; that the preservation exceptions be reorganised by reference to whether works had been lawfully disseminated to the public (rather than published); and that the three-copy limit for preservation copying be abandoned in favour of copying as reasonably necessary. In recommending these changes, the Copyright Office stated that it 'remains firm in its belief that section 108 needs to be updated so that libraries, archives, and museums have a robust, comprehensible, and balanced safe harbour in order to fulfil their missions'.[104]

Interestingly, in both reports the analysis of fair use was relatively brief. Whilst the Study Group included a description of fair use in its background analysis,[105] once it turned to its substantive analysis of section 108 there were only passing references to the role of arguments under section 107. The Copyright Office engaged more closely with the utilisation of fair use by cultural institutions, including via an observation that in its 'summer 2016 stakeholder meetings ... the Copyright Office heard many variations on the assertion that section 108 did not need to be revised because any gaps are easily and legally filled by fair use'.[106] Its response to this argument was that

> fair use remains a fact-based, case-by-case analysis, and there remain many essential library and archives activities that may not be authorized by fair use if they are not covered by section 108 – specifically in the area of distribution of copies of works to users. ... Furthermore, there remain other activities where fair use may apply, but which have simply not been tested in court, such as exceeding the three-copy limit for preservation, research, or replacement copies, or making preservation copies of all categories of published works. Resolution of many of these issues may therefore require long-term litigation that would be beyond or drain the resources of many smaller institutions.[107]

---

[103] Section 108 Study Group, *The Section 108 Study Group Report: An Independent Report sponsored by the United States Copyright Office and the National Digital Information Infrastructure and Preservation Program of the Library of Congress* (March 2008); United States Copyright Office, *Section 108 of Title 17: A Discussion Document of the Register of Copyrights* (United States Copyright Office, September 2017).
[104] United States Copyright Office, ibid., p. 1.
[105] Section 108 Study Group, n. 103 above, especially pp. 21–22.
[106] United States Copyright Office, n. 103 above, p. 14.   [107] Ibid., pp. 15–16.

Drafting Copyright Exceptions 335

This raises an interesting final question for this book: what happens where the recommendation is for specific exceptions to be reformed *in the backdrop of fair use*. For instance, whilst it may seem absurd to exclude museums from the ambit of section 108, the empirical research with US interviewees was equivocal regarding the need for, and likely effect of, the expansion of section 108 to include museums. Although some interviewees said that greater certainty in the application of exceptions had attractions,[108] or that fair use was at times 'so flexible that it leads to people throwing up their hands and doing nothing',[109] they also lauded the ability of fair use to apply in a range of scenarios,[110] and – most importantly – appeared relatively confident in invoking fair use for activities of a type covered by section 108.[111] One interviewee observed that 'it would be good to extend the institutions to which section 108 applies, but we have survived this far without it'.[112]

Importantly, too, the reported experiences of US participants did not suggest there were glaring holes in the current legal framework. To the extent that museums were engaged in practices covered by section 108 – preservation and request-based copying – these were frequently on a lower scale than libraries and archives, and could be dealt with through fair use and licensing. For instance, it has been seen that copyright law was not described as an impediment to preservation copying,[113] and nor did those handling external requests express concern about the different legal regulation of text-based works in library and archival collections (for which sections 108(d) and (e) are applicable) and other types of material (which are excluded from these provisions). The main copyright issues for museums instead related to online uses – activities largely outside the ambit of section 108, even if expanded as per the somewhat broader recommendations of the Copyright Office. As one interviewee observed in relation to the earlier Study Group Report, it did not appear that extending section 108 to museums 'would authorise us to do anything different to what we're already doing'.[114] The fieldwork therefore raised

---

[108] E.g., 7G, 10L, 26G, 45M.   [109] 36M.
[110] E.g., 3X, 7G, 9M, 16G, 19L ('ambiguity is our friend'), 26G, 33G, 36M, 39L, 43M, 48G, 50G, 53G; also 47X.
[111] For instance, fair use was described as relevant to preservation activities and the supply of reproductions in response to external requests: see Chapter 5.
[112] 54M. Similar: 39L (reform of section 108 not all that important because of section 107).
[113] See Chapters 4 and 5.   [114] 43M.

the question of whether allowing museums to invoke section 108 would facilitate new outcomes.[115]

One response that may be levelled against this point is that expanding section 108 is a no-risk option as it can extend the reach of those provisions and remove anomalous wording whilst leaving fair use arguments intact. This view is supported by subsection 108(f)(4), the relevant portion of which states that nothing in section 108 'in any way affects the right of fair use as provided by section 107'.[116] It may be that, even if reform to section 108 did not lead to a turning of the page, there are nevertheless benefits to revising the statute, for instance in relation to the legitimacy of the law; to provide greater legal clarity for institutions with fewer resources and/or higher levels of risk aversion; and to further reduce the possibility of litigation. On the other hand, if reform is made along the lines suggested in the Copyright Office's discussion paper, it is important to ask whether such changes might send the message that institutions have been overestimating the reach of fair use. One risk with expansion of section 108 is that it might be used to support the view that broader understandings of fair use are misguided. If this is not intended, then any reform to section 108 may benefit from explicit clarification regarding not only the availability of fair use but that the revised provisions may overlap with existing fair use interpretations.

IV Conclusion

One of the key themes underlying Burrell and Coleman's *Copyright Exceptions: The Digital Impact* was to question whether fair use was a viable solution to the problems commonly associated with detailed, closed-ended drafting. This book, through its analysis of the law in action, provides support for fair use, albeit not as a panacea that can and should be rolled out universally. This reflects the lesson that determining the best form of legislative drafting is a deeply empirical matter, being informed by a range of factors including promulgation costs, the costs of learning about the law, user characteristics and the costs of enforcement. In the cultural institution context, for example, the fieldwork suggested that interpretations of exceptions were influenced by staff knowledge, internal management structures, institutional attitudes to

---

[115] E.g., 7G (describing section 108 as 'not an extremely helpful statute' and observing that it seemed intuitively to be about the operation of a library) and 43M (noting the perception that section 108 is about 'crumbling books in libraries').

[116] The Copyright Office stated, in no uncertain terms, that this savings clause must be retained in any new iteration of section 108: United States Copyright Office, n. 103 above, pp. 42–43.

Conclusion

risk, relationship management concerns, ethical understandings of best practices and historical effects. One could make the case that, if there was sufficient appetite amongst users, jurisdictions such as Australia and (depending on the form of Brexit) the United Kingdom should move to fair use. That said, the UK experience, and to a degree that in Canada, also supported expanded fair dealing as a way to improve considerably on the status quo, casting doubt on the characterisation of fair dealing reform as 'very much a second-best option'.[117]

There are complications to the foregoing analysis. User interpretations are not fixed in time, and in this research changed not just in response to legal developments but to a range of internal and external matters. In addition, one observation from the standards and rules literature is that the classification of an exception cannot be discerned from its face,[118] and the empirical work likewise came across instances of rule-like provisions being read in standard-like ways, and of cases where copyright had not been internalised as a relevant consideration for certain institutional practices. But it may be that these instances of divergence from the statutory text should themselves inform our consideration of the content and form of exceptions. For instance, the simplification of preservation copying exceptions via the removal of subject-matter and quantitative limits would seem to be sound, both as a normative matter and as a matter of legal drafting.

Finally, this research provides lessons about how the law in books translates to the law in action, and the range of matters to which legislators should have regard when implementing copyright reform. There may be compelling arguments that, in some countries, fair use is a viable way to future-proof the copyright statute for technological change and that it has other attractions when compared with other models, for instance in its strong signalling effects. But for reform to lead to meaningful change, users need to embrace any new provision, and it may therefore be necessary to consider additional legal and non-legal measures to support the utilisation of any new fair use exception, for instance via statements in the explanatory materials, remedies limitations for some users, and by ensuring that public institutions receive adequate funding for copyright management. Indeed, the latter is important not only for exceptions but to ensure other elements of copyright management are

---

[117] Sentiment expressed in a number of submissions to the ALRC, n. 88 above, para. 6.20. The ALRC seemed to accept that expanded fair dealing would not have all the benefits of fair use, describing it as a 'pragmatic second-best option': para. 6.40.

[118] C. Sunstein, 'Problems with Rules' (1995) 83 *California Law Review* 953, 959–960.

undertaken properly, including licensing arrangements with copyright owners.

In conclusion, with concerns in many jurisdictions that, when it comes to the drafting of exceptions, '[r]igidity is the rule' and every exception must be 'defined precisely and confined within high and immutable walls',[119] it is unsurprising that fair use remains in the minds of those involved in copyright policy. Fair use has come to represent a new vision for copyright and a rejection of existing interpretative paradigms. Whether it would exhibit these qualities in practice depends not only on doctrinal matters but the interpretations of copyright stakeholders. For those interested in expanding the ground covered by free exceptions, it may be that new fair dealing purposes are just as effective. Furthermore, for some widespread and fairly homogenous behaviours, there are obvious efficiency benefits from well-drafted rules. Thus, whilst it would be wrong to treat fair use as a universal panacea to cure the ills of closed-ended drafting, it might be one cure, along with a number of other legal and non-legal interventions that together ensure greater correspondence between the normative goals of exceptions, their articulation in the law in books and their manifestation in the law in action.

---

[119] H. Laddie, 'Copyright: Over-Strength, Over-Regulated, Over-Rated?' (1996) 18 *European Intellectual Property Review* 253, 258.

Appendix   Empirical Methodology

The methodology used in this book was summarised in Chapter 3. The aim of the Appendix is to describe more fully the empirical work, especially in relation to the fieldwork conducted from 2007 onwards. The methodology used in the first tranche of Australian fieldwork in 2004 and 2005 has been described elsewhere,[1] although the underlying approach remained largely the same. Relevant differences are noted in the text that follows.

The results of the first Australian project raised a number of questions about the role and content of free exceptions, including whether the existing provisions were in need of reform and, if so, the form those reforms should take. While it was relatively easy to find analysis of the philosophy of exceptions, interpretations in the case law and predicted outcomes of different drafting styles, it was much harder to find empirical analysis of day-to-day copyright practices. This made it difficult to compare Australian experiences with those of other countries, or to use overseas practices to help draw conclusions regarding the merits of different reform options. One aim of the research conducted from 2007 onwards was to help respond to this gap. As noted in Chapter 3, the second phase of research was undertaken for my doctorate, and examined experiences in Canada and the United States. This was followed by a third phase of research that added the United Kingdom as a jurisdiction and included new and comprehensive fieldwork in Australia.

This Appendix describes the thinking behind: (1) the selection of countries for study; (2) the decision to use semi-structured interviews; (3) the target institutions and interviewees; and (4) the conduct and content of the interviews. Broader questions regarding the role and weaknesses of qualitative research – including the reliability and validity

---

[1] E. Hudson and A. Kenyon, 'Digital Access: The Impact of Copyright on Digitisation Practices in Australian Museums, Galleries, Libraries and Archives' (2007) 30 *University of New South Wales Law Journal* 12, especially 15–17.

of data, and the use of interviews to generate data – have been addressed elsewhere and are not repeated here.[2] However, the Appendix concludes with some comments on the status of the data and the strength of the conclusions that can be drawn from this research.

1 Selection of Countries

In thinking about the design of this empirical research project, an initial matter was the country or countries that would be selected for comparative analysis with Australia. This resulted in the decision to study Canada, the United States, and, subsequently, the United Kingdom. Reasons that influenced this choice included the following:

(a) *Similarities in cultural institution practices.* In all four countries, there has been a push for cultural institutions to embrace digital technologies as part of their institutional activities. It was therefore thought that they would face common issues in relation to copyright management.
(b) *Doctrinal indications.* Whilst the overarching structure of copyright law is broadly similar between Australia, Canada, the United Kingdom and the United States, individual doctrines and principles differ in their scope and interpretation. For instance, doctrinal analysis suggested that the following might be particularly significant to practices in the United States and Canada: the presence of fair use in section 107 of the US Copyright Act; the Supreme Court of Canada decision in *CCH Canadian Ltd* v. *Law Society of Upper Canada*[3] in relation to fair dealing; and the emphasis given to collective management in Canadian law. The United Kingdom was later introduced with the aim of analysing the experiences of a jurisdiction that shared a legal history with the three other countries, but which also formed part of the European Union, and which could provide some indications of the influence of European harmonisation on the themes in this book. It was also of interest that the United Kingdom revised and expanded exceptions in 2014.
(c) *Privileges afforded to cultural institutions.* The statutes of all four countries include detailed sector-specific exceptions along with fair use or fair dealing. This is consistent with acceptance that cultural

---

[2] See, e.g., L. Epstein and A. Martin, *An Introduction to Empirical Legal Research* (Oxford: Oxford University Press, 2014), pp. 46–57; C. Seale, 'Research Quality' in C. Seale, *Researching Society and Culture*, 4th edition (London: Sage, 2018); N. King, C. Horrocks and J. Brooks, *Interviews in Qualitative Research*, 2nd edition (London: Sage, 2019).
[3] [2004] 1 SCR 339.

institutions should be afforded some special privileges in copyright law. However, it was also observed that there are differences in the legislative history of these provisions, and in the precise acts that would seem to fall within their ambit.

(d) *Practical considerations.* Whilst some continental European countries were considered for study, it was thought that language issues might prove difficult for both the doctrinal and empirical aspects of this project. Access to legal materials was also considered, including the availability in Australia and the United Kingdom of large subscription databases including much US and Canadian content.

2 Use of Semi-Structured Interviews

Another preliminary question was whether the post-2007 fieldwork should follow the methodology of the first batch of Australian research by using semi-structured interviews. This included consideration of alternative empirical techniques, such as a written questionnaire.[4] It was decided to retain an interview-based approach, with responses supplemented by documentation provided by interviewees (such as boilerplate copyright deeds and licences) and information obtained from publicly available sources (such as institution websites). The research did not involve unsupervised analysis of internal files or databases – the only internal documents considered were those voluntarily supplied or shown by interviewees. Nor did it involve the observation of interviewees in situ. Experiences are therefore those reported in the interviews.

The decision not to use a questionnaire was based on a number of factors. Perhaps the most compelling reason was that a questionnaire seemed far less likely to elicit the sort of information being sought in this research.[5] The aim of the fieldwork was to gain an understanding of the decision-making processes used by cultural institutions in their management of copyright. There was therefore a need to ask questions about a range of matters; and it was predicted that responses could be detailed and involved. Comparing the respective merits of interviews and questionnaires, it was thought that interviews had a number of advantages (e.g., the ability to clarify questions and to probe for further information), and that the research questions would not fit well within a survey

---

[4] See C. Seale, 'Questionnaires and Interviews' in C. Seale, *Researching Society and Culture*, 4th edition (London: Sage, 2018).
[5] For similar reasoning, see A. Kenyon, *Defamation: Comparative Law and Practice* (London: UCL Press, 2006), p. 394.

environment and may also encourage a low response rate.[6] In addition, given the subject of the interviews involved discussion of potentially sensitive matters in relation to copyright but would often require the disclosure of personally identifying information, it was considered that concerns about anonymity and confidentiality might be better allayed through interviews than a written questionnaire.[7]

In addition to these concerns, a further reason to use semi-structured interviews was to retain continuity between the Australian and later research, thus aiding the comparative aspects of the project. The success of the Australian fieldwork made it attractive as a model for the later research, albeit with some specific changes to reflect that work's themes and target participants.

3 Selection of Institutions

The initial tranche of Australian research was divided into two stages, the first of which comprised in-depth fieldwork at six major cultural institutions. The aim of this first stage was to develop a comprehensive understanding of legal and non-legal aspects of digitisation practices. The second stage of the Australian research involved copyright-oriented interviews at a range of institutions and peak bodies and was intended to 'assess experiences across the sector'.[8] The second stage therefore included institutional participants of various sizes and from both urban and regional locations.

In contrast with the initial Australian fieldwork, the research subsequently focused on larger institutions in major cities. There were a number of factors that influenced this decision. First, given the research was interested in the utilisation of copyright exceptions – including some detailed questions about decision-making and the emergence of new copyright norms – the cohort needed to include institutions that would be considering these questions. In this regard, the earlier research in Australia suggested that smaller institutions tended to have 'fewer resources to dedicate to copyright compliance' and therefore showed a much lower level of engagement with the law than their larger counterparts.[9] Second, it was thought that leading institutions would be most likely to be at the forefront of trends and practices across the sector, for instance by sharing information about their copyright management practices and taking a leading role in debates about reform to law and

---

[6] Seale, 'Questionnaires and Interviews', n. 4 above, p. 182.
[7] Some similar concerns supported the use of interviews in Kenyon's study, n. 5 above.
[8] Hudson and Kenyon, n. 1 above, 15.   [9] Ibid., 36.

practices. It was also expected that interviewees would have an idea of how their institution's practices compared with those of other institutions, thus giving an indirect analysis of broader approaches. Third, whilst conducting fieldwork at institutions in a mix of regional and metropolitan locations was achievable in Australia, it was anticipated that this would be far more challenging to accomplish overseas given the resources available for a PhD project and, later, research conducted alongside standard academic duties.

Prior to the fieldwork, a target was set to conduct fieldwork at 20 bodies in any given country. This figure was set in the light of the Australian research, which suggested that it would: be sufficient to gain an understanding of the range of approaches taken to copyright management and the utilisation of exceptions; enable analysis of common issues and practices; and (for the North American work) was appropriate for the scale of research needed in a doctoral project. Statistics regarding the fieldwork are contained Chapter 3, Table 1.

4 Selection of Interviewees

Target interviewees were staff whose responsibilities included managing copyright and/or setting copyright policy. Where such people were employed, this project sought to interview in-house legal counsel and full-time copyright officers. At many institutions, interviews were conducted with two or more people and, in some instances, these took place in small groups rather than individually. Speaking with more than one interviewee was attractive to get a sense of practices throughout the institution, for instance where a copyright officer could speak to the handling of external requests and a registrar could discuss copyright procedures at acquisition.

Potential participants were identified in a number of ways. Some institutions were approached on the basis of information available from publicly available sources, in particular from institution websites. There were also some institution staff who had indicated a willingness to participate in the research following presentations given at conferences and workshops. Finally, it was common for interviewees to suggest other individuals who might be interested in the research. In that way, there was a strong snowball effect as the fieldwork was conducted. Potential participants were approached in writing (via email) and were supplied with copies of the Plain Language Statement and consent form prior to the interview taking place.

Interviewees were all aged over 18 years and were asked to provide written consent to participate. The methodology was reviewed and given ethical approval in accordance with policies for research with humans set by the University of Melbourne, University of Oxford and King's College London. One of the key ethical matters related to the confidentiality and anonymity of responses.[10] Whilst procedures in relation to confidentiality related primarily to the accessibility and storage of data (which was undertaken in accordance with the relevant privacy and data protection laws), interviewees were also told that they could identify certain responses as confidential (i.e., that those responses would not form part of the reported data set at all). In order to encourage interviewees to speak openly about their experiences, it was also decided to present all data anonymously. This means that in this book, all interviewees are referred to by a pseudonym, and any references to names, institutions or other identifying information has been removed.

5   Conduct of Interviews

The interviews were semi-structured and generally lasted between one and two hours. Interviews were generally conducted face-to-face, but in instances where this was not possible, interviews were conducted using remote video or, on occasion, telephone. In addition to taking notes using a computer, discussions were audio-recorded (where permission was given) in order to permit a full and accurate record of what was said. The contemporaneous interview notes were later checked against the audio recordings but were not necessarily transcribed in full, as it was often enough to have summary notes rather than an exact transcript.[11] That said, for areas where an interviewee's precise form of words were important or they were being quoted in this book, a verbatim transcript was generated. Analysis of interview data was facilitated by the NVivo software, which permitted coding and other forms of data manipulation.

All interviews commenced with a series of background questions that were designed to learn more about the interviewee and his or her institution. These included the interviewee's title or position; the length of time they had worked at the institution; relevant previous employment and/or study (including any legal training); key duties; and an overview of the institution's collection, activities and resourcing of copyright. The latter included the types of staff whose duties included copyright, and whether there were staff with copyright expertise and/or a centralised unit to oversee copyright.

---

[10] See King, Horrocks and Brooks, n. 2 above, pp. 44–48.
[11] See B. Byrne, 'Qualitative Interviewing' in C. Seale, *Researching Society and Culture*, 4th edition (London: Sage, 2018), p. 233. A further consideration was the resource-intensiveness of producing a full transcript from the audio recordings, particularly where there was not funding for such support.

Appendix

The body of the interview was structured around experiences of the following five categories of activity:

(1) *administration and collection management,* such as creating internal collection management databases, documenting loans and obtaining insurance;
(2) *preservation,* especially creating access copies (to reduce the day-to-day handling of original items) and archival copies (which may eventually become the repository of content should original items disintegrate);
(3) *external requests,* including from researchers, publishers and media organisations, and other institutions (including under interlibrary supply schemes);
(4) *onsite public access,* for instance as part of exhibitions, interactive displays, intranet facilities and on signage; and
(5) *offsite public access,* including in publications, marketing materials, online databases and on websites.

These categories were selected because they are points on a spectrum ranging from purely internal activities through to those creating outputs that can be accessed by patrons outside the physical premises of the institution. It must be emphasised that the content of each interview was tailored to reflect the experiences, expertise and legal knowledge of the participant. For instance, an interview with a publications manager would generally focus on a narrower band of activity than one with in-house legal counsel. Furthermore, a degree of flexibility was required in the order of the topics covered, as it was important that discussions flow naturally rather than be shoehorned into a fixed set of pre-prepared questions. With this in mind, the sort of questions asked in the body of the interview related to:

(1) *the nature of digitisation practices*: e.g., the types of projects being undertaken and their goals; the ways collection items were being used; the number and type of collection items being used; technical standards; whether external funding was obtained; and the accessibility of content;
(2) *copyright subsistence and ownership,* e.g., the copyright status of works being used for these projects; and whether copyright status was relevant to the selection of items to be used;
(3) *decision-making around using third-party copyright works,* e.g.:
   a. whether thought was given to copyright; and
   b. if so, how copyright was dealt with (e.g., via licensing or assignment, reliance on an exception, and/or risk management); and

(4) *further information about those strategies*, e.g.:
 a. for licensing and assignment practices: how and when those licences were negotiated; usual licence terms; the relevance (if any) of collective models of administration; and whether the institution sought copyright assignments;
 b. for exceptions: which exception(s) were relied upon; the sources used to inform understanding of those provisions; the ease or difficulty in ascertaining their content; and the relevance and impact of any case law; and
 c. for risk management: the circumstances in which risk management was used; and the factors that were relevant to such decision-making.

Interviews often concluded with some general questions in relation to copyright, for instance in relation to orphaned works; risk preferences and relationship management; experiences with copyright collectives; the overall impact of copyright on institutional activities; thoughts on the drafting of exceptions and fair use as a reform option; and whether there were particular areas in which reform to law or practice would be desirable.

6 Concluding Remarks

This final section addresses the status of the data and the strength of the conclusions that can be drawn from this research. These questions are often associated with the concepts of 'reliability' and 'validity'. As explained by Clive Seale, 'validity refers to the truth-value of a research project; can we say whether the reported results are true' whilst 'reliability … concerns the consistency with which research procedures deliver their results (whether or not these are true)'.[12] There are criticisms of these concepts, which seem to draw from a particular understanding of the scientific method and which may be seen to presume the existence of some objectively ascertainable truth.[13] However, it would be difficult to deny the general proposition that it is proper to identify the sort of conclusions that can be drawn from a particular project, whether based on realist or idealist understandings of the importance of research.

---

[12] Seale, 'Research Quality', n. 2 above, p. 568.
[13] Ibid; see also C. Seale, 'Philosophy, Politics and Values' in C. Seale, *Researching Society and Culture*, 4th edition (London: Sage, 2018).

The aim of this project was to develop an in-depth understanding of decision-making in relation to copyright management (including the utilisation of exceptions), in order to compare these with indications that arise from a purely doctrinal analysis. As noted above, the institutions who participated were generally prominent institutions located in major cities. An effort was made to ensure there was a balance between different types of institution and collection genre, with participants including academic and public libraries, social history museums, galleries and art museums, and archives. In Australia, Canada and the United States, interviews were conducted at a number of different cities in case there were regional variations in approaches to copyright; in the United Kingdom, there was likewise a mix of London and non-London participants. Interviews were also undertaken with other entities, such as peak bodies, creator representatives and other professional organisations, in order to get the perspectives of those working closely with the sector. Where possible, internal documentation and publicly accessible information was also analysed to supplement interview responses.

Amongst all participants, a coherent picture emerged of copyright practices and understandings. Interviewees were often aware of approaches adopted by different institutions, and those who were using (or pressing for) new or less common strategies would generally explain this as part of their responses. Atypical approaches were therefore very clear. The method of presenting the data, in particular the extensive use of interviewee pseudonyms in the footnotes, was intended to give more transparent indications to the reader regarding the weight that could be afforded to various propositions, thus helping protect against claims of anecdotalism.[14]

Since the initial Australian fieldwork, the sample has not included small institutions (as judged by collection size and staff numbers). However, the aim of the study was not to provide a comprehensive survey of sector-wide practices but rather to gain an understanding of the types of factors that drive institutional decision-making. Larger, metropolitan institutions were particularly attractive because of their engagement with these issues and their likely place as leaders in the field. Given the size and importance of their collections, and their participation in many large-scale digitisation projects, their practices are extremely important in preserving and providing access to content. However, this is not to

---

[14] See also Kenyon, above n. 5, p. 400.

suggest that work with other institutions would not be a valuable focus of future research; on the contrary, this research was intended to demonstrate the importance of empirical considerations, and suggests that research with various members of the copyright community (e.g., authors, publishers, artists, educators, cultural institutions and so forth) will be important for ongoing discussions about copyright.

Bibliography

Scholarly books, articles and similar

Adams, K., 'The Library Exceptions' in H. Knopf (ed), *The New Copyright Act: Managing the Impact* (Toronto: Insight Press, 1997).

Africa, M., 'The Misuse of Licensing Evidence in Fair Use Analysis: New Technologies, New Markets, and the Courts' (2000) 88 *California Law Review* 1145.

Alberts Carson, C., 'Laser Bones: Copyright Issues Raised by the Use of Information Technology in Archaelogy' (1997) 10 *Harvard Journal of Law & Technology* 281.

Allan, R., 'After *Bridgeman*: Copyright, Museums, and Public Domain Works of Art' (2007) 155 *University of Pennsylvania Law Review* 961.

Amineddoleh, L. 'The Role of Museums in the Trade of Black Market Cultural Heritage Property' (2013) 18 *Art Antiquity and Law* 227.

Aplin, T., 'Contemplating Australia's Digital Future: The *Copyright Amendment (Digital Agenda) Act*' (2001) 23 *European Intellectual Property Review* 565.

'Confidential Information as Property?' (2013) 24 *King's Law Journal* 172.

Aplin, T. and L. Bently, 'Displacing the Dominance of the Three-Step Test: The Role of Global, Mandatory Fair Use' in H. Sun, S. Balganesh and W. Ng-Loy (eds), *Comparative Aspects of Limitations and Exceptions in Copyright Law* (New York: Cambridge University Press, forthcoming).

Appel, S., 'Copyright, Digitization of Images, and Art Museums: Cyberspace and Other New Frontiers' (1999) 6 *UCLA Entertainment Law Review* 149.

Ariely, D., *The (Honest) Truth About Dishonesty* (London: Harper, 2012).

Arnold, R. and E. Rosati, 'Are National Courts the Addressee of the InfoSoc Three-Step Test?' (2015) 10 *Journal of Intellectual Property Law & Practice* 741.

Austin, G., 'Four Questions about the Australian Approach to Fair Dealing Defenses to Copyright Infringement' (2010) 57 *Journal of the Copyright Society of the USA* 611.

'The Two Faces of Fair Use' (2012) 25 *New Zealand Universities Law Review* 285.

'This Is a Complex Issue: A Few More Questions about Fair Use' (2018) 28 *Australian Intellectual Property Journal* 97.

Axelrod, R., *The Evolution of Cooperation* (New York: Basic Books, 1984).

Band, J. and B. Butler, 'Some Cautionary Tales about Collective Licensing' (2013) 21 *Michigan State International Law Review* 687.
Bartow, A., 'Electrifying Copyright Norms and Making Cyberspace More Like a Book' (2003) 48 *Villanova Law Review* 13.
Becker, G., 'Crime and Punishment: An Economic Analysis' (1968) 78 *Journal of Political Economy* 169.
Beebe, B., 'An Empirical Study of U.S. Copyright Fair Use Opinions' (2008) 156 *University of Pennsylvania Law Review* 549.
Bell, A., and Parchomovsky, G., 'The Dual-Grant Theory of Fair Use' (2016) 83 *University of Chicago Law Review* 1051.
Bell, T., 'Fair Use vs Fared Use: The Impact of Automated Rights Management on Copyright's Fair Use Doctrine' (1998) 76 *North Carolina Law Review* 557.
Bently, L., 'Trade Secrets: "Intellectual Property" but Not "Property"?' in H. Howe and J. Griffiths (eds), *Concepts of Property in Intellectual Property Law* (Cambridge: Cambridge University Press, 2013).
Bently, L. and T. Aplin, 'Whatever Became of Global, Mandatory, Fair Use? A Case Study in Dysfunctional Pluralism' in S. Frankel (ed), *Is Intellectual Property Pluralism Functional?* (Cheltenham: Edward Elgar, 2019).
Bently, L. and B. Sherman, *Intellectual Property Law*, 3rd edition (Oxford: Oxford University Press, 2009).
Bently, L., B. Sherman, D. Gangjee and P. Johnson, *Intellectual Property Law*, 5th edition (Oxford: Oxford University Press, 2018).
Besek, J. and P. Loengard, 'Maintaining the Integrity of Digital Archives' (2008) 31 *Columbia Journal of Law and the Arts* 267.
Besser-Jones, L., 'The Role of Justice in Hume's Theory of Psychological Development' (2006) 32 *Hume Studies* 253.
Bouchard, M., 'Collective Management in Commonwealth Jurisdictions: Comparing Canada with Australia' in D. Gervais (ed), *Collective Management of Copyright and Related Rights* (Alphen aan den Rijn: Kluwer Law International, 2006).
Bowrey, K. and J. Anderson, 'The Politics of Global Information Sharing: Whose Cultural Agendas Are Being Advanced?' (2009) 18 *Social & Legal Studies* 479.
Bowrey, K., M. Handler, D. Nicol and K. Weatherall, *Australian Intellectual Property Law: Commentary, Law and Practice*, 2nd edition (South Melbourne: Oxford University Press, 2015).
Brannon, P., 'Reforming Copyright to Foster Innovation: Providing Access to Orphaned Works' (2006) 14 *Journal of Intellectual Property Law* 145.
Breakey, H., 'Natural Intellectual Property Rights and the Public Domain' (2010) 73 *Modern Law Review* 208.
Brennan, D., 'Copyright and Parody in Australia: Some Thoughts on *Suntrust Bank v Houghton Mifflin Company*' (2002) 13 *Australian Intellectual Property Journal* 161.
  'The Copyright Tribunal as Exception-Maker: Are Both Flexibility and Certainty Achievable' (2018) 28 *Australian Intellectual Property Journal* 83.

Brooks, D. 'Rectifying Fair Use After *Cariou v. Prince*: Reviving the Forgotten Statutory Text and Requiring that Unauthorized Copying Be Justified, rather than Merely "Transformative"' (2016) 15 *Chicago-Kent Journal of Intellectual Property Law* 93.

Burrell, R., 'Reining in Copyright Law: Is Fair Use the Answer?' [2001] *Intellectual Property Quarterly* 361.

Burrell, R. and A. Coleman, *Copyright Exceptions: The Digital Impact* (Cambridge: Cambridge University Press, 2005).

Burrell, R. and K. Weatherall, 'Exporting Controversy? Reactions to the Copyright Provisions of the U.S.-Australia Free Trade Agreement: Lessons for U.S. Trade Policy' [2008] 2 *University of Illinois Journal of Law, Technology and Policy* 259.

Burroughs & Co, *Canadian Encyclopedic Digest Western*, 2nd edition, volume 5 (Calgary: Burroughs & Co, 1958).

Butler, B., 'Transformative Teaching and Educational Fair Use After Georgia State' (2015) 48 *Connecticut Law Review* 475.

Calabresi, G. and A. Melamed, 'Property Rules, Liability Rules, and Inalienability: One View of the Cathedral' (1972) 85 *Harvard Law Review* 1089.

Capell, L., 'Digitization as a Preservation Method for Damaged Acetate Negatives: A Case Study' (2010) 73 *The American Archivist* 235.

Carrier, M., 'Cabining Intellectual Property through a Property Paradigm' (2004) 54 *Duke Law Journal* 1.

Carroll, M., 'Fixing Fair Use' (2007) 85 *North Carolina Law Review* 1087.

Chapdelaine, P., 'The Property Attributes of Copyright' (2014) 10 *Buffalo Intellectual Property Law Journal* 34.

Copyright User Rights: Contracts and the Erosion of Property (Oxford: Oxford University Press, 2017).

Christie, A., 'Making It Simple: How Copyright Legislation Can Be Simplified' (2011) 6 *New Zealand Intellectual Property Journal* 783.

'Maximising Permissible Exceptions to Intellectual Property Rights' in A. Kur and V. Mizaras (eds), *The Structure of Intellectual Property Law: Can One Size Fit All?* (Cheltenham: Edward Elgar, 2011).

Cloonan, M., 'W(h)ither Preservation?' (2001) 71 *The Library Quarterly: Information, Community, Policy* 231.

Coase, R., 'The Problem of Social Cost' (1960) 3 *Journal of Law & Economics* 1.

Cohen, J., 'What Kind of Property Is Intellectual Property?' (2014) 52 *Houston Law Review* 691.

Conrad, S., 'Analog, the Sequel: An Analysis of Current Film Archiving Practice and Hesitance to Embrace Digital Preservation' (2012) 34 *Archival Issues* 27.

Conway, P., 'Overview: Rationale for Digitization and Preservation' in M. Sitts (ed), *Handbook for Digital Projects: A Management Tool for Preservation and Access* (Andover, MA: Northeast Document Conservation Center, 2000).

Cooter, R., 'Expressive Law and Economics' (1998) 27 *Journal of Legal Studies* 585.

Corbett, S., 'Copyright Norms and Flexibilities and the Digitisation Practices of New Zealand Museums' (2013) 29 *Law in Context: A Socio-Legal Journal* 55.

Cornish, G., 'The New United Kingdom Copyright Act and Its Implications for Libraries and Archives' (1991) 83 *Law Library Journal* 51.
Cornish, W., D. Llewellyn and T. Aplin, *Intellectual Property: Patents, Copyright, Trade Marks and Allied Rights*, 8th edition (London: Sweet & Maxwell, 2013).
Cowan, T., 'Rule or Standard in Tort Law' (1955) 13 *Rutgers Law Review* 141.
Craig, C., 'The Changing Face of Fair Dealing in Canadian Copyright Law: A Proposal for Legislative Reform' in M. Geist (ed), *In the Public Interest: The Future of Canadian Copyright Law* (Toronto: Irwin Law, 2005).
  'Globalizing User Rights-Talk: On Copyright Limits and Rhetorical Risks' (2017) 33 *American University International Law Review* 1.
Crews, K., *Copyright, Fair Use, and the Challenge for Universities: Promoting the Progress of Higher Education* (Chicago: University of Chicago Press, 1993).
  'Electronic Reserves and Fair Use: The Outer Limits of CONFU' (1999) 50 (14) *Journal of the American Society for Information Science* 1342.
  Copyright Law for Librarians and Educators: Creative Strategies and Practical Solutions, 2nd edition (Chicago: American Library Association, 2006).
  'Museum Policies and Art Images: Conflicting Objectives and Copyright Overreaching' (2012) 22 Fordham Intellectual Property, *Media & Entertainment Law Journal* 795.
Dagan, H., 'Property and the Public Domain' (2006) 18 Supplement *Yale Journal of Law and the Humanities* 84.
D'Agostino, G., 'Healing Fair Dealing? A Comparative Analysis of Canada's Fair Dealing to U.K. Fair Dealing and U.S. Fair Use' (2008) 53 *McGill Law Journal* 309.
Dalton, J., 'Electronic Reserves and the Copyright Challenge in Canada' (2007) 17 *Journal of Interlibrary Loan, Document Delivery & Electronic Reserve* 97.
Davison, M., A. Monotti and L. Wiseman, *Australian Intellectual Property Law*, 3rd edition (Melbourne: Cambridge University Press, 2016).
Deazley, R., 'Copyright and Parody: Taking Backward the Gowers Review?' (2010) 73 *Modern Law Review* 785.
de Beer, J. and M. Bouchard, *Canada's "Orphan Works" Regime: Unlocatable Copyright Owners and the Copyright Board* (1 December 2009).
Depoorter, B., 'Technology and Uncertainty: The Shaping Effect on Copyright Law' (2009) 157 *University of Pennsylvania Law Review* 1831.
Dewey, J., *Theory of the Moral Life (1932)* (New York: Irvington Publishers, 1996).
de Zwart, M., 'A Historical Analysis of the Birth of Fair Dealing and Fair Use: Lessons for the Digital Age' [2007] 1 *Intellectual Property Quarterly* 60.
  'The Copyright Amendment Act 2006: The New Copyright Exceptions' (2007) 25 *Copyright Reporter* 4.
Di Valentino, L., 'Laying the Foundation for Copyright Policy and Practice in Canadian Universities' (PhD Thesis, The University of Western Ontario, 2016) https://ir.lib.uwo.ca/etd/4312.

Dias Pereira, A., 'Levies in EU Copyright Law: An Overview of the CJEU's Judgments on the Fair Compensation of Private Copying and Reprography' (2017) 12 *Journal of Intellectual Property Law & Practice* 591.

Dinwoodie, G. and R. Dreyfuss, *A Neofederalist Vision of TRIPS* (New York: Oxford University Press, 2012).

Drassinower, A., 'Taking User Rights Seriously' in M. Geist (ed), *In the Public Interest: The Future of Canadian Copyright Law* (Toronto: Irwin Law, 2005).

'Exceptions Properly So-Called' in A. Drassinower and Y. Gendreau (eds), *Language and Copyright* (Montréal: Carswell, 2010).

Duxbury, N., *Patterns of American Jurisprudence* (Oxford: Clarendon Press, 1997).

Dworkin, G., 'Reports of Committees: The Whitford Committee Report on Copyright and Designs Law' (1977) 40 *Modern Law Review* 685.

Ehrlich, I. and R. Posner, 'An Economic Analysis of Legal Rulemaking' (1974) 3 *The Journal of Legal Studies* 257.

Elkin-Koren, N. and O. Fischman-Afori, 'Rulifying Fair Use' (2017) 59 *Arizona Law Review* 161.

Ellickson, R., *Order without Law: How Neighbors Settle Disputes* (Cambridge: Harvard University Press, 1991).

'Law and Economics Discovers Social Norms' (1998) 27 *Journal of Legal Studies* 537.

Fagundes, D., 'Crystals in the Public Domain' (2009) 50 *Boston College Law Review* 139.

Favale, M., M. Kretschmer and P. Torremans, 'Is There an EU Copyright Jurisprudence? An Empirical Analysis of the Workings of the European Court of Justice' (2016) 79 *Modern Law Review* 31.

Ficsor, M., *Collective Management of Copyright and Related Rights* (Geneva: World Intellectual Property Organization, 2002).

The Law of Copyright and the Internet (Oxford: Oxford University Press, 2002).

Fisher III, W., 'Reconstructing the Fair Use Doctrine' (1988) 101 *Harvard Law Review* 1659.

Fitzgerald, B., 'Underlying Rationales of Fair Use: Simplifying the Copyright Act' (1998) 2 *Southern Cross University Law Review* 153.

Fox, H., *The Canadian Law of Copyright* (The University of Toronto Press, 1944).

The Canadian Law of Copyright and Industrial Designs, 2nd edition (Carswell Company Limited, 1967).

Fraser, M., 'Fair Is Foul and Foul Is Fair: From Analogue to Digital Fair Dealing' (1998) 9 *Journal of Law and Information Science* 93.

Füller, J., 'Article 13 Limitations and Exceptions' in P. Stoll, J. Busche and K. Arend (eds), *WTO—Trade-Related Aspects of Intellectual Property Rights* (Leiden: Brill, 2009).

Gangjee, D. and R. Burrell, 'Because You're Worth It: *L'Oréal* and the Prohibition on Free Riding' (2010) 73 *Modern Law Review* 282.

Garnett, K., 'Copyright in Photographs' (2000) 22 *European Intellectual Property Review* 229.

Gasaway, L., 'Library Reserve Collections: From Paper to Electronic Collections' in L. Gasaway (ed), *Growing Pains: Adapting Copyright for Libraries, Education, and Society* (Littleton: Fred B. Rothman & Co, 1997).

'Values Conflict in the Digital Environment: Libraries versus Copyright Holders' (2000) 24 *Columbia-VLA Journal of Law and the Arts* 115.

'Libraries, Digital Content, and Copyright' (2010) 12 *Vanderbilt Journal of Entertainment and Technology Law* 755.

'Libraries and Copyright at the Dawn of the Twentieth Century: The 1909 Copyright Act' (2010) 11 *North Carolina Journal of Law & Technology* 419.

Geiger, C., 'From Berne to National Law, Via the Copyright Directive: The Dangerous Mutations of the Three-Step Test' (2007) 29 *European Intellectual Property Review* 486.

'Promoting Creativity through Copyright Limitations: Reflections on the Concept of Exclusivity in Copyright Law' (2010) 12 *Vanderbilt Journal of Entertainment and Technology Law* 515.

Geiger, C., D. Gervais and M. Senftleben, 'The Three-Step Test Revisited: How to Use the Test's Flexibility in National Copyright Law' (2014) 29 *American University International Law Review* 581.

Geiger, C., J. Griffiths and R. Hilty, 'Towards a Balanced Interpretation of the "Three-Step Test" in Copyright Law' (2008) 30 *European Intellectual Property Review* 489.

Geist, M., 'Fairness Found: How Canada Quietly Shifted from Fair Dealing to Fair Use' in M. Geist (ed), *The Copyright Pentalogy: How the Supreme Court of Canada Shook the Foundations of Canadian Copyright Law* (Ottawa: University of Ottawa Press, 2013).

Gervais, D., 'Collective Management of Copyright and Neighbouring Rights in Canada: An International Perspective' (2002) 1 *Canadian Journal of Law and Technology* 21.

'Canadian Copyright Law Post-*CCH*' (2004) 18 *Intellectual Property Journal* 131.

'A Uniquely Canadian Institution: The Copyright Board of Canada' in Y. Gendreau, *An Emerging Intellectual Property Paradigm: Perspectives from Canada* (Cheltenham: Edward Elgar, 2008).

'Fair Use, Fair Dealing, Fair Principles: Efforts to Conceptualize Exceptions and Limitations to Copyright' (2010) 57 *Journal of the Copyright Society of the USA* 499.

'Collective Management of Copyright: Theory and Practice in the Digital Age' in D. Gervais (ed), *Collective Management of Copyright and Related Rights*, 3rd edition (Alphen aan den Rijn: Wolters Kluwer, 2015).

Giblin, R., 'Stranded in the Technological Dark Ages: Implications of the Full Federal Court's Decision in *NRL v Optus*' (2012) 34 *European Intellectual Property Review* 632.

Gibson, J., 'Risk Aversion and Rights Accretion in Intellectual Property Law' (2007) 116 *Yale Law Journal* 882.

Ginsburg, J., 'Toward Supranational Copyright Law? The WTO Panel Decision and the "Three-Step Test" for Copyright Exceptions' (2001) 187 *Revue Internationale du Droit D'Auteur* 3.

'Legal Protection of Technological Measures Protecting Works of Authorship: International Obligations and the US Experience' (2005) 29 *Columbia Journal of Law and the Arts* 11.

Goebel, J., 'Rules and Standards: A Critique of Two Critical Theorists' (1992) 31 *Duquesne Law Review* 51.

Goldstein, P., 'Copyright's Commons' (2005) 29 *Columbia Journal of Law and the Arts* 1.

'Fair Use in Context' (2008) 31 *Columbia Journal of Law and the Arts* 433

Goldstein on Copyright Volume II (New York: Aspen Publishers, 2008).

Gordon, W., 'Fair Use as Market Failure: A Structural and Economic Analysis of the Betamax Case and Its Predecessors' (1982) 82 *Columbia Law Review* 1600.

'A Property Right in Self-Expression: Equality and Individualism in the Natural Law of Intellectual Property' (1993) 102 *Yale Law Journal* 1533.

'On the Economics of Copyright, Restitution, and "Fair Use": Systematic Versus Case-by-Case Responses to Market Failure' (1997) 8 *Journal of Law and Information Science* 7.

'Excuse and Justification in the Law of Fair Use: Commodification and Market Perspectives' in N. Elkin-Koren and N. Netanel (eds), *The Commodification of Information* (The Hague: Kluwer Law International, 2002).

'The "Why" of Markets: Fair Use and Circularity' (2007) 116 *Yale Law Journal Pocket Part* 358.

Gould, T., T. Lipinski and E. Buchanan, 'Copyright Policies and the Deciphering of Fair Use in the Creation of Reserves at University Libraries' (2005) 31 *Journal of Academic Librarianship* 182.

Gracy, K., 'Ambition and Ambivalence: A Study of Professional Attitudes towards Digital Distribution of Archival Moving Images' (2013) 76 *The American Archivist* 346.

'The Evolution and Integration of Moving Image Preservation Work into Cultural Heritage Institutions' (2013) 48 *Information & Culture* 368.

Griffiths, J., 'Preserving Judicial Freedom of Movement – Interpreting Fair Dealing in Copyright Law' [2000] *Intellectual Property Quarterly* 164.

'The "Three-Step Test" in European Copyright Law: Problems and Solutions' [2009] *Intellectual Property Quarterly* 428.

'Fair Dealing after Deckmyn – The United Kingdom's Defence for Caricature, Parody or Pastiche' in M. Richardson and S. Ricketson (eds), *Research Handbook on Intellectual Property in Media and Entertainment* (Cheltenham: Edward Elgar 2017).

Guibault, L. and S. Schroff, 'Extended Collective Licensing for the Use of Out-of-Commerce Works in Europe: A Matter of Legitimacy vis-a-vis Rights Holders' (2018) 49 *International Review of Intellectual Property and Competition Law* 916.

Haight Farley, C., 'No Comment: Will *Cariou v. Prince* Alter Copyright Judges' Taste in Art?' (2015) 5 *IP Theory* 19.

Handler, M., 'Continuing Problems with Film Copyright' in F. Macmillan (ed), *New Directions in Copyright Law, Volume 6* (Cheltenham: Edward Elgar, 2007).

Handler, M. and E. Hudson, 'Fair Use as an Advance on Fair Dealing? Depolarising the Debate' in H. Sun, S. Balganesh and W. Ng-Loy (eds), *Comparative Aspects of Limitations and Exceptions in Copyright Law* (New York: Cambridge University Press, forthcoming).

Handler, M. and D. Rolph, '"A Real Pea Souper": *The Panel Case* and the Development of the Fair Dealing Defences to Copyright Infringement in Australia' (2003) 27 *Melbourne University Law Review* 381.

Harris, L., *Canadian Copyright Law*, 3rd edition (Toronto: McGraw-Hill, 2001).

Hazucha, B., 'Private Copying and Harm to Authors – Compensation versus Remuneration' (2017) 133 *Law Quarterly Review* 269.

Hedstrom, M., 'Digital Preservation: A Time Bomb for Digital Libraries' (1998) 31 *Computers and the Humanities* 189.

Helberger, N. and P. Hugenholtz, 'No Place Like Home for Making a Copy: Private Copying in European Copyright Law and Consumer Law' (2007) 22 *Berkeley Technology Law Journal* 1061.

Helfer, L., 'World Music on a U.S. Stage: A Berne/TRIPS and Economic Analysis of the Fairness in Music Licensing Act' (2000) 80 *Boston University Law Review* 93.

Heymann, L., 'Everything Is Transformative: Fair Use and Reader Response' (2008) 31 *Columbia Journal of Law and the Arts* 445.

Hirtle, P., 'Research, Libraries, and Fair Use: The Gentlemen's Agreement of 1935' (2006) 53 *Journal of the Copyright Society of the USA* 545.

'The History and Current State of Digital Preservation in the United States' in *Metadata and Digital Collections: A Festschrift in Honor of Thomas P. Turner* (Cornell University Library, online resource).

Hohfeld, W., 'Some Fundamental Legal Conceptions as Applied in Legal Reasoning' (1913) 23 *Yale Law Journal* 16.

Holmes, O., 'The Path of the Law' (1897) 10 *Harvard Law Review* 457.

Hudson, E., 'Copyright and Publicly Located Artistic Works: The End of an Exception?' (2006) 19 *Intellectual Property Law Bulletin* 106.

'The Copyright Amendment Act 2006: The Scope and Likely Impact of New Library Exceptions' (2006) 14 *Australian Law Librarian* 25.

'Copyright Exceptions: The Experiences of Cultural Institutions in the United States, Canada and Australia' (PhD Thesis, University of Melbourne, November 2011).

'Implementing Fair Use in Copyright Law: Lessons from Australia' (2013) 25 *Intellectual Property Journal* 201.

'*Phillips v Mulcaire*: A Property Paradox' in S. Douglas, R. Hickey and E. Waring (eds), *Landmark Cases in Property Law* (Oxford: Hart, 2015).

'The Pastiche Exception in Copyright Law: A Case of Mashed-Up Drafting?' [2017] *Intellectual Property Quarterly* 346.

'The Georgia State Litigation: Literal Copying in Education' (2019) 82 *Modern Law Review* 508.

'Copyright and Invisible Authors: A Property Perspective' in A. Johnston and L. Talbot (eds), *Great Debates in Critical Commercial and Corporate Law* (Basingstoke: Palgrave, forthcoming).

Hudson E., and Burrell, R., 'Abandonment, Copyright and Orphaned Works: What Does It Mean to Take the Proprietary Nature of Intellectual Property Rights Seriously?' (2011) 35 *Melbourne University Law Review* 971.

Hudson, E. and A. Kenyon, 'Communication in the Digital Environment: An Empirical Study into Copyright Law and Digitisation Practices in Public Museums, Galleries and Libraries' (Working Paper No 15/05, Intellectual Property Research Institute of Australia, July 2005).

Copyright and Cultural Institutions: Guidelines for Digitisation (Melbourne: University of Melbourne, 2005).

'Digital Access: The Impact of Copyright on Digitisation Practices in Australian Museums, Galleries, Libraries and Archives' (2007) 30 *University of New South Wales Law Journal* 12.

'Without Walls: Copyright Law and Digital Collections in Australian Cultural Institutions' (2007) 4 *SCRIPTed* 197.

Hugenholtz, P., 'Flexible Copyright: Can the EU Author's Rights Accommodate Fair Use' in R. Okediji (ed), *Copyright Law in an Age of Limitations and Exceptions* (New York: Cambridge University Press, 2017).

Hughes, J., 'Fair Use Across Time' (2003) 50 *UCLA Law Review* 775.

'The Photographer's Copyright – Photograph as Art, Photograph as Database' (2012) 25 *Harvard Journal of Law & Technology* 339.

'Fair Use and Its Politics – at Home and Abroad' in R. Okediji (ed), *Copyright Law in an Age of Limitations and Exceptions* (New York: Cambridge University Press, 2017).

Hughes, R., 'Evolution of the Concept of Fair Dealing in Canadian Copyright Law' (2008) 26 *Copyright Reporter* 44.

Hunter, D., 'American Lessons: Implementing Fair Use in Australia' (2014) 24 *Australian Intellectual Property Journal* 192.

Iljadica, M., *Copyright Beyond Law: Regulating Creativity in the Graffiti Subculture* (Oxford: Hart, 2016).

'Copyright and the Right to the City' (2017) 68 *Northern Island Legal Quarterly* 59.

Jacques, S., 'Are National Courts Required to Have an (Exceptional) European Sense of Humour?' (2015) 37 *European Intellectual Property Review* 134.

Jaszi, P., 'Copyright, Fair Use and Motion Pictures' (2007) *Utah Law Review* 715.

Johns, A., *Piracy: The Intellectual Property Wars from Gutenberg to Gates* (Chicago: University of Chicago Press, 2009).

Kalimo, H., T. Meyer and T. Mylly, 'Of Values and Legitimacy – Discourse Analytical Insights on the Copyright Case Law of the Court of Justice of the European Union' (2018) 81 *Modern Law Review* 282.

Kaplow, L., 'Rules versus Standards: An Economic Analysis' (1992) 42 *Duke Law Journal* 557.

'A Model of the Optimal Complexity of Legal Rules' (1995) 11 *Journal of Law, Economics & Organization* 150.

Kaplow, L. and S. Shavell, 'Property Rules versus Liability Rules: An Economic Analysis' (1996) 109 *Harvard Law Review* 713.

Katz, A., 'Spectre: Canadian Copyright and the Mandatory Tariff – Part I' (2015) 27 *Intellectual Property Journal* 151.

'Spectre: Canadian Copyright and the Mandatory Tariff – Part II' (2015) 28 *Intellectual Property Journal* 39.

Kennedy, D., 'Form and Substance in Private Law Adjudication' (1976) 89 *Harvard Law Review* 1685.

Kenyon, A. and E. Hudson, 'Copyright, Digitisation and Cultural Institutions' (2004) 31 *Australian Journal of Communication* 89.

Kenyon, A. and R. Wright, 'Whose Conflict? Copyright, Creators and Cultural Institutions' (2010) 33 *UNSW Law Journal* 286.

Knopf, H., 'Limits on the Nature and Scope of Copyright' in G. Henderson (ed), *Copyright and Confidential Information Law of Canada* (Toronto: Carswell, 1994).

Koelman, K., 'Fixing the Three Step Test' (2006) 28 *European Intellectual Property Review* 407.

Kogan, T., 'Photographic Reproductions, Copyright and the Slavish Copy' (2012) 35 *Columbia Journal of Law and the Arts* 445.

Korobkin, R., 'Behavioral Analysis and Legal Form: Rules vs. Standards Revisited' (2000) 79 *Oregon Law Review* 23.

Korobkin, R. and T. Ulen, 'Law and Behavioral Science: Removing the Rationality Assumption from Law and Economics' (2000) 88 *California Law Review* 1051.

Laddie, H., 'Copyright: Over-Strength, Over-Regulated, Over-Rated?' (1996) 18 *European Intellectual Property Review* 253.

Lahore, J., 'Photocopying in Australian Libraries: Developments in Copyright Law' (1976) 4 *International Journal of Law Libraries* 32.

Landes, W. and R. Posner, 'An Economic Analysis of Copyright Law' (1989) 18 *Journal of Legal Studies* 325.

Laughlin, G., 'Digitization and Democracy: The Conflict between the Amazon Kindle License Agreement and the Role of Libraries in a Free Society' (2010) 40 *University of Baltimore Law Review* 3.

Leenheer Zimmerman, D., 'Can Our Culture Be Saved? The Future of Digital Archiving' (2007) 91 *Minnesota Law Review* 989.

Lemley, M., 'Property, Intellectual Property, and Free Riding' (2005) 83 *Texas Law Review* 1031.

'Should a Licensing Market Require Licensing?' (2007) 70 *Law and Contemporary Problems* 185.

Leval, P., 'Toward a Fair Use Standard' (1990) 103 *Harvard Law Review* 1105.

Lindsay, D., 'Fair Use and Other Copyright Exceptions: Overview of Issues' (2005) 23 *Copyright Reporter* 4.

Litman, J., 'Copyright, Compromise, and Legislative History' (1987) 72 *Cornell Law Review* 857.

'Copyright Legislation and Technological Change' (1989) 68 *Oregon Law Review* 275.

'Copyright as Myth' (1991) 53 *University of Pittsburgh Law Review* 235.

'Revising Copyright Law for the Information Age' (1996) 75 *Oregon Law Review* 19.

Loring, C., 'Library Reserves and Copyright: Thirty Years on and Still Changing' (1997) 21 *Library Acquisitions: Practice & Theory* 29.

Lunney, G., 'Copyright Collectives and Collecting Societies: The United States Experience' in D. Gervais (ed), *Collective Management of Copyright and Related Rights*, 3rd edition (Alphen aan den Rijn: Wolters Kluwer, 2015).

Madison, M., 'Rewriting Fair Use and the Future of Copyright Reform' (2005) 23 *Cardozo Arts & Entertainment Law Journal* 391.

Malaro, M., and I. DeAngelis, *A Legal Primer on Managing Museum Collections*, 3rd edition (Washington, DC: Smithsonian Books, 2012).

Matz, R., '*Bridgeman Art Library, Ltd* v *Corel Corp*' (2000) 15 *Berkeley Technology Law Journal* 3.

Matusiak, K. and T. Johnston, 'Digitization for Preservation and Access: Restoring the Usefulness of the Nitrate Negative Collections at the American Geographical Society Library' (2014) 77 *The American Archivist* 241.

Marshall, D., 'Access to the Law: Should Copyright Play a Role?' in H. Knopf (ed), *The New Copyright Act: Managing the Impact* (Toronto: Insight Press, 1997).

Maurice Hyam, G., 'The Working Paper on Copyright: A Preliminary Response' (Summer 1977) 4 *Archivaria* 188.

McAdams, R., 'The Origin, Development, and Regulation of Norms' (1997) 96 *Michigan Law Review* 338.

 'Beyond the Prisoners' Dilemma: Coordination, Game Theory, and Law' (2009) 82 *Southern California Law Review* 209.

McCutcheon, J., and Holloway, S., 'Whose Fair Dealing? Third-Party Reliance on the Fair Dealing Exception for Parody or Satire' (2016) 27 *Australian Intellectual Property Journal* 54.

McKeown, J., *Fox Canadian Law of Copyright and Industrial Designs*, 3rd edition (Toronto: Carswell, 2000).

Melamut, S., 'Pursuing Fair Use, Law Libraries, and Electronic Reserves' (2000) 92 *Law Library Journal* 157.

Menell, P., 'Knowledge Accessibility and Preservation Policy for the Digital Age' (2007) 44 *Houston Law Review* 1013.

Merges, R., 'Are You Making Fun of Me: Notes on Market Failure and the Parody Defense in Copyright' (1993) 21 *AIPLA Quarterly Journal* 305.

Minow, M. and T. Lipinski, *The Library's Legal Answer Book* (Chicago: American Library Association, 2003).

Morrison, C., 'Illustration for Instruction and the UK Higher Education Sector' (MA dissertation, King's College London, 2018).

Mossoff, A., 'Is Copyright Property?' (2005) 42 *San Diego Law Review* 29.

Mumford, M., 'Copyright in Canadian Archives: An Evolving Challenge' (2006) 31 *Canadian Law Library Review* 238.

Murray, L. and S. Trosow, *Canadian Copyright: A Citizen's Guide* (Toronto: Between the Lines, 2007).

Murray, L., S. Piper and K. Robertson, *Putting Intellectual Property in Its Place: Rights Discourses, Creative Labor, and the Everyday* (New York: Oxford University Press, 2014).

Netanel, N., 'Copyright and a Democratic Civil Society' (1996) 106 *Yale Law Journal* 283.
  'The Next Round: The Impact of the WIPO Copyright Treaty on TRIPS Dispute Settlement' (1997) 37 *Virginia Journal of International Law* 441.
  'Making Sense of Fair Use' (2011) 15 *Lewis & Clark Law Review* 715.
Nimmer, D., '"Fairest of Them All" and Other Fairy Tales of Fair Use' (2003) 66 *Law and Contemporary Problems* 263.
Nimmer, M., and D. Nimmer, *Nimmer on Copyright* (LexisNexis, online resource).
Nordemann, W., K. Vinck, P. Hertin and G. Meyer, *International Copyright and Neighbouring Rights Law* (Weinheim: VCH, 1990).
Oakley, R., 'Preservation and Copyright' in L. Gasaway (ed), *Growing Pains: Adapting Copyright for Libraries, Education, and Society* (Littleton, Colorado: Fred B. Rothman & Co, 1997).
Okediji, R., 'Towards an International Fair Use Doctrine' (2000) 39 *Columbia Journal of Transnational Law* 75.
Oliver, J., 'Copyright in the WTO: The Panel Decision and the Three-Step Test' (2002) 25 *Columbia Journal of Law and the Arts* 119.
Ong, B., 'Fissures in the Façade of Fair Dealing: Users' Rights in Works Protected by Copyright' [2004] *Singapore Journal of Legal Studies* 150.
Owen, V., 'The Librarian's Perspective on Collecting Societies' (Paper presented at the World Library and Information Congress: 73rd IFLA General Conference and Council, Durban, South Africa, 19–23 August 2007).
Padfield, T., *Copyright for Archivists and Users of Archives*, 2nd edition (London: Facet Publishing, 2004).
Pallante, M., 'Orphan Works & Mass Digitization: Obstacles & Opportunities' (2012) 27 *Berkeley Technology Law Journal* 1251.
Pallas Loren, L., 'Redefining the Market Failure Approach to Fair Use in an Era of Copyright Permission Systems' (1997) 5 *Journal of Intellectual Property Law* 1.
Pantalony, R., *Illustrating Options: Collective Administration of Intellectual Property for Canadian Cultural Heritage Institutions* (Canadian Heritage Information Network, 1999).
Patry, W., *The Fair Use Privilege in Copyright Law*, 2nd edition (Washington, DC: BNA Books, 1995).
  Patry on Copyright, Volume 4 (Thomson Reuters, online resource, updated to March 2018).
Patterson, L., 'Free Speech, Copyright, and Fair Use' (1987) 40 *Vanderbilt Law Review* 1.
  '*Folsom v Marsh* and Its Legacy' (1998) 5 *Journal of Intellectual Property Law* 431.
Patterson, L. and S. Lindberg, *The Nature of Copyright: A Law of Users' Rights* (Athens: University of Georgia Press, 1991).
Pessach, G., 'Museums, Digitization and Copyright Law: Taking Stock and Looking Ahead' (2007) 1 *Journal of International Media & Entertainment Law* 253.
Petri, G., 'Copyright and Reproductions of Two-Dimensional Works of Art' (2014) 12 *Journal of Conservation and Museum Studies*.

Pila, J., 'Pluralism, Principles and Proportionality in Intellectual Property' (2014) 34 *Oxford Journal of Legal Studies* 182.

Pila, J. and P. Torremans, *European Intellectual Property Law* (Oxford: Oxford University Press 2016).

Posner, R., 'When Is Parody Fair Use?' (1992) 21 *Journal of Legal Studies* 67.

Posner, E., 'Standards, Rules, and Social Norms' (1997) 21 *Harvard Journal of Law and Public Policy* 101.

Law and Social Norms (Cambridge: Harvard University Press, 2000).

Pound, R., 'Hierarchy of Sources and Forms in Different Systems of Law' (1933) 7 *Tulane Law Review* 475.

Purday, J., 'Intellectual Property Issues and Europeana, Europe's Digital Library, Museum and Archive' (2010) 10 *Legal Information Management* 174.

Reese, A., 'Photographs of Public Domain Paintings: How, If at All, Should We Protect Them' (2009) 34 *Journal of Corporation Law* 1033.

Reese, R., 'The Story of Folsom v. Marsh: Distinguishing between Infringing and Legitimate Uses' in R. Dreyfuss and J. Ginsburg (eds), *Intellectual Property Stories* (New York: Foundation Press, 2006).

'Transformativeness and the Derivative Work Right' (2008) 31 *Columbia Journal of Law and the Arts* 467.

Ricketson, S., 'Simplifying Copyright Law: Proposals from Down Under' (1999) 21 *European Intellectual Property Review* 537.

Rendas, T., 'Advocate General Szpunar in Spiegel Online (or Why We Need Fair Use in the EU)' (2019) 14 *Journal of Intellectual Property Law & Practice* 265.

Ricketson, S. and C. Creswell, *Law of Intellectual Property: Copyright, Design and Confidential Information* (Legal Online, electronic resource).

Ricketson, S. and J. Ginsburg, *International Copyright and Neighbouring Rights: The Berne Convention and Beyond Volume I*, 2nd edition (Oxford: Oxford University Press, 2006).

Rieger, O., *Preservation in the Age of Large-Scale Digitization: A White Paper* (February 2008).

Rimmer, M., 'Canadian Rhapsody: Copyright Law and Research Libraries' (2004) 35 *Australian Academic & Research Libraries* 193.

Rosati, E., 'CJEU says that Member States May Grant Public Libraries the Right to Digitize Works in Their Collections' (2015) 10 *Journal of Intellectual Property Law & Practice* 6.

Copyright in the EU: In Search of (in)flexibilities' (2014) 9 *Journal of Intellectual Property Law & Practice* 585.

Rose, C., 'Crystals and Mud in Property Law' (1988) 40 *Stanford Law Review* 577.

Rothman, J., 'The Questionable Use of Custom in Intellectual Property Law' (2007) 93 *Virginia Law Review* 1899.

Russell, C., *Complete Copyright: An Everyday Guide for Librarians* (Chicago: American Library Association, 2004).

Sag, M., 'God in the Machine: A New Structural Analysis of Copyright's Fair Use Doctrine' (2005) 11 *Michigan Telecommunications and Technology Law Review* 381.

'The Google Book Settlement and the Fair Use Counterfactual' (2010/11) 55 *New York Law School Law Review* 19.

'Predicting Fair Use' (2012) 73 *Ohio State Law Journal* 47.
Samuelson, P., 'Unbundling Fair Uses' (2009) 77 *Fordham Law Review* 2537.
'Possible Future of Fair Use' (2015) 90 *Washington Law Review* 815.
'Justifications for Copyright Limitations and Exceptions' in R. Okediji, *Copyright Law in an Age of Limitations and Exceptions* (New York: Cambridge University Press, 2017).
'The Relative Virtues of Bottom-Up and Top-Down Theories of Fair Use' (2017) 83 *University of Chicago Law Review Online* 206.
Scassa, T., 'Recalibrating Copyright Law? A Comment on the Supreme Court of Canada's Decision in *CCH Canadian Limited et al v Law Society of Upper Canada*' (2004) 3 *Canadian Journal of Law & Technology* 89.
Schlag, P., 'Rules and Standards' (1985) 33 *UCLA Law Review* 379.
Seale, C., 'Validity, Reliability and the Quality of Research' in Clive Seale (ed) *Researching Society and Culture* (London: Sage Publications, 2nd edition, 2004).
Senftleben, M. *Copyright, Limitations and the Three-Step Test: An Analysis of the Three-Step Test in International and EC Copyright Law* (The Hague: Kluwer Law International, 2004).
'The Perfect Match: Civil Law Judges and Open-Ended Fair Use Provisions' (2017) 33 *American University International Law Review* 231.
Sherman, B. and L. Bently, *The Making of Modern Intellectual Property Law* (Cambridge: Cambridge University Press, 2002).
Sherman, B. and L. Wiseman, 'Fair Copy: Protecting Access to Scientific Information in Post-War Britain' (2010) 73 *Modern Law Review* 240.
Sims, A., 'Abundant Pest or Endangered Species? The Future of Fair Dealing in Copyright Law' (2008) 14 *New Zealand Business Law Quarterly* 231.
'Strangling Their Creation: The Courts' Treatment of Fair Dealing in Copyright Law Since 1911' [2010] *Intellectual Property Quarterly* 192.
Singh, S., M. Blake and J. O'Donnell, 'Digitizing Pacific Cultural Collections: The Australian Experience' (2013) 20 *International Journal of Cultural Property* 77.
Sites, B., 'Fair Use and the New Transformative' (2016) 39 *Columbia Journal of Law and the Arts* 513.
Skone James, F., and Skone James, E., (eds), *Copinger and Skone James on the Law of Copyright*, 9th edition (London: Sweet & Maxwell, 1958).
Spence, M., 'Intellectual Property and the Problem of Parody' (1998) 114 *Law Quarterly Review* 594.
Intellectual Property (Oxford: Oxford University Press, 2007).
Spence, M. and T. Endicott, 'Vagueness in the Scope of Copyright' (2005) 121 *Law Quarterly Review* 657.
Sterk, S., 'Intellectualizing Property: The Tenuous Connections between Land and Copyright' (2005) 83 *Washington University Law Quarterly* 417.
'Property Rules, Liability Rules, and Uncertainty About Property Rights' (2008) 106 *Michigan Law Review* 1285.
Sterling, J., *World Copyright Law*, 3rd edition (London: Street & Maxwell, 1998).
Stewart, A., P. Griffith, J. Bannister and A. Liberman, *Intellectual Property in Australia*, 5th edition (Chatswood NSW: LexisNexis Butterworths, 2014).

Stewart, S., *International Copyright and Neighbouring Rights*, 2nd edition (London: Butterworths, 1989).
Stokes, S., '*Graves' Case* and Copyright in Photographs: *Bridgeman v. Corel (USA)*' in D. McClean and K. Schubert (eds), *Dear Images: Art, Copyright and Culture* (London: Ridinghouse and Institute of Contemporary Arts, 2002).
Sullivan, K., 'The Justices of Rules and Standards' (1992) 106 *Harvard Law Review* 22.
Sun, H., 'Copyright and Responsibility' (2013) 4 *Harvard Journal of Sports & Entertainment Law* 263.
Sunstein, C., 'Problems with Rules' (1995) 83 *California Law Review* 953.
Tamaro, N., *The Annotated Copyright Act 1992* (Toronto: Carswell, 1992).
  The 1997 Annotated Copyright Act (Toronto: Carswell, 1996).
  The 1999 Annotated Copyright Act (Toronto: Carswell, 1999).
  The 2002 Annotated Copyright Act (Toronto: Carswell, 2002).
  The 2009 Annotated Copyright Act (Toronto: Carswell, 2008).
Tamura, Y., 'Rethinking Copyright Institution for the Digital Age' (2009) 1 *WIPO Journal* 63.
The Canadian Encyclopedic Digest (Western), Fourth Edition, Volume 8, Title 35, 'Copyright' (title current to November 2008).
Trosow, S., 'Bill C-32 and the Educational Sector: Overcoming Impediments to Fair Dealing' in M. Geist (ed), *From "Radical Extremism" to "Balanced Copyright": Canadian Copyright and the Digital Agenda* (Toronto: Irwin Law, 2010).
Trosow, S., S. Armstrong and B. Harasym, 'Objections to the Proposed Access Copyright Post-Secondary Tariff and Its Progeny Licenses: A Working Paper' (14 August 2012).
Tushnet, R., 'Copy This Essay: How Fair Use Doctrine Harms Free Speech and How Copying Serves It' (2004) 114 *Yale Law Journal* 535.
Vanderschraaf, P., 'The Informal Game Theory in Hume's Account of Convention' (1998) 14 *Economics & Philosophy* 215.
Vaver, D., *Copyright Law* (Toronto: Irwin Law, 2000).
  'Canada's Intellectual Property Framework: A Comparative Overview' (2004) 17 *Intellectual Property Journal* 125.
van Gompel, S., 'Formalities in the Digital Era: An Obstacle or Opportunity?' in L. Bently, U. Suthersanen and P. Torremans (eds), *Global Copyright: Three Hundred Years since the Statute of Anne, from 1709 to Cyberspace* (Cheltenham: Edward Elgar, 2010).
Warner, P., 'Reserves, Electronic Reserves and Copyright in Canada' (2006) 1 *Canadian Online Library and Archives Journal*.
Weinrib, L., 'Fair's Fair: A Comment on the Fair Use Doctrine' (1990) 103 *Harvard Law Review* 1137.
Williams, M., 'Recent Second Circuit Opinions Indicate that Google's Library Project Is Not Transformative' (2007) 25 *Cardozo Arts & Entertainment Law Journal* 303.
Wiseman, L., 'Beyond the Photocopier: Copyright and Publishing in Australia' (2002) 7 *Media and Arts Law Review* 299.

Law Reform Reports and Submissions, Industry Reports and Similar

American Library Association, *Model Policy Concerning College and University Photocopying for Classroom, Research and Library Reserve Use* (1982).

Attorney-General's Department, *Fair Use and Other Copyright Exceptions: An Examination of Fair Use, Fair Dealing and Other Exceptions in the Digital Age* (May 2005).

'Major Copyright Reforms Strike Balance', Media Release 088/2006 (14 May 2006).

Australian Copyright Council (ACC), *Special Case Exception: Educations, Libraries, Collections: A Practical Guide*, B130v01 (December 2007) (text attributed to Ian McDonald).

2006 Copyright Amendments: A Practical Guide (December 2007)

Australian Law Reform Commission, *Copyright in the Digital Economy: Discussion Paper*, DP 79 (May 2013).

Copyright and the Digital Economy: Final Report, Report No. 122 (November 2013).

Australian Libraries Copyright Committee (ALCC) and the Australian Digital Alliance (ADA), *A User's Guide to the Flexible Dealing Provision for Libraries, Educational Institutions and Cultural Institutions: Section 200AB of the Copyright Act 1968 (Cth)* (2008) (text attributed to Laura Simes).

Bergström, S., 'Report on the Work of Main Committee I (Substantive Provisions of the Berne Convention: Articles 1 to 20) in WIPO, *Records of the Intellectual Property Conference of Stockholm*, Volume II (WIPO, 1971).

Bently, L., 'Exploring the Flexibilities Available to UK Law', submission to the Hargreaves Review of Intellectual Property and Growth (3 March 2011).

Besek, J., Copyright and Related Issues Relevant to Digital Preservation and Dissemination of Unpublished Pre-1972 Sound Recordings by Libraries and Archives (Council on Library and Information Resources and Library of Congress, March 2009).

Besek, J., J. Ginsburg, P. Loengard and Y. Lev-Aretz, 'Copyright Exceptions in the United States for Educational Uses of Copyrighted Works', submission in response to the ALRC Issues Paper (2012).

Burrell, R., M. Handler, E. Hudson and K. Weatherall, 'ALRC Inquiry into Copyright and the Digital Economy: Submission in response to Issues Paper No. 42' (14 December 2012).

'ALRC Inquiry into Copyright and the Digital Economy: Submission in response to Discussion Paper No. 79 (DP 79)' (31 July 2013).

Canadian Library Association, *CLA Objection to the Access Copyright Post Secondary Tariff* (27 July 2010), http://cla.ca/wp-content/uploads/CLA_Tariff_objections_jul2010_final.pdf.

Classroom Guidelines, HR Rep No 94-1467, 94th Congress, 2nd Session (1976).

Commission of the European Communities, *Proposal for a European Parliament and Council Directive on the Harmonization of Certain Aspects of Copyright and Related Rights in the Information Society*, 97/0359 (COD).

Committee to Consider the Law on Copyright and Designs (Whitford Committee), *Report on Copyright and Designs Law*, Cmnd 6732 (1977).
Copyright Committee (Gregory Committee), *Report of the Copyright Committee*, Cmd 8662 (1952).
Copyright in Cultural Institutions (CICI), *Flexible Dealing and Cultural Institutions: Statement of Principles Regarding the Use of Section 200AB of the Copyright Act (1968): An Industry Standard and User Guide for the Cultural Sector* (September 2010) (text attributed to Sarah Waladan).
Copyright Law Committee on Reprographic Reproduction (Franki Committee), *Report of the Copyright Law Committee on Reprographic Reproduction* (AGPS, 1976).
Copyright Law Review Committee (Spicer Committee), *Report of the Committee Appointed by the Attorney-General of the Commonwealth to Consider What Alterations Are Desirable in the Copyright Law of the Commonwealth* (CGP, 1959).
Copyright Law Review Committee, *Simplification of the Copyright Act 1968 Part 1: Exceptions to the Exclusive Rights of Copyright Owners* (September 1998).
Economic Council of Canada, *Report on Intellectual and Industrial Property* (Information Canada, January 1971).
Erola, J. and F. Fox, *From Gutenberg to Telidon: A White Paper on Copyright: Proposals for the Revision of the Canadian Copyright Act* (Department of Consumer and Corporate Affairs and Department of Communications, 1984).
Favale, M., F. Homberg, M. Kretschmer, D. Mendis and D. Secchi, *Copyright, and the Regulation of Orphan Works: A Comparative Review of Seven Jurisdictions and a Rights Clearance Simulation* (IPO, 2013).
Federal Cultural Policy Review Committee, *Report of the Federal Cultural Policy Review Committee* (Information Services, Department of Communications, Government of Canada, 1982).
Gowers, A., *Gowers Review of Intellectual Property* (HM Treasury 2006).
Hargreaves, I., *Digital Opportunity: A Review of Intellectual Property and Growth* (May 2011).
Hébert, M., *Copyright Act Reform* (Library of Parliament, 25 October 1982 revised 9 January 1990).
  Background Paper: Copyright Reform (Library of Parliament, March 1996).
  Bill C-32: An Act to Amend the Copyright Act (Library of Parliament, 17 May 1996 revised 21 March 1997).
Hinze, G., P. Jaszi and M. Sag, 'The Fair Use Doctrine in the United States – A Response to the Kernochan Report', submission in response to ALRC Discussion Paper 79 (26 July 2013).
House of Commons Standing Committee on Communications and Culture, Sub-Committee on the Revision of Copyright, *A Charter of Rights for Creators* (Minister of Supply and Services Canada, October 1985).
HR Report No 89-2237 (1966).
HR Report No 94-1476, 94th Congress, 2nd Session (1976).
Hudson, E., T. Aplin and R. Burrell, 'Submission to the Copyright Consultation: Department of Communications and the Arts' (4 July 2018).

Bibliography

Ilsley Report: Royal Commission on Patents, Copyright, Trade Marks and Industrial Designs, *Report on Copyright* (Queen's Printer, 1957).

Intellectual Property Office, *Exceptions to Copyright: Guidance for Creators and Copyright Owners* (IPO, 2014).

Intellectual Property Office, *Exceptions to Copyright: Libraries, Archives and Museums* (May 2014).

Joint Standing Committee on Treaties (JSCOT), Parliament of Australia, *Report 61: Australia-United States Free Trade Agreement* (23 June 2004).

Keyes, A. and C. Brunet, *Copyright in Canada: Proposals for a Revision of the Law* (Consumer and Corporate Affairs Canada, April 1977).

Latman, A., *Study No 14: Fair Use of Copyrighted Works* (March 1958), reproduced in Committee Print, 86th Congress, 2nd Session, Studies 14-16 (United States Government Printing Service, 1960).

Liberal Party of Australia, *Strengthening Australian Arts* (2004).

Library of Congress, US Copyright Office, *Library Reproduction of Copyrighted Works (17 U.S.C. 108): Report of the Register of Copyrights* (Library of Congress, 1983).

National Commission on New Technological Uses of Copyrighted Works, *Final Report of the National Commission on New Technological Uses of Copyrighted Works, July 31, 1978* (Library of Congress, 1979).

Phillips Fox, *Digital Agenda Review: Report and Recommendations* (January 2004).

Rasenberger, M. and C. Weston, 'Overview of the Libraries and Archives Exception in the Copyright Act: Background, History, and Meaning', attached as Appendix K to the Section 108 Study Group.

Register of Copyrights, *Report of the Register of Copyrights on the General Revision of the US Copyright Law*, 87th Congress, 1st Session (Comm Print, 1961).

Royal Commission on Patents, Copyright, Trade Marks and Industrial Designs ('Ilsley Report'), *Report on Copyright* (Queen's Printer, 1957).

Secker, J., E. Gadd and C. Morrison, *Understanding the Value of the CLA Licence to UK Higher Education* (Universities UK/Guild HE Copyright Negotiation and Advisory Committee, July 2019).

Second reading speech of the Attorney-General: Commonwealth, *Parliamentary Debates*, House of Representatives, 19 October 2006 (Philip Ruddock).

Section 108 Study Group, *The Section 108 Study Group Report: An Independent Report sponsored by the United States Copyright Office and the National Digital Information Infrastructure and Preservation Program of the Library of Congress* (March 2008).

Senate Select Committee on the Free Trade Agreement between Australia and the United States of America, Parliament of Australia, *Final Report on the Free Trade Agreement between Australia and the United States of America* (5 August 2004).

Torno, B., *Fair Dealing: The Need for Conceptual Clarity on the Road to Copyright Revision* (Consumer and Corporate Affairs, 1981).

Varmer, B., *Study No 15: Photoduplication of Copyrighted Material by Libraries* (May 1959), reproduced in Committee Print, 86th Congress, 2nd Session, Studies 14–16 (United States Government Printing Service, 1960).

Bibliography 367

United States Copyright Office, *Report on Orphan Works: A Report of the Register of Copyrights* (Washington DC: Library of Congress, 2006).
Orphan Works and Mass Digitization: A Report of the Register of Copyrights (United States Copyright Office, June 2015).
Section 1201 of Title 17: A Report of the Register of Copyrights (United States Copyright Office, June 2017).
Section 108 of Title 17: A Discussion Document of the Register of Copyrights (United States Copyright Office, September 2017).
WIPO, *Records of the Intellectual Property Conference of Stockholm*, Volume 1 (Geneva: WIPO, 1971).

Newspaper Articles, Blog Posts and Similar

Albanese, A., 'GSU Prevails (Again) in Key Copyright Case', *Publishers Weekly* (1 April 2016), www.publishersweekly.com/pw/by-topic/digital/copyright/article/69830-gsu-prevails-again-in-key-copyright-case.html.
Austin, G. and E. Hudson, 'Why the Not-for-Profit Cultural Sector Needs Tailor-Made Copyright Safe Harbours', *The Conversation* (13 February 2018), http://theconversation.com/why-the-not-for-profit-cultural-sector-needs-tailor-made-copyright-safe-harbours-89564.
Beck B., and von Werder, K. 'German Federal Court of Justice Confirms Copyright in Photographs of Public Domain Paintings', *All About IP* (21 March 2019), www.allaboutipblog.com/2019/03/german-federal-court-of-justice-confirms-copyright-in-photographs-of-public-domain-paintings/.
Berkowitz, P., 'Majority of Canadian Universities Sign Licence with Access Copyright', *University Affairs* (9 July 2012), www.universityaffairs.ca/news/news-article/majority-of-canadian-universities-sign-licence-with-access-copyright/.
Brown, J., 'Copyright Board Warns Universities They Can't Dodge Copying Tariff', *Canadian Lawyer* (29 August 2011), www.canadianlawyermag.com/author/jennifer-brown/copyright-board-warns-universities-they-cant-dodge-copying-tariff-1311/.
Butler, B., 'My GSU Hot Take' (1 April 2016), http://brandonbutler.info/post/142052963020/my-gsu-hot-take.
Courtney, K., 'GSU e-Reserves Decision | Peer to Peer Review', *Library Journal* (12 May 2016), https://lj.libraryjournal.com/2016/05/opinion/peer-to-peer-review/gsu-e-reserves-decision-peer-to-peer-review/.
Cox, K., 'Authors Guild v. HathiTrust Litigation Ends in Victory for Fair Use', *ARL Policy Notes Blog* (8 January 2015), http://policynotes.arl.org/?p=837.
Di Valentino, L., 'Access Copyright's New Offerings and the Collective's Future with Universities', *Fair Dealing in Education* (5 January 2016), https://fairdealingineducation.com/2016/01/05/access-copyrights-new-offerings-and-the-collectives-future-with-universities/.
'Access Copyright Renewals Update', *Fair Dealing in Education* (updated 8 February 2016), https://fairdealingineducation.com/2015/10/15/access-copyright-renewals-update/.

'Access Copyright Renewals Update 2019', *Fair Dealing in Education* (updated 21 February 2019), https://fairdealingineducation.com/2019/05/21/access-copyright-renewals-update-2019/#more-790.

Esmail, P., 'CCH Canadian Ltd v Law Society of Upper Canada: Case Comment on a Landmark Copyright Case' (2005) 10 *Appeal* 13.

Geist, M., 'Low-tech Case Has High-tech Impact', *Toronto Star* (22 March 2004), www.michaelgeist.ca/resc/html_bkup/mar222004.html.

'Access Copyright and AUCC Strike a Deal: What It Means for Innovation in Education', *Michael Geist* (17 April 2011), www.michaelgeist.ca/2012/04/access-copyright-and-aucc-deal/.

'The Access Copyright Interim Tariff Opt-Out List', *Michael Geist* (29 July 2011), www.michaelgeist.ca/2011/07/access-copyright-opt-out-list/.

'Ignoring the Supreme Court: Federal Court Judge Hands Access Copyright Fair Dealing Victory', *Michael Geist* (13 July 2017), www.michaelgeist.ca/2017/07/ignoring-supreme-court-trial-judge-hands-access-copyright-fair-dealing-victory/.

Katz, A., 'The Voice of Canadian Universities?', *Arial Katz* (24 April 2012), https://arielkatz.org/the-voice-of-canadian-universities/.

Knopf, H., 'Access Copyright's Excessive $45 per University Student Proposed Tariff – August 11, 2010 Deadline', *Excess Copyright* (8 August 2010), http://excesscopyright.blogspot.com/2010/08/access-copyrights-excessive-45-per.html.

'AUCC Follows UofT & Western and Capitulates to Access Copyright's Copyright Bullying – And It Still "Ain't Over"', *Excess Copyright* (19 April 2012), http://excesscopyright.blogspot.com/2012/04/aucc-follows-uoft-western-and.html.

'Access Copyright v. York U – The Federal Court of Appeal Hearing Is March 5 and 6, 2019', *Excess Copyright* (4 March 2019), http://excesscopyright.blogspot.com/2019/03/access-copyright-v-york-u-federal-court.html.

'U. of T. and Western Capitulate to Access Copyright', *Excess Copyright* (31 January 2012), http://excesscopyright.blogspot.com/2012/01/u-of-t-and-western-capitulate-to-access.html.

Lorinc, J., 'Universities in Dispute with Copyright Collective Over Fees', *University Affairs* (16 August 2010), www.universityaffairs.ca/news/news-article/universities-in-dispute-with-copyright-collective/.

Smirke, R., 'European Court Rules in Favor of Kraftwerk in 20 Year-Long Copyright Dispute', *Billboard* (29 July 2019), https://www.billboard.com/articles/business/8524267/kraftwerk-european-court-justice-ruling-metall-auf-metall.

Smith, K., 'Here We Go Again: Latest GSU Ruling an Odd Victory for Libraries' (1 April 2016), https://blogs.library.duke.edu/scholcomm/2016/04/01/fgo-latest-gsuruling-odd-victory-libraries/.

Somers, J., 'Torching the Modern-Day Library of Alexandria', *The Atlantic* (20 April 2017), www.theatlantic.com/technology/archive/2017/04/the-tragedy-of-google-books/523320/.

Trosow, S., 'Compilation of Announcements for Institutions Opting-Out of Model Licence', *Sam Trosow* (29 June 2012), https://samtrosow.wordpress.com/2012/06/29/compilation-of-annoucements-for-institutions-opting-out-of-model-license/.

Zhang, S., 'The Real Cost of Knowledge', *The Atlantic* (4 March 2019), at www.theatlantic.com/science/archive/2019/03/uc-elsevier-publisher/583909/.

Index

Access Copyright
 blanket licensing by, 235, 255, 267–275, 287, 302–303
 dispute with York University, 69, 173, 266, 274–275, 301–306, 327
 establishment, 235
 university withdrawal from blanket licence, 83–84, 259, 267–275, 298
administrative use. *See* collection management
American Alliance of Museums, 145, 313
American Library Association, 195
Aplin, Tanya, 277–278
archives, defining, 123–128
Association of Universities and Colleges of Canada (AUCC), 269–274
Australia
 administrative purposes exception, 37, 113, 143–145, 313
 ALRC Review of 2013, 31
 approach to exceptions, 9–10
 collective management in, 81–84
 compulsory licences for education, 86, 111
 eligibility for sector-specific exceptions, 124–125
 fair dealing in, 9–10, 28, 211–214, 227, 232–235
 Fair Use Review of 2005, 208–215, 332
 history of sector-specific exceptions, 110–111, 113, 130–131
 onsite consultation of preservation copies, 152
 preservation copying exceptions, 41, 128–132, 137–139, 213, 313, 333
 request-based copying exceptions, 38, 148–151
 risk management in, 88–91, 220–221, 224–229, 293–294, 299–300, 324, 328
 section 200AB. *See* section 200AB (Australia)

Simplification Review of 1998, 30–31
US-Australia Free Trade Agreement, 208–210
Australian Copyright Council, 110, 215–217
Australian Digital Alliance, 211, 213, 215–217
Australian Film Commission, 212
Australian Law Reform Commission (ALRC), 31
Australian Libraries Copyright Committee, 215–217
Australian Vice-Chancellors' Committee, 211
Australian War Memorial, 213
authorship and copyright, 48–49

Beebe, Barton, 40, 171, 174, 187
behavioural economics, 29, 49
 biases, self-serving, 51–52, 301
 deterrence, 49, 51
Bently, Lionel, 277–278
Berne Convention
 quotation and, 276–278, 282–284, 333
 three-step test and, 14–19
best practice norms. *See* institutional norms
Bibendum (the Michelin Man), 321
Blackboard, 195
Bouchard, Mario, 81, 94
Brexit, copyright law and, 19, 23, 92, 95, 100–101, 337
British Film Institute, 96
British Library, 97–98
Burrell, Robert
 on exceptions, 9–10, 308–310
 on fair use, 158, 308–310, 336
 on the ISD Directive, 25, 112
 on the UK libraries and archives provisions, 112–113
Butler, Brandon, 201

370

Index

Canada
- approach to exceptions, 9–10
- collection management exception, 143–145, 296, 313
- collective management in, 80–84, 118–119, 317–319. *See also* Access Copyright
- Copyright Modernization Act (Canada), 12, 121, 268, 273, 307, 332
- eligibility for sector-specific exceptions, 127–128
- history of fair dealing, 319–321
- history of sector-specific exceptions, 117–121, 317–319
- onsite consultation of preservation copies, 151–152
- preservation copying exceptions, 130, 136–137
- request-based copying exceptions, 147, 254
- risk management in, 88–91, 323
- section 77 scheme for unlocatable copyright owners, 92–94
- withdrawal of universities from Access Copyright licence, 83–84, 259, 267–275, 298

caricature, parody and pastiche, 287–292
- CJEU on parody, 291
- Intellectual Property Office definitions, 290
- Information Society Directive and, 289
- meaning of pastiche, 290–292
- 2014 UK Reforms, 275, 287–289
- relevance to institutions, 287–289

CCH Canadian Ltd. v. Law Society of Upper Canada
- academic commentary on, 5–6, 231, 248–252, 325–326
- application in later cases, 242–248
- application to electronic reserves and VLEs, 257–259, 267–268, 302
- application to user request services, 253–257
- definition of library, 127–128
- definition of research, 240–241, 246–247, 325
- fairness factors and, 172–173, 241–242, 246–247, 250, 305
- legal issues in, 236
- litigation background, 4–5, 235–238
- reconceptualisation of Canadian copyright law by, 5–6, 249–250, 322–323
- response from cultural institutions, 6, 252–261, 325–326
- users rights' language and, 5, 239, 248–250

certainty. *See* standards and rules analysis

Coasean analysis, 52

Coleman, Allison
- on exceptions, 9–10, 308–310
- on fair use, 158, 308–310, 336
- on the ISD Directive, 25, 112
- on the UK libraries and archives provisions, 112–113

collection management
- in Australia, 37, 113, 143–145, 313
- in Canada, 143–145, 296, 313
- drafting of sector-specific exceptions, 143–144
- fair use and, 145–146, 177–179
- institutional norms and, 57, 144–147, 157, 312–313
- lessons for drafting of, 147
- practices, 74–88, 144–147
- sector-specific exceptions, 143–144
- in the United Kingdom, 146–147, 313
- in the United States, 145–146, 177–179, 313

collective management, 80–84. *See also* Access Copyright, Copyright Licensing Agency and orphaned works
- advantages of, 80, 82–83
- in Australia, 81–84
- in Canada, 80–84, 118–119, 317–319
- extended collective licensing. *See* extended collective licensing (ECL)
- defining, 80
- disadvantages of, 80, 82–83
- mechanisms of, 80
- in the United Kingdom, 81–84
- in the United States, 81–83

compliance with copyright
- costs, 48–50, 57–58
- free exceptions, cultural institutions and, 86–88
- negotiation-based approaches, 74–84
- options for cultural institutions, 63–64, 70–71
- selection-based approaches, 71–74

compulsory licenses, 84–86, 111

CONTU rule of 5, 150

Cooter, Robert, 53

Copibec, 255

copyright
- absence of formalities, 76
- balance within, 8–9, 243–245
- Brexit and, 19, 23, 92, 95, 100–101, 337
- duration, 101
- European harmonisation and, 19–25

Index

copyright (cont.)
  exceptions. *See* exceptions
  expansion of, 8–9
  international treaties and, 13–19, 23–25
  justifications for. *See* justifications
  originality, 72–73, 236–238
  property right, 63–64, 78, 118, 318–319
  relevance to cultural institutions, 70–71
Copyright Agency Limited (CAL), 212
Copyright Board of Canada, 80, 92–94, 246–247
Copyright Clearance Center, 81
Copyright in Cultural Institutions Group (CICI), 211–212, 215–218
Copyright Law Review Committee, 30–31
Copyright Licensing Agency (CLA), 84, 286
Copyright Office (US)
  on fair use, 334–335
  on preservation, 129, 153–154, 334
  on reform to section 108, 126, 129, 148, 153–154, 334–336
Copyright Tribunal (UK), 95
costs, award of in litigation, 58, 200, 203
Côte d'Or chocolate bars, 243
Courtney, Kyle, 204
Cowan, Thomas, 32
Craig, Carys, 5, 250
CREATe, 96
Creative Commons, 286
Crews, Kenneth, 195, 197
cultural institutions
  accreditation of, 140, 145, 313
  best practices and. *See* institutional norms
  centralisation of copyright management, 177, 295, 315–316
  copyright management techniques, 156–157, 176–177, 293–301, 315–316
  custodianship and, 73–74
  importance of, 7, 65–66
  industry guidelines, 41, 108–109, 150, 215–218
  options for copyright compliance, 63–64, 70–88
  public domain works and, 71–74
  reasons for empirical study of, 65–66
  risk preferences of. *See* risk preferences
  selection of institutions for empirical study, 342–343, 347–348
  social norms and, 181, 312–315, 328–329
  virtual institution, expectations of, 70–71, 328–329
  workflows within, 75, 79, 99, 133, 149, 156–157, 274–275, 280, 325–326

D'Agostino, Pina, 251–252
dedicated terminals exception, 152–156
de Beer, Jeremy, 94
digital technologies
  disruptive effects of, 65–66, 70–71, 183
  onsite consultation and, 151–156, 182–183
  power of, 70–71, 183, 194–195
digitisation
  mass, 65, 71, 98, 133–134, 185, 223, 253
  as preservation technique, 132–134
Directive on Copyright in the Digital Single Market (DSM Directive)
  contracting out and, 142
  harmonising exceptions, 20, 23–25, 287
  out-of-commerce works and, 82–83, 92, 130, 147
  preservation copying and, 153
  works of visual art in the public domain, 72–73
Di Valentino, Lisa, 274
Drassinower, Abraham, 248, 251

educational copying
  Access Copyright v. *York* litigation, 6, 69, 173, 266, 274–275, 301–306, 327
  Alberta v. *Access Copyright* litigation, 271–273
  compulsory licences, 84–86, 111
  electronic reserves. *See* electronic reserves
  fair use and course packs, 173
  fair dealing for education (Canada), 86, 268, 273, 332
  fair dealing for illustration for instruction (United Kingdom), 284–287, 333
  Georgia State litigation, 150, 161, 172, 194–205, 329
  photocopying revolution and, 109–113
  relationship between exceptions and licensing, 286
  section 200AB (Australia), 87, 213–214
  transformative use and, 171–172
  virtual learning environments. *See* virtual learning environments (VLEs)
Ehrlich, Isaac, 32, 36, 38, 49–50
Electronic Frontiers Australia, 211
electronic reserves, 194–195
  in Canada, 257–259, 267–268, 302
  fair use and, 194–205

Index

eligibility, for sector-specific exceptions, 122–128
Ellickson, Robert
  on controllers of rules of behaviour, 53, 56, 312
  on sanctions, 54
  on social norms, 53, 55
empirical methodology. *See also* interviews and interviewees
  anecdotalism, 347
  anonymity, 67, 344
  Plain Language Statement, 343
  reliability, 346
  selection of institutions, 342–343
  selection of countries, 343–344
  semi-structured interviews versus questionnaires, 341–342
  snowball effect, 343
  use of pseudonyms, 66–67, 347
  validity, 346
Endicott, Timothy
  on precision, 33–34, 62
  on tort law, 34
  on uncertainty, 52
enforcement costs, 57–58, 329–330
ethics. *See* institutional norms
European Commission, 25
European Union
  DSM Directive. *See* Directive on Copyright in the Digital Single Market (DSM Directive)
  and fair use, 20–21
  harmonisation, 19–23
  Information Society Directive. *See* Information Society Directive (ISD)
  single market, 24
European Union Intellectual Property Office (EUIPO), 95–96, 98–99
exceptions. *See also* sector-specific exceptions
  artworks in public places, 87–88
  autochthonous drafting, 87, 207, 214, 228, 323–325
  contractual exclusion of, 75, 142
  closed list versus open list, 8–13, 20–21, 28–29, 61–62, 308, 330–332, 338
  defining, 9–10, 84
  drafting approaches, 9–11
  DSM Directive. *See* Directive on Copyright in the Digital Single Market (DSM Directive)
  existing scholarship, 3–4
  fair balance, 22–23, 279, 291, 292
  future-proofing, 26–27, 310, 327, 337
  harmonisation of, 23–25

Information Society Directive. *See* Information Society Directive
  justifications for, 8, 84–85
  overview of exceptions most relevant to cultural institutions, 85–86
  as part of copyright compliance framework, 64
  private copying, 46–48
  prohibitions on contracting out, 142–143
  terminology, 248–250
  three-step test. *See* three-step test
  time-shifting, 47–48
  as users' rights, 5, 239, 248–250
  verbosity of, 11
extended collective licensing (ECL), 27, 80–83, 92, 100–101, 299
external requests. *See* request-based copying

Fair Copying Declaration of 1950, 108
fair dealing
  10 per cent rule, 233, 304
  Access Copyright v. *York* litigation, 69, 173, 266, 274–275, 301–306, 327
  agency arguments, 234–235, 237, 240–241
  in Australia, 9–10, 211–214, 227, 228, 232–235
  in Canada, 4–6, 117, 230–262, 267–275, 298, 319–326
  caricature, parody and pastiche. *See* caricature, parody and pastiche
  CCH Canadian Ltd. v. *Law Society of Upper Canada*. *See* CCH Canadian Ltd. v. *Law Society of Upper Canada*
  classification as standard or rule, 36–38, 230
  Copyright Act of 1911 and, 9–10, 108, 230, 233, 309
  Copyright Modernization Act and, 121, 268, 273, 332
  costs of learning about, 50, 315–316, 327–328
  criticism and review, 37, 227, 233–234
  criticisms of, 11, 233–235, 309
  defining, 10, 86–87, 230
  education. *See* educational copying
  expanded (new purposes), 266, 332–333, 336–337
  extended (open-ended), 10, 30–31, 112, 231
  fairness factors (Canada), 241–242, 246–247, 250
  illustration for instruction. *See* educational copying

374   Index

fair dealing (cont.)
  news reporting, 86, 227, 233–234
  quotation. *See* quotation exception
  research, meaning of, 234, 240–241,
    246–247, 325
  researcher requests. *See* request-based
    copying
  sufficient acknowledgement, 37, 266,
    276, 286
  in the United Kingdom, 9–10, 108–109,
    275–292, 309–310, 315–316, 328, 332
fair use
  as bargaining tool in licensing
    negotiations, 189
  compliance with three-step test, 14,
    212
  collection management and, 145–146,
    177–179, 313
  costs of learning about, 50, 60–61,
    315–316, 327–328
  classification as standard, 36–38, 40,
    58–59, 163, 175–177
  criticisms of, 12–13, 60, 161, 212, 335
  defining, 9, 36–37, 87, 162–163
  fairness factors, 162, 165–167, 176,
    186–188, 193–194, 198–200, 202–205
  Georgia State litigation, 150, 172,
    194–205, 329
  HathiTrust litigation, 161, 168, 192–194,
    329
  'leading cases' approach, 28
  market effect (harm) and, 60, 166–167,
    172–175, 187–188, 190, 193–194,
    199, 203–205
  orphaned works and, 189–191
  overview of practices, 161, 175–177
  as panacea. *See* fair use panacea
  preservation and, 134–135, 180
  promulgation costs and, 327, 329, 330
  request-based copying, and, 181–182
  relevance to online and offsite uses,
    184–189
  relevance to onsite consultation, 182–183
  role of case law, 28, 40, 163–164, 176,
    329–330
  section 108 reforms and, 333–335
  statutory language of, 9, 162–163, 312
  thumbnails cases, 164–167
  transformativeness and, 165–172, 179,
    186, 193–194
  Williams & Wilkins litigation and, 115–116
fair use panacea, 7–13, 26, 158–159, 162,
  308–310, 330, 333, 336–338
Fair Use Review of 2005 (Australia),
  209–215, 332

Information Society Directive and,
  20–23
section 200AB (Australia) and, 87,
  207–215, 227, 331–332
social norms and, 329–330
signaling effect of, 330–331, 333
Fair Use Review of 2005, 209–215, 332
Federal Cultural Policy Review Committee,
  318
fieldwork. *See* empirical methodology;
  interviews and interviewees
First Amendment, 209, 309
flexibility. *See* standards and rules analysis
format-shifting, 46, 215, 225
Franki Committee, 110, 112, 113
free riding, 78, 202, 205

Geist, Michael, 231
Gentleman's Agreement of 1935, 108
Georgia State litigation, 150, 172, 194–205,
  329
Gervais, Daniel, 250–251
Gibson, James, 51
Ginsburg, Jane, 282–284
Glasgow Museums, 97
Goldstein, Paul, 3–4, 170, 317
Google Books Project, 65–66, 192
Gowers Review, 112
Great Library at Osgoode Hall, 5, 127, 235,
  257
Gregory Committee, 109–110, 117

Hargreaves Review, 112
harmonisation
  European Union and, 19–25
  of exceptions, 13–14, 23–25
  national implementation and, 21
  under Information Society Directive,
    19–23
Harris, Lesley Ellen, 322
HathiTrust litigation, 161, 168, 192–194,
  329
Hébert, Monique, 119
Hirtle, Peter, 108, 142
Hohfeldian analysis, 249
Holmesian 'bad man', 44
House Report of 1976, 58
Hugenholtz, Bernt, 317
Humanist Library and Archives, 96–97
Hume, David, 52, 56
Hungary, 96

Iljadica, Marta, 55
illustration for instruction. *See* educational
  copying

Index

Imperial War Museum, 95–96
Impressions Gallery, 97
Internet Industry Association, 211
incentivisation
  copyright law and, 48–49, 52, 79–98
  fair use and, 174–175
  free riding and, 202, 204–205
  in standards and rules analysis, 43
indigenous content, 73
individual rights negotiation, 74–79
Information Society Directive (ISD), 13–14
  amendment by DSM Directive, 20
  caricature, parody or pastiche, 289–291
  dedicated terminals, 152–153
  fair use and, 20–23
  harmonisation of rights under, 19–20
  legislative history of, 25
  logic of harmonisation and, 21–23
  national implementation and, 21–23
  permitted cases (Article 5), 19–23, 112–113, 275, 332–333
  quotation, 276, 280, 282
  reproductions by libraries, museums and archives, 112, 152–153
  three-step test and, 17–18, 23
  transposition to domestic law, 21–23
infringement
  analogy to trespass, 319
  by authorisation, 70, 236, 238
  secondary infringement, 243–244
institutional norms
  best practice, 40–41, 56–57, 61, 107, 131, 135–142, 157–158, 178–180, 312–315, 323, 336–337
  codes and guidelines, 40–41, 56–57
  collection management and, 56–57, 144–147, 157, 178–179, 313
  changes in, 63, 265–267, 307, 323, 326–327
  closed exceptions and, 157–159, 313–314
  Ellickson's 'controllers' of rules of behaviour, 53, 56, 312
  ethics and, 56–57, 314
  fair use and, 313–314
  limitations of, 314–315
  public-facing use and, 185–186, 314
  preservation and, 41, 135–142, 157–158, 180, 313–314
Intellectual Property Office (IPO) (United Kingdom)
  definitions of caricature, parody and pastiche, 290
  orphaned works licensing scheme, 96–101, 299–301

interlibrary supply
  in Australia, 149–151
  in Canada, 253–254
  complexity, 148–149
  CONTU rule of 5, 150
  drafting of sector-specific exceptions, 147–149
  general exceptions and, 151, 253–254
  in the United Kingdom, 149–151
  in the United States, 149–151
international treaties, 13–19, 23–25
  Berne Convention. *See* Berne Convention
  Marrakesh Treaty, 23, 105
  TRIPS. *See* TRIPS (Trade-Related Aspects of Intellectual Property)
Internet
  cloud copying services, 46–48
  changes in attitudes to, 328–329
  electronic reserves. *See* electronic reserves
  music previews and fair dealing, 246–248
  online uses by institutions. *See* online and offsite public access
  search engines and fair use, 164–167, 170
  subscription databases, 123, 142, 258–259, 267–269, 274, 286
  virtual institutions, 70
  VLEs. *See* virtual learning environments
Internet Industry Association, 211
interviews and interviewees. *See also* empirical methodology
  aims of fieldwork, 7, 339
  anonymity of interviewees, 67, 344
  allocation of pseudonyms, 67, 68
  preliminary case studies, 66–67
  conduct of interviews, 66–67, 339–340, 344–346
  fieldwork phases, 67–70
  Plain Language Statement, 343
  reasons for using interviews, 341–342
  reasons for studying cultural institutions, 65–66
  recording of interviews, 66–67
  selection of countries, 340–341
  selection of interviewees, 343–344
  selection of institutions, 342–343, 347–348
  structure of interviews, 344–346

Jaguar Daimler Heritage Trust, 96
Joint Libraries Committee on Copyright, 115
justifications
  copyright, 48–49, 183, 202, 238–239, 243–246, 320

justifications (cont.)
  exceptions, 8, 84–85
  free riding. *See* free riding
  incentives. *See* incentivisation
  legitimate economic interests, 244
  Lockean justifications, 239
  sector-specific exceptions, 106
  time-shifting exceptions, 47

Kaplow, Louis, 35, 42
  on classification as standard or rule, 39–40
  on legal knowledge, 49
Katz, Ariel, 270
Keyes and Brunet Report, 118, 318
King's College, Cambridge, 96–97
Knopf, Howard, 270

Laddie, Hugh, 10
Leddy Library, 257–258
Leeds Museums and Galleries, 97
legal commands, audiences of, 39
legal knowledge. *See also* standards and rules analysis
  acquisition of, 48
  change over time, 220, 292–293, 298
  costs of acquiring, 48, 327–328
  frontline staff and, 149–150, 156–157
Leval, Pierre, 167
libraries
  Australian law reform and, 109–113
  Canadian law reform and, 117–121
  defining, 123–124
  Franki Committee on, 110–111
  overlaps with other cultural institutions, 123–124
  photocopiers and, 107–112, 114–118, 235
  UK law reform and, 109–113
  US law reform and, 114–117
libraries and archives provisions.
  See sector-specific exceptions
licensing by cultural institutions
  with Access Copyright, 235, 255, 267–273, 287, 302–303
  centralised licensing; *see* orphaned works
  challenges of individual negotiation, 75–78
  collective management and. *See* collective management
  by the Copyright Board of Canada; *see* orphaned works
  efficiency of individual negotiation, 75

experiences of individual negotiation, 74–79, 101–102
extended collective licensing. *See* extended collective licensing
by the Intellectual Property Office (United Kingdom); *see* orphaned works
market failure and, 75–76
preservation copying and, 134, 135, 136, 138, 140, 180
request-based copying and, 150–151
similarities between different countries, 74
subscription databases and, 123, 142, 258–259, 267–269, 274, 286
transactions costs of, 75–80
Linen Hall Library, 97
Lipinski, Tomas, 173, 197
Litman, Jessica, 48–49
LSE Library, 96
Lunney, Glynn, 81

Madison, Michael, 60
management norms. *See* institutional norms
market effect (harm)
  fair dealing and, 172–173, 241–242, 305–306
  fair use and, 60, 166–167, 172–175, 187–188, 190, 193–194, 199, 203–205
  meta-factor in fair use, 174, 187
market failure, 12, 75–76, 84–85, 106, 185, 266–267
Marrakesh Treaty. *See* international treaties
metadata, 153, 190
Minow, Mary, 173, 197
Moodle, 195
monopolies, 10, 80, 110, 172–173
moral rights, 245
Murray, Laura, 120, 249–250
Museum of the Order of St. John, 96, 97

National Archives of Australia, 213
National Film and Sound Archive, 212
National Institutes of Health, 115
National Library of Medicine, 115
negligence, 34
neoliberalism, 85
the Netherlands, 96
news reporting exceptions, 10, 86, 227, 233–234
nonresponsive copyright owners, 76, 300
norms. *See* institutional norms; social norms
Northern Ireland Screen, 96

Index   377

online and offsite public access
  in Canada, 259–261
  fair use and, 184–191, 314
  fair dealing and, 259–261
  online collection databases, 55–56, 83, 186–188, 228
  in the United States, 183–191, 314
onsite consultation
  in Australia, 152
  in Canada, 151–152
  digital technology and, 151
  drafting of sector-specific exceptions, 151–154
  fair use and, 182–183
  practices, 154–156
  in the United Kingdom, 152–153, 154–156
  in the United States, 153–154, 182–183
open access, 75, 84, 151, 269, 286
Optus, 46–47
originality, 72–73, 236–238
orphaned works
  in Australia, 208–209, 218–221, 225–227
  in Canada, 92–94, 261
  centralised licensing of, 92, 102
  challenges of, 76–77, 299
  EU exception, 94–101
  fair use and, 189–191
  licensing scheme (UK Intellectual Property Office), 96–98
  limitations of fair use approach, 191
  lobbying around EU exception, 100
  remedies limitations, 88–92
  risk management and, 88–92, 190–191, 300
  section 200AB (Australia) and, 209, 218–220, 225–228, 299–300
  in the United Kingdom, 94–101, 299–300
  in the United States, 189–191
  unlocatable copyright owners scheme (Canada), 92–94

parody; *see* caricature, parody and pastiche
pastiche; *see* caricature, parody and pastiche
Patry, Bill, 170
Pentalogy, 268, 271, 307
photocopying, 71, 107–109
  fair dealing and, 254–255
  libraries and, 107–112, 114–118, 194
photographs, originality of, 72–73
Pila, Justine, 20
Poland, 96
Posner, Eric, 55
Posner, Richard, 32, 36, 38, 49–50
Pound, Roscoe, 32

preservation copying
  in Australia, 41, 128–132, 137–139, 213, 313, 333
  in Canada, 130, 136–137
  Copyright Office (United States) on, 129, 153–154, 334
  defining, 128
  digitisation as preservation technique, 132–133
  drafting of sector-specific exceptions, 128–132
  DSM Directive and, 113, 130
  fair use and, 134–135, 180, 193
  future of, 142
  institutional norms and, 135–142
  practices, 132–142
  publication status and, 129–131
  synergies with access, 133–134
  three-copy limit, 41, 131, 135, 138, 157, 313–314, 334
  in the United Kingdom, 129–132, 139–141
  in the United States, 128–129, 134–136
Prisoner's Dilemma, 54–55
private copying, 46–48
profit-making enterprises, sector-specific exceptions and, 124, 127
promulgation costs of legislation, 42–48, 105, 327
  cultural institutions and, 327
  fair use and, 327, 330
property rights
  copyright as property, 118–119, 318–319
  property-style rights in copyright law, 52, 63, 78, 99–100
property rules, 78, 85, 92
proportionate use, 20–21
public access. *See* onsite uses and offsite public access
public domain works
  DSM Directive and, 72–73
  restricting access to, 72–74
  intellectual property issues and, 72–73
  prioritising use of works in, 71, 78–79, 101, 184, 259

quotation exception
  application to unpublished works, 281–284
  Berne Convention on, 276–278, 282–284, 333
  collection management and, 146
  CJEU on, 278–280, 281–282, 284

quotation exception (cont.)
  Information Society Directive and, 20, 276–277
  meaning of, 277–280
  in the United Kingdom, 276–284

reasonable person, in tort law, 33–34
relationship management; *see also* reputation
  relevance of, 52–56, 181, 182–183, 312–315, 328–329
  social norms, and, 52–56
replacement copying, sector-specific exceptions and, 128–142; *see also* preservation
reproduction right
  Berne Convention and, 14–15
  Information Society Directive and, 19–20
  CJEU on right to digitise, 152–153
  meaning of reproduction, 245, 254, 320
reputation. *See also* relationship management
  ethics and, 56–57, 329
  relevance of, 79, 91, 323, 328–329
  social norms and, 52, 56
request-based copying. *See also* interlibrary supply
  in Australia, 38, 148–151
  in Canada, 147, 253–257
  CCH Canadian Ltd. v. *Law Society of Upper Canada* and, 253–257
  complexity of sector-specific exceptions, 147–149
  drafting of sector-specific exceptions, 147–149
  fair dealing and, 253–257
  fair use and, 181–182
  suitability for rule-like drafting, 149, 156–157
  in the United Kingdom, 148–151
  in the United States, 147–151, 181–182
reserve collection, 194–195; *see also* electronic reserves
Ricketson, Sam, 282–284
Rimmer, Matthew, 249
risk preferences, 26, 51–52, 60, 88–92, 292–301, 328
  growing risk tolerance in Australia and the United Kingdom, 90–92, 293, 297–301, 328
risk management, 88–92, 298–301
  circumstances in which used, 89–90, 289–299
  decision-making and, 88–89
  orphaned works. *See* orphaned works

  relevance to drafting of exceptions, 266–267, 336–337
  remedies limitations and, 64, 92, 300–301
  standards and rules and, 51–52, 296–297
  section 200AB (Australia) and, 220–221, 225–227
Roman Roads Research Association, 96
Rose, Carol, 35
rules. *See also* standards and rules analysis
  clarity of, 38
  complexity of, 37–38, 50, 149
  costs of learning about, 49–50
  defining, 28–30
  enforcement of, 57–58, 329–330
  Holmesian 'bad man' and, 44
  legislative process in drafting, 44–45, 105
  prescriptiveness of, 31–35
  risk preferences and, 51–52, 296–297
  social norms and, 55
Russell, Carrie, 197

Sag, Matthew, 40
Samuelson, Pamela, 40
Scassa, Teresa, 231, 251
Schlag, Pierre, 33–35
Seale, Clive, 346
section 200AB (Australia), 207–230
  aims of, 207–208, 213–214
  awareness of, 220
  challenges in understanding, 221–224, 312, 314–315
  complexity of, 221–223, 323–324
  critiques of, 221–225
  defining, 87, 207–208
  drafting of, 207–208, 214–215, 328
  failure of, 227–229, 323, 324, 331–332
  fair use and, 87, 207–215, 227, 331–332
  future of, 323–325
  history of, 209–215
  interpretative guides, 215–218
  orphaned works and, 209, 218–219, 225–228, 299–300
  practices, 218–227
  risk management and, 220–221, 225–227
  special case requirement, 223
  standards and rules and, 208–209, 217–218, 220, 225, 228
  three-step test language and, 17, 207–209, 214, 216–217, 224, 228, 312, 324–325
sector-specific exceptions. *See also* exceptions
  aims of, 106

Index

classification as standard or rule, 37, 39
collection management. *See* collection management
defining, 86
dedicated terminals, 152–156
eligibility for, 123–128
external requests. *See* request-based copying
history of, 107–122
interlibrary supply. *See* interlibrary supply
preservation. *See* preservation copying
profit-making enterprises and, 124–127
Sheffield Museums, 97
Sherman, Brad, 108
Smith, Kevin, 203
social norms, 52–56. *See also* relationship management and reputation
cultural institutions and, 181, 312–315, 328–329
defining, 52–54
Ellickson's five controllers of rules of behaviour, 53, 56
game theory, 54–55
request-based copying, and, 181
sanctions and, 53–54
standards and rules and, 55–56
Society of Authors, Composers and Music Publishers of Canada (SOCAN), 246
Spence, Michael
on precision, 33–34, 62
on tort law, 34
on uncertainty, 52
Spicer Committee, 110
standards. *See also* standards and rules analysis
complexity of, 37–38
costs of learning about, 49–50, 60–61
defining, 28–30
enforcement of, 57–58, 329–330
fair use as, 36–37, 38, 162–163, 175–176
intuitive elements of, 50, 60–61
judicial rule-making and, 36, 163
prescriptiveness of, 31–35
risk preferences and, 51–52, 296–297
section 200AB (Australia) and, 208–209
social norms and, 55
vagueness of, 51–52
standards and rules analysis, 6–7
certainty, 33–35, 42, 43, 51–52, 59–60, 106, 212–213
chronological heterogeneity, 45–46, 327, 330
clarity of language, 38
complexity of language, 37–38, 50, 58, 157
crystals and mud, 35

decision timing, 35–36
deterrence effect of law, 49
flexibility, 33–35, 42, 59–60, 175–176
gradations between standards and rules, 36–37
guidance value of precise laws, 33
intellectual origins, 28–30
interpretive practices, relevance to classification as standard or rule, 39–41, 160–161, 310
knowledge, 49–50
private copying exceptions and, 46–48
property law and, 35
predictions arising from, 60–61
process value of precise laws, 33
promulgation costs. *See* promulgation costs of legislation
relevance to copyright law, 28–31
reputational concerns and, 52–56
risk preferences and, 51–52, 60
selecting between standards and rules, 42–58, 310, 316
social norms and, 55–56, 157–158
speeding offences, 32, 35–36, 37
vulgar behaviour, 39–40
Standing Committee on Canadian Heritage, 119
statutory damages, 58, 311
statutory licenses. *See* compulsory licences.
Stirling Council Archives, 96
Stockholm Conference 1967, 15
subscription databases, 123, 142, 258–259, 267–269, 274, 286
Sunstain, Cass, 39

Tamaro, Normand, 250, 322
technological protection measures, 142, 210, 217
three-copy limit, 41, 131, 135, 138, 157, 313–314, 334
three-step test, 14–19
Declaration on a Balanced Interpretation of, 18
fair dealing and, 231
institutional understandings of, 224, 228, 324–325
section 200AB (Australia) and, 17, 207–209, 214, 216–217, 224, 312, 324–325
terminology in domestic legislation, 324–325
time-shifting, 46
exceptions, 47
Toblerone chocolate bars, 243
Torremans, Paul, 20

380   Index

tort law
  reasonable person in, 33–34
transaction costs
  free exceptions and, 12, 85
  of licensing, 52, 75–81, 188
transformativeness, 165–172, 179, 186, 193–194
TRIPS (Trade-Related Aspects of Intellectual Property), 207–208
three-step test and, 14–19, 230–231
  terminology in domestic legislation, 217, 324–325
  WTO Panel decision on section 110(5), 15–17
Trosow, Samuel, 120, 249–250
Tushnet, Rebecca, 171
Twain, Shania, 321

uncertainty. *See* standards and rules analysis
United Kingdom
  approach to exceptions, 9–11
  caricature, parody or pastiche, 287–292
  collection management in, 146–147, 313
  collective management in, 81–84
  dedicated terminals and, 152–156
  eligibility for sector-specific exceptions, 122–124
  exceptions reform of 2014, 20–21, 112–113, 275
  fair dealing in, 9–10, 108–109, 275–292, 309–310, 315–316, 328, 332
  illustration for instruction, 284–287, 333
  interlibrary supply in, 149–151
  non-commercial research, private study, and, 288
  orphaned works, 94–101, 299–300
  permitted acts, 10
  preservation copying exception, 129–132, 139–141
  quotation and, 276–284
  request-based copying exceptions, 148–151
  risk management in, 88–92, 293, 297–301, 328
United States
  approach to exceptions, 9
  collection management in, 145–146, 177–179, 313
  collective management in, 81–83
  eligibility for sector-specific exceptions, 125–126
  fair use. *See* fair use
  onsite consultation in, 153–154, 182–183
  preservation copying exceptions, 128–129, 134–136
  request-based copying exceptions, 147–151, 181–182, 335–336
  risk management in, 189–191, 326, 336
  section 108, reform of, 126, 129, 148, 153–154, 180, 334–336
University of Kent, 96
University of Melbourne, 67–68
University of Reading Art Collection, 97
user requests. *See* request-based copying services
users' rights, 5, 239, 248–250

Varmer, Borge, 114
Vaver, David
  on exceptions as users' rights, 239, 249
  on fair dealing, 251
  on sector-specific exceptions, 120, 127
virtual learning environments (VLEs)
  in Canada, 257–259, 267–268, 302
  fair use and, 194–205
  in United Kingdom, 285–286

Wellcome Trust, 96
Whitford Committee, 111–112
Williams & Wilkins litigation, 115–116
Wiseman, Leanne, 108
works located in public places, free exceptions and, 87–88
World Trade Organization
  WTO Panel decision on section 110(5), 15–17

CAMBRIDGE INTELLECTUAL PROPERTY AND INFORMATION LAW

Titles in the Series (formerly known as Cambridge Studies in Intellectual Property Rights)

BRAD SHERMAN and LIONEL BENTLY *The Making of Modern Intellectual Property Law*
IRINI A. STAMATOUDI *Copyright and Multimedia Products: A Comparative Analysis*
PASCAL KAMINA *Film Copyright in the European Union*
HUW BEVERLY-SMITH *The Commercial Appropriation of Personality*
MARK J. DAVISON *The Legal Protection of Databases*
ROBERT BURRELL and ALLISON COLEMAN *Copyright Exceptions: The Digital Impact*
HUW BEVERLY-SMITH, ANSGAR OHLY and AGNÈS LUCAS-SCHLOETTER *Privacy, Property and Personality: Civil Law Perspectives on Commercial Appropriation*
CATHERINE SEVILLE *The Internationalisation of Copyright Law: Books, Buccaneers and the Black Flag in the Nineteenth Century*
PHILIP LEITH *Software and Patents in Europe*
GEERTRUI VAN OVERWALLE *Gene Patents and Clearing Models*
LIONEL BENTLY, JENNIFER DAVIS and JANE C. GINSBURG *Trade Marks and Brands: An Interdisciplinary Critique*
JONATHAN CURCI *The Protection of Biodiversity and Traditional Knowledge in International Law of Intellectual Property*
LIONEL BENTLY, JENNIFER DAVIS and JANE C. GINSBURG *Copyright and Piracy: An Interdisciplinary Critique*
MEGAN RICHARDSON and JULIAN THOMAS *Framing Intellectual Property: Legal Constructions of Creativity and Appropriation 1840–1940*
DEV GANGJEE *Relocating the Law of Geographical Indications*
ANDREW KENYON, MEGAN RICHARDSON and NG-LOY WEE-LOON *The Law of Reputation and Brands in the Asia Pacific Region*
EDSON BEAS RODRIGUES JR *The General Exception Clauses of the TRIPS Agreement: Promoting Sustainable Development*
ANNABELLE LEVER *New Frontiers in the Philosophy of Intellectual Property*
SIGRID STERCKX and JULIAN COCKBAIN *Exclusions from Patentability: How the European Patent Office Is Eroding Boundaries*
SEBASTIAN HAUNSS *Conflicts in the Knowledge Society: The Contentious Politics of Intellectual Property*
HELENA R. HOWE and JONATHAN GRIFFITHS *Concepts of Property in Intellectual Property Law*
ROCHELLE COOPER DREYFUSS and JANE C. GINSBURG *Intellectual Property at the Edge: The Contested Contours of IP*
NORMANN WITZLEB, DAVID LINDSAY, MOIRA PATERSON and SHARON RODRICK *Emerging Challenges in Privacy Law: Comparative Perspectives*
PAUL BERNAL *Internet Privacy Rights: Rights to Protect Autonomy*
PETER DRAHOS *Intellectual Property, Indigenous People and Their Knowledge*
SUSY FRANKEL and DANIEL GERVAIS *The Evolution and Equilibrium of Copyright in the Digital Age*

Edited by Kathy Bowrey and Michael Handler *Law and Creativity in the Age of the Entertainment Franchise*
SEAN BOTTOMLEY *The British Patent System and the Industrial Revolution 1700–1852: From Privileges to Property*
SUSY FRANKEL *Test Tubes for Global Intellectual Property Issues: Small Market Economies*
JAN OSTER *Media Freedom as a Fundamental Right*
SARA BANNERMAN *International Copyright and Access to Knowledge*
ANDREW T. KENYON *Comparative Defamation and Privacy Law*
PASCAL KAMINA *Film Copyright in the European Union (second edition)*
TIM W. DORNIS *Trademark and Unfair Competition Conflicts*
GE CHEN *Copyright and International Negotiations: An Engine of Free Expression in China?*
DAVID TAN *The Commercial Appropriation of Fame: A Cultural Critique of the Right of Publicity and Passing Off*
JAY SANDERSON *Plants, People and Practices: The Nature and History of the UPOV Convention*
DANIEL BENOLIEL *Patent Intensity and Economic Growth*
JEFFREY A. MAINE and Xuan-Thao Nguyen *The Intellectual Property Holding Company: Tax Use and Abuse from Victoria's Secret to Apple*
MEGAN RICHARDSON *The Right to Privacy: Origins and Influence of a Nineteenth-Century Idea*
MARTIN HUSOVEC *Injunctions against Intermediaries in the European Union: Accountable but Not Liable?*
ESTELLE DERCLAYE *The Copyright/Design Interface: Past, Present and Future*
MAGDALENA KOLASA *Trade Secrets and Employee Mobility: In Search of an Equilibrium*
PÉTER MEZEI *Copyright Exhaustion: Law and Policy in the United States and the European Union*
GRAHAM GREENLEAF and DAVID LINDSAY *Public Rights: Copyright's Public Domains*
OLE-ANDREAS ROGNSTAD *Property Aspects of Intellectual Property*
ELENA COOPER *Art and Modern Copyright: The Contested Image*
PAUL BERNAL *The Internet, Warts and All: Free Speech, Privacy and Truth*
SEBASTIAN FELIX SCHWEMER *Licensing and Access to Content in the European Union: Regulation between Copyright and Competition Law*
DANIELA SIMONE *Copyright and Collective Authorship: Locating the Authors of Collaborative Work*

Lightning Source UK Ltd.
Milton Keynes UK
UKHW010745250620
365545UK00013B/295